(Conti...

German Baroque Writers, 1580–1660

Dictionary of Literary Biography® • Volume One Hundred Sixty-Four

German Baroque Writers, 1580–1660

Edited by
James Hardin
University of South Carolina

A Bruccoli Clark Layman Book
Gale Research Inc.
Detroit, Washington, D.C., London

The paper used in this publication meets the minimum requirements
of American National Standard for Information Sciences–Permanence
Paper for Printed Library Materials, ANSI Z39.48-1984. ∞ ™

Library of Congress Cataloging-in-Publication Data

German Baroque writers, 1580–1660 / edited by James Hardin.
    p. cm. – (Dictionary of literary biography; v. 164)
"A Bruccoli Clark Layman book."
Includes bibliographical references and index.
ISBN 0-8103-9359-X (alk. paper)
1. German literature – Early modern, 1500–1700 – Bio-bibliography – Dictionaries. 2. Baroque
literature – Bio-bibliography – Dictionaries. 3. Authors, German – Early modern, 1500–1700 –
Biography – Dictionaries. I. Hardin, James N. II. Series.
PT271.G47   1996
830.9'004 – dc20   96–2337
                                                                                                  CIP
[B]

10 9 8 7 6 5 4 3 2 1

For Anne, editor par excellence

Contents

Contents

Plan of the Series

. . . Almost the most prodigious asset of a country, and perhaps its most precious possession, is its native literary product — when that product is fine and noble and enduring.

Mark Twain*

The advisory board, the editors, and the publisher of the *Dictionary of Literary Biography* are joined in endorsing Mark Twain's declaration. The literature of a nation provides an inexhaustible resource of permanent worth. We intend to make literature and its creators better understood and more accessible to students and the reading public, while satisfying the standards of teachers and scholars.

To meet these requirements, *literary biography* has been construed in terms of the author's achievement. The most important thing about a writer is his writing. Accordingly, the entries in *DLB* are career biographies, tracing the development of the author's canon and the evolution of his reputation.

The purpose of *DLB* is not only to provide reliable information in a convenient format but also to place the figures in the larger perspective of literary history and to offer appraisals of their accomplishments by qualified scholars.

The publication plan for *DLB* resulted from two years of preparation. The project was proposed to Bruccoli Clark by Frederick C. Ruffner, president of the Gale Research Company, in November 1975. After specimen entries were prepared and typeset, an advisory board was formed to refine the entry format and develop the series rationale. In meetings held during 1976, the publisher, series editors, and advisory board approved the scheme for a comprehensive biographical dictionary of persons who contributed to North American literature. Editorial work on the first volume began in January 1977, and it was published in 1978. In order to make *DLB* more than a reference tool and to compile volumes that individually have claim to status as literary history, it was decided to organize volumes by topic, period, or genre. Each of these free-standing volumes provides a biographical-bibliographical guide and overview for a particular area of literature. We are convinced that this organization — as opposed to a single alphabet method — constitutes a valuable innovation in the presentation of reference material. The volume plan necessarily requires many decisions for the placement and treatment of authors who might properly be included in two or three volumes. In some instances a major figure will be included in separate volumes, but with different entries emphasizing the aspect of his career appropriate to each volume. Ernest Hemingway, for example, is represented in *American Writers in Paris, 1920–1939* by an entry focusing on his expatriate apprenticeship; he is also in *American Novelists, 1910–1945* with an entry surveying his entire career. Each volume includes a cumulative index of the subject authors and articles. Comprehensive indexes to the entire series are planned.

With volume ten in 1982 it was decided to enlarge the scope of *DLB*. By the end of 1986 twenty-one volumes treating British literature had been published, and volumes for Commonwealth and Modern European literature were in progress. The series has been further augmented by the *DLB Yearbooks* (since 1981) which update published entries and add new entries to keep the *DLB* current with contemporary activity. There have also been *DLB Documentary Series* volumes which provide biographical and critical source materials for figures whose work is judged to have particular interest for students. One of these companion volumes is entirely devoted to Tennessee Williams.

We define literature as the *intellectual commerce of a nation:* not merely as belles lettres but as that ample and complex process by which ideas are generated, shaped, and transmitted. *DLB* entries are not limited to "creative writers" but extend to other figures who in their time and in their way influenced the mind of a people. Thus the series encompasses historians, journalists, publishers, and screenwriters. By this means readers of *DLB* may be aided to perceive literature not as cult scripture in the keeping of intellectual high priests but firmly positioned at the center of a nation's life.

*From an unpublished section of Mark Twain's autobiography, copyright by the Mark Twain Company

DLB includes the major writers appropriate to each volume and those standing in the ranks immediately behind them. Scholarly and critical counsel has been sought in deciding which minor figures to include and how full their entries should be. Wherever possible, useful references are made to figures who do not warrant separate entries.

Each *DLB* volume has a volume editor responsible for planning the volume, selecting the figures for inclusion, and assigning the entries. Volume editors are also responsible for preparing, where appropriate, appendices surveying the major periodicals and literary and intellectual movements for their volumes, as well as lists of further readings. Work on the series as a whole is coordinated at the Bruccoli Clark Layman editorial center in Columbia, South Carolina, where the editorial staff is responsible for accuracy of the published volumes.

One feature that distinguishes *DLB* is the illustration policy – its concern with the iconography of literature. Just as an author is influenced by his surroundings, so is the reader's understanding of the author enhanced by a knowledge of his environment. Therefore *DLB* volumes include not only drawings, paintings, and photographs of authors, often depicting them at various stages in their careers, but also illustrations of their families and places where they lived. Title pages are regularly reproduced in facsimile along with dust jackets for modern authors. The dust jackets are a special feature of *DLB* because they often document better than anything else the way in which an author's work was perceived in its own time. Specimens of the writers' manuscripts are included when feasible.

Samuel Johnson rightly decreed that "The chief glory of every people arises from its authors." The purpose of the *Dictionary of Literary Biography* is to compile literary history in the surest way available to us – by accurate and comprehensive treatment of the lives and work of those who contributed to it.

The *DLB* Advisory Board

Introduction

German baroque literature comprises writings in German and in Latin – primarily prose fiction and poetry but also religious tracts, works by theologians and mystics, and a vast body of alchemical, astrological, and quasi-scientific literature – published in the Holy Roman Empire of the German Nation from around 1580 to around 1720. One is, unfortunately, forced to deal in this arbitrary fashion with a literature that defies the application of any single stylistic or thematic link that might more precisely define it – though there has been no lack of efforts to find a satisfying linking principle. German baroque literature was neglected by scholars in the nineteenth century; the recognition that German literature of the period between the Reformation and the Enlightenment had much to offer not only as an invaluable commentary on the life and culture of the time but also as art in its own right (though one that subscribed to different aesthetic norms from those of the nineteenth and twentieth centuries) did not come until the first decade of the twentieth century, and bibliographies, critical editions, and biographies – not to speak of overarching literary histories of the period – were few and unreliable until after the midpoint of the century. The German baroque period was generally treated, if at all, with some embarrassment as the mannered and formless product of a time whose mores and sense of balance had been devastated by war and whose cultural and linguistic independence had been severely damaged by the incursions of foreign soldiers and the influences of stronger cultures. Nineteenth-century literary histories tended to dismiss most of the literature of the baroque in condescending clichés and generalizations copied from earlier histories. To be sure, the importance and literary genius of such seminal figures as Martin Opitz, Hans Jakob Christoffel von Grimmelshausen, and Andreas Gryphius were recognized even in the mid nineteenth century – but they were, it was thought, the exceptions that proved the rule.

Modern literary scholarship has come to a more differentiated and favorable view of the period. Precisely because the German baroque offered, until relatively recently, such a profusion of scholarly problems and tasks undone – unidentified authors, lack of bibliographical and biographical reference works, the literary works themselves (even the most important ones) not only unedited but largely unavailable except in rare copies in obscure libraries – a great amount of scholarly energy, time, and talent has been devoted to research on German literature of the seventeenth century. And in exactly those areas that had been most neglected, and where the most grievous lacunae existed – critical editions, descriptive and annotated bibliographies, biographical studies – there now exists a respectable number of basic tools that make research incomparably more convenient and less frustrating than it was as recently as the 1960s. In addition, hundreds of scholarly monographs and articles on virtually every aspect of this variegated literature and culture have been published. Of special interest have been the studies that treat the historical and sociological aspects of the period and that uncover the rich and little-understood interconnections between the court and the middle-class writer. German baroque literature is still a fertile, if difficult, area for research, and a great deal remains to be done before scholars will be able to recognize clearly, much less analyze, the historical and social forces behind the literature of the period. For that reason, this introduction can offer no consensus of scholarly opinion as to what constitutes the German baroque; one can merely sketch out some of the historical, philosophical-theological, and social issues that underlay the literature of the time and consider some of the themes that preoccupied it.

No one even knows how the term *baroque* itself arose. One suggestion is that it derives from the Portuguese *baroco,* meaning an irregularly shaped pearl; another is that it comes from a medieval rhetorical term. The etymology does not matter, in the last analysis, since the word *baroque* is used more as a convenience than as a descriptive term; it is obvious to anyone familiar with German literature of the seventeenth century that many works do not possess any of those stylistic characteristics – irregularity, heaping up of words for rhetorical effect, mannered descriptive techniques that emphasize the grotesque, overuse of adornment to the point of bombast, and the like – that are associated with the "baroque." Richard Alewyn says that the term is altogether inappropriate for most seventeenth-century literature and should be reserved for the visual art and music of the period. There are, however, examples in German literature, especially in the second half of the century, of the kind of mannered style and use of recondite, elaborate, inflated language and metaphor that is clearly "baroque" in the narrow (mannerist) sense of the word. What is and what is not baroque is still a much-debated question; the term will be used here, as it is commonly used in German studies, to designate the literature and art that arose between, roughly, 1580 and 1720.

Literature in Germany at the beginning of this period was based on models from languages other than German. There were three reasons for this phenomenon. First, the German vernacular – and, therefore, the literature written in German – lagged behind those of England, France, Italy, and Spain by approximately a century; one need only compare William Shakespeare's English with the best German being written around 1590 to see the contrast between the languages. Unlike Spain, France, and England, Germany had no major Renaissance writer in the vernacular of whom it could boast; this situation was to obtain throughout the seventeenth century, although Gryphius and Grimmelshausen were writers of great talent and lasting influence. The learned Germans who comprised the writing class of the baroque era felt this shortcoming keenly. It was for this reason that Martin Opitz prescribed translation from the classics and from works by major writers of the other vernacular languages as a means for German writers to produce great literature. Opitz himself set a great example: among his many achievements along these lines were an adaptation of Sophocles' *Antigone* (1636); translations of Seneca's *Trojan Women* (1625) and John Barclay's long courtly novel *Argenis* (1626); and a revision of an earlier German translation of Sir Philip Sidney's *Arcadia* (1638). Second, much European literature in this period derived from the Neo-Latin writing of the German humanists of the sixteenth century. In Germany itself, the Latin poetry of the humanists led, in the seventeenth century, to an erudite, sometimes erotic poetry that had little to do with any native German literary traditions. Third, while in the sixteenth century the city had been the center, by and large, of German culture, with the rise of absolutism in the seventeenth century the cultural center moved to the courts of the various German principalities. The new writer class of this period constituted the bureaucracy of the court; it consisted of middle-class scholars, teachers, secretaries, and clergymen, all of whom were united in their ability to read and write Latin, sometimes Greek, and usually one or more vernacular languages. This new learned class, steeped in the litera-

ture of antiquity, was attuned to foreign literature in a way unheard of in the sixteenth century. It is, therefore, not surprising that many of the most important works in German literature of the first half of the seventeenth century are adaptations or translations of works from other languages. The task of German poets was to prove that the German language was capable of the nuances possible in the other vernaculars. Germany's great literary and cultural efflorescence was to come in the second half of the eighteenth century, but the linguistic and literary developments of the seventeenth century were a necessary stage on the way to the sophistication of the German used by Johann Wolfgang von Goethe and his contemporaries.

One can learn a great deal about German literature and its ambitions in the early and mid seventeenth century by looking at works of German poetics, even though the actual practice of German writers often ran contrary to the poetic theory. The poetics handbook was a highly significant genre in Germany throughout the seventeenth century; based ultimately on classical poetics and rhetoric but more directly on the works of the sixteenth-century Italian humanist Julius Caesar Scaliger, the German poetics were intended to be used by anyone who might be called on to compose poetry for occasions such as births, christenings, weddings, dedications of buildings, awarding of academic degrees, and deaths. It was one of the duties of the educated middle-class man to be able to compose such "occasional" poetry, and a large proportion, perhaps a majority, of German literary works of the seventeenth century were poetry of this type.

But the books of poetics, particularly the early ones, had another, less immediately practical and more idealistic purpose: to promote the growth and beauty of German language and literature. The first full-blown German poetics, and one of the most significant works in the history of German literature, is Opitz's *Buch von der deutschen Poeterey* (Book of German Poetry, 1624). This slender but pithy volume, which discusses all of the genres of literature that were known to classical antiquity (the novel is ignored), was authoritative, albeit in modified form, for the rest of the seventeenth century and into the eighteenth. Opitz, using a topos at least as old as Plato, justifies literature as a kind of *verborgene Theologie* (hidden theology) and argues, following Horace, that poetry's first aim is to instruct and its second is to delight. Like the many poetics that followed, the *Buch von der deutschen Poeterey* emphasizes clarity and the use of elegant diction, metaphor, and epithet. The poet should create composite words or circumlocutions, such as *die arbeitströsterinn* (work consoler) for *night,* and should use words appropriate to the mood and atmosphere being described. Unlike many authors of succeeding poetics, Opitz warns that poets are born, not made by the mere observance of rules. But talent alone is not enough, either. Opitz insists that the metrical stress in poetry should correspond to the way German syllables are accented in ordinary speech; odd as it may seem, German vernacular literature up to Opitz's time had not observed this rule. He recommends the use of a "high style" for tragedy; a "middle style," not too elaborate or ornate, for the pastoral; and a "lower" style for comedy. Poetics books published in Germany later in the seventeenth century prescribed more and more ornamentation, going far beyond Opitz's recipes, until, toward the end of the century, a new vogue for simplicity can be documented in the writings of influential theoreticians, such as Christian Weise, who were calling for a more sober, lucid use of language and for verse that differed little from prose. Around the same time, works such as Johann Beer's *Printz Adimantus und Ormizella* (1678) were satirizing the ornate qualities of much baroque literature.

The recommendations found in the German poetics correspond well to the actual stylistic tendencies practiced in succeeding periods of the baroque. For the baroque style, among those writers who partook of it, did evolve: some scholars speak of a prebaroque or early baroque style, followed by high baroque toward 1650, and then a time of stylistic decadence – overadornment, preciosity, and elephantine heaviness – in the 1670s and 1680s. The highly elaborate style of some works late in the century gave a bad name to the whole of German baroque literature. One now distinguishes between the early baroque, perhaps up to Opitz's translation of *Antigone* in 1636, and the increasingly ornate style and *Schwulst* (bombast) found in some writers of the end phase of baroque literature. It would, therefore, be a misconception to associate the overly ornate, overblown language of a Daniel Casper von Lohenstein with all German baroque literature. While it is true that the majority of German works of the baroque period are characterized by a highly embellished style, it is also true that a significant number are rather sober and straightforward.

Closely related to the German poetics is the rise of the *Sprachgesellschaften* (linguistic societies), whose immediate purpose was the improvement of German language, literature, and taste. The societies were also concerned, however, with broader ethical and political issues having to do with the tradition of republicanism and the ethos of true nobility, the nobility of the soul or the pen. The creation of such patriotic societies was part of a general European movement that began in Italy in the fifteenth century and, in Germany, traced its roots specifically to the founding of the *Accademia della crusca* in Florence in 1582. The first German Sprachgesellschaft was the famous Fruchtbringende Gesellschaft (Fruit-bringing Society), founded in 1617 by Duke Ludwig of Anhalt-Köthen. Other Sprachgesellschaften were founded in rapid succession, such as the Aufrichtige Gesellschaft von der Tannen (Upright Society of the Pine Tree), founded in 1633 in Strasbourg; the Teutsch-Gesinnte Genossenschaft (Society for Promotion of German Culture), founded in 1643 in Hamburg; and the Löblicher Hirten- und Blumenorden an der Pegnitz (Eminent Order of Shepherds and Flowers on the Pegnitz), founded in 1644 in Nuremberg. While most of the original members of the Fruchtbringende Gesellschaft were noblemen, the membership increasingly came to consist of middle-class intellectuals and writers. The Sprachgesellschaften were created for the primary purpose of "cleansing" German of foreign loan words and neologisms, many of which had penetrated the language as a result of the chaotic conditions that prevailed during the Thirty Years' War of 1618 to 1648. But such matters as grammar, syntax, orthography, and style were also important to the linguistic societies, and although certain of them, such as Philipp von Zesen's Teutsch-Gesinnte Genossenschaft, undoubtedly went absurdly far in the attempt to eliminate foreign terms, the overall effect of the societies' efforts was beneficial. It led in the same direction as the consciousness-raising efforts of the German poetics, pointing toward other languages and literatures as examples to be followed by German literature.

The Thirty Years' War was the decisive occurrence in Germany in the seventeenth century. Based in the beginning on religious considerations – in effect, a continuation and rekindling of the issues and emotions that had brought about the Reformation and Counter Reformation in the preceding century – the war developed into a struggle for territorial aggrandizement. The armies of Sweden, France, Spain, and the Holy Roman Empire were engaged in the ruthless and bloody conflict, but most of the fighting took place on German soil. The result was the devastation of the German economy and culture. It has been variously estimated that the population of Germany during the Thirty Years' War declined from around eighteen million to twelve or even six million. Germany, which had been the richest nation on the Continent in 1600, was plunged into a period of chaos and turmoil from which it only slowly and painfully emerged during the second half of the century. The experience of the Thirty Years' War was central to all Germans living in the first half of the century, and one often distinguishes among German writers whose works appeared before the war, those who wrote during the war, and those who were productive after the war and knew about it only indirectly. The war had its most conspicuous and well-known influence on the century's greatest novel, Grimmelshausen's *Der abentheuerliche Simplicissimus Teutsch* (The Adventurous Simplicissimus German, 1669), much of which describes actual events that occurred during the phase of the war in which Grimmelshausen served for several years as a secretary to a high-ranking officer. The novel has been called the greatest history of the Thirty Years' War; the characterization is misleading, because the work is by no means a mere account but a highly stylized, carefully structured, profound treatment of the human condition that brings together virtually every important contemporary literary theme and social issue. The influence of the Thirty Years' War can also be seen in the emphasis of many of the writers of the first half of the century on the vanity of earthly things and on the afterlife as the only reality: the pessimistic, angst-ridden nature of much German literature of the period, particularly the works of Gryphius, has much to do with the horrendous memories left behind by the war.

It has been theorized that the desire for law and order after the turmoil of war was one reason for acquiescence in the absolutistic form of government that had increasingly made its way through most of continental Europe (with the notable exception of Holland). A similar desire for order in literature has been noted in connection with the poetics and Sprachgesellschaften. Germany, unlike England, Spain, and France, was never politically or culturally unified in the seventeenth – or, for that matter, in the eighteenth – century but remained a loose confederation of cities and principalities. There was never a city that played a central role in German culture in the way that Paris and London did in French and English culture, respectively; culture was centered in courts throughout Germany, a situation that has resulted in the continuing decentralization of German culture to this day. The other European countries had no interest in a unified Germany, and the political checkerboard of the Holy Roman Empire would not be simplified until Napo-

leon Bonaparte consolidated his rule over the area in 1806.

The cities in seventeenth-century Germany were integrated into the absolutistic state; their loss of autonomy led to a loss of political power by the middle class, whose literature had dominated the sixteenth century. Middle-class culture was not totally submerged in the courtly culture; the old folk literature, such as the chapbook (a well-known example of which is the *Historia von D. Johann Fausten* [History of Dr. Johann Faust, 1587]), remained popular through the seventeenth and into the eighteenth century. But to a great extent, middle-class authors accepted the cultural hegemony of the courts. Literature, music, and architecture at the court were produced, with a few notable exceptions, by the middle class; therefore, the literature of the absolutistic German courts was a mixture of middle-class and aristocratic taste and thought. (The theoreticians of absolutism, such as Thomas Hobbes in England, were, after all, of middle-class origin.)

Even so, the culture of the court (and also of many cities) was dominated by a strict code of etiquette of Romance origin and by a strict system of ceremony and precedence that placed all social classes in a clearly defined hierarchy. People were expected to act, dress, and speak in a manner appropriate to their social rank. This expectation regarding strict decorum is particularly striking in two literary genres: in the tragedy, which was considered the highest literary art form of the time, and in the courtly novel. But it is also found in poetry, including the voluminous occasional poetry that arose at court and in the cities. It is significant that those literary forms most closely associated with the courts ceased to have any influence after the baroque period. The courtly novel, with perhaps one exception – Heinrich Anselm von Zigler und Kliphausen's *Die Asiatische Banise* (The Asian Banise, 1689) – found few readers in the eighteenth century. Today only scholars of the German baroque read the courtly novel; the baroque tragedy likewise lost its influence as early as the late seventeenth century. Only those works that have strong folk elements and characteristics associated with literary "realism" (portrayal of the poor, use of everyday slang and obscenity, emphasis on description of contemporary places and conditions) have survived. These are largely picaresque works. The best examples of these works are Grimmelshausen's *Der abentheuerliche Simplicissimus Teutsch* and some of the novels of Beer. Some of the poetry of the German baroque has survived, particularly that of Gryphius, whose sonnets are known to German students.

Genres of Baroque Literature

Poetry

Poetry in Germany, as previously mentioned, arose largely from foreign influences: Latin verse, which had been the poetic medium of the learned class in the previous century; Dutch writers, most notably Daniel Heinsius, a classicist and leading scholar of the age and a strong influence on Opitz; and the Romance Renaissance poets. Another source of German poetry was the song, which was an adaptation of Italian texts and can be compared to the Elizabethan madrigal. These songs introduced new stanzaic forms that permitted considerably more freedom than the relatively hidebound German verse of the sixteenth century. Latin verse was based on such classical models as Catullus and Propertius; Opitz and his most important successor, Paul Fleming, saw it as their highest goal to reproduce in German the meter and thematics of the Latin models. Opitz and Fleming also continued, of course, to write poetry in Latin, as did many other German writers; they did so not only because Latin was a lingua franca that made their work "European" and not merely relevant in Germany but also because of the perception that Latin was still a superior linguistic tool, capable of subtler modes of expression than German.

One of the most important works in German poetry of the first half of the century was Opitz's *Teutsche Poemata* (German Poetics, 1624). This work, often reprinted, provided examples of the types of poetry that, Opitz argued, could serve as models for German literature. He provides translations from the Greek Anthology, Propertius, Neo-Latin poets such as Scaliger, and Petrarch. The collection includes poems in a variety of genres: odes, epigrams, eclogues, epitaphs, and love songs. Though the forms of the poetry are varied, they tend to stress virtuosity at the expense of profundity and emotion. Fleming, who has been called the greatest lyrical poet of the century, was one of the few German poets who could breathe real feeling into the new forms imported from abroad. His poems reflect the entire Petrarchan love system: love is slavery; the beloved woman stands at a distance, commanding, and on a pedestal; she is not only beautiful but also virtuous; and so on. Lyric poetry toward the middle of the century, however, as found in the collections of Zesen, Georg Philipp Harsdörffer, and Johann Klaj, is rich in its formal aspects – its playfulness, puns, virtuosity, varied and daring rhythms and rhymes, and neologisms and experimentation – but has been faulted for its lack of genuine emotion. The poetry strikes one as a game rather than an evocation of a deeply felt experience. This criticism is, of course, a projection of tastes that did not come into being until the mid eighteenth century onto a period that set no store by such subjective criteria. Adherents of the New Criticism, who, like most nineteenth-century German critics, find in German baroque poetry only the promise of great works to come in the eighteenth century, and scholars of the German baroque, who wish not to judge the poetry of that age according to criteria that belong to other periods of literature, will never agree in their assessment of German poetry of the seventeenth century. However one may judge this virtuoso poetry, with its verbal exuberance, it shows the continuing evolution of German as an expressive, sophisticated literary language. Stylistic tendencies in poetry toward the end of the seventeenth century followed the stylistic tendencies in the other genres toward less ornate language.

The Novel

Early baroque poetics, including Opitz's, did not touch on the novel. Only after the publication of Andreas Heinrich Buchholtz's *Des Christlichen Teutschen Groß-Fürsten Herkules und der Böhmischen Königlichen Fräulein Valiska Wunder-Geschichte* (The Marvelous Story of the Christian German Great Prince Hercules and the Bohemian Royal Maiden Valiska, 1659, 1660) and Duke Anton Ulrich's five-volume *Die durchleuchtige Syerinn Aramena* (The Illustrious Syrian Princess Aramena, 1669–1673) were the so-called *Romainen* (novels) treated as a genre in the poetics. In 1682, for example, Eberhard Werner Happel printed the German translation of an essay by Pierre D. Huet, *Traité de l'origine des romans* (Essay on the Origin of Novels, 1670), one of the first European theoretical works on the novel. In that same year the polyhistorian Daniel Georg Morhof, citing French critics, referred to the novel as a serious literary form; he mentioned in particular the novels of Anton Ulrich and Buchholtz as being on a par with foreign models.

In the first half of the century, however, the novel in Germany was dominated by translations of foreign models. The three chief genres were the *Schäferroman* (pastoral novel), the *Staatsroman* (courtly novel or novel of state), and the *Schelmenroman* (picaresque novel). The pastoral novel can trace its origins at least as far back as Jacopo Sannazaro's Italian work *Arcadia* (1502), the first significant pastoral novel of the Renaissance; it was followed in Spain by Jorge de Montemajor's *Diana* (1541), which was partially translated or adapted by Hans Ludwig von Kuffstein in 1619 from a Latin translation. Another much-respected pastoral novel, Sidney's *Arcadia* (1590, 1593), was translated into German in 1629; in 1638 the translation was much improved by Opitz.

In pastoral novels the costume of the shepherd serves as a disguise or persona for the characters, who bear names from Greek and Roman antiquity so that they may discuss politics and moral philosophy in a distanced setting that presumably has nothing to do with contemporary times. Topics could thus be taken up that would otherwise be controversial and that might even lead to censorship. The novel also allows for lengthy discourses on friendship, love, religion, and education. This attempt to make of the novel a work that instructs and that contains seemingly peripheral information anticipates the encyclopedic tendency of the novel of state, which was prominent in the second half of the century. Another important influence on the pastoral novel was Honoré d'Urfé's five-volume novel *L'Astrée* (1607–1627), part of which was translated into German in 1619. This work remained popular throughout the seventeenth century and served as a kind of guidebook for the courtier in matters of deportment, language, dress, and ethics.

The first native German pastoral work was created by Opitz: the relatively short *Schäferey von der Nimpfen Hercinie* (The Pastoral of the Nymph Hercinie, 1630) is a prose eclogue, a hybrid of the pastoral novel and the verse eclogue. The verse eclogue derives most prominently from the eclogues of Virgil, which largely followed the models of Theocritus. The prose eclogue, like its verse forerunner, often has a satiric element and comments on current events and issues; it goes back as far as Boethius's *The Consolation of Philosophy* (circa 524). Opitz's *Schäferey von der Nimpfen Hercinie* follows the pastoral tradition: the poet journeys through the mountains in his shepherd costume and carries on long conversations with friends about love, the supernatural, friendship, and the like. The "shepherds" encounter Hercinie, who, following a motif found in Sannazaro's *Arcadia*, leads them through magnificent grottoes. The work, which includes songs and poems, takes place in an idyllic bucolic setting that has been translated from Arcadia to the rural landscape of Silesia. The work draws on Silesian folklore, a topic that fascinated Opitz, and is, therefore, not merely an imitation of foreign models; the settings for subsequent German pastoral works were, likewise,

rural villages and the forests of landed estates. *Schäferey von der Nimpfen Hercinie* inspired later prose eclogues by such prominent writers as Harsdörffer, Klaj, Fleming, Johann Hellwig, and Sigmund von Birken.

The courtly novel tends to be much longer than the pastoral and takes place at court, not in the countryside. The characters are idealized types of kings, queens, princes, and princesses; the language of these novels is correspondingly elevated. Affairs of the heart are combined with affairs of state, so that one usually finds a highly placed couple, rather than a single hero, at the center of the novel. The couple is typically separated by hostile forces, shipwreck, or abduction, and only after enduring a succession of severe trials, both physical and moral, and going through a series of disguises and adventures, sometimes involving the supernatural, are the still-pure lovers reunited. Typically the courtly novel ends with the marriage of the protagonists, celebrated with all the pomp and ceremony one would expect of the baroque court, often followed by the marriages of their retainers.

The courtly or state novels are complex in structure and action, and the chief exemplars are voluminous and labyrinthine. Their structure is made all the more difficult by the typical use of delayed revelation – that is, explaining what appear to be inexplicable actions and mysterious acts only after the reader has puzzled over them for several chapters – and by the practice of beginning a novel in medias res. This technique requires the reader to work actively to weave together the disparate threads of the plot and to keep straight the many dozens of figures introduced. Such novels were obviously intended for an upper-class or learned audience that had the leisure to read them and the money to purchase them. One of the most important foreign models for the Staatsroman was the series of novels titled *Amadís de Gaula*, which had arisen in Portugal or Spain in the fifteenth century. The first book was published by Garci Rodríguez Montalvo in a Spanish version around 1508; it was translated into French and expanded into eight books by Herberay des Essarts in 1527. The German version, which came out between 1569 and 1595, was the most voluminous of all, consisting of twenty-four books. The *Amadís* novels' popularity is easily explained: they combine erotic adventure, tales of knighthood, supernatural happenings, and magic. The importance of the German translation of the work, aside from its role in providing themes and material for many future novels, was that it showed the capability of the German language to express complicated and ornate figures of speech. In spite of this achievement, the novels were extremely unpopular with the clergy, who attacked the works' supernatural and magical elements even more violently than their eroticism.

Another important model for the Staatsroman was Barclay's *Argenis,* originally published in Latin in 1621 and translated into German by Opitz in 1626. The novel makes use of a historical setting to allow the author to discuss contemporary events and issues, particularly in France of the Valois. Examples of political wisdom and foolishness are mingled with courtly intrigues and love stories. Unlike the *Amadís,* Barclay's novel avoids the fantastic and titillating, stressing instead statecraft and the idea that the passions must be overcome by good sense and reason.

The first original German Staatsroman was Buchholtz's *Des Christlichen Teutschen Groß-Fürsten Herkules und der Böhmischen Königlichen Fräulein Valiska Wunder-Geschichte,* which was so popular that a sequel, *Der Christlichen Königlichen Fürsten Herkuliskus und Herkuladisla auch ihrer Hochfürstlichen Gesellschaft anmuthige Wunder-Geschichte* (The Christian Royal Prince Herkuliskas and Herkuladisla, also Their Princely Society, Charming Marvelous Story) appeared in 1665 and went through many reprints, the last of which appeared as late as 1744. Buchholtz was a pastor; his goal in the two works was to provide a Christian antidote to the erotic *Amadís* novels. But he follows the model in other ways: in their original editions the two novels run to 1,793 pages and 1,460 pages, respectively, with a register in *Herkuliskus und Herkuladisla* providing the names of 450 characters. In *Herkules und . . . Valiska* Hercules, a German prince living shortly after the time of Christ, is kidnapped and sold as a slave in Rome, where he converts to Christianity. After undergoing incredible tribulations he is reunited with his fiancée, the Bohemian princess Valiska, who had herself been kidnapped on her way to the wedding. Her virtue is still intact, and hero and heroine are united in a magnificent wedding. The sequel tells the story of their sons. Buchholtz's heroes are not only courageous but also pious: before setting off on an adventure or taking part in a battle they take time to pray. The complicated plots and large number of figures follow the foreign precedents and set the stage for the even more complex courtly novels of Duke Anton Ulrich and Lohenstein in the second half of the century. But the piety of Pastor Buchholtz's novel did not detract from its contemporary appeal and lasting popularity: in Goethe's *Wilhelm Meisters Lehrjahre* (1795–1796; translated as *Wilhelm Meister's Apprenticeship,* 1824) the woman identified as the *schöne Seele* (beautiful soul) speaks with great admiration of the then 150-year-old novel.

The picaresque novel, or Schelmenroman, evolved from German adaptations and translations of Spanish and French novels of roguery early in the seventeenth century. These novels are written in realistic, even naturalistic, prose; are relatively short; are episodic; and present either figures from the lower classes or upper-class figures who are in a state of decline. The genre was introduced into Germany by Aegidius Albertinus, who translated Mateo Alemán's *Guzmán de Alfarache* (1599) in 1615. The seventeenth-century high points of the novel of roguery are Grimmelshausen's *Der abenteuerliche Simplicissimus Teutsch* and the lighter novels of such writers as Beer and Johann Kuhnau in the latter half of the century.

Drama

The drama in sixteenth-century Germany had undergone no development similar to that which occurred in England during the Elizabethan Renaissance. The century's best German dramatist, the Nuremberg shoemaker Hans Sachs, wrote in a somewhat mechanical and jerky verse form (*Knittelvers*) that was not well suited to express emotion or to deal with profound issues. The German theater of the seventeenth century, therefore, had little on which to build and was not nearly as highly developed as those of England, France, or Spain. Neither were there professional actors, nor, until the end of the century, were theaters established exclusively for the performance of plays. Again, Germany looked to foreign models, one of the most important of which was the *englische Komödianten* — professional English actors who journeyed to Germany to perform plays in castles and courthouses across the region. The plays they put on were well known on the British stage and included *King Lear, Romeo and Juliet,* and a crude and much-truncated version of *Hamlet.* The plays were at first given in English with the "Hans Wurst" or clown figure providing a running commentary in German; in later years the English players learned German or added German actors so that dialogue could be delivered in German. English actors came to Germany as early as 1586 and continued playing there, off and on, into the second half of the seventeenth century. A published collection of the plays given by one troupe appeared in 1620. In the second half of the century the English troupes performed plays by German authors such as Gryphius and Lohenstein.

The rather simple theater of the English players, which required little stage machinery and few actors, was well suited for the generally primitive German stage.

One of the earliest German playwrights influenced by the English actors was Jakob Ayrer, who wrote, like his predecessor Sachs, in the wooden Knittelvers typical of the sixteenth century. Ayrer, who, like Sachs, came from Nuremberg, was a prolific dramatist; he wrote more than one hundred plays, of which many are still extant. His plays are reminiscent of those of Sachs, except that they are longer. Some of his plays are based on dramas performed by the English actors, including Thomas Kyd's *The Spanish Tragedy* (circa 1585–1590). Ayrer is better known for his industriousness than for his poetic talent.

A more significant figure in the history of baroque drama in Germany is Duke Heinrich Julius of Brunswick. The English actors, who came to his court several times, must have stimulated his desire to write dramas. Composed in the last decade of the sixteenth century, and not in Knittelvers but in prose, his play about Nero, *Von einem ungeratenen Sohn* (Concerning a Spoiled Son, 1594) prefigures later baroque dramas about cunning, violent villains, such as those by Gryphius and Lohenstein. The horrific Senecan scenes and the style point forward to the high baroque period.

The Jesuit theater, another important aspect of German drama in the first half of the seventeenth century, had begun as early as the 1560s. The Jesuit dramas, given in Latin, drew for the most part on materials from the Old Testament and from the history of classical antiquity, especially of the Roman and Byzantine Empires. The primary purpose of the plays was to influence the audience to accept the Jesuit interpretation of history. The theory of Jesuit theater was based on Scaliger, and the chief influence was that of the Roman poet Seneca. At the beginning of the seventeenth century the Jesuit plays were performed in public places, but later in the century they made increasing use of complicated stage machinery and effects such as moving heavenly bodies, airborne chariots, and the like, intended to impress and strike awe in the audience, and required specialized theater buildings. In the second half of the century Italian opera influenced Jesuit theater, and music and ballet played increasing roles.

One of the most important writers in this genre was the Jesuit priest and teacher Jacob Bidermann. *Cenodoxus,* his first play and one of his best, was performed in Munich in 1602 and is based on the legend of the conversion of Saint Bruno. The play, like so many other Jesuit dramas, was intended to frighten the audience into adopting the Catholic point of view. A primary theme of these plays, which was to be taken up in Gryphius's plays around the middle of the century, was the inconstancy of fortune, the transitoriness of glory and happiness. The same theme occurs in Protestant drama, showing its pervasiveness in the seventeenth century. The style of Protestant drama is also similar to that of Jesuit drama, though the Protestants wrote in German rather than in Latin.

Ever since Opitz's translation of Seneca's *Trojan Women* as *Die Trojanerinnen* (1625), the preferred verse form of the German tragedy was the alexandrine, a long line with a caesura or pause in the middle that approximated the antique hexameter. At the time of Opitz's translation serious drama was not being written or produced in Germany. Opitz's translations and adaptations were possibly the most important influences on the development of German baroque tragedy. The first significant German tragedian was the Protestant Gryphius, who had a profound knowledge of classical and European theater, including Dutch drama; for this reason his works depart utterly from the unsophisticated folk drama of sixteenth-century Germany. His plays were written for performance not on the professional stage but on the stage of the Protestant gymnasium, one of the primary settings for the performance of drama in the mid to late seventeenth century. The presence of large numbers of students, whose training included rhetoric and its use in dramatic performance, made possible the production of dramas with large casts of characters. In Gryphius's first tragedy, *Leo Armenius* (1646), the title character is the Byzantine general who deposed the emperor Michael I in 813 and was murdered seven years later. The drama demonstrates that evil will be punished on earth. The language of the play is dignified, rhythmic, and solemn and reveals that German is capable of a subtlety and dignity seldom found in earlier literature. Gryphius's other tragedies share these characteristics. His *Ermordete Majestät oder Carolus Stuardus* (Murdered Majesty; or, Charles Stuart, 1657) deals with one of the most horrendous events of the century from the German standpoint, the beheading of King Charles I of England in 1649. The greatest German tragedian of the century was also the greatest writer of comedies; his *Absurda Comica oder Peter Squentz* (1658) makes use of materials from classical antiquity that were used by Shakespeare in his *A Midsummer Night's Dream* (circa 1595–1596). It is remarkable that a poet capable of producing such solemn and gruesome scenes as those found in *Catharina von Georgien* (Catharina of Georgia, 1657) and *Leo Armenius* was also capable of writing lighthearted comedies that remain entertaining and performable today. Gryphius's tendency toward ornate language and his use of learned apparatus – his plays were carefully researched – pointed the way for the baroque drama of the second half of the century, especially the plays of Lohenstein.

In this volume, as in preceding *DLB* volumes treating German literature, the attempt has been made to avoid the use of terms that are not comprehensible to the general reader. Titles of works mentioned in the text of each entry are translated into English the first time they occur, as are non-English words and quotations. As in all *DLB* volumes, a high priority has been the preparation of a thorough and accurate primary bibliography of the works covered. This has been a particular problem in the case of German baroque authors, owing to the length of the titles of most of their works. It was a practice of the publishers of the seventeenth century to use the title pages of books as advertisements for the books; the title pages were, in effect, the dust jackets of the time. For that reason baroque titles are excessively long; it would have made this volume much too long if they had been reproduced in their entirety, so they have, in many cases, been truncated. In the bibliographies the orthography of the originals, such as *j* for *i* and *v* for *u,* have been retained, as have upper-case initial letters that normally would be lower case (adjectives, for example) if they were apparently used for emphasis or because of social or rhetorical conventions of the time. If such words were capitalized simply because they were the first word on a line of the title page, however, the upper-case initial letters have usually not been retained. In the text of each entry the orthography both of titles and quotations has been regularized. In both titles and quotations the baroque virgules (forward slash marks) have been replaced with commas.*

– *James Hardin*

*The works cited in the Books for Further Reading at the end of this volume by Richard Alewyn, Curt von Faber du Faur, Roy Pascal, Marian Szyrocki, Hans Wagener, and Frank Warnke, as well as Harald Steinhagen's introductory essay in his and Benno von Wiese's *Deutsche Dichter des 17. Jahrhunderts: Ihr Leben und Werk* (German Writers of the Seventeenth Century: Their Lives and Works, 1984), have been especially useful in the writing of this introduction.

Acknowledgments

This book was produced by Bruccoli Clark Layman, Inc. Karen L. Rood is senior editor for the *Dictionary of Literary Biography* series. Philip B. Dematteis was the in-house editor.

Production coordinator is James W. Hipp. Photography editors are Julie E. Frick and Margaret Meriwether. Photographic copy work was performed by Joseph M. Bruccoli. Layout and graphics supervisor is Emily Ruth Sharpe. Copyediting supervisor is Laurel M. Gladden. Typesetting supervisor is Kathleen M. Flanagan. Systems manager is George F. Dodge. Laura Pleicones and L. Kay Webster are editorial associates. The production staff includes Phyllis A. Avant, Ann M. Cheschi, Melody W. Clegg, Patricia Coate, Joyce Fowler, Stephanie C. Hatchell, Rebecca Mayo, Kathy Lawler Merlette, Jeff Miller, Pamela D. Norton, Delores Plastow, Lisa A. Stufft, William L. Thomas Jr., and Allison Trussell.

Walter W. Ross and Steven Gross did library research. They were assisted by the following librarians at the Thomas Cooper Library of the University of South Carolina: Linda Holderfield and the interlibrary-loan staff; reference-department head Virginia Weathers; reference librarians Marilee Birchfield, Stefanie Buck, Stefanie DuBose, Rebecca Feind, Karen Joseph, Donna Lehman, Charlene Loope, Anthony McKissick, Jean Rhyne, Kwamine Simpson, and Virginia Weathers; circulation-department head Caroline Taylor; and acquisitions-searching supervisor David Haggard.

German Baroque Writers,
1580–1660

Dictionary of Literary Biography

Aegidius Albertinus

(circa 1560 – March 1620)

Lawrence S. Larsen
University of Oklahoma

BOOKS: *Der Kriegßleut Weckvhr begreifft zween Theyl* (Munich: Printed by Nicolaus Heinrich, 1601);

Haußpolicey, begreifft vier vnterschidtliche Theyl (Munich: Printed by Nicolaus Heinrich, 1602);

Fünffter, Sechster vnd Sibender Theyl Der Haußpolicey (Munich: Printed by Nicolaus Heinrich, 1602);

Himlisch Frawenzimmer (Munich: Printed by Anna Berg, published by Raphael Sadler, 1611); enlarged as *Himmelisch Frawenzimmer . . . Anjetzt aber mit sonderm Fleiß corrigiert vnd gantz ernewert* (Munich: Johann Jäcklin, 1675);

Der Teutschen recreation oder Lusthauß, 4 volumes (Munich: Printed by Nicolaus Heinrich, published by Johann Kruger in Augsburg, 1612–1613);

Triumph Christi, Begreifft sehr schöne andächtige Betrachtungen von der Geburt, Leyden, Sterben, Aufferstehung vnd Himmelfahrt Christi (Munich: Printed by Anna Berg, widow, published by Raphael Sadler, 1612);

Der Welt Thurnierplatz (Munich: Printed by Nicolaus Heinrich, 1614);

Lucifers Königreich vnd Seelengejaidt, Acht Theil begreiffendt (Munich: Printed by Nicolaus Heinrich, 1616);

Vnser L. Frauen Triumph: Erstlich jhr Leben begreiffent. Folgents wirdt erwiesen, daß der jenig, der ein wahre Andacht zu jhr hat, außerwählt vu [sic] fürsehen seye (Munich: Printed by Anna Berg, 1617);

Christi vnsers Herrn Königreich vnd Seelengejaidt (Munich: Printed by Nicolaus Heinrich, 1618);

Hiren schleifer (Munich: Printed by Nicolaus Heinrich, 1618);

Aegidius Albertinus; copper engraving by Lucas Kilian

Himmlische Cammerherrn Oder Leben der heiligen Aposteln, Euangelisten, Griechischen vnd Lateinischen Kirchenlehrern, wie auch anderer fürnembster Heyligen, nit allein mit sonderm fleiß beschriben sonder auch, neben kurtzen andächtigen Gebettlein zu jedem Heyligen . . . für Augen gestellt (Munich: Printed by Andreas Aperger, published by Nicolaus Heinrich in Munich, 1645).

Editions and Collections: *Lucifers Königreich vnd Seelengejaidt,* edited by Rochus Freiherr von Liliencron, Deutsche Nationalliteratur, no. 26 (Berlin: Spemann, 1884; reprinted, Tübingen, 1974);

Hirnschleiffer, edited by Lawrence S. Larsen (Stuttgart: Hiersemann, 1977);

Christi Königriech vnd Seelengejaidt, edited by Rainulf A. Stelzmann (Bern: Peter Lang, 1983);

Verachtung des Hoflebens und Lob des Landlebens, edited by Christoph E. Schweitzer (Bern: Peter Lang, 1987).

TRANSLATIONS: Jean de Cartigny, *Deß Jrrenden Ritters Raiß. Der Welt Eitelkeit, vnd den Weg zu der ewigen Seligkeit begreiffend* (Munich: Printed by Adam Berg, 1594);

Antonio de Guevara, *Zwey schöne Tractätl, dern das eine: Contemptvs Vitæ Avlicæ, & Laus Ruris: intitulirt, Darinn mit zierlichen warnungen vnd exempeln erklärt wird, warumb das Burgerliche vnd Ainsame leben auffm Landt, besser vnd sicherer sey, als das Hofleben, vnd was diß für vngelegenheiten auff sich hat* (Munich: Printed by Nicolaus Heinrich, 1598);

Guevara, *Guldene Sendtschreiben,* 3 volumes (Munich: Printed by Adam Berg, 1598–1599);

Guevara, *Speculum Religiosorum & exercitium Virtuosorum oder: Der Geistliche Spiegel* (Munich: Printed by Adam Berg, 1599);

Guevara, *Lustgarten vnd Weckvhr,* 3 volumes (Munich: Printed by Nicolaus Heinrich, 1599);

Antonius van Hulst, *Der Geistlich Wettlauffer: Welcher vns herrliche Lehr vnd schöne Exempel gibt, was für einen weg, auff was weiß, vnd auß was vrsachen wir rennen vnd lauffen müssen, zu erlangung deß allerköstlichisten Kleinots der ewigen Seligkeit. Vnd was vns an glücklicher vollendung solches Lauffs verhindere vnd zuruck halte* (Munich: Printed by Nicolaus Heinrich, 1599);

Guevara, *Der Fürsten und Potentaten Sterbkunst* (Munich: Printed by Nicolaus Heinrich, 1599);

Guevara, *Speculum Religiosorum & exercitium Virtuosorum Oder: Der Geistliche Spiegel* (Munich: Printed by Adam Berg, 1599);

Guevara, *Institvtiones Vitae Avlicae, Oder HofSchul* (Munich: Printed by Nicolaus Heinrich, 1600);

Pedro de Rivadeneira, *Fons Vitae et consolationis: Der Brunn deß Lebens vnd Trostes. Begreifft die general vnd particular Trübseligkeiten der jetzigen Welt, vnd wie sich der Mensch in allen denselbigen zuuerhalten, damit er einen ersprießlichen Trost vnd inwendige Ruhe haben möge* (Munich: Printed by Nicolaus Heinrich, 1600);

Guevara, *Mons Calvariæ* (Munich: Printed by Nicolaus Heinrich, 1600);

Guevara, *Ander Theil deß Bergs Calvariae* (Munich: Printed by Nicolaus Heinrich, 1600);

Jean Gerson, *Ars Contemplandi siue Theologia mistica. Oder Das gulden büchlein der wahren Weißheit* (Munich: Printed by Nicolaus Heinrich, 1600);

Juan de Avila, *Trivmph, Vber die Welt, das Fleisch, vnd den Teufel* (Munich: Printed by Nicolaus Heinrich the Younger, 1601);

Agostino de Vivos, *Stvdivm Verae Sapentiae. Die vbung der wahren Weißheit,* 2 volumes (Munich: Printed by Nicolaus Heinrich, 1601);

Salvador Pons, *Histori Von dem Leben vnd Wunderwercken deß heyligen Raymundi de Penia forte, Predigers Ordens. Sampt zweyen schönen Predigen von der solitudine oder Einsambkeit vnser lieben Frawen* (Munich: Printed by Nicolaus Heinrich, 1602);

Francisco de Osuna, *Flagellum Diaboli: Oder Deß Teufels Gaißl.* (Munich: Printed by Adam Berg, 1602);

Osuna, *Trost der armen vnd Warnung der Reichen* (Munich: Printed by Nicolaus Heinrich, 1602);

Pedro de Medina, *Das Buech der Warheit. Begreifft drey Thail* (Munich: Printed by Adam Berg, 1603);

Luis de Escobar, *Der Zeitkürtzer. Begreifft allerley natürliche, moralische, Politische vnd Theologische Fragen sambt derselben außlegung* (Munich: Printed by Nicolaus Heinrich & Adam Berg, 1603);

Osuna, *Spiegel der Reichen* (Munich: Printed by Nicolaus Heinrich, 1603);

Luis de Malvenda, *Von den sonderbaren Geheimnussen deß Antichristi* (Munich: Printed by Adam Berg, 1604);

Malvenda, *Ander theil vom Antichristo welcher Rosetum Christianorum genent* (Munich: Printed by Adam Berg, 1604);

Malvenda, *Spiegel eines Christlichen Fürsten. Begreifft drey Theil* (Munich: Printed by Adam Berg, 1604);

Pedro Malón de Chaide, *Ein Geistreiches Tractätlein: Von dem dryfachen standt der H. Mariae Magdalenae* (Munich: Printed by Nicolaus Heinrich, 1604);

Juan de la Cerda, *Paedia Religiosorum: Oder Der Religiosen Mans- vnd Weibspersonen Schulzucht* (Munich: Printed by Nicolaus Heinrich, 1605);

Alonso de Orozco, *Hortus Sacer oder Der Heilig Garten* (Munich: Printed by Nicolaus Heinrich, 1605);

Orozco, *Das Buch der Geistlichen Vermählung. Allen Closter-jungkfrawen vnd andern Religiosen vast annemblich vnd nutzlich zulesen* (Munich: Printed by Nicolau Heinrich, 1605);

Cerda, *Weiblicher Lustgarten. Begreifft vier Theil* (Munich: Printed by Nicolaus Heinrich, 1605);

Lorenzo de Zamora, *Nosce te Ipsum. Oder, Kenn dich selbst* (Munich: Printed by Nicolaus Heinrich, 1607);

Diego de Pantoja, *Histori vnd eigentliche beschreibung, erstlich was gestalt, vermittelst sonderbarer Hülff vnd Schickung deß Allmächtigen, dann auch der Ehrwürdigen Vätter der Societet Iesu gebrauchten Fleiß, vnd außgestandener Mühe, Arbeit vnd Gefahr, numehr vnd vor gar wenig Jahren hero, das Euangelium vnd Lehr Christi in dem grossen vnd gewaltigen Königreich China eingeführt, gepflantzt vnd geprediget wirdt* (Munich: Printed by Adam Berg, 1608);

Saint Bonaventura, Pierre de Blois, and Lucas Pinellus, *Der Geistliche Seraphin* (Munich: Printed by Adam Berg, 1608);

Pedro Sanchez, S. J., *Das Buch Vom Reich Gottes, Acht Theyl begreiffendt* (Munich, 1609);

Historische Relation. Was sich inn etlichen Jaren hero, im Königreich Iapon, so wol im geist als auch weltlichem Wesen, namhafftes begeben vnd zugetragen (Munich: Printed by Nicolaus Heinrich, 1609);

Giovanni Botero, *Allgemeine historische Weltbeschreibung* (Munich: Printed by Nicolaus Heinrich, published by Anthony Hierat, 1611);

Antonio Gallonio, *Histori vnd Leben deß seligen Vatters Philippi Nerij von Florentz, stiffters der Congregation deß Oratorij zu Rom* (Munich: Printed by Nicolaus Heinrich, 1611);

Ambrogio Frigerio, *Das wunderbarliche Leben, hohe vnd vnerhörte Wunderwerck deß H. Nicolai von Tolentin, vnd der seligen Jungkfrawen Clarae von Montefalco, beyde der Einsidler S. Augustini Ordens* (Munich: Printed by Nicolaus Heinrich, 1611);

Petrus Berchorius, *Der Welt Tummel: vnd Schaw-Platz. Sampt der bitter: süssen Warheit* (Munich: Printed by Nicolaus Heinrich, published by Hans Kruger in Augsburg, 1612);

Florimond de Rémond, *Historia vom Vrsprung, auff- vnd abnemmen der Ketzereyen, vnd was sie seyter Anno 1500. schier aller orten in der Welt, sonderlich aber in Teutschland, Böheimb, Vngern, Sibenbürgen, Poln, Dennemarcken, Schweden, Norwegen, Engellandt vnd Franckreich für wunderbarliche vëranderungen, weitläuffigkeiten, jammer, noth, vnd höchste gefarlichheiten verursacht* (Munich: Printed by Nicolaus Heinrich, 1614);

Mateo Alemán, *Der Landtdstörtzer: Gusman von Alfarche oder Picaro genannt, dessen wunderbarliches abenthewrlichs vnd possirlichs Leben, was gestallt er schier alle ort der Welt durchloffen allerhand Ständt, Dienst vnd Aembter versucht, vil guts vnd böses gegangen vnd außgestanden, jetzt reich, bald arm, vnd widerumb reich vnd gar elendig worden, doch letztlichen sich bekehrt hat hierin beschriben wirdt*, translated and enlarged by Albertinus (Munich: Printed by Nicolaus Heinrich, 1615);

Pierre de Bessé, *Postill oder Außlegung aller Sonn- Fest vnd feyrtäglichen Euangelien, durch das gantze Jar, Aduent vnd Fasten* (Munich: Printed by Nicolaus Heinrich, 1616);

Bessé, *Der Seelen Compaß. Das ist: Von den Vier letsten dingen deß Menschen: Nemblich vom Todt, Jüngsten Gericht, der Höllen vnd Ewigen Leben* (Munich: Printed by Nicolaus Heinrich, 1617);

Bessé, *Von dem wunderbarlichen, herrlichen vnd fürtrefflichen Pancket, welches Christus vnser Herr kurtz vor seinem End mit seinen Jüngern auff Erden gehalten: Jn acht Predigen auff die acht Tag in der heiligen Marterwochen gerichtet* (Munich: Printed by Nicolaus Heinrich, 1618);

Adriaen de Witte, *Newes zuuor vnerhörtes Closter- vnd Hofleben, je lenger je lieber: Sambt artlicher Beschreibung aller derselben Diener, Officier, Beambten, herrlichen Priuilegien vnd Hochheiten* (Munich: Printed by Nicolaus Heinrich, 1618).

Aegidius Albertinus was one of the most prolific, important, and successful writers of the German Counter Reformation. With his translations of works of Antonio de Guevara and with his pioneering 1615 translation of Mateo Alemán's *La Vida del Pícaro Guzmán de Alfarache* (1599) – the first picaresque novel rendered into German – Albertinus is recognized as the foremost translator of devotional and inspirational works from the *siglo de oro*, the Spanish literature of the sixteenth century. Although Albertinus began to write relatively late, at age thirty-four, his output was copious, averaging two titles per year from his first work in 1594 until his death in 1620. Of his approximately fifty-two works – there is still some doubt as to the precise number – Albertinus adapted twenty-two works from Spanish, six from French, and eleven from Latin and Italian sources. His influence on the religious thought of Hans Jacob Christoffel von Grimmelshausen was considerable.

Several ironies are evident in the life and writings of Albertinus. A native of the Netherlands, whose mother tongue was Dutch, he was a master of German style. Although foreign-born, he is remembered as the father of the German picaresque novel. A mildly misogynistic moralist, he was the head of a large and financially burdensome family. And although he never took religious orders, most of his writings might be characterized as collections of homilies and short sermons.

Concerning Albertinus's life, little is known of the years before he was appointed on 19 February 1593 to the position of secretary at the ducal court of William V, "the Pious," in Munich. His first work, *Deß Irrenden Ritters Raiß* (The Knight Errant's Journey), was a translation of an allegorical *Ritterroman* (knightly novel), *Le voyage du chevalier errant* (1557), by Jean de Cartigny. Albertinus's advancement at court was steady: in 1596 he became secretary of the Privy Council, and in 1604 he added to this position the duties of librarian to Duke Maximilian I; in 1618 he was named "Hof- und geistlicher Ratssekretär" (court and spiritual privy secretary).

Probably because of his complete mastery of German, scholarly doubts were expressed as late as 1932 about the author's Dutch origins. While no proof of these origins is available, early evidence includes the copperplate engraving of Albertinus executed ten years after his death by Lucas Killian: the Latin in the oval border surrounding the portrait states that Albertinus was born in Deventer. Albertinus himself says in prefaces to several of his works that German was not his native tongue. In his penultimate work, *Hiren schleifer* (Brain-Whetter, 1618), the last to be published during his lifetime, he refers to the difficulties he encountered in trying to unlearn his native tongue – presumably for the purpose of perfecting his writing style in German.

Judging from the strict and largely humorless moral tone of his oeuvre, from certain often-recurring tenets of faith expressed in his works, and from the encyclopedic knowledge revealed in them, one can surmise that in his youth Albertinus was subjected to the rigorous schooling of the Jesuits. This surmise is supported by his lifelong interest in the Society of Jesus. Albertinus expended a great deal of time and effort and exhibited deep dedication in his translations of the histories of two Jesuit missionary expeditions: Diego de Pantoja's *Histori und eigentliche beschreibung, erstlich was gestalt, vermittelst sonderbarer Hülff und Schickung deß Allmächtigen, dann auch der Ehrwürdigen Vätter der Societet Iesu gebrauchten Fleiß, und außgestandener Mühe, Arbeit und Gefahr, numehr und vor gar wenig Jahren hero, das Evangelium und Lehr Christi in dem grossen und gewaltigen Königreich China eingeführt, gepflantzt und geprediget wirdt* (History and Actual Description of How, a Few Short Years Ago, the Gospel and Teachings of Christ Were Introduced, Planted, and Preached in the Kingdom of China, through Great Diligence, Tribulations Overcome, Labor and Danger by the Reverend Fathers of the Society of Jesus, with the Aid and Providence of the Almighty) in 1608, and, from various sources, *Historische Relation: Was sich inn etlichen Jaren hero, im Königreich Iapon, so wol im geistals auch weltlichem Wesen, namhafftes begeben vnd zugetragen* (Historical Relation: Concerning the Notable Events Which Occurred a Few Years Ago in the Kingdom of Japan in Both the Spiritual and the Secular Spheres) in 1609. These works recount details of the ultimately unsuccessful attempts by the Jesuits to establish missionary footholds in China, Japan, and other Asian and African countries.

Scholars speculate that Albertinus's family fled religious persecution in Deventer between 1570 and 1580, a violent period of enforced introduction of the Reformation to the Netherlands. Albertinus may have lived for several years in Münster; another possibility is that he found his way to the southern Netherlands and thence to Spain before continuing on to Salzburg and finally settling in Munich.

In 1593 Albertinus married Maria Glöckler, the sister of the abbot of the cloister at Hohenaltaich. In 1602 Albertinus purchased a house on a Munich street that is variously referred to as Schäfflergasse, Schrammengässl, and Schäfflerstraße. He no doubt lived there with his family until his death on 9 March 1620, for court records exist relating to the disposal of the property by his widow in that year. It is also known that, with the duke's blessing and financial support, Albertinus journeyed to Rome in 1605 on matters pertaining to the Anger Cloisters.

In latinizing his name, Albertinus adhered to the practice common among the literati of the day. His Dutch name may have been Giles, or Jelle, Albertszoon. Despite the name by which he is known, and unlike his contemporaries, Albertinus did not write in Latin. Although by 1700 he had fallen into a long period of obscurity, the fact that his works were so popular during his lifetime and beyond – not only in Catholic areas but among Protestants as well – may be attributable to his practice of writing exclusively in the vernacular. A gifted, facile polyglot and a prolific writer, Albertinus frequently quotes from his sources in their original languages. With many of these sources, Albertinus appends German subtitles to the foreign-language titles that he has retained, as in his translation of Antonio de Guevara's *Institutiones Vitae Aulicae, oder HofSchul* (Institutions of Courtly Life; or, Court-School, 1600), or he makes up his own Latin-German titles, as in *Nosce te Ipsum: Oder, Kenn dich selbst* (Know Thyself, 1607), derived from a much longer Spanish work, *Monarchia mystica de la Iglesia* (1598), by Lorenzo de Zamora. As with his titles, Albertinus provides immediate "running" translations of the many foreign quotations in his texts. Exceptions to this practice are found in his twin hagiographic works, *Himlisch Frawenzimmer* (Saintly Women, 1611) and *Himmlische Cammerherrn* (Saintly Gentlemen, 1645), where only Latin verse accompanies and identifies the portraits of the saints.

Albertinus's influence on the German language of his day was considerable. Rochus Freiherr von Liliencron says that

> Albertinus schreibt nicht das Deutsch, welches Luther auf der Grundlage der sächsischen Kanzleisprache gebildet und für die gebildete Welt durchgesetzt hatte . . . sondern er schreibt Oberdeutsch. . . . Aber er schreibt dabei nicht etwa einen rohen Dialekt, sondern eine wenn auch nicht konsequent durchgeführte, so doch im ganzen wohlgebildete Schriftsprache. Man irrt schwerlich in der Annahme, daß dies mit Bewußtsein und Absicht betrieben worden sei; die Gegenreformation wollte auch äußerlich nicht in dem Sprachgewande der Reformation erscheinen.

> (Albertinus does not write the German that Luther had created for the educated on the basis of the language of the Saxon court . . . rather, he writes High German. . . . But in doing so he does not write in some raw dialect, but for the most part, if not with complete consistency, he writes an educated literary language. One would hardly err in the assumption that he did this consciously and intentionally; the Counter-Reformation did not wish to appear, even outwardly, in the linguistic garments of the Reformation.)

Karl von Reinhardstöttner comments: "Nun hat aber Albertinus für Bayern das spezielle Inter-

esse, daß seine Sprache ein treues Abbild der damals gesprochenen Mundart ist, und daß speziell der Münchener in ihr sofort sein heimatliches Idiom erkennt" (Albertinus is of special interest to Bavaria in that his language is a true picture of the dialect spoken then, and that the citizen of Munich immediately recognizes in it his native idiom). Albertinus's great popularity and his importance for the history of German literature lie in the fact that he wrote German at a time when almost all other scholars were writing in Latin.

Albertinus's style is, judged by the standard of his day, sober, serious, accessible, and eminently readable. He recognized that a readable style was an important weapon of communication in the Counter Reformation. His intended readers were, as he says on occasion, the educated middle-class citizens of Bavaria, not the scholar, the cleric, or the nobility, although these groups, too, were addressed in some of his writings.

Albertinus reveals himself in his writings to be deeply committed to Jesuit doctrine and a loyal soldier in the battle that the church was waging to recover its losses in property and members. His earnest, colloquial style is well suited to his purpose. His is not the pyrotechnic, neologistic style of the Lutheran satirist Johann Fischart, although echoes of the latter's "Worttrunkenheit" (word drunkenness) can be sensed in an occasional Albertinian sentence where synonymic adjectives, verbs, or nouns accumulate. While Albertinus has a predilection for lengthy and hypotactic sentences, the meaning of such sentences is clear and easily grasped. He is also capable of the dramatically succinct phrase. Albertinus's major fault may be his overgenerous use of Latin and latinate vocabulary. This stylistic element is noticeable on nearly every page, and it may have contributed to the author's having been largely forgotten by the beginning of the eighteenth century, when Latin began to lose its primacy as the required language of instruction in schools and universities.

In his *Zur Sprache des Aegidius Albertinus* (On the Language of Aegidius Albertinus, 1901), Gebhard Himmler deals at length with Albertinian orthography and syllabification. (His comments are based on Albertinus's *Lucifers Königreich und Seelengejaidt* [Lucifer's Kingdom and Soul-Hunt, 1616], but this work is representative in language and style of the author's oeuvre.) It can be difficult to distinguish Albertinus's orthography from the idiosyncratic spelling of typesetters and compositors, who tended to place considerations of type justification or a temporary scarcity of a letter in a font above the details of an author's manuscript. Nevertheless, certain consistent orthographic and dialect aspects of Albertinus's language and style can be observed. Monophthongs and diphthongs that are either archaic or belong to the Bavarian dialect are used frequently. They include *e* for modern *ö* (*leschen* [extinguish], *gewehnen* [accustom], *schweren* [swear]); *e* for modern *ä* (*verechtlichste* [most-despised], *erzehlte* [related], *underthenig* [subordinate]); *u* for modern *o* (*Wull* [wool], *Almusen* [alms]); *ai* for modern *ei* (*Verzaichnuß* [register], *zaigen* [show, indicate], *haist* [be named], *laider* [unfortunately]); *eu* for modern *ie* (*verdreust* [vexes], *fleuhet* [flees], *verleurt* [closes], *scheust* [shoots]); *eu* for modern *au* (*geseugt* [sucked, suckled], *weitleuffigkeit* [spaciousness, lengthiness]), *eu* for modern *ü* (*betreugt* [betrays]); *ö* for modern *e* (*Wöhr* [defense]); *üe* for modern *ü* (*hüeten* [defend], *süeß* [sweet], *müed* [tired], *Barfüesser* [barefoot monk]); *ue* for modern *u* (*Rueß* [soot], *Rueder* [rudder], *zuthuen* [do, be done], *zue Bueß* [as penance, do penance]); and *ie* for modern *ü* (*betrieglich* [deceptive, deceitful], *liege* [lie, falsehood]). Albertinus uses the diphthongs *ey, ay, ei,* and *ai* interchangeably, and the semivowels *h* and *y* both as consonants and as vowels: *h* for modern *g* (*zohen* [pulled]), *y* for modern *ie* (*schrye* [shouted]). Voiced and unvoiced consonants in initial and medial position are often used interchangeably, reflecting pronunciation in the Bavarian dialect: *p* for modern *b* (*Prunnen* [fountain], *Pueckel* [hunchback]); *b* for modern *p* (*Babst* [pope], *butzen* [polish], *brangen* [glitter]); *d* for modern *t* (*undüchtig* [inept], *undertrucken* [oppress]); and *t* for modern *d* (*Tach* [roof], *Trachen* [dragon], *undertrucken*).

Although they were not uncommon in Albertinus's time, certain prefixes and suffixes deriving from Upper Bavarian are noteworthy insofar as they deviate from standard German. Frequently the suffixes *-heit* and *-keit* are interchanged, as in *Dapferheit* (courage). The forms *ig, igk,* and *g* variously occur in spellings such as *gemeinglich, gemeingklich, gemeiniglich,* and *gemainigklich* (commonly). Albertinus always uses the suffix *-nuß,* as in *Gefaengnuß* (prison) and *Verzaichnuß,* in lieu of the standard *-nis.* The prefix *be-* is used occasionally in place of the more common *ge-,* as in *benügen* (suffice) and *beschehen* (happen). The superlative suffix *-st* occurs also as *-ist* and *-est,* as in *niederigiste* (lowest) and *allerhöcheste* (highest of all). Almost without exception the prefix *vor-* is written *für-,* as in *fürnemblich* (chiefly, especially), *fürsicht* (foresight, caution) and *herfürgehet* (proceed, emerge from). Albertinus also commonly uses such Upper Bavarian words as *Natter* (viper), *Lefftzen* (lips), *Butzen* (glowing coals), *greinen* (weep), *Klumse* (hole, tear), *Luck* (lid) and *Almusen.*

Albertinus often neglects to distinguish between the present and imperfect tenses of weak verbs, a common practice at that time – for example, *sagt* (says) and *sagte* (said) have the same meaning. At times he uses a singular verb with multiple subjects. The older, fuller forms of the verb in the third-person singular, such as *saget* or *wehret* (defends, defended), will not confuse readers familiar with the period. The *zu* (to) of dependent infinitives and infinitive phrases is attached to the verb, as with *zuempfinden* (to sense, to feel). Past participles of some strong verbs appear with weak forms, as in *erhebt* (raised), *angerufft* (called to) and *verderbt* (ruined). The past participle of *verderben* is, however, when used adjectivally, rendered *verdorben.* Albertinus also uses archaisms and unusual phrases that were not coined by him. Among them are *sambt were es* (as if it were); *es ist nit ohne, daß* (nevertheless); *ob nun wol dem allem also* (be that as it may); *weder wann* (even if); and *sintemal* or *seytemal* (since, as). A passage from *Hiren schleifer* illustrates his highly readable and compelling style:

Ob aber schon dem allem also, vnd die Seel das allerköstlichste Kleinot im Menschen ist, so wirdt sie doch vilmals vbel vnnd spöttlich gehalten vnd verwahrlost. Dann wann wir vns in der Gefahr deß Schiffbruchs vnnd deß Vngewitters befinden, so lauffen wir geschwindt zu Gott, betten vnnd verloben sonderbare Walfahrten: Wann vns ein Fieber, ein Widerwertigkeit, Vnglück vnd verlust der zeitlichen Guter zustehet, so seufftzen, achetzen, heulen, klagen vnd wainen wir, wann vns nur die Fußsolen oder Kopff oder der Bauch wehe thut, so trawret die seel, vnd hat ein mitleiden: man schicket geschwind vmb den *Medicum* oder Artzten, der muß vns sirupiren, purgiren vnnd zur Ader lassen. Wann vns ein Kind stirbt so trawren vnd bekümmern wir vns schier zu todt. Aber wann die Seel kranck wird, vnd durch ein todsünd stirbt, so thun wir gar nichts, oder aber sehr langsam vnd schläfferig darzu, damit ihr geholffen werde.

(Be that as it may, the soul is the most precious jewel of all in mankind, yet it is often neglected, ill considered and ridiculed, for when we find ourselves in danger of shipwreck and storm, we run quickly to God, pray and promise special pilgrimages. When we suffer from fever, from anything disgusting, from misfortunes and the loss of our worldly goods, we sigh, complain, howl, and weep. If our feet, head, or stomach pain us, the soul is saddened and has sympathy. One quickly sends for the physician or doctor, who must serve us a treacly concoction, purge and bleed us. If a child of ours dies, we mourn and complain to the heavens. But if the soul sicken and die in mortal sin, then we do nothing at all or react very slowly and sleepily, in order that it [the soul] be given aid.)

While Albertinus aimed at a broad public, "allen Catholischen Christen Teutscher Nation zum besten" (for the good of Catholic Christians of the German Nation"), an occasional work was directed at a specific group such as courtiers, noblemen, or novitiates. To the former two he directed his translations of Antonio de Guevara's *Der Fürsten und Potentaten Sterbkunst* (Princes' and Potentates' Art of Dying, 1599), Louis de Malvenda's *Spiegel eines Christlichen Fürsten* (Mirror of a Christian Prince, 1604) and Guevara's *Institutiones Vitae Aulicae, oder HofSchul.* To novitiates he directed his translations of Juan de la Cerda's *Paedia Religiosorum* (Schools for the Religious, 1605), Alonso de Orozco's *Hortus Sacer* (Sacred Garden, 1605) and the hagiographical works *Himlisch Frawenzimmer* and *Himmlische Cammerherrn.* Albertinus was eminently successful in judging his audience, for many of his works enjoyed multiple editions during his lifetime and well beyond. An edition of *Hiren schleifer* that appeared in 1758, nearly 140 years after his death, signaled a minor revival of interest in an author who had been in eclipse since around 1700.

By today's standards, and in today's terminology, Albertinus would be considered a workaholic. In addition to his considerable professional duties as a highly placed court official in increasingly prestigious capacities, he wrote at a feverish pace. So successful was he in his secretarial positions at court, his literary pursuits, and his ability to win the favor of wealthy and influential patrons by dedicating his works to them that he incurred the envy of other high court officials. Accused of neglecting his official duties because of "unfleis und unbesonnenheit" (lack of industry and consideration), he defended himself in a letter to Duke Maximilian I dated 1614 – apparently successfully, for he continued both writing and serving at court until his death. In the letter he says that the accusation is "nur ein pur lautere malevolentz unnd von denen herrüret, die mich gern vorlengst ruinirt hetten" (nought but pure malevolence stirred up by those who have long wished my ruin) and tells the duke: "Sie wollen ihnen hinfüran nit glauben, noch auch sich so leichtlich zu so scharpfen verweisen ... sonnder mich zuvor mit meiner verantwortung vernemen und mir meine delatores vor augen stellen laßen" (You will not wish to believe them nor to be moved easily to such sharp reproaches ... but rather will desire to hear my response and to let me confront my detractors). Albertinus's prolific authorship was motivated by his fervent and proselytizing Christianity. He intended always to caution, warn, and inspire his readers to rededicate them-

Title page for Albertinus's only emblem book

selves to Christian living; to instruct them in pious living; to win back to the Catholic Church those who had been converted to Lutheranism and other Protestant confessions; and to bring backsliders to a state of grace. A second, more mundane motivation for Albertinus's writing was his need to lighten the financial burden of his large family: he augmented his income by obtaining favor from wealthy or noble patrons through the time-honored practice of dedicating his books to them. A third reason may simply have been his love of knowledge, books, and publishing. In 1618 he suffered an illness that he did not expect to survive; in his introduction to *Hiren schleifer* he poignantly refers to this work as "den Colophonem meiner Arbeit" (the colophon of all my work). He was partly correct in this supposition, for *Hiren schleifer* was, indeed, his last work to be published during his lifetime; his final work, *Himmlische Cammerherrn,* was published posthumously. (As there has been no research on the stylistics involved either in this or other posthumously expanded versions of his works, scholars are in doubt concerning whether Albertinus was the author of *Himmlische Cammerherrn* or whether his publisher of many years, Nicolaus Heinrich, wrote or commissioned the work to capitalize on Albertinus's popularity. The practice of adding to a popular work after its author's death was common. Albertinus's *Himlisch Frawenzimmer,* which in the first edition of 1611 comprised fifty-two chapters, was expanded to more than eighty in the posthumous edition of 1675.)

Guillaume van Gemert has divided Albertinus's writings into four broad groups. The "speculum" (mirror) group teaches and informs directly, without exempla. A mirror is, so to speak, held up to the readers, wherein they see reflected both the good and the evil of which humankind is capable. This category includes *Spiegel eines Christlichen Fürsten* and the translation of Cerda's *Weiblicher Lustgarten* (Female Pleasure Grounds, 1605). The second category is "Exempelschriften," works that teach by exempla, through the depiction of historic events and biographies, both true and invented, as in Petrus Berchorius's *Der Welt Tummel: und Schawplatz* (The World's Playground and Theater, 1612), the picaresque *Gusman von Alfarche,* and the translation of Pedro Sanchez's *Das Buch Vom Reich Gottes* (Book of the Empire of God, 1609). "Trost- und Sterbebücher" (instructional books of consolation), which deal in part with how to die well in the grace of the Lord, constitute the third category, a small one. In these works moral and ascetic tenets are presented for the edification and moral improvement of the reader. Here are to be found such works as the translation of Ambrogio Frigerio's *Das wunderbarliche Leben, hohe vnd unerhörte Wunderwerck deß H. Nicolai von Tolentin, und der seligen Jungkfrawen Clarae von Montefalco, beyde der Einsidler S. Augustini Ordens* (The Miraculous Life, Great and Unprecedented Miracles of Saint Nicolas of Tolentin and the Blessed Virgin Clara of Montefalco, Both of the Anchorite Order of Saint Augustine, 1611) and the translation of Pedro de Medina's *Das Buech der Wahrheit* (The Book of Truth, 1603), as well as the hagiographical works. The fourth group is also a small one. While exhibiting elements of the other three groups, the works in this category can be considered primarily a compendium of homilies or sermons. Although he never took religious orders, Al-

bertinus was by nature a proselytizer. In this group is included his unique *Hiren schleifer,* the only product of his pen purporting to be an Emblembuch (book of emblems). Albertinus's writings are didactic, not dramatic or epic, so – except for the picaresque *Der Landtstörtzer* (The Vagabond, 1615) – they do not contain what might be called a narrative story line. Although those rare works in which his name appears as author rather than as translator cannot be viewed as emanating from the mind of a deep or original thinker, Albertinus, an eclectic writer par excellence, may be considered a creatively gifted borrower. He had a finely honed gift for gathering materials from various sources and turning them into something uniquely his own.

The work to which Albertinus owes much of his lasting fame in German literary history came toward the end of his life with *Der Landtstörtzer,* his genial adaptation of Alemán's great picaresque novel *La Vida del Pícaro Guzmán de Alfarache.* Albertinus's work is not merely a *Verteutschung* (germanization) of Alemán's novel but is, as he says on the title page, "theils auß dem Spanischen verteutscht, theils gemehrt vnd gebessert" (partly translated into German from the Spanish, partly expanded on and improved). In addition to germanizing the hero's name from Guzmán de Alfarache to Gusman von Alfarche, Albertinus alters the Spanish novel in many ways, adding elements he deems useful and omitting those he considers inimical to his purposes: for example, he suppresses any criticism of the Catholic Church. He uses episodes from only the first part of the original and adds scenes from Juan Marti's continuation of Alemán's novel. He transforms the Spanish picaro into a German vagabond, thief, servant, and rogue who operates in a German culture. He has changed Alemán's complex work into a dualistic allegory of sin and of mercy, an erring pilgrim's progress, what Hans Gerd Rötzer calls an allegorical novel of penitence. Its influence on Grimmelshausen's great novel *Der abenteuerliche Simplicissimus Teutsch* (The Adventurous Simplicissimus German, 1699) is clear.

Albertinus's religious thought is derivative; much of his source material is to be found in Vincent de Beauvais's thirteenth-century compendium *Speculum naturale, doctrinale, morale et historicum* (Natural, Doctrinal, Moral and Historical Mirror, circa 1255) and in the *Livre du Trésor* (circa 1265) by Vincent's contemporary, Brunetto Latini. Jesuitical asceticism and quietism characterize Albertinus's religious thought. His eclecticism is not heretical in any way; he follows in the traditions and history of the church, which have been those of accommodation and compromise. Albertinus advocated, as the best means by which the sinful Christian might obtain grace, complete withdrawal from the world, preferably within cloistered walls. Christians are exhorted to withdraw from the temptations of secular life to practice the "Exercitium Spirituale," that rigorous, never-ceasing exercising of mind and soul demanded by Saint Ignatius Loyola. Mixed with this Jesuitical asceticism that emphasizes complete suppression, castigation, and denial of the flesh and its appetites is the concept of quietism, with its concommitant inward-turning mysticism and its emphasis on the "unio mistica," a personal, individual relationship with the deity. Quietism, however, includes certain attitudes not to be found in Jesuit thought: Albertinus views God as a loving and gracious Father more than as a jealous deity who is quick to exact vengeance, and he conceives of sin as a dishonoring and wounding of God the Father more than as an abomination. One tenet of quietism is the idea that beauty is wedded to virtue, a viewpoint later espoused by Johann Wolfgang von Goethe: a person's physical countenance reflects his or her inner goodness – a "schöne Seele" (beautiful soul) housed in a lovely body. Conversely, sinfulness is expressed by an ugly countenance.

In an age of misogyny, which found one of its expressions in the hunting down and executing of thousands of women identified as witches (few warlocks – male "witches" – were executed), Albertinus sometimes displays a surprisingly gentle, if not precisely modern, attitude toward women. In *Hiren schleifer* he distinguishes, for example, varying degrees of sinfulness in young women, particularly in regard to virginity or the lack thereof: "Underschiedliche Jungfrawen werden gefunden, die ersten seyn Jungfrawen am Leib vnnd im Gemüt, welche dermassen behutsam in geberden seyn, dass sie der Männer Seelen nit an sich ziehen, noch auch jhrer begeren, vnd dergleichen Jungfrawen werden billich vor andern geehrt" (Various kinds of virgins are to be found. The first are virgins both of body and of mind. They are so careful in their deportment that they neither entice men's spirits nor have any lustful desire for men. Such virgins are justly honored above other virgins). He honors next those who are pure in spirit but have been defiled against their will; although they are considered by society to be sullied and violated, they are unspoiled in the eyes of God. The third category comprises those who are virginal in body only, having lacked the opportunity to realize their illicit desires. These are the virgins who are "wider ihrer willen Jungfrawen: solche Jungfrawen seind gleichwol vor den Men-

schen Jungfrawen, aber nit vor Gott, dann die reinigkeit dess Leibs hillft wenig, wofern das Gemüt vnrein vnd beflekt ist" (virgins against their wills; such virgins are pure in the sight of man but not before God, for purity of the body is of little avail insofar as the mind is impure and stained). Albertinus directs scorn at impure women who attempt to retain an undeserved reputation of innocence.

In *Himlisch Frawenzimmer,* a recounting of the lives and deeds of women, both historical and legendary, who have attained sainthood, Albertinus presents a hierarchy of virtue. Foremost in sanctity are, in Albertinus's view, those who are mentioned in the New Testament: Mary, Anna, Elisabeth, Sarah, and Mary Magdalene. The next highest category comprises those who, like Saint Theodora and Saint Dympna, have elected to suffer martyrdom rather than submit to acts of unchastity. The third group consists of those, such as Saint Anastasia of Rome, who, in dedication to God, preserved their chastity even in marriage. Saints who were wives, widows, and mothers and suffered martyrdom are placed on a somewhat lower level because they no longer retain the laurel of chastity. Albertinus reveres, next, those women of high birth who established cloisters, lived exemplary lives, and performed miracles. Lowest among the blessed are – with the exception of Mary Magdalene – those who, like Saint Afra of Augsburg, turned from a life of prostitution to Christianity, thereafter leading exemplary lives or suffering martyrdom.

One also encounters in Albertinus, who does not attempt to reconcile diverse, even contradictory ideas, a theme that contrasts strongly with quietism: that of *nosce te ipsum* (know thyself). Albertinus used this phrase as the title of his 1607 condensation of Zamora's devotional work *Monarquia mistica de la iglesia.* This *nosce te ipsum* is not the familiar Greek anthropocentric concept that was carved above the portal of the temple at Delphi. It expresses, rather, the medieval insistence that human beings be ever mindful that they are vile sinners, conceived in iniquity and born in sin, and that they may gain grace through acts of penance: by self-castigation and denying their mortal flesh. Albertinus's exhortation to know oneself is to realize that one was conceived in sin, was born in iniquity, and possesses a body that is a vile and repulsive thing, a stinking cadaver, fit only to be food for worms.

Bibliographies:

Manfred Kremer, "Zur Aegidius Albertinus-Bibliographie," *Argenis: Zeitschrift für Mittlere Deutsche Literatur,* 2, no. 1–4 (1978): 309–315;

Gerhard Dünnhaupt, *Personalbibliographien zu den Drucken des Barock,* volume 9, part 1 (Stuttgart: Hiersemann, 1991), pp. 191–238.

References:

Käte Fuchs, *Die Religiosität des Johann Jakob Christoffel von Grimmelshausen,* Palaestra, no. 202 (Leipzig: Mayer & Müller, 1935);

Guillaume van Gemert, "Übersetzung und Kompilation im Dienste der Katholischen Reformbewegung: Zum Literaturprogramm des Aegidius Albertinus (1560–1620)," *Daphnis: Zeitschrift für Mittlere Deutsche Literatur,* 8, no. 3/4 (1979): 123–142;

Gemert, *Die Werke des Aegidius Albertinus (1560–1620)* (Amsterdam: APA-Holland University Press, 1979);

Gebhard Himmler, *Zur Sprache des Aegidius Albertinus: Beiträge zur Geschichte der Münchener Literatur- und Drucksprache am Beginn des 17. Jahrhunderts. I. Teil* (Munich: Programm der K. Wilhelmsgymnasium, 1902);

Himmler, *Zur Sprache des Aegidius Albertinus. II. Teil* (Passau: Program des K. humanistischen Gymnasiums, 1903);

Gerhart Hoffmeister, "Das Spanische Modell: Aleman's *Guzman de Alfarache* und die Albertinische Bearbeitung," in *Chloe Beihefte zum Daphnis,* volume 5: *Der deutsche Schelmenroman im Europäischen Kontext: Rezeption, Interpretation, Bibliographie,* edited by Hoffmeister (Amsterdam: Rodopi, 1987), pp. 29–48;

Hoffmeister, ed., *German Baroque Literature,* (New York: Ungar, 1983), pp. 80–85;

Lawrence S. Larsen, *Aegidius Albertinus's "Hirnschleiffer": Kritische Ausgabe* (Stuttgart: Hiersemann, 1977);

Larsen, "A Critical Edition and an Appreciation of Aegidius Albertinus's Emblematic Work 'Hirnscheleiffer,'" dissertation, University of Texas at Austin, 1971;

Hans Pörnbacher, *Die Literatur des Barock* (Munich: Süddeutscher Verlag, 1986), pp. 11–19;

Karl von Reinhardtstöttner, "Aegidius Albertinus, der Vater des deutschen Schelmenromans," *Jahrbuch für Münchener Geschichte,* 2 (1888): 13–86;

Hans Gerd Rötzer, *Picaro – Landstörtzer – Simplicius* (Darmstadt: Wissenschaftliche Buchgesellschaft, 1972);

Herbert Walz, *Der Moralist im Dienste des Hofes: Eine vergleichende Studie zu der Lehrdichtung von Antonio de Guevara und Aegidius Albertinus* (Frankfurt am Main, Bern & New York: Peter Lang, 1984).

Johann Valentin Andreae

(17 August 1586 – 27 June 1654)

Stanley W. Beeler
University of Calgary

BOOKS: *Panegyricvs, De Joh. Schermario, Ivreconsvlto, et Patritio Ulmensi: Ad Senatvm Cives Vlmenses* (Tübingen: Printed by Johann Alexander Cellius, 1609);

Geistliche Gemähl (Tübingen, 1612);

Allgemeine vnd General Reformation, der gantzen weiten Welt. Beneben der Fama Fraternitatis, deß Löblichen Ordens des Rosenkreutzes, an alle Gelehrte vnd Häupter Europae geschrieben, anonymous (Cassel: Printed by Wilhelm Wessel, 1614);

Collectaneorvm Mathematicorvm Decades XI. Centum & decem tabulis aeneis exhibitae (Tübingen: Printed by Johann Alexander Cellius, 1614);

Doctrinae Christianae Summa: Ex Magni et Celeberrimi Theologi, Matthiæ Hefenrefferi, Locis communibus contracta (Tübingen: Printed by Johann Alexander Cellius, 1614);

Fama Fraternitatis R. C.: Das ist, Gerücht der Brüderschafft des Hochlöblichen Ordens R. C. An alle Gelehrte vnd Häupter Europae (Cassel: Wilhelm Wessel, 1615);

Fama Fraternitatis oder Entdeckung der Brüderschafft deß löblichen Ordens deß RosenCreutzes, beneben der Confession oder Bekanntnis derselben Fraternitet, an alle Gelehrte und Häupter in Europa geschrieben (Danzig: Printed by Andreas Hünefeld, 1615) – includes "Confessio Fraternitatis";

Hercvlis Christiani Lvctæ XXIV, anonymous (Strasbourg: Published by Lazarus Zetzner, 1615);

Sendschreiben oder Einfältige Antwort an die Hocherleuchte Brüderschafft deß hochöblichen Ordens deß RosenCreutzes (Frankfurt am Main: Johann Bringer, 1615);

Vom Besten vnd Edelsten Beruff. Des wahren Dienst Gottes wider der Welt verkehrtes vnd vnbesonnenes Vrtheil, anonymous (Strasbourg: Lazarus Zetzner, 1615);

De Christiani Cosmoxeni Genitvra, Ivdicivm, by Andreae and Matthias Haffenreffer (Montbéliard: Printed by Jacob Foillet, 1615);

Johann Valentin Andreae at age sixty-two

Theca Gladii Spiritvs, anonymous (Strasbourg: Printed by Conrad Scher, published by Lazarus Zetzner, 1615);

Tvrbo, Sive Moleste et Frvstra per Cuncta Divagans. Ingenivm, anonymous (Strasbourg, 1616);

Chymische Hochzeit: Christiani Rosencreutz. Anno 1459, anonymous (Strasbourg: Printed by Conrad

Scher, published by Lazarus Zetzner, 1616);
translated by E. Foxcroft as *The Hermetick Romance; or, The Chymical Wedding* (London: A. Sowle, 1690);

Invitatio Fraternitatis Christi (Strasbourg: Lazarus Zetzner, 1617);

Menippus sive dialogorum satyricorum centuria (Strasbourg, 1617);

Veri Christianismi solidaeque Philosophiae libertas (Strasbourg: Lazarus Zetzner, 1618);

Invitationis ad fraternitatem Christi pars altera (Strasbourg: Lazarus Zetzner, 1618);

Peregrini in Patria Errores, anonymous (Strasbourg: Lazarus Zetzner's heirs, 1618);

Civis Christianus, sive Peregrini Quondam errantis restitutiones (Strasbourg: Lazarus Zetzner's heirs, 1619);

Memorialia, Benevolentium Honori, Amori et Condolentiae (Strasbourg: Lazarus Zetzner's heirs, 1619);

Mythologia christiana (Strasbourg: Lazarus Zetzner's heirs, 1619);

Turris Babel sive Judiciorum de Fraternitate Rosaceae Crusis Chaos, anonymous (Strasbourg: Lazarus Zetzner's heirs, 1619);

Republicæ Christianopolitanæ Descriptio, anonymous (Strasbourg: Lazarus Zetzner's heirs, 1619); translated by F. Emil Held as *Christianopolis: An Ideal State of the 17th Century* (New York: Oxford University Press, 1916);

Practica Leonis Viridis, das ist, Der Rechte Wahre Fussteig zu dem Königlichen HochzeitSaal F.C.R., anonymous (Frankfurt an der Oder: Thieme, 1619);

Die Christenburger Schlacht (Strasbourg: Lazarus Zetzner's heirs, 1620);

De Curiositatis Pernicie Syntagma ad singularitatis Studiosos (Stuttgart: Printed by Johann Weyrich Rösslin, 1620);

Christiani amoris dextera porrecta (Tübingen, 1620); translated by John Hall as *The Right Hand of Christian Love Offered* (Cambridge, 1647);

Christliche Evangelische Kinder-Lehr (Tübingen, 1621);

Ehrenrici Hohenfelderi Equitis Austrij, Flos Virtvtvm (Strasbourg: Lazarus Zetzner's heirs, 1623);

Veritatis lacrymae sive Euphormionis Lusinini continuatio, as Alitophilus (N.p., 1625);

Christenburg, das ist: Ein schön geistlich Gedicht (Freiburg, 1626);

Christliche Leichpredig, bey der Begräbnus, deß Weilund Ehrwürdigen, Hochgelehrten Herren, Pavli Rvckheri, Fürstlichen Württembergischen Raths vnd Prälaten deß Closters Hirsaw, Welcher den 9. Tag Januarij . . . entschlaffen, vnd den folgenden 12. . . . bestattet worden (Tübingen: Printed by Dietrich Werlin, 1627);

Peregrinatio Ecclesiae. Das ist: Biblische Kirchen-Historien (Strasbourg: Lazarus Zetzner's heirs, 1628);

Veræ Unionis in Christi Jesu Specimen, Selectißimis ac Probatissimis Amicis Sacrum (Nuremberg, 1628);

Fama Andreana Reflorescens, sive Jacobi Andreae Waiblingensis Theol. Doctoris. Vitae, Funeris, Scriptorum, eregrinationum, et Progeniei (Strasbourg: Printed by Johann Repp, 1630);

Ecclesia militans das ist Kurtze Kirchen Hystori. von den H. Aposteln an. biß auff gegenwartige Zeit (Strasbourg: Lazarus Zetzner's heirs, 1630);

Ein Kinder-Spil auff das 1630. Jar, von viertzehn Personen. Nemlich: Der Jungfrauen Maria vnd jhrem ChristKindlein (Nuremberg: Caspar Fuld, 1630);

Verzeichnuß wie in Anno 1630. die Aempter in Calw besetzet gewesen (Strasbourg, 1630);

Duæ Orationes Funebres De Vita et Obitu: . . . Erasmi Grüningeri (Tübingen: Printed by Theodor Werlin, 1632);

Das Leben, Lehr und Leiden Christi. Sambt Summarischem Lauff der Christlichen Kirchen. Auch andern geistlichen Stücken. Zu einer Kinderkurtzweil zugericht (Strasbourg: Printed by Johann Repp, 1632);

Johannis Valentini Andreæ in Bene Meritos Gratitudo (Strasbourg: Lazarus Zetzner's heirs, 1633);

Opuscula aliquot de Restitutione Reipub: Christianae in Germania, occasione temporum istorum huc collecta (Nuremberg: Printed by Wolfgang Endter, 1633);

Klaglied, vber der Stadt Calw laidigem Vntergang (Strasbourg, 1635);

Threni Calvensis, Quibus Urbis Calvæ Wirtembrgicæ Bustum, Sors Præsens Lamentabilis et Innocentia Expressa (Strasbourg: Lazarus Zetzner's heirs, 1635);

Sol Veritatis sive Religionis Christianæ Certitudo (Tübingen: Printed by Philibert Brunn, 1641);

Harmonia Vitæ Jesu Christi, Theantropi (Tübingen: Printed by Philibert Brunn, 1641);

Arca Noha sive Domus Dei in Hoc Mundi Pelago Fluctuantis. Oeconomia (Tübingen: Printed by Philibert Brunn, 1641);

Oculus eruditis sive rerum universitatis compendiosa contemplatio (Tübingen, 1642);

Rei Christianæ et Literariæ Subsidia (Tübingen: Printed by Philibert Brunn, 1642);

Amicorum singularium classimorum funera (Lüneburg: Johann & Heinrich Stern, 1642);

Honor Doctoralis Theologicus (Tübingen: Printed by Philibert Brunn, 1642);

In natalem augustum Augusti Ducis Brunovicens (N.p., 1643);

Virgae Divinae Urbi Calvæ Wirtemberg (Stuttgart: Printed by Johann Weyrich Rößlin, 1643);

Deo Triuno opt. max. quod Augustam . . . in avitam regiam Guelpherbütum . . . restituerit (N.p., 1643);

Florentissimi ingenii . . . Anthonio Ulrico Brunovicensi . . . gratulatur (N.p., 1643);

Augustus Principis Exemplum. In Plausum natalis sexagesimi sexti felicissimi Expositus (Stuttgart: Printed by Rudolph Kautt, 1644);

Johannis Cunradi Goebelii in Augusta Vindelic: Ecclesia Senioris benè meriti Theologi laudati Vita in Exemplum exposita (Stuttgart: Printed by Johann Weyrich Rösslin, 1644);

Johan: Valentin Andreae, T. D. Vnd Agnes Elisabeth, geborner Grüningerin. Eheleut, GeschlechtRegister (Stuttgart: Printed by Johann Weyrich Rösslin, 1644);

Johannes Sauberti Theologi, Umbra Delineata (Stuttgart: Matthias Kautt, 1647);

Theophilus, Sive de Christiana Religione sanctius colenda, Vita temperantius instituenda, Et Literatura rationabilius Consilium (Stuttgart: Printed by Matthias Kautt, 1649);

Seleniana Augustalia (Ulm: Balthasar Kühn, 1649);

Theologi Vita Expositore Leui Sutoria (Lüneburg: Johann & Heinrich Stern, 1649);

Sereniss. Domus Augustae Selenianae Princip. Juventutis Utriusque Sexus Pietatis, Eruditionis, Comitatisque Exemplum sine pari in perfectae Educationis et Institutionis normam expositium (Ulm: Balthasar Kühn, 1654);

Vita ab ipso conscripta (Winterthur: Steiner, 1799); translated by David Christoph Seybold as *Selbstbiographie* (Winterthur: Steiner, 1799).

OTHER: Johann Arndt, *Christianismvs genuinus,* commentary by Andreae (Strasbourg: Printed by Theodosius Glaser, published by Paul Ledertz, 1615);

Geistliche Kurtzweil: Zu Ergetzlichkeit einfältiger Christen mitgetheilt, edited by Andreae (Strasbourg: Lazarus Zetzner's heirs, 1619);

Justus Lipsius, *Admiranda Oder Wundergeschichten, Von der vnaußsprächlichen Macht, Herrlich: vnd Großmächtigkeit der Statt Rom, und Römischen Monarchey,* translated by Andreae (Strasbourg: Lazarus Zetzner's heirs, 1620);

Christoph Vischer, *Kinder-Postill,* edited by Andreae (Strasbourg, 1626);

Guillaume de Saluste, Chevalier du Bartas, *Triumph deß Glaubens in hoch Teutsch gebracht,* translated by Andreae (Strasbourg, 1627);

Teutsche Handbibel, nach D. Luthers Uebersezung, edited by Andreae (Tübingen: Eberhard Wild, 1627);

Juan Luis Vives, *Zwey Bücher Iohannis Lodovici Vivis Valentini. Welche in sich begreiffen, wie man solle die Armen vnderhalten,* translated by Andreae (Durlach: Senfft, 1627);

Lucas Osiander the Elder, *Kurtze Kirchen-Historia,* edited by Andreae and Johann Bernhard Wagner (Strasbourg: Lazarus Zetzner's heirs, 1630);

Die Augspurgische Confession auff das einfältigste in ein Kinderspiel gebracht, adapted by Andreae (Strasbourg, 1631);

Johannes Saubert, *Zuchtbüchlein der Evangelischen Kirchen,* foreword by Andreae (Nuremberg: Wolfgang Endter the Elder, 1633);

Cynosura oeconomiae ecclesiasticae Wirtembergicae: oder: Summarischer Extract deren in dem Herzogthum Würtemburg zu Erhaltung Evangelischer Kirchenzucht und Ordnungen nach ausgeschriebener Hochfürstlichen Rescripten, Decreten und Resolutionen, edited by Andreae (Stuttgart: Printed by Johann Weyrich Rösslin, 1639);

Michael Maestlin, *Sinoptica Chronologia,* edited by Andreae (Tübingen: Printed by Philibert Brunn, 1642);

Teutsche Bibel, edited by Andreae (Lüneburg: Johann & Heinrich Stern, 1653).

One of the most intriguing literary figures of baroque Germany is the Lutheran theologian, utopian, and mystic writer Johann Valentin Andreae. Andreae is known not only for the substantial corpus of his acknowledged works but also for anonymous works that have been attributed to him. Because he admitted authorship of *Chymische Hochzeit: Christiani Rosencreutz* (1616; translated as *The Hermetick Romance,* 1690), many believe that he was also the author of the *Fama Fraternitatis* (1615) and the "Confessio Fraternitatis" (1615). These three texts are collectively called the *Rosencreutzer Schriften* (Rosicrucian Writings) and form the foundation for a literary tradition, as well as for a fraternal organization that is still active. Andreae's *Reipublicæ Christianopolitanæ Descriptio* (1619; translated as *Christianopolis,* 1916) is an important example of utopian literature with far-reaching literary and social effects. His writings on theological subjects are of great significance in the history of the Lutheran Church, and many consider Andreae's work influential in the development of German Pietism.

Andreae was born in the small town of Herrenburg in Württemberg on 17 August 1586.

His grandfather, Jakob Andreae, the rector of the University of Tübingen, was a signatory of the Formula of Concord in 1580. This document was the first official statement of the Lutheran religion and was highly significant in the further development of that faith. At the time of Andreae's birth his father, Johannes, was pastor of the Herrenburg church. Andreae's mother was Maria Andreae, née Moser.

In 1601 Johannes Andreae died of dropsy at the age of forty-seven, forcing Maria Andreae to support her family of seven by serving as a court apothecary in Tübingen. It may have been this early contact with seventeenth-century chemistry that later inspired Johann Valentin Andreae to write on the subject of alchemy; his father had also been noted for a weakness for alchemical charlatans. During the family's journey to Tübingen in midwinter, Andreae fell under the wagon while running to keep warm and was permanently scarred.

Andreae demonstrated an early interest in such diverse subjects as mathematics, mechanics, painting, music, and languages. He received his baccalaureate from the University of Tübingen on 13 April 1603 and, two years later, the master of arts. The detailed notes in Andreae's autobiography (1799) concerning his teachers at Tübingen have fueled speculation concerning the possibility of a clandestine mystical movement at the university: commentators who believe that Andreae was involved in the production of *Fama Fraternitatus* and "Confessio Fraternitatis" maintain that he was involved with a circle of professors and students interested in mystical theology.

Andreae's initial literary efforts were dramas. Between 1602 and 1605 he wrote two plays, *Esther* and *Hyacinth,* comedies based on his observations of the efforts of traveling English actors. These plays have not survived. During this period he also wrote *Chymische Hochzeit* and perhaps the other two original Rosicrucian texts. One argument against Andreae's authorship of all three works is that the texts are by no means consistent in theme or literary form. The first, *Fama Fraternitatis,* deals with the journey to the Middle East, during the fifteenth century, of a character known only as C. R. It details his creation of a secret society dedicated to the improvement of the lot of humanity using the alchemical knowledge that he brought back from his wanderings. The tale ends with the discovery of C. R.'s tomb more than a hundred years after his death. The tomb is filled with wonders and is illuminated by a permanent artificial light. This marvelous tomb is a literary topos that is still present in fiction about the Rosicrucian Society in the twentieth century. The "Confessio

Fraternitatis" seems to be primarily concerned with the affirmation of the essentially Protestant character of the Rosicrucian Society, which was at this point, as far as is known, still a literary fiction. The "Confessio" is most notable for a passage that has given rise to a great deal of confusion concerning the Rosicrucian myths: "Wehre es nicht ein köstlich Ding, daß du köndtest alle Stunde also leben als wenn du von Anfang der Welt bißher gelebet hettest, und noch ferner biß ans Ende derselben leben soltest?" (Would it not be precious if you could live each hour as if you had lived from the beginning of the world and further as if you would live until the end of it?). Although this text is phrased in the subjunctive and seems to be advocating a philosophical attitude toward life, it has been interpreted as holding forth to the members of the Rosicrucian Society the promise of eternal life in a physical body. This attitude became so pervasive that much of the later literature concerning the Rosicrucians considers this to be the most important element of the myth.

The third work of the series, *Chymische Hochzeit: Christiani Rosencreutz,* is the only one of the three texts Andreae acknowledged as his work. The character C. R. becomes Christian Rosencreutz and presents a first-person narrative of his experiences at an allegorical wedding ceremony. Unlike the two earlier Rosicrucian texts, *Chymische Hochzeit* does not have the flavor of a manifesto but has the form and structure of a novel. It begins with Rosencreutz receiving an invitation to a royal wedding from an angel-like figure. He journeys to a castle, where he is measured and weighed physically and morally and is deemed fit to take part in the reanimation of the king and queen, who have been ritually executed. Before Rosencreutz goes to the tower in which this procedure is to take place, he is taken to the castle vaults and sees the unclothed body of Venus. He then takes part in a series of alchemical procedures intended to form new bodies for the souls of the king and queen. After the souls have been installed in these laboriously created bodies, Rosencreutz goes off with his fellow alchemists to receive his just reward. During the reward ceremony he learns, much to his chagrin, that the doorkeeper was once a famous astrologer who lost his place in the august society for the crime of viewing Venus in a state of undress. Rosencreutz confesses, and the story ends with a surprising literary device: the reader is informed by a new narrator that after some time in service as a doorkeeper Rosencreutz was permitted to return home; the narrator goes on to say that two quarto leaves of the text are missing and that Rosencreutz's fate is not known.

16

In his autobiography Andreae says that this work of his youth was a joke and was greatly overrated by some of its readers. It certainly caused him problems within the Lutheran Church: he was dogged for the rest of his life by suspicions that ranged from simple professional jealousy to accusations of authorship of heretical writings, and he opens his autobiography with a declaration of his innocence of the heresies of which he has been accused. The rather defensive tone of this document demonstrates the persistence of the rumors of Andreae's involvement in mystical societies.

The effect of the Rosicrucian texts was remarkable: soon after their appearance Germany was inundated with publications related to the Rosicrucian Society. Many writers sought to establish contact with the alchemical organization mentioned in the texts, while others expressed disapproval of it or disbelief in its existence. This flood of publications had an influence that has lasted until the twentieth century: many writers on Andreae are concerned primarily with his involvement with the Rosicrucian myth; some are convinced that he was a member of a mystical society, and others vigorously defend his reputation as an orthodox Lutheran. Whatever the truth of the matter, it is amazing that *Chymische Hochzeit,* which was written while Andreae was still a boy, has had such a strong effect on the reception of his entire body of publications.

In 1606 Andreae was condemned by the university, along with several others, for association with prostitutes. Andreae claims in his autobiography that he was not directly involved but was forced to suffer with the guilty students by order of the university chancellor, Mattias Enzlin. Some commentators, such as Paul Arnold, believe that Andreae's condemnation was an expression of the chancellor's proabsolutist sentiments, since the Andreaes were prominent members of the new Lutheran nonaristocratic leadership. In any case, Andreae, having lost his scholarship and the possibility of a pastoral position, left Württemberg and went to Strasbourg, where he became acquainted with Lazarus Zetzner, a printer of alchemical texts who later became Andreae's publisher. In 1608 he returned to Tübingen, where he earned a living as a tutor. During this time he learned to play the lute and the zither, as well as clockmaking and other handcrafts. In 1610 he left Tübingen, prompted by the onset of the plague in that city. Traveling through Switzerland, he was greatly impressed by the Calvinist rule in the city of Geneva. Andreae's experience in Geneva may have influenced the ideal society he would depict in his *Reipublicæ Chris-*

tianopolitanæ Descriptio. After traveling through France he returned to Tübingen, where he again worked as a tutor. Collaborating with his friend Matthias Haffenreffer, he wrote *De Christiani Cosmoxeni Genitura* (On the Formation of a Christian Pilgrim, 1615), a description of the Christian as a pilgrim in the world.

In 1612 Andreae traveled through Austria and Italy; he had learned Italian from his friend Christoph Besold, who had earlier assisted him in his acquisition of French. Although he was favorably impressed by the artistic life of Italy, his visit to Rome left him with the firm belief that the Lutheran religion was superior to Roman Catholicism. On his return to Tübingen, Andreae took up residence at the Tübinger Stift, the foundation for the support of scholars at the university, and studied for ordination as a Lutheran pastor. It was during his residence at the Stift that Andreae wrote *Collectaneorum Mathematicorum Decades XI* (Eleven Decades of the Collected Mathematics, 1614), a work that demonstrates his scientific as well as his literary gifts.

On 25 February 1614 Andreae was ordained and began work as an assistant pastor in Vaihingen. During his first year there he met and married Agnes Elisabeth Grüninger. Three of his children were born in the town: Maria in 1616, Concordia in 1617, and Agnes Elisabeth in 1618; the last two died in infancy.

In 1616 Andreae published *Turbo,* a Latin teaching play he had written while staying with Haffenreffer in 1611. Dismayed with the progress of his university education, Turbo gives up his formal studies and goes to France to learn about life firsthand. He has an unhappy love affair and returns home to apprentice himself to an alchemist. *Turbo* has elicited much interest because of its superficial similarities to the Faust legend; commentators have also noted the similarities between Turbo's adventures and Andreae's life and have considered the play to be a dramatized autobiography. The work has also been viewed as a critique of university life in Andreae's day.

During his time in Vaihingen, Andreae wrote many theological tracts, as well as verse based on Christian themes. *Menippus* (1617) is a collection of short satires, several of which were translated from the Latin by Johann Gottfried Herder in volume five (1793) of his *Zerstreute Blätter* (Scattered Leaves, 1785–1797). (Herder also wrote an introduction to a collection of translations of Andreae's poetry [1786].) In his autobiography Andreae characterizes *Menippus* as an invitation to Christian brotherhood and a counter to the "game of Rosicrucians." Despite this nod in the direction of Lutheran orthodoxy, there was a reaction against the book that included published denunciations of it. In 1619 Andreae edited *Geistliche Kurtzweil* (Spiritual Pastime), a collection of poetry.

In the same year Andreae also published his utopia, *Reipublicæ Christianopolitanæ Descriptio*. Cosmonexus Christianus is shipwrecked on the island of Caphar Salama, which is under religious rule. On his arrival, Cosmonexus is subjected to a moral examination reminiscent of the examination Christian Rosencreutz undergoes in *Chymische Hochzeit*. After Cosmonexus has been accepted by the inhabitants of Christianopolis he is taken on a tour of the city. The first level he sees is the material organization – public projects, agriculture, and day-to-day labor. The inner circle of the city is dedicated to education, justice, and religion. Christianopolis is based on the intelligent study of the physical world as a form of divine worship, and the most important social class in the city consists of scientist-artisans. Andreae recognized that science requires a practical side if it is not to fall into the idle speculation that characterized preindustrial studies of nature. The clearer understanding of nature that the work of these scientist-artisans provides is, in Andreae's opinion, the key to freedom from the mundane world. In *Reipublicæ Christianopolitanæ Descriptio* Andreae proposes an educational system that, unlike the education of his own day, does not rely on corporal punishment as an incentive to scholarly excellence and in which both male and female students are instructed in the classical languages. Much of Andreae's reputation as a writer is founded on *Reipublicæ Christianopoliæ Descriptio*.

Like many of his contemporaries, Andreae suffered greatly from the effects of the Thirty Years' War. He endeared himself to his flock through his efforts toward the rebuilding of Vaihingen after it was burned in the winter of 1617 and again in the winter of 1618. His home and library were lost in the second destruction of the town.

In 1620 Andreae was given the position of chief pastor of the town of Calw, near Stuttgart. During his time in Calw, Andreae founded the Färberstift (Dyer's Charitable Institution), a benevolent organization for the support of craftsmen, students, the poor, and the infirm; most of the members were employed in the cloth industry. He also wrote *Theophilus,* which was not published until 1649; it is considered to be influential in the development of German Pietism. While in Calw, Andreae and his wife had six children; only two, a sec-

ond daughter named Agnes Elisabeth, born in 1620, and Gottlieb, born in 1622, survived childhood.

In 1634 Calw again fell victim to the horrors of the Thirty Years' War when it was attacked by Swedish troops; Andreae's home was razed. Once again he lost his library, as well as manuscripts of his own writings and an art collection that included works by Albrecht Dürer and Hans Holbein. His ten-year-old, mentally handicapped son, Ehrenreich, died from the rigors of the family's flight from the town. Andreae put aside his own losses and worked diligently for the relief of his flock. Calw was attacked again in 1638, and Andreae was forced to flee to Nuremberg.

In 1639 Andreae was appointed court pastor for Württemberg by Duke Eberhard, moving to Stuttgart to take up the post. During his tenure Andreae brought out *Cynosura oeconomiae ecclesiasticae Wirtembergicae* (Württemberg Guide to Ecclesiastical Management, 1639), which presented standards for church practices and regulations in Württemberg. He also worked for the enhancement of the Tübinger Stift and the Stuttgart Gymnasium. In 1641 he was promoted to doctor of theology by Duke August of Brunswick. He pleaded for release from his position as court pastor in 1646, and although his petition was unsuccessful he was given a reduction in duties. Nevertheless, Andreae presented one thousand sermons during his tenure in Stuttgart. In 1646 he joined the Fruchtbringende Gesellschaft (Fruit-bringing Society), an association for the promotion of the German language as a literary medium, taking the societal name Der Mürbe (The Moss). Andreae may have been too much a Latinist for the ideals of the society, but he was an important addition to the literary credentials of the group.

In 1650 Andreae was released from his duties at the Stuttgart court and became abbot at the Lutheran school of Bebenhausen. In 1653 his longtime patron Duke August invited Andreae, whom he had never met face to face, to visit him in Wolfenbüttel. Although the duke sent a large party of two riders, six horses, and three servants to transport him, Andreae was too ill to make the journey.

The next year Andreae was appointed abbot of Adelburg, a burned abbey. With this purely nominal post as a source of income, Andreae retired to the house in Stuttgart that had been given to him by Duke August. He died there on 27 June 1654.

Bibliography:
Gerhard Dünnhaupt, *Personalbibliographen zu den Drucken des Barock,* volume 9, part 1 (Stuttgart: Hiersemann, 1990), pp. 255–293.

References:

Paul Arnold, *Histoire des Rose-Croix et les origines de la Franc-Maçonniere* (Paris: Mercure de France, 1955);

Stanley W. Beeler, *The Invisible College: A Study of the Three Original Rosicrucian Texts* (New York: AMS, 1991);

William Begeman, *Die Fruchtbringende Gesellschaft und Johann Valentin Andreae* (Berlin: Mittler, 1911);

Klaus Conerman, *Die Mitglieder der Fruchtbringenden Gesellschaft 1617–1650* (Leipzig: VCH, 1985);

Richard van Dülmen, *Die Utopie einer christlichen Gesellschaft: Johann Valentin Andreae* (Stuttgart: Frommann-Holzboog, 1978);

Roland Edighoffer, "Johann Valentin Andreae: Vom Rosenkreuz zur Pantopie," *Daphnis,* 10, no. 2/3 (1981): 211–239;

Richard Kienast, *Johann Valentin Andreae und die vier echten Rosencreutzer-Schriften* (Leipzig: Mayer & Müller, 1926);

Frank E. Manuel and Fritzie P. Manuel, *Utopian Thought in the Western World* (Cambridge, Mass.: Harvard University Press, 1979), pp. 289–308;

John Warwick Montgomery, *Cross and Crucible* (The Hague: Martinus Nijhoff, 1973);

Will-Erich Peuckert, *Pansophie: Ein Versuch zur Geschichte der weißen und schwarzen Magie* (Berlin: Erich Schmidt, 1957);

Peuckert, *Das Rosenkreutz* (Berlin: Erich Schmidt, 1973);

Hans Schick, *Das ältere Rosenkreuzertum: Ein Beitrag zur Entstehungsgeschichte der Freimaurerei* (Berlin: Nordland, 1942);

Arthur Edward Waite, *The Brotherhood of the Rosy Cross: Being the Records of the House of the Holy Spirit in Its Inward and Outward History* (London: Rider, 1924);

Frances A. Yates, *The Rosicrucian Enlightenment* (London: Routledge & Kegan Paul, 1972).

Nicolaus Avancini

(1 December 1611 – 6 December 1686)

Lawrence S. Larsen
University of Oklahoma

BOOKS: *S. Franciscus Xaverius Indiarum Apostolus Acta Ludis Litterariis Serenissimo Ferdinando Francisco Augustissimorum Caesarium Ferdinandi III. Et Mariae Primogenito Cum in Caesareo et Academico Collegio Soc. Jesu Viennae Victoribus litteriis Austriaca liberalitate praemia partiretur,* anonymous (Vienna: Printed by Maria Formicinus, widow, 1640);

Fortunæ Tragoedia Sive Emmanuel Sosa Naufragus; Acta Viennae Ludis Paschalibus Literariis (Vienna: Printed by Matthäus Cosmerovius, 1643);

Euphonema heptaphonon, Quo LI. Philosoph. Baccalaureis Cum ad debitatam supremi in Philosophia Magisterii oleam capessendam inducebantur (Vienna, 1646);

Chlodoaldus, anonymous (Vienna, 1647); republished in Latin as *Chlodoaldus* (Vienna, 1647);

Adeliches FrawenKlayd jn den Exequien der Hoch- vnd Wolgebornen Grafin . . . Durch die LeichPredig im S. Michaelis Kirchen zu Wienn den 17. Julii (Vienna: Printed by Matthäus Cosmerovius, 1648);

Ioseph von seinen Brüdern wiederumb erkennt, anonymous (Vienna: Printed by Matthäus Cosmerovius, 1650);

Conclusiones theologicae De Verbo Incarnato (Vienna: Printed by Matthäus Cosmerovius, 1651);

Epitome Dramatis Quo D. Franciscum Xaverium Philosophorum Patronum, anonymous (Vienna: Printed by Matthäus Cosmerovius, 1651);

Theses Theologicae De Iustitia et Iure (Vienna: Printed by Matthäus Cosmerovius, 1651);

Assertiones theologicae De Deo Uno et Trino (Vienna: Printed by Matthäus Cosmerovius, 1652);

Assertiones Theologicae De Deo Trino et Uno (Vienna: Printed by Matthäus Cosmerovius, 1652);

Assertiones Theologicae seu Quinquaginta conclusiones ex universa Theologie explicatae (Vienna: Printed by Matthäus Cosmerovius, 1652);

Bertulphus durch Ansberta von Ottomani Gefängnuß: Das Römisch Reich durch Oesterreich vom Joch Martis erlöset (Vienna: Printed by Johann Jacob Kürner, 1652);

Tractatus de Incarnatione, Gatia, Fide (Vienna, circa 1654);

Elogium D. Leopoldo a consilio et industria Felicissimo Principi (Vienna: Printed by Johann Jacob Kürner, 1655);

Poesis Dramatica Nicolai Avancini e Sociatete Iesv. Pars I. (Vienna: Printed by Matthäus Cosmerovius, 1655);

Orationes Nicolai Avancini, è Soc. Iesv, In tres Partes divisae, 3 volumes (Vienna: Printed by Johann Jacob Kürner, 1656–1660);

Sapientia Terrarum Coelique Potens. Sive Panegyricvs Funebris, Ad Solennes Exequias Avgvstissimi, invictissimi, ac Principvm Sapientissimi Ferdinandi III. (Vienna: Printed by Matthäus Cosmerovius, 1657);

Effigies, ac elogie quinquaginta Germanico-Romanorum Caesarum (N.p., 1658);

Imperium Romano-Germanicum, a Carolo Magno Primo Romano-Germanico Cæsare, per Qvadraginta Novem Imperatores et Germaniæ Reges, et ex his per XIV. Avstriacos, ad Augustissimum et Invictissimum Rom. Imperatorem Leopoldvm Hungariæ Bohemiæque Regem, &c. . . . ab Antiquissima ac Celeberrima Vniversitate Avstriaco-Viennensi, anonymous (Vienna: Printed by Matthäus Cosmerovius, 1658);

Obsigende Gottseeligkeit das ist Flavius Constantinus der Grosse nach vberwundenen Tyrann Maxentio Sighafft, anonymous (Vienna: Printed by Matthäus Cosmerovius, 1659);

Pietas Victrix, sive Flavius Constantinus Magnus. De Maxentio Tyranno Victor (Vienna: Printed by Matthäus Cosmerovius, 1659);

Poesis Lyrica (Vienna: Printed by Matthäus Cosmerovius, 1659);

Evergetes et Endoxa Honori Reverendissimi & Celsissimi Principis ac Domini D. Wenceslai Dei & Apostolicae Sedis gratia Episcopi Passaviensis, anonymous (Passau: Printed by Georg Höller, 1665);

Leopoldi Gvilielmi, Archidvcis Avstriæ, Principis Pace et Bello Inclyti, Virtvtes (Antwerp: Printed by Balthasar Moretus, 1665);

Vita et Doctrina Jesu Christi, ex Quatuor Evangelistis Collecta, et in Meditationum materiam ad singulos totius anni dies Distributa (Vienna: Printed by Matthäus Cosmerovius, 1665); translated by F. E. Bazalgette as *Meditations on the Life and Doctrine of Jesus Christ*, 2 volumes (London: Burns & Oates, 1875); translated by B. E. Kenworthy-Browne as *The Life and Teaching of Our Lord Jesus Christ Taken from the Gospel and Arranged for Daily Meditation by Nicolaus Avancini, S.J.* (New York: Kenedy, 1961);

Nucleus Rhetoricus, in quo Tanquam in Compendio delitescunt, I. Fontes Descriptionum, II. Potiora lumina, quibus oratio efflorescit, III. Variae variorum stylorum Descriptiones, IV. Variae, variorum Dispositionum Formulae. In gratiam Eloquentiae studiosorum, publicae luci datus (Sulzbach: Printed by Abraham Lichtenthaler, 1666);

Eheliche Trewgeflissenheit oder Ansberta Jhres Gemahels Bertulfi Auß harter Gefangeschafft trewe Erlöserin Zu schuldigisten Ehren Bayder Kays: Mayestäten Leopoldi vnd Margaritae von der studirenden Jugendt in dem Kays: Academischen Collegio der Societät Jesu in Wienn auff offentlichen theatro vorgestellt den . . . Tag Augusti Anno 1667 (Vienna: Printed by Matthäus Cosmerovius, 1667);

Fides conjugalis, sive Ansberta seui Conjugis Bertulfi e dura captivitate liberatrix, anonymous (Vienna: Printed by Matthäus Cosmerovius, 1667);

Fortuna Naufraga Emmanvelis Sosæ Sepul Vedæ. Betaurliches Vnglück Emmanuelis Sosa. Zu einem Schawspil fürgestelt, Von der studierenden Jugent, deß Churfürstlichen Gymnasij der Societet Jesu Jn Chur-Fürstlicher Haupt-Statt München (Munich: Printed by Lucas Straub, 1668);

Poesis Dramatica Nicolai Avancini è Societate Iesu Pars II. (Vienna: Printed by Johann Jacob Kürner, 1669);

Poesis Dramataica Nicolai Avancini e Societate Jesv. Pars III. (Vienna: Printed by Matthäus Cosmerovius, 1671);

Cyrus: Ludus nuptialibus Augustissimi Romanorum Imperatoris Leopoldi & Claudiae Felicis (Graz: Printed by Ferdinand Widmanstetter's heirs, 1673); German version published as *Cyrus zu Hochzeitlichen Ehren-Spihl Jhro Kayserlichen Majestäten Leopoldo I. vnd Claudiae Felici* (Graz: Printed by Ferdinand Widmanstetter's heirs, 1673);

Poesis Dramatica Nicolai Avancini e Societate Jesu Pars IV. (Prague: Printed by the Karl-Ferdinand University, 1678);

Poesis Dramatica Nicolai Avancini e Societate Jesu Pars V. (Cologne: Printed by Johann Wilhelm Friessem Jr., 1679);

Compendium virtutum ac miraculorum S. Francisci Xaveri Apostoli (Vienna: Printed by Leopold Voigt, 1680);

Ferdinandus Quintus Rex Hispaniae Maurorum Domitor: Drama des Wiener Jesuitenkollegs anläßlich der Befreiung von den Türken 1683, Latin text attributed to Avancini, German translation by Karl Plepilits, music by Johann Bernhard Staudt, edited by Walter Pass, Publikationen der Gesellschaft zur Herausgabe der Denkmäler der Tonkunst in Oesterreich, volume 132 (Graz: Akademische Druck- und Verlagsanstalt, 1981).

OTHER: *Hecatombe odarum Libris V.,* paraphrased by Avancini (Vienna: Printed by Matthäus Cosmerovius, 1651);

Francesco Sbarra, *Tyrannis Idokerdi seu Privati commodi vulgo Interesse dicti, Tragoedia politico-moralis,* translated by Avancini (Vienna: Printed by Matthäus Cosmerovius, 1671);

Scipione Sgambata, S.J., *Compendium Vitae & Miraculorum S. Franccici Borgiæ,* translated by Avancini (Vienna: Printed by Matthäus Cosmerovius, 1671);

Henri Marie Boudon, *Deus solus sue Confoederatio inita Ad honorem solius Dei promovendum Opusculum,* translated by Avancini (Vienna: Printed by Matthäus Cosmerovius, 1672).

Nicolaus Avancini's writings are associated with the pinnacle of the development of the Jesuit theater, which coincided with the literary high baroque era of the second half of the seventeenth century. His oeuvre is unfailingly didactic. Self-expression was a minor consideration for him, although late in life he addressed the question of his mission as a dramatist and poet. Avancini viewed his lyrical, dramatic, devotional, and oratorical writings as humble offerings in service to the church and to the state. As a teacher he strove to inculcate in his students a mature knowledge of Latin, and in his dramas, orations, and odes he endeavored to instruct his public in Christian morality and in patriotic dedication to Austria. The dramas further served his order and the church in their campaign to reclaim Saxony. Avancini glorified and adulated the state as embodied in its emperors, especially Ferdinand III and Leopold I.

No one exceeded Avancini in his masterly use of all the devices of the stage. He exploited fully its pageantry of sight and sound and took advantage of every advancement and improvement. His *ludi caesarei* (emperor plays) equaled in splendor the sumptuous Italianate operas of the day. He has been called "der vollendetste Theatermann der gesamten Jesuitenbühnenentwicklung" (the most perfect man of the theater of the entire Jesuit development of the stage), the "erfolgreichster Dramatiker des lateinischen Jesuitendramas" (most successful dramatist of Jesuit Latin drama), and "the greatest dramatist after [Jacob] Bidermann." In his rhetorical, lyrical, metrical, and linguistic mastery; in the lucidity and orderliness of his thought in prose and poetry; in his effulgent use of imagery and learned allusion, which encompassed Christian, heathen, allegorical, and mythic elements, Avancini exhibited a special quality of style that was so revered by his contemporaries that it was referred to as "Avancinismus." His dramas are the epitome of the florid style demanded by court and church. The works of his successor in Vienna, Johann Baptist Adolph, exhibit transitional characteristics that differentiate them from the high baroque qualities of the "Age of Absolutism."

The son of a wealthy nobleman, Avancini was born on 1 December 1611 in the south Tyrolean town of Brez; the family name is Italian in origin. Avancini went to school in Graz, and then, following in the footsteps of several relatives, he began his novitiate in the Society of Jesus on 14 October 1627.

Finishing his novitiate in 1629, Avancini returned to Graz. In 1630 he began philosophical studies at the University of Graz, completing them in 1633 and assuming the post of professor of grammar at the Jesuit school in Trieste in 1634. In the following year he taught grammar and rhetoric at schools in Agram and Laibach. He undertook the four-year Jesuit course of studies in theology at the University of Vienna from 1636 until 1640, after which he became professor of rhetoric, then of philosophy, and finally of morals and dogma at the university. On 1 November 1646 he recited his fourth special vow of obedience to the pope.

In 1657 Avancini was named dramaturge and vice dean of the theological faculty at the University of Vienna. Saddened by the death of Ferdinand III that year, Avancini determined to stop writing for the stage – a decision that proved short-lived. Subsequent to this decision he wrote an ode, "Author

Poesin valere jubet, severioribus studiis occupatus" (The Author, Gripped by a Great Zeal, Orders Poetry to Prevail), in which he listed all of his dramas; it can be found in his *Poesis Lyrica* (Lyric Poetry, 1659). In 1658, on the occasions of Leopold I becoming the fiftieth emperor of the Holy Roman Empire and of the commencement of the fifth century of Hapsburg rule, he wrote an adulatory poem to the new emperor and to the House of Hapsburg: *Effigies, ac elogie quinquaginta Germanico-Romanorum Caesarum* (Images and Mottoes on Fifty Holy Roman Emperors).

Avancini's responsibilities as professor and dean included the presenting of orations and sermons, both in Latin and German, on many ceremonial occasions at court, in the colleges, and on special religious occasions. Frequently of modest religious content, these orations served primarily to inculcate in his audiences a high sense of morality and to exhibit his rhetorical skills as models to be emulated by his students. Between 1656 and 1660 Avancini collected and published his sermons and orations in three volumes. For these collections he had those of his speeches that had originally been delivered in German translated into Latin. The first two volumes comprise ceremonial orations, the third quotidian sermons. Many of his public orations were directed to students on the occasion of the beginning or close of a school year or the granting of degrees; other speeches were delivered on important ceremonial occasions of jubilation or mourning, often in Saint Stephen's Cathedral in Vienna.

From the beginning of his pedagogical career Avancini's duties included the writing of Latin school dramas. Jesuit school dramas were the responsibility of teachers of rhetoric; their purposes were to instruct the pupils in the proper use of Latin and to advance their moral education – purposes of which Avancini never lost sight, for even the grandiose ludi caesarei that glorified the emperors embody these elements. The latter dramas include *Saxonia conversa sive Clodualdus Daniae princeps cum tota familia a Carolo Magno, superato Vitigindo, conversus* (Saxony Converted; or, Clodoaldus, Ruler of Denmark, Converted with His Entire Family by Charlemagne after the Vitigindi Had Been Conquered, 1647), *Curae Caesarum pro Deo et populo sive Theodosius Magnus* (The Cares of the Emperors on Behalf of God and for the People; or, Theodosius the Great, 1653), both of which were included in the first part of his *Poesis Dramatica* (1655), and his magnum opus, *Pietas Victrix, sive Flavius Constantinus Magnus. De Maxentio Tyranno Victor* (Piety Victorious; or, Flavius

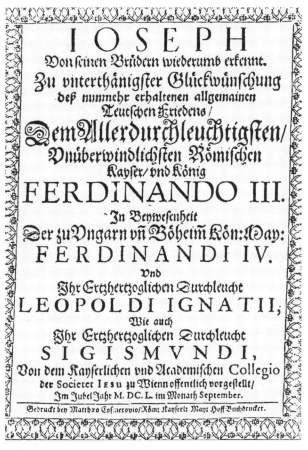

Title page for the German-language Periocha, or summary, of
Nicolaus Avancini's Latin play Pax imperii anno Domini
1650 sive Joseph a fratribus recognitus

Constantine the Great. Victor over Maxentius the Tyrant, 1659). Avancini's plays often included scores of roles – musical, pantomime and acting – so that as many pupils as possible might profit from performing. *Pietas Victrix,* for example, has forty-six speaking roles.

Avancini served as rector of the Jesuit college in Passau from 23 November 1664 until 5 May 1666, when he returned to Vienna. From 7 February 1672 until November 1675 he was rector of the Jesuit college in Graz. In November 1675 he became visitator for the province of Bohemia. From 15 December 1676 until August 1680 he acted as provincial of Austria.

On the death of the Jesuit general Gian Paolo Oliva on 26 November 1681 Avancini was sent to Rome as the Austrian delegate for the election of the order's twelfth general. Avancini was named adjunct for Germany in the curia there. While in Rome, Avancini occupied himself with editing his writings, publishing his dramas in five volumes (1655–1679), and scientific studies. He became vice

general of the order, assuming the duties of the ill Gen. Charles de Noyelle – whom, ironically, he preceded in death by six months. Avancini died in Rome on 6 December 1686. For all of his devotional and exhortatory plays, poems, and orations he was esteemed by his contemporaries as a second Thomas à Kempis.

The poems of this "Hofpoet der Ferdinande" (Court Poet to the Ferdinands) were mostly occasional odes dedicated to specific events at court, church, school, or college, such as births, marriages, deaths, battles, and dedicatory and pedagogical ceremonies. He wrote many paeans to the Virgin Mary that contained strong patriotic elements, and he composed panegyric adulatory verse dedicated to individual sovereigns of Austria and of the Holy Roman Empire.

A term that has been anachronistically applied – in both its positive and negative intimations – to Avancini's style is *Übervollsaftigkeit* (overwrought ornateness in language and rhetoric). Avancini stood at the apex of a particularly intricate, florid form of expression and on the brink of a reaction against such a style. That Avancini appreciated the mystical and linguistic innovations within Catholicism is evidenced by his approbation of a masterwork of Angelus Silesius (Angel of the Silesians), the pseudonym of the physician Johann Scheffler, who had recently converted to Catholicism. In 1657, just after being installed as dean of the theological faculty, Avancini championed with pen and tongue Scheffler's mystical *Geistreiche Sinnund Schlussreime* (Witty and Sensible Rhymes), which appeared that year.

The only work of Avancini that continues to be popular today is *Vita et Doctrina Jesu Christi* (Life and Teaching of Jesus Christ, 1665), which is written in Latin prose; it was translated into English as *Meditations on the Life and Doctrine of Jesus Christ* (1875). Avancini's meditations, according to William H. McCabe, have proven their staying power and "rank high among Christian aids to mental prayer. They are uplifting but always practical, warm but never sentimental, at once encouraging and severely exacting." The popularity of Avancini's *Vita et Doctrina Jesu Christi* is because of its lucid style, its clear and simple arrangement, and the genial insights of Avancini's inspired and learned commentary.

Vita et Doctrina Jesu Christi is primarily an allegorical interpretation of Scripture. The daily meditations are brief – each requiring no more than three minutes to read – and readily comprehended. On the many occasions where several thoughts concerning a passage occur to him, Avancini numbers his reflections. The work urges the reader toward pious contemplation and devotion, not through scholarly or pedantic exegesis but through a deep appreciation of details in the life and ministry of Christ. The arrangement is chronological through the church year, except for the first few pages, which refer to Genesis, and a section at the end that reflects on Christ's parables. While Christ is at the center of the work, the traditional Catholic reverence for Mary is strongly evident. The meditations are tripartite in arrangement: each begins with a thematic statement of the contents, followed by a quotation or series of quotations from the Bible or from an office of the church; Avancini's ruminations constitute the third element. An example of Avancini's approach is his meditation on the Feast of the Holy Name, celebrated on 2 January. He lists three considerations that might have motivated Christ in his willingness to undergo the Jewish rite of circumcision: to show that he, although exempt from the law, "had taken a real body and not one

that was a phantasm"; "that He might declare Himself a Son of Abraham, to Whom the law had been first given"; and "that He might show His love for us even as an Infant, for the highest test of love is willingness to suffer for the beloved." In his meditation for 2 January, Avancini lists and expounds on the chief virtues (obedience, humility, and charity) that Christ showed by his submission to this Old Testament law.

By his own admission Avancini was indebted to Seneca in the drama, especially in regard to metrics and rhetoric. Yet he paid little attention to the classical dramatic unities, referring to dramatists who closely observed them as "scrupulous" and "superstitious"; his plays span long periods of time and include subplots. Historical realities are subordinated to dramatic verities; many characters and some events in his dramas are pure inventions.

Avancini was not driven to write by what the baroque theorist Martin Opitz called "*furor poeticus*"; rather, he looked on his dramas as tasks that were assigned him by his superiors and were to be conscientiously completed. Reviewing his dramas on the occasion of collecting them for publication, Avancini was mindful that his choice to write for immediate goals rather than for posterity might well preclude personal literary immortality. His deliberations afford a fascinating glimpse into his reflections on the differences, as he viewed them, between writing for the stage and writing for the page. His deep knowledge of the dramatic arts is evidenced in the first volume of his *Poesis Dramaticus*. With poignancy and clarity he discusses in it the options open to him in his long career as a dramatist and lists the reasons for choosing to write for the immediate needs of society and the church. He says that he places great value on the ability of sight and sound to inspire; he writes for the present, hoping that spectators and performers alike will receive inspiration to lead more moral and more godly lives under a benign and wise sovereign. The Jesuit theater was a mixture of entertainment and religious and political instruction; its motto was "*ducere cum delectare*" (to educate by means of entertainment).

Avancini took full advantage of the advances that were being made in stage technology. The transitional stage permitted him to include many rapidly changing scenes within each act. He availed himself of the often ponderous but effective engines that the new stage in Vienna offered; these mechanical devices made possible depictions of land and sea battles, fireworks, thunder and lightning, smoke and fire, intricate displays of light and darkness, flight through the air, sudden appearances and dis-

Illustration from Avancini's Pietas Victrix *showing Constantine's army storming Rome*

appearances, collapsing bridges, army encampments, clouds, dream sequences, and hellish and celestial hordes. Because Jesuit dramas were written in Latin, they used dance, vocal and instrumental music, pantomime, and broad gestures to aid the spectators in understanding the events and to ensure that the underlying messages were clear. Jesuit dramatists had some advantage over secular playwrights in their access to ornate liturgical furniture for such scenes as might require it and to generous monetary aid from church and court.

Much more than a playwright, Avancini was also a stage director, ballet master, choir director, librettist, and sound technician. His great court spectacles rivaled the popular Italian opera, with which they vied in opulence. There is reason to believe that Avancini possessed, in addition to his talents as dramatist, great diplomatic skills, which, aside from his noble birth, enabled him for many years to negotiate the hazards and intrigues of the Viennese court and to attain the de facto position of court

dramatist to Emperor Leopold I. Educated by Jesuits, Leopold I undertook an intense and deliberately calculated program of marshaling the strengths of the drama to reinforce the concepts of absolute rule, the divine right of kings, and unquestioning obedience to one's sovereign in peace and war, and to impress the spectators with the power and grandeur of the emperor. In his historical dramas Avancini frequently depicts the Roman god of war, Mars, as an instrument of God in the righteous warfare of the faithful against heathendom.

Pietas Victrix was first performed in the great Aula theater of the University of Vienna in the presence of three thousand spectators – including Leopold I, who frequently attended such great secular and religious spectacles with his entire retinue. The occasion was Leopold's accession to the imperial throne. *Cyrus* (1673), another festal drama, was one of three great ceremonial and laudatory works performed in Graz to celebrate Leopold's marriage to Claudia Felicitas (the others were *Ibrahim Sultan*

[Ibrahim the Sultan], by Daniel Caspar von Lohenstein, and the pastoral *Die sinnreiche Liebe Oder Der Glückseelige Adonis Und die Vergnügte Rosibella* [Meaningful Love; or, Blissful Adonis and Happy Rosibella], by Johann Christian Hallmann). *Cyrus* had speaking, singing, and instrumental parts for 140 men. The total number of dramas Avancini wrote is not known but is estimated to be near forty. Twenty-seven are included in his five-volume collection, but only the titles of five other dramas are known: *Justus peremptus* (That Which Is Just Has Been Annihilated); *Trebellius; Andronikus; Tilly oder die Eroberung Magdeburgs* (Tilly; or, The Conquest of Magdeburg); and *Felicianus*.

Avancini's plays are of five distinct kinds. The biblical dramas include *Pax imperii anno Domini 1650 sive Joseph a fratribus recognitus* (The Peace of the Empire A.D. 1650; or, Joseph Recognized by His Brothers); *Susanna Hebraea* (Susanna the Hebrew); *David de Golia Victor* (David, Victor over Goliath); *Sidrach, Misach et Abednago* (Shadrach, Meshach and Abednego); and *Fiducia in Deum sive Bethulia liberata* (Trust in God; or, Bethulia Liberated). The historical dramas are *Alfons von Spanien* (Alphonse of Spain); *Artaxerxes; Olavus Magnus Norvegiae rex* (Olaf the Great, King of Norway); *Ambitio sive Sosa Naufragus* (Ambition; or, Sosa the Shipwrecked); *Canutus*; and *Saxonia conversa sive Clodualdus Daniae princeps cum tota familia a Carolo Magno, superato Vitigindo, conversus*. The legendary dramas include *Eugenia Romana* (The Roman Eugenia); *Suspicio sive pomum Theodosii* (Suspicion; or, The Fruit of Theodosius); and *Idda*. The allegorical drama is titled *Connubium Meriti et Honoris sive Euergetes et Eudoxia* (The Marriage of Merit and Honor; or, Evergetes and Eudoxia), and the mythical drama is *Fides coniugalis sive Ansberta sui coniugis Bertulfi e dura captivitate liberatrix* (Conjugal Fidelity; or, Ansberta, Liberator of Her Husband Bertulfus from Dire Captivity). Avancini's ludi caesarei, such as *Pietas Victrix, Jason* (which was staged for the glorification of Leopold's activities in Belgium), *Cyrus, Fides conjugalis sive Ansberta,* and *Dei bonitas de humana pertinacia victrix sive Alphonsus X* (The Grace of God Victorious over Human Stubbornness; or, Alphonsus X), may fit into more than one of these five categories. As was the case with most serious Jesuit dramas, Avancini's usually have double titles, the first dealing with the moral purpose of the work, the second identifying the protagonist.

In baroque historical dramas there are no innocent victims. Either the protagonists are evil rulers whose evil actions or sins cause their downfall, or they are heroic and positive rulers, guided by Providence to victory against all odds. Some of these dramas contained only one type of monarch; *Pietas Victrix* and Lohenstein's *Cleopatra* (1656) contain both types.

Pietas Victrix depicts the victorious siege of Rome by Constantine the Great in 312. In an example of poetic justice, the cruel and devious tyrant Maxentius is killed in the battle at the 420-year-old Milvian Bridge, which Maxentius had undermined in the hope of luring Constantine and his army to cross it to their destruction. The play recounts Constantine's vision of the cross in the sky with the flaming words "in hoc signo vinces" (in this sign you will conquer) and his consequent promise to become a Christian, a faith to which he was already inclined. This scene runs contrary to historical report: Avancini has the Apostles Peter and Paul reveal the sign in the heavens to Constantine. *Pietas Victrix* is offered as a prefiguration both of Leopold's battles with the Turks and of the church's forceful recatholicization of Protestant lands, Silesia in particular. Constantine is likened to Moses, Maxentius to the evil Pharaoh.

The play's classically structured five acts contain a total of forty-one scenes; only the last act has no chorus. The 101 stage directions are indicative of Avancini's attention to detail. Taking full advantage of the baroque stage, Avancini creates moments of theatrical spectacle and dramatic tension that follow hard on each other: for example, the first two parallel/contrastive dream-sequence scenes, where Maxentius's defeat is prophesied to him and where Constantine learns of his forthcoming victory; the third and fourth scenes, where each ruler relates his dreams to his trusted counselor (Saint Nicolaus and Maximus, respectively); scenes where each seeks his son's aid; and scenes portraying events in the headquarters of the protagonists and their reactions to changing fortune. Angelic and demonic figures are richly represented, including angels appearing in a fiery cloud and Pluto, king of the underworld. Maxentius's evil sorcerer, Dymas, calls forth Satan's legions; Dymas can fly through the air and transform himself into the likeness of Constantine to confuse the emperor's armies.

Major and minor, legendary and mythical, saintly and ghostly, allegorical and abstract figures abound, both in allegorical settings and in interaction with historical personages. Appearing to Constantine in a dream, his mother, Saint Helena, who is absent from Rome, reveals his fate, which she had learned when the Mother of God appeared to her in a vision. She predicts the death of Constantine's son Crispin and Constantine's victory over Maxentius. In a dialogue between Saint Helena and an angel, following Helena's revelation of Constantine's fate, the line of the House of Hapsburg is recited, with a brief description of each emperor's virtues, beginning with Rudolf and culminating in a glorification of Leopold I. In reply to Helena's question concerning the future of the Hapsburgs, the angel promises that the German Empire will never retreat from Austria and that the Hapsburg line will endure as long as time exists. Flying dragons appear, as do mythic and allegorical figures and divinities of antiquity such as Neptune, Mars, Pluto, Victoria, Pax, Industria, Fama, Consilium, Nemesis, and the Water God of the Tiber. In the four allegorical choruses that conclude the first four acts the conflict between Impietas and Pietas results in the latter's victory.

A subplot involves Maximus and his son, Selius. Discovering that Maximus has plotted to deliver the city over to Constantine, Maxentius compels Selius to kill his father with an arrow. Selius chooses martyrdom instead, and Maximus escapes to Constantine's camp.

Although no textual study has been undertaken to compare *Ferdinandus Quintus* (Ferdinand the Fifth, written in 1630, first published in 1981) stylistically or metrically with Avancini's other writings for the stage, there is good reason to believe that he wrote the text to the opera, which was composed by the Jesuit-educated Johann Barnhard Staudt in Vienna. Though *Ferdinandus Quintus* was written and performed in Vienna in 1684, at a time when the aged Avancini was occupied with weighty matters in Rome, elements that point to his authorship include the expert use of music, dance, and pantomime; the masterful Latin verse; the interspersing of allegorical scenes throughout the work; the contrasting parallel scenes alternating between the camps of the two sovereigns; the antithetical qualities of the rulers – the duplicitous and treacherous machinations of the Moorish king, Boabdilis, so like those of Maxentius, are in stark contrast to the honest, wise, and moral actions of Ferdinandus and Constantine; the fact that, like Avancini's other festal dramas, the opera depicts a historical occurrence (Spain's victorious war with the Moors in 1492 under the leadership of King Ferdinand V) as a prefiguration of an event under Austria's emperor; and the adulatory verse predicting Hapsburg's enduring glory and, more immediately, Austria's triumphs over the Moslem Turks.

Bibliographies:

Johannes Müller, S.J., *Das Jesuitendrama in den Ländern deutscher Zunge vom Anfang (1555) bis zum Hochbarock (1665),* Schriften zur deutschen Literatur, volume 8 (Augsburg: Filser, 1930);

Gerhard Dünnhaupt, *Personalbibliographien zu den Drucken des Barock,* volume 9, part 1 (Stuttgart: Hiersemann, 1990), pp. 357–377.

References:

Kurt Adel, "Handschriften von Jesuitendramen in der österreichischen Nationalbibliothek in Wien," *Jahrbuch der Gesellschaft für Wiener Theaterforschung,* 12 (1960), pp. 83–112;

Adel, *Das Jesuitendrama in Oesterreich,* Oesterreich-Reihe, volume 39/40 (Vienna: Bergland, 1957), pp. 17–25;

Judith P. Aikin, *German Baroque Drama* (Boston: Twayne, 1982), pp. 19–20, 86–87;

Robert J. Alexander, *Das deutsche Barockdrama* (Stuttgart: Metzler, 1984), pp. 59, 78, 84–86;

Wili Flemming, ed., *Das Ordensdrama* (Leipzig: Reclam, 1930), pp. 26–27;

René Fülöp-Miller, *The Power and Secret of the Jesuits,* translated by F. S. Flint and D. F. Tait (New York: Viking, 1930), p. 420;

Robert Arthur Griffin, *High Baroque Culture and Theatre in Vienna* (New York: Humanities Press, 1972);

W. Gordon Marigold, "Überlegungen zu einigen Jesuitenhuldi-gungen," in *Grenzgänge: Literatur und Kultur im Kontext,* edited by Guillaume van Gemert and Hans Ester (Amsterdam & Atlanta, 1990), pp. 33–50;

William H. McCabe, S.J., *An Introduction to the Jesuit Theater: A Posthumous Work,* edited by Louis J. Oldani, S.J. (Saint Louis: Institute of Jesuit Sources, 1983), pp. 39, 49, 53, 184;

Nikolaus Scheid, S.J., *Wissenschaftliche Beilage zum 22. Jahresberichtes des Privatgymnasiums Stella Matutina in Feldkirch* (Düsseldorf: Sausgruber, 1913);

Scheid, "Der Verfasser des Wiener Genovefa-Dramas," *Euphorion,* 13 (1906): 757–764;

George C. Schoolfield, "The Eagle of the Empire," in *Literary Culture in the Holy Roman Empire, 1555–1720,* edited by James A. Parente and others, University of North Carolina Studies in Germanic Languages and Literatures, no. 113 (Chapel Hill & London: University of North Carolina Press, 1991), pp. 109–125;

Franz Günter Sieveke, "Actio scaenica und persuasorischer Perfektionismus: Zur Funktion des Theaters bei Nikolaus Avancinus S.J.," in *Die Österreichische Literatur: Ihr Profil von den An-*

faengen im Mittelalter bis ins 18. Jahrhundert (1050-1750), 2 volumes, edited by Herbert Zeman (Graz: Akademische Druck und Verlagsanstalt, 1986), II: 1255-1282;

Sieveke, "Avancini," in *Literatur Lexikon: Autoren und Werke deutscher Sprache,* edited by Walther Killy (Gütersloh & Munich: Bertelsmann, 1990), pp. 260-261;

Elida Maria Szarota, *Das Jesuitendrama im deutschen Sprachgebiet: Eine Periochen-Edition. Texte und Kommentare,* 4 volumes (Munich: Fink, 1979);

Marian Szyrocki, *Die Deutsche Literatur des Barock: Eine Einführung* (Reinbeck bei Hamburg: Rowohlt, 1968), pp. 193-194;

Rolf Tarot, "Schuldrama und Jesuitentheater," in *Handbuch des deutschen Dramas,* edited by Walter Hinck (Düsseldorf: Bagel, 1980), pp. 35-47;

Eugen Thurnher, "Nikolaus Avancinus: Die Vollendung des Jesuitentheaters in Wien," *Jahrbuch des Südtyrolischen Kulturinstituts,* 2 (1962): 250-269;

Jean-Marie Valentin, "Programme von Avancinis Stücken," in *Literaturwissenschaftliches Jahrbuch: Im Auftrag der Görres-Gesellschaft,* new series, 12 (1971): 1-42;

Valentin, *Le Théâtre des Jésuites dans les Pays de Langue Allemande: Repertoire Chronologique des Pièces représentées et des Documents conservés (1555-1773), Première Partie* (Stuttgart: Hiersemann, 1983);

Valentin, "'Virtus et solium indissociabili, Vivunt conjugio': Zu Avancinis lyrischem und dramatischem Werk," in *Die Österreichische Literatur,* edited by Zeman, II: 1237-1254;

Valentin, "Zur Wiener Auffuhrung des Avancinischen 'Sosa Naufragus' (1643)," in *Humanistica lovaniensia,* volume 37 (Louvain: Louvain University Press, 1977), pp. 220-227;

Ruprecht Wimmer, *Jesuitentheater: Didaktik und Fest. Das Exemplus des ägyptischen Joseph auf den deutschen Bühnen der Gesellschaft Jesu* (Frankfurt am Main: Klostermann, 1982).

Jacob Balde

(3 or 4 January 1604 – 9 August 1668)

George C. Schoolfield
Yale University

BOOKS: *Panegyricvs Eqvestris Illvstrissimo Comiti Generosissimo Heroi Othoni Henrico Fvggero Eqviti Avrei Velleris, Comiti Khirchbergae et Weissenhornij, Dynastae Grönenbachij,* anonymous (Munich: Printed by Cornelius Leysser, 1628);

Maximilianus Primus Austriacus Redivivus, anonymous (Ingolstadt: Gregor Hänlin, 1631);

Epithalamion quod Serenissimus conjugibus Maximiliano, Bojariae Duci, Domitis Palatini Rheni, Sac. Rom. Imp. Septemviro Archidapifero, & Mariae Annae, Austriacae, Sacratissimi & Augustissimi Imperatoris Ferdinandi II (Munich: Cornelius Leysser, 1635);

Batracho-Myomachia Homeri (Ingolstadt: Gregor Hänlin, 1637);

Hecatombe seu Ode Nova de Vanitate Mundi, Centum Strophis Latinis, totidemque Germanicis absoluta (Munich: Nicolaus Heinrich, 1636); enlarged as *Poema de Vanitate Mundi* (Munich: Cornelius Leysser, 1638);

Templvm honoris a Romanis conditvm Apertvm virtvte Ferdinandi III. Serenissimi & Potentissimi Hungariae & Bohemiae Regis &c. (Ingolstadt: Printed by Gregor Hänlin, 1637);

Ode Dicta Agathyrsvs de Solatio Macilentorvm (Munich: Cornelius Leysser, 1638); republished, with German translation by Balde, Johannes Khuen, Joachim Meychl, Thomas König, and others, as *Agathyrsvs Teutsch. Teutscher Poeten Eyferig: vnd lustiges nachsinnen vber das trostreiche ehren Lied, Agathyrs genannt, vom Lob vnd Wolstandt der Dürr oder Mageren Gesellschaft. Anfänglich Lateinisch beschriben* (Munich: Printed by Lucas Straub, published by Johann Wagner, 1647);

Ehrenpreiß der Allerseligisten Jungfrawen vnd Mutter Gottes Mariæ. Auff einer schlechten Harpffen jhres vnwürdigen Dieners gestimbt vnd gesungen, anonymous (Munich, 1640); republished, with Latin translation by Balde, Simon Mair, Ernst Bidermann, Michael Pexenfelder, Karl Sonnenberg, as *Olympia Sacra in Stadio Mariano Lvdis*

Jacob Balde; oil painting by an unknown artist (Verwaltung der staatlichen Schlösser, Gärten und Seen, Munich)

Apollinaribvs Celebrata. Sive Certamen Poeticvm de Lavdibvs B. Mariae Virginis svper Ode Parthenia Germanica, anonymous (Munich: Printed by Lucas Straub, 1648);

Lyricorvm Lib. IV. Epodon Lib. vnus (Munich: Cornelius Leysser's heirs, 1643; corrected and enlarged edition, Cologne: Jodocus Kalckhoven, 1645);

Sylvarvm Libri VII (Munich: Cornelius Leysser's heirs, 1643; enlarged as *Sylvae Lyricae* (Cologne: Jodocus Kalckhoven [i.e., Amsterdam: Ludwig Elzevier?], 1646);

29

Paraphrasis Lyrica in Philomelam D. Bonaventurae doct. Ecclesiae (Munich: Published by Johann Wagner, 1645);

Poesis Osca sive Drama Georgicvm (Munich: Published by Johann Wagner, 1647);

De Laudib'. B. Mariae V. Odae Partheniae (Munich: Published by Johann Wagner, 1648);

Chorea Mortvalis sive Lessvs in Obitu Avgvstissimæ Imperatricis Leopoldinæ Ferdin. Vrbanæ Serenissimorvm Archidvcvm Leopoldi Com. Tyrol. et Clavdiæ Medicae F. Caesari Ferdinando III. Nuptae, by Balde and Khuen (Munich: Published by Johann Wagner, 1649);

Medicinae Gloria per Satyras XXII. Asserta (Munich: Printed by Lucas Straub, 1651);

Jephtias: Tragoedia (Amberg: Georg Haugenhofer, 1654);

Eleonorae Magdalenae Theresiae, Serenissimorum Principum Philippi Wilhelmi, Comitis Palatini Rheni, Bavariae, Juliae, Cliviae, Montium, Ducis, &c., &c. Et Elisabethae Amaliae, Landgraviae Hassiae, Comitis in Catzenelenbogen &c. &c. Dulcissimae filiolae, Principi ac primogenitae, ipso festo trium Regum hoc geniale carmen in persona trium Gratiarum Observantiae ergo accinuit (Ingolstadt: Gregor Hänlin, 1655);

Satyra contra Abvsvm Tabaci (Ingolstadt: Johannes Ostermayr, 1657);

Antagathyrsus sive Apologia Pingvium adversus Agathyrsum sive Exsultantem Congregationem (Munich: Published by Johann Wagner, 1658);

Vultuosae Torvitatis Encomium (Munich: Printed by Lucas Straub, sold by Johann Wagner, 1658);

Poemata, 4 volumes (Cologne: Johann Busaeus, 1660);

Solatium Podagricorvm (Munich: Published by Johann Wagner, 1661);

De Eclipsi Solari Anno M. DC. LIV. Die XII. Augusti, in Europa, a pluribus spectata Tvbo Optico (Munich: Printed by Lucas Straub, published by Johann Wagner, 1662);

Urania Victrix (Munich: Printed by Johann Wilhelm Schell, sold by Johann Wagner, 1663); translated anonymously as *Urania, die Siegerin* (Nuremberg, 1679);

Expeditio Polemica-Poëtica: Sive Castrvm Ignorantiae (Munich: Printed by Johann Wilhelm Schell, published by Johann Wagner, 1664);

Paean Parthenivs, sive Hymnvs in honorem SS. Ursulae & sociarvm eivs Virg. & Mart. (Cologne: Johann Busaeus, 1664); translated anonymously as *Triumphierlichs Lobgesang zu Ehren der ailff Tausendt Junckfrawen S. Vrsulae vnd jhrer Heyligen Gesellschaft* (Ingolstadt, 1664);

Magnus Tillius redivivus, sive M. *Tilli Parentalia,* anonymous (Munich: Printed by Sebastian Rauch, 1678);

Poemata de Vanitate Mundi (Cologne: Franz Metternich, 1717–1718);

Poematum Heroica (Cologne: Franz Metternich, 1718);

Poematum Satyrica (Cologne: Franz Metternich, 1718);

Opera Poetica Omnia Magnam partem nunquam edita; è MM.SS. Auctoris Nunc primum collecta, 8 volumes (Munich: Printed by Johann Lucas Straub, 1729).

Collections and Editions: *Jacobi Balde a Societate Jesu Carmina Selecta,* edited by Johann Conrad Orelli (Zurich: Orelli, Füßli, 1805; revised, 1818);

Carmina Selecta, edited by Franciscus Rohn (Vienna: Bauer, 1824);

Bavarias Musen in Jakob Balde's Oden, 4 volumes, translated by Johann Baptist Neubig (volumes 1 & 2, Munich: Giel, 1828, 1829; volume 3, Kempten: Kösel, 1830; volume 4, Auerbach: Neubig, 1843);

Jakob Balde's Oden und Epoden in fünf Büchern, translated by Joseph Aigner (Augsberg: Rieger, 1831);

Medizinische Satyren, translated by Neubig (Munich: Giel, 1833);

Carmina Selecta, edited by Carl Clesca (Neuburg an der Donau: Griessmayer, 1843);

Carmina Lyrica, edited by Benno Müller (Munich, 1844; revised edition, Regensburg: Coppenrath, 1884; reprinted, Hildesheim & New York: Olms, 1977);

Carmina Lyrica, edited by Franciscus Hipler (Müster: Theising, 1856);

Die Marien-Gesänge aus den Büchern der Oden und dem der Epoden, translated by C. B. Schlüter (Paderborn: Schöningh, 1857);

Krieg der Frösche und Mäuse, ein Vorspiel des dreißigjährigen Krieges, translated by Max Joseph Berchem (Münster: Coppenrath, 1859);

Geschichtliche Oden der ersten Bandes seiner gesammelten Werke, translated by Franz Xaver Binhack (Neuburg: Griessmeyer, 1868);

Renaissance: Ausgewählte Dichtungen, translated by Johannes Schrott and Martin Schleich (Munich: Lindauer, 1870);

Geschichtliche Oden des zweiten Bandes seiner gesammelten Werke, translated by Binhack (Amberg: Von Train, 1871–1874);

Der wieder zum Leben erwachte große Tilly, oder Des großen Tilly Totenfeier, edited and translated by Joseph Böhm (Munich: Lindauer, 1889);

Interpretatio Somnii de Cursu Historiae Bavaricae, edited by Joseph Bach (Regensburg, 1904);

Dichtungen, Lateinisch und Deutsch, edited and translated by Max Wehrli (Cologne & Olten: Hegner, 1963);

Choix de Poèmes Lyriques, edited and translated by Andrée Thill (Mulhouse: Université de Haute Alsace: Centre de Recherches et d'Etudes Rhénanes, 1981);

Deutsche Dichtungen: "Ode nova dicta Hecatombe de vanitate mvndi," 1637, "Ehrenpreiß," 1640, edited by Rudolf Berger (Amsterdam & Maarssen: APA–Holland University Press, 1983);

Odes (Lyrica). Livres I–II, translated with commentary by Thill (Mulhouse: Université de Haute Alsace: Centre de Recherches et d'Etudes Rhénanes, 1987).

OTHER: "Interpretatio Poematis quod Somnium inscribitur De Cursu Historiae Bavaricae," in *Sammlung historischer Schriften und Urkunden,* volume 4, edited by Max Freyherr von Freyberg (Stuttgart & Tübingen: Cotta, 1834), pp. 179–220;

Jocus Serius Theatralis, edited by Jean-Marie Valentin, *Euphorion,* 66 (1972): 412–436.

Jacob Balde occupied a key but paradoxical position in Germany's literary life during the seventeenth century. He was the most gifted of the many Neo-Latin poets in the baroque age and on this account achieved international fame. He was a political commentator in verse who had a close relationship with a major participant in the Thirty Years' War, Maximilian of Bavaria, and he was the most trenchant poetic voice of the Catholic forces in that conflict. As late as the nineteenth century he was celebrated as a Bavarian bard, a role to which several translations of his odes and other poems attest. With the decline of classical studies, however, the virtuoso Latinity for which he was celebrated in his day served to push him more and more to the sidelines of popular and literary interest, and today he is frequently referred to but seldom read. It is true that the penetration of his work can be difficult because of his ornate Latin and his use of codes; nor is it easy to make a fair appraisal of the intellectually keen but severely self-limiting world of Jesuitism in which he lived. Yet the effort to achieve an understanding of his work will be rewarded: while much of his religious verse offers orthodox and expect-

able attitudes, his secular poetry is subtle, ambiguous, and full of illuminations and surprises.

Balde's father, Hugo Balde, came from Giromagny, near Belfort in the Vosges mountains, but was *Kammer- und Gerichtssecretarius* (chamber and court secretary) in Ensisheim, the capital of the Hapsburg possessions in Upper Alsace and thus an important element in the administrative unity of Vorderösterreich, created by the Emperor Maximilian I at the end of the fifteenth century. In his adopted town, Hugo Balde married Magdalena Wittenbach; Jacob Balde, born at the end of 1603 or the beginning of 1604 (he was baptized on 4 January 1604), was the second of their eight children. At the age of nine he was packed off to Belfort – ostensibly to learn Bourgignon, a French-Burgundian dialect that would be useful to him in an administrative or judicial career; but perhaps he was sent away to spare him the horror of the execution of his maternal grandmother, Ursula Wittenbach, who was burned in September 1613 after confessing under torture to witchcraft. (Forty-five women suffered this fate in Ensisheim between 1551 and 1622.) After about three years in Belfort Balde returned to Ensisheim to enter the newly opened Jesuit gymnasium. His father died on 3 March 1617. In 1620 Balde entered the Jesuit university in Molsheim in Lower Alsace.

In 1621 when Molsheim, the property and residence of the bishop of Strasbourg, was threatened by anti-imperial troops under the command of Ernst von Mansfeld, Balde moved to the University of Ingolstadt in Bavaria. He received the doctorate of philosophy in 1623. His plans to pursue a career in the law were changed by an episode that became central to the Balde legend: he was serenading a baker's daughter beneath her window when he was interrupted by the sound of midnight psalms from a Franciscan cloister across the street; taking the chant as a sign from God, Balde smashed his lute, crying, "Cantatum satis est! Frangito barbiton!" (There has been enough singing! Let the lyre be broken!). The next morning he appeared before the provincial of the Jesuit order, Walther Mundbrot, who, in his previous capacity as rector of the university, had apparently gotten to know Balde as something of a rowdy. He at first refused to listen to the young man's announcement of his sudden desire to enter the Society of Jesus but relented after repeated pleas from Balde.

Balde was received into the order on 1 July 1624 and underwent his probationary period at Landsberg on the Lech; two years later he was sent to teach at the Jesuit gymnasium in Munich, taking his simple vows at this time. The gymnasium had a strong literary tradition: Jacob Bidermann, the greatest of Germany's Jesuit dramatists, had been professor of rhetoric there from 1605 to 1614, and his *Cenodoxus* (1602) and *Belisarius* (1607) had been written for performance by its pupils. Balde quickly began to move in the ecclesiastical-intellectual circles of the Bavarian capital. His special mentor was the rector of the gymnasium, Father Jakob Keller, known for his plays *Alexis* (1600) and *Mauritius Imperator* (1603) and as an adviser to Maximilian. When the professor of rhetoric, Paul Gabler, was called away in February 1628 Balde, as his substitute, undertook two large pieces of Latin poetry (professors of rhetoric were expected to write plays or other pieces of literature for performance or recitation by their students): *Panegyricus Equestris* (Knightly Panegyric, 1628) for the soldier Otto Heinrich Fugger and *Batracho-Myomachia Homeri* (The Homeric War of the Frogs and the Mice), a comical beast epic. Full of contemporary allusions, the latter work was not published until 1637, with considerable additions dealing with events of the intervening decade.

Later in 1628 Balde was transferred to the Jesuit academy at Innsbruck to teach rhetoric. There he tried his hand at theatrical writing with the comedy *Jocus Serius Theatralis* (Serious Theatrical Jest), composed for performance on 1 October 1629 in connection with the baptism of Archduchess Clara Isabella, the daughter of Leopold V, archduke of the Tyrol, and Claudia dei Medici. (The work was not published until 1972.)

In 1630 Balde went back to Ingolstadt to finish his studies in theology. During this stay he completed a quasi epic, a mixture of prose and verse titled *Maximilianus Primus Austriacus Redivivus* (Maximilian I, Austrian Reborn, 1631), and witnessed the brief siege of the city by the Swedish army of Gustav Adolf (Gustav II). After his victory over Count Johannes Tserclaes Tilly at Breitenfeld in September 1631, Gustav Adolf had invaded Bavaria. He crossed the Danube at Donauwörth on 7 April 1632 and, in one of the most heroic exploits of the Thirty Years' War, on 14–15 April his Finnish shock troops established a beachhead on the Bavarian side of the river Lech; Tilly, who was in command of Bavarian and imperial forces, was mortally wounded in the action and transported to the fortified city of Ingolstadt. On 30 April, Tilly, the greatest of the imperial commanders in the war's first decade, died while the unsuccessful siege of the city by the Swedes was under way. Balde kept a diary of events both inside and outside the walls, which he

incorporated into his long and fascinating valedictory for Tilly, *Magni Tillii Parentalia* (Obsequies of the Great Tilly), another mixture of verse and prose, which was not published until 1678 – a work bearing witness not only to Balde's dedication to the Catholic cause but also to his fear of the Swedish and Finnish "barbarians," principal targets in his subsequent poetry about the war.

Balde was consecrated a priest in Ingolstadt on 24 September 1633. He was appointed professor of rhetoric at the university in 1635; that year his *Epithalamion* for the marriage of the aged Electoral Prince Maximilian to Maria Anna of Austria, the daughter of Ferdinand II, Maximilian's major ally, was published in Munich. In 1636 he wrote a *Panegyricus* for the emperor's son, Ferdinand, king of Bohemia and Hungary and just crowned in Regensburg as the "King of the Romans" on 22 December; after Ferdinand II died on 15 February 1637 Balde used the introduction and epilogue of this work in the much grander prose and verse work *Templum Honoris* (Temple of Honor) to celebrate the succession of the younger Ferdinand as emperor. Also, although it was not published until 1654, his students at Ingolstadt produced his sole venture into the realm of Jesuit tragedy, *Jephtias,* based on the story in Judges 11 about the father compelled by a vow to sacrifice his daughter; Balde drew on the play *Jephtes* (1557), by the Scottish humanist George Buchanan. More important for Balde's growing reputation was his *Hecatombe seu Ode Nova de Vanitate Mundi* (Hecatomb; or, New Ode concerning the World's Vanity, 1636), to which he made extensive additions two years later as *Poema de Vanitate Mundi* (Poem Concerning the World's Vanity, 1638), a poetic cycle in the form of a dance of death separated into one hundred scenes, each comprising an eight-line Latin strophe and an eight-line rhymed German strophe. Here, as everywhere in Balde's work, the Latin is sophisticated, the German at a more primitive level, resulting – in the words of Curt von Faber du Faur – in "a remarkable amalgam of South German Exuberance with the finely chiselled Jesuit culture." Often reprinted, it became the most widely distributed of all of Balde's works. Still another fruit of this stay in Ingolstadt was the publication of the expanded *Batracho-Myomachia Homeri,* with its references to Tilly's destruction of Magdeburg, of which Balde approved, and to the assassination in 1634 of the ambitious imperial general Albrecht von Wallenstein.

In October 1637 Balde returned to Munich as professor of rhetoric at the Jesuit gymnasium, the beginning of what Eckart Schäfer has called his "lyric decade" – following the tradition established in 1868 by Balde's biographer Georg Westermayer, who divided Balde's career into "epic morning" (1626 to 1637), "lyric noon" (1637 to 1649), "satirical evening" (1649 to 1662), and "elegiac twilight" (1662 to 1668). In all likelihood the return to Munich occurred at the behest of Duke Albrecht VI, the younger brother of Maximilian, who wished to acquire the gifted Jesuit as a tutor for his son, Albrecht Sigismund. On the death in 1638 of Maximilian's court preacher, Jeremias Drexelius, Balde was appointed to the position. That year he published for a Marian sodality *Ehrenpreiß der Allerseligisten Jungfrawen und Mutter Gottes Mariæ. Auff einer schlechten Harpffen ihres unwürdigen Dieners gestimbt und gesungen* (Praise of the Most Blessed Virgin and Mother of God Maria. Tuned and Sung on the Simple Harp of Her Unworthy Servant). The work praises the Virgin Mary in thirty-eight eight-line stanzas, together with an envoi in which the poet says that he is "froh / Daß d'Lauten sey zertrimmert" (happy / That the lyre has been smashed) and will no longer concern himself with "Saitenspiel" (the playing of strings). The poem was so popular that in 1648 five Jesuit poets, including Balde himself, competed to see who could make the best Latin translation of it; the result was the curious *Olympia Sacra in Stadio Mariano Ludis Apollinaribus Celebrata* (Sacred Olympiad in the Marian Stadium, Celebrated in Apollonian Games). While in Munich, Balde – following the practice common among humanistically trained men in the sixteenth and seventeenth centuries and reflected in Germany's language societies and the poetic circles of Nuremberg and Königsberg (today Kaliningrad, Russia) – formed his own club, the Congregatio Macilentorum (Society of Thin People), whose purpose was to oppose the gluttony and drinking on which Balde blamed many of Germany's troubles. In 1638 Balde, who was himself quite lean, published *Ode Dicta Agathyrsus de Solatio Macilentorum* (Ode Named Agathyrsus concerning the Consolation of the Thin), a satiric poem of eighty-five eight-line strophes that he had probably written in Ingolstadt; the Agathyrsi were an ancient Scythian tribe who would only choose a gaunt person as their ruler. Later Balde would write *Antagathyrsus sive Apologia Pingvium adversus Agathyrsum* (Antagathyrsus; or, The Defense of the Fat against Agathyrsus, 1658), a feigned argument in Latin hexameters in favor of the corpulent.

Balde held the post of court preacher until he was named court historiographer in 1640; on 31 July of that year he took his final priestly vows at the Church of Saint Michael in Munich. His Munich years were productive ones, during which his fame spread throughout Catholic and, to an extent, Protestant Germany. The Munich climate, however, was bad for him; he was frequently ill, and his Ode 2:35 tells, in humorous but nasty detail, about his battle with catarrh, "Viscosa pulmonum teredo et / Pernicies Eribique spuma" (Slimy termites of the lungs, and bane and spittle-foam of hell). He grew steadily unhappier in his position as court historiographer, evidently because he could not reconcile his own love of historical truth with the propagandistic intents of the Wittelsbach dynasty.

In 1643 Balde brought out the work on which his fame throughout the Latin-reading world of Germany and beyond would be based: *Lyricorum Lib. IV. Epodon Lib. unus* (Four Books of Odes, One Book of Epodes); more than anything else he ever wrote – and Westermayer asserts that he composed some eighty thousand lines of Latin verse, making him the most prolific Latin poet of all time – it placed him, in Wilhelm Kühlmann's judgment, among "den wenigen deutschen Barockdichtern von internationaler Ausstrahlung und . . . den bedeutendsten Autoren lateinischer Zunge" (the few German baroque poets of international reputation . . . and the most important authors in the Latin tongue). The original Munich edition was followed in 1645 by a corrected and augmented one.

The same year as the first edition of the odes Balde also published *Sylvarum Libri VII* (Seven Books of *Silvae*), poems of varied content written in imitation of the Roman poet Publius Papinius Statius; "poetische Wälder" (poetic forests), with lyric "trees" of many shapes and sizes, were a standard division of vernacular verse collections from the baroque century, as they had been in the poems of the Neo-Latin poets of the Renaissance. A second edition, *Sylvae Lyricae* (Lyrical Forests, 1646), was enlarged by the addition of two books. Unlike the odes, which contain occasional minicycles such as the heroic poems near the end of the first book but otherwise do not seem to have any clear order, the poems in *Sylvae Lyricae* are carefully laid out by theme: book 1 is composed of allegorical poems on hunting, distantly modeled on the "Cynegetica" of Nemesianus; book 2 consists of pastoral poems, a cycle on bees and bee-keeping – both with religious overtones – and poems to the Virgin Mary; book 3 is a jeremiad on the decline of German morals; book 4 consists of laments on the horrors of the war; book 5 comprises short poems of mixed content, including comments on Balde's own poetry; book 6, assumed to be a youthful work, is a poetic dispute between a giant and a dwarf; book 7 con-

Engraving by Wolfgang Kilian for Balde's Poemata de
Vanitate Mundi

sists of poems of a reflective nature, including one of Balde's several cemetery poems; book 8 contains, in contrast, "Genialia," poems of a lighthearted nature; book 9 is dedicated to Claude de Mesmes, Comte d'Avaux – a key figure in the diplomacy of the Thirty Years' War – and expresses hope for the end of hostilities. Of the poems in *Sylvae Lyricae,* the best known are the threnodies of book 4, written in the summer of 1640.

Moving to more-spiritual matters, in 1645 Balde published *Paraphrasis Lyrica in Philomelam D. Bonaventurae doct. Ecclesiae* (Lyric Paraphrase on the *Philomela* of Saint Bonaventura, Doctor of the Church), the story of the Christian nightingale that, sensing the approach of death, sings with increasing intensity each hour until, its throat bursting, it dies – at the ninth hour, like Christ on the cross. Balde accepted the tradition that the author of the

original *Philomela* (Nightingale), a lyrical meditation laid out in accordance with the seven liturgical hours, was the thirteenth-century Franciscan theologian Giovanni di Fidanza, canonized in 1482 as Saint Bonaventura; recent scholarship, however, attributes the poem to John Peckham, Bonaventura's pupil and eventually archbishop of Canterbury. In contrast to the original, Balde's poem is a great metrical display, each section having its own form (Archilochians, Glyconics, Phalaecians, dactylic tetrameters, iambs). The seventy poems of *De Laudibus B. Mariae V. Odae Partheniae* (Concerning the Praises of the Blessed Virgin Mary, 1648) are another showcase of metrical virtuosity.

With *Poesis Osca sive Drama Georgicum* (Oscan Poetry; or, Rustic Drama, 1647) Balde demonstrated his linguistic ability by writing a peasant drama partly in an "Oscan" dialect constructed by the poet himself on the basis of surviving inscriptions in this tongue, which had once been the chief language of central Italy. After a long prelude consisting of five dialogues between the poet and his muse, the former is transformed into an Oscan bard when he drinks from a giant stone covered with cryptic inscriptions in the Oscan alphabet. All this preliminary matter is in standard Latin; the Oscan drama itself begins with a conversation between a pair of peasants from the region of Ulm, discussing the horrors of war. In the second part of the drama Mercury appears, disguised as a goatherd, and explains the reasons for Bavaria's withdrawal from the conflict in complex terms that the peasants do not understand; he then repeats his explanation in Oscan, revealing himself as a god. The grand finale is a pastoral festival celebrating the peace. An appendix provides the inscriptions from the stone, a hymn of praise in Oscan to the Queen of Heaven, and a Sapphic ode directed to the Comte d'Avaux in which the poet announces his intention to return to classical Latin. The work was no doubt written at the command of the electoral prince Maximilian, who wanted a justification of the separate – and, as it would turn out, highly injudicious – peace he had concluded with the French and the Swedes in 1647; but while the surface argument of the play supports Maximilian's neutrality, it has been conjectured that the work actually betrays Balde's lack of enthusiasm for his master's policy: the feigned inscriptions adjure the Germans to act in unity, precisely what Maximilian had not done with respect to his imperial allies. Balde may, then, have rejoiced at the resumption of Maximilian's longstanding alliance with Ferdinand III, even though that switch in policy turned out disastrously for Bavaria.

The death in childbed of Ferdinand's consort, the empress Leopoldina Ferdinanda Urbana, after only a year of marriage was lamented by Balde and his associate Johannes Khuen in *Chorea Mortualis* (Dance of Death, 1649), a poem of thirty-three eight-line strophes in which the first four lines in each strophe are in Latin, by Balde, and the second four in German, by Khuen. It was intended to be sung and has accompanying music. Another work from Balde's late Munich years, not published until Balde's *Opera Poetica Omnia* (Complete Poetic Works) appeared in 1729, is in honor of a hero of the resurgent empire and resurgent Catholicism: "Arion Scaldicus, sive Celeusema Triumphale, Decantatum Honoribus Alexandri Farnesii" (The Arion of the Scheldt; or, Triumphant Command Sung in Honor of Alexander Farnese) memorializes the Spanish governor of the Netherlands, Alessandro Farnese, who, taking Antwerp after a fourteen-month siege in 1584–1585, put the seal on the conquest of the southern provinces for Spain. Westermayer suggests that the work, composed in haste in the summer of 1649, was written at the request of a Jesuit college in Belgium.

The request from the college may have been only an internal Jesuit matter; but Balde's connections with the international world of Neo-Latin humanism, the *respublica litteraria* (republic of letters), had been on the increase for some time – a sign not only of the quality of his work, particularly the odes and the *Sylvae Lyricae,* but also of how swiftly the fame of Neo-Latin poets moved from country to country since there was no need of translations. Of Balde's foreign admirers, one of the most important was the Comte d'Avaux, to whom Balde had dedicated the ninth book of the *Sylvae Lyricae* and who arranged for a gift of gold from Louis XIV to the Bavarian priest. Other foreign correspondents of Balde's included the Dutch poet, Latinist, and Calvinist Caspar Barlaeus; the papal nuncio Fabio Chigi, who became Pope Alexander VII in 1651; and Ferdinand von Fürstenburg, the scion of an ancient Westphalian noble family. The humble Balde had a talent for finding his way into the favor of the powerful.

Balde's loyalty to Munich was notable: he remained when the capital was almost captured in 1646 and again in 1648. Relieved of his duties as historiographer in 1648, he described his difficulties in the position in his "Interpretatio Poematis quod Somnium Inscribitur De Cursu Historiae Bavaricae" (Interpretation of a Poem Titled "The Dream concerning the Course of Bavarian History"), a prose explication of a mysterious poem, "Somnium" (The Dream), in the seventh book of his *Sylvae Lyricae.* The commentary was completed in 1649 but not published until 1834. Balde says that he was denied permission by Maximilian's "despotica censura" (despotic censorship) to publish a work he had written in the course of his official duties, "Expeditio Donawerdana," about Maximilian's occupation of the rebellious city of Donauwörth in 1608 – an episode that foreshadowed the great war to come. (The manuscript for the work has not survived.) Balde appears to have been subjected to considerable criticism from Maximilian's courtiers and some members of Balde's own order, but he enjoyed the constant support of Duke Albrecht.

On 8 May 1649 the relics of the saints Cosmas and Damian, martyred in Cilicia in 303, had been brought to Munich by Maximilian, who had obtained them from Protestant Bremen, and placed in the high altar of Saint Michael's Church. Since the saints had been physicians and were the patrons of the medical profession, Balde, whose friends included many prominent Munich doctors, conceived the notion of writing *Medicinae Gloria per Satyras XXII Asserta* (The Glory of Medicine, Stated in 22 Satires), which was not published until 1651. It is clear that he was thoroughly imbued with the works of such satiric authors of classical antiquity as Horace, Persius, Martial, and Juvenal. The literary historian Daniel Georg Morhof said in the posthumous edition of his *Polyhistor* (1708) that Balde was one of the few modern satirists to have attained the level of the ancients: "Satyrici post Veteres non adeo multi occurrunt, inter recentiores, qui magnopere commendari possint, praeter Jacobum Balde, qui in Satyricis suis . . . mire vetustae dictionis Satyricae genium exprimit" (Since the ancients, satirists who could be recommended do not appear in any great number among moderns, save for Jacob Balde, who in his satires .. splendidly expresses the spirit of the old satiric poetry). Satire was a form of literary expression that allowed Balde to give vent to the robust side of his considerable sense of humor.

Balde's medical satires range from sixteen to some two hundred verses; for all the variety of their examples, they have a single theme, the separating of good doctors from bad – a distinction foolish patients can seldom make – and a single moral purpose, as Balde says in his introduction: "Satyra animos intrat, eiectisque vitiis morum temperiem quaerit inducere" (Satire invades the spirits [of people], and with vices thrown out, wishes to bring about a moderation of manners and morals). But the amusement of the book, which immediately became popular among physicians, lies in the way it makes fun of malpractice and malpractitioners and their often willing victims. It demonstrates the harmfulness of the water cure; the avarice of physicians; the stupidity of rich patients; and the prevalence of quacks, Jews, poison mixers, and gypsies. (In his anti-Semitism, Balde was following prevailing attitudes of his time.) Interspersed are portraits of responsible physicians. Satire 20 prefigures a popular cause of the late twentieth century in its warning against the use of tobacco. In seventeenth-century literature smoking was often praised as a pleasant and civilizing institution; equally, it was condemned as a practice of crude soldiers or degenerate Frenchmen. With more wittiness than zealotry Balde stood on the antitobacco side, as he would later show again in his *Satyra contra Abvsvm Tabaci* (Satire against the Abuse of Tobacco, 1657).

The Munich period ended for Balde in the spring of 1650, when, for reasons of health, he was transferred to Landshut to serve as preacher in the collegiate church of Saint Martin. His longtime master, Maximilian, died on 27 September 1651. Balde left Landshut after three years to become city preacher in Amberg in the Upper Palatinate, where the Jesuits had the task of converting the Reformed or Lutheran populace. There he revised, expanded, and added extensive notes to his Ingolstadt play, *Jephtias,* published in Amberg in 1654. The main event of his year in Amberg was an eclipse of the sun, which would lead in 1662 to *De Eclipsi Solari Anno 1654 die XII Augusti* (Concerning the Solar Eclipse of 12 August 1654), a prose satire criticizing astrology, contemporary events, manners, and public affairs." (The etchings accompanying the text represent suns hidden – eclipsed – by human masks.)

In the autumn of 1654 Balde became court preacher and chaplain to the Count Palatine Philipp Wilhelm at Neuburg on the Danube. A former pupil of the Jesuits, Philipp Wilhelm had acceded on 20 March 1653 to the throne of the principality of Pfalz-Neuburg and the duchies of Jülich and Berg on the Rhine, and he wanted the distinguished poet as an ornament of his eastern court. Balde's journey southward from Amberg to Neuburg turned out to be a triumphal procession: in Protestant Nuremberg he was greeted by a special deputation of the city council, and at Altdorf, Nuremberg's nearby university town, he was accorded a reception by the academic senate. In Neuburg itself the wealthy painter Joachim Sandrart is said to have impressed the citizens before Balde's arrival with stories of the poet's fame in the distant Netherlands.

Balde's duties in Neuburg were not heavy. The count was absent much of the time in his other capital, Düsseldorf, far away on the Rhine. To celebrate the birth in Düsseldorf of the count's first child, Balde wrote *Eleonorae Magdalenae Theresiae . . . geniale carmen* (Birthday Poem of Eleonora Magdalena Theresia, 1655), which would get him a reputation as a prophet: in the course of the work's 125 hexameters Balde predicted that many crowned suitors would compete for the girl's hand and that she would give birth to an imperial heir. In fact, she would become the third wife of the Emperor Leopold I in 1676 and would produce not one but two emperors, Joseph I and Karl VI. The count and his family were in residence in Neuburg from August 1655 to October 1656; they did not return until August 1661, when Balde was appointed Philipp Wilhelm's personal confessor. Occasionally he had to carry out the duties of a court poet; otherwise, much of what Balde published while in Neuburg had its origins in an earlier time – the satire against the misuse of tobacco; the *Antagathyrsus*; the *Solatium Podagricorum* (Consolation of Those with Podagra, 1661), an offshoot of the medical satires; and the book about the eclipse of 1654 (to which Balde added, at the conclusion of its first book, an enthusiastic description of Peter Paul Rubens's painting of the Last Judgment on the high altar of the Jesuit court church in Neuburg, a treasure that has since been moved to the Pinakothek in Munich). But there were also works that had, apparently, both their conception and completion at the court. *Vultuosae Torvitatis Encomium* (Praise of Facial Ugliness, 1658) is an attempt to prove that bad looks are a sign of intellectual gifts; its most important part, however, is the introductory "Dissertatio de studio poetico" (Essay Concerning Poetic Matters), in which Balde argues that a poet must have a thorough philosophical and historical training, but that no one may hope to become a true poet simply by grammatical, linguistic, or other knowledge: "Nimirum Philosopho, veritatem amanti, novitas interdicitur: a poeta, figmentis delectante, exposcitur, fidibus et fidiculis" (To the philosopher, the lover of truth, novelty is prohibited; from the poet, arousing the pleasure through inventions, it is required, from lyres great and small). The novelty should be sophisticated rather than simple and, by its style and elegant nature, reminiscent of the ancients but not slavishly devoted to them. In another poetological work, *Expeditio Polemico-Poëtica: Sive Castrum Ignorantiae* (Polemic-Poetic Expedition; or, The Camp of Ignorance, 1664), Balde compares the value of modern (that is, Neo-Latin) poets to that of the poets of antiquity in storming the camp of ignorance.

The work Balde regarded as the peak of his career was *Urania Victrix* (Urania the Victress, 1663), a long allegorical poem (and the first part of a planned trilogy) begun in 1656, about the worldly employment, or abuse, of the arts and sciences. Urania (Heavenly Love) refuses her hand to all her suitors – the arts and sciences – who approach her one by one, demanding of them the complete sacrifice of any fame of their own so that the soul, using them in a purified form and itself purified, may reach heaven and get the eternal crown of victory. The Jesuit censorship, deeming Balde's commentary explaining the work unnecessary, would not allow it to be published; the manuscript has been lost. *Urania Victrix* was translated into German by an unknown hand in 1679. Balde's last work, *Paean Parthenius* (Virginal Paean, 1664), found an anonymous translator in the year of its Latin publication; the German title, fully describing the subject, is *Triumphierlichs Lobgesang zu Ehren der ailff Tausendt Junckfrawen S. Ursulae und ihrer Heyligen Gesellschaft* (Triumphant Song of Praise in Honor of the Eleven Thousand Virgins, Saint Ursula and Her Holy Society). Fittingly, the Latin version of this story of the mass martyrdom of the eleven thousand virgins by Attila and his Huns at Cologne was published in that city, while the German translation came out in Ingolstadt. It was an appropriate end for Balde's career as a devout German Catholic poet.

Philipp Wilhelm and his entourage left Neuburg on 5 November 1664. On 24 September 1665 Balde took a symbolic farewell of poetry by hanging a golden medallion with Alexander VII's portrait (a gift in response to Balde's dedication of *Urania Victrix* to the pope) on his favorite altar in the court church as he said mass; it was meant as a votive offering to the Virgin Mary, whose statue adorned the altar. He is supposed to have spent the rest of his life in seclusion, leaving his room only to carry out his priestly functions. He died on 9 August 1668; that evening Philipp Wilhelm's children returned from Düsseldorf to find their beloved Father Balde dead. He was buried in the vault of the court church, but the location of his grave has been lost. He had left behind a feigned epitaph in the seventh book of the *Sylvae Lyricae,* written in lapidary style: "Heic. Jacet. Alsata. Poeta. Quondam. Non. Sine. Laureis" (Here lies an Alsatian poet, formerly not without laurels), to which he had subjoined the lines: "O vanitas! expurge rursus, / Si jaceam, satis est, quiete" (Oh vanity, erase it again. / If I may lie in peace, that suffices). There is a small memorial tablet to Balde in the church's left nave.

Balde's fame did not abate for some decades after his death; a story often told is that of the effort of a Nuremberg city councillor to obtain one of Balde's pens, which he then had encased in silver. Largely because of Balde's German verse, however, dissenting voices were soon raised: in *De Poëtis Germanicis* (Concerning German Poets, 1695) Erdmann Neumeister and Friedrich Grohmann wrote: "sed quam in Latini felix, tam infelix ac plane miser, linguae maternae faber" (however felicitous a poet he was in Latin, he was equally an infelicitous and simply wretched maker of his mother tongue). In *Unterricht von der Teutschen Sprache und Poesie* (Instruction concerning the German Language and Poetry, 1682) Morhof, who praised Balde as a Latin satirist in *Polyhistor,* put him among the Bavarians, Tyroleans, and Austrians who have "keine sonderliche Art im Poetisieren" (no special skill in writing poetry) because of their homely language; Morhof calls Balde's poem about human vanity "unförmlich und hart" (clumsy and hard). Three volumes of Balde's works, "in usum studiosae juventutis" (a selection for school use), appeared in 1717–1718; in the latter year a volume of his satiric writings and a volume of his heroic poems came out. These were followed in 1729 by the most complete edition of his oeuvre, the *Opera Poetica Omnia* (Complete Poetic Works), in eight volumes; for all its inclusiveness, it has been criticized as less dependable than the "Ausgabe letzter Hand" (author's final edition), *Poemata,* which had been published in four volumes in 1660.

In spite of these editions, Balde's works, save in Bavaria and other Catholic parts of Germany, were less read during the eighteenth century than they had been in the seventeenth. A rediscovery occurred in 1795–1796 with Johann Gottfried Herder's *Terpsichore,* which presented Balde's work to the world of German classicism through appreciative essays and free translations. Impressed by Herder's renderings, Johann Wolfgang von Goethe wrote to Charlotte von Kalb on 29 April 1794: "Die Bekanntschaft mit diesem vergessenen Landsmann wird bei jedem Epoche machen, der Poesie liebt und Menschheit ehrt" (The acquaintanceship with this forgotten fellow countryman will create a sensation with everyone who loves poetry and honors humanity). (Goethe's use of the term *Landsmann* [fellow countryman] is perhaps an effort to bridge the gap between Protestant and Catholic cultures that had so long prevailed in German-speaking lands.) August Wilhelm Schlegel's interest was also aroused by Herder's work; in his essay "Jakob Balde, ein Mönch und Dichter des siebzehnten Jahrhunderts" (Jacob Balde, a Monk and Poet of the Seventeenth Century), Schlegel agreed with Herder that Balde was a "Dichter Deutschlands für alle Zeiten" (poet of Germany for the ages). Schlegel, however, who persisted in calling Balde a monk – at that time a pejorative anti-Catholic term – was convinced that the limitations Balde's priestly life imposed, and the fact that he wrote in Latin, had kept him from achieving a full poetic maturity: "Vielleicht waren hier Anlagen zu einem großen Dichter vorhanden; nur eine dichterische Welt und eine dichterische Muttersprache fehlten" (Perhaps all the necessary personal qualities for a great poet were present here; only a poetic world and a poetic mother tongue were lacking). In a review of *Terpsichore* that same year, however, Schlegel paid more attention to the refined Latin verse of "den wackern vaterländischen Dichter" (the excellent patriotic poet), although he said that he found Balde much too long-winded.

In the nineteenth century Balde remained a "Lokalgröße" (local hero) or, more elegantly, "der Bayrische Nationalsänger" (the Bavarian national bard). The translations of his poems that appeared were the work of Bavarians, including Johann Baptist Neubig's translations of the odes and some epodes (1828–1843); Joseph Aigner's selection from the odes (1831); Neubig's rendering of the medical satires (1833); Franz Xaver Binhack's translations of "historical odes" and of the third and fourth books of *Sylvae Lyricae* (1868, 1871–1874); and the selection, titled *Renaissance,* by Johannes Schrott and Martin Schleich in 1870. Schrott and Schleich admit that "Baldes Werke bilden für unsere Zeitgenossen eine kaum dem Namen nach bekannte Gegend; daß sie größten Theils lateinisch geschrieben, ist nicht die einzige Ursache" (for our contemporaries Balde's works comprise a region scarcely known even by name; that they are for the most part written in Latin is not the only cause). Other reasons they cite for Balde's lack of popularity among modern critics are the Jesuit order to which he belonged, the fiercely religious time in which he lived, the ultraconservative part of Germany in which he was active, and the devotion with which he clung to Maximilian. Some enthusiasm for Balde existed in Catholic Westphalia, where C. B. Schlüter prepared translations of Balde's "Mariengesänge" (Songs to the Virgin Mary, 1857) from the odes and epodes and Max Joseph Berchem translated the satiric *Krieg der Frösche und Mäuse* (War of the Frogs and Mice, 1859).

The tricentennial of Balde's birth inspired another spurt of writing about him: for example, Father Nikolaus Scheid's essay on Balde as a dramatist (1904), J. Knepper's on Balde as a medical satirist (1905), and Joseph Bach's *Jakob Balde: Ein religiös-patriotischer Dichter aus dem Elsass* (Jacob Balde: a Religious-Patriotic Poet from Alsace, 1904), a semi-scholarly work emphasizing the poet's devotion to a German empire. The "German" Balde and the incorporation of Alsace into the Hohenzollerns' realm a generation and a half earlier inspired Anton Heinrich's *Die lyrischen Dichtungen Jakob Baldes* (The Lyrical Poems of Jacob Balde, 1915).

Despite the blossoming of German baroque studies that began in the 1920s, little attention was paid to Balde's work until the Zurich Germanist Max Wehrli's fine selection from Balde's poetry in Latin and German was published in 1963. Since Wehrli's book appeared, studies by Wehrli's stu-

*Title page for the collection of Latin poems that established
Balde's international reputation; engraving by Wolfgang
Kilian, after a drawing by Hanns Jerg*

dents Martin Heinrich Müller, Urs Herzog, and Rudolf Berger; by scholars in Germany, such as Dieter Breuer, Günter Hess, Wilhelm Kühlmann, and Eckart Schäfer; and by Jean-Marie Valentin and Andrée Thill in France have contributed much to the knowledge and interpretation of Balde, perceiving complexities and connotations of which earlier enthusiasts did not dream. Yet for all the attention paid to Balde by recent scholarship, his place in the essential canon of the German baroque is still not firm: anthologies of German baroque poetry do not always include specimens of his work, and two widely disseminated volumes of short biographies, *Deutsche Dichter des 17. Jahrhunderts: Ihr Leben und Werk* (German Poets of the 17th Century: Their

Life and Work, 1984), edited by Benno von Wiese and Harald Steinhagen, and *Reformation, Renaissance und Barock* (Reformation, Renaissance and Baroque, 1988), the second volume of *Deutsche Dichter* (German Poets), edited by Gunter E. Grimm and Rainer Marx, do not include Balde – no doubt on the basis that he is not primarily a "deutschsprachiger Autor" (German-language author). Balde, whose comments on Wallenstein are extensive, was even ignored by Golo Mann in his massive 1971 biography of the warlord.

Over the centuries attention has rightly been centered on Balde's odes and, to a somewhat lesser extent, the *Sylvae Lyricae*. Balde was given a central position in the growing historical study of Neo-

Latinity in 1805, when – doubtless urged on by Herder's *Terpsichore* – the Zurich pastor Johann Conrad Orelli brought out *Jacobi Balde a Societate Jesu Carmina Selecta* (Selected Odes of Jacob Balde, S.J.) at the distinguished Swiss house of Orelli, Füssli – an edition, with extensive commentary, inspired by Orelli's belief that Balde was one of the classics of Neo-Latin poetry; it included a copious selection from the four books of odes, four of the epodes, poems from books 3 to 5 and 7 to 9 of *Sylvae Lyricae,* and a piece from *Paraphrasis Lyrica in Philomelam D. Bonaventurae doct. Ecclesiae;* the second edition (1818) added two more odes, several more poems from *Sylvae Lyricae,* a selection from the *Poema de Vanitate Mundi,* and samples of the German poetry. The Catholic camp responded with selections for school and amateur use – two volumes titled *Carmina Selecta,* one edited by Francis Rohn in 1824 and the other by Carl Clesca in 1843 – and two complete editions of the odes with commentaries, one by Benno Müller in 1844 and the other by Francis Hipler in 1856. Although both of these editions are dependent to a considerable extent on Orelli, Müller's, since it is complete and Orelli's is not, has become the standard edition of Balde's central work.

Balde's 190 odes and 21 epodes were modeled on the 103 odes and 17 epodes of Horace and were written in competition with the *Lyricorum Libri IV. Epoden Liber Unus* (Four Books of Lyrics; One Book of Odes, 1632) of the Polish Jesuit Matthias Casimirus Sarbievius (Maciej Kazimierz Sarbiewski), which comprises 121 odes and 12 epodes. The eroticism sometimes present in Horace's work is, for obvious reasons, absent from that of his Jesuit imitators; but the writings of all three include poems to friends and on friendship, commentaries on political developments, moral instructions and exhortations, and reflections on journeys and social pleasures and on nature. The elements of Greco-Roman religion and mythology with which Horace so frequently toys are mostly replaced in the Jesuits' poetry by Christian-devotional odes, especially to the Virgin Mary – to whom Balde accords even more reverence than does his Polish predecessor. Both Balde and Sarbievius exhibit great metrical virtuosity, employing the meters – Alcaic, Sapphic, Adonic, Asclepiadean, and Archilochian – that are the technical trademark of the Horatian tradition.

The troublesome "meandering" style and complex syntax of Horace are also apparent (but in Sarbievius's poems less than in Balde's), as is the highly coded language, in which mythological allusion has a particularly great role. Balde's odes range from the simplicity in word and image of the two-strophe poem on the Egyptian Mary (ode 2:16 in Müller's edition), in which the atoning woman says "Aegyptus in me sicca squallet: / Vos, lacrymae, meus este Nilus" (Egypt turns into dust in my drought: / Tears, be now my Nile); or the Christmas ode (4:32) on the Virgin Mary, "Speculum sine macula" (Mirror without Blemish); to the difficulty of the "Ludus Palamedis" (Game of Palamedes, ode 3:13), on chess as an emblem of the vagaries of fortune, with its almost despairing and epigrammatic ending, "Ludus vivitur et sumus" (Living is a game, and so are we); or the prophetic "Omni parentis Naturae Iusta querela Adversus ingratos mortaleis" (Justified Lament of the All-Mother Nature against an Ungrateful Humanity, ode 4:9), whose "Quae simul iunxi, male separantur" (What I have joined, it is ill to separate) is a reminder of humanity's insignificance in the presence of nature and of the harm that human beings do that looks forward to the lyrics of Goethe and Friedrich Gottlob Klopstock, and well beyond.

Balde, whose attitude toward the contemporary events he describes is much more nuanced than that of his Polish predecessor, offers many more nuts than does Sarbievius for the interpreter to crack. Though he was absolutely convinced of the justice of the Catholic-imperial cause, Balde's delineations of events through classical circumlocutions allow the reader to suspect a certain ambivalence of intention or standpoint, as in the emotionally complex "Auctoris Melancholia" (Melancholy of the Author, ode 1:36), about the fall of the key imperial stronghold of Breisach on the Upper Rhine to the forces of Bernhard von Weimar in December 1638, or in the short, violent, and punning salute "Ad Aquilam Romani Imperii" (To the Eagle of the Roman Empire, ode 1:38). How much Balde revealed of himself in "Melancholia" (ode 4:36), with its opening "Semper ego inclusus Germanae finibus orae / In Bavara tellure senescam" (I am forever enclosed within the boundaries of Germany / I shall grow old on Bavarian soil) and its tribute to freedom of the mind, "Libera mens tamen est" (The mind, nonetheless, is free), or in the vision of a journey through the heavens in the ode (3:1) to Sabinus Fuscus; or in the ode (2:36) to sleep, "Mansete Mortis frater, eburneae / Dynasta portae" (Oh calm brother of death, prince of the ivory gate) will remain a matter of speculation. One wonders to what extent the ode (1:28) to Paul Waltenhofer, on "philautia" (self-love) is a general statement on this flaw, so warned against in Jesuit dramas, and to what extent it is a self-analysis. One also wonders about the short, harsh ode (4:31) dedicated to the Stoic Christoph Immola but subtitled "De se ipso" (Concerning Himself), with its contempt for the mob. On the other hand, his poems on the death in 1632 of the imperial general Gottfried Heinrich, Graf zu Pappenheim (ode 1:19), on the anniversary of the Catholic-imperial (for Balde, the Bavarian) victory over "torva" (savage) Bohemia at White Mountain (ode 2:3), on the Alsatian exiles (odes 3:20 and 3:34), and on the Bavarian country girl who protected her chastity from the lustful Swedes by means of a ruse (ode 3:26) leave no doubt about their intentions: they are propaganda pieces.

The many Marian odes may seem on cursory reading to be an almost monotonous expression of devotion. Some of them, however, while unimpeachable in their fervor, have a playful and pagan hue: for example, the brief and graceful ode (3:2) to the Blessed Virgin of Ettal, with its Horatian opening; the transformation of Mary into a nymph of the grotto in an ode (2:11) written on a visit to the shrine at Maria-Waldrast, near Innsbruck; or the ode (3:11) written in anticipation of an excursion to the Jesuit retreat at Ebersberg, in which the poet turns the Mother of God into the "latitiae parens" (parent of joy) and, thinking of a quiet sail on the Ebersberg pond, gives her the name, Cymodoce, of one of Virgil's sea nymphs.

A commentator on the Catholic baroque culture of the seventeenth century, Benno Hubensteiner, senses that a tension lay at the basis of Balde's career: the absorption of the "weinfrohen, spottsüchtigen Elsässer" (the wine-loving Alsatian, given to mockery) into "die rauhere, derbere Art Altbayerns" (the cruder, rougher way of Old Bavaria), an uprooting and replanting from which Balde never fully recovered and to which he creatively reacted. Balde provides a telling example of the gifted exile's fate, even though he was nurtured and cultivated by the host society. His work, like himself, may actually be homeless, or, as Hubensteiner puts it, "ein ungeheuer erratischer Block, der seither fast unverrückbar in unserer Geistes- und Literatur-geschichte liegt" (a huge erratic block, that, since then, lies almost unmovable in our intellectual and literary history).

Letters:

Wilhelm Kühlmann, "Jacob Baldes Korrespondenz mit Ferdinand von Fürstenberg: Text-Übersetzung-Erläuterungen," *Euphorion,* 76 (1982): 133–155.

Bibliography:

Gerhard Dünnhaupt, *Personalbibliographien zu den Drucken des Barock,* volume 9, part 1 (Stuttgart: Hiersemann, 1990), pp. 378–400.

Biographies:

Georg Westermayer, *Jacobus Balde, sein Leben und seine Werke: Eine literärhistorische Skizze* (Munich: Lindauer, 1868);

Wilhelm Beemelmans, "Der Hexenprozess gegen die Grossmutter des Dichters Jakob Balde," *Zeitschrift für Geschichte des Oberrheins,* 20 (1905): 359–388;

Dieter Breuer, "Princeps et poeta: Jacob Baldes Verhältnis zu Kurfürst Maximilian I. von Bayern," in *Um Glauben und Recht: Kurfürst Maximilian I. Beiträge zur bayrischen Geschichte und Kunst 1573–1657,* edited by Hubert Glaser (Munich & Zurich: Piper, 1980), pp. 341–352;

Wilhelm Kühlmann, "Jacob Balde," in *Literatur-Lexikon,* edited by Walther Killy, volume 1 (Gütersloh & Munich: Bertelsmann, 1988), pp. 296–298;

Wilfried Stroh, " 'Zerbrich das Saitenspiel': Die Lebensgeschichte des Jacobus Balde S.J. (1604–1668) nach dem Neuburger Nekrolog," *Literatur in Bayern,* 11 (1988): 9–13.

References:

Joseph Bach, *Jakob Balde: Ein religiös-patriotischer Dichter aus dem Elsaß* (Freiburg im Breisgau: Herder, 1904);

Barbara Bauer, "Apathie des stoischen Weisen oder Ekstase der christlichen Braut?: Jesuitische Stoakritik und Jacob Baldes *Jephtias,*" in *Res Publica Litteraria: Die Institution der Gelehrsamkeit in der frühen Neuzeit,* edited by Sebastian Neumeister and Conrad Wiedemann (Wiesbaden: Harrassowitz, 1987), pp. 453–474;

Alexander Baumgartner, "Urban VIII, Sarbiewski und Balde," in his *Die lateinische und griechische Literatur der christlichen Völker,* volume 1 (Freiburg im Breisgau: Herder, 1900), pp. 637–656;

Wolfgang Beitinger, "Thomas Morus in einer Ode Jakob Baldes (Carmen.Lyr. I, 3)," *Anregung,* 31 (1985): 312–321;

Beitinger and others, *Jakob Balde Festschrift: Zur 300. Wiederkehr seines Todestages am 9. August 1968* (Neuburg an der Donau: Heimatverein, 1969);

Rudolf Berger, *Jacob Balde: Die deutschen Dichtungen* (Bonn: Bouvier Verlag Herbert Grundmann, 1972);

Joseph Böhm, *Jakob Balde: Der wider zum Leben erwachte große Tilly oder des großen Tilly Totenfeier. In den Hauptzügen zum erstenmal übersetzt und erklärt* (Munich: Lindauer, 1889);

Richard Boschan, "Jakob Balde: Ein patriotischer Dichter des XVII. Jahrhunderts," *Deutsche Geschichtsblätter: Monatsschrift für Erforschung deutscher Vergangenheit auf landesgeschichtlicher Grundlage,* 18, no. 1 (1917): 1–16;

Dieter Breuer, "Besonderheiten der Zweisprachigkeit im katholischen Oberdeutschland während des 17. Jahrhunderts," in *Gegenreformation und Literatur: Beiträge zur interdisziplinären Erforschung der katholischen Reformbewegung,* edited by Jean-Marie Valentin (Amsterdam: Rodopi, 1979), pp. 145–163;

Breuer, "Goethes christliche Mythologie: Zur Schlußszene des Faust," *Jahrbuch des Wiener Goethevereins,* 84–85 (1980–1981): 7–24;

Breuer, *Oberdeutsche Literatur 1565–1650: Deutsche Literaturgeschichte und Territorialgeschichte in frühabsolutistischer Zeit* (Munich: Beck, 1979);

C. J. Classen, "Barocke Zeitkritik in antikem Gewande: Bemerkungen zu den medizinischen Satiren des 'Teutschen Horatius' Jacob Balde S.J.," *Daphnis,* 5, no. 1 (1976): 67–125;

Curt von Faber du Faur, *German Baroque Literature* (New Haven: Yale University Press, 1958), pp. 252–255;

Gérard Freyburger, ed., *De Virgile à Jacob Balde: Hommage à Mme. Andrée Thill* (Paris: Les Belles Lettres, 1987);

Jürgen Galle, "Das Genovefa-Motiv in der Lyrik: Die lateinische Ode Jacob Baldes und ihre deutschen Versionen im 17. Jahrhundert," in Gerhart Hoffmeister, *Europäische Tradition und deutscher Literaturbarock* (Bern & Munich: Francke, 1973), pp. 117–134;

Galle, *Die lateinische Lyrik Jacob Baldes und die Geschichte ihrer Übertragungen* (Münster: Aschendorff, 1973);

G. Gietmann, S.J., "Jakob Balde: Zum dritten Zentenar (4. Januar 1904)," *Stimmen aus Maria Laach,* 66 (1904): 1–20;

Reinhard Häussler, "Drei Gedichte an den Schlaf: Statius-Balde-Hölderlin," *Arcadia,* 13, no. 2 (1978): 113–145;

Anton Heinrich, *Die lyrischen Dichtungen Jakob Baldes* (Strasbourg: Trübner, 1915);

Johann Gottfried Herder, *Terpsichore,* 3 volumes (Lübeck: Bohn, 1795–1796);

Urs Herzog, *Divina Poesis: Studien zu Jacob Baldes geistlicher Odendichtung* (Tübingen: Niemeyer, 1976);

Herzog, "Lyrik und Emblematik: Jacob Baldes 'Heliotropium' Ode," in *Deutsche Barocklyrik: Gedichtinterpretationen von Spee bis Haller,* edited by Martin Bircher and Alois Haas (Bern & Munich: Francke, 1973), pp. 65–95;

Günter Hess, "Fracta Cithara oder Die zerbrochene Laute: Zur Allegorisierung der Bekehrungsgeschichte Baldes im 18. Jahrhundert," in *Formen und Funktionen der Allegorie: Symposium Wolfenbüttel 1978,* edited by Walter Haug (Stuttgart: Metzler, 1980), pp. 606–631;

Hess, "Ut pictura poesis: Jakob Baldes Beschreibung des Freisinger Hochaltarbildes von Peter Paul Rubens," in *Handbuch der Literatur in Bayern: Vom Frühmittelalter bis zur Gegenwart: Geschichte und Interpretationen,* edited by Albrecht Weber (Regensburg: Pustet, 1987), pp. 207–220;

Benno Hubensteiner, *Vom Geist des Barock: Kultur und Frömmigkeit im alten Bayern* (Munich: Süddeutscher Verlag, 1967), pp. 159–172;

Jozef IJsewijn, "Jacob Baldes 'Choreae Mortuales,' " in *Republica Guelpherbytana: Wolfenbütteler Beiträge zur Renaissance- und Barockforschung: Festschrift für Paul Raabe,* edited by August Buch and Martin Bircher (Amsterdam: Rodopi, 1987), pp. 69–77;

Werner Kohlschmidt, "Die Choreae Mortuales des Jakob Balde: Ein Gedicht des Hochbarock in vergleichender Betrachtung," *Orbis Litterarum,* 25–26 (1970–1971): 157–170;

Albert Knapp, "Ueber des Dichters Jakob Balde Leben und Schriften," in his *Sechs Lebensbilder* (Stuttgart: Steinkopf, 1875), pp. 1–73;

J. Knepper, "Ein deutscher Jesuit als medizinischer Satiriker: Zum Jubiläum Baldes am 4. Januar 1904," *Archiv für Kultur-Geschichte,* 2 (1905): 38–59;

Gisbert Kranz, "Zu Jacob Baldes Bildgedichten," *Archiv für Kulturgeschichte,* 60 (1978): 305–325;

Andreas Kraus, "Bayern unter Kurfürst Maximilian I. (1598–1651)," in his *Geschichte Bayerns* (Munich: Beck, 1983), pp. 226–269;

Wilhelm Kühlmann, "Georg Westermayer und die bayrische Balde-Rezeption des 19. Jahrhunderts: Die Briefe Westermayers an Otto Voggenreiter (1872/73)," *Daphnis,* 23, no. 1 (1994): 85–108;

Kühlmann, "Jacob Balde: Cum de Alberti Wallensteinii . . . funesto exitu verba fecisset: 'Magna fabula nominis': Jacob Baldes Meditationen über Wallensteins Tod," in *Gedichte und Interpretationen I: Renaissance und Barock,* edited by Volker Meid (Stuttgart: Reclam, 1982), pp. 190–197;

Jürgen Leonhardt, "Philologie in Baldes 'Drama Georgicum,' " in Sebastian Neumeister and Conrad Wiedemann, eds., *Res Publica Litteraria: Die Institution der Gelehrsamkeit in der frühen Neuzeit* (Wiesbaden: Harrassowitz, 1987), pp. 475–484;

Daniel Georg Morhof, *Polyhistor Literarius, Philosophicus et Practicus* (Lübeck: Published by Peter Böckmann, 1708);

Morhof, *Unterricht von der Teutschen Sprache und Poesie,* second enlarged edition (Lübeck & Frankfurt am Main: Published by Johann Wiedemeyer, 1700);

Martin Heinrich Müller, *"Parodia Christiana": Studien zu Jacob Baldes Odendichtung* (Zurich: Juriz, 1964);

Karl August Neuhausen, "Immer mehr oder immer weniger wollen: Zu einer Sentenz bei Ovid (fast.1, 212) und ihrer Antithese in Baldes Programmgedicht (lyr. 1, 1, 34)," *Antike und Abendland,* 32 (1986): 125–135;

Erdmann Neumeister and Friedrich Grohmann, *De Poëtis Germanicis hujus Seculii Præcipuis Dissertatio Compendiaria* (N.p., 1695);

Hildegard Pfanner, "Horazische Gedanken bei Jakob Balde," *Innsbrucker Beiträge zur Kulturwissenschaft,* 4 (1956): 39–43;

Luzian Pfleger, "Unediertes von und über Jakob Balde," *Zeitschrift für die Geschichte des Oberrheins,* new series 19 (1904): 69–79;

Hans Pörnbacher, "Eigenheiten der katholischen Barockliteratur dargestellt am Beispiel Bayerns," in Jean-Marie Valentin, ed., *Gegenreformation und Literatur: Beiträge zur interdisziplinären Erforschung der katholischen Reformbewegung* (Amsterdam: Rodopi, 1979), pp. 71–92;

Karl Pörnbacher, *Jeremias Drexel: Leben und Werk eines Barockpredigers* (Munich: Seitz, 1965);

Pörnbacher, "Nachwort," in *Sigmund von Birken, Die truckene Trunkenheit, mit Jakob Baldes "Satyra Contra Abusum Tabaci,"* edited by Pörnbacher (Munich: Kösel, 1967), pp. 205–224;

Walther Rehm, *Europäische Romdichtung* (Munich: Hueber, 1960), pp. 149–154;

Eckart Schäfer, *Deutscher Horaz: Conrad Celtis, Georg Fabricius, Paul Melissus, Jacob Balde: Die Nachwirkung des Horaz in der neulateinischen Dichtung Deutschlands* (Wiesbaden: Steiner, 1976), pp. 109–260;

Nikolaus Scheid, "J. Balde als Dramatiker: Ein Beitrag zur 300-jährigen Geburtstagsfeier des Dichters, 4. Januar 1604," *Historisch-politische Blätter für das katholische Deutschland,* 133 (1904): 19–39;

August Wilhelm Schlegel, "Jakob Balde, ein Mönch und Dichter des siebzehnten Jahrhunderts," in his *Kritische Schriften,* volume 1 (Berlin: Reimer, 1828), pp. 325–330;

Schlegel, "Terpsichore, von J. G. Herder," in his *Sämmtliche Werke,* volume 10, edited by Eduard Böcking (Leipzig: Weidmann, 1846), pp. 376–413;

Peter L. Schmidt, " 'The Battle of the Books' auf Neulatein: Jacob Baldes 'Expeditio polemico-poetica,' " *Der altsprachliche Unterricht,* 27, no. 6 (1984): 37–48;

George C. Schoolfield, "The Eagle of the Empire," in *Literary Culture in the Holy Roman Empire, 1555–1720,* edited by Schoolfield, James A. Parente Jr., and Richard Schade (Chapel Hill: University of North Carolina Press, 1991), pp. 109–125;

Schoolfield, "Jacob Balde and Breisach's Fall," in *Opitz und seine Welt: Festschrift für George Schulz-Behrend,* edited by Barbara Becker-Cantarino and Jörg-Ulrich Fechner (Amsterdam & Atlanta: Rodopi, 1990), pp. 435–454;

Mauriz Schuster, "Catull und Tibull bei Jakob Balde," *Philologische Wochenschrift,* 8 February 1936, pp. 173–174;

Schuster, "Jakob Balde und die horazische Dichtung," *Zeitschrift für deutsche Geistesgeschichte,* 1 (1935): 194–206;

Felix Stieve, "Die 'Expeditiones Donawerdanae' der Dichter Jakob Balde und Jakob Bidermann," *Oberbayrisches Archiv für vaterländische Geschichte,* 35 (1875–1876): 58–76;

Joseph Stiglmayer, S.J., "Jakob Balde S.J., der 'deutsche Horaz': Zur 250. Wiederkehr des Todestages des Dichters," *Stimmen der Zeit: Katholische Monatsschrift für das Geistesleben der Gegenwart,* 95 (1918): 467–488;

Wilfried Stroh, " 'An Senat und Volk von München': Die Münchener Mariensäule und ihr Dichter Balde," *Literatur in Bayern,* 11 (1988): 2–13;

Andrée Thill, "Un avatar Baroque du ciel de Phaeton (Jacob Balde, Lyr. 15-Ovide, Met. II 1 sqq.)," *Filologia e forme letterarie: Studi offerti a Francesco della Corte, Universita degli studi di Urbino,* 5 (1988): 589–606;

Thill, "Balde-Forschung seit 1968," in *Das Ende der Renaissance: Europäische Kultur um 1600,* edited by August Buck and Tibor Klaniczay (Wiesbaden: Harrassowitz, 1987), pp. 221–230;

Thill, "Cimitière et Champs Elysées: Jacob Balde, *Choreae Mortuales (Lyrica* II, 33) et Virgile, *Enéide,* VI" in *Hommage à Jean Granarolo: Philologie, littératures, et histoire ancienne,* edited by René Braun (Paris: Les Belles Lettres, 1985), pp. 339–347;

Thill, "L'élégie néolatine de Jacob Balde," in *Actes du Colloque international "L'élégie romaine: Enracinement, Thèmes, Diffusion" (Mulhouse, mars 1979),* edited by Thill (Paris: Ophrys, 1980), pp. 159–177;

Thill, "Jacob Balde, poète baroque," *Dix-septième siècle,* 37 (1985): 7–16;

Thill, "Jacob Balde (1604–1668) et Virgile," *Humanistica Lovaniensia,* 32 (1983): 325–341;

Thill, "Jacob Balde (1604–1668): Un poème de l'exil (Lyrica III:34)," in *Etudes rhénanes: Mélanges offerts à Raymond Oberlé* (Paris & Geneva: Slatkine, 1983), pp. 108–120;

Thill, "Jacob Balde und der Humanismus: Praxis und Hassliebe," *Daphnis,* 19, no. 2 (1990): 293–302;

Thill, "Marie, muse chrétienne de Jacob Balde," in *Hommage à Robert Schilling,* edited by Hubert Zehnacker and Gustave Hentz (Paris: Les Belles Lettres, 1982), pp. 413–422;

Thill, "Mort et vanité dans le lyrisme de Jacob Balde (1604–1668)," *Revue des études latines,* 62 (1984): 326–343;

Thill, "La Philomela de Jacobus Balde: Création poétique dans une 'paraphrase' néolatine," *Revue des études latines,* 58 (1980): 428–448;

Thill, "Vergil-Rezeption im Werke Jacob Baldes (1604–1668)," *Würzburger Jahrbücher für Altertumswissenschaft,* new series 8 (1982): 129–136;

Jean-Marie Valentin, "*Hercules moriens. Christus patiens:* Baldes *Jephtias* und das Problem des christlichen Stoizismus im deutschen Theater des 17. Jahrhunderts," *Argenis,* 2, no. 1 (1978): 37–72;

Valentin, "Jakob Baldes *Jocus serius theatralis* (1629)," *Euphorion,* 66, no. 4 (1972): 412–436;

Valentin, ed., *Jacob Balde und seine Zeit: Akten des Ensisheimer Kolloquiums 15–16 Oktober 1982* (Bern, Frankfurt am Main & New York: Lang, 1986);

Max Wehrli, "Jacob Balde und die Ode 'An Sabinus Fuscus,' " in *Rückschau und Ausblick: Jakob Hegner zum 80. Geburtstag* (Cologne & Olten: Hegner, 1962), pp. 116–122;

Wehrli, "Jacob Balde: Zum 300. Todestag des Dichters," *Stimmen der Zeit,* 182 (1968): 157–166;

Wehrli, "Lateinisch und Deutsch in der Barockliteratur," *Jahrbuch für Internationale Germanistik,* 2 (1976): 134–149;

F. W. Wentzlaff-Eggebert, *Dichtung und Sprache des jungen Gryphius: Die Überwindung der lateinischen Tradition und die Entwicklung zum deutschen Stil* (Berlin: Verlag der Akademie der Wissenschaften, in Kommission bei Walter de Gruyter, 1936), pp. 71–103;

Wentzlaff-Eggebert, *Der triumphierende und der besiegte Tod in der Wort- und Bildkunst des Barock* (Berlin & New York: De Gruyter, 1975), pp. 70–106;

Hermann Wiegmann, "Ingenium und Urbanitas: Untersuchungen zur literaturgeschichtlichen Position Jacob Baldes," *Germanisch-Romanische Monatsschrift,* 63 (1982): 22–28.

Papers:

Jacob Balde's papers are in the Bavarian State Archives, Munich; the library of the University of Munich; and the archive of the Archbisopric's General Vicariate, Paderborn.

Jacob Bidermann

(1577 or 1578 – 20 August 1639)

Thomas W. Best
University of Virginia

BOOKS: *Epigrammatvm Libri Tres* (Dillingen: Printed by Melchior Algeyer, 1620);

Herodiados. Libri Tres, siue D.D. Innocentes Christo-Martyres, ab Herode Tyranno crudeliter coesi (Dillingen: Printed by Ulrich Remy, 1622);

Reverendvs et Religiosvs F. Lvdovicvs Meris Ordinis Cisterciensis, in Celebri Coenobio S. Vrbani Professvs (Dillingen: Printed by Ulrich Remy, 1624);

Prolvsiones Theologicæ (Dillingen: Printed by Ulrich Remy, 1624);

Agonisticωn Libri Tres, Pro Miracvlis (Dillingen: Printed by Jacob Sermodi, 1626);

Herovm Epistolae (Antwerp: Printed by Balthasar Moret, 1630);

Vbaldinvs (Rome: Printed by Guilielmo Facciotti's heirs, 1633);

Sylvulæ Hendecasyllaborvm (Rome: Printed by Pietro Antonio Facciotti, 1634);

Deliciae Sacrae (Rome: Printed by Francesco Caballi, 1636);

Heroidum Epistolae (Rome: Pietro Antonio Facciotti, 1638);

Vtopia Didaci Bemardini, edited by Georg Stengel (Dillingen: Printed by Caspar Suter, 1640);

Aloysivs (Munich: Printed by Cornelius Leysser, 1640);

Acroamata Academicorvm (Lucerne: Printed by David Haut, 1642);

Ludi Theatrales Sacri. Sive Opera Comica Posthuma (Munich: Printed by Johann Wilhelm Schell, 1666) – comprises *Belisarius, Cenodoxus, Cosmarchia, Josephus,* and *Macarius; Cenodoxus* translated by D. G. Dyer and Cecily Longrigg (Edinburgh: Edinburgh Bilingual Library / Austin: Texas University Press, 1974); *Cosmarchia* translated by Thomas W. Best (Bern: Lang, 1991);

Operum Comicorum . . . Pars Altera (Munich: Printed by Johann Wilhelm Schell, 1666) – comprises *Philemon Martyr, Jacobus Usurarius, Joannes Calybita, Josaphatus, Stertinius.*

OTHER: Pedro de Rivadeneira, *Res à B. Ignatio Loiola Societatis Iesv Parente gestæ,* translated by Bidermann (Munich: Printed by Anna Berg, 1612);

Petrus Frank, S.J., *Certamen Poeticvm,* translated by Bidermann, Matthäus Rader, Rudolph Mattmann, and Jermias Drexel (Munich: Printed by Anna Berg, 1615);

Himmel Glöcklein, das ist Catholische außerlesene geistliche Gesäng Auff alle Zeit des Jahrs (Augsburg: Printed by Georg Willer, 1621);

Cicero, *Narrationvm selectarvm M. Tvllii Ciceronis libri tres,* 2 volumes, edited by Bidermann (Dillingen: Printed by Ulrich Remy, 1621, 1622).

Jacob Bidermann is generally considered the best of the Jesuit dramatists not only in his native Germany but also throughout Europe. Each of his many literary works – which include lyric poems and prose stories, as well as plays – is written in Latin, the language of the Catholic Church. Their purpose was to edify the students in Jesuit schools while sharpening their linguistic skills; by being performed, the plays were intended to have the same effects on the educated public. Bidermann's preeminence as a dramatist is because of the liveliness of his characters, and making the characters interest his audience was his chief artistic concern. The characters draw the spectator into the plays so that he or she will heed the works' religious messages. For the same purpose Bidermann combined humorous and serious elements in his dramas, which are anything but Aristotelian. Loosely constructed, they include not only comedy and tragedy but also song and dance. The Latin in which they are composed is easy to follow, in contrast to the rather Senecan or manneristic style of most Jesuit drama.

Little is known about Bidermann's life. He was born in the Catholic Swabian town of Ehingen, but the date of his birth has not been preserved. Since he is reliably reported to have entered the

Jesuit Order at age sixteen, on 23 February 1594, he must have been born in 1577 or early 1578. His father may have been a caretaker in the employ of the church. At about eight Bidermann began attending the Jesuit school at Augsburg. After becoming a Jesuit in 1594 he served a two-year novitiate at Landsberg. He studied philosophy in Ingolstadt from 1596 to 1600, then taught Latin at the Jesuit school at Augsburg until October 1602. In the latter year he composed his first two plays, *Cenodoxus* (translated, 1974) and the no-longer-extant *Cassianus*.

Cenodoxus dramatizes the legend of Saint Bruno, who founded the Carthusian Order in 1082; but instead of focusing on Bruno, Bidermann makes Bruno's law professor in Paris, who is nameless in the legend, the protagonist. In the legend, when the venerated teacher died and was about to be buried his corpse rose from its bier three times – to the consternation of his mourners – and ultimately announced that his soul had been damned. Because the teacher seemed to be a model of virtue as well as of wisdom, Bruno decided to flee from civilization to escape whatever seductions must have corrupted the professor. In his most original dramatic endeavor Bidermann created a secretly sinful personality for Bruno's mentor, thereby explaining the latter's condemnation, which is left a mystery in the legendary source. Bidermann makes the professor a complacent pretender who believes that he is good if people take him to be so; thus, Bidermann calls him Cenodoxus, Greco-Latin for "vainglorious." The conflict of the play is between the supernatural forces of good and evil that vie for the title figure's soul as he wavers between them. Invariably, however, the agents of hell persuade Cenodoxus that he is a saint because of his apparent altruism, even though all he cares about is basking in adulation. The climax occurs as he lies on his deathbed in act 4, scene 5 and definitively sides with the allegorical figure Hypocrisy rather than with his guardian angel, who warns that good deeds do not earn salvation if they do not derive from humility. Cenodoxus succumbs as he has lived, endorsing appearance rather than substance.

In act 5, as his body reposes for three days on its bier, Cenodoxus is judged in heaven by a stern, unyielding Christ. On the first day the corpse sits up for a moment to announce that its soul has been accused; on the second day it proclaims that its soul has been judged; and on the third day it wails that its soul has been banished to hell. The play concludes with Bruno and some followers deciding to become hermits to escape whatever temptations ruined their baffling former master.

Probably in late 1602 Bidermann returned to Ingolstadt for four years of training in theology. On 20 May 1606 he was ordained a priest, and in October he was sent to the large Jesuit college in Munich to teach rhetoric. The death of the Belgian humanist Justus Lipsius in 1606 caused Bidermann to lament in a letter having been attracted to Christian Stoicism, which Lipsius had popularized. At Munich, Bidermann wrote and staged at least five plays. One of them, *Stertinius,* is just a skit whose precise date is unknown. The titles and dates of the other dramas that definitely date from Bidermann's Munich period are *Adrianus* (1606), *Belisarius* (1607), *Macarius* (1613), and *Josephus* (1615). In addition, Bidermann is likely to have composed the comedy *Philemon Martyr* in Munich. His first published work, a translation into Latin of a Spanish biography of Saint Ignatius Loyola, the founder of the Jesuit order, appeared in 1612.

Though *Adrianus* has been lost, playbills summarizing its plot have survived: Adrianus, a convert to Christianity, is encouraged by his wife, Natalia, to suffer martyrdom for his new faith. *Belisarius* teaches that good fortune depends on virtue, for God controls the world, distributing punishments and rewards according to behavior. Belisarius, the leading general of the Eastern Roman emperor Justinian, exemplifies this precept. In the first three acts he triumphs over the perfidious Vandal ruler Gilimer, but Gilimer's fate anticipates Belisarius's. In acts 4 and 5 Belisarius sins against Pope Silverius at the behest of Justinian's wife and is blinded by Justinian because the emperor accepts false accusations against him: the general is rightly chastised but for the wrong crime. Whereas Adrianus resists fear, Belisarius yields to it, though he differs from Cenodoxus by learning how he has erred before it is too late.

In *Macarius,* another story of a saint, the protagonist is a boy who, to preserve his virginity, runs away from his wealthy Roman family on his wedding day and becomes a hermit in a distant forest. He is tortured by homesickness and finally is overwhelmed by it. When he realizes that he has been tricked by a devil he is mortified, but the archangel Raphael consoles him: in the future Macarius will be more resolute in resisting temptation.

Josephus enacts the Genesis narrative of Jacob's favorite son being sold into Egyptian slavery by his older brothers, being falsely accused by Potiphar's libidinous wife, correctly administering Egypt as Pharaoh's sagacious viceroy, and reuniting his family there. What unifies the string of biblical episodes is the conflict between Josephus and his initially envious siblings. They, together with Potiphar and the latter's spouse, plus several minor characters invented by Bidermann, represent irreligious worldlings whom the Christian must learn to outsmart. Joseph falls victim to his brothers and to Potiphar's wife because he is naive. After earning his release from prison by accurately interpreting Pharaoh's dreams, Joseph knows how to deal with people, as he proves in his handling of grain during the seven years of famine that bring his brothers unwittingly to him. He tests them by arresting them as spies. One of them he holds as a hostage while the others fetch the youngest family member, Benjamin. Joseph has his golden goblet hidden in the grain that Benjamin is to carry back to Hebron. The ostensible culprit is arrested, and his brothers stand by him, showing that they have mellowed during the years since they mistreated Josephus. Josephus reveals his identity to them and sends them for their father, Jacob. In both his private and public life the erstwhile simpleton Josephus has grown successful because he has acquired astuteness to complement the virtue that he has always possessed. Thus, he resembles Macarius but contrasts with Belisarius, who combined the two traits before losing virtue.

Philemon Martyr is a comedy about the power of divine grace, which can almost nullify the freedom of the human will. Philemon is a pagan minstrel in the ancient Egyptian city of Antinoe. When everyone is required by Emperor Diocletian to pay homage to Jupiter, the Christian leader Apollonius, who fears martyrdom, hires Philemon to perform the pagan rite while impersonating him. Wearing Apollonius's clothes, Philemon is heading for Jupiter's altar when his guardian angel frightens him away and then persuades him, partly with a serenade by fellow angels, to become the Christian that he merely feigns being. He is converted so completely that nothing will change his mind once he is unmasked and found to be in earnest rather than jesting, as hitherto has been his wont. He is sentenced to be shot with arrows, but he wards them off by shouting "Jesus!" When the Roman governor Arrianus goes to observe the miracle, an arrow that has hung suspended in the air plunges into his eye. Summoned to restore Arrianus's sight, Philemon tells the governor to sprinkle the stricken eye with dust from Philemon's grave after the mime has been martyred and to pronounce Christ's name at the same time. These instructions lead not only to Arrianus's physical cure but also to his spiritual conversion, ending the local persecution of Christians. Grace, in the form of Philemon's angel, has far-reaching effects.

Frontispiece for Jacob Bidermann's unfinished, posthumously published Utopia

Bidermann spent several months at Ebersberg late in 1614 to complete his novitiate. In October 1615 he was transferred to the Jesuit college at Dillingen as professor of philosophy. Three years later he completed his doctorate in theology and began to teach that subject at the Dillingen school. In all likelihood he remained there until he was called to Rome in 1626. In Dillingen, where he was raised to the highest level of the Jesuit order on 31 July 1619, Bidermann probably wrote four plays: *Cosmarchia* (translated, 1991), *Jacobus Usurarius* (Jacob the Usurer), *Joannes Calybita* (1618), and *Josaphatus. Cosmarchia* and *Jacobus Usurarius* can tentatively be dated 1617, and *Josaphatus,* Bidermann's last drama, originated not long before he went to Rome, according to the editor of his collected plays, published in 1666. Unlike Bidermann's other plays, *Joannes Calybita, Jacobus Usurarius,* and *Josaphatus* are not in verse but in prose arranged like verse; *Cos-*

marchia, perhaps a transitional drama in regard to form, contains a couple of passages in verselike prose. While at Dillingen, Bidermann published three literary works: a collection of religious epigrams in 1620; *Herodias,* an epic poem based on Matthew 2:13–21, in 1622; and *Agonisticon,* a dialogue concerning miracles, in 1626.

Cosmarchia, which is by far Bidermann's shortest play except for the rudimentary *Stertinius,* was probably meant to be performed during Shrovetide. It is a reworking of a parable on the transitoriness of life in the Byzantine novel *Barlaam and Joasaph,* believed to have been written in the seventh century and to have been put into final form by Saint John of Damascus in the eighth century. In the parable the kings of a certain country are enthroned for a year and then are banished to a barren isle, but one of them learns of his fate in time to send much of his wealth ahead so that he will continue to live in comfort. His forwarded riches allegorically represent good deeds that will make his otherwise unpleasant afterlife a paradise. In *Cosmarchia* exile no longer symbolizes death, for King Promethes returns from it with a conquering army. Cosmarchia, his perfidious kingdom, stands for the irreligious world, and his triumph over it warns Christians that this world must be fought, as it was by the Jesuits. Christians dare not trust it, as Promethes trusts his subjects before his immediate forerunner returns to disillusion him. Like Joseph, Promethes, whose descriptive name means "cautious," becomes wise to the world's deceptiveness.

Jacobus Usurarius celebrates the Virgin Mary by expanding on the legend of a wealthy and stingy moneylender, Jacob, who abused his fellowmen for the sake of pelf but ritually said his rosary every day. When he died and was about to go to hell, Christ's mother rescued him on account of his devotion to her, despite its hollowness. Bidermann adds a subplot that overshadows the story of Jacob's crimes and reward. In this supposedly subordinate tale Jacob's extravagant son, Morellus, attempts, like many a young rake in the Roman comedies of Plautus and Terence, to trick his father out of money. Morellus's servant, Sagario, hires robbers to ambush Jacob, but Jacob eludes them. Then Sagario steals from a blind man, only to be outsmarted by his victim. In act 5 Jacob is reformed by the knowledge of his impending death. At the trial of his soul his selfish misdeeds greatly outweigh his meager benefactions until Mary casts his rosary onto the scales.

In *Joannes Calybita,* as in *Macarius,* the title figure is a young patrician who runs away to avoid marriage and becomes a hermit racked by homesickness. Joannes differs from Macarius, however, in returning unrecognized to his parents' residence shortly before his demise and establishing himself outside their front door as a beggar in a little hut (*kalybe* in Greek). Like a Jesuit, he is *in* the secular world but not *of* it; and unlike Macarius, he has resisted temptation by compromising with it. As he dies he reveals his identity to his father and mother, terminating his conflict with them.

Josaphatus dramatizes the novel *Barlaam and Joasaph,* from which Bidermann borrowed the apologue that he used for *Cosmarchia.* Josaphatus is an Indian prince whose father, Abennus, raises him in the luxurious confines of the royal palace to thwart predictions that the boy will eventually become a Christian. As a fifteen-year-old, Josaphatus wants to venture beyond the palace walls and finally obtains permission to do so. During his excursion he encounters three physically afflicted men who cause him to question his artificial lifestyle. Subsequently, a clever Christian, Barlaam, gains entrance to the palace and acquaints the disenchanted prince with Jesus. Thus, Josaphatus's predestined conversion comes about in spite of his father's misguided efforts to prevent it. When Abennus tries to trick Josaphatus by having an impersonator of Barlaam pretend to recant, Josaphatus turns the tables on him by threatening to roast the impostor alive if the latter claims that he lied to royalty. Abennus accepts his son's Christianity, so that a kingdom is won for True Religion, as in *Philemon Martyr.* Like Joseph and Promethes, Josaphatus has learned to protect himself against deceit.

While Bidermann was living in Rome and functioning as a Church censor, four of his nondramatic literary works were published. Two were collections of fictional letters in elegiac couplets, patterned after Ovid's *Heroides. Heroum Epistolae* (1630) consists of letters ascribed to men, and *Heroidum Epistolae* (1638) offers letters allegedly written to women. Each collection is divided into three books, and both works are meant to edify. *Sylvulæ Hendecasyllaborum* (1634) is a collection of poems in eleven-syllable verses, and *Deliciae Sacrae* (Sacred Delights, 1636) is a compilation of religious stories in prose.

Besides his surviving plays, which were printed in 1666, two other literary works by Bidermann appeared after his death from a stroke on 20 August 1639. In 1640 the first edition of his *Utopia* was published, having been written in 1604. It is an unfinished collection of secular anecdotes narrated by three friends. One of the trio purports to be the author, Didacus Bemardinus, whose first name is the equivalent of Jacob and whose last name is an anagram of Bidermanus, the Latin form of Bidermann. Bidermann's *Acroamata Academicorum* was published in 1642. It is a collection of moralizations illustrated with stories.

Letters:

Richard van Dülmen, ed., "Die Gesellschaft Jesu und der bayerische Späthumanismus," *Zeitschrift für bayerische Landesgeschichte,* 37 (1974): 393–415.

Bibliographies:

Carlos Sommervogel, *Bibliothèque de la Compagnie de Jésus,* volume 1 (Brussels: Schepens, 1890), pp. 1443–1456;

Gerhard Dünnhaupt, *Personalbibliographien zu den Drucken des Barock,* volume 9, part 1 (Stuttgart: Hiersemann, 1990), pp. 550–581.

References:

Thomas W. Best, *Jacob Bidermann* (Boston: Twayne, 1975);

Best, "Jacob Bidermann's *Cenodoxus* and Tirso de Molina's *El mayor desengaño,*" in *Opitz und seine Welt: Festschrift für George Schulz-Behrend,* edited by Barbara Becker-Cantarino and Jörg-Ulrich Fechner (Amsterdam: Rodopi, 1990), pp. 57–70;

Berchtold Bischof, *Jakob Bidermanns Joannes Calybita (1618)* (Engeberg: Stiftsdruckerei, 1932);

Denys G. Dyer, "Jacob Bidermann, a Seventeenth-Century German Jesuit Dramatist," dissertation, University of Cambridge, 1950;

Naphtali Lebermann, *Belisar in der Litteratur der romanischen und germanischen Nationen* (Nuremberg: Gutmann, 1899);

Karl von Reinhardstöttner, "Zur Geschichte des Jesuitendramas in München," *Jahrbuch für Münchener Geschichte,* 3 (1889): 53–176;

Meinrad Sadil, "Jakob Bidermann, ein Dramatiker des 17. Jahrhunderts aus dem Jesuitenorder," *Jahresbericht des k. u. k. Ober-Gymnasiums zu den Schotten in Wien* (1898–1899): 3–32; (1899–1900): 3–48;

Jean-Marie Valentin, *Le théâtre des Jésuites dans les pays de langue allemande, Répertoire bibliographique,* 2 volumes (Stuttgart: Hiersemann, 1983–1984), II: 1027–1028;

Max Wehrli, "Bidermann, *Cenodoxus,*" in *Das deutsche Drama,* volume 1, edited by Benno von Wiese (Düsseldorf: Bagel, 1958), pp. 13–34.

Sigmund von Birken

(5 May 1626 – 12 June 1681)

John Roger Paas
Carleton College

BOOKS: *Fortsetzung der Pegnitz-Schäferey, behandlend, unter vielen andern rein-neuen freymuhtigen Lust-Gedichten und Reimarten, derer von Anfang des Teutschen Krieges verstorbenen tugend-berümtesten Helden Lob-Gedächtnisse,* by Birken and Johann Klaj (Nuremberg: Wolfgang Endter, 1645);

Der Pegnitz Hirten FrülingsFreude, Herrn M. Andre Jahnens und Jungfer Marien Simons Myrtenfeste gewidmet, by Birken, Klaj, and Georg Philipp Harsdörffer (Nuremberg, 1645);

Lustgedicht zu hochzeitlichem Ehrenbegängniß Herrn D. Johann Röders, und Jungfer Maria Rosina Schmiden, auf der siebenröhrigen Schilffpfeiffen Pans wolmeinend gespielet, by Birken, Klaj, Harsdörffer, and others (Nuremberg: Wolfgang Endter, 1645);

Dannebergische Helden-Beut, in den jetzischen Blum-Feldern beglorwürdiget, anonymous (Hamburg: Printed by Jacob Rebenlein, 1648);

Floridans des Pegnitzschäfers niedersächsische Letze, seinen Wehrten und Geehrten Hausgenossen und andern Gutgönnern und Freunden zu Dankbarer Erwiederung und Gutem Andenken hinterlassen jn Dannenberg (Hamburg: Printed by Jacob Rebenlein, 1648);

Pegnesisches Schäfergedicht, in den Nördgauer Gefilden, angestimmet, by Birken, Klaj, and Anton Burmeister (Nuremberg, 1648);

Kurtze Beschreibung deß schwedischen Friedensmahls, gehalten in Nürnberg den 25. Herbstmonats Anno 1649, anonymous (Nuremberg: Jeremias Dümler, 1649);

Krieges- und Friedensbildung; in einer, bey hochansehnlicher volkreicher Versammelung, öffentlich vorgetragenen Rede, aufgestellet, nebenst einer Schäferey (Nuremberg: Wolfgang Endter, 1649);

Teutscher Kriegs Ab- und FriedensEinzug, jn etlichen Aufzügen bey allhier gehaltenem hochansehnlichen Fürstlichen Amalfischen Freudenmahl, Schauspielweiß vorgestellt (Nuremberg, 1650);

Sigmund von Birken; etching by Jacob von Sandrart, 1664

Teutschlands Krieges-Beschluß, und FriedensKuß, beklungen und besungen jn den Pegnitzgefilden von dem Schäfer Floridan. Eigentliche Beschreibung, auch Grund- und Perspectivischer Abriß des Frjed- und Freudenmahls, Schauspiel und Feuerwerks (Nuremberg: Jeremias Dümler, 1650);

Der Dorus aus Istrien, Hoher Nymfen und Schöner Hirtinnen, am Donaustrand, edler Belober und Liebhaber, anonymous (Nuremberg, 1651);

Kurzer Entwurf eines neuen Schauspiels, darinnen ausgebildet wird das Vergnügte, Beklagte und Widerbefridigte Teutschland (Nuremberg, 1651);

50

Des Friedens Vermählung mit Teutschland, in etlichen Kupfern ausgebildet, und poetisch beschrieben (Nuremberg: Wolfgang Endter the Elder, 1651);

Die Fried-erfreuete Teutonie. Eine Geschichtschrifft, von dem Teutschen Friedensvergleich (Nuremberg: Jeremias Dümler, 1652);

Geistlicher Weihrauchkörner oder Andachtslieder I. Dutzet; samt einer Zugabe XII Dutzet kurzer Tagseufzer, anonymous (Nuremberg: Jeremias Dümler, 1652);

Neues Trauerspiel Psyche, ausbildend den Zustand der Seele (Nuremberg, 1652);

Schäfer Floridans, Poetischer Liebes-Blumen I. Sträußlein, gepflücket und gebunden an der Pegnitz (Nuremberg: Sold by Jacob Pillenhofer, 1653);

Klag-Lied, über des Allerglorwürdigsten Röm: Keys: auch zu Hung: und Beheim Kön: May: Ferdinand III. unverhofften höchst betraurerlichen Todes-Hintritt den 2. Apr. St. N. A. 1657 ist gesetzt auf die Singweise deß Klaggesangs der Keyserin Leopoldina, anonymous (Nuremberg: Michael Endter, 1657);

Ostländischer Lorbeerhäyn, ein Ehrengedicht, von dem höchstlöbl. Erzhaus Oesterreich: Einen Fürsten-Spiegel, in XII. Sinnbildern, und eben so vielen Keyser- und Tugend-Bildnissen (Nuremberg: Michael Endter, 1657);

Feld-Gedicht zu des Wohl-Edlen und Gestrengen Herrn Christoph Fürers von Haimendorff in Wolckersdorff. Und der Wohl-Edlen Viel-Ehrn-Tugendreichen Jungfrauen Ann-Lucien, gebohrne Löffelhölzin von Colberg, hochzeitlichem Ehren-Fest, anonymous (Nuremberg: Printed by Wolfgang Eberhard Felsecker, 1659);

Pegnesjsche Lämmer-Vereinbarung, zwischen dem Höchstpreißwürdigen Hirten Luzjdor und der unvergleichlichen Schäferinn Luzjana, anonymous (Nuremberg: Printed by Wolfgang Eberhard Felsecker, 1661);

Singspiel, betitelt Sophia: zu des Durchleuchtigsten Fürsten und Herrn, Herrn Christian-Ernstens Markgravens zu Brandenburg . . . mit der Durchleuchtigsten Chur Princessinn, Freulein Sophien-Erdmuht, Herzoginn zu Sachßen, Gülich, Cleve und Berg. . . . Hochfürstlichen Beylager, anonymous (Bayreuth: Printed by Johann Gebhard, 1662);

Ballet der Natur, welche mit ihren Vier Elementen, frölich und Glückwünschend sich vernehmen lässt, bey hochansehnlichster Heimführung und höchstgewünschter Ankunfft in die Hochfürstliche Brandenburgische Residenz Bayreuth der Durchlauchtigsten Fürstin und Frauen Frauen

Erdmuht-Sophien, geborner Princessin zu Sachsen, Jülich, Cleve und Berg, anonymous (Bayreuth: Printed by Johann Gebhard, 1662);

Der Donau-Strand mit allen seinen Ein- und Zuflüssen, angelegenen Königreichen, Provinzen, Herrschaften und Städten, auch dererselben Alten und Neuen Nahmen, vom Ursprung bis zum Ausflusse: in Dreyfacher LandMappe vorgestellet (Nuremberg: Jacob von Sandrart, 1664);

Pegnesische Gesprächspiel-Gesellschaft von Nymfen und Hirten: bey dem Windischgrätz-Oettingischen HochGräflichen Beylager, aufgeführt durch den Erwachsenen (Nuremberg: Michael & Johann Friedrich Endter, 1665);

Abgebrochener Hoch-Fürstlich Oesterreichischer Regenten-Zweig, anonymous (Nuremberg: Printed by Wolfgang Eberhard Felsecker, 1665);

HochFürstlicher Brandenburgischer Vlysses: oder Verlauf der Länder-Reise, welche der Durchleuchtigste Fürst und Herr, Herr Christian Ernst, Marggraf zu Brandenburg . . . durch Teutschland, Frankreich, Jtalien und die Niderlande, auch nach den Spanischen Frontieren, hochlöblichst verrichtet (Bayreuth: Printed by Johann Gebhard, 1668);

Guelfis oder NiderSächsischer Lorbeerhayn (Nuremberg: Printed by Christoph Gerhard, published by Johann Hoffmann, 1669);

Todes-Gedanken und Todten-Andenken, by Birken and others (Nuremberg: Published by Johann Kramer, printed in Bayreuth by Johann Gebhard, 1670);

Pegnesjs: oder der Pegnitz Blumgenoß-Schäfere Feld-Gedichte in neun Tagzeiten, by Birken and others, edited by Birken (Nuremberg: Wolfgang Eberhard Felsecker, 1673);

Der Norische Metellus oder Löffelholzisches Ehrengedächtnis, des glückhaften vördersten Regentens der Weltberühmten Norisburg, by Birken and others (Nuremberg, 1675);

Der Norische Parnaß und jrdische HimmelGarten (Nuremberg: Printed by Christoph Gerhard, 1677);

Chur- und Fürstlicher Sächsischer Helden-Saal; oder Kurze jedoch ausführliche Beschreibung der Ankunft, Aufnahme, Fortpflanzung und vernemster Geschichten dieses höchstlöblichen Hauses, samt Dessen Genealogie, Wappen und Kupfer-Bildnisen (Nuremberg: Printed by Christoph Gerhard, published by Johann Hoffmann, 1677);

Pegnesis Zweyter Theil: begreifend acht Feldgedichte der Blumgenoß-Hirten an der Pegnitz, by Birken and others (Nuremberg: Wolfgang Eberhard Felsecker, 1679);

Teutsche Rede-bind- und Dicht-Kunst, oder kurze Anweisung zur Teutschen Poesy, mit Geistlichen Exempeln (Nuremberg: Printed by Christoph Gerhard, published by Christoph Riegel, 1679);

Margenis oder Das vergnügte bekriegte und wiederbefriedigte Teutschland (Nuremberg: Georg Scheurer, 1679);

Heiliger Sonntags-Handel und Kirch-Wandel (Nuremberg: Printed by Christian Sigmund Froberger, published in Nuremberg by Johann Jacob von Sandrart and in Frankfurt am Main by David Funck, 1681);

Die Tagebücher des Sigmund von Birken, 2 volumes, edited by Joachim Kröll (Würzburg: Schöningh, 1971, 1974).

Editions: *Fortsetzung der Pegnitz-Schäferey* (Tübingen: Niemeyer, 1966);

Teutsche rede- bind- und Dicht-Kunst, oder kurze Anweisung zur Teutschen Poesy, mit Geistlichen Exempeln (Hildesheim: Olms, 1973);

Prosapia/Biographia, edited by Dietrich Jöns and Hartmut Laufhütte, Werke und Korrespondenz, volume 14 (Tübingen: Metzler, 1988);

Unbekannte Gedichte und Lieder des Sigmund von Birken, edited by John Roger Paas (Amsterdam: Rodopi, 1990).

OTHER: Jacob Masen, *Neues Schauspiel, betitelt Androfilo oder Die Wunderliebe,* translated and revised by Birken (Wolfenbüttel: Printed by Johann Bissmarck, 1656);

Jacob Balde, *Die truckene Trunkenheit,* translated by Birken (Nuremberg: Michael Endter, 1658; reprinted, Munich: Francke, 1967);

Johann Amos Comenius, *Orbis Sensualium Pictus,* translated and revised by Birken (Nuremberg: Michael Endter, 1658; reprinted, Osnabrück: Zeller, 1964);

Christian Ernest, margrave of Brandenburg, *Kunst-Rede,* translated by Birken (Bayreuth: Printed by Johann Gebhard, 1660);

Franz Graf von Nadasdi, *Mausoleum Potentissimorum ac Gloriosissimorum Regni Apostolici Regum & Primorum Militantis Ungariæ Ducum,* translated by Birken (Nuremberg: Michael & Johann Friedrich Endter, 1664);

Simon Wolder, *Türckischer Untergang,* edited by Birken (Nuremberg: Wolfgang Eberhard Felsecker, 1664);

Johann Jacob Fugger (i.e., Clemens Jäger), *Spiegel der Ehren des Hochlöblichsten Kayser- und Königlichen Ertzhauses Oesterreich,* revised and edited by Birken (Nuremberg: Michael & Johann Friedrich Endter, 1668).

Living most of his life in Nuremberg, a leading center of German culture and book production in the seventeenth century, Sigmund von Birken was at the heart of literary activity in the city for three decades. His influence, however, reached far beyond the city, for he maintained an extensive network of literary contacts that included nobles as well as commoners. More through his untiring managerial and editorial efforts and his facility in composing poetry virtually on demand than through any great gift of poetic inspiration, he achieved a position of high esteem among his contemporaries. Birken was a true poet of his age; but at the same time he was unique, in that he was one of the first German poets before Gotthold Ephraim Lessing to make his living by his pen alone. At the time of his death he was widely recognized as a master of German literary style and was favorably compared by some of his fellow poets to Virgil and Horace; but by the end of the seventeenth century he fell out of fashion and was subsequently relegated to a position of literary-historical insignificance. This situation promises not to be permanent, however, for Birken documented his professional, social, and personal activities like no other European literary figure in the seventeenth century. He will never regain his reputation as a first-rate poet; but the literary and cultural information preserved in his unpublished manuscripts, personal diaries, diaries of correspondence, and voluminous correspondence itself may one day return him to a prominent position among German baroque poets.

Birken was born Sigmund Betulius on 5 May 1626 in the Bohemian village of Wildstein near Cheb; an ancestor had followed the practice common among scholars in the Renaissance and latinized the name from Birkener to Betulius (*Birken* and *betula* both mean "birch tree"). Sigmund was the fourth of six children of Daniel Betulius, the village pastor in Wildstein, and Veronica Betulius, née Khobelt, a native of Nuremberg. By the time he was three years old the Thirty Years' War had been raging for ten years, and in that first decade of conflict the Catholics had routed the "Winter King," Friedrich V of the Palatinate, and his Calvinist supporters from Bohemia and were on the verge of driving all Protestant forces from the empire. In 1629 Emperor Ferdinand II felt sufficiently secure militarily to promulgate the Edict of Restitution, which required the Protestants in the empire to restore to the Catholics all lands taken since the Peace of Augsburg (1555). As devout Lutherans, Daniel and Veronica Betulius had little choice but to flee Bohemia with their children, and after finding tem-

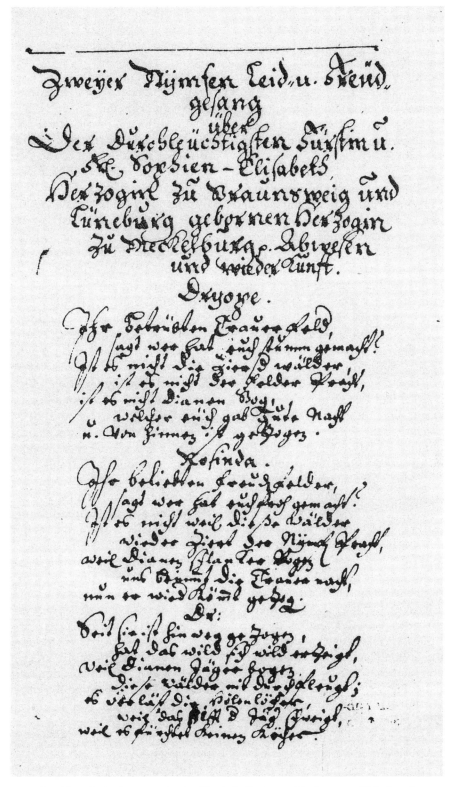

Leaf from Birken's manuscript for "Poetische Lorbeerwälder," an unpublished work
(Germanisches Nationalmuseum, Nuremberg)

porary shelter with relatives in Hohenberg and Bayreuth they settled in late 1632 in Nuremberg, the primary haven for Protestant refugees from Hapsburg lands.

In 1633 Birken lost his mother, and in 1642 his father died; despite an existence dominated by poverty, however, he was able to gain an excellent education. He received instruction and encouragement from experienced teachers such as Daniel Wülfer, a noted theologian, and Adam Zanner, who had a strong interest in the German language. He also came to the attention of Johann Michael Dilherr, one of the most respected and influential German theologians and scholars of his time, who had been engaged by the Nuremberg town councillors in 1642 to oversee the rejuvenation of Christian life in the city. In addition to having impeccable professional qualifications, Dilherr was an accomplished Neo-Latin poet with a deep appreciation of high vernacular literature. He took Birken into his home and became his mentor.

Birken matriculated at Dilherr's alma mater, Jena University, in the fall of 1643. He initially studied law but, as he admitted later, he had little success in this subject and soon switched to theology. Although his father had wished him to become a Lutheran clergyman, Birken wanted to be an independent religious scholar whose devotional works could help to strengthen his fellow Christians' religious commitment. A lack of funds forced him to leave the university after three semesters, and in early 1644 he went back to Nuremberg in search of employment.

Birken's return to Nuremberg coincided with a sudden burst of poetic energy among the literary elite of the city. Because Nuremberg poets had been slower than their counterparts in Strasbourg, Leipzig, and Hamburg in accepting the reform of German verse begun by Martin Opitz in 1624, there had been no significant poetic activity in the city for years. This situation changed fundamentally when the patrician Georg Philipp Harsdörffer, an authority on German verse, and Johann Klaj, a poetically gifted student of theology, founded the Pegnesischer Blumenorden (Order of the Flowers on the Pegnitz River). This society or club shared with other contemporary German language societies a commitment to the elevation of German as a literary medium, but underlying this artistic goal in Nuremberg was piety: the Nuremberg poets pursued their literary interests for the greater glory of God.

The founding of the society is traditionally marked by the publication of *Das Pegnesische Schäfer-gedicht* (The Shepherd Poem of the Pegnitz), which Harsdörffer and Klaj wrote ostensibly to commemorate a double patrician wedding in October 1644. It is a pastoral in the tradition of the Virgilian eclogues, but it consists of prose as well as verse. Although its motifs follow closely those in Opitz's *Schäfferey von der Nymfen Hercinie* (Shepherd Poem of the Nymph Hercinie, 1630), each poem experiments with a different poetic meter or verse form. *Das Pegnesische Schäfergedicht* was a seminal work that institutionalized the form of the German pastoral for years to come and served as a model for more than a hundred works in that genre by Nuremberg poets. The best of these pastorals are inspired and full of poetic virtuosity; the weakest are frivolous, contrived, and confusing. Yet whether good or bad, they are generally innovative and engaging.

In 1645 Birken joined the society under the name Floridan, and in the same year he collaborated with Klaj in writing *Fortsetzung der Pegnitz-Schäferey* (Continuation of the Shepherd Poem of the Pegnitz), which includes the "official" account of the society's founding. It is set in the area surrounding Nuremberg, and the loosely structured plot with allegorical descriptions offered Birken ample opportunity to include poems of all types and meters. His poetic language is lively, and the work quickly won the admiration of his fellow poets in Nuremberg.

Birken was, however, unable to secure a well-paying position in Nuremberg. Harsdörffer, a widely traveled and well-connected literary figure, acted as his patron, turning to contacts outside the city to find a suitable situation for him. As a result of Harsdörffer's recommendation to the noted grammarian Justus Georg Schottelius, Birken was offered a post in Wolfenbüttel as tutor to Anton Ulrich and Ferdinand Albrecht, sons of Duke August the Younger of Brunswick-Lüneburg, an inveterate bibliophile with one of the most important libraries in Europe. He was to receive free room and board and an annual salary of one hundred talers. Birken took up residency in Wolfenbüttel toward the end of 1645 and within a short time established himself in the intellectual community at the court. His poetic ability was readily apparent, and in early 1646 he was crowned a *poeta laureatus caesareus* (imperial poet laureate), an honor to which every ambitious young poet aspired.

Birken had a good rapport with his pupils, especially Anton Ulrich; the two would remain in friendly contact for the rest of Birken's life. But Birken's stay in Wolfenbüttel was cut short when his involvement in petty court intrigues led to his abrupt dismissal in October 1646. Traveling north with addresses provided by Harsdörffer, he made contacts with poets in various northern German cities. In Hamburg he stayed for an extended period of time with Johann Rist and met Philipp von Zesen, the head of the Teutschgesinnte Genossenschaft (German-minded Society). He moved on in 1647 to Dannenberg, where he once again took a position as tutor. A short pastoral from this time, *Dannebergische Helden-Beut* (The Elite of the Dannenberg Heroes, 1648), sheds some light on Birken's feelings about how bad luck had kept him from staying in Wolfenbüttel with his friends, but essentially the work is an allegorical glorification of Anton Ulrich, to whom it is dedicated. In early 1648 Birken traveled to the old Hanseatic port of Rostock, where he met Andreas Tscherning, poet and professor of rhetoric.

At this time the peace negotiations to end the Thirty Years' War were drawing to a successful conclusion in Münster and Osnabrück. Many details, however, remained to be worked out, and the delegates decided to move to Nuremberg to complete the negotiations, sign the treaty, and celebrate their accomplishments. The city councillors were less than enthusiastic about having two powerful opposing armies camped outside their walls, but the poets were of a different mind. The lavish celebrations that were planned and the presence of nobles from all over Europe offered the Nuremberg poets an unparalleled opportunity to display their talents in a European arena. Quick to grasp the significance this situation could have for his career, Birken hurried back to Nuremberg. The negotiations and ceremonies were not scheduled to begin until April 1649, but when Birken arrived on 20 November 1648 he found that Harsdörffer and Klaj had already aligned themselves with the Swedes. If Birken wished to further his literary career and find generous patrons, he had little choice but to seek his fortunes in the Catholic camp.

A series of works for the celebrations flowed rapidly from Birken's pen. The first, a speech titled *Krieges- und Friedensbildung* (A Depiction of War and Peace, 1649) that he delivered to an assembly of the imperial delegates and Nuremberg patricians in early 1649, is an allegorical description of the victory of Peace over War, with Piety, Justice, and Prosperity reigning in the end. Birken was paid ten talers for the work, but the speech was so well received that he quickly received other commissions. His *Kurtze Beschreibung deß schwedischen Friedensmahls* (A Short Description of the Swedish Banquet, 1649) is an account of the lavish dinner that the Swedes hosted in the Nuremberg city hall to commemorate

the end of the Thirty Years' War. *Teutscher Kriegs Ab- und FriedensEinzug* (The Departure of War and Entrance of Peace in Germany, 1650) is a short allegorical dramatic work in honor of Ottavio Piccolomini, Duke of Amalfi, the head of the Catholic delegation. The play, which was performed during festivities on 4 July 1650 and for which Birken received fifty talers, celebrates the end of war on German soil. Mars gives way to Venus, who says with confidence that the Germans will now be more interested in virtuous love than in destructive war. The hope is expressed that old German loyalty will once again reign in the country. Birken's *Teutschlands Krieges-Beschuluß, und FriedensKuß* (Germany's End to War and Kiss of Peace, 1650) describes in prose and verse the banquet, play, and fireworks display hosted by the duke of Amalfi in August 1650 in honor of his past adversary, Carl Gustaf of Sweden. The play, Birken's own *Teutscher Kriegs Ab- und FriedensEinzug,* was performed after the banquet, with members of Nuremberg's patrician families in the leading roles; it was followed by the fireworks display, in which a large mock castle was set afire and burned to the ground with Discordia inside; all that remained intact was a column with Peace standing confidently on top.

Although the peace celebrations in Nuremberg concluded in 1650, Birken wrote several more works on the subject. *Des Friedens Vermählung mit Teutschland* (The Wedding of Peace and Germany, 1651) is a collection of seven illustrated broadsheets about the most memorable events during the celebrations. *Die Fried-erfreuete Teutonie* (Teutonia, Delighted in Peace, 1652), which Birken calls a "Geschichtschrift" (poetic representation of history), is an allegorical account of the peace celebrations in prose and verse that includes expanded parts from some of his earlier works on the subject. The plot is straightforward. When Princess Teutonia (Germany) hears of the end of the war, she goes to Norisburg (Nuremberg) and asks the Tesping (Pegnitz) Shepherds to compose poetic works to commemorate the occasion. Among the military who attend the celebrations are the duke of Filama (the duke of Amalfi) and Prince Vagusto (Carl Gustaf) of Deusien (Sweden). They host sumptuous banquets, and in the end all depart in peace. Birken began a further allegorical play at this time, *Margenis oder Das vergnügte bekriegte und wiederbefriedigte Teutschland* (Margenis; or, Happy, Embattled, and Once Again Peaceful Germany), in which the leading character represents Germany (*Margenis* is an anagram for *Germanis*); but other projects postponed its completion, and it did not appear in print until 1679.

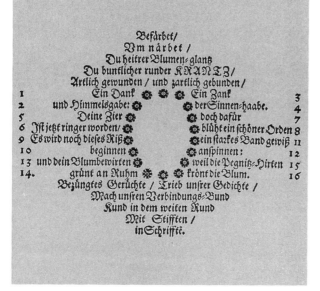

Dem spielerischen Gestaltungswillen der Nürnberger entsprach auch das Verfassen von Figurengedichten, wo die Strophenform als bildliche Wiedergabe des beschriebenen Gegenstandes galt. Die Pegnitz-Schäfereien enthalten zahlreiche Beispiele davon. Wir zitieren eins aus der von Sigmund von Birken und Johann Klaj verfaßten Fortsetzung der ursprünglichen Pegnitz-Schäferei (1645). Im Zusammenhang mit dem Bericht von der Gründung des Ordens beschreibt Klaj den Ursprung des blumenbestickten Seidenbandes, das als Kennzeichen von den Mitgliedern getragen wurde. Die Worte sind Strefon (Harsdörffer) in den Mund gelegt.

Figure poem from Fortsetzung der Pegnitz-Schäferey, *by Birken and Johann Klaj. The poem is set in the form of the object it describes: the flower-embroidered silk band worn by the members of the Pegnesischer Blumenorden.*

The works Birken wrote during the peace celebrations brought him recognition not only in Nuremberg but across the empire, but they did not immediately improve his precarious financial situation. His elegant eulogizing of the imperial side did, however, bring him to the attention of high-ranking Austrians, who began to take an interest in furthering the young poet's career. Baron (later Count) Gottlieb von Windischgrätz, an influential nobleman at the imperial court in Vienna who fancied himself a poet of sorts, sought Birken's help in polishing some of his own writings. Impressed by Birken's talents and pleased with the outcome of the work, he soon became Birken's patron. It was primarily through his intercession with Emperor Ferdinand III that Birken was ennobled on 15 May 1655 in recognition of the works he had written in praise of the Hapsburgs. To the hereditary patricians in Nuremberg, however, he would always be a commoner dependent on their goodwill.

With the honor of ennoblement came some monetary remuneration, but not enough to make Birken financially independent. For the rest of his life he would have to seek employment as an editor of other people's works and sell his services as an occasional poet. The diaries he kept for most of the last two decades of his life reveal how filled his time was with commissions for occasional poetry and various larger projects; hardly a month passed when he was not writing verse for a birth, marriage, promotion, death, or some other occasion, and frequently he had to divide his time among several different commissioned works. It is clear from the diaries that Birken valued these poems as highly as he did any of his literary work, and when he received a commission for an occasional poem it usually took precedence over other long-term projects in which he was already engaged. Once he did commit himself to composing an occasional poem, he tended to complete it in one day, no matter how long it might be.

Birken's ties to the imperial court continued to grow and were strengthened with the appearance in 1657 of his *Ostländischer Lorbeerhäyn* (Eastern Laurel Grove), dedicated to the future Emperor Leopold I. A genealogical eulogy in the garb of a prose eclogue, it is set in a typical pastoral scene along the Pegnitz River. Floridan and three fellow shepherd-poets, walking in the forest, meet the nymph Noris, who leads them to a beautiful temple dedicated to the glory of the House of Hapsburg and filled with ornate genealogical monuments to the Hapsburg emperors from Rudolf I to Birken's time. The praise of the Hapsburgs is continued in an appendix, which includes many panegyric poems dedicated to noble and nonnoble families, some of whom had helped Birken to further his career.

Birken had established his reputation as a literary figure and was in correspondence with influential people throughout the empire, yet he had still not achieved financial security. A common way to improve one's economic position was through a calculated marriage, and in 1658 Birken married Margaretha Magdalena Müleck, née Göring, a landed woman twice widowed and sixteen years his senior whom he had met in Creussen, near Bayreuth. The marriage was one of convenience rather than of love, and their years together were marked by constant strife, some of it physical in nature. Having been ennobled, Birken was theoretically the equal of his wife; but with no wealth of his own, he was dependent on her for any fundamental improvement in his material circumstances. Unfortunately for him, however, the tribulations of her earlier life had taught her to guard her assets carefully, and thus Birken remained responsible for covering all household expenses out of his own income. In accordance with his wife's wishes, they lived for a few months on her estate in Creussen and then moved to Bayreuth, where the margrave of Brandenburg held court. Although there was little chance of Birken's obtaining lucrative commissions in this provincial court town, he would have had little choice but to continue living in Bayreuth had his connections with Vienna not necessitated his return to Nuremberg in 1660.

In this age of absolute rulers, representations of their power and wealth in art and literature had the important function of legitimizing their dynastic claims, and at the imperial court there was keen interest in having a written history of the glories of the House of Hapsburg. The decision was, therefore, made in Vienna to update and publish *Das Österreichische Erenwerk* (The Austrian Work of Honor), a chronicle of the house that had been completed in 1555 by Clemens Jäger (though it was commonly attributed to Johann Jacob Fugger). The publication of such a monumental work had to be overseen by a well-established publisher, and Michael Endter in Nuremberg was chosen. An astute businessman, he was of the opinion that the text had to be modernized to conform to contemporary literary taste. Birken had not yet produced any historical work of significance, but Endter was well acquainted with his literary abilities and arranged, along with Birken's influential contacts in Vienna, to have Birken engaged as the editor. For Birken, an opportunity to work for the imperial court was a godsend.

The literary atmosphere in the Nuremberg to which Birken returned was profoundly different from what it had been only ten years earlier. Klaj, who had shown such poetic promise in the mid 1640s, had dissipated his talents and had died in 1656. Harsdörffer, who had been the driving force behind much of the literary activity in the city since the early 1640s, had lost interest in the Pegnesischer Blumenorden after the first few years and had died in 1658. No one had come forward to take his place, and the society was on the verge of dissolving. It thus fell to the energetic and ambitious Birken to revive Nuremberg as a literary center. The Pegnesischer Blumenorden had been without a *Präses* (head) for four years when the few remaining members selected Birken to fill the office in 1662, and he immediately set about rebuilding the society. Whereas during Harsdörffer's fourteen years of leadership only fifteen members had joined the society (and almost all of these before 1650), in the nineteen years of Birken's guidance almost four

times as many new members were admitted. He also altered the earlier constituency of almost exclusively male commoners by admitting thirteen women and five nobles. Under Birken's leadership the shepherd-poets in the *Pegnesischer Blumenorden* continued to cultivate an interest in the refinement and elevation of the German language, and for some – especially for Birken – a strong personal piety also shows through in the poetry. Most of the pastorals that the members in Nuremberg produced were communal works in which poems and individual verses are woven into a loose narrative structure. Birken collected some of these poems in a two-volume anthology, *Pegnesys* (Pegnesis, 1673).

Birken was elected in 1658 into the Fruchtbringende Gesellschaft (Fruit-bringing Society), the oldest and most influential of the German language societies, under the name Der Erwachsene (The Adult). His stature continued to grow during the 1660s as he undertook some of his most ambitious projects and established his reputation as one of the most respected literary figures in the empire. He continued to compose occasional poems and pastorals, but his primary interest turned increasingly to longer geographical and historical works. The first was *Der Donau-Strand* (The Banks of the Danube, 1664), which appeared at a time when there was intense interest in the Ottoman Empire because of widespread unrest in Hungary. Birken's stated objective was to describe all of the cities and lands along the Danube from its source at Donaueschingen to its end near Constantinople (today Istanbul, Turkey), and the work is a compilation of material from various earlier travel accounts and histories by other authors. The language throughout is elegant and literary, whereas the content and tone vary from objective listings and descriptions to blatant Christian polemics against the Turks. Birken shared with his compatriots a deep-seated hatred of the Turks, who in 1529 had advanced as far as Vienna and who remained a threat to Christian Europe. There was both fear of and fascination with the Turks, and in this atmosphere works such as *Der Donau-Strand* enjoyed great popularity. It was reprinted many times and was enlarged by other hands and reprinted several more times into the early eighteenth century. As part of his interest in the Turkish archenemy Birken also edited Simon Wolder's *Türckischer Untergang* (Turkish Demise, 1664) and translated Graf von Franz Nadasdi's *Mausoleum potentissimorum ac Gloriosissimorum Regni Apostolici Regum & Primorum Militantis Ungariæ Ducum* (Mausoleum for the Most Powerful and Most Glorious Kings of the Christian Kingdom and for the Foremost Military Leaders of Hungary, 1664).

Birken's edition of Jäger's chronicle appeared in 1668 as *Spiegel der Ehren des Hochlöblichsten Kayser- und Königlichen Ertzhauses Oesterreich* (Mirror of Honors of the Most Praiseworthy Royal and Imperial House of Austria). Jäger's manuscript had ended with the death of Emperor Maximilian I in the early sixteenth century, so Birken's main task was to bring it up to date; he also made revisions in Jäger's commentary and polished the prose. Following the accepted norm of scholarly writing at the time, he relied heavily on the work of others for his new material. In one section, for example, only one of fourteen folio pages contains material by Jäger; the remaining thirteen are a compilation of excerpts from various other sources. Birken stresses in his introduction that his work is impartial, but he is clearly a pro-Austrian chronicler rather than an objective historian. He was required to send his drafts to Vienna to be studied by the censors, who deleted any comments that might reflect negatively on the House of Hapsburg, the pope, the clergy in general, Venice, Bavaria, or other Catholic lands and rulers. The monumental work that Birken produced is, consequently, a prime example of biased, if not fanciful, baroque historiography. It is of only limited historical use to modern scholars, though it was highly valued by those who had commissioned it.

In the same year, Birken's *HochFürstlicher Brandenburgischer Ulysses* (The Prince of Brandenburg as Ulysses), commissioned by Christian Ernst, margrave of Brandenburg, was published in Bayreuth. After his departure from Bayreuth, Birken had continued to maintain close contacts with the court, primarily through his correspondence with Caspar von Lilien, the most influential of the margrave's advisers. In 1662 Birken had written two works in celebration of the margrave's marriage to a Saxon princess that were so well received that Birken became the unofficial court poet. He continued to write occasional poems for various people at the court, and it was natural for him to be engaged to write the literary account of the margrave's grand tour. It was widely believed at the time that a grand tour was necessary for princes if they were to rule their lands wisely, and Birken argues in his introduction that such travels were undertaken not simply to see curiosities but to learn useful things through firsthand observation of people and customs in other lands. Christian Ernst had traveled from 1656 to 1661 through Germany, France, Italy, and the Netherlands, and, based on his travel journals and the reports that he had sent back to his

court in Bayreuth, Birken wrote an encomiastic account of his peregrinations and compared him in exaggerated fashion to Ulysses. Birken's diaries and letters reveal how closely the poet worked with the court in Bayreuth while composing this work. He was required to submit a draft of each section to Lilien, who discussed the text with the margrave before returning the emended manuscript to Birken. Though the biased nature of work vitiates any value it might have for historians, it shows clearly Birken's ability to transform rather mundane material into a pleasing literary narrative.

The following year Birken wrote *Guelfis oder NiderSächsischer Lorbeerhayn* (Guelfis; or, Lower Saxon Laurel Grove), a panegyrical prose eclogue similar to his *Ostländischer Lorbeerhäyn* of twelve years earlier. He dedicated the work to Anton Ulrich, his former pupil, who was then the ruling duke of Brunswick-Lüneburg. Written in prose and verse, the work follows closely the format of the earlier genealogical work. The nymph Guelfis takes the author to a grotto filled with monuments to members of the Brunswick-Lüneburg house, giving him the opportunity to develop an idealized genealogy of the house from the first Guelph ruler to the death of Duke August the Younger in 1666. The appendix includes many pages of celebratory poetry and family trees.

In 1670 Birken's wife died, and although the childless marriage had been filled with arguments about the most trivial matters, he genuinely grieved for her. In her memory he wrote a funerary pastoral, "Floridans Lieb- und Lob-Andenken seiner seelig-entseelten Margaris" (Floridan's Thoughts of Love and Praise for His Dearly-Departed Margaris), which was printed at the end of his *Todes-Gedanken und Todten-Andenken* (Thoughts of Death and Remembrances of Those Who Are Deceased, 1670). Birken was understandably preoccupied at this time with thoughts of human mortality. The devout Christian belief in the vanity of human endeavors and in the transitoriness of all earthly objects is the basic theme of much of baroque poetry, and Birken's purpose in this work is to help people prepare in a Christian way for the end of their earthly existence. The work is a collection of thirteen daily preparations for death on such subjects as remembering human mortality, thanking the Lord for his kindness, and repenting for sinful behavior. Each section is a mixture of prayer, devotional prose, and devotional poetry; some of the poems were borrowed from other poets.

Birken's experience in his first marriage might have moved him to remain single, but his health

Title page for a wedding poem by Birken, Klaj, and
Anton Burmeister

had been so adversely affected by his drinking that he needed a wife to help him carry out his daily affairs. He considered marrying Catharina Margaretha Schweser, a talented eighteen-year-old Bayreuth poet who was also a member of the Pegnesischer Blumenorden, but she showed no interest in marriage. He eventually found a suitable partner in Nuremberg, and in 1673 he married Clara Catharina Weinmann, née Bosch, a fifty-eight-year-old widow. It was, once again, a marriage of convenience that brought him little contentment.

Although the later stage of his life was not particularly happy, Birken's productivity continued and his fame grew. He became involved in several large editorial projects. His former pupil, Anton Ulrich, had continued to develop his literary interests, and as he worked on his multivolume novels he turned to Birken for assistance as an editor and as his literary agent in Nuremberg, where the novels were to be printed. As early as 1664 Birken was revising and correcting drafts of Anton Ulrich's *Die Durchleuchtige Syrerinn Aramena* (The Illustrious Syrian Woman Aramena, 1669–1673), and from 1672 until the spring of 1673 this project entailed almost

daily work. No sooner had this project concluded than his editorial work on Anton Ulrich's *Octavia: Römische Geschichte* (Octavia: A Roman Story, 1677–1679) began. At about the same time he was also involved in editing Joachim von Sandrart's monumental *Teutsche Academie der Edlen Bau- Bild- und Mahlerey-Künste Pittura* (The German Academy of the Noble Arts of Architecture, Sculpture, and Painting, 1675–1679). In all of these editorial projects Birken's stylistic revisions show a penchant for linguistic economy rather than complexity. In contrast to the high-flown rhetorical style common at the time, Birken's is one of naturalness, verisimilitude, and simplicity. By placing more weight on reason than on fantasy Birken was pointing in his own way toward the style of the early Enlightenment.

At this time Birken also returned to his historiographical work, and in 1677 he finished *Chur- und Fürstlicher Sächsischer Helden-Saal* (Gallery of Saxon Electoral and Princely Heroes), in which he depicts the lives and deeds of Saxon rulers from the time of Harderich, around 70 B.C., up to his own time. His stated purpose was to bring together material from disparate sources to give a unified account of the

Saxon house, and he succeeded in producing not a scholarly historical work but a highly readable chronicle of the Saxon rulers. The work was so popular that it was expanded anonymously in the early eighteenth century and reprinted until the middle of the century.

The most important work of Birken's later life is *Teutsche Rede-bind- und Dicht-Kunst, oder kurze Anweisung zur teutschen Poesy, mit Geistlichen Exempeln* (German Art of Poetry; or, A Short Introduction to German Verse, with Religious Examples), which he had begun many years earlier but did not complete for publication until 1679. It is a learned treatise on German poetics based on the idea that literature has primarily a Christian, moralistic role to play. The earliest poets, for him, were biblical figures such as Moses and David, and, therefore, he concludes that pastoral poetry is the oldest and most noble type of poetry. All poetry comes directly from God, and its ultimate purpose is to praise God. Birken was not blind to the merits of classical poetry, but he found the new vernacular poetry to be theologically superior and, therefore, suitable to replace classical poetry as the norm. For example, he rejects Aristotle's dictum that the purpose of a tragedy is to produce and purge feelings of pity and fear; in its place he demands that plays praise God and move Christians to do good deeds. By rejecting any classical norm for poetry he puts the Christian poet in the position of superseding his pagan predecessors. This line of reasoning was ultimately a legitimation of his own role as a writer of the new vernacular poetry.

Birken's theory of the Christian function of literature determined much of the poetry that he wrote, especially in later life. Throughout his career he devoted much of his energy to devotional poetry, and many of these songs, hymns, and poems appeared in works by other authors, such as Johann Michael Dilherr. After his second wife's death in 1679 he was beset with growing concerns about his own mortality and concentrated his efforts on writing devotional poetry and preparing it for publication. His "Psalterium Betulianum" (Birken's Psalter), a collection of devotional songs, and "Todten-Andenken und Himmelsgedanken" (Remembrances of the Dead, and Thoughts of Heaven), a collection of poems of mourning, were never published as books, although many of the poems in them had previously been printed individually. A collection of his devotional poems did appear shortly before his death as *Heiliger Sonntags-Handel und Kirch-Wandel* (Solemn Sunday Devotion and Church Conduct, 1681).

Throughout his life Birken had not been in the best of health, and in later years his diet, his sedentary work habits, and his alcoholism contributed to his becoming so obese that he was unable even to climb stairs unassisted. In his diary he complained about attacks of gout and rheumatism, and he became increasingly aware of his approaching end. In early June 1681 he complained of health problems, and on 12 June he died of a heart attack. He was mourned by friends and fellow poets throughout the empire.

Birken is a prime example of the occasional poet, one who with equal facility could mourn a death or celebrate a marriage. He is also *the* pastoral poet of the seventeenth century, who was equally comfortable writing for commoners or for nobles. From the 1650s to the time of his death he was a key figure in German literary life, and at the height of his success his web of contacts stretched across the empire. His need for recognition, money, and power, however, led many critics to characterize Birken reproachfully as an opportunistic and servile poet whose work lacks true poetic inspiration or commitment. Such judgments may be accurate if one accepts the Romantic emphasis on poetic inspiration, but it may be argued that they are misplaced when applied to poets in the seventeenth century. If he is viewed as an example of an accomplished occasional poet of his age, Birken deserves more widespread attention than he has thus far received, for an understanding and appreciation of his well-documented activities offers insights into the social value of poetry and its production in the seventeenth century.

Bibliographies:

Richard Mai, "Bibliographie zum Werk Sigmund von Birkens," *Jahrbuch der Deutschen Schillergesellschaft,* 13 (1969): 577–640;

Gerhard Dünnhaupt, "Sigmund von Birken," in his *Personalbibliographien zu den Drucken des Barock,* volume 9, part 1 (Stuttgart: Hiersemann, 1990), pp. 582–671.

References:

Jeremy Adler, "Arcadian Semiotics: The Visual Poetry of Sigmund von Birken (1626–1681)," in *The German Book 1470–1750: Studies Presented to David L. Paisey* (London: British Library, 1995), pp. 213–231;

Adler, "Pastoral Typography: Sigmund von Birken and the 'Picture Rhymes' of Johann Helwig," *Visible Language,* 20 (Winter 1986): 121–135;

Judith P. Aikin, "Happily Ever After: An Alternative Affective Theory of Comedy and Some Plays by Birken, Gryphius, and Weise," *Daphnis,* 17, no. 1 (1988): 55–76;

Frans Blom and Guillaume van Gemert, "Ein Stammbucheintrag Sigmund von Birkens aus dem Jahre 1649," *Wolfenbütteler Barock-Nachrichten,* 10 (October 1983): 458–463;

Hermann Braun, *Zum 300. Todestag von Sigmund von Birken,* Schriftenreihe der Volkshochschule Marktredwitz, no. 41 (Marktredwitz: Volkshochschule, 1981);

Carl August Hugo Burckhardt, "Aus dem Briefwechsel Sigmund von Birkens und Georg Neumarks 1656–1669," *Euphorion,* supplement 3 (1897): 12–55;

Rudolf Endres, "Das Einkommen eines freischaffenden Literaten der Barockzeit in Nürnberg," in *Quaestiones in musica: Festschrift für Franz Krautwurst zum 65. Geburtstag,* edited by Friedhelm Brusniak (Tutzing: Schneider, 1989), pp. 85–100;

Horst Helge Fassel, "Sigmund von Birken und Siebenbürgen," *Wolfenbütteler Barock-Nachrichten,* 5 (May 1978): 140–142;

Fassel and Klaus H. Schroeder, "Das Rumänienbild bei Sigmund von Birken (1626–1681)," *Südost-Forschungen,* 31 (1972): 164–177;

Klaus Garber, "Edition der Schäferdichtungen im Rahmen der 'Sämtlichen Werke' Sigmund von Birkens," *Jahrbuch für Internationale Germanistik,* 4 (1972): 71–72;

Garber, "Private literarische Gebrauchsformen im 17. Jahrhundert: Autobiographika und Korrespondenz Sigmund von Birkens," in *Wolfenbütteler Arbeiten zur Barockforschung,* volume 6, edited by Hans-Henrik Krummacher (Hamburg: Hauswedell, 1978), pp. 107–138;

Garber, "Sigmund von Birken: Ein Geleitwort zur Edition seiner Werke," *Wolfenbütteler Barock-Nachrichten,* 15 (December 1988): 78–84;

Garber, "Sigmund von Birken: Städtischer Ordenspräsident und höfischer Dichter: Historisch-soziologischer Umriß seiner Gestalt – Analyse seines Nachlasses und Prolegomenon zur Edition seines Werkes," in *Wolfenbütteler Arbeiten zur Barockforschung,* volume 7, edited by Martin Bircher and Ferdinand van Ingen (Hamburg: Hauswedell, 1978), pp. 223–254;

Garber, "Die Tagebücher Sigmund von Birkens: Einige Erwägungen anläßlich ihrer Edition," *Euphorion,* 68, no. 1 (1974): 88–96;

Garber and Dietrich Jöns, "Der Nachlaß Sigmund von Birkens," *Wolfenbütteler Barock-Nachrichten,* 6 (June 1979): 266–267;

Wolfgang Harms, "Anonyme Texte bekannter Autoren auf illustrierten Flugblättern des 17. Jahrhunderts: Zu Beispielen von Logau, Birken und Harsdörffer," *Wolfenbütteler Barock-Nachrichten,* 12 (August 1985): 49–58;

Wilhelm Hauenstein, "Der Nürnberger Poet Siegmund von Birken in seinen historischen Schriften," *Mitteilungen des Vereins für Geschichte der Stadt Nürnberg,* 18 (1908): 197–235;

Johann Herdegen, *Historische Nachricht von deß löblichen Hirten- und Blumen-Ordens an der Pegnitz Anfang und Fortgang* (Nuremberg: Riegel, 1744), pp. 79–158;

Ferdinand van Ingen, "Georg Philipp Harsdörffer und die Pegnitz-Schäfer Johann Klaj und Sigmund von Birken," in *Deutsche Dichter,* volume 2, edited by Gunter Grimm (Stuttgart: Reclam, 1989), pp. 206–211;

Adam Christof Jobst, "Sigmund von Birkens 'Amalfis,'" *Unser Egerland,* 18 (1914): 17–20, 42–44;

Dietrich Jöns, "Auftrag und Ausführung: Sigmund von Birkens Gedicht auf die Hochzeit von Christoph Fürer von Haimendorf mit Anna Lucia Löffelholz von Colberg am 13. September 1659," in *Bausteine zu einem transatlantischen Literaturverständnis; Views on Literatur in a Transatlantic Context,* edited by Hans W. Panthel and Peter Rau (Bern: Lang, 1994), pp. 131–149;

Jöns, "Sigmund von Birken: Zum Phänomen einer literarischen Existenz zwischen Hof und Stadt," in *Literatur in der Stadt,* edited by Horst Brunner (Göppingen: Kümmerle, 1982), pp. 167–187;

Jöns and Hartmut Laufhütte, "Sigmund von Birken: Werke und Briefe. Zum Stand der Arbeiten an der Abteilung 'Autobiographica und Briefe,'" *Wolfenbütteler Barock-Nachrichten,* 14 (July 1987): 9–11;

Jean-Daniel Krebs, "La poésie de circonstance à l'honneur: Les belles inconnues de Sigmund von Birken (1626–1681)," *Etudes germaniques,* 46 (July–September 1991): 357–360;

Joachim Kröll, "Bayreuther Barock und frühe Aufklärung, Teil 2: Die Briefe der Bayreuther General-Superintendent Caspar von Lilien an den Nürnberger Dichter Sigmund von Birken," *Archiv für Geschichte von Oberfranken,* 56 (1976): 121–234;

Kröll, "Der Dichter Sigmund von Birken in seinen Beziehungen zu Creußen und Bayreuth,"

Archiv für Geschichte von Oberfranken, 47 (1967): 179–276;

Kröll, "Die Erasmus-Bearbeitung Birkens: Ein Beitrag zur Fürstenspiegel-Literatur," *Archiv für Geschichte von Oberfranken,* 63 (1983): 147–218;

Kröll, "Sigmund Birken (1626–1681)," *Fränkische Lebensbilder,* 9 (1980): 187–203;

Kröll, "Sigmund von Birken dargestellt aus seinen Tagebüchern," *Jahrbuch für Fränkische Landesforschung,* 32 (1972): 111–150;

Hartmut Laufhütte, "Floridans Silvia: Transformation einer Liebesbeziehung; neue Erkenntnisse zur Biographie Sigmund von Birkens," *Archiv für Kulturgeschichte,* 73 (1991): 85–134;

Laufhütte, "Der gebändigte Mars: Kriegsallegorie und Kriegsverständnis im deutschen Schauspiel um 1648," in *Ares und Dionysos: Das Furchtbare und das Lächerliche in der europäischen Literatur,* edited by Laufhütte and Hans-Jürgen Horn (Heidelberg: Winter, 1981), pp. 121–135;

Laufhütte, "Der literarische Nachlaß Sigmund von Birkens als Gegenstand neuesten Forschungsinteresses," *Mitteilungen des Vereins für Geschichte der Stadt Nürnberg,* 76 (1989): 349–353;

Laufhütte, "Ein Schriftstellerleben im 17. Jahrhundert: Überlieferung und Wirklichkeit. Zur bevorstehenden Publikation der Autobiographie Sigmund von Birkens," *Literatur in Bayern,* 12 (1988): 40–45;

Wolfgang Lockemann, *Die Entstehung des Erzählproblems: Untersuchungen zur deutschen Dichtungstheorie im 17. und 18. Jahrhundert* (Meisenheim am Glan: Hain, 1963), pp. 60–76;

Richard Mai, "Das geistliche Lied Sigmund von Birkens," dissertation, University of Munich, 1968;

Fritz Martini, *Der Tod Neros: Suetonius, Anton Ulrich von Braunschweig, Sigmund von Birken oder: Historischer Bericht, erzählerische Fiktion und Stil der frühen Aufklärung* (Stuttgart: Metzler, 1974);

Heinrich Meyer, *Der deutsche Schäferroman des 17. Jahrhunderts* (Dorpat: Mattiesen, 1928), pp. 34–59;

Jane Ogden Newman, "Institutions of the Pastoral: The Nuremberg Pegnesischer Blumenorden," dissertation, Princeton University, 1983;

Newman, *Pastoral Conventions: Poetry, Language, and Thought in Seventeenth-Century Nuremberg* (Baltimore & London: Johns Hopkins University Press, 1990);

John Roger Paas, "In Praise of Johann Michael Dilherr: Occasional Poems Written in 1644 by Sigmund von Birken, Georg Philipp Harsdörffer, and Johann Klaj," *Daphnis,* 21, no. 4 (1992): 601–613;

Paas, "Jacob von Sandrarts gedruckte Reiterbildnisse mit Versen des Sigmund von Birken," *Philobiblon,* 38 (1994): 16–32;

Paas, "The Publication of a Seventeenth-Century Bestseller: Sigmund von Birken's *Der Donau-Strand* (1664)," in *The German Book 1450–1750,* pp. 229–241;

Paas, "Sigmund von Birken and Gabrielle Charlotte Patin," *Daphnis,* 18, no. 3 (1989): 569–575;

Paas, "Sigmund von Birken (1626–1681): A Microliterary Study of a German Baroque Poet at Work," in *The Image of the Baroque,* edited by Aldo Scaglione, Studies in Italian Culture, no. 16 (Bern: Lang, 1995), pp. 157–174;

Paas, "Sigmund von Birkens anonyme Flugblattgedichte im Kunstverlag des Paul Fürst," *Philobiblon,* 34 (1990): 321–339;

Paas, "Sigmund von Birken's *Des Friedens Vermählung mit Teutschland,*" *Wolfenbütteler Barock-Nachrichten,* 17 (December 1990): 82–89;

Paas, "Unknown Verses by Sigmund von Birken on Maps by Jacob von Sandrart," *Wolfenbütteler Barock-Nachrichten,* 21 (June 1994): 7–9;

Paas, ed., *Der Franken Rom: Nürnbergs Blütezeit in der zweiten Hälfte des 17. Jahrhunderts* (Wiesbaden: Harrassowitz, 1995);

Gustav Quedefeld, *Über Sigmund von Birken* (Freienwalde: Cohn, 1878);

August Schmidt, "Sigmund von Birken, genannt Betulius," in *Festschrift zur 250jährigen Jubelfeier des Pegnesischen Blumenordens,* edited by Theodor Bischoff and August Schmidt (Nuremberg: Schrag, 1894), pp. 477–532;

Blake Lee Spahr, *Anton Ulrich and Aramena: The Genesis and Development of a Baroque Novel,* University of California Publications in Modern Philology, 76 (Berkeley & Los Angeles: University of California Press, 1966), pp. 52–79;

Spahr, *The Archives of the Pegnesischer Blumenorden,* University of California Publications in Modern Philology, no. 57 (Berkeley & Los Angeles: University of California Press, 1960), pp. 75–91;

Spahr, "*Dorus aus Istrien:* A Question Answered," *Modern Language Notes,* 72 (December 1957): 591–596;

Spahr, "*Dorus aus Istrien:* A Question of Identity," *PMLA,* 68 (December 1953): 1056–1067;

Spahr, "The Pastoral Works of Sigmund von Birken," dissertation, Yale University, 1952;

Julius Tittmann, *Die Nürnberger Dichterschule: Harsdörffer, Klaj, Birken* (Wiesbaden: Sändig, 1965);

Michael Titzmann, "Zur Dichtung der Nürnberger 'Pegnitz-Schäfer': 'O Pan / der du in Wäldern irrest.' Ein Gedicht von Birken und Klaj und sein Kontext," in *Handbuch der Literatur in Bayern,* edited by Albrecht Weber (Regensburg: Pustet, 1987), pp. 221–234;

Jean-Marie Valentin, "Birken et Boccace: La comédie de *Sylvia,*" in *Barocker Lust-Spiegel: Studien zur Literatur des Barock. Festschrift für Blake Lee Spahr,* edited by Martin Bircher and others (Amsterdam: Rodopi, 1984), pp. 115–138;

Theodor Verweyen, "Daphnes Metamorphosen: Zur Problematik der Tradition mittelalterlicher Denkformen im 17. Jahrhundert am Beispiel des 'Programma Poeticum' Sigmund von Birkens," in *Rezeption und Produktion zwischen 1570 und 1730: Festschrift für Günther Weydt,* edited by Wolfdietrich Rasch and others (Bern: Francke, 1972), pp. 319–379;

Mara Wade, *The German Baroque Pastoral Singspiel* (Bern: Lang, 1990);

Franz X. von Wegele, *Geschichte der Deutschen Historiographie seit dem Auftreten des Humanismus* (Munich & Leipzig: Oldenbourg, 1885), pp. 693–696;

Conrad Wiedemann, "Sigmund von Birken 1626–1681," in *Fränkische Klassiker,* edited by Wolfgang Buhl (Nuremberg: Nürnberger Presse, 1971), pp. 325–336.

Papers:

Sigmund von Birken bequeathed his entire library and all his manuscripts to the Pegnesischer Blumenorden; except for some books that were lost during World War II, all of this material is in the Germanic National Museum in Nuremberg. Manuscripts include an autobiography in Latin up to the year 1656, diaries for almost all of the years from 1660 through 1679, diaries of his correspondence, more than two thousand letters to and by Birken, and several works, some of which were ready for publication at the time of Birken's death.

Jakob Böhme
(1575 – 16 or 17 November 1624)

Albrecht Classen
University of Arizona

BOOKS: *Der Weg zu Christo. Jn zweyen Büchlein* (Görlitz: Johann Rhamba, 1624); republished as *Tevtonici Philosophi* (Amsterdam: Heinrich Betke [i.e., Frankfurt am Main: Jacob Gottfried Seyler], 1624); translated by John Sparrow(?) as *The Way to Christ Discovered* (London: Printed by Matthew Simmons for H. Blunden, 1648); translated by John Joseph Stoudt as *Jacob Boehme's The Way to Christ: In a New Translation* (New York & London: Harper, 1947);

Iosephus Redivivus, edited by Abraham von Franckenberg (Amsterdam: Veit Heinrichs, 1630);

Avrora das ist: MorgenRöthe im Auffgang vnd Mutter der Philosophiae. Oder: Beschreibung der Natur (Amsterdam: Johannes Jansson, 1634); translated by Sparrow as *Avrora. That Is, The Day-Spring, or Dawning of the Day in the Orient, or Morning-Rednesse in the Rising Svn. That Is, the Root or Mother of Philosophie, Astrologie & Theologie from the True Ground* (London: Printed by John Streater for Giles Calvert, 1656);

De Signatvra Rervm: Das ist, Bezeichnung aller dingen, wie das Jnnere vom Eusseren bezeichnet wird (Amsterdam?, 1635); translated by John Ellistone as *Signatura Rerum, or the Signature of All Things, Shewing the Sign and Signification of the Severall Forms and Shapes in the Creation, and What the Beginning, Ruin, and Cure of Everything Is* (London: Giles Calvert, 1651);

Trost-Schrift, von vier Complexionen. Daß ist: Vnterweisung in zeit der anfechtung, fur ein stetz trauriges angefochtenes Hertze (Amsterdam, before 1636); translated by C. Hotham as *A Consolatory Treatise of the Four Complexions, That Is, an Instruction in the Time of Temptation for a Sad and Assaulted Heart* (London: Printed by T. W. for H. Blunden, 1654);

Vier Episteln des Erläuchten vnd von Gottes Geist getriebenen Mannes Jabob Bühmens. Von dem Wesen aller Wesen (N.p., 1639?);

Jakob Böhme; oil painting on wood, attributed to C. G. Rymann, dating from the first half of the eighteenth century. No authentic pictures of Böhme are known to exist (Stadt- und Kreismuseum, Kamenz).

Zween seher schöne SendBrieff, darinnen Das Leben eines wahren Christen beschrieben wird, was ein Christ sey, vnd wie Er ein Christ werde? Neben Andeutung waß ein TitelChrist sey? Was Jhrer beyder Glauben vnd Leben sey? (N.p., 1639); translated anonymously as *Two Theosophicall Epistles: Wherein the Life of a True Christian Is Described* (London: Printed by Matthew Simmons for B. Allen, 1645);

Bedencken vber Essaiae Stieffels Büchlein: Von Dreyerley Zustandt des Menschen, vnnd dessen Newen Geburt. Geschrieben Anno Christi 1621. (Amsterdam, 1639);

Mysterivm Magnvm, oder Erklärung vber das Erste Buch Mosis, von der Offenbahrung Göttlichen Worts durch die drey Principia Göttliches Wesens, vnd vom Vrsprunge der Welt und der Creation: Darrinen das

Reich der Natur, vnd das Reich der Gnaden erkläret wird (Amsterdam: Johann Jansson, 1640); translated by Ellistone and Sparrow as *Mysterium Magnum; or, an Exposition of the first Book of Moses called Genesis. Concerning the Manifestation or Revelation of the Divine Word through the Three Principles of the Divine Essence; also of the Originall of the World and the Creation. Wherein the Kingdome of Nature, and the Kingdome of Grace, Are Expounded* (London: Printed by Matthew Simmons for H. Blunden, 1654);

Von Christi Testamenten 2. Büchlein, edited by Heinrich Prunius (Dresden: Printed by Anastasio Morgenroth, 1642); translated by Sparrow as *Of Christ's Testaments, viz. – Baptisme and the Supper* (London: Matthew Simmons, 1652);

The Clavis, or Key. Or, An Exposition of Some Principall Matters, and Words in the Writings of Jacob Behmen, Very Usefull for the Better Apprehending, and Understanding of the Booke, Written in the German Language, in March and Aprill, Anno., 1624, translated by Sparrow (London, 1647); German version published as *Clavis oder Schlüssel etlicher vornehmen Puncten und Wörter, so in allen des Authoris Büchern zufinden, deutlicher erkläret* (Amsterdam: Printed by Christoph Conrad, published by Heinrich Betke, 1662);

XL. Questions concerning the Soule. Propounded by Dr. Balthasar Walter. And Answered, by Jacob Behmen . . . Written in the Germane Language Anno. 1620, translated by Sparrow (London: Printed by Matthew Simmons, 1647); German version published as *Viertzig Fragen von der Seelen Vrstand, Essentz, Wesen, Natur vnd Eigenschafft, was sie von Ewigkeit sey?,* edited by Balthasar Walther (Amsterdam: Hans Fabel, 1648);

The Second Booke. Concerning the Three Principles of the Divine Essence of the Eternall, Dark, Light, and Temporary World. Shewing What the Soule, the Image and the Spirit of the Soule Are, translated by Sparrow (London: Printed by Matthew Simmons for H. Blunden, 1648); German version published as *Beschreibung der drey Principien Göttliches Wesens,* edited by Prunius (Amsterdam: Heinrich Betke, 1660);

Dialogus oder Gespräch, einer hungerigen, dürstigen Seelen, nach der Quell des Lebens (der süssen Liebe Jesu Christi) vnd einer erleuchteten Seelen (Amsterdam: Printed by Hans Fabel, 1649);

The Third Booke of the Author, Being the High and Deepe Searching out of the Threefold Life of Man through (or according to) the Three Principles. By Jacob Behmen, Alias Teutonicus Philosophus. Written in the Germane Language, Anno 1620, trans-

lated by Sparrow (London: Printed by Matthew Simmons for H. Blunden, 1650); German version published as *Hohe und tieffe Gründe von dem dreyfachen Leben des Menschen, nach dem Geheimnüß der dreyen Principien Göttlicher Offenbarung* (Amsterdam: Heinrich Betke, 1660);

Concerning the Election of Grace. Or, Of Gods Will towards Man. Commonly Called Predestination. That Is, How the Texts of Scripture Are to Be Understood Which Treat of Fallen Lost Adam, and of the New Birth from Christ . . . Written in the German Tongue, Anno 1623, translated by Sparrow (London: Printed by John Streater for Giles Calvert & John Allen, 1655); German version published as *Von der Gnaden-Wahl, oder dem Willen Gottes über die menschen* (Amsterdam: Printed by Christoph Conrad, published by Heinrich Betke, 1665);

Theosophische Send-Schreiben des von Gott in Gnaden Erlächteten Jacob Böemens von Alt-Seidenburg. Darinnen allerhand Gottsehlige Ermanungen zu wahrer Buß und besserung: Wie auch einfältiger Bericht vom hochwürdigem Erkändtnüs Göttlicher und Natürlicher Weisheit. Nebst rechter prüfung itziger Zeit, edited by Abraham von Franckenberg (Amsterdam: Heinrich Betke, 1658); translated by Sparrow as *Theosophick Letters; or, Epistles of the Man, from God Enlightened, in Grace* (London: Printed by Matthew Simmons for Giles Calvert, 1661);

The Fifth Book of the Authour, in Three Parts. The First, of the Becoming Man or Incarnation of Jesus Christ the Sonne of God. That Is, concerning the Virgin Mary, What She Was from Her Original, and What Kinde of Mother She Came to Be in the Conception of Her Sonne Jesus Christ, and How the Eternal Word is Become Man. A Second Part, Is of Christ's Suffering, Dying, Death, and Resurrection, and How We May Enter Thereunto. The Third Part, Is of the Tree of Christian Faith, Shewing What True Faith Is, translated by Sparrow (London: Printed by John Macock for Lodowick Loyd, 1659); German version published as *Von der Menschwerdung Jesu Christi, wie das Ewige Wort sey Mensch worden. Und von Maria der Jungfrawen, wie sie sey von ihrem Urstand gewesen, und was sie sey in der Empfängnüß ihres Sohnes Jesu Christi für eine Mutter worden. Jn drey Theil abgetheilet* (Amsterdam: Heinrich Betke, 1660);

The Sixt Booke of the Authour. Being a High and Deep Searching of the Great Six Points, translated by Sparrow (London: Lodowick Lloyd, 1661); German version published as *Vom sechs Puncten hohe und tieffe Gründung* (Amsterdam: Printed by Christoph Conrad, published by Heinrich Betke, 1665);

A Fundamentall Instruction Concerning the Earthly and Concerning the Heavenly Mystery. How they Do Stand in One Another; and How in the Earthly the Heavenly Becometh Manifested of Revealed. Comprised in Nine Texts. By Jacob Behme Otherwise Called the Teutonick Philosopher. Written the 8. May 1620. in High Dutch, translated by Sparrow (London: Printed by Matthew Simmons for Lodowick Lloyd, 1661); German version published as *Gründlicher Bericht, vom Jrrdischen und Himmlischen Mysterio, wie dieselbe ineinander stehen: Was das Jrrdische und Himmlische offenbahret werde. Alles gantz ernstlich und treulich gegeben aus dem Erkentniß des großen Mysterii. Verfasset in Neun Texte, und geschrieben von Jacob Böhmen, den 8. Maji, 1620* (Amsterdam: Printed by Christoph Conrad, published by Heinrich Betke, 1676);

An Apologie concerning Perfection: Being a Fundamentall Answer and Reply upon Esaiah Stiefel His Exposition of Four Texts of the Holy Scripture, translated by Sparrow (London: Printed by Matthew Simmons for Giles Calvert, 1661); German version published as *Apologia, betreffend die Vollkommenheit des Menschen. Das ist, eine gründliche Antwort auff die Auslegung Esaiae Stiefels, über vier unterschiedliche Texte der H. Schrifft. Geschrieben im Jahr, 1622. geendigt den 6. Aprilis* (Amsterdam: Printed by Christoph Conrad, published by Heinrich Betke, 1676);

An Apologie or Defence for the Requisite Refuting of the Shamefull, Disgracefull Writings and Horrible Libell against the Book of True Repentance and of True Resignation, Which Gregor Rickter, Primate of Goerlits, Hath Spread Abroad against It, in Open Print. Answered in the Year of Christ, 1624, translated anonymously (London: Printed by Matthew Simmons for Giles Calvert, 1661); German version published as *Apologia oder Schutz-Rede zu gebührlichen Verantwortung und Ablehnung des schrecklichen Pasquils und Schmähkarten, wider das Bächlein, der Weg zu Christo genandt, jtem von der wahren Buß und Gelassenheit, welches Pasquil Herr Gregor. Richter, obrist Pfarrherr zu Görlitz darwider ausgesprenget hat* (Amsterdam: Heinrich Betke, 1675);

An Explanation or Exposition of the Table of the Three Principles of the Divine Revelation, Shewing How God, Is to Be Considered How He Is without Nature, in Himself, and Then in Nature, according to the Three Principles. Also, What Heaven and Hell,

the World, Time, and Eternity Are, together with All Creatures? Out of What All Is Existed. What the Visible and Invisible Are. By Jacob Behme Teutonicus Philosophus. Written in February, 1624, translated by Sparrow (London: Printed by Matthew Simmons for Lodowick Lloyd, 1661); German version published as *Betrachtung Göttlicher Offenbahrung, was Gott, Natur und Creatur, so wohl Himmel, Hölle, und Welt, samt allen Creaturen sind? Woher alle Dinge in der Natur ihren Uhrsprung genommen haben; und wozu Gott dieselbige geschaffen hat. Sonderlich von dem Menschen, was Adam und Christus sey. Durch den gantzen Proceß und Lauff der Welt, biß ans Ende, und in die Ewigkeit geführet; und jn 177. Theosophische Fragen vorgestelt. Zu mehrerm Nachdenken, was der Mensch sey, auß rechtem wahrem Theosophischen Grunde. Angefangen zu beantworten, jedoch nicht vollendet, im Jahr 1624.* (Amsterdam: Printed by Christoph Conrad, published by Heinrich Betke, 1677);

The first Apologie to Balthazar Tylcken, Being an Answer of the Authour, concerning his Booke the Avrora . . . This Answer Written Anno 1621, translated by Sparrow (London: Printed by Matthew Simmons for Giles Calvert, 1666); German version published as *Jacob Böhmens Erste Apologia wider Balthasar Tilken. Eine Verantwortung des Authoris, wegen seines Buchs Aurora; durch einen feindlichen Paßquill angefochten, im Jahr 1621* (Amsterdam: Printed by Christoph Conrad, published by Heinrich Betke, 1676);

Das umgewante Auge, welches handelt von der Seelen und ihrer Bildniß, und dan von der Turba, welche die Bildniß zerstöret (Amsterdam: Printed by Christoph Conrad, published by Heinrich Betke, 1676);

Eine kurtze Erklärung von Sechs Puncten, I. Vom Blut und Wasser der Seelen. II. Von der Gnaden-Wahl, vom Guten und Bösen. III Von der Sünde: Was Sünde sey? und wie es Sünde sey? IV. Wie Christus das Reich seinem Vater überantworten werde. V. Von der Magia; was Magia ist, und was der Magische Grund sey? VI. Vom Mysterio, was dasselbige ist? (Amsterdam: Heinrich Betke, 1676);

Jacob Böhmens Andere Apologia wider Balthasar Tilken, handelenda von dem ewigen Fürsatz und Gnadenwahl Gottes; wie auch von der Menschwerdung und Persohn Christi, und von Maria der Jungfrauen. Geschrieben im Jahr 1621. (Amsterdam: Printed by Christoph Conrad, published by Heinrich Betke, 1676).

Editions and Collections: *Des Gottseeligen Hoch-Erleuchteten Jacob Böhmens Teutonici Philosophi*

Alle Theosophischen Wercken, 15 volumes, edited by Johann Georg Gichtel (Amsterdam, 1682);

Theosophja Revelata. Das ist: Alle Göttliche Schriften des Gottseligen und Hocherleuchteten Deutschen Theosophi Jacob Böhmens, 2 volumes, edited by Johann Otto Glüsing (Hamburg: Hermann Heinrich Holle, 1715);

Christosophia. Das ist: Der Weg zu Christo (Hamburg: Hermann Heinrich Holle[?], 1718);

Theosophisches Hand-Buch, genannt: Der Weg zu Christo (Hamburg[?], 1730);

Theosophja Revelata. Das ist: Alle Göttliche Schriften des Gottseligen und Hocherleuchteten Deutschen Theosophi Jacob Böhmens, 14 volumes, edited by Johann Wilhelm Überfeld (Leiden or Amsterdam, 1730); facsimile reprint, 11 volumes, edited by A. Faust and W. E. Peuckert (Stuttgart: Frommann, 1955–1961);

Jakob Böhme's sämmtliche Werke, 7 volumes, edited by K. W. Schiebler (Leipzig: Barth, 1831–1847);

Jakob Böhmes Werke: Studienausgabe in Einzelbänden, edited by Gerhard Wehr (Freiburg: Aurum, 1975).

Editions in English: *Dialogues on the Supersensual Life,* translated by William Law and others, edited by Bernard Holland (London: Methuen, 1901);

The Signature of All Things, with Other Writings, edited by Clifford Bax (London: Dent / New York: Dutton, 1912);

Six Theosophic Points, and Other Writings, translated by John Rolleston Earle (London: Constable, 1919; New York: Knopf, 1920);

The Confessions of Jacob Boehme, edited by W. Scott Palmer (London: Methuen, 1920; New York: Knopf, 1920);

Jacob Boehme's The Way to Christ, in a New Translation, translated by John Joseph Stoudt (New York & London: Harper, 1947).

Christian mysticism was a major force in Europe throughout the Middle Ages, reaching its peak in the thirteenth and fourteenth centuries. Nevertheless, it continued to exert a strong influence on cultural life far into the sixteenth and seventeenth centuries. One of the major landmarks of German mystical writing is the oeuvre of Jakob Böhme, a simple seventeenth-century shoemaker, whom his contemporaries and many intellectuals of the Romantic movement admired as the "Teutonicus Philosophus" (German Philosopher).

Böhme was born in 1575 in Alt-Seidenberg, south of Görlitz in Silesia; the precise date is unknown. His father, Jakob, and his mother, Ursula, were peasants who had achieved a stable economic position by the time Jakob was born. As a boy he claimed to have discovered a cave in which stood a cauldron filled with gold; afraid, he ran out of the cave, and he could not find it again when he returned in the company of other children.

Because his physical condition was too weak for farming, his parents apprenticed him to a cobbler. He had his second mystical experience when a man entered the shop to buy a pair of shoes. Since Böhme was alone in the shop and had no commission from his master to sell shoes, he asked an unusually high price – which was, to his astonishment, paid immediately. After the customer left the shop he called Böhme out into the street and, holding his hand and calling him by his first name, told him that he would become a man of importance and that he should study the Bible arduously, be pious, and fear God.

After completing his apprenticeship Böhme began his years of wandering as a journeyman. Legend has it that he experienced other visions during those years, perhaps triggered by reading about Manichaean and Paracelsian ideas. He returned to Görlitz in 1592 and gained the rank of master cobbler in 1594. On 14 April 1599 Böhme acquired citizenship in Görlitz and bought a shoemaker's workshop. He also purchased a *Schuhbank* (shoe stand) at the city market. On 10 May of that year he married Katharina Kuntzschmann, the daughter of a butcher, and on 21 August he bought a house outside the city gates. On 29 January 1600 their son Jakob was born, followed by three other sons in 1602, 1603, and 1611. The second son appears to have become a victim of one of the many plague epidemics.

In 1600 Böhme had a mystical vision while looking at a pewter cup: he believed that he was able to see into the inner core of all things. Confused, he left the house to clear his mind; the vision continued to impress itself on him as he walked in the countryside. When the same vision recurred in 1610 he decided to write down what he had seen and learned. The major part of the manuscript, which Böhme called "Morgenröte im Aufgang" (Dawn in the East), was completed between January and Pentecost in 1612; it was published posthumously in 1634 as *Aurora das ist: MörgenRöthe im Auffgang und Mutter der Philosophiae* (translated as *Aurora. That Is, The Day-Spring, or Dawning of Day in the Orient,* 1656). Here Böhme merely describes his visions, refraining from the astrological and cabalistic arguments that would characterize his later treatises; this was one reason the nineteenth-century

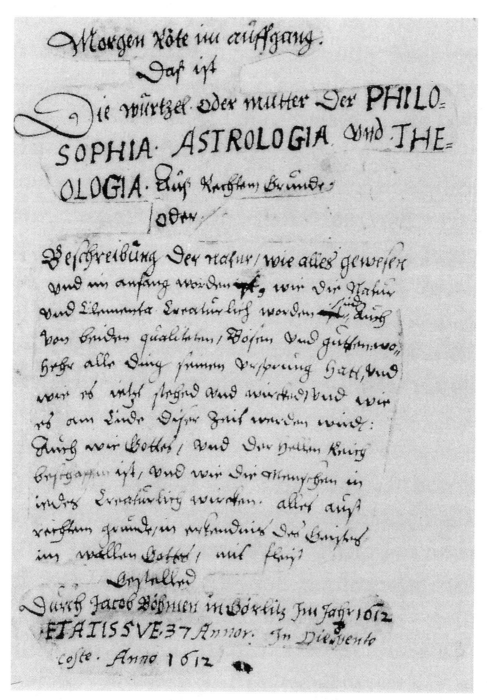

Title page of the manuscript for Böhme's first work, written in 1612 but not published until 1634

philosopher Georg Wilhelm Friedrich Hegel would hail this text as Böhme's masterpiece. At the beginning of the work Böhme characterizes philosophy, astrology, and theology as branches of one and the same tree, a tree deeply rooted in the soil of God's garden. The garden represents the world; the soil, nature; the tree trunk, the stars; the branches, the elements; the fruit, human beings; the sap, the Godhead. The study of nature will allow a person to receive a vision through which he or she can understand God's greatness and the secrets of the universe. Like many mystics before and after him, Böhme reports his inner struggles and his victories over the devil. Bursting through the gates of hell, he says, he reached the center of the universe – God – an experience that no words can express.

In spite of his mystical experiences, Böhme continued to conduct his business in a normal fashion, even becoming actively involved in a dispute between the shoemakers' and tanners' guilds. He eventually told friends about the manuscript; one of them was Count Karl of Sercha, a follower of the Protestant mystic Kaspar von Schwenckfeld, who borrowed it and secretly had a copy made. In a similar way, most of Böhme's later writings would be copied and distributed among his followers. With the exception of *Der Weg zu Christo* (1624; translated as *The Way to Christ Discovered,* 1648), his works would find their way into print only after his death.

Unfortunately for Böhme, the primate of the Protestant church in Görlitz, Gregor Richter, was strongly opposed to the heretical ideas that he perceived in Böhme's treatise. (Martin Luther had taken pains to distance himself from mystics such as Schwenckfeld.) On 28 July 1613 Richter attacked Böhme in his Sunday sermon as a drunkard, a heretic, a perjurer, and a disgrace to the church and the country. Böhme, who attended the service, was shocked by this sudden lashing out against him; ministers often used the pulpit to criticize the Catholic Church but rarely targeted members of their own community. On 30 July Böhme was ordered to defend himself before the city council. Despite his plea of innocence, he was exiled from Görlitz without even being allowed to see his family. The next morning the council voted again on the matter, decided that an injustice had been committed, and allowed the shoemaker to return. A few days later the council ordered him never to write about his visions again. Richter, however, continued his vitriolic attacks on Böhme. In March 1613 Böhme sold his shop and began a yarn trade that required him to travel extensively. Although he continued to be attacked in his hometown, these travels enabled him

to acquire many friends and supporters and to spread his ideas widely.

Among these friends and believers were Dr. Balthasar Walther of Glogau and Christian Bernhard of Sagan. The former, an expert in the alchemical, mystical, and scientific writings of Paracelsus who had traveled extensively in the Near and Middle East to acquire secret knowledge from the Jews, Arabs, and Persians, persuaded Böhme to document on paper his visions and how they were to be interpreted. In 1618, after a prolonged illness, Böhme witnessed the collapse of the Neiße bridge at Görlitz, which was for him a sign of divine intervention in human destiny. Also in 1618 what was to become the Thirty Years' War broke out in Bohemia; Böhme predicted that it would tear Germany apart and wreak havoc on large parts of its population, as is known from a letter to his friend Gottfried Freudenhammer dated 17 October 1621. Such experiences strengthened his resolve to resume his writing.

His second work, *Beschreibung der drey Principien Göttliches Wesens* (translated as *The Second Booke. Concerning the Three Principles of the Divine Essence of the Eternall, Dark, Light, and Temporary World,* 1648; published in German, 1660), completed in 1619, elucidates his concept of the tripartite structure of the world. The first principle, or cosmic sphere, is God's anger, in the form of fire, filling the universe. The second principle is the creation by God of his Son, in whom the principle of wrathful fire is transformed into light and love. The third principle is the divine creation, the transformation of divinity into material essence and human nature: all objects in the physical and the supernatural worlds are interrelated, and all share in God's power. Humanity, in particular, is an image and parable of God and is made out of the qualities of darkness, light, and the elements of the physical world. Adam is the corporeal representation of all three principles. When he fell asleep in the Garden of Eden, the spirit of joy, which Böhme calls Sophia, escaped from him, and it has been waiting for him ever since. Sophia is the fourth part of the Holy Trinity – or part of all three persons of the Trinity – and human beings are called on to reunite with this esoteric essence by reaching back to God. Alchemical elements and Lutheran thinking merge in Böhme's visionary imagery.

The next year Böhme wrote *Hohe und tieffe Gründe von dem dreyfachen Leben des Menschen, nach dem Geheimnüß der dreyen Principien Göttlicher Offenbarung* (translated as *The Third Booke of the Authour, Being the High and Deepe Searching out of the Threefold Life of Man* through [or according to] the Three Principles, 1650; German version published 1660), in which he says that God's nature reveals itself in the creation of humanity. Here is found Böhme's androgynous concept of the human being as comprising male and female elements, as shown by Eve's creation from Adam's rib. The sexes were separated by Original Sin, but the coming of Christ and the redemption of sin through his Crucifixion made possible their reunification. All people desire to return to the original undivided state of being, which explains the sexual attraction between men and women. The Virgin Mary is a symbol of the reunification of the two forces, since she gave birth to God's son. At the resurrection sexual differences will disappear. The world is a *mysterium magnum* (great miracle), a holistic unity in which nothing is left to chance but everything is ordered according to God's will; God created the world so that his nature would be visible. The world is in chaos because of Lucifer's fall, but hope remains because God's Spirit is reified in the world and can be observed in it. Böhme expresses similar views in three other works written in 1620: *Viertzig Fragen von der Seelen Urstand, Essentz, Wesen, Natur und Eigenschafft, was sie von Ewigkeit sey?* (translated as *XL. Questions concerning the Soule. Propounded by Dr. Balthasar Walter. And Answered, by Jacob Behmen,* 1647; German version published 1648); *Von der Menschwerdung Jesu Christi* (translated as *The Fifth Book of the Authour, in Three Parts. The First, of the Becoming Man or Incarnation of Jesus Christ the Sonne of God,* 1659; German version published 1660); and *Vom sechs Puncten hohe und tieffe Gründung* (translated as *The Sixt Booke of the Authour. Being a High and Deep Searching of the Great Six Points,* 1661; German version published 1665).

Concurrently Böhme was carrying on an extensive correspondence in which he discussed his visions and his interpretations of biblical texts; he also reflected on the approaching fronts of the Thirty Years' War. Instead of returning to his cobbler's workbench to produce footwear, which was in high demand because of the war, he continued his prolific outpouring of manuscripts and letters while his family labored to maintain the yarn business.

Opponents who criticized Böhme's writings included the Silesian nobleman Balthasar Tilke. Böhme responded in 1621 in a polemic titled "Schutzschriften wider Balthasar Tilke" (translated as *The first Apologie to Balthazar Tylcken,* 1666; German version published as *Jacob Böhmens Erste Apologia wider Balthasar Tilken,* 1676). In 1623 followed, in the same vein but in a more moderate tone, *Von der*

Gnaden-Wahl (translated as *Concerning the Election of Grace,* 1655; German version published 1665), in which he accused Tilke of being influenced by Calvinism. Böhme goes so far as to challenge the traditional view of the Creation as defended by the church. The original, unfathomable Will, which is neither evil nor good, is the "ewige Vater" (eternal Father). The born Will is his "eingeborene Sohn" (only begotten Son), an entity that establishes a foundation in a foundationless world. The medium for this creation process is *Geist* (Spirit). The result of the process is the happiness of Father, Son, and Spirit, a kind of mirror in which all three reflect themselves, which Böhme calls "Gottes Weisheit" (God's wisdom) or Sophia. Sophia emanates from God's words and constitutes material existence, as the Evangelist John stresses at the beginning of his testament.

Böhme was never able to overcome his opponents in public debates; one of these disputations, which took place in 1622 at the residence of Johann Theodor von Tschesch, was hardly to Böhme's credit. There, however, he met Abraham von Franckenberg, who was to edit some of his works. He made at least six major trips through the Lusatia region between 1621 and 1624, visiting the cities of Breslau, Striegau, Glogau, Bunzlau, and Liegnitz. In 1622 he wrote the enigmatic *De Signatura Rerum: Das ist, Bezeichnung aller dingen* (1635; translated as *Signatura Rerum, or the Signature of All Things,* 1651), possibly in an endeavor to impress the urban intelligentsia. Despite its intricacies, the work attracted a large audience and was copied many times by Böhme's followers before it appeared in print. The work is an ambitious attempt to discover order in a chaotic, war-torn world by revealing the divine scheme. God's language is written in living letters in every stone, plant, and animal and can be read by human beings; all parts of the cosmos share in the same characteristics and, thus, may understand each other. The universe consists of evil and good forces, which interact to create cosmic harmony.

In *Mysterium Magnum, oder Erklärung uber das Erste Buch Mosis* (1640; translated as *Mysterium Magnum; or, an Exposition of the first Book of Moses called Genesis,* 1654), which was completed by 11 September 1623 and would comprise nine hundred pages in printed form, Böhme completed the cycle of his major writings by creating a sophisticated symbolism that remains largely impenetrable. One reason for his choice of this enigmatic language was his conviction that it is impossible to talk about God in a rational way. Böhme anticipates the coming of the new human being, who will reintegrate the old

Adam into Christ and thereby leave the material world and linear time to enter the world of God's essence. Böhme argues that humanity has to relearn the true language, to return to the time before the building of the Tower of Babel, to become the mouthpiece for God's words.

Böhme's decisive battle with the Lutheran Church began when *Der Weg zu Christo* was published in January 1624; the printing, by Johann Rhamba in Görlitz, was financed by Johann Sigismund von Schweinichen without Böhme's knowledge. It was the first time any of his works had appeared in print; until then all his texts had been circulated in handwritten copies. Richter condemned the work as blasphemous and heretical and vilified the mystical writer vehemently. Böhme, who was away on a business trip, heard about Richter's pasquinade (as Böhme called it) but remained calm. In a letter to Martin Moser in Goldberg, dated 5 March 1624, he said that Richter's criticism would help his own work to attract a wide readership.

On 26 March Böhme returned to Görlitz and was summoned to defend himself before the city council for defying its prohibition against writing about his visions. Several members of the council supported Böhme but were afraid to speak up against Richter, and no decision was made. Böhme evaluated his appearance before the council as positive, since the members had been forced to read his other texts in preparation for it. Nevertheless, he and his family were exposed to the persecutions and ridicule of the citizens. Böhme composed *Apologia oder Schutz-Rede zu gebührlichen Verantwortung und Ablehnung des schrecklichen Pasquils und Schmähkarten, wider das Bächlein, der Weg zu Christo genandt, item von der wahren Buß und Gelassenheit, welches Pasquil Herr Gregor. Richter, obrist Pfarrherr zu Görlitz darwider ausgesprenget hat* (translated as *An Apologie or Defence for the Requisite Refuting of the Shamefull, Disgracefull Writings and Horrible Libell against the Book of True Repentance and of True Resignation, Which Gregor Rickter, Primate of Goerlits, Hath Spread Abroad against It, in Open Print,* 1661; German version published 1675), rebutting all points brought forth by the primate. Like many Reformation writers before him, Böhme stresses that the Holy Spirit can talk to anyone and is not bound to the institution of the church. He accuses Richter of being ignorant of his works and, hence, of lacking any authority to judge them. Most important, however, he appeals to Richter to exercise Christian love toward him. Böhme claims that he has been selected to be God's mouthpiece, whereas Richter might turn out to be the Antichrist. Insult is exchanged with insult as Böhme responds

Title page for a collection of Böhme's letters

to Richter's accusation that he is an alcoholic by making the same charge against Richter; but Böhme points out his own poverty would allow him only to drink cheap beer, whereas the minister had to be carried home on several occasions because he was drunk from wine or spirits. The city council, fearing that the clash between the two might lead to riots, asked Böhme to leave town for a time. His friend Benedict Hinckelmann, court physician and alchemist, invited him to be his guest in Dresden.

On 10 May 1624 Böhme traveled to the court in Dresden, where he met state officials and military officers, among them the Superior Court priest Höe von Höenegg, but it is uncertain whether the shoemaker ever met Duke August I of Saxony. His worst enemy, Richter, died on 24 August, at a time when Böhme was composing a new treatise, *Betrachtung Göttlicher Offenbahrung* (Meditation on Divine Revelation, 1677). During the writing he fell ill with fever and dropsy; he returned home on 7 November and died on 16 or 17 November after telling his family and friends that he had heard some divine music and was now going to paradise. The local clergyman refused to officiate at the burial in the public cemetery of Görlitz at the burial and had to be ordered by the magistrate to carry out his duty; he began his sermon by saying that he was following orders, and he rejected his fee. A monument at the cemetery in honor of Böhme was destroyed by a mob.

As in the case of his earlier writings, Böhme's final manuscript was quickly copied by hand; the copies prepared by Christian Bernhard and Michael Ender are considered the most reliable ones. In the Netherlands, where Böhme had a wide circle of followers, Heinrich Betke published some individual texts between 1568 and 1678. The Regensburg lawyer Johann Georg Gichtel assumed the task of editing Böhme's complete works beginning in 1682. Böhme's original manuscripts were lost or are indistinguishable from the copies; only in 1934 would Werner Buddecke discover the original of *MorgenRöthe im Auffgang,* which had been kept by a small group of Böhme's followers in Linz am Rhein.

As early as in 1620 an unidentified Latin writer had labeled Böhme "Teutonicus Philosophus" (German Philosopher) because of his influence on his contemporaries. In the seventeenth century Johannes Scheffler, "Angelus Silesius" (the Silesian Angel), was one of the first German poets to reflect Böhme's philosophy in his work; he was soon followed by Quirinus Kuhlmann. In Germany, the Romantics Ludwig Tieck, Friedrich von Schlegel, Friedrich von Hardenberg, and Johann Wolfgang von Goethe; in England, John Milton and Sir Isaac Newton; in France, Louis Claude de Saint Martin; and in Russia, Vladimir S. Solovjov and Nicolay A. Berdyayev testified to the enormous influence Böhme's work exerted on them, and the American philosopher and poet Ralph Waldo Emerson showed Böhme's influence. Philosophers such as Hegel, Friedrich Wilhelm Joseph von Schelling, and Ernst Bloch admired Böhme's dialectical worldview. Wilhelm Raabe created a portrait of Böhme in his novel *Der Hungerpastor* (1864; translated as *The Hunger-Pastor,* 1885), and Erwin Guido Kolbenheyer composed a historical novel about the shoemaker-mystic, *Meister Joachim Pausewang* (1910; translated as *A Winter Chronicle,* 1938). The writers Gerhart Hauptmann and Hermann Hesse expressed their deep admiration for Böhme, who also influenced the theologian Martin Buber; the physicist, mathematician, and philosopher Albert Einstein; and the psychologist Carl Gustav Jung.

Letters:

The Epistles of Jacob Behmen, Aliter, Tevtonicvs Philosophvs. Very Usefull and Necessary for Those That Read His Writings, and Are Very Full of Excellent and Plaine Instructions How to Attaine to the Life of Christ, translated by John Ellistone (London: Printed by Matthew Simmons for Giles Calvert, 1649).

Bibliography:

Gerhard Dünnhaupt, *Personalbibliographien zu den Drucken des Barock,* volume 9, part 1 (Stuttgart: Hiersemann, 1990), pp. 672–702.

Biographies:

Willy-Erich Peukert, *Das Leben Jakob Böhmes* (Jena: Diederichs, 1924);

Heinrich Bornkamm, *Luther und Böhme* (Bonn, 1925);

Gerhard Wehr, *Jakob Böhme in Selbstzeugnissen und Bilddokumenten* (Reinbek bei Hamburg: Rowohlt, 1971);

Ernst Heinz Lemper, *Jakob Böhme, Leben und Werk* (Berlin: Union, 1976);

Hans Tesch, *Jakob Böhme: Mystiker und Philosoph* (Munich: Delp, 1976).

References:

Franz von Baader, *Vorlesungen und Erläuterungen zu Jakob Böhmes Lehre,* volume 13, part 1 of his *Sämmtliche Werke,* edited by Franz Hoffmann and others (Leipzig: Bethmann, 1855);

Ernst Bloch, *Vorlesungen zur Philosophie der Renaissance,* second edition (Frankfurt am Main: Suhrkamp, 1972);

Heinrich Bornkamm, "Renaissancemystik, Luther und Böhme," *Luther-Jahrbuch,* 9 (1927): 156–197;

Werner Buddecke, *Verzeichnis von Jakob Böhme-Handschriften* (Göttingen: Häntzschel, 1934);

Wolfgang Buddecke, "Die Jakob-Böhme-Autographen: Ein historischer Bericht," *Wolfenbütteler Beiträge,* 1 (1972): 61–87;

Gerd Haensch, "Über die naturphilosophischen Anschauungen Jakob Böhmes," *Deutsche Zeitschrift für Philosophie,* 23, no. 3 (1975): 415–426;

Paul Hankamer, *Jakob Böhme: Gestalt und Gestaltung* (Bonn: Friedrich Cohen, 1924);

Elisabeth Hurth, "The Uses of a Mystic Prophet: Emerson and Boehme," *Philological Quarterly*, 70 (Spring 1991): 219–236;

Russell H. Hvolbek, "Being and Knowing: Spiritualist Epistemology and Anthropology from Schwenckfeld to Böhme," *Sixteenth Century Journal*, 22 (Spring 1991): 97–110;

Frans A. Janssen, "Böhme's 'Wercken' (1682): Its Editor, Its Publisher, Its Printer," *Quaerendo*, 16 (1986): 137–141;

Wolfgang Kayser, "Boehmes Natursprachenlehre und ihre Grundlagen," *Euphorion*, 31 (1930): 521–562;

Friedhelm Kemp, "Jakob Böhme in Holland, England und Frankreich," *Wolfenbütteler Arbeiten zur Barockforschung*, 11 (1983): 211–226;

Eberhard H. Pältz, "Zum Problem Glaube und Geschichte bei Jakob Boehme," *Evangelische Theologie*, 22 (1962): 156–160;

Pältz, "Zur Eigenart des Spiritualismus Jakob Boehmes," in *Wort und Welt: Festgabe Erich Hertzsch*, edited by Manfred Weise (Berlin: Evangelische Verlagsanstalt, 1968), pp. 251–261;

Michael John Petry, "Behmenism and Spinozism in the Religious Culture of the Netherlands, 1660–1730," *Wolfenbütteler Studien zur Aufklärung*, 12 (1984): 111–147;

Lawrence M. Principe and Andrew Weeks, "Jacob Boehme's Divine Substance 'Salitter': Its Nature, Origin, and Relationship to Seventeenth Century Scientific Theories," *British Journal for the History of Sciences*, 22 (March 1989): 53–61;

Peter Schäublin, *Zur Sprache Jakob Böhmes* (Winterthur: Keller, 1963);

T. Schipflinger, "Die Sophia bei Jakob Böhme," *Una Sancta*, 41 (1986): 195–210;

John Joseph Stoudt, *Sunrise to Eternity: A Study in Jakob Boehme's Life and Thought* (New York: Seabury, 1957);

Herman Vetterling, *The Illuminate of Görlitz or Jakob Böhme (*1575–✝ 1624). Life and Philosophy: A Comparative Study* (Leipzig: Markert & Petters, 1923; reprinted, Hildesheim: Gerstenberg, 1978);

D. Walsh, *The Mysticism of Innerworldly Fulfillment: A Study of Jakob Böhme* (Gainesville: University Presses of Florida, 1983);

Andrew Weeks, *Boehme: An Intellectual Biography of the Seventeenth-Century Philosopher and Mystic* (Albany: State University of New York Press, 1991);

Viktor Weiss, *Die Gnosis Jacob Böhmes* (Zurich: Origo, 1955).

Papers:

Jakob Böhme's papers are in the Herzog August Bibliothek Wolfenbüttel (Slg. 2405).

Augustus Buchner

(2 November 1591 – 12 February 1661)

Judith P. Aikin
University of Iowa

BOOKS: *Ehren Gedicht, an den Wolweisen vnd Achtbarn Herrn, Michael Hornenn, bißhero gewesenen Stadtrichter, nunmehr aber rechtmessig erwehleten vnd bestättigten Bürgemeister zu Witberg* (Wittenberg: Printed by Job Wilhelm Fincelius, 1628);

Nachtmal des Herrn. Nebenst etlichen andern Christlichen Getichten (Wittenberg, 1628);

Weynacht-Gedanken (Wittenberg, 1628);

De Philosophia Ecloga (Wittenberg: Printed by Salomon Auerbach's heirs, 1630);

In Theophania, sive Natalem Domini, Edyllia duo, quorum prius bucolicum, Ioas, inscribitur (Wittenberg, 1631);

Dissertatio Gemina de Exercitatione Styli: Instituta pro more in Panegyri Philosophicâ et publicè pronunciata (Wittenberg: Printed by Johann Röhner, 1635);

Die Bußfertige Magdalena, anonymous (Dresden: Gimel Bergen, 1636);

Trostschrifft an Heinrich Schützen, sächs. Capellmeister zu Dresden, über den Tod seiner Tochter (Wittenberg: Tobias Mevius's heirs, 1638);

Zwey TrostSchrifften an unterschiedene Personen, und unterschiedlich geschrieben, jetzo aber zusammen gebracht (Wittenberg: Printed by Johann Hake, published by Balthasar Mevius, 1644);

Gedicht auf Absterben des HochEdlen Gestrengen vnd Vesten Herrn Hansen Lösers vff Pretsch, Salitz, Hänichen und Nenckersdorff (N.p., 1644);

Dissertationum Academicarum, sive Programmatum Publico Nomine Editorum (Wittenberg: Johann Seelfisch, 1650);

Kurzer Weg-Weiser zur Deutschen Tichtkunst, aus ezzlichen geschriebenen Exemplarien ergänzet, mit einem Register vermehret, und auff vielfältiges Ansuchen der Studierenden Jugend izo zum ersten mahl hervorgegeben, edited by Georg Göze (Jena: Georg Sengenwald, 1663);

De Commutata Ratione Dicendi Libri Duo: Qvibus in Fine Adjuncta Dissertatio Gemina de Exercitatione Styli,

Augustus Buchner; engraving by Johann Dürr after a painting by Christoph Spetner

edited by Praetorius (Wittenberg: Printed by Matthius Henckel for Buchner's heirs, 1664);

Anleitung zur Deutschen Poeterey, wie Er selbige kurtz vor seinem Ende selbsten übersehen, an unterschiedenen Orten geändert, und verbessert hat, edited by Otho Praetorius (Wittenberg: Printed by Michael Wendt for Buchner's heirs, 1665);

Poet aus dessen nachgelassener Bibliothek heraus gegeben, edited by Praetorius (Wittenberg: Printed by Michael Wendt for Buchner's heirs, 1665);

Orationes Panegyricae, Habitae in Academia Wittenbergensi. Annexae sunt Ejusdem Orationes

Funebres, quas in Exequiis Clarissimorum virorum, aliorumque honestissimorum hominum, et civium Academicorum Habuit, edited by Praetorius (Kleve: Johann Mauritius, 1668; enlarged edition, Wittenberg: Printed by Michael Wendt for Buchner's heirs, 1669);

Epistolæ Opus posthumum (Dresden: Published by Martin Gabriel Hübner, printed by Melchior Bergen's heirs, 1679);

Orationum Academicarum Volumina Duo; Qvorum prius Auctius Multò, quam Hactenus Fuit, Panegyricas, posterius nunquam antehac in lucem editum, Festas continet, edited by Johann Jacob Stübelius (Dresden: Published by Martin Gabriel Hübner, printed by the widow and heirs of Melchior Bergen, 1682);

Poetae et Oratoris Celeberrimi Poemata Selectiora, nunc primum edita (Leipzig & Frankfurt am Main: Printed by Johann Heinrich Richter, published by Martin Gabriel Hübner in Dresden, 1694);

Poemata Elegantissima, nunc altere vice multo correctiora quam antea, edited by Stübelius (Leipzig & Frankfurt am Main: Martin Gabriel Hübner, 1720).

Editions: *Anleitung zur Deutschen Poeterey. Poet (1665),* edited by Marian Szyrocki, Deutsche Neudrucke, Reihe Barock, 5 (Tübingen: Niemeyer, 1966);

Kurtzer Wegweiser zur Deutschen Tichtkunst (Leipzig: Zentralantiquariat, 1977).

OTHER: Philipp Melanchthon, *Grammatica Latina Philippi Melanchthonis,* edited by Buchner (Wittenberg: Printed by Hiob Wilbel, 1622);

Basilius Faber, *Thesaurus Eruditionis Scholasticæ,* edited by Buchner (Wittenberg, 1623);

"Wer ist, Herr Nüßler doch, so bisher Venus Bogen . . . ," in *Herren Bernhardt Wilhelm Nüßlers vnd Jungfrawen Justinen Gierlachinn Hochzeitlieder* (N.p., 1624);

Venantius Honorius Clementianus Fortunatus, *Hymnus de Resurrectione Domini, cum animadversionibus Augusti Buchneri,* edited by Buchner (Wittenberg, 1627);

Quintus Horatius Flaccus, *Ars poetica,* commentary by Buchner (Wittenberg, 1628);

Titus Maccius Plautus, *Comoediæ XX. superstites,* edited by Buchner (Wittenberg: Printed by Johann Röhner for Zacharias Schüer's heirs, 1640);

Gabriel Naudé, *Bibliographia Politica,* edited by Buchner (Wittenberg: Published by Balthasar Mevius, printed by Johann Röhner, 1641);

Virgil, *Oratio de Quarta Virgilii Ecloga: Vtrumne id carmen de Christo Servatore Poëta condiderit,* commentary by Buchner (Wittenberg: Printed by Johann Röhner, 1641);

König Davids vornembster Danck-Psalm, verse paraphrase by Buchner (Altenburg: Printed by Otto Michael, 1642);

Aurelius Prudentius Clemens, *Hymnus de Christi Domini et Salvatoris Nostri Natali,* edited by Buchner (Wittenberg: Published by Balthasar Mevius, printed by Johann Hake, 1643);

Petrus Cunaeus, *Orationes Argumenti Varii,* edited by Buchner (Wittenberg: Printed by Johann Röhner, published by Melchior Klosemann in Frankfurt an der Oder, 1643);

Cajus Plinius Caecilius Secundus, *Epistolarum Libri X.,* commentary by Buchner (Frankfurt an der Oder: Melchior Klosemann, 1644);

Lucius Annaeus Seneca, *Consolationem ad Helviam,* preface by Buchner (Wittenberg: Printed by Johann Hake for Balthasar Mevius, 1655);

"Der schöne Tag bricht an," in *Neu-erfundene Geistliche Wasser-quelle,* edited by Johann Niedling (Frankfurt an der Oder: Johann Ernst, 1658), p. 96;

Wolfgang Franz, *Historia Animalium,* preface by Buchner (Wittenberg: Published by Balthasar Mevius, printed by Johann Bauer in Leipzig, 1659);

Gotthilf Treuer, *Deutscher Daedalus begreiffendt ein vollständig außgeführtes poetisch Lexicon und Wörter-Buch,* foreword by Buchner (Berlin: Rupert Völcker, 1660);

Cornelius Nepos, *Vitæ excellentium Imperatorum,* commentary by Buchner (Hamburg, 1674);

John Barclay, *Icon Animorum, Celeberrimi Viri,* commentary by Buchner (Dresden: Printed by Christian Bergen for Martin Gabriel Hübner, 1680);

C. Cornelius Tacitus, *Agricolae Vita,* commentary by Buchner (Leipzig: Printed by Christoph Günther for Martin Gabriel Hübner, 1683);

Theophrastus, *Characteres Morum. Cum nova versione Latina,* edited by Johann Conrad Schwartz, commentary by Buchner (Coburg, 1739).

Augustus Buchner, "the father of the German dactyl" and one of the most significant literary figures of the second quarter of the seventeenth century in Germany, was neither an extraordinarily talented poet nor a particularly prolific one. Most of his poems, whether in Latin or in German, were published only in pamphlets produced for particular occasions; unlike many of his contemporaries, he never put together a collected edition of his poetry. Even his *Anleitung zur Deutschen Poeterey* (Introduction to German Poetics, 1665), his claim to any lasting fame, was not published during his lifetime. Yet, as Joachim Rachel wrote in a literary satire shortly after Buchner's death, two lines of verse by Buchner outweighed entire books written by others. And aside from the *Buch von der Deutschen Poeterey* (Book of German Poetry, 1624), by Buchner's friend Martin Opitz, Buchner's treatise – which was widely distributed in manuscript form and was the basis for Buchner's lectures at the University of Wittenberg, where he was professor of poetics – appears to have been the single most influential work on the subject. Also, beginning in the 1630s and for the next hundred years, Buchner's Latin prose and verse were seen as the ultimate models for Neo-Latin style.

Buchner was born in Dresden on 2 November 1591 into an old Dresden family that had long produced military men. He was the youngest son of Paul Buchner the *Oberzeugmeister* (director of munitions and fortifications), and Maria Buchner, née Kroes, whose father was mayor of Dresden and important courtier at the electoral court. The oldest son, Paul, followed their father in the Oberzeugmeister post; but Augustus, following tutoring and schooling in Dresden, enrolled at the celebrated school in Schulphorta in 1604 and at the University of Wittenberg in 1610. At the university, where he had originally intended to study law, he came under the spell of Friedrich Taubmann, a classical philologist and Neo-Latin poet. Buchner turned to philosophy, which included philology and poetry, and gained from Taubmann an abiding interest not only in Latin poets but also in the German-language poets of the Middle Ages. In 1616, three years after Taubmann's death, Buchner was named to succeed him as professor of poetics in the philosophy faculty. In 1631 the chair in rhetoric would be added to his duties.

Also in 1616 Buchner married Elisabeth Krause, the daughter of a theology professor. The marriage produced eleven children, of whom seven would survive their father. The three sons would take up the military careers traditional in Buchner's family; two of the daughters would marry professors, and a third would marry a lawyer. Buchner declined offers of rectorships at Schulphorta and at the gymnasium in Hamburg and of a professorship at Uppsala to remain at Wittenberg. He was rector in 1618, 1632, and 1654 and acting rector in 1642 and 1648; dean of the philosophy faculty every three to five years; and senior professor of his faculty in 1638 and of the university in 1649 – the latter appoint-

ments were a particular sign of distinction since he was by no means literally the eldest or most "senior" professor.

Buchner, like his mentor and predecessor Taubmann, was both a classical philologist and a Neo-Latin poet; but Buchner was also interested in German-language poetry. For Buchner, as for German poetry in general, 1624 was a major turning point. After expressing his enthusiasm for Opitz's recently published first collection of German poetry, *Teutsche Poemata*, he received from Opitz an advance copy of the *Buch von der Deutschen Poeterey*. Buchner immediately perceived the pivotal significance of this treatise and moved to promote both its tenets and its author, particularly with the influential Fruchtbringende Gesellschaft (Fruit-bringing Society), an academy founded by Prince Ludwig of Anhalt-Köthen for the purpose of championing and purifying the German language. Although the new rule-based poetics, particularly its insistence on an accentual rather than a quantitative basis for poetic meter, was resisted for a time, the conservative society eventually acknowledged the value of the treatise; Opitz himself was admitted into the society in 1629. Opitz's poetics formed the basis for Buchner's lectures on German poetry, the notes for which eventually coalesced into his own treatise.

Opitz's work also seems to have inspired Buchner to try his hand at German-language poetry. During the decade following his introduction to Opitz's theories he wrote German poems for special occasions and to recommend the books of others; he also wrote German hymns and religious songs. One of the earliest poems, published in 1624 in a collection of wedding poems, was addressed to Opitz, "den Phoenix der Teutschen Poeten" (the phoenix of German poets)

> WAnn diese meine Reim, euch ohngefehr zu lesen,
> Herr Opitz kämen für, bitt ich, ihr wollet nicht
> Die Augen brauchen gantz: Dann wann uff sie gericht
> Würden all derer Strahln, müsten sie stracks verwesen.

> (If these my verses accidentally come,
> Mr. Opitz, before your sight, I beg that you will not
> Fully employ your eyes: For if you look too closely,
> They'd fall right apart.)

The excessive anxiety about his own work that this epigram exhibits is typical of Buchner and is not to be taken as a mere modesty topos.

Most of Buchner's German-language honorific and memorial poetry is in the elegant alexandrines preferred by Opitz; but Buchner also began to write strophic songs, again modeled on examples pro-

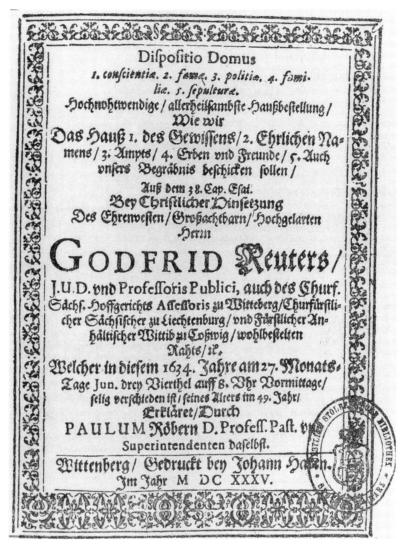

Title page for a eulogy by Paul Röber for Gottfried Reuter that includes a poem and an oration

vided in Opitz's book, for such occasions and for general use by pious laypersons. One of his hymns, "Der schöne Tag bricht an" (The beautiful day breaks, 1658) has been republished in many anthologies of sacred songs. Two short collections of Buchner's sacred songs, *Nachtmal des Herrn* (The Lord's Supper) and *Weynacht-Gedancken* (Christmas Thoughts), appeared in 1628. But his published German-language lyric poetry after this date is limited to a few memorial pamphlets and some poems introducing the works of others; his poetic oeuvre after 1628 consists largely of Latin epicedia (mourning poems), epistles, and orations. It is not known when he wrote the examples of German poems that appear in his treatise; the most notable of these poems are "Alle Tage" (Every Day) and "Zu Nacht und Tage" (Night and Day), as examples of trochaic

and iambic poetry with varying line lengths, and "Nichtige Freuden" (Vain Pleasures) and "Lasset uns, lasset uns mindern im Garten" (Let us, oh let us pluck in the garden), as examples of dactylic poetry.

The treatise appears to have been a product of the early 1630s, and references to a complete manuscript that Buchner sent to various acquaintances occur in letters and documents dating from 1638 to 1642. For the most part Buchner's treatise agrees with parallel passages in Opitz's, and Opitz is the poet whose lines occur most frequently as examples to be emulated. Although Buchner's use of the symbols for long and short syllables, inherited from Latin and Romance-language poetics, as well as of the terms *lang* (long) and *kurtz* (short), apparently contradict Opitz's position that German is a language of accent, not of quantity, Buchner defines his usage in a way that demonstrates his adherence to Opitz's emphasis on accent: "Die Sylben sind entweder lang oder kurtz: welche ihre Beschaffenheit in unser deutschen Poeterey bloß und allein aus der Ausrede und dem Thone zu ermessen" (The syllables are either long or short, which in our German metrics depends entirely on the way it is pronounced and on the loudness [of each syllable]).

In one instance, however, Buchner clearly deviates from Opitz: whereas Opitz found dactylic meter unsuited to German-language verse, Buchner not only defines it and offers examples but also actively promotes its use. He points out that rather than avoiding a three-syllable word with the accent on the first syllable, such as *nichtige* (vain, futile), or syncopating it – against Opitz's rules – as *nicht'ge,* it is better to admit dactylic meter as a natural rhythmic pattern of the German language. Furthermore, when one fits together a trochaic word and an iambic word, such as *leichtes Geräusch* (soft sound), the result is essentially dactylic. He also raises the possibility of considering certain variants of dactylic rhythm as anapestic meter. In other words, although Buchner accepted and promoted Opitz's revolutionary emphasis on accented and unaccented syllables as the basis for versification in German, he rejected Opitz's exclusive reliance on binary meters. In the late 1630s and 1640s his "invention" of dactylic verse attracted ardent followers such as Philipp von Zesen, Justus Georg Schottelius, Georg Philipp Harsdörffer, Johannes Klaj, and Sigmund von Birken, some of whom further refined the form. But he also found himself under attack by the head of the conservative Fruchtbringende Gesellschaft (Fruit-bringing Society). Buchner sent a manuscript copy of his treatise to Prince Ludwig in 1638; the prince's response was highly critical, and the main point of contention was the issue of dactylic meter. Publication was not feasible under those circumstances. Manuscript copies circulated, however, and Buchner was named as the originator of dactylic verse in every reference to the form throughout the remainder of the century.

During the 1630s the Thirty Years' War had a major impact on daily life in Saxony. Travel became difficult; consumer goods were not always readily available; and the university, although it never closed its doors, was in a nearly constant state of crisis. Stipends to professors were suspended for a time, and Buchner had to support his large family from student fees and from writing poetry or giving orations for special occasions. The deaths from the plague of two of his children and, in 1639, of his friend Opitz were additional blows during this difficult decade.

In addition to those poets who followed him in using dactylic verse in their poetry and advocating it in their own poetical treatises, Buchner found an ally in Heinrich Schütz, kapellmeister at the elector's court in Dresden. Schütz wanted German-language texts suitable for musical settings of the sorts he had found richly developed in Italy during his visits there in 1621 and 1628–1629. Buchner had acted as Schütz's agent in 1626–1627 in procuring Opitz's participation in such a project: the musical drama *Dafne* (1627), written for the wedding of a daughter of the elector, is known as the first German-language opera. Schütz's second Italian journey had exposed him to further developments in opera and in the spiritual cantata and inspired him to introduce the innovations in new works to be performed at Dresden. With Opitz no longer readily available, and Buchner apparently short of funds and seeking commissions, a new collaboration was born, which produced two works: a cantata in dramatic form, *Die Bußfertige Magdalena* (The Repentant Magdalen) in 1636 and a *Singballet* (opera with extensive balletic scenes), *Orpheus und Euridice,* in 1638. Since the former uses only a single soloist and an angel chorus of perhaps four – possibly accompanied by little more than basso continuo – and would have demanded minimal costuming and scenery, it would have formed a suitable entertainment during a time of financial constraint. The *Singballet,* designed for the occasion of another dynastic marriage, on the other hand, is a full-fledged spectacle; cost seems not to have been an issue in this case. The two texts, the only large-scale works from Buchner's pen, form the acme of his German-language poetic oeuvre. Schütz's compositions do not survive.

Die Bußfertige Magdalena comprises three scenes, each consisting of a strophic song sung by an angel to introduce the background narrative, followed by a long monologue in madrigalian verse by Magdalena. In the first scene she recounts the effect Christ's sermon in the Temple had on her, and she removes her finery and jewels – the outward signs of her previous sinful life – as she renounces her past life. The second scene is her plea to Christ, when she has followed him into the house of Simon, to forgive her for her sins, and it culminates in the singing of a psalm of repentance (the Fifty-first Psalm, as versified by Cornelius Becker). In the final scene Magdalena rejoices in Christ's mercy and resolves to lead a blameless life, and the chorus of angels provides a finale. The poet has prefaced the text, which was published anonymously in a festive edition, with a short note to the reader on what he saw as significant in his creation: a continuation of the development of what later came to be called madrigalian verse – the mixed meters, variable line lengths, and scattered rhymes characteristic of Italian recitative – and the use of dactylic verse in the finale.

The balletic opera *Orpheus und Euridice* uses a similar mixture of strophic and madrigalian verse forms for its much more complex fabric of characters, plot, and dramatic scene changes that, united with music and dance, form an early *Gesamtkunstwerk* (total work of art). This favorite opera plot, which incorporates the archetypal singer, Orpheus, into a medium in which everyone sings, provided ample opportunity for composer, poet, singers, and dancers. The finale is, again, in dactylic meter. Dactylic finales were common in operas after 1640, a practice apparently begun by Buchner in these two works of the 1630s.

That Buchner, at the time of the performance of *Orpheus und Euridice,* was sensitive about the rejection of his new verse form by the Fruchtbringende Gesellschaft, is clear from a letter of 19 November 1639 to Prince Ludwig of Anhalt-Köthen in which he excuses its inclusion by referring to the express wishes of Schütz, who, Buchner claims, considered it one of the poetic forms most suitable for musical composition; triple meter in music, the meter most natural for dance, works best with dactylic verse. It appears that the use of madrigalian verse in these works, as well as in Opitz's *Dafne,* was also at the explicit request of the composer. Thus, both of Buchner's chief contributions to German-language poetry, dactylic verse and an improved madrigalian verse, appear to have been intimately related to his collaborations with the most important German composer of the age, but both were quickly incorporated by others into poetic works not designed for musical presentation.

In spite of their quarrel over dactylic meter, Prince Ludwig continually consulted Buchner on matters of poetics. Buchner was finally invited to become a member of the Fruchtbringende Gesellschaft, under the name Der Genossene (The pleasurebringer), in 1641 – in time to witness the triumph of the "Buchnerart" (Buchner meter), as dactylic verse came to be called, during the 1640s, especially in the works of the Nuremberg poets Harsdörffer and Klaj. Not until 1643, however, did Ludwig grudgingly allow that dactyls could be used in German poetry. In 1645 Schottelius's *Teutsche Vers- oder Reimkunst* (The Art of German Verse or Rhyme) appeared; it included a discussion of dactylic verse, so Buchner did not bother to publish his own treatise, which would appear posthumously in 1665. Students from all over the German-speaking world and the Netherlands assembled in Wittenberg to hear Buchner's lectures on poetics, and the powerful and the famous consulted him about manuscripts and begged for his dedicatory poems to grace their own products. As Paul Fleming had written shortly after Opitz's death, Buchner had taken over where Opitz had left off: "Ist Buchner nur nicht tot, so lebet Opitz noch" (As long as Buchner is not dead, Opitz still lives). The "phoenix of German poets" had risen from the ashes in the person of Buchner.

Rather than write poetry, however, Buchner preferred to devote himself to academic life. He was known for his devotion to his students, and he continued to mentor them long after they had left Wittenberg. He wrote innumerable memorial orations for colleagues and for university festivities, and he accepted administrative duties regularly. Even his philological publications – editions and annotations of works by ancient authors – are more like the textbook editions of a devoted teacher than like the more arcane scholarship of many of his contemporaries.

Although he was often consulted as the greatest living expert on German-language poetics, his position as professor of poetics and rhetoric meant that he was also considered a master of Neo-Latin style. Collections of his Latin orations and epistles were published later in the century, and the epistles went through eight editions between 1679 and 1720. His poetry, both German and Latin, was collected for posthumous publication in 1694.

Thus Buchner, who wrote relatively little poetry and published even less, achieved lasting fame as the father of German dactylic poetry; but he was also known in his own century as a master of Latin style and a model for the art of writing letters. He helped Opitz's ideas about the accentual basis of German-language verse gain the upper hand, but his collaborations with Schütz also achieved a rapprochement between the new German verse and German music. Above all, perhaps, Buchner was the hub for all those exploratory efforts that advanced the cause of German-language poetry in the first half of the seventeenth century.

Buchner died on 12 February 1661 and was buried a week later in the Schloßkirche (castle church) in Wittenberg. The memorial pamphlet prepared by Andreas Kunad, rector of the theology faculty, forms the basis for later biographies.

Letters:

Cl. Viri Augusti Buchneri Epistolæ Opus posthumum
(Dresden: Printed by Christian Bergen II, sold
by Martin Gabriel Hübner, 1679);

Gottlieb Krause, ed., *Der fruchtbringenden Gesellschaft
ältester Ertzschrein* (Leipzig: Dyk, 1855), pp.
228–231;

Alexander Reifferscheid, ed., *Briefe G. M. Lingelsheims,
M. Berneggers und ihrer Freunde,* Quellen zur
Geschichte des geistigen Lebens in Deutschland,
no. 1 (Heilbrunn: Henninger, 1889).

Bibliographies:

Karl Goedeke, *Grundriß zur Geschichte der deutschen
Dichtung aus den Quellen,* volume 3 (Dresden:
Ehlermann, 1887), pp. 55–57;

Curt von Faber du Faur, *German Baroque Literature:
A Catalogue of the Collection in the Yale University
Library* (New Haven: Yale University Press,
1958), pp. 69–70;

Gerhard Dünnhaupt, *Personalbibliographien zu den
Drucken des Barock,* volume 9, part 2 (Stuttgart:
Hiersemann, 1990), pp. 855–910.

Biographies:

Wilhelm Buchner, *August Buchner, Professor der Poesie
und Beredsamkeit zu Wittenberg, sein Leben und
Wirken* (Hannover, 1863);

Walter Friedensburg, *Geschichte der Universität
Wittenberg* (Halle: Niemeyer, 1917), pp. 471–
492.

References:

Judith P. Aikin, "Augustus Buchner's *Die
Bußfertige Magdalena* (1636)," *Daphnis: Zeitschrift für Mittlere Deutsche Literatur,* 2, no. 1
(1993): 1–26;

Edward Bialek and Wojciech Mrozowicz, "Die
Eintragungen von August Buchner in den
Stammbüchern der Universität Wittenberg,"
Wolfenbütteler Barock-Nachrichten, 14 (August
1987): 68–71;

Hans Heinrich Borcherdt, *Augustus Buchner und seine
Bedeutung für die deutsche Literatur des siebzehnten
Jahrhunderts* (Munich: Beck, 1919);

Karl Borinski, *Die Poetik der Renaissance und die
Anfänge der literarischen Kritik in Deutschland* (Berlin: Weidmann 1886), pp. 131–150;

Heinrich Hoffmann von Fallersleben, "August
Buchner," *Weimarisches Jahrbuch für Deutsche
Sprache, Litteratur und Kunst,* 2 (1855): 1–39;

F. Hahne, "Paul Gerhardt und August Buchner,"
Euphorion, 15 (1908): 19–34;

Andreas Heusler, *Deutsche Versgeschichte,* volume 3
(Berlin: De Gruyter, 1929), pp. 189–192;

Käte Lorenzen, "August Buchner," in *Die Musik in
Geschichte und Gegenwart: Allgemeine Enzyklopäpie
der Musik,* edited by Friedrich Blume, volume
2 (Kassel: Bärenreiter, 1952), cols. 416–418;

Bruno Markwardt, *Geschichte der deutschen Poetik,* volume 1 (Berlin: De Gruyter, 1937), pp. 55–64,
368–370.

Daniel Czepko

(23 September 1605 – 9 September 1660)

Hans-Gert Roloff
Freie Universität Berlin

Translated by Gunther J. Holst

BOOKS: *Viro Reverendo et Clarissimo Dn Danieli Czepkio Ecclesiae Marian. apud Svid. Pastor. fideliss. post triennal. Arthritid. contumaciam, divinitùs, mitigat. Vires & Sanitat. indies recuperanti, Gratiae hujus divin. consummat. animis & Musis honori ejus devotissimis Gratulabundi comprecant. Nonnulli Pietat. & Bonarum art. Studiosi.,* by Czepko and others (Schweidnitz: Printed by Johann Jäger, 1622);

Zwo Glükwünschungs-Oden an den Wolehrnvesten vnd Hochgelahrten Herren Matthiasen Berneggern, vornehmen Professorn in Straßburg (Breslau: Georg Baumann, 1626);

Xenia Viro eruditiß Baltha-Sari Venatori, Philologo & Poetae, oblata (Breslau: Georg Baumann, 1626);

Trochæus Amoribus Flaschnerianis Scriptus (Breslau: Georg Baumann, 1627);

Ode vber den kläglichen Vntergang, Christoph von Panwitzen als Er von seinen Reisen nach Hause gedacht, vnd in einem außgang der Weeser zu schiff in der vberfahrt geblieben (Brieg, 1630);

Danckgedichte an Herren Friedrich Echarden, Artzney Doctorn, vnd der Fürstlichen Stadt Brieg wolverordneten Phisicum; Als er jhn einer gefehrlichen Kranckheit glücklichen curiret. Sambt anden zwo Oden (Brieg, 1630);

Trophæum Bibranum De Pace Imperatoriae Domus Austriacae, Erectum Suidnici, d. 2. Julij (Breslau: Printed by Georg Baumann, 1635);

Pierie (Breslau, 1636);

Auff deß Wohlgebohrnen Herren Herren Hans Georg Czigan, Freyherrn von Schlupska, Herrn auff Freystadt, Dobroslawitz vnd Sacraco in Gott seeligen Abschied. So geschehen den 16. Jenner deß 1640. Jahres. (Breslau: Printed by Georg Baumann, 1640);

Clarissimo Viro Severino Fuchsio Philosoph: & Med: Doctori Svidnitii Anno M DC XL. d. XIV. April: cum annum ageret XXXI. usibus & rebus humanis exempto Medico et Amico Suo Sostrum Ultimum

Daniel Czepko

solvit (Breslau: Printed by Georg Baumann, 1640);

Triumph Bogen, welche Jhr Röm: Kayserl: auch zu Hungarn vnd Böhaimb Königl: Maytt: Ferdinand dem Dritten, allzeit Mehrern der Reich, dem Fromen vnd Gerechten Fürsten vnd Vater der Deutschen Lande, vnter dem Schutz vnd Schirm deß Wolgebornen Herren, Herren Georg Ludwigen, Herren von Stahremberg [sic] *&c. aus Vnterhänigster Andacht vnd gehorsambster Demuth, zu Glükseligem Eintritt deß M. DC. XLI. Jahres setzet vnd heiliget* (Breslau: Printed by Georg Baumann, sold by Christoph Jacobs, 1641);

Panegyricus de Asserta Svidnicio Illustriss.⁰ Heroi Georgio Ludovico Starhembergio Dictus (Breslau: Printed by Georg Baumann, 1641);

Aquila Peracta Translationis Solennitate in Suednicense Districtu Capta et Chartaceo Aviario Inclusa. Sereniss.⁰Q. Principi Ferdinando Quarto Hung:' et Bohæm: Regi Ducatuum Suidnicensis et Javorensis Duci Clementiss⁰ ut Felix Omen Imperi Insigne Fulminis Hæres Dictata A. C. M DC XLIX. IV Idus Nov. (Schweidnitz, 1649);

βασιλικον Δωρον *abs Optimo Principe Ferdinadno Quarto, Hung. & Bohaem. Rege Suprema Præfectura Illustrissimo Domino Othoni L. B. Nosticio Domino de Rothkittnitz, Seifersdorf, Mangschuz & Herzog Waldau; Sacr. Caesar. Reg.q; Majest. Consil. & Ducat. hact. Vratisl. Capitan. ut Ipsi Justitiæ Reduci Decreta et Confirmata Ducatibus Suidnicensi ac Javorensi Exhibitum et Consecratum A.C. M DC. LI. Cal. Jan.* (Breslau: Printed by Gottfried Gründer, 1651);

Nostitziches Freudenfest über der Römischen Königlichen Wahl und Krönung Ferdinand des Heiligen Römischen Reiches, wie auch zu Hungarn und Bohaimb Königes, Ertzhertzogs zu Osterreich, von Otto Freiherren von Nostitz, Jhr Röm: Kayserl.: auch Röm: Königl.: Majest: Rath und Kämmerern, der Fürstenthümber Schweidnitz und Jawer Vollmächtigen Landeshaubtmann, wie inn Fürstenthümern gesambt geschehen, also vor sich im Hirschbergischen Warmen Bronnen am Tage S. Johannis des Teuffers jm Jahr Christi 1653. mit eifriger Feyerung vollzogen und gehalten, anonymous (Schweidnitz: Printed by Samuel Rosypalius Wltawsky, 1653);

Ferdinandinum Quatuor Columnis suspensum & Divinae Memoriae Ferdinandi Quarti Sacri Romani Imperi nec non Hungariæ ac Bohoemiæ nunc Æternitatis Regis Opt. Max. omnium in Dvcatibvs Suidnicensi ac Javorensi Dicatum Consecratum. A.C. M DC LIV. VI. Cal. Augusti, anonymous (Breslau: Printed by Gottfried Gründer for Georg Baumann's heirs, 1654);

Dreyfache vom Vaterlande aus dem Nostitz-Seyffersdorffischen Hause erhaltene Ehre (N.p., 1655);

Der Fürstenthümer Schweidnitz und Januar unter Freyherrlicher Nostitzischer Lands-Hauptmannschafft, auff beyder Hoch-Gräffl. Gn. Herrn, Herrn Graff Christoff Leopold Schaffgotsch genand, und Frauen, Frauen Agnes verwittibten Gräffin von Promnitz, Wolgeborner Freyin von Ragknitz. Jn Breßlaw den 28. Hornung deß 1656. Jahres gehaltenes Hoch-Gräffliches Beylager, von einem unwürdigen Mitgliede entworffen, anonymous (N.p., 1656);

Divi Cæsaris Augusti Ferdinandi Tertii P. P. Principis Omnium Mortalium Immortalibus Lachrumis ac Laudibus ob Pacem Publ. Restitutam Dignissimi. Inscriptio Sepulchralis, anonymous (Brieg: Printed by Christoph Tschorn, 1657);

Statua Gabrieli ab Hund Principis Lignicensis Bregensis Wolaviensis Christiani Consiliaris et Caputaneo Bene Merito, ob Felicia Nominis Anniversaria (N.p., 1658);

Rede auß der Seeligkeit welche die Seelig Verstorbene Frau Eva Tscheschwitzin, gebohrne von Borwizin, an jhren EheHerrn Herren Christoph von Tscheschwitz und Weissig, auf Kunitz Fürstl. Brieg. HoffMarschall, bey jhrer volckreichen Leichbestattung gethan Brieg den 19. Februar. Anno 1659, anonymous (N.p., 1659);

Abdanckung nach vollendetem Leichbegängnüß der Durchlauchtigen, Hochgebornen Fürstin und Freile Louise gebohrner Hertzogin in Schlesien, zur Liegnitz, Brieg und Wohlau, im Fürstl: Zimmer zur Ohlaw jm Jahr Christi, 1660. den 17. Martij gehalten von Dan: von Czepkon Röm: Käy: Maytt: wie auch Fürstl: Wohlauischen Regierungs-Rathe (Steinau: Printed by Wigand Funck, 1660);

Dan. von Czepko Röm. Kayserl. Mayt. Wie auch Fürstl. Liegnitzischen, Briegischen, Wohlauischen Regierungs-Rathes, Rede auß seinem Grabe, welche er, annoch bey guter Gesundheit, doch nicht so gar unlängst vor seinem, den 8. Septembr. dieses noch lauffenden 1660sten Jahres, erfolgten Ableben auffgesetzet (Breslau: Printed by Gottfried Gründer for Georg Baumann's heirs, 1660);

Sieben-Gestirne königlicher Busse, das ist, Die Sieben Buß-Psalmen, des Königs und Propheten Davids, edited by Christian Deodat von Czepko (Brieg: Printed by Christoph Tschorn, 1671);

Auff proßkawer FreyHerrliche Hochzeit Frewde, anonymous (N.p., n.d.);

Dan: Cepconis Alter-Idem sivè Intimatio Amicitiæ ad Virum Nobiliss: Franciscum Scholtetum (Breslau: Printed by Georg Baumann, n.d.);

Faces Nuptiales ex Promisso L.M.Q. Accendit et Lucet Dn. Zachariæ Richtero, Pastori Libstadtensi &c. (Dresden: Bergen, n.d.).

Collections and editions: *Geistliche Schriften,* edited by Werner Milch (Breslau: Historische Kommission für schlesischen Geschichte, 1930; reprinted, Darmstadt: Wissenschaftliche Buchgesellschaft, 1963);

Weltliche Dichtungen, edited by Milch (Breslau: Historische Kommission für schlesischen Geschichte, 1932; reprinted, Darmstadt: Wissenschaftliche Buchgesellschaft, 1963);

Sämtliche Werke, 7 volumes, edited by Hans-Gert Roloff and Marian Szyrocki (Berlin & New York: De Gruyter, 1980–1986).

The Silesian poet Daniel Czepko is one of the most significant figures in seventeenth-century German literature, but only in the last few decades of the twentieth century have literary historians become fully aware of the high level of his linguistic skill, his mastery of the formal aspects of writing, and the intellectual independence manifest in his poetic, religious, and political ideas. This late recognition is because of the way his work was passed on. Aside from the play *Pierie* (1636), only eighteen relatively insignificant occasional poems were published during his lifetime because he was always in conflict with the censors. The bulk of his work was spread in manuscript form in copies made by friends or scribes; all of the originals are lost. Some of these works were published for the first time in the early 1930s as *Geistliche Schriften* (Spiritual Writings, 1930) and *Weltliche Dichtungen* (Worldly Poems, 1932). Some of the manuscript copies were lost during World War II, and others suffered water damage during the war and have since been in a state of irreversible deterioration. To save these works from oblivion, a seven-volume definitive edition of Czepko's complete works was initiated in 1980. For the first time scholars will be able to assess Czepko properly, especially in his roles as social critic and regional politician.

Czepko was born on 23 September 1605 in Koischwitz in the principality of Liegnitz to the Protestant pastor Daniel Czepko and Anna Czepko, née Kretzinski. His father became pastor at the Marienkirche (Church of Saint Mary's) in Schweidnitz in 1606. Czepko started attending Latin school in Schweidnitz in 1612; at first he was a poor student, but in puberty he started writing prose and poetry. In 1622 he published a collection of Latin poems dedicated to his father, who died the following year. In the winter semester of 1623 Czepko enrolled at the University of Leipzig to study medicine, but the next year he went to Strasbourg to study law with Matthias Bernegger, one of the most prominent scholars of his time, who called his attention to Martin Opitz's *Teutsche Pöemata* (German Poetics, 1624). Czepko's years in Strasbourg were interrupted by trips to France, Switzerland, the high court in Speyer, Heidelberg, and Leipzig.

In December 1626 Czepko returned to Schweidnitz. In May 1628 he moved to Brieg to escape the Counter-Reformation measures enforced by the Austrian army. For some time thereafter he was engaged as a private tutor to aristocratic families in Upper Silesia and, beginning in 1633, to the barons Czigan in Dobroslawitz, near Cosel. In 1634, in the vicinity of Hultschin, Czepko lost all his possessions – including his manuscripts – to marauding Croats. He returned to Schweidnitz in 1635. On 16 February 1637 he married the wealthy Anna Catharina Heinitz. They had seven children, four of whom died young.

Toward the end of 1639 the Thirty Years' War reached Schweidnitz when the Swedes laid siege to the city; on 3 July 1642 the imperial commandant surrendered. Czepko, a Protestant who had remained loyal to the Catholic Hapsburg Empire, was caught in the middle: the Swedish troops had laid waste to his estate outside the city, and the imperial civil servants considered him a rebel. Czepko described the events in the essays "Einfältiger Bericht, welchermaßen die Stadt Schweidnitz Ao. 1642. an den Feind kommen" (Simple Report on How the City of Schweidnitz Fell to the Enemy in the Year 1642) and "Schildbachs Defensions-Schrift" (Schildbach's Defense).

In 1656 Anna Czepko died; her final illness was documented by Czepko in great detail in his "Historia morbi uxoris" (History of the Death of His Wife). In the same year his efforts to become a member of the nobility, begun in the late 1630s, came to fruition when he was allowed to add the honorific "von Reigersfeld" to his name. He energetically promoted the construction of the Protestant Friedenskirche (Church of Peace) in Schweidnitz, which was consecrated in 1657; he helped formulate its ritual. Those efforts did not keep the orthodox Protestant censorship, represented by the Breslau pastor Ananias Weber, from forbidding him to publish "Sexcenta Monodisticha Sapientium" (Six Hundred Single Couplets of Wise Men), dedicated to Duke William of Saxe-Weimar, the head of the literary society Fruchtbringende Gesellschaft (Fruit-bringing Society), because he thought it contained hidden Calvinist and mystical ideas.

In March 1657 Czepko was appointed privy councillor by Duke Christian of Liegnitz, Brieg, and Wohlau. In that capacity he was sent to the imperial court as a member of the delegation that was charged with renegotiating the conditions of the ducal succession. His "Gesandtschaffts-Relation" (Ambassadorial Report) is a colorful account of the negotiations that depicts the political and courtly culture of the Hapsburg Empire. At the court Emperor Leopold I appointed him imperial councillor. In 1659 Czepko became ill, probably of scurvy. The following year, while inspecting the mines of

Reichenstein, Czepko was poisoned by methane gas; he died on 9 September in Wohlau. He was buried in Schweidnitz.

In his political and historical essays Czepko developed proposals for the civil and social order of the Silesian estates, but these works go beyond the immediate occasions that prompted them because they are important discussions of the problems of absolutism. In them practical experience, philosophy, and religiosity combine in an appeal for a utopia based on morality and guided by Christian piety. In his "Rede . . . von Ursachen der Verterbung und Auffrichtung der Städte" (Speech . . . on the Ruination and Restoration of the Cities), written in 1648, he proceeds from the principle of natural law that *salus populi suprema lex esto* (the welfare of the people is the supreme law). The civic authorities are to consider the general welfare as the supreme law guiding all their actions; in return, the people owe obedience to the authorities.

In the age of absolutism discussions of statecraft were not the sole province of constitutional lawyers and scholars but were also carried on in literature. This literary "laboratory" made it possible to develop utopian models of society. The extent to which Czepko considered rational thought and tolerance the foundations of a peaceful social order is evident in his drama *Pierie,* which he began writing around 1629 and published in 1636, and especially in his voluminous verse composition "Coridon und Phyllis."

The plot of *Pierie,* in which a young girl succeeds in making peace between two warring cities, is taken from Plutarch's *De Mulierum virtutibus* (The Virtue of Women) and Polyaenos's *Strategica* (Strategies). Because of the hostilities the women of Myos can make their pilgrimage to Miletus to worship the gods only on certain holidays. On one of these pilgrimages Pierie, the daughter of Pytes of Myos, meets Phrygius, the young ruler of Miletus, who falls in love with her. Pierie asks him to make it possible for her to go to Miletus more frequently and in large groups; Phrygius understands that she is asking for peace, and so he ends the war. In this undramatic story Czepko stresses the absurdity of war and shows how easily peace could be made. Conflict is not imposed by the gods but caused by human beings; it can, therefore, be ended by rational procedures. The play is in three acts, without prologue or epilogue; contrary to tradition, the audience is given no help in comprehending the intent of the work. It is presented in the simplest linguistic forms: monologue, dialogue, and choral recitation. The play was dedicated to Duke Heinrich Wenzel

zu Münsterberg and his wife on the occasion of their wedding.

Czepko's massive pastoral epic "Coridon und Phyllis" comprises 9,222 lines. The text was handed down in only two copies from the eighteenth century; the 1723 copy was lost at the end of World War II, so only the 1722 manuscript exists. The shepherd Coridon maintains his independence from a court that is morally corrupt; he also criticizes the nobility, the church, the academic world, the judicial system, and the moral lapses of the common people. Toward the end of the second book Czepko recalls the decline of the Roman Empire – "wie die Macht / Ihre Kinder umbgebracht, Die der Welt Gesetze gaben" (how power / killed its children, who gave laws to all the world) – and appeals to the reader to "Ehret unser Österreich" (Honor our Austria). The Hapsburgs' imperial reign guarantees a peaceful life if all can be united under the imperial house; but for their part the emperors have a duty to exercise tolerance and make provisions for their subjects. The third book begins by celebrating the victory of the imperial troops over the Swedes at Nördlingen in 1634 and continues with a discourse on the cultivation of a perfect rural estate. The lovingly detailed description of agriculture functions as a contrast to war.

Czepko's extensive lyric output consists of poems in German and Latin; the Latin songs constitute about a quarter of the poetry as it exists today. The manuscript containing his juvenilia has been missing since 1945; it included, in addition to the fragmentary pastoral epic "Sylvie aus dem Elsaß" (Sylvia from Alsace), occasional poems and light verses for the delectation of Czepko's friends in the Hochansehnlichen Ordens einsamer Gedancken (Eminent Order of Lonesome Thoughts) in Birava and Dobroslawitz. An example of the latter is "XIII. Gesetze der Liebe" (The Thirteen Laws of Love), written in 1632 in six-line stanzas. Similarly conceived was "Drey Rollen verliebter Gedancken" (Three Rolls of Amorous Thoughts), written in 1634, the manuscript for which Czepko, as he reports, saved from the ashes after the Croats burned his possessions. These are short poems, mostly in two lines, expressing with restrained eroticism the amorous games of aristocratic society. Of the three volumes of "Unbedachtsame Einfälle" (Careless Ideas), written at about the same time, only the first volume has survived. They are poems on a variety of topics, written in an attempt to prove the purity and poetic suitability of the German language. The collection "Kurtze satyrische Gedichte" (Short Satiric Poems), comprising six volumes and written in

Schweidnitz, lashes out against the vices and follies of the bourgeois and the lower aristocracy, such as dandyism, fads, the immorality of courtiers, city life, lovesickness, vanity, and hypocrisy.

Czepko's earliest known cycles of sacred verses, "Gegenlage der Eitelkeit" (The Opposite of Vanity) and "Inwendige Himmel Reich" (The Inner Kingdom of Heaven), were composed in Dobroslawitz and reflect the mysticism and spiritualism of the circle associated with the barons Czigan; scholars disagree about the extent of Czepko's indebtedness to medieval or Spanish mysticism or to the ideas of Jakob Böhme, Johannes Tauler, Paracelsus, Valentin Weigel, Kaspar von Schwenckfeld, or Abraham von Franckenberg. The topic of the poems is the supreme bliss of the union of the human soul with the divine, which can happen only by suppression of the demands of the body. The cycle "Gegenlage der Eitelkeit" points out the path from vanity to truth in a series of questions and religious instructions. The poem "Consolatio ad Baronissam Cziganeam" (Consolation for the Baroness Czigan), written in 1633, manifests a kind of mystical pantheism in which "die Natur nicht allein ihm gleich, sondern auch die Ewigkeit selbst sey" (nature is not only a likeness of him [God] but is eternity itself). The work became the stimulus for Johannes Scheffler's (Angelus Silesius's) *Cherubinischer Wandersmann* (Cherubic Wayfarer, 1675).

In 1657, on the occasion of the dedication of the Friedenskirche in Schweidnitz, Czepko wrote a libretto for an oratorio that is unique for the genre; it is unknown whether this libretto, "Semita Amoris Divini" (The Path of Divine Love), subtitled "Das Heilige Dreyeck" (The Holy Triangle), was ever set to music. It is divided into three parts: "Tag der Menschwerdung" (The Day of Incarnation), "Tag der Kreuzigung" (The Day of Crucifixion), and "Tag der Auferstehung" (The Day of Resurrection). The structural elements include a full choir, a partial choir, and solo parts consisting of recitatives and arias. The recitatives are in alexandrines, the arias in facile tetrameters. One of the richest in content of all oratorios in German, the work would not be equaled until the eighteenth century. The annotations include abundant references to patristic literature and reveal Czepko's extensive knowledge of church literature. He calls for the emulation of Christ: "Lerne an dieser Auffgabe alle Tage, alle Stunden, alle Augenblicke, dann sie darff nur einmahl auffgesaget werden. Kanst du Sie, dir ist geholffen: wo nicht: Du bist verlohren. Nicht säume dich: Es hänget an einem kurtzen Augenblick" (Learn to fulfill this task every day, every hour, every moment,

for it can be set only once. If you succeed, you will be helped. If not, you will be lost. Do not tarry. It all depends on one brief moment). The oratorio concludes with the recitative:

Das Christus Aufferstehn des unsern
　　　　　　　　　　　　　vorspiel sey.
Bringt durch Natur und Schrifft der Heilge
　　　　　　　　　　　　　Geist uns bey.
Mensch, glaube dieser Schrifft, so wird
　　　　　　　　　　　　dir die Natur
In ihrer Heimlichkeit auch zeigen diese
　　　　　　　　　　　　Spur.
Doch was Schrifft? was Natur? wann
　　　　　　　　　　es der Geist nicht thut.
(Ach! nim ihn an) ist hier Natur und
　　　　　　　　　　　Schrifft nicht gut.

(That Christ's Resurrection is the
　　　　　　　　prelude to ours
Is taught to us through nature and scripture
　　　　　　　　by the Holy Ghost.
Man, if you believe these scriptures, then
　　　　　　　　to you will nature
Reveal its secret and also show you that
　　　　　　　　this is so.
But what good is Scripture? What good nature? if
　　　　　　　they are not wrought by the Holy Ghost
(Oh! do accept him) neither nature nor the
　　　　　　　Scriptures will do us any good.)

Czepko continued writing sacred texts with *Sieben-Gestirne königlicher Busse* (The Pleiades of Royal Penance, 1671), an adaptation of the seven Psalms for the pardon of sins (numbers 6, 32, 38, 51, 102, 130, and 143), in which he interprets each of the Psalms in many stanzas. Czepko continued to work on the Psalms until he died. The poems on the Psalms are among the most impressive of their kind; they constitute the crowning glory of his work.

Bibliography:

Gerhardt Dünnhaupt, *Personalbibliographien zu den Drucken des Barock*, volume 9, part 2 (Stuttgart: Hiersemann, 1990), pp. 983–995.

References:

Judith P. Aikin, "Creating a Language for German Opera: The Struggle to Adapt Madrigal Versification in Seventeenth-Century Germany," *Deutsche Vierteljahresschrift für Literaturwissenschaft und Geistesgeschichte*, 62 (June 1988): 266–289;

Ruth K. Angress, *The Early German Epigram: A Study in Baroque Poetry* (Lexington: University Press of Kentucky, 1971);

Hans Heinrich Borcherdt, "Beiträge zur Geschichte der Oper und des Schauspiels in Schlesien bis zum Jahre 1740," *Zeitschrift des Vereins für Geschichte Schlesiens,* 43 (1909): 217–242;

Robert M. Browning, *Deutsche Lyrik des Barock 1618–1723,* edited by Gerhart Teuscher (Stuttgart: Kröner, 1980);

Ernst Fritze, "Daniel Czepko: Ein Dichter und seine Kirche," *Schlesien,* 12 (1967): 103–105;

Burckhard Garbe and Gisela Garbe, "Ein verstecktes Figurengedicht bei Daniel von Czepko: 'Das treuhertzige Creutze' als krypto-technopaignie eines Hymnus von Venantius Fortunatus," *Euphorion,* 69, no. 1 (1975): 100–106;

Bernard Gorceix, "Natur und Mystik im 17. Jahrhundert: Daniel Czepko und Catharina Regina von Greiffenberg," in his *Epochen der Naturmystik* (Berlin: Erich Schmidt, 1979), pp. 212–226;

Ingrid Guentherodt, "Frühe Spuren von Maria Cunitia und Daniel Czepko in Schweidnitz 1623," *Daphnis,* 20, no. 3/4 (1991): 547–584;

Hans Heckel, "Die Mystik von Schwenckfeld bis Böhme," in his *Geschichte der deutschen Literatur in Schlesien,* volume 1: *Von den Anfängen bis zum Ausgange des Barock* (Breslau: Ostdeutsche Verlagsanstalt, 1929), pp. 152–279;

Gerhard Hultsch, "Daniel Czepko von Reigersfeld, 1605–1660," *Jahrbuch für Schlesische Kirchengeschichte,* 39 (1960): 91–113;

Friedhelm Klöhr, "Daniel Czepko von Reigersfeld (1605–1660) – Historiograph und Mystiker," in *Schweidnitz im Wandel der Zeiten,* edited by the Stiftung Kulturwerk Schlesien, revised by Werner Bern and Ulrich Schmilewski (Würzburg: Korn, 1990), pp. 218–221;

Wilhelm Kühlmann, "Ein schlesischer Dichter am Oberrhein. Unbekannte Gedichte aus der Straßburger Studienzeit Daniel von Czepkos," *Zeitschrift für die Geschichte des Oberrheins,* 129 (1981): 323–338;

Volker Meid, *Barocklyrik* (Stuttgart: Metzler, 1986), pp. 108–111;

Annemarie Meier, *Daniel Czepko als geistlicher Dichter* (Bonn: Bouvier, 1975);

Werner Milch, "Daniel Czepko von Reigersfeld," *Schlesische Monatshefte,* 6 (1929): 532–536;

Milch, "Daniel Czepkos Bericht über Krankheit und Tod seiner Frau," *Sudhoffs Archiv für Geschichte der Medizin,* 26 (1965): 146–165;

Milch, *Daniel von Czepko: Persönlichkeiten und Leistung* (Breslau: Trewendt & Granier, 1934);

Milch, "Drei zeitgenössische Quellen zur Biographie Daniel von Czepkos," *Euphorion,* 30 (1929): 257–281;

Milch, "Schlesische Sonderart im deutschen Schrifttum," *Zeitschrift für Deutschkunde,* 45 (1931): 566–581;

Milch, "Unveröffentlichtes von Daniel Czepko, 1605–1660," *Schlesische Monatshefte,* 6 (1929): 531;

Hermann Palm, "Daniel von Czepko von Reigersfeld: 1605–1660," *Archiv für die Geschichte deutscher Sprache und Dichtung,* 1 (1874): 193–211;

Will-Erich Peuckert, "Czepko," in his *Pansophie: Ein Versuch zur Geschichte der weißen und schwarzen Magie* (Berlin: Erich Schmidt, 1956), pp. 403–410;

Hans-Gert Roloff, "Daniel Czepkos 'Pierie,'" *Chloe,* 7 (1988): 599–613;

Roloff, "Daniel Czepkos 'Poema germanicum': Edition und Interpretation," in *Textkritik und Interpretation: Festschrift für Karl Konrad Polheim,* edited by Heinro Reinitzer (Bern: Peter Lang, 1987), pp. 95–141;

Hans-Gerd Rundstedt, "Ein unbekanntes Czepko Gedicht," *Zeitschrift der Vereins für Geschichte Schlesiens,* 72 (1938): 375–379;

Sibylle Rusterholz, "Rhetorica mystica: Zu Daniel Czepkos Parentatio auf die Herzogin Louise," in *Leichenpredigten als Quelle historischer Wissenschaften,* volume 2, edited by Rudolf Lenz (Marburg: Schwarz, 1979), pp. 235–253;

Wilhelm Schiller, "Große Liegnitzer: Daniel Czepko von Reigersfeld," *Liegnitzer Heimatbrief,* 4 (1952): 11–12;

Michael Schilling, "Daniel Czepko von Reigersfeld: Sexcenta Monodisticha Sapientum," in *Kindlers neues Literaturlexikon,* volume 4, edited by Walter Jens (Munich, 1989), pp. 359–361;

Ulrich Seelbach, "Hohberg und Czepko," *Daphnis,* 16, no. 4 (1987): 711–716;

Max Stebler, "'Aus Waffen Sensen schmieden': Krieg und Frieden in 'Corydon et Phyllis,'" *Germanica Wratislaviensia,* 85 (1989): 189–194;

Stebler, "Kannte der Steller von 'Fragen eines lesenden Arbeiters' 'Coridon et Phyllis?,'" *Germanica Wratislaviensia,* 69 (1986): 174–180;

Stebler, "Zur Wertung Daniel Czepkos in der Literaturgeschichte," *Germanica Wratislaviensa,* 85 (1989): 189–194;

Theodorus Cornelis van Stockum, *Zwischen Jakob Böhme und Johann Scheffler: Abraham von Franckenberg (1593–1652) und Daniel Czepko von Reigersfeld (1605–1660)* (Amsterdam: Noord-Holl. Uitg. Maatsch, 1967);

Siegfried Sudhof, "Daniel von Czepko," in his *Deutsche Dichter des 17. Jahrhunderts: Ihr Leben und Werk* (Berlin: Erich Schmidt, 1984), pp. 227–241;

Marian Szyrocki, "Daniel Czepko. Ungedruckte Gedichte. Aus: Kurtzer satyrischer Gedichte drittes Buch," *Germanica Wratislaviensia,* 36 (1980): 225–236;

Szyrocki, "Daniel Czepko von Reigersfeld," in *Literaturlexikon: Autoren und Werke deutscher Sprache,* volume 2, edited by Walther Killy (Gütersloh & Munich: Bertelsmann, 1989), pp. 501–503;

Szyrocki, "Social-politische Probleme in der Dichtung Czepkos," *Germanica Wratislaviensia,* 2 (1959): 57–67;

Szyrocki, "Ungedruckte satirische Gedichte von Daniel Czepko," *Germanica Wratislavensia,* 31 (1978): 123–129; 32 (1979): 135–147; 36 (1980): 225–236;

Erich Trunz, "Daniel von Czepko und die Barockforschung (Sammelrezension zur Ausgabe und zur Darstellung von Werner Milch)," *De Weegschaal,* no. 2 (1936/1937): 17–20; no. 3 (1936/1937): 33–38;

Friedrich Wilhelm Wentzlaff-Eggebert, *Deutsche Mystik zwischen Mittelalter und Neuzeit: Einheit und Wandlung ihrer Erscheinungsformen,* second edition (Berlin: De Gruyter, 1944), pp. 208–221, 268;

Wentzlaff-Eggebert, "Joy in This World and Confidence in the Next: On Mysticism as Speculation in the Works of Daniel von Czepko," in *Yearbook of Comparative Criticism,* volume 4: *Anagogic Qualities of Literature,* edited by Joseph P. Strelka (London & University Park: Pennsylvania State University Press, 1971), pp. 308–318.

Simon Dach
(29 July 1605 – 15 April 1659)

George C. Schoolfield
Yale University

SELECTED BOOKS: *Auff Herrn Hans-Ernst Ad-ersbachen Kläglichen und frühzeitigen zwar jedoch seeligen Abschied* (Königsberg, 1632);

Abschieds-Lied dem ehrenvesten vornehmgeachteten vnd in vieler Lehr vnd Kunst wolgeübten H. Robert Robertihn alß er im Augustus-Mond des 1634. Jahres auß Preussen in die Marck zu ziehen gedachte (Königsberg, 1634);

Musicalisches Ehrengedechtniß deß weiland GroßAcht-baren, Ehrenvesten vnd Wolgelahrten Herren Hiobi Lepneri, Trewen vnd wolverdienten ProConsulis der Churfürstl: Altenstadt Königsberg: Des gar vnvergleichlichen Liebhabers vnd Beförderets der löbichen Music-Kunst, auffgerichtet bey dessen Leichbegengnüß jhme, als biß in den Todt wolverspürten Patrono vnd alten Freunde (Danzig: Printed by Georg Rhete, 1635);

Ehrengedicht über den tödtlichen Abschiedt des . . . Herrn Mauritii Güttich, Bürgern vnd Kannegiessern im Kneiphoff (Königsberg, 1635);

Cleomedes der allerwehrteste vnd lobwürdigste trewe Hirt der Crohn Polen, anonymous, music by Heinrich Albert (Königsberg, 1635);

Anke van Tharaw öß de my geföllt, attributed to Dach (Königsberg, 1636);

Als Martin Opitz von Boberfeld &c. naher Königsberg kommen, seine guten Freunde daselbst zu ersuchen, ist Jhme von Simon Dachen vnd mir diese wenige Music durch hülffe etlicher Studiosorum praesentirt worden, den 29. Tag des Hewmonats im Jahr 1638, by Dach and Albert (Königsberg, 1638);

Schuldigste Dienst-Erweisung dem Durchläuchtigsten . . . Herren Georg Wilhelmen, Marggraffen zu Branden-burg . . . durch einen Musicalischen Auffzug zu Königsberg in Preussen von denen sämptlichen Studioisis dero Churfürstl. Durchläuchtig. Vniversitet daselbst Vnterhänigst bezeuget. Jm Jahr 1638. den 7. Tag des Wintermonats (Königsberg: Printed by Lorenz Segebade's heirs, 1638);

Vber J. Elisabeth Reimerinnen seligen Abschied (Königsberg, 1638);

Simon Dach; copperplate engraving, executed in 1730, after an oil painting in the Wallenrodt Library in Königsberg that was destroyed in an air raid in 1944

Auff Hn. Robert Robertihns, Churf. Durchl. zu Brand. Preuss. Hofgerichts Secretarii vnd J. Vrsula Vogtin Hochzeit (Königsberg, 1639);

Sterb-Lied bey seligem Ableiben Fr. Annä Gebohrnen von Weinbeer Hr. Christoff Schimmelfennigs vielgeliebten Haußfrawen, gesungen (Königsberg, 1639);

Todesgedancken bey seligem Hintritt Hn. Wilhelm Perssen, welcher den 7. Nov. entschlaffen, und den 11. zur Erden bestetiget worden (Königsberg, 1640);

Denckmal, dem . . . H. Michael Aderßbachen . . . auffgerichtet (Königsberg, 1640);

Vber dem seligen Ableiben der . . . Frawen Agnes
Möllerinn, des Weiland Ehrwürdigen . . . Herrn
Georg Weissels, Pfarrers auff dem Roßgarten Hinter-
lassenen Wittwen geschrieben 1641. Den 24. Martij.
(Königsberg: Printed by Johann Reusner, 1641);

Wander-Lied, nach den [sic] Maß vnd auff die Weise des
79. Psalms im Lobwasser. Von Simon Dachen vnd
Iohanne Stobaeo, geschrieben vnd mit 5. Stimmen
gesetzet, als die beyde Eheleut Robert Roberthin vnd
Vrsula Vogtin eine newe Wohnung bezogen im Mayen
des 1641 sten Jahres (Königsberg: Printed by
Pasche Mense, 1641);

Denckmal dem Weyland Durchleuchtigsten Hochgebohrnen
Fürsten vnd Herren Georg Wilhelmen, Marggraffen
zu Brandenburg, . . . vnd Churfürsten, in Preussen . . . Bey dessen Churfürstliche [sic] Leichen
höchstfeyerlichen Beysetzung zu Königsberg
(Königsberg: Printed by Johann Reusner,
1642);

Christliches Trawer-Lied. Mit fünff Stimmen gesetzet durch
Johannem Stobaeum (Elbing: Wendelin Bodenhausen, 1642);

Vnterricht: Das Schauspiel Prussiarchus welches zum
Beschluß des Jubelfests der löblichen hohen Schul zu
Königsberg in Preussen gespielt werden soll, desto
besser zu verstehen, anonymous (Königsberg:
Printed by Johann Reusner, 1644);

Danck-Reyme an einen Hochweisen Raht der Löblichen
Stadt Kneiphoff Königsbergk, als derselbte aus
rühmlicher Gunst gegen die Gelarten mir jhrer an
Pregel-Strom im Thum gelegenen Wohnungen eine
hochgünstig eingereumet (Königsberg, 1644);

Auff die glückselige Heyrath des HochEdlen Gestrengen
vnd Vesten Hn. Johan von Höverbecken . . . vnd der
Hoch Edlen . . . Jungfrawen Annen Sophien, des . . .
Herren Wolff Dieterich von Rochawen des Eltern . . .
Tochter (Königsberg: Printed by Johann Reus-
ner, 1644);

Christliches Denkmal dem . . . Hn. Urban Lepnern, der
altstädtischen Gemeine Seelsorgern, welcher den 3.
Christmonats entschlaffen, vnd den 7. darauff
beygesetzt (Königsberg, 1645);

Klag-Lied bey hochbetrawrlichem Ableiben des
hochberühmten Musici Hn. Johann Stobaei, Churfl.
Capellmeistern, meines gewesenen lieben vnd werthen
Freundes (Königsberg, 1646);

Hochzeit-Lied. Auff . . . Hn. Georg Andressen vnd Maria
Salbertinnen Hochzeit (Königsberg, 1647);

Glückwüntzschung an Herrn Heinrich Schützen (Dresden,
1648);

Schuldige Auffwartung durch welche des Erlauchten Hochgebohrnen vnd Großmächtigen Herrn Gerharden,

Graffen zu Dönhoff, Pomerellischen Wojewoden, der
Lande Preussen Schatzmeistern, Starosten zu
Marienburgk . . . &c&c . . . Seines gnädigen Herrn
hochgültige Gnade zu erhalten sich bemühet dessen
gehorsamer Simon Dach (Königsberg, 1648);

Bittere Klage vber des weiland GrosAchtbaren,
Hochgelarten vnd Weitberühmten H. Robert
Roberthins . . . Vnverhofften vnd recht
hochbetrübtem aber seeligem Hintritt aus dieser
Welt . . . geführet . . . 1648. 10. Ostermonats-Tag
(Königsberg, 1648);

Christliche Todes Errinnerung des Weyland Groß —
Achtbarn . . . Herrn Robert Roberthns . . . Auff
dessen Begehren schon vor etzlichen Jahren
geschrieben von Simon Dachen vnd anitzo bey seinem . . . Ableiben . . . jn 5. Stimmen gesetzet von
Heinrich Alberten. Den 7. Oster-MonatsTag im Jahr
1648 (Königsberg: Printed by Pasche Mense,
1648);

Christliche Trost-Schrifft bey Christlicher vnd ansehnlicher
Leich-Bestattung Der . . . Fr. Maria, gebohrnen
Ridelinn, welche . . . 1648. 21. Mey selig
eingeschlaffen, vnd den 24. drauff . . . eingesencket
an dero Hochbetrübten hinterlassen Witwer . . . Hn.
Johann Schmeissen (Königsberg: Printed by Johann Reusner, 1648);

Vber dem seligen Abschied des HochEdlen Herrn Georg von
der Gröben. . . . Klag-Lied jn der Person der
Hochbetrübten Fraw Wittwen (Königsberg, 1649);

Christliche Klag- vnd Trost-Reime . . . Hn. Georg von der
Gröben . . . welcher 1648. 7. Herbstmonats sein
Leben geschlossen, vnd 1649. 26. Newjahrsmo-
nats . . . eingesenckt worden (Königsberg, 1649);

Hirten Liedchen zu vermehrung der Hochzeitlichen Ehren-
Frewden Herrn Johann Fauljochs . . . vnd der Ehr-
vnd Tugendreichen Frawen Maria Fischerin . . . auff
Nach-ahrtung eines von Hrn. Eccardo mit 4. Stim-
men verfertigen vnd dem Herrn Bräutigamb
wolbekandten Leides fünffstimmig componiret von
Heinrich Alberten (Königsberg: Printed by
Pasche Mense, 1649);

Der 128. Psalm, bey Hochzeitlichem Ehrentage des . . . Hn.
Johann Melhorn vnd der . . . J. Anna Koese
(Königsberg, 1649);

Braut-Tanz (Königsberg, 1649);

Trost-Reimchen dem . . . Hn. Johann Reusnern, Buchdruc-
ker zu Königsberg, als er seinen lieben Sohn Johannem daselbst begraben ließ (Königsberg:
Printed by Johann Reusner, 1650);

Rechte Heyrats-Kunst, bey Hochzeitlichen Ehren-Frewden
des . . . Herrn Christoff Pohl . . . vnd der Viel-Ehr
vnd Tugendsamen Jungfrauen Vrsulen, des . . .
Christophori Stangenwaldes . . . Tochter, jn 5. Stimmen gesetzet von Heinrich Alberten. Angestellet zu

Welau den 9. Maij-Monats jm Jahr Christi 1650.
(Königsberg: Printed by Pasche Mense, 1650);
Vnbewegter Trost der wahren Christen, auch mitten im
Tode, aus Paulo Rom. 8. v. 35 bey hochseligem
Ableiben des Hoch- und Wolgebornen Herrn, Herrn
Achatii, Burggraffen und Graffen zu Dhona . . .
welcher in standhaffter Zuversicht auff Gott durch
Christum 1651. den 16. Hornungs selig diese Welt
gesegnet, und den 7. Brachmonats hochansenhlich und
Christlich . . . beygesetzet worden, geschrieben von
Simon Dachen, und nach der Melodey des
berühmbten Gudimels über den 130. Psalm in 5.
Stimmen gesetzt von Heinrich Alberten (Kö-
nigsberg: Printed by Johann Reusner, 1651);
Sanfftmuth der Männer ihren EheFrawen zu erweisen bey
der Leichbestattung der . . . Frawen Anna
Winnefenniginn . . . Herrn Johann Sanden . . .
Hauß Frawen. . . . geschrieben von Simon Dachen.
1651. 23. Augustmonats (Königsberg: Printed
by Johann Reusner, 1651);
Christliches Sterb-Liedchen bey seligem Abschied . . . Hn.
Greger Werners . . . geschrieben von Simon Dachen
vnd mit 5. Stimmen verfertiget durch Iohannem
Stobaeum (Königsberg: Printed by Johann
Reusner, 1652);
Letzte Ehre dem . . . H. Gregor Wernern . . . 1652. 21.
Mertz (Königsberg: Printed by Johann Reus-
ner, 1652);
Letzter Ehrendienst dem . . . Herrn Ambrosio Scala, des
Churfl. Br. Hoffgerichts in Preussen Advocaten, den
hochbetrübten Hinterbliebenen zu Trost erwiesen
(Königsberg, 1652);
Letztes Ehren-Gedächtnüs der . . . Frawen Anna Koesin . . .
des . . . Hn. Johann Melhorns . . . Ehegenossen,
welche 1652. 18. Augustm. . . . eingeschlaffen, und
den 21. der Erden eingebracht worden (Königs-
berg: Printed by Johann Reusner, 1652);
Einfältige Hochzeit-Reimchen, der . . . Heyrath des . . . Hn.
Johann Sand[en] . . . vnd der . . . Jungfrawen
Sophien . . . Herrn M. Joachim Babaten . . . Tochter
1654. 4. Mey . . . gehalten (Königsberg: Printed
by Johann Reusner, 1654);
Einfältiger Trost . . . bey . . . Ableiben des . . . Hn. Johann
Sand[en] . . . welcher . . . 1654. 18. Hewmon. . . .
eingeschlaffen (Königsberg: Printed by Johann
Reusner, 1654);
Letztes und wolverdientes Ehren-Gedächtnuß welches dem . . .
Herrn H. Ludwigen von Kanitz welcher 1654. . . .
3. April zu Berlin selig eingeschlaffen, und daselbst
22. Herbstm. . . . der lieben Erden eingebracht
worden . . . gestiftet (Berlin: Printed by
Christoph Runge, 1654);
Hertzlicher und vielleicht letzter Segen welchen bey
Gelegenheit der Liebreichen Heyraht Hn. Johann

Christoph Rehefelden . . . mit der . . . Jungf. Annen . . .
Cörbers 1655. 18 Newjahrsm. . . . der löblichen
Statt Mümmel, seinem geliebten Vaterlande
hinterlassen Simon Dach (Königsberg, 1655);
Auff . . . Ableiben . . . Hn. Michael Kreuschners &c. wel-
cher . . . 1655. 8. Herbst-mon. . . . eingeschlaffen,
vnd 12. darauf . . . eingebracht worden
(Königsberg: Printed by Johann Reusner,
1655);
Mors est sine conjuge vita Das ist einfältige Reime der
liebreichen Heyrath des . . . Hn. Christoff Göbels . . .
vnd der . . . Jungfr. Barbaren, Herrn Heinrich
Mewii . . . hinterlassenen Ehleiblichen Tochter,
welcher Hochzeitlicher Ehren-Tag 1655. 5.
Weinmon. . . . gehalten worden (Königsberg:
Printed by Johann Reusner, 1655);
Sidera sunt voti portio sola mei. Oder Christliches
Sterbelied, so die . . . Fraw Vrsula Vogtinn . . .
Herrn Jacobi Bolii . . . Hertzliebe HausFraw, welche
im 37.sten Jahr, 22.sten Tag ihres Alters, 1655.
30. Weinm. . . . eingeschlaffen, schon . . . 1649. 3.
Brachmon. . . . zuverfertigen begehret, geschrieben
von Simon Dachen, vnd mit 5. Stimmen gesetzet von
Heinrich Alberten (Königsberg: Printed by Jo-
hann Reusner, 1655);
Omnia possideat non possidet aethera Mundus. Oder Die
Selige Ewigkeit, welche der . . . Frawen Sophien
gebohrnen Schwartzin, des . . . Herrn Johann
Schimmelpfennings . . . Hertzliebsten Haußfrawen . . .
Welche 1656. 10. Hornung im 39. Jahr ihres Alters . . .
selig eingeschlaffen . . . zu einem Begräbnüß-Liede . . .
geschrieben . . . vnd mit fünff Stimmen gesetzt von
Christoph Kaldenbach (Königsberg: Printed by
Johann Reusner, 1656);
Letztes Ehren-Gedächtniß dem weiland Ehrnvesten. . . Hn.
Joachim Bellach, Churfl. Brand . . . Kammer-
Diener, Welcher im fünff und dreyssigsten Jahr
seines Alters 1656. 13. Herbstmon. selig
eingeschlaffen, vnd 17. . . . eingesencket worden (Kö-
nigsberg: Printed by Johann Reusner, 1656);
Unterricht des Schawspiels Prussiarchus, Welches zum
Beschluß des Jubelfests der löblichen hohen Schul zu
Königsberg in Preussen 1644 gespielet worden, auch
nachmahln im jetztlauffenden 1656. Jahr . . .
wiederholet . . . ward (Königsberg: Johann Reusner, 1656);
Fidentem nescit deseruisse Deus. Oder: Christliche
Freudigkeit . . . bey seligem Ableiben des . . . Hn. M.
Martini Wolderi . . . welcher . . . 1657. 27. Brachm. . . .
eingeschlaffen, vnd . . . 3. Hewmonat . . . der Erden
eingeleibet worden, geschrieben von Simon Dachen,
vnd mit fünff Stimmen zu singen vnd spielen gesetzt
von Conrado Matthaei, Altstädtischen Cantore
(Königsberg: Printed by Johann Reusner, 1657);

Funera non tedas cantet morbosa senectus oder Einfältige
Hochzeit-Reime Hn. Christoff Tetschen . . . vnd Jfr.
Gertruden Weger (Königsberg, 1657);
Vnterthänigste gedoppelte Trew vnd Frewde bey dem höchst-
erwünschten Gebuhrts-Tage Sr. Sr. Churfürstl. vnd
Chur-Printzl. Durchl. Durchl. zu Brandenburg Hn.
Hn. Friedrich Wilhelmen vnd Carl Æmyls . . . vnsers
gnädigsten Churfürsten vnd Chur-Printzen des 6./16.
Hornung 1658. (Königsberg, 1658);
Hochzeit-Reime . . . Hn. Hans Heinrich Perband[s] . . .
vnd Fr. Anna Höpnerin (Königsberg, 1659);
Christliches Ehrengedächtnis dem . . . Hn. Heinrich De-
chant . . . welcher 1659. 3. Newjahrsmonat selig
eingeschlaffen, vnd den 10. . . . der Erden
eingebracht worden (Königsberg: Printed by Johann Reusner, 1659);
Freüdigmachender Trost der Wunden Jesu; welchen kurtz
vor seinem Ende der Weyland . . . Herr Simon Dach
dem . . . Hn. Johann Reüsnern Churfl. Durchl. Vnd
Deroselben Vniversität . . . Buchdruckern . . . auff-
gesetzt: Vnd von Sel. Joh. Weichmann jn eine
Melodey gebracht, jtzo aber mit mehr Stimmen
bekleidet, nebst einer Sinfoni von Joh. Sebastiani
(Königsberg: Printed by Friedrich Reusner,
1666);
Chur-Brandenburgische Rose, Adler, Löw und Scepter
(Königsberg: Printed by Friedrich Reusner's
heirs, 1681; enlarged edition, 2 volumes, circa
1690); republished as *Poetische Wercke, bestehend*
in heroischen Gedichten, denen beygefüget zwey seiner
verfertigten poetischen Schau-Spiele, anitzo auf
vielfältiges Verlangen zum Druck herausgegeben, 1
volume (Königsberg: Printed by Friedrich
Reusner's heirs, published by Heinrich Boye,
1696).

Collections and Editions: *Simon Dach,* edited by
Hermann Oesterley (Tübingen: Literarischer
Vereins, 1876; reprinted, Hildesheim & New
York: Olms, 1977);
Gedichte 1–4, 4 volumes, edited by Walther Ziese-
mer (Halle: Niemeyer, 1936–1938);
Poetische Wercke (Hildesheim & New York: Olms,
1970);
Simon Dach und der Königsberger Dichterkreis, edited by
Alfred Kelletat (Stuttgart: Reclam, 1986).

OTHER: "Wer wird in der Engel Chor / Gott, dich
ewig singen?," in *Schuldiges Danck- und Denck-*
Mahl, welches dem Hn. Johanni Stobaeo . . .
außgefertigt, by Georg Colbe (Königsberg:
Printed by Johann Reusner, 1646).

Among the German-language poets of the seventeenth century, Simon Dach has long been popular because of a handful of poems that have assumed almost the status of folk songs. Dach was a
master of direct, appealing, and sometimes homely
poetic diction in a time that customarily set far
greater store by excessive verbal ornament. Further,
sentimental legends have been attached to his life,
transforming him into a traditional and beloved national type – the good-hearted, naive, pious, and
musically gifted German – and he has appeared as
such in plays, narrative poems, and operettas. Until
the late twentieth century, however, literary scholarship had not accorded him a respect commensu-
rate with his public stature. At last, greater appreciation of occasional verse and its poetological and sociological functions has led to scrutiny of Dach's
enormous production of epithalamic, funerary, and
other purposeful poems. In this process, regard for
his poetic gifts has been enhanced rather than di-
minished.

Dach was born on 29 July 1605 in Memel
(today Klaipeda, Lithuania), a city at the extreme
northeastern tip of the Duchy of Prussia that had
been founded in 1252 by the Teutonic Knights at
the outlet of the river Dange into the Kurisches Haff,
a lagoon sheltered by a strip of coastal islands; its fortress, the Memelburg, controlled the passage from the
Baltic into the Haff and, on land, governed the important coastal road leading northward from
Königsberg, Prussia's capital, to Kurland. Dach's father, Simon Dach the elder, served as an interpreter of
Polish, Lithuanian, and Latvian in the courts; he also
worked as a mercantile translator, and the younger
Dach seems to have acquired a knowledge of the
world of customs and trade that would later be evidenced in his poems. Low German was the lingua
franca of the region, but by Dach's time it had long
since lost its social status and – thanks not least to Lutheran pastors speaking Martin Luther's High German from the pulpit – had ceased to function as a literary tongue, save for comic or peasantlike effect.

In the epithalamium for Johann Christoph
Rehefeld and Anna Cörber, the daughter of the late
pastor of the fortress and city of Memel (1655),
Dach gives an exceptional verse picture of the city
of his boyhood. Notably, his mother, Anna, née
Lepler, is mentioned only in passing: she had died
young, and his father had remarried. In the poem
Dach imagines that he and members of his family
are taken on a stroll by his late father through
places that are now much changed; he speaks of
boyhood games but neither of his education nor of
his main interest as a boy: music. He had taught
himself to play the *Knie-Geige* (viola de gamba), and
his passion for the instrument, and for music, would

never leave him. At fourteen he was sent off to the cathedral school in Königsberg (today Kaliningrad, Russia). There he lodged with his maternal aunt, Hedwig, and her husband, Johannes Vogler, a deacon at the cathedral. His musical talent made him a favorite of the school's rector, Peter Hagen, a well-known writer of hymns. His stay in Königsberg was brief: an outbreak of the plague, in which Hagen died, drove him back to Memel. By Easter 1621 he was once more in Königsberg; but he soon left again as a famulus of the theologian Martin Wolder, whom he had met in the Vogler household. (Wolder would eventually marry Dach's cousin, Anna Vogler, and become pastor of the church in the Königsberg Altstadt [Old Town]; in 1657 Dach would write an *epicedium* [mourning poem] on his death that begins "Wer seinen Sinn auff Gott nicht Einig stellt" [Who does not turn his mind to God alone], celebrating Wolder's piety.) Accompanying Wolder to the heart of German Lutheranism, Wittenberg, Dach was enrolled for three years in the city school while Wolder completed his studies at the university. Then Dach moved on to the Latin school in Magdeburg, where he lived with Archdeacon Christian Vogler, another relative. He completed his studies in 1625 with a treatise in Greek, a compendium of statements about astrology from Scripture, the classics, the church fathers, and the founders of Lutheranism, Martin Luther, Andreas Osiander, and Philipp Melanchthon; it is dedicated to Johannes and Christian Vogler and to Wolder.

The next year the threat of conflict – the Lower Saxon–Danish phase of the Thirty Years' War had just begun, and Magdeburg was threatened – and an outbreak of the plague caused Dach to flee to the relative safety of the northeast by way of Lüneburg, Hamburg, and, by sea, to Königsberg (today Kaliningrad, Russia). On 21 August 1626 he was enrolled at the Albertina, the university founded in Königsberg in 1544 by Duke Albrecht, who had given it his name. Dach would never leave the city again, except for brief excursions into its immediate hinterland. Königsberg was actually a combination of three independent boroughs, each with its own government, privileges, and character: the Altstadt, with the castle; the Kneiphof, with the university and cathedral; and the Löbenicht, with the dwellings of artisans and truck farmers.

At the Albertina, Dach's studies were at first in theology; but he soon turned to the humanities and the composition of Latin and German verse. His earliest preserved texts in both languages are from 1630: they are occasional poems, as almost all of Dach's subsequent verse would be, written for special occasions – in this instance a wedding – and for pay. Dach supported himself at first as resident tutor in the home of a member of the Kneiphof council, Christian Polikein, who in 1633 found Dach a position as assistant teacher at the cathedral school where Dach had once been a pupil; in 1636 he was promoted to corector of the school. Despite his advancement, Dach detested the work, and in a long autobiographical poem, "Danckbahrliche Auffrichtigkeit an Herrn Robert Roberthin" (Thankful Sincerity to Mr. Robert Roberthin), written in 1647 and first published by Walther Ziesemer in *Euphorion* in 1924, he described his reaction to the dirty, crowded, and airless classrooms; the careless and noisy pupils; and the monotony of the rote teaching. Indeed, Dach halfway attributed the asthma that racked him for years to the conditions at the cathedral school:

> Die Schule sey vielleicht die Vrsach meiner Pein,
> Ich mag vielleicht so schwach auch wohl gebohren
>   seyn.

> (The school may well have been the true cause of my
>   pain,
> My weakness may as well in me from birth have lain.)

Another depressing aspect of his job as assistant teacher was the responsibility for leading the school's poor boys to the graveyard as they accompanied the coffins of the departed – many of whom had died from the plague – with song.

During his years at the school Dach wrote – if he wrote it – the best known of his poems, *Anke van Tharaw* (Anke from Tharau, 1636). The song achieved its initial popularity when Heinrich Albert included it in the fifth volume (1648) of his *Arien oder Melodeyen Etlicher theils Geistlicher theils Weltlicher, zu guten Sitten vnd Lust dienender Lieder* (Arias or Melodies of Some Songs, Partly Spiritual, Partly Secular, Serving Good Morals and Pleasure, 1638–1659) as "Aria incerti autoris" (Aria of an Uncertain Author). The legend surrounding the work, which praises the girl's charms and virtues, stems from the church chronicle of the village of Tharau, which says that Simon Dach, the "Berühmte Preussische Poet . . . welcher damahlen noch ein Studiosus gewesen" (the famous Prussian poet, who at the time was still a student), composed the song for the wedding in 1636 of Anna Neander, the daughter of the late vicar, to Johann Portatius, pastor in Trempen (after his death she would marry and outlive two of his successors in the post). The chronicle was composed in 1723; the same year Dach's first biographer, Theophil Siegfried Bayer, wrote a more poignant account, according to which Dach had been in love with Anna, she had been taken away from him, and the song was a piece of self-consolation. The song was translated from Low into High German by Johann Gottfried Herder in his *Stimmen der Völker in Liedern* (Voices of the Peoples in Songs, 1778–1779); Herder's translation, with the last seven strophes omitted, was included in the Romantic verse collection *Des Knaben Wunderhorn* (The Boy's Magic Horn, 1805), by Achim von Arnim and Clemens Brentano; this version was given a more singable melody by the composer Friedrich Silcher and became one of the successes of his *Sammlung deutscher Volkslieder* (Collection of German Folk Songs, 1825). The sad story told by Bayer gave rise to *Ännchen von Tharau* (1829), a drama by the "German Walter Scott," Willibald Alexis (pseudonym of Heinrich Georg Wilhelm Häring); to an epyllion by Franz Hirsch, *Aennchen von Tharau: Ein Lied aus alter Zeit* (Aennchen von Tharau: A Song from Olden Times, 1882); and to several novels and stage works in the twentieth century. Dach's authorship has been much debated; it was accepted by Hermann Oesterley in his edition of Dach's poems (1876) and rejected by Ziesemer in his much fuller collection. Ziesemer attributed the poem to Albert, arguing that Albert, a non-Prussian, made errors in the Low German that Dach, a native speaker of the dialect, could not have committed. Ziesemer seems not to have wanted to lay the last seven strophes of the poem, with their robust diction, at Dach's door; but he was well aware that Dach had written the even stronger "Grethke-Lied" (Grethke Song), which had not been printed during Dach's lifetime and was discovered and published in 1912. Also, in the autobiographical poem to Roberthin, Dach boasts of having written "Anke van Tharaw." The balance of the circumstantial evidence points to Dach as the author. As a student of Latin literature Dach knew that broad jokes were an accepted part of epithalamic poetry, and the references in the song's latter strophes to Anke as "mihn Dühfkin myn Schahpken mihn Hohn" (my dovelet, my sheeplet, my chicken) are mild indeed. The poem could have been a "bridal dance" to amuse the wedding guests; as such, it could be considered part of Dach's huge professional production of marriage poetry.

In any event, Dach enjoyed social events and had a genius for friendship. The primus inter pares of his friends was Roberthin, the son of a pastor in Saalfeld, who had been sent abroad to study at the universities of Leipzig and Strasbourg; at the latter university he was first the student and then the as-

sociate of Matthias Bernegger, the noted philologist and historian who had also been the mentor of Martin Opitz. A second scholarly tour, after a stint as a tutor in his homeland, took Roberthin to the Netherlands, England, Paris, and Strasbourg, and a third, in 1633, back to France and the Netherlands and to Italy. By this time Roberthin and Dach were fast friends. When Roberthin left for the Mark Brandenburg in 1634 to be secretary of the Protestant branch of the Knights of Saint John, Dach bade him farewell in an *Abschieds-Lied* (Departure Song): "Ihr zieht, Herr Robert, auch nun hin, / Und ich hab' euch mein Hertz verpfändet" (And now, Sir Robert, you depart, / And I have pledged my heart to you) – sentiments that led Oesterley to characterize their relationship as a "hingebende, fast liebeglühende freundschaft" (devoted friendship almost glowing with love). In 1636 Roberthin, much favored by Georg Wilhelm, the elector of Brandenburg, returned to Königsberg as a member of the Prussian *Hofgericht* (high court of justice). When Roberthin married Ursula Vogt in 1639, Dach composed an extensive poem in the couple's honor. Still a bachelor, Dach appears to have lived for a time in the newlyweds' home: "Ursulchen, deine Lust, daß Muster theurer Sitten, / Hat deinetwegen mich im Hause gern gelitten" (Little Ursula, your delight, deportment's model true, / Has gladly suffered me at home because of you), he says in "Danckbahrliche Auffrichtigkeit an Herrn Robert Roberthin." Dach's relationship to Roberthin was one of dependency, devotion, and sheer admiration; as he says in the same poem, his friend, who had enjoyed the excellent international education Dach himself never received, was also his scholarly model; not without a trace of envy, Dach remarks: "Mein VaterGut war schlecht, sonst wär auch ich gezogen / Dem weisen Leiden zu" (My father's funds were small, else I too would have gone / To learned Leyden). Furthermore, Roberthin inspired Dach to undertake poetry, giving him books, giving him the courage to write, and even, according to the same poem, copying out Dach's verses and passing them along to others.

Dach may have met Roberthin through Albert, a cousin of the great composer Heinrich Schütz and Schütz's sometime pupil in Dresden; after law studies in Leipzig, Albert entered the university at Königsberg on 21 August 1626, the same day as Dach. By 1630 he was provisional organist at the Königsberg cathedral; the post was made permanent in 1631, and Albert would hold it until his death. Dach would probably not have achieved his large reputation in his own time had it not been for Albert's eight-volume song collection, *Arien*. Of the al-

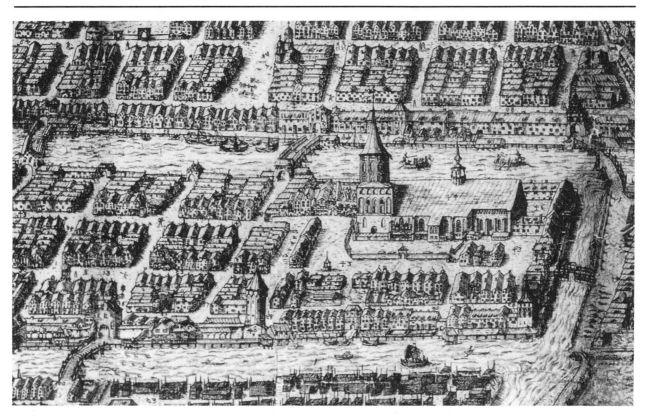

Detail from an aerial view of Königsberg, engraved in 1613 by Joachim Bering. Part of the Altstadt and the Löbenicht can be seen at the top; the Kneiphof, with the cathedral, is in the middle.

most 200 poems set to music by Albert, "the creator of the modern German song," 126 are by Dach, followed by Roberthin and Albert himself with 18 apiece. Apart from the *Arien,* Albert put together another document of consequence for modern knowledge of the so-called Königsberger Dichterkreis (Königsberg Poets' Circle): the cantata *Musicalische Kürbs-Hütte, welche uns erinnert Menschlicher Hinfälligkeit* (Musical Pumpkin Hut, Which Reminds Us of Human Decrepitude), dated 1641 but not published until 1645. Albert had been given a small plot of land by the council of the Kneiphof in which he and the assistant who pumped the organ at the cathedral planted the "hortulus Alberti" "Albert's little garden." The garden lay outside the Kneiphof proper, on the southern arm of the Pregel, at a spot where a fortification guarding the city's eastern flank had once stood. The site had thus been transformed into a place of peace and joy, as Dach said in his lament (written on 13 January 1641; first published by Ziesemer in 1924 in *Altpreußische Forschungen* and in *Euphorion*) after the garden was destroyed to make way for a road. Albert reports in the introduction to *Kürbs-Hütte* that he had conceived the idea of carving or writing the names of his friends, and, for each, a corresponding short verse, on the pumpkins

or gourds that were the garden's main plants, so that, as they grew, the names and messages would grow, too. Roberthin then argued that it would enhance the reputation of the garden if the words could be sung, and so Albert's cantata was created. The identities of the twelve whose names were inscribed on the pumpkins is not altogether clear; Oesterley suggests that they may be the ten people, plus Roberthin and Albert, who congratulated Dach when he received the master's degree at the Albertina in 1641. If so, they would have been the core of the Königsberger Dichterkreis. According to Oesterley, "Außer den genannten gehörte dem freundeskreise noch eine reihe anderer begabter und ausgezeichneter männer an, die . . . allmählig zu einem förmlichen dichterbunde zusammenwuchsen" (Apart from those [already] named, a series of other gifted and excellent men belonged to the circle of friends, who . . . gradually grew into an actual poets' society). They held meetings, according to Oesterley, on the model of the Italian academies and the German Fruchtbringende Gesellschaft (Fruit-bringing Society).

The Königsberg group was distinguished by its strong emphasis on competent musical performance of its texts, of which Albert's *Arien* gives the best sampling. It obviously partook of the seventeenth century's passion for the *locus amoenus* (pleasant place) of the garden in which poetry, friendship, and, sometimes, love could flourish – examples would be, in fiction, the suburban garden of Philipp von Zesen's *Adriatische Rosemund* (Adriatic Rosemund, 1645), and in real life, the Nuremberg *Poetenwäldchen* (poets' little forest) and the *Irrgarten* (maze) of the so-called Pegnitz Shepherds (including Georg Philipp Harsdörffer, Johann Klaj, and Sigmund von Birken). The circle also used some of the fanciful shepherd names common in such groups, and in pastoral novels and poetry of the time, such as "Chasmindo" and "Sichamond" for Dach, "Damon" for Albert, "Berrintho" for Roberthin, "Barchedas" for Andreas Adersbach, and "Celadon" for Christoph Kaldenbach. But maintenance of a slight pastoral pose and the enjoyment of sociability were not the only concerns of the group; more important was the constant awareness of human mortality – a skull surmounted by an hourglass is at the center of the lower edge of the frontispiece to *Kürbs-Hütte*. Further, as Albrecht Schöne has pointed out, the pumpkin or gourd that, in Jonah 4:6–10, came up in a night and perished in a night at Nineveh, is the emblem of human life – rapidly growing and rapidly decaying, "*cito nata, cito pereunt*" (quickly born, they perish quickly). To Schöne's observation, Alfred Kelletat adds that death in Albert's garden and in the verses of his cantata is neither the wages of sin nor "der herrscherliche Tod der pompösen barocken Grabmäler" (the imperious death of pompous baroque mausoleums) but a "sanfte Naturnotwendigkeit" (gentle necessity of nature), a prefiguration of Johann Wolfgang von Goethe's "Stirb und werde" (Die and become). Kelletat also adds that the activities of the Königsberg poets prefigure the sentimental friendship cults of the eighteenth century. In his lament, Dach sees the destruction of the garden as a sign of the triumph of time – "Waß mit der Zeit entsteht, fährt mit der Zeit auch hin" (Whatever with time does grow, in time does pass away) – and equally a sign of the vanity of human endeavor. Yet the products of the human spirit endure and defy time:

> Wir zwingen ihren Zwang, sie wüte wie sie kan,
> Sie greifft nicht vnsern Geist, noch seine Gaben an
> (We force the force of time, let it rage as it will,
> It cannot do our soul or do its gifts aught ill).

The lines are a rendering of the thoughts from Horace's ode 3:30, "Exegi monumentum aere perennius" (I have erected a monument outlasting bronze) and "Non omnis moriar" (I shall not altogether die), in which the humanistic and posthumanistic age took such consolation. In this respect Dach was more or less right: literary history, if not the general public, still remembers the names and some of the accomplishments of the men associated with Albert's miniature garden – not just Dach, Albert, and Roberthin but also the diplomat Adersbach, a member of a prominent Königsberg family, whose father opened his house to the group; Kaldenbach, probably the group's most gifted member after Dach and the most versatile, an active poet in several languages and professor of Greek at the university; Johann Stobaeus, the cantor of the Kneiphof and, from 1626, the court Kapellmeister (orchestra conductor), who set several of Dach's texts to music; Georg Mylius, who died in his twenties; and Valentin Thilo, professor of eloquence at the Albertina and, like his pastor father, the author of many chorales.

In June 1635, when King Vladislav IV of Poland came to Königsberg to receive its formal pledge of loyalty, Dach and Albert were called on to produce text and music for a festival opera, *Cleomedes,* to celebrate his visit. The libretto is disingenuous: Cleomedes, who represents Vladislav – *der allerwehrteste und lobwürdigste trewe Hirt der Crohn Polen* (the most worthy and most praiseworthy faithful shepherd of the crown of Poland), as the subtitle calls him – protects the nymphs Venda (Poland) and Herophile (Sweden) from the satyrs Agathyrsus, Zantybius, and Polyphobus (the Muscovites, the Turks, and the Tartars, respectively). The short opera ends with a choral celebration of "Edler Friede, Gold der Zeiten" (Noble peace, gold of the ages) and of the vastly gifted Vladislav himself. A few months after the performance, on 12 September, the Peace of Stuhmsdorf was concluded in the presence of representatives of Brandenburg, England, France, and the United Netherlands – all of which countries appear as extras in the cast – between the combatants of the first Swedish-Polish War. Dach's talent for poetic celebration was again employed on 29 July 1638, when Opitz, the reigning prince of German poetry, came to Königsberg, at Roberthin's invitation, from Danzig (today Gdansk, Poland), where he resided as Vladislav's court historiographer and royal secretary. Dach's poem to Opitz, with Albert's music, quite expectedly praises Opitz to the skies, proclaiming that Germany owes it to "Sir Opitz" alone that the deference shown to foreign tongues had begun to fade, "Und man nunmehr ins gemein / Lieber Deutsch begehrt zu sein" (And now people generally, / German much prefer to be). Opitz, it would seem, got to know something about the bachelor Dach's private life; writing in Latin to Roberthin after the visit, he sent his greetings to Dach but added that Dach should not fall in love with a Miss Brodine because she was too lively for him; of course, Opitz concluded, he may compose a song for her.

Also in 1638 a still more important figure, the elector Georg Wilhelm, came to Königsberg to stay; he was accompanied by his son, Friedrich Wilhelm, and Dach welcomed them with a grand poetic salute whose burden came near its end:

> Laß uns keiner Frewde sparen!
> Die ihr geht mit greisen Haren,
> Die ihr an den Brüsten seyt,
> Mütter, Jüngling' und Jungfrawen,
> Arm und Reich, ihr müsset schawen,
> Nach gewünschter Fröligkeit
>
> (Let us keep no joy away,
> You who walk with hair of gray,
> You who suckle at the breast,
> Mothers, youths, and maidens fair,
> Poor and rich, see that you share
> In the wished-for joyfulness).

As a matter of fact, Georg Wilhelm had come to Königsberg almost as a refugee, and in considerable disgrace.

Georg Wilhelm promised Dach the chair of poetry at the university whenever it fell vacant; its holder, Christoff Eiland, almost immediately died, and it went to Dach on 1 August 1639. As he held no advanced academic degree, he had to obtain a hasty master of arts. He did so in April 1640, arguing three theses: that poetry is concerned with truth and poems are not fictions, that a tragedy may have a happy ending, and that the writer of immoral verses does not deserve fame. (The disputation is said to have been defended at table, amid wine and other refreshments.) His duties were to lecture on Latin authors (Horace, Ovid, Seneca, Juvenal), to provide Latin verse for solemn academic occasions (many of his surviving 259 Latin poems were intended for this purpose), and to inspect the Latin poetry of other members of the faculty. He became sufficiently popular with his colleagues – and with Friedrich Wilhelm – to be named dean of the philological faculty five times and once, in 1656, rector of the university.

Dach's most notable poetic contribution to the university was the festival opera, or pageant, written in 1644 for the hundredth anniversary of the Albertina's founding; the enrollment had at last exceeded a thousand, and the institution had become a favorite place of study for youths not only from regions more or less close by but even from Hungary and particularly from the German-language is-

land of Transylvania. *Prussiarchus* – retitled *Sorbuisa* when it was printed in the second volume of the collection *Chur-Brandenburgische Rose, Adler, Löw und Scepter* (Elector Brandenburg's Rose, Eagle, Lion, and Scepter, circa 1690) – with music by Albert, was performed by students in the auditorium maximum on 21 September 1644; it was repeated in 1645 at the court, in the presence of Friedrich Wilhelm's aunt, Maria Eleonora, the widow of the Swedish king Gustav Adolph, as a ceremonial sign of the restored relations between Sweden and Brandenburg-Prussia. In 1656 it was given once more, in the presence of Friedrich Wilhelm and his first wife, Luise Henrietta, the daughter of Frederik Hendrik of Orange.

Sorbuisa, representing the Duchy of Prussia, realizes that she has become an object of mockery because of her playmate Wustlieb, "Die Preußische Barbarey" (Prussian barbarism); she is urged on by Pollentius (Georg von Polent, bishop of Samland, a contemporary of Duke Albrecht who had embraced the Reformation in the 1520s). Pollentius advises Prussiarch (Albrecht) to bring Apollo and the Nine Muses to Sorbuisa, and Sabnius (Georg Sabinus, the son-in-law of Melanchthon, a distinguished Neo-Latin poet, and the first rector of the Albertina) is selected to lead them on their trip to the north. In this project Prussiarch is encouraged by Cimbrina (Albrecht's wife, Anna Dorothea, the daughter of Fredrik I of Denmark). The offensive Wustlieb tries once again to make merry with Sorbuisa but, rejected, turns for aid to Wurschkaytes, "Ein Heydnischer Götzen-Pfaf" (a heathen idolatrous priest), for aid. Wustlieb is transformed into the form of Sabnius by pagan magic, and sows "eitel Barbarey, Zanck, und Zwietracht" (nothing but barbarism, strife, and disunity). Prussiarch becomes "hefftig verwirret und zornig" (violently confused and angry), a patent allusion to the theological squabbles that rent the Albertina; but the genuine Sabnius is able to unmask his double, and Wustlieb and Wurschkaytes depart "mit Ach und Weh" (with loud lamentations), while Apollo and his band take possession of the Prussian Helicon amid general rejoicing. In the finale, after a salute to Albrecht, Dach praises Albrecht's son, Albrecht Friedrich; Georg Friedrich, the margrave of Brandenburg-Ansbach and Bayreuth, who came to the feeble-minded ruler's aid with "Sorg und Väterliche Trew" (care and paternal loyalty); the electors Joachim Friedrich and Johann Sigismund, noted for their "Trew und Wachsamkeit" (loyalty and vigilance); and the "Muht und klugen Sinnen" (courage and wise mind) of Georg Wilhelm, who receives a whole stanza, with Apollo predicting that a golden age begins with him. The climax of this rousing ending belongs to Friedrich Wilhelm, "Der Völcker Trost, der Länder Rhue" (the people's balm, the nations' peace). Only the cast of characters, résumés of the five acts, and the texts, without the music, of some choruses and arias have survived. The loss of the full text is particularly regrettable because it contained the seriocomic inlays or entr'actes with Wustlieb, his wife, Domdeyke, and Wurschkaytes, which might have revealed something more about Dach's knowledge of the duchy's aboriginal population. The elector was fond of Dach; in an often-quoted passage Bayer says that Friedrich Wilhelm learned many of Dach's poems by heart and never came to Königsberg without having the poet brought to the castle. He was so conversant with Dach's style that he could tell whether an unfamiliar poem was by Dach or someone else.

With the professorship and the favor of the house of Brandenburg-Prussia in hand, Dach had at last been able to marry: he had wed Regina Pohl on his thirty-sixth birthday. The event was celebrated in song and music by Roberthin and Albert. The union with "Pohlinchen" was both happy and fruitful; Dach wrote warmly of the pleasures of hearth and home, for example, in an epithalamium of 22 January 1647, in which he tells the newlyweds – a member of the elector's chancellery, Georg Andressen, and his bride, Maria Salbertin – how he likes to come in from the snowy fields beside the Pregel to his children and his wife: "Steinern ist, dem dies nicht Rhue / Oder Frewde kan erwecken" (He's of stone whom this cannot / Give a sense of peace and gladness).

The Dachs had seven children: the first, Christoph, born on 13 August 1642, died about a year later – after his father, not very encouragingly, had told the infant in a *genethliacon* (poem celebrating a birth) that life was "Wanckelmuth und reiche Betteley, / Der Freiheit Dienst, ein Hauß der Siechheit und der Sünden" (Fickleness and moneyed beggary / Free slavery, a house of sickness and of sinning). Their sixth child and fifth son, Johann, born in 1650, also did not survive infancy.

In 1644 the town council of the Kneiphof gave Dach a house, free for life, in the Magistergasse, for which Dach richly thanked it and, as was his poetic-pedantic wont, provided an exact description of its site:

Wo nach des Thumes Brücken
Der Pregel See-warts fährt,
Vnd seinen krummen Rücken
Stracks nach der Rechten kehrt

(Where after the cathedral bridge
The Pregel flows to the sea
And turns its wavy surface
To the right hand instantly).

In the spring of 1650 the council gave Dach a garden with a storehouse near the site of Albert's garden, a kind of life insurance for his wife and children. Dach had been ailing for years, and some of his most affecting verse describes his illnesses. For example, a sonnet of 1647 (first published in Oesterley's edition), written "des Nachts, da ich vor Engbrüstigkeit nicht schlaffen können, auff dem Bette" (at night in bed, when I could not sleep because of angina pectoris), is an appeal for release from suffering: "Wie? ist es denn nicht gnug, gern einmal sterben wollen? / Natur, Verhängnüs, Gott, waß haltet ihr mich auff?" (What? Does it not suffice, one willing death to have? / Why, nature, fortune, God, shall you thus hold me fast?). In a strophic verse of 1650 (first published in Oesterley's edition), when a constriction of the breast again would not let him sleep, he writes: "Die Glocken hör ich schlagen: / Zwölff, eines, zwey, drey, vier" (I hear the clocks, their chiming: / Twelve, one, two, three, and four). Frequently his complaints enter into his occasional poetry, as in an epithalamium of 24 September 1657:

Bey dem Keichen, bey dem Hust,
Bey mit Schlamm erfüllter Brust
Ist es schlecht zu singen

(With my cough, my panting chest,
With my phlegm-distended breast,
It is hard to sing).

Another apparently inappropriate message for a bridal couple came on 7 January 1659, a few months before Dach's death:

Meines wilden Durstes Noht
Ist schier ärger als der Tod,
Tantals Straff ist nicht zu achten:
So muß einer Schnecken seyn,
Wenn sie für der Hitze Pein
In dem Sommer muß verschmachten

(And my raging thirst's despair
Almost is worse than death to bear,
Tantalus had no such anguish:
This is what a snail must know

When, beneath the cruel glow
Of the summer, it must languish).

Several conclusions can be drawn from the references to the poet's illness. Their painfully out-of-place appearance in marriage poems shows how enormously popular Dach had become as a purveyor of occasional poetry; their personal quality increased their prestige value for the families that had ordered them. Also, although the illness poem was scarcely an unknown subgenre of the lament at the time (as in the bitter *derniers vers* [last verses] of Pierre de Ronsard or the self-portraits from the sickbed of Andreas Gryphius), Dach's poems on his condition have a frankness and a readiness to employ almost clinical detail that make them unusual, if not unique. Furthermore, the poems of affliction offer still another reminder of the appalling medical conditions of the time and of the omnipresent threat of death, even in a place, such as Prussia, that was at peace. Dach was ill with the plague in 1650, a year after one of those frightful eruptions of the disease that laid waste to Prussia. Prussia had the distinction of being one of the most plague-ridden sections of Europe in the seventeenth century, and Dach provided terrifying pictures of its ravages in his poetry – for example, in the *Christliches Denckmal* (Christian Monument) of December 1645 for Urban Lepner, pastor in the Altstadt: "Kein Hauß fast war befreyt vom ubel dieser Seuchen. / Der Tag ist viel zu kurtz die grosse Zahl der Leichen / Zu bringen in das Grab" (Almost no house was free from this plague's cruel contagions. / The day is much too short, the corpses in their legions / To carry to their grave). Dach's friends were carried off: Albert in 1651; Ambrosius Scala, a court lawyer, "Mit dem ich jung nach Liebes-Brauch / Mich Brüderlich verschworen" (To whom I, young, in loving's way / Had pledged myself as a brother), in 1652. Stobaeus and Roberthin had gone before, of other causes: the musician in 1646, the diplomat in 1648. Roberthin's death of a stroke had given rise to Dach's *Bittere Klage* (Bitter Lament, 1648), which ends with the conceit that the poet's tears mixed with his ink and erased everything he wrote from his tablet.

To these personal losses must be added, in the 1650s, Dach's awareness of new perils besetting Prussia from without, especially during the second Swedish-Polish War of 1655 to 1660. When Friedrich Wilhelm's efforts to maintain an armed neutrality came to naught, the elector was compelled to participate in the war on the Swedish side, joining Carl X Gustaf at the battle of Warsaw in July 1656.

In revenge, a Polish army, strengthened by Lithuanian and Tartar units, invaded Prussia, carrying out a campaign of atrocity; the Tartar mercenaries were particularly vicious as they ravaged the southern part of the duchy. These events contributed to the anxiety and despair in which Dach wrote the epicedium for Michael Kreuschner, who died in his twentieth year in 1655. Here, in one of the relatively rare classical allusions in his vernacular verse, Dach refers to the maxim of Posidippus in the Greek Anthology that it would be better never to have been born. Likewise, the dead are fortunate:

Jetzt müssen wir bekennen
Wie selig die zu nennen
So hier der Seuchen zwangk
Gebracht in ihre Kammer,
Sie hören keinen Jammer
Und keiner Waffen Klangk.

(Indeed, we must confess
How greatly those are blest
Who forced by sickness' lash
in death's still chamber languish,
They hear no cries of anguish,
Nor hear the weapons' clash.)

Concerned about his family's lot after his demise, sometime in 1657 or early 1658 Dach directed an "Unterthänigste letzte Fleh-Schrifft" (Most Devoted, Final Supplication) to the elector in which he said that even an old warhorse was put out to pasture as its reward, that "Ja kein alter Hund verdirbet, / Der uns trewlich hat bewacht" (Yes, no old dog's left to hunger / Which has faithfully kept guard). The plea seems to have worked, for on 16 February 1658 – the elector's thirty-eighth birthday and his son, Carl Emil's, fourth – the elector bestowed on the poet a property of ten and a half acres near Kuikeim, in the Kaymen section northeast of Königsberg. In a birthday poem Dach thanked father and son for the gift.

It is difficult to imagine Dach's prouder contemporaries, such as Opitz, Paul Fleming, or Georg Rudolf Weckherlin, comparing themselves to worn-out steeds and aged dogs; in the "Fleh-Schrifft," however, Dach also makes a claim for the eternity of art and his role in its creation:

Phoebus ist bey mir daheime,
Diese Kunst der Deutschen Reime
Lernet Preussen erst von mir,
Meine sind die ersten Seiten,
Zwar man sang vor meinen Zeiten,
Aber ohn Geschick und Zier.

(Phoebus has in me his dwelling,

And this art of German rhyming
Prussia has first learned from me,
My strings were the first that sounded –
Of course, before, crude song abounded,
But without skill and elegancy.)

The deed for the property was made out and signed on 3 September. (The farm existed until the expulsion by the Soviet Union of the German population of East Prussia in 1945; a commemorative tablet recorded Dach's ownership.) The elector had good reason to be in a generous frame of mind: by clever maneuvering, he had steered Prussia through the latter stages of the Swedish-Polish War and had attained his family's long-cherished goal, independence from even nominal Polish rule over Prussia, by the Treaty of Wehlau in 1657. The opening of the "Fleh-Schrifft" may contain an allusion to this diplomatic triumph when Dach addresses the hero, at whose feet "Länder liegen, Ströme fliessen" (lands are lying, streams are flowing). The peace is certainly mentioned in the epithalamium for Christoff Tetsch and Gertrud Meyer of 24 September 1657, the poem that opens with Dach's detailed description of the condition of his lungs and his advanced age. (To Dach's financial advantage, marriages were as common as funerals among his middle-class customers; epithalamia by Dach for the nobility are rare.) The poet's spirits rise when he thinks of the happier world in which the couple has established its union, a world adorned once again by the golden crown of peace. Dach confesses that he had thought of fleeing to Holstein, but "Da sich Mars auch dorthin wandt" (When Mars also turned that way) – that is, when the Swedes, under Carl X Gustaf, marched through Holstein on their way to Jutland – he planned instead to go to Mitau (today Jelgava, Latvia), the capital of Kurland. (That would have been a bad idea, too, since the next year Swedish forces occupied Kurland and imprisoned Duke Jakob, Friedrich Wilhelm's brother-in-law, not releasing him until after the Peace of Oliva of 3 May 1660 finally brought the conflict in the northeast to an end.) Dach is glad that God has given Prussia calm once more so that the couple, like the poet himself, may someday be buried there undisturbed.

Dach's death, of tuberculosis, on 15 April 1659 was followed by a small scandal: Georg Kolbe, the clergyman to whom he made his final confession, claimed that Dach had said he wished that his life had been purer and that he particularly regretted having composed his "Bauer-Lied" (the Low German "Grethke-Lied"). The family published *Ehrenrettung S. Hoch-Achtbarkeit Herrn M. Simonis*

Dachii usw. und Georgii Colbii (Salvation of the Honor of the Highly Respectable Mr. Simon Dach, etc., and Georg Kolbe), arguing that Dach's conscience was bothered by having written epicedia in remembrance of people who did not deserve respect, but that he was blameless in the matter because he had been given incorrect information by the survivors.

Despite the absence of a collection of his verse, Dach's reputation grew as the century approached its end, for he possessed an almost unique voice that was all the rarer since German baroque poetry, particularly in the hands of the Silesians Hofmann von Hofmannswaldau and Daniel Casper von Lohenstein, became ever more artful. A faithful Opitzian, Dach had maintained straightforward metrical patterns, sticking to the iamb and the trochee and avoiding more-complex feet, such as the dactyl and the anapest, made popular by the members of the Nuremberg school during the last decade and a half of Dach's life; his rhetorical figures were pellucid, and he had eschewed learned references. At length, his verses for the house of Brandenburg-Prussia appeared in a single volume, *Chur-Brandenburgische Rose, Adler, Löw und Scepter,* published in 1681 for the fortieth anniversary of the beginning of the Friedrich Wilhelm's reign and reprinted with a second volume around 1690, after Friedrich Wilhelm's death; but an edition of Dach's collected works was conspicuous by its absence.

Meanwhile, his admirers carried on a kind of missionary work. The Zittau schoolmaster and pastor Balthasar Kindermann's *Der Deutsche Poët* (The German Poet, 1664), a poetic treatise and, thanks to its many examples, a semianthology, draws fairly heavily on Dach, and Gryphius quoted Dach in his *Dissertationes Funebres, oder Leichabdankungen* (Funeral Orations, 1667). Dach's friend Kaldenbach, who had moved to Tübingen in 1656 as professor of poetry, eloquence, and "histories," employed many examples from Dach in his handbook of German poetry, *Poetice Germanica, seu de ratione scribendi Carminis Teutonici Libri Duo* (German Poetics; or, Two Books concerning the Rules of Writing German Song, 1674). Earlier, in his *Sylvae Tubingenses* (Tübingen Sylvae, 1667), Kaldenbach had included a Latin ode saluting his former colleague as possessing all the gifts of the gods: Memel played the role of Mantua, Virgil's birthplace, and Dach was the Maro of the Prussians. In the so-called first history of German literature, *Unterricht von der Teutschen Sprache und Poesie* (Instruction concerning German Language and Poetry, 1682), Daniel Georg Morhof wrote that "Die Preussischen Lieder, insonderheit des

Simon Dachs sind sehr gut, insonderheit auff die Music gerichtet" (The Prussian songs, especially those of Simon Dach, are very good, especially set to music). Erdmann Neumeister, in his biographical-bibliographical compendium *De Poetis Germanicis* (Concerning German Poets, 1695), lamented that the works of Dach, "spiritus ubique et succi pleno" (full everywhere of spirit and strength), were not to be had in a single volume: he referred curious readers to Albert's anthologies, *Poetisches Lust-Gärtlein* (Poetic Little Garden of Pleasure, 1645) and *Poetisch-Musicalisches Lust-Wäldlein* (Musical Little Grove of Pleasure, 1648), and to Kaldenbach's poetics. In his great anthology, *Herrn von Hoffmannswaldau und andrer Deutschen auserlesener und biszher ungedruckter Gedichte erster Theil* (First Part of Selected and Hitherto Unprinted Poems of Mr. von Hoffmannswaldau and Other Germans, 1697), the Silesian Benjamin Neukirch wrote that Dach was "unvergleichlich in geistlichen liedern und ungemein glücklich in übersetzung der Psalmen, und ist nur schade, daß man seine sachen der welt nicht mehr bekandt gemacht" (incomparable in spiritual songs and uncommonly felicitous in the translation of the Psalms, and it is simply too bad that his products have not been made better known to the world). In the fifth volume of the anthology (1710), probably compiled by another Silesian, Gottlieb Stolle-Leander, there are twenty-nine poems by Dach, mostly under the rubric of "Galante und Verliebte Arien" (Gallant and Amorous Arias), together with an epithalamium, several funeral poems, a poem to Georg Wilhelm, and four "Vermischte Arien" (Mixed Arias), including the well-known "Der Mensch hat nichts so eigen" (Mankind has naught so special), under the title "Lob der Freundschafft" (Praise of Friendship). The Silesians, who had long maintained connections with Königsberg, continued to show their interest with the assembly of Dach's singly printed works and manuscripts by Johann Caspar Arlet, a Breslau polyhistor and rector of the venerable Elisabeth Gymnasium, whose love of Opitz's poetry had led him to Dach. As early as 1748 Arlet called for a genuine collection of Dach's poetry, but he never carried out the task himself.

Dach's fellow Prussian, Johann Christoph Gottsched, was also troubled by the lack of an edition of Dach's works. In the mid eighteenth century the Royal German Society of Königsberg announced that, more than twenty years before, it had sent a collection of Dach's poems to the critic; the collection had been put together with great zeal by Heinrich Bartsch, the Königsberg city secretary and archivist, but Gottsched claimed that he had never received the package. In his *Kurzgefasste historische Nachricht von den bekanntesten preußischen Poeten* (Brief Historical Report of the Best-Known Prussian Poets, 1747) Gottsched had written that Dach was "der erste, der diesen Namen in einem vortrefflichern Grade verdient" (the first who deserved this name in a more excellent way). Herder contributed to the transformation of Dach's texts into popular songs with his *Stimmen der Völker in Liedern,* where he included not only "Ännchen von Tharau" but also "Der Mensch hat nichts so eigen" (here titled "Lied der Freundschaft" [Song of Friendship]) with the notation "Schon die treuherzige Sprache dieses Dichters verdient Bekanntmachung und Liebe" (The openhearted language of this poet deserves to be known and loved).

Among the Romantics, the folk-song quality of Dach's poetry captured the attention of Ludwig Rhesa, professor of theology at Königsberg, director of the university's Lithuanian seminar, and the major collector and translator of Lithuanian folk songs, who dedicated a poem to Dach in his *Prutena oder Preußische Volkslieder und andere vaterländische Dichtungen* (Prutena; or, Prussian Folk Songs and Other Songs of the Fatherland, 1809), in which the nymph of the river Dange puts a wreath on Dach's image, an indication that Rhesa may have sensed a Lithuanian heritage in the poet. More important for Dach's reputation in Germany was the selection of poems by Dach, Roberthin, and Albert that the poet Wilhelm Müller published in 1823 as the fifth volume in his *Bibliothek deutscher Dichter des siebzehnten Jahrhunderts* (Library of German Poets of the Seventeenth Century), for which Albert's *Arien* was a main source. In Müller's opinion,

> Dach gehört zu den besten Liederdichtern, nicht nur seines Jahrhunderts, sondern der Deutschen aller Jahrhunderte. . . . Mehrere von Dach's lyrischen Gedichten haben den Ton des Volksliedes sehr glücklich getroffen, und werden deutsche Volkslieder in der ächten Bedeutung dieses Wortes bleiben, so lange es, wenigstens in Wort und Gesang, noch ein deutsches Volk giebt.

> (Dach belongs to the best song-poets not only of his own century but of the Germans of all centuries. . . . Several of Dach's lyrical poems have struck the tone of the folk song altogether successfully and will remain German folk songs in the true sense of this word as long as a German people exists, at least in word and song.)

Dach also wrote texts for church songs, a side of his talents that made him popular in Lutheran circles. This popularity is reflected in August Gebauer's anthology, *Simon Dach und seine Freunde als Kirchenliederdichter* (Simon Dach and His Friends as Poets of Church Songs, 1828), and continued into the twentieth century.

However well known Dach was as a writer of quasi-folk songs and hymns, his reputation in literary history and criticism suffered, as Wulf Segebrecht has argued, from the circumstance that he was overwhelmingly an occasional poet, which led to condescension or neglect in a time when the Goethean *Erlebnislyrik* (lyric of experience) was a critical ideal. When Oesterley published his collection of 413 German texts, and the initial lines of 1,002 German and 259 Latin poems in 1876, he felt the need to justify the inclusion of so much occasional verse: the many personal interjections in the bridal and burial poems, he says, give "langen reihen von gelegenheitsgedichten, die im übrigen ohne jede bedeutung sind, einen hohen werth für die kenntnis von Dachs leben und charakter" (long series of occasional poems, which otherwise are quite without importance, a high value for the knowledge of Dach's life and character). The Oesterley edition served scholarship well for some sixty years. In the 1920s and 1930s the Königsberg Germanist Ziesemer, who had already made important discoveries of Dach manuscripts (including the poem on the destruction of the pumpkin hut and the long autobiographical poem to Roberthin), undertook a full scholarly edition of Dach's works using all available sources, especially those in the Königsberg state archives. His edition, published from 1936 to 1938, was completed just in time: Soviet troops took Königsberg by storm on 10 April 1945, then sacked and razed the city, destroying archival holdings. (Ziesemer escaped to the West, where he died in 1951.) Königsberg was renamed Kaliningrad and repopulated with Russians.

The gentle persona reflected in Dach's poems, combined with the total and brutal disappearance of the city in which he had lived, gave the poet an attraction for creative writers of the postwar world. Johannes Bobrowski, who had been a student at the gymnasium descended from Dach's cathedral school, referred to Dach in several prose works and included in a handwritten florilegium of favorite poems Dach's sonnet on his illness; and Günter Grass, from nearby Danzig, selected a fictionalized Dach to give the final, irenic speech for the assembled German baroque authors in his literary-historical fantasy *Das Treffen in Telgte* (1979; translated as *The Meeting in Telgte,* 1981).

In modern anthologies of German poetry certain of Dach's poems appear again and again: above

all, "Der Mensch hat nichts so eigen," "Ännchen von Tharau," one or another of the spring songs, and the sonnet on his illness. None of these poems can be firmly identified as occasional poetry in the sense of being written on order, for pay, and for a special purpose or occasion; but it is likely that, except for the sonnet, all of them were. Segebrecht notes that Dach's poetry is mostly directed to specific recipients: "Dachs Gedichte begleiteten . . . die Angehörigen des gehobenen Königsberger Bürgertums und teilweise auch des Adels von der Wiege bis zur Bahre" (Dach's poems accompanied . . . the members of the upper Königsberg bourgeoisie and, partly, of the nobility as well, from the cradle to the grave). Of the about fifteen hundred poems that survive, Segebrecht reckons that more than half are for occasions of mourning, about a third for weddings, and the rest for court, academic, and other "organized" purposes. Into this last, miscellaneous category would fall poems of imprecation or gratitude, a few poems written for births, and the familiar social songs. In his 1986 selection of Dach's poetry Kelletat, following Ziesemer, divides the poems into two categories: worldly and spiritual.

Dach's many Leichengedichte (funeral poems [literally, corpse poems]) are further separated into two groups by Irmgard Scheitler. The first group includes the *Sterbe-Lied* (death song), also called *Trost-Lied* (song of consolation); the *Begräbnis-Lied* (funeral song); and the *Abschieds-Lied* (farewell song). Such poems were either commissioned in advance, when the death was foreseen, or quickly requested by the bereaved family, when it was unexpected. Most of these poems are fairly brief, are stanzaic, have short lines in three- or four-foot iambic meter, and are singable; set for five voices, they were customarily sung by the poor boys of the cathedral school. Dach could also, however, essay the classical Sapphic-and-Adonic strophe of antiquity; this Horatian form had long been employed in Protestant vernacular hymn writing.

Often two poems were produced for the same affluent departed: the Sterbe-Lied would be followed by a poem of the second type, the grander true epicedium, called variously *poetisches Denckmal* (poetic monument), *Klage* (lament), *Gedächtnis* (in memoriam), or *Reime* (verses), that was customarily declaimed at graveside. These poems are longer, do not have music, and, in keeping with the higher socioeconomic status of the deceased, may abandon the plain stanzaic form for the complex "Pindaric" ode or use alexandrines in stichic verse. As Dach's career advanced, the introductory strophes in the epicedia began to include personal reflections by

Dach – for example, contrasting his own fragility with the apparent robustness, *ante mortem,* of the departed. An example is the *Letztes und wolverdientes Ehren-Gedächtnüß* (Last and Well-Deserved Commemoration of Honor, 1654) for the official and nobleman Ludwig von Canitz, who died "in der besten Blüte seines Alters" (in the best blossom of his age) at twenty-eight:

> Ich geh' ein Schiem allhier,
> Mich möcht ein Wind umbwehen,
> Du pflagst herein zu gehn
> Wie wir die Fichten sehen
> In ihren Wäldern stehn.
>
> (I walk along, a shade,
> I'd fall if wind did blow,
> But you were wont to go
> The way fir trees, we know,
> Stand in their forest row.)

The spiritual poetry is less inventive than the poems in the worldly category: Dach's gift for colorful expression was hampered by the necessity of giving appropriate voice to the lament or consolation; he appears at first to have been much more hesitant about making his fascinating personal comments in poems intended to be read or sung in church or at the graveside. Also, having spent his life in a Lutheran milieu, where theological convention was the order of the day, while serving unofficially a house that belonged to the Reformed church, he was limited to a relatively unadventurous set of religious formulations and thoughts. Thus, several of his spiritual poems readily entered the hymnal or, at least, were altogether appropriate in a church setting. For example, the *Musicalisches Ehrengedechtniß* (Musical Commemoration of Honor, 1635) for Hiob Lepner, which begins "O wie Seelig seydt jhr doch, Ihr Frommen" (Oh how blessed are you now indeed), became one of Dach's best-known hymns and is the only one that survives today in the *Evangelisches Kirchengesangbuch* (Evangelical Hymnbook). Other examples include the *Christliches Todes Errinnerung* (Christian Reminder of Death, 1648) for Roberthin, beginning "Ich bin ja, Herr, in deiner Macht" (Oh Lord, I am indeed within your power), commissioned and written "schon vor etzlichen Jahren" (some years before); *Sidera sunt voti portio sola mei. Oder Christliches Sterbelied* (The Stars Are the Sole Portion of My Prayer; or, Christian Death Song, 1655), beginning "Schöner HimmelsSaal" (Fair heavenly hall), commissioned in 1649 by Roberthin's widow (who had remarried) and performed after her death on 30 October 1655, "nach

ausgestandenem vielem Creutz und Kranckheit, in beständiger Anruffung ihres Erlösers sanfft und selig eingeschlafen" (after the endurance of much pain and sickness, while constantly calling on her redeemer, gently and blessedly gone to sleep); the *Unbewegter Trost der wahren Christen* (Unwavering Consolation of the True Christians, 1651), beginning "Ich bin bey Gott in Gnaden" (I am in God's good graces), based on Romans 8:35, for Achatius von Dohna; and the *Christliches Sterb-Liedchen* (Little Death-Song, 1652) for Greger Werner, beginning "Wir sprechen sonst: je größre Noth" (We elsewise say: the greater woe).

Over the years Dach's techniques became more sophisticated. The 1635 poem on the death of the pewtersmith Mauritius Güttich opens with a description of decay that closely resembles those in the works of other poets of the time, such as Gryphius:

> Das welcke Fleisch, die blosse Haut
> Deß Körpers, den Ihr vor euch schawt,
> Das starren in den stieffen Sehnen,
> Der tieffen Augen Finsternüß
>
> (The withered flesh, the skin all bare
> Of the corpse you see before you there,
> The stiffening in the rigid muscles,
> The darkness of the deep-set eyes).

According to the simple argument of this *Ehrengedicht,* the body is merely a container or sheath for which no tears should be shed. The same naive directness can be seen in the first of the two poems in the *Todesgedancken* (Death Thoughts) for Wilhelm Pärß, who died on 7 November 1640. The departed speaks – an early employment of a device that would be much favored by Dach later on – and his words are horrifying for modern sensibilities. As the dry earth swallows the rain without leaving a trace, so our bodies vanish into it: "Also schluckt das weite Grab / Uns sein Mast-Vieh, stets hinab" (Thus the gaping grave does eat / Us, its cattle, as its feed) – a gruesomely effective, if mixed, metaphor. The second poem for Pärß is a feigned speech of thanks, again delivered by the deceased, for his release from earthly life.

A pair of poems on the death in 1646 of the Kapellmeister Stobaeus, appropriately, include musical references. The first, "Wer wird in der Engel Chor / Gott, dich ewig singen?" (Who will in the angels' choir / God, sing of you forever?), a hymn, bestows on Stobaeus the position of "Pracht / Himmlicher Kapellen" (adornment of / Heavenly orchestras). The second, a *Klag-Lied,* gives moving

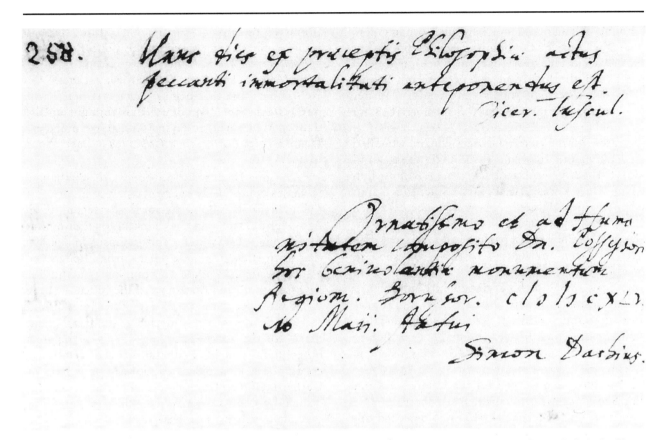

Inscription by Dach, dated 1645, in an album kept by Johannes Salzwedel (Herzog August Bibliothek Wolfenbüttel, Cod. Guelf. 29 Noviss. 12°, page 258)

expression to Dach's grief at the loss of his musical "father." For the *Trost-Reimchen* (Little Consolatory Rhyme, 1650) commissioned by the Königsberg printer and publisher Johann Reusner for the death of his son, Dach dips into another technical vocabulary to say that humanity is but a product of the print shop of God: we are "Fast ein Buchstaben gleich: / Denn Gott hat uns gegossen" (Almost like unto the letters / For God has cast our form). Several poems tell a good deal about Königsberg's mercantile society; for example, the second poem written for the death of Werner gives more individual details than the preceding hymnlike poem: "Er war ein auserlesen / Glückhaffter Bürgersmann" (He was a most distinguished / and happy citizen), and "Gerecht war stets sein Handel" (His dealings all were honest). The *Christliches Ehrengedächtnis* (Christian Pious Memory, 1659) for Heinrich Dechant says that the forty-year-old apothecary made extensive travels – to Poland, Moscow, Lübeck, Hamburg, Stockholm, Venice, and Padua – to increase his knowledge, but they now avail him nothing; neither the journeys nor all the medicines in his shop could save him from death. The survivors must find strength in God; as for Dechant himself, "Er muste

nur erkalten, / Hie war sein Stündelein" (He was compelled to perish, / Here was his final hour).

The poems to members of the nobility have, understandably, greater formality and reveal greater respect for their subjects. In *Uber dem seligen Abschied des HochEdlen Herrn Georg von der Gröben* (On the Blessed Departure of the Honorable Lord Georg von der Gröben, 1649), which begins "Du hast mich wund geschlagen" (Thou hast dealt wounds unto me), Dach writes a lament addressed to someone whom, in all likelihood, he did not know, and who in station was far above Pärß, Stobaeus, Werner, and Dechant; the poem is spoken in the person of the widow, who asks the Almighty to help her to be "Gedultig und bescheiden" (Patient and modest) in her suffering. A poem in Dach's own voice follows it, addressed to the widow; it is a detailed account of the accomplishments of both von der Gröben and his wife – they had traveled widely in Germany, the Netherlands, England, France, Spain, and Italy and were multilingual: "Er kuntte, so wie du, in allen Sprachen rein / Ein Welscher, ein Frantzoß und auch ein Spanier sein" (He could, just as you, in every language be / A Frenchman, Spaniard too, someone from Italy). Erich Trunz detects a larger amount of rhetorical or "baroque" ornament in poems written for the nobility; Schöne points out that Dach often had longer to work on funeral poems for the highly placed because much time elapsed before their tombs were ready. Von der Gröben, for example, died on 7 September 1648 but was not buried until 26 January 1649. Such was also the case with the elector Georg Wilhelm, who died on 1 December 1640 but was not laid to rest until March 1642, when Dach's *Denckmal* – with its flattering if not necessarily accurate line, "Dieß sind Glieder eines Helden" (These are members of a hero) – was presumably read at the interment. Georg Wilhelm's actual passing had been memorialized by Dach in a *Klag-Lied* (first published in Albert's *Arien*) that begins, "Was für Unmut, Pein und Sorg / Hat dich, Preussen, itzt umgeben?" (What despair and pain and care / Do, oh Prussia, now surround you?). Yet if Dach's social distance from the blue-blooded dead sometimes resulted in perfunctory formulas, on other occasions his poetic inventiveness was stimulated; such is the case in the memorable poem written for the funeral of Anna von Schlieben (first published in Albert's *Arien*), who died on 6 February 1645. The departed addresses the earth that bore her – "Du, O getrewe Mutter, Erde" (Thou, oh faithful mother, Earth) – and that now takes her back. The poem perhaps conjures up the pagan Baltic world of the *dainos*, (Lithuanian folk songs) yet the word *Christlich* is carefully injected into the final strophe: "was weint jhr so, jhr lieben kinder! / Begrabt mich Christlich, als jhr thut" (Why, dear children, do you weep so? / Bury me Christianly, as you do).

Beyond the mass of poems on death, there is a much smaller group of poems that have a religious tone but are intended for happier – or, at least, less gloomy – events: a moving-day song, *Wander-Lied* (1641), written for Roberthin and his wife; the evening song beginning "O Christe, Schutz-Herr deiner Glieder" (Christ, protector of your members), first published in volume five (1642) of Albert's *Arien*, and "Abend-Lied am Sonntage" (Evening Song on Sunday), beginning "Der Tag hat auch sein Ende" (The day too has its ending), both of which were included in the Prussian hymnal of 1657; seasonal songs such as "Frülings Lob-Lied" (Song in Praise of Spring), "In kalter Winters-Zeit" (In Cold Wintertime); and songs of atonement in times of pestilence or war, which may well have been used for church ceremonies. But these other "spiritual songs" are few, measured against the funeral songs and poems that, together with the epithalamia, were Dach's major source of income. Dach had a large

following of satisfied customers: in June 1649 he wrote a church song based on the 128th Psalm and a *Braut-Tantz* (Bridal Dance) for the wedding of Johann Melhorn and Anna Koese; the latter text is the well-known one that begins "Wer erst den Tantz hat auffgebracht" (Whoever first thought up the dance). When Anna died in 1652, at age nineteen, Dach wrote *Letztes Ehren-Gedächtnüs* (Last Pious Memory) for her.

Among Dach's worldly poems, the epithalamic verses comprise as overwhelming a majority as the funeral poems do in the spiritual category. A biographer of Dach must be thankful for the amount of personal observations and glimpses of the age that Dach wove into these poems, from thoughts of his domestic happiness to complaints about his illnesses, and from snapshots of life in Königsberg to manifold fears about the city's fate. In addition, though, to the broad and rich epithalamic vein, there are the several begging poems to persons other than Friedrich Wilhelm, gauged in tone according to the recipient: an application of 1648 to Gerhard, Graf zu Dönhof, has an overture in Latin distichs and, in its German main body, is careful to cast a flattering light on Gerhard's patronage of the late Opitz. Dach's request is not specific but simply for "eine Stelle . . . / In deinen Hochberühmten Gnaden" (a place . . . / In your far-famed good graces). Moving a bit downward on the social ladder, Dach speaks more to the point, asking Johann Schimmelpfennig for firewood and listing other citizens of Königsberg who have been or might be generous. Nor does he blush to ask Johann Reimann, the commander of the fortress at Ragnit, for money: "Traw es mir, ich leide Noht, / Und geniesse kaum noch Brod" (Believe you me, I suffer need, / And now scarcely still have bread). One wonders whether Dach's financial situation – the latter poem was written in 1646, when he was at the height of his popularity – was actually as dire as he made it out to be. The thankful verses written in November 1652 (first published in Oesterley's edition) to Friedrich von Schlieben, the commander at Tilsit, for the gift of a beef ox, including a bloody description of the animal's slaughter, would indicate that Dach's day-to-day existence was precarious even as his local fame was at its zenith.

The literary historian Josef Nadler thought that Dach's poetry was "gänzlich unbarock" (completely unbaroque); it has, beyond question, a directness that is distinctive for its time, a quality Ulrich Maché has called a "bemerkenswerte Offenheit" (notable openness). Yet the apparent simplicity can deceive; in the interpretation of single poems, Segebrecht, Eberhard Mannack, and Joachim Dyck have demonstrated how Dach proceeds with unostentatious skill and rhetorical cunning. And he is not without slyness: both the poem on Adersbach's garden and his plea to the gentlemen of Friedrich Wilhelm's superior council, "Ihr Seulen dieser Lande" (You Pillars of These Lands) end with his name, "Dach," literally in the sense of the "roof" (*Dach*) of the world: "Bis an der Sternen Dach" (Unto the stars' own roof) and "Bis an des Himmels Dach" (Unto the heavens' roof), respectively. Yet it is also a signature, and not a wholly modest one.

Bibliography:

Gerhard Dünnhaupt, *Personalbibliographien zu den Drucken des Barock,* volume 9, part 2 (Stuttgart: Hiersemann, 1990), pp. 996–1230.

Biographies:

Theophil Siegfried Bayer, "Das Leben Simonis Dachii eines Preußischen Poeten," in *Erleutertes Preußen,* volume 1, edited by Michael Lilienthal (Königsberg: Martin Hallervord, 1723), pp. 159–195;

Kurt Quecke, "Der Dichter Simon Dach (1605–1659): Eine medizin-historische Studie zu seinem 300. Todestage," *Medizinische Monatsschrift,* 13 (1959): 592–596;

Lotte Bartsch, "Simon Dachs Leben, Familie, Zeit und Wirkung," *Jahrbuch der Albertus-Universität zu Königsberg,* 17 (1967): 305–333;

Walter Schlusnus, "Simon Dach," in *Große Deutsche aus Ostpreussen,* edited by Wilhelm Matull (Munich: Gräfe & Unzer, 1970), pp. 28–38;

Harald Edel, "Simon Dach: Das Leben des Dichters, sein Verhältnis zum kurfürstlichen Haus und seine finanzielle und materielle Situation 1–2," *Nordost-Archiv,* 14, no. 61–62 (1981): 13–29; no. 63–64 (1981): 5–20;

Wulf Segebrecht, "Simon Dach und die Königsberger," in *Deutsche Dichter des 17. Jahrhunderts: Ihr Leben und Werk,* edited by Harald Steinhagen and Benno von Weise (Berlin: Erich Schmidt, 1984), pp. 242–269;

Alfred Kelletat, "Simon Dach," in *Deutsche Dichter,* volume 2: *Reformation, Renaissance and Barock,* edited by Gunter E. Grimm and Frank Rainer Max (Stuttgart: Reclam, 1988), pp. 174–183;

Ulrich Maché, "Simon Dach," in *Literatur-Lexikon,* volume 2, edited by Walther Killy (Gütersloh & Munich: Bertelsmann, 1988), pp. 505–507.

References:

Wilfried Barner, "Einleitung," in Christoph Kaldenbach, *Auswahl aus dem Werk,* edited by Wilfried Barner (Tübingen: Niemeyer, 1977), pp. xii–lii;

Joachim Dyck, "'Lob der Rhetorik und des Redners' als Thema eines Casualcarmens von Simon Dach für Valentin Thilo," *Wolfenbütteler Barock-Nachrichten,* 5 (1978): 133–140;

Fritz Gause, *Die Geschichte der Stadt Königsberg in Preußen,* volume 1: *Von der Gründung der Stadt bis zum letzten Kurfürsten* (Cologne & Graz: Böhlau, 1965);

August Gebauer, *Simon Dach und seine Freunde als Kirchenliederdichter* (Tübingen: Osiander, 1828);

Werner Hoffmeister, "Dach, Distel und die Dichter: Günter Grass 'Das Treffen in Telgte,'" *Zeitschrift für deutsche Philologie,* 100, no. 2 (1981): 274–287;

Günther Kraft, ed., *Festschrift zur Ehrung von Heinrich Albert (1604–1651)* (Weimar, 1954);

Hans-Henrik Krummacher, "Das barocke Epicedium: Rhetorische Tradition und deutsche Gelegenheitsdichtung im 17. Jahrhundert," *Jahrbuch der Deutschen Schillergesellschaft,* 18 (1974): 89–147;

Ivar Ljungerud, "Anke von Tharau," *Niederdeutsche Mitteilungen,* 5 (1949): 113–135;

Ljungerud, "Ehren-Rettung M. Simonis Dachii," *Euphorion,* 61 (1967): 36–83;

Eberhard Mannack, "Barocke Lyrik als Medium der 'Redekunst': Simon Dach: Perpetui coelum tempora veris habet," *Deutschunterricht,* 37, no. 5 (1983): 15–24;

Helmut Motekat, *Ostpreußische Literaturgeschichte mit Danzig und Westpreußen* (Munich: Schild, 1977), pp. 67–79;

Wilhelm Müller, "Über das Leben und die Schriften Simon Dach's, Robert Roberthin's und Heinrich Albert's," in *Auserlesene Gedichte von Simon Dach, Robert Roberthin und Heinrich Albert,* edited by Müller, Bibliothek deutscher Dichter des siebzehnten Jahrhunderts, volume 5 (Leipzig: Brockhaus, 1823), pp. xiii–xxxvi;

Joseph Müller-Blattau, "Die Musik im Zeitalter der Reformation und des Barock," in his *Geschichte der Musik in Ost- und Westpreußen* (Wolfenbuttel & Zürich: Möseler, 1968), pp. 21–74;

Müller-Blattau, "Heinrich Albert und das deutsche Barocklied," *Deutsche Vierteljahrsschrift für Literaturwissenschaft und Geistesgeschichte,* 25 (1951): 401–414; reprinted in his *Von der Vielfalt der Musik: Musikgeschichte, Musikerziehung,*

Musikpflege (Freiburg im Breisgau: Rombach, 1966), pp. 51–70;

Müller-Blattau, ed., *Preußische Festlieder: Zeitgenössische Kompositionen zu Dichtungen Simon Dachs* (Kassel: Bärenreiter, 1939);

Josef Nadler, *Literaturgeschichte des Deutschen Volkes: Dichtung und Schrifttum der deutschen Stämme und Landschaften,* fourth edition, volume 1 (Berlin: Propyläen, 1938), p. 698;

Otto Nicolai, "Ueber das alte Lied 'Ännchen von Tharau' nebst einer abschweifenden Bemerkung über lyrische Texte," in his *Musikalische Aufsätze,* edited by Georg Richard Kruse, Deutsche Musikbücherei, volume 10 (Regensburg: Busse, n.d.), pp. 93–103;

David L. Paisey, "A Hitherto Unattributed German Elegy on the Death of Simon Dach, 1659," *British Library Journal,* 2 (Autumn 1976): 177–178;

Matilde de Pasquale, "Alcuni interrogativi su: Simon Dach, 'Klage über den endlichen Untergang und Ruinierung der musicalischen Kürbs-Hütte und Gärtchens,'" *Studi Germanici,* new series 9 (1971): 208–222;

Georg Christoph Pisanski, *Entwurf der Preussischen Litterärgeschichte während des 17. Jahrhunderts,* edited by Friedrich Adolph Meckelburg (Königsberg: Koch, 1853), pp. 235–260;

Robert Priebsch, "Gretke, war umb heffstu mi: Das 'Bauer-Lied' Simon Dachs," in *Miscellany Presented to Kuno Meyer,* edited by Osborn Bergin and Carl Marstrander (Halle: Niemeyer, 1912), pp. 65–78;

Irmgard Scheitler, *Das geistliche Lied im deutschen Barock* (Berlin: Duncker & Humblot, 1982), pp. 199–229;

Albrecht Schöne, *Kürbishütte und Königsberg: Modellversuch einer sozialgeschichtlichen Entzifferung poetischer Texte. Am Beispiel Simon Dach* (Munich: Beck, 1982);

George C. Schoolfield, "Cupio dissolvi: Deathbed Poems of the German Baroque," in *Images of the Baroque,* edited by Aldo Scaglione (Frankfurt am Main, Bern & New York: Peter Lang, 1994), pp. 179–193;

Schoolfield, "Memory's Lane: Simon Dach's Memel Epithalamium of January 18, 1655," in *Life's Golden Tree: Studies in German Literature from the Reformation to Rilke,* edited by Schoolfield and Thomas Kerth (Columbia, S.C.: Camden House, 1990), pp. 64–100;

Rudolf Alexander Schröder, "Simon Dach," in his *Gesammelte Werke,* volume 3 (Frankfurt am Main: Suhrkamp, 1952), pp. 685–722;

Bruno Schumacher, *Geschichte Ost- und Westpreußens,* sixth edition (Würzburg: Holzner, 1972);

Wulf Segebrecht, *Das Gelegenheitsgedicht: Ein Beitrag zur Geschichte und Poetik der deutschen Lyrik* (Stuttgart: Metzler, 1977);

Segebrecht, "Simon Dach: Unterthänigste Fleh-Schrift: Die Dialektik des rhetorischen Herrscherlobs," in *Gedichte und Interpretationen I: Renaissance und Barock,* edited by Volker Meid (Stuttgart: Reclam, 1982), pp. 198–209;

Götz von Selle, *Geschichte der Albertus-Universität zu Königsberg in Preußen,* second edition (Würzburg: Holzner, 1956);

Johannes Sembritzki, *Geschichte der königlich preussischen See- und Handelstadt Memel* (Memel: F. W. Siebert/Memeler Dampfboot Aktien-Gesellschaft, 1926);

Elida Maria Szarota, "Dichter des 17. Jahrhunderts über Polen (Opitz, Dach, Vondel, La Fontaine, und Filicaia)," *Neophilologus,* 55 (October 1971): 359–374;

Erich Trunz, "Der deutsche Späthumanismus um 1600 als Standeskultur," in *Deutsche Barockforschung: Dokumentation einer Epoche* edited by Richard Alewyn (Cologne & Berlin: Erich Schmidt, 1965), pp. 147–181;

Trunz, "Simon Dach, Gedichte 1. Bd.," *Deutsche Literaturzeitung,* 57 (July–December 1936): 2176–2180;

Trunz, "Simon Dach, Gedichte 2. Bd.," *Deutsche Literaturzeitung,* 58 (July–December 1937): 1954–1958;

Trunz, "Simon Dach, Gedichte 3. und 4 Bd.," *Deutsche Literaturzeitung,* 60 (January–June 1939): 154–160;

Erich Weise, *Handbuch der historischen Stätten: Ost- und Westpreußen* (Stuttgart: Kröner, 1966);

Walther Ziesemer, "Der Anteil des deutschen Ostens an der niederdeutschen Literatur," *Jahrbuch des Vereins für niederdeutsche Sprachforschung,* 71–73 (1948–1950): 147–157;

Ziesemer, "Geistiges Leben im 16. und 17. Jahrhundert," in *Deutsche Staatenbildung und deutsche Kultur im Preußenlande,* edited by Paul Blunk (Königsberg: Gräfe & Unzer, 1931), pp. 205–220;

Ziesemer, "Neues zu Simon Dach," *Euphorion,* 25 (1924): 591–608;

Ziesemer, "Simon Dach," *Altpreußische Forschungen,* 1 (1924): 23–56.

Paul Fleming

(5 October 1609 – 2 April 1640)

Anthony J. Harper
University of Strathclyde

SELECTED BOOKS: *Jesu Christo S. Natalitium* (Leipzig: Printed by Abraham Lamberg's heirs, 1631);

Johannes Zeidleri . . . Casus XXII De Tussi Quem . . . offert Pauli Flemming (Leipzig: Johann Albert Minzel, 1631);

Promus Miscellaeorum Epigrammatum & Odarum, Omnem nuperorum dierum historiae penum abundanter extradens (Leipzig: Printed by Gregor Ritsch, 1631);

Taedæ Schönburgicæ (Leipzig: Printed by Abraham Lamberg's heirs, published by Elias Rehefeld, 1631);

Germaniae Exsulis ad Suos Filios sive Proceres Regni Epistola (Leipzig: Printed by Friedrich Lanckisch's heirs, 1631);

Rubella, seu Suaviorum Liber I (Leipzig: Printed by Friedrich Lanckisch's heirs, 1631);

Klagegedichte vber das vnschüldigste Leiden vnsers Erlösers vnd Todt Jesu Chrjstj (Leipzig: Published by Elias Rehefeld, printed by Abraham Lamberg's heirs, 1632);

Gymnasium Revaliense (Revel: Printed by Christoph Reusner, 1635);

Gedichte auff des Ehrnvesten vnd Wolgelarten Herrn Reineri Brocmans, der Griechischen Sprache Professorn am Gymnasio zu Reval, vnd der Erbarn, Viel Ehren vnd Tugendreichen Jungfrawen Dorotheen Temme, Hochzeit (Revel: Printed by Christoph Reusner, 1635);

Lieffländische Schneegräffinn, auff H. Andres Rüttings, vnd Jungfr. Annen von Holten Hochzeit (Revel: Printed by Christoph Reusner, 1636);

Disputatio Medica Inauguralis De Lue Venerea . . . (Leiden: Printed by Wilhelm Christian, 1640);

Poetischer Gedichten so nach seinem Tode haben sollen herauß gegeben werden, Prodromus, edited by Adam Olearius (Hamburg: Printed by Hans Gutwasser, published by Tobias Gundermann, 1641);

Teutsche Poemata, edited by Olearius (Lübeck: Published by Laurentz Jauch, 1646); republished

Paul Fleming

as *Geist- und Weltliche Poemata* (Jena: Printed by Georg Sengenwald, 1651);

Epigrammata Latina ante hac non edita, edited by Olearius (Amsterdam: Johannes Blaeu, 1649).

Collections: *Lateinische Gedichte,* edited by Johann Martin Lappenberg (Stuttgart: Hiersemann, 1863; reprinted, Amsterdam: Rodopi, 1969);

Deutsche Gedichte, 2 volumes, edited by Lappenberg (Stuttgart: Hiersemann, 1865; reprinted, Darmstadt: Wissenschaftliche Buchgesellschaft, 1965);

Deutsche Gedichte, edited by Volker Meid (Stuttgart: Reclam, 1986).

Editions in English: *The Penguin Book of German Verse,* translated by Leonard Forster (London: Penguin, 1957), pp. 119–125;

Frank J. Warnke, *European Metaphysical Poetry* (New Haven & London: Yale University Press, 1961), pp. 170–183;

The German Lyric of the Baroque in English Translation, translated by George C. Schoolfield (New York: AMC Press, 1966), pp. 96–105;

The Baroque Poem: A Comparative Survey, edited by Harold B. Segel (New York: Dalton, 1974), pp. 164, 245–246, 272–273.

OTHER: *Davids, des Hebreischen Königs vnd Propheten Bußpsalme, vnd Manasse, des Königs Juda Gebet, als er zu Babel gefangen war,* verse paraphrase by Fleming (Leipzig: Elias Rehefeldt, 1631);

Giovanni Battista Guarini, *Pastor Fido oder Die allerschönste Tragicomoedia. Der Getrewe Hürt genant,* translated by Fleming (Schleusingen: Printed by Peter Schmidt, sold by Johann Birckner in Erfurt, 1636).

Paul Fleming is one of the most important German poets of the seventeenth century. His earliest poetry, much of it written in Latin, shows the usual stamp of rhetorical training at school and university; later, his German verse flourished under the influence of his main model, Martin Opitz. He used European conventions, such as the pastoral tradition, to good effect in his work, a good deal of which was written for occasions in the lives of his friends and acquaintances. His religious poetry combines intensity of expression with balance, while in his love poetry he fuses the Petrarchan tradition with a stress on Stoic fortitude, fidelity, and constancy, creating at times an immediacy of impact that is attractive to the modern reader. His sonnets are usually traditional in form, while in his songs he exploits a wide variety of verse lines and demonstrates a rhythmic facility that is without equal in the German poetry of his time. Fleming's adventurous life, his travels, and his romances with the Niehusen sisters, together with his early death, have encouraged a romantic view of him and his poetry (novels have been written about him), but a more valid verdict would be that his work represents a high point in what could be achieved within the conventions of the period.

The first child of Abraham Fleming, schoolmaster and later pastor in the little town of Hartenstein in the Erzgebirge, and Dorothea Fleming, née Müller, Paul Fleming was born on 5 October 1609 (Old Style). His godmother was Katharina von Schönburg, whom Dorothea had served as a maid; the patronage of the Schönburgs, who were the local *Landesherren* (lords of the manor), helped to support Fleming's education. In the early summer of 1615 the Flemings moved to Topfseidersdorf, near Rochlitz, where Abraham had been offered the post of pastor. On 17 February of the following year Dorothea Fleming died; on 2 November, Abraham Fleming married the widow Ursula Köhler, née Zehler, of Freiberg, whose maternal love Fleming later remembered with affection. She would live until late 1633, the year of Fleming's departure on his travels; Abraham would outlive his son, dying on 5 October 1649.

In 1616 Fleming was sent to the Latin school in Mittweida, about six miles from Topfseidersdorf; it is not known whether he walked there each day or had lodgings in the town. In the spring or early summer of 1622 his father, ambitious for his only son, sent him to the celebrated Thomasschule (Saint Thomas's School) in Leipzig. Thus Fleming found himself in a lively and thriving center that, despite its deprivations later during the Thirty Years' War, was to retain its cultural importance.

The Thomasschule, situated next to the Thomaskirche (Saint Thomas's Church), was a school for local poor boys and a boarding school for those who lived at a distance. Music played a large role in the life of the school, as it did in that of the city, and the boys received instruction in music and provided the choir for church services, including accompanying funeral corteges to the cemetery, and for public music in the town. The church cantors carried major responsibilities as teachers and musical directors; the best known would be Johann Sebastian Bach, but in Fleming's time the cantor was Johann Hermann Schein, whose multipart songs, full of Italianate artifice, belonged to a tradition that was destined to be replaced by the solo song established through the influence of Opitz. Schein's witty verse may have contributed to the development of Fleming's poetry.

In the winter semester of 1623 Fleming matriculated at the University of Leipzig as a *non iuratus* — that is, he registered his intent to matriculate fully at a later point. As a pupil in the higher grades at the Thomasschule he was allowed to attend lectures at the university. In the summer of 1628 he received a five-year scholarship from the elector of Saxony to study in the faculties of arts and medicine; at that time all students began in the arts faculty before proceeding to one of the three higher faculties: theology, law, or medicine. In the winter semester of 1628 he took the oath and was registered as a full student.

Among the more important and talented of the many friends Fleming made at the university were Georg Gloger from Habelschwerdt and Martin Christenius from Jägerndorff, Silesians who encouraged Fleming to try his hand at poetry in German by stressing the insight of their countryman Opitz, whose *Buch von der Deutschen Poeterey* (Book of German Poetry, 1624) had advocated the importance of the coincidence of metrical and natural stress – a fundamental point for the new German poetry that, until then, had not been obvious. Among Fleming's Saxon friends were Adam Olearius of Achersleben and Gottfried Finckelthaus and Christian Brehme, both of Leipzig. All of these men would create an atmosphere in which interest in German culture and the writing of poetry in German would increase.

At first, though, Fleming followed the pattern of the humanist poet by composing in Latin. On 1 February 1631 he recited in the philosophical auditorium of the university his poem on the birth of Christ; in the summer he was composing love poems to a Leipzig girl named Rubella, whose death from the plague he lamented in a poetic cycle of the same name. Other Latin works of the period comment on the political events of the day, including the Thirty Years' War. On 25 January 1632 he was crowned an imperial poet laureate (by that time, however, the distinction was becoming somewhat overused). On 9/10 March he was awarded the baccalaureate, the lowest academic degree; he attained the magister degree on 2 May 1633. During his time in Leipzig Fleming also wrote poetry in German, mainly short occasional pieces for the many funerals and weddings in war-torn and disease-ridden Leipzig but also longer works such as *Klagegedichte uber das unschüldigste Leiden unsers Erlösers und Todt Jesu Christi* (Lament on the Most Innocent Suffering of Our Savior and Death of Jesus Christ), which was published in March 1632 and sent the following month to the well-known professor of poetics at the University of Wittenberg, Augustus Buchner.

In 1633 Fleming undertook the first of a series of travels that would last until his death. Through Olearius he learned of a trade mission that Otto Brüggemann and Philipp Kruse were to lead to Russia and Persia on behalf of Friedrich III, Duke of

Holstein-Gottorp, to negotiate an overland trade route. He applied to join the mission and was accepted as a scholar and travel poet. He left Leipzig with Olearius in August to join the mission in Hamburg, and on 9 November 1633 the group embarked from Travemünde on the Baltic.

They arrived at Riga, Latvia, on 14 November and traveled by sledge to Narva. From there the expedition, under Fleming's leadership, went on to Novgorod on Lake Ilmen. There he composed the long, reflective travel poem "In Groß-Neugart der Reußen" (In Novgorod of the Russians); its idyllic description of the life of the Russian people is based partly on personal observation and partly on literary models such as Horace's second epode and Opitz's *Zlatna* (1623). The reunited mission proceeded to Moscow, arriving on 14 August. The negotiations with the czar achieved some success, but the czar required further documentation from Duke Friedrich before letting them proceed to Persia. The group left Moscow on Christmas Eve 1634 to return to the Baltic, arriving in Revel (today Tallinn), Estonia, on 10 January 1635. From there the ambassadors returned by land to Holstein, while the main body of the group, including Fleming, remained in Revel.

Although Revel was distant from the Germany of the Holy Roman Empire and was under Swedish rule, it was a member of the Hanseatic League and had connections with northern German towns. German influence was strong; most of the books printed there were in German or Latin, and many of the middle-class merchant families and the teachers at the gymnasium were German. Fleming swiftly came to feel at home in the town; his first publication in Revel, the short Latin collection of poetry *Gymnasium Revaliense* of April 1635, was written for the professors at the local school, and another publication of the same month was a pastoral for the wedding of the professor of Greek, Reiner Brockmann. In spite of its local reference, the latter work was reprinted the same year in Leipzig. Fleming was well known in Revel society, and he soon began to write occasional verse for events in the town. A vivid description of a Revel wedding is given in a poem of February 1636, *Lieffländische Schneegräffinn* (Livonian Snow-Countess), where the dancing and the flirtations of the young people are attractively depicted.

Among the local families Fleming got to know well were the Niehusens, who had moved to Revel in 1633 from Hamburg. Heinrich Niehusen, a well-to-do merchant, had three unmarried daughters, all of whom feature in Fleming's poetry. The eldest

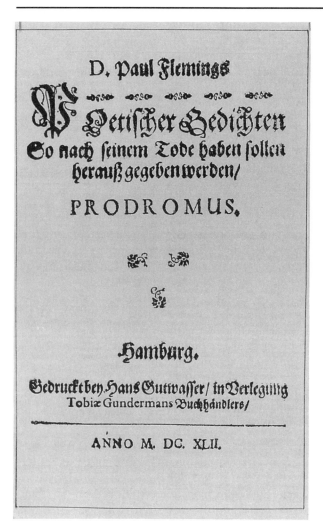

D. Paul Flemings

Poetischer Gedichten
So nach seinem Tode haben sollen
herauß gegeben werden/

PRODROMUS.

Hamburg.

Gedruckt bey Hans Gutwasser/ in Verlegung
Tobiæ Gundermans Buchhändlers/

ANNO M. DC. XLII.

Title page for the second edition of the first posthumous collection
of Fleming's German poems

was Elisabeth, called by Fleming "die Keusche" (the Chaste One); the middle sister, Elsabe, "die Schöne" (the Fair One), was the one with whom Fleming first fell in love. The third daughter, Anna, "die Fromme" (the Good One), would become Fleming's betrothed shortly before his death.

The romance between Fleming and Elsabe probably began in the spring of 1635. Apart from possessing standard accomplishments for a well-educated young lady from the wealthier bourgeoisie, such as sewing and painting, she shared Fleming's interest in music: she could play the spinet and sing and was also a composer. Many of Fleming's best-known poems were written for her; she appears under such names as Elsgen and Basilene, and the poems often include acrostics for both names. There was a surplus of marriageable girls in the town, and several members of the trade mission formed attachments; but with the exception

of the senior member, Kruse, none became betrothed. Betrothal meant a commitment of marriage in the near future, and the dangers of the impending journey made the delegates' safe return uncertain. Another obstacle in the case of Fleming and Elsabe was that it would have been unusual for a second daughter to become engaged before the first. His departure from Revel, by early March 1636, heralded the end of their relationship, although an understanding between them still existed when he left.

Many of Fleming's songs and sonnets operate within the Petrarchan tradition of love poetry, with its convention of the suffering lover dying of the pain inflicted by his hard-hearted lady. Into this tradition Fleming introduces other themes and tones: the stress on mutual love that can be found in his epithalamiums; the emphasis on fidelity and fortitude from the Neo-Stoic tradition that informs so much of his poetry; and, from outside the humanist tradition, the German folk song, with its constant reiteration of separation and fidelity. It is in his "odes" – that is, songs – that this attractive fusion of themes is most noticeable, modifying the Petrarchan tradition without abandoning it. Songs such as "An Basilenen, nachdem er von ihr gereiset war" (To Basilene, after He Had Parted from Her), "Das getreue Elsgen" (Faithful Elsgen), "Elsgens treues Hertz" (Elsgen's Faithful Heart), "An Elsabe" (To Elsabe), "Treue Pflicht" (Faithful Duty), and "Standhaftigkeit" (Constancy) are magnificent achievements in an apparently simple song form. His love sonnets, by contrast, are usually written in the more formal alexandrine verse line and seem closer to conventional Petrarchism, as can be seen in "An Osculanen" (To Osculane), where the girl expresses feigned annoyance at a snatched kiss, and in "An Amenen, als sie sich mit Angeln erlustirete" (To Amene, When She Took Pleasure in Angling). Common to both songs and sonnets are witty, rhythmic phrases and a sharp and polished style that handles emotion in the best humanist tradition. This polish links his love poetry to the occasional verses he wrote for events in the lives of others.

In the spring of 1636 Fleming departed with the other delegates. They spent the period between March and July in Moscow, and on 30 July they began the voyage to Persia down the Volga, pausing in September–October in Astrakhan and arriving at the Caspian Sea in November. Between January and March 1637 Fleming fell ill in Shemakha, near Baku, where the news reached him that Elsabe had become betrothed to the former family tutor, Magister Salomon Matthias. In the sonnet "Zur Zeit seiner Verstoßung" (At the Time of His Rejection) he expresses his reaction to the news of the loss of Elsabe with traditional analogies and rhetoric. His belated official poem of congratulation on the wedding of Elsabe and Matthias, which took place on 12 June 1637, was not written until June 1638.

In the spring of 1638 the trade group made a difficult and dangerous march from Esfahan, the Persian capital, through Dagestan, and in the fall they returned to Astrakhan. During the whole journey Fleming composed poetry regularly: occasional verse for, or in the name of, other members of the party; poetic epistles about the places they were visiting; or poems relating to events at home in Germany. Finally the group started back northward, arriving in Revel on 13 April 1639.

It had been more than three years since Fleming's departure from Revel; he had aged through sickness, and Elsabe was married and no longer lived in the town. All the same, his health and spirits improved in the familiar surroundings. Elsabe's sister Anna was old enough to be courted; he turned his attentions to her, and a new phase of love poetry ensued, including the ode "Anemone" – in which he seems to relate his love for Anna to that for her sister, using a couplet from an earlier song to Elsabe, "An Anemonen, nachdem er von ihr gereiset war" (To Anemone, after He Had Traveled from Her) – and "An Anna aus der Ferne" (To Anna, from Afar). On 8 July 1639 he and Anna became betrothed. To obtain his doctorate in medicine he sailed for Germany on 11 July, stopping in Hamburg, then proceeding to Leiden, the Netherlands, where he enrolled at the university on 29 October.

On 23 January 1640 Fleming was confirmed as a doctor of medicine with the dissertation *De Lue Venerea* (On Venereal Disease). He was unable to return to Revel immediately because sea voyages were impossible in January and February, but on 7 March he left Leiden on the first stage of his journey. On his arrival in Hamburg on 20 March he was ill and had to take to his bed; he composed his own epitaph on 27 March. He died on Maundy Thursday, 2 April 1640. The funeral service and burial took place on Easter Monday, 6 April, in the Katharinenkirche, where the Niehusen family vault was situated.

A small selection of Fleming's German poetry appeared in 1641; it was edited by Olearius, who brought out a full edition in 1646 and an edition of the Latin poems in 1649. In these volumes the full range of Fleming's achievement can be seen – a range that extends from magnificent religious sonnets such as "An meinen Erlöser" (To My Redeemer) to reflective poetic epistles from the Russian and Persian journeys; poems about his homeland, such as "Er beklaget die Aenderung und Furchtsamkeit itziger Deutschen" (He Complains at the Mutability and Timidity of Today's Germans) and "An Deutschland" (To Germany); Stoic and philosophical poetry, such as "Gedancken über die Zeit" (Thoughts about Time) and "An sich" (To Himself); and a wide range of occasional poetry, friendship and love songs, and sonnets. The most complete modern editions of Fleming's German and Latin poetry are those produced by Johann Martin Lappenberg in the 1860s, which were reprinted in the 1960s.

Bibliographies:

Karl Goedeke, *Grundriß zur Geschichte der deutschen Dichtung aus den Quellen,* second edition, volume 3 (Dresden: Ehlermann, 1887), pp. 58–63;

Curt von Faber du Faur, *German Baroque Literature: A Catalogue of the Collection in the Yale University Library* (New Haven: Yale University Press, 1958), pp. 82–84;

Gerhard Dünnhaupt, *Personalbibliographien zu den Drucken des Barock,* volume 9, part 2 (Stuttgart: Hiersemann, 1990), pp. 1490–1513.

Biographies:

Karl August Varnhagen von Ense, "Paul Flemming," in his *Ausgewählte Schriften,* volume 10 (Leipzig: Brockhaus, 1872), pp. 1–115;

Heinz Entner, *Paul Fleming: Ein deutscher Dichter im Dreißigjährigen Krieg* (Leipzig: Reclam, 1989).

References:

Ferdinand Ambacher, "Paul Fleming and 'Erlebnisdichtung,'" dissertation, Rutgers University, 1972;

Barbara Becker-Cantorino, "Drei Briefautographen von Paul Fleming," *Wolfenbütteler Beiträge: Aus den Schätzen der Herzog August Bibliothek,* 4 (1981): 191–204;

Manfred Beller, "Thema, Konvention und Sprache der mythologischen Ausdrucksformen in Paul Flemings Gedichten," *Euphorion,* 67, no. 2 (1973): 157–189;

A. G. de Capua, "Paul Fleming," in his *German Baroque Poetry: Interpretative Readings* (Albany: State University of New York Press, 1973), pp. 51–57;

Jörg-Ulrich Fechner, "Paul Fleming," in *Deutsche Dichter des 17. Jahrhunderts: Ihr Leben und Werk,* edited by Benno von Wiese (Berlin: Schmidt, 1984), pp. 365–384;

Klaus Garber, "Paul Fleming in Riga: Die wiederentdeckten Gedichte aus der Sammlung Gadebusch," in *Daß eine Nation die ander verstehen möge: Festschrift für Marian Szyrocki zu seinem 60. Geburtstag,* edited by Norbert Honsza and Hans-Gert Roloff, Beihefte zum *Daphnis,* no. 7 (Amsterdam: Rodopi, 1988), pp. 255–308;

Gerhart Hoffmeister, "Paul Fleming," in *Deutsche Dichter 2. Reformation, Renaissance und Barock,* edited by Günter E. Grimm and Frank Rainer Max (Stuttgart: Reclam, 1988), pp. 212–224;

G. L. Jones, "The Mulde's 'Half-Prodigal Son.' Paul Fleming, Germany and the Thirty Years' War," *German Life and Letters,* 26 (January 1973): 125–136;

Peter Krahé, "Persönlicher Ausdruck in der literarischen Konvention: Paul Fleming als Wegbereiter der Erlebnislyrik?," *Zeitschrift für deutsche Philologie,* 106 (1987): 481–513;

Wilhelm Kühlmann, "Selbstbehauptung und Selbstdisziplin: Zu Paul Flemings 'An Sich,'" "Sterben als heroischer Akt: Zu Paul Flemings 'Grabschrifft,' " and "Ausgeklammerte Askese: Zur Tradition heiterer erotischer Dichtung in Paul Flemings Kußgedicht," in *Gedichte und Interpretationen,* volume 1: *Renaissance und Barock,* edited by Volker Meid (Stuttgart: Reclam, 1982), pp. 160–166, 168–175, 177–186;

Hans Pyritz, *Paul Flemings Liebeslyrik: Zur Geschichte des Petrarkismus* (Göttingen: Vandenhoek & Ruprecht, 1963);

Kyra Robert, "Pauli Flemingi raamatupärandist Eesti TA Raamatukogus," and "Über Paul Flemings Büchernachlaß in der Bibliothek der Estnischen Akademie der Wissenschaften," in her *Raamatutel on oma Saatus* (Tallinn: Eesti Teaduste Akademia Raamatukogu, 1991), pp. 66–76, 158–159;

Dietmar Schubert, "'Man wird mich nennen hören . . .': Zum poetischen Vermächtnis Paul Flemings," *Weimarer Beiträge,* 30, no. 10 (1984): 1687–1706;

Marian R. Sperberg-McQueen, *The German Poetry of Paul Fleming: Studies in Genre and History,* University of North Carolina Studies in the Germanic Languages and Literature, no. 110 (Chapel Hill & London: University of North Carolina Press, 1990);

Sperberg-McQueen, "Leipzig Pastoral: Two Epithalamia by Martin Christenius, with a Note on Paul Fleming," *Chloe,* 10 (Fall 1990): 489–503;

Sperberg-McQueen, "Paul Fleming: A Report on a Newly-Found Poem and Imprints in Zwickau and Wroclaw," *Michigan Germanic Studies,* 12 (1986): 105–132;

Sperberg-McQueen, "Paul Fleming's Inaugural Disputation in Medicine: A 'Lost' Work Found," *Wolfenbütteler Barock-Nachrichten,* 11, no. 1 (1984): 6–9;

Liselotte Supersaxo, *Die Sonette Paul Flemings: Chronologie und Entwicklung* (Singen: Steinhauser, 1956);

Theodor Weevers, "The Influence of Heinsius on Two Genres of the German Baroque," *Journal of English and Germanic Philology,* 37 (1938): 524–532;

Stephen Zon, "Imitations of Petrarch: Opitz, Fleming," *Daphnis: Zeitschrift für Mittlere Deutsche Literatur,* 7, no. 3 (1978): 497–512.

Papers:

Manuscripts by Paul Fleming are in the Herzog August Bibliothek, Wolfenbüttel, and in the Ratsschulbibliothek, Zwickau.

Paul Gerhardt
(12 March 1607 – 27 May 1676)

Erika A. Metzger
State University of New York at Buffalo

BOOKS: *Trawerklagen, vber den frühzeitigen und jämmerlichen Hintritt des frommen Knabens Joachim Friedrich Spenglers . . . welcher . . . den 28. Decemb. . . . in die ewige Frewde versetzet worden* (Berlin: Printed by Christoph Runge, 1650);

Leich-Sermon, dem weyland WolEhrenvesten VorAchtbaren und Wolvornehmen Herrn Joachim Schrödern, des Churfürst. Brandenb. Ampts Zossen gewesenen wolbestalten auch wolverdienten Amptschreibern, als derselbe den 17. Maij dieses 1655. Jahres in der Kirchen zu Zossen Christlich und ehrlich zur Erden bestattet wurde, aus dem von ihme selbst zum Leich-Text erwehlten 9. vers. des 71. Psalms: Verwirff mich nicht in meinem Alter, verlaß mich nicht, wenn ich schwach werde. In bemeldter Kirchen zu Zossen gehalten (Berlin: Printed by Christoph Runge, 1655);

Leich-Sermon, dem Weyland . . . Nicolao Wernicken, gewesenen Churförstl. Brandenburg . . . Vice-Registratori . . . aus den 7. 8. 9. vers. des 7. Cap. Propheten Micha (Berlin: Printed by Christoph Runge, 1659);

Leich-Sermon dem in der Zucht und Vermahnung zum Herren wohl auffgezogenen und nunmehr Seeligen Knaben, Friederich Ludowig Zarlangen, Herrn Michael Zarlanges, Wolverdienten BürgerMeisters dieser löblichen Residentz-Stadt Berlin, eintzigen Hertzlieben Sohne, als derselbe am 13. Augusti dieses 1660ten Jahres . . . abgeschieden und sein Leichnam den folgenden 19. Augusti . . . zu S. Nicolai allhier beygesetzt . . . wurde. Aus dem 27. v. des 89. Ps. in besagter Kirche gehalten (Wittenberg: Printed by Johann Hake, 1660);

Leich-Sermon der . . . Fr. Anna Flörings, des . . . M. Georgii Webers Wohlverdienten Burger-Meisters dieser löblichen Residentz-Stadt Berlin . . . hertzgeliebten Hauß-Ehre, als dieselbe am 31. Januarij dieses 1661. Jahres . . . entschlaffen. Auß dem 11. Vers des 86. Psalms Davids (Wittenberg: Printed by Johann Röhner, 1661);

Castæ Castissimorum Manium Inferiæ . . . cum digna Feralia Virgunculæ delicatissimae Margarethæ,

Paul Gerhardt; painting by an unidentified artist (Paul-Gerhardt-Kirche, Lübbe)

Filiolæ . . . dn. Michael Zarlangius, Reip. Berl. Consul . . . die XXIV. Februarii pararet (Berlin, 1667);

Pauli Gerhardi Geistliche Andachten bestehend in hundert und zwantzig Liedern, auff hoher und vornehmer Herren Anfoderung in ein Buch gebracht, der göttlichen Majestät zu foderst zu Ehren, denn auch der werthen und bedrängten Christenheit zu Trost, und einer jedweden gläubigen Seelen zu Vermehrung ihres Christenthums also dutzendweise mit neuen sechsstimmigen Melodeyen gezieret, edited by Johann Georg Ebeling (Berlin: Printed by

113

Christoph Runge, 1667; revised edition, Stettin: Printed by Daniel Starck, 1669; revised, 1671); revised as *Evangelischer Lust-Garten* (Stettin: Printed by Daniel Starck, 1671).

Editions: *Geistreiche Hauß- und Kirchen-Lieder zur Ubung und Gebrauch des singenden Gottesdienstes vormahls zum Druck befördert; jetzo aber nach des sel. Autoris eigenhändigen revidirten Exemplar mit Fleiß übersehen, auch samt einem kurtzen, doch nöthigen Vorbericht bey dieser ersten und gantz neuen verbesserten und vermehrten Aufflage,* edited by Johann Heinrich Feustking (Zerbst: Printed by Samuel Tietze, published by Carl Anton David, 1707);

Leben und Lieder von Paulus Gerhardt, edited by E. C. G. Langbecker (Berlin: Reimer, 1841);

Paulus Gerhardts geistliche Lieder: Getreu nach der bei seinen Lebzeiten erschienenen Ausgabe wiederabgedruckt, second edition (Stuttgart: Liesching, 1849; reprinted, Bern: Lang, 1974);

Paul Gerhardts geistliche Lieder, edited by Johann Friedrich Bachmann (Berlin: Oehmigke, 1866);

Paul Gerhardts Geistliche andachten in hundert und zwanzig liedern (Berlin: Nicolai, 1869);

Gedichte von Paulus Gerhardt, edited by Karl Goedeke (Leipzig: Brockhaus, 1877);

Paulus Gerhardt als prediger, vier leichenpredigten desselben aus den jahren 1655, 1659, 1660 und 1661, edited by O. Willkomm (Zwickau: Hermann, 1906);

Paulus Gerhardts Geistliche Lieder, edited by Philipp Wackernagel, ninth edition, edited by W. Tuempel (Gütersloh: Bertelsmann, 1907);

Paul Gerhardts Geistliche Lieder, edited by Karl Gerok, seventh edition (Leipzig: Amelang, 1911);

Ich singe Dir mit Herz und Mund (Lahr: Schweickart, 1957);

Ein Botschafter der Freude: Dokumente und Gedichte aus Paul Gerhardts Berliner Jahren, edited by Kurt Ihlenfeld (Berlin: Merseburger, 1957);

Dichtungen und Schriften, edited by Eberhard von Cranach-Sichart (Munich: Müller, 1957);

Gedichte, edited by Albrecht Goes (Frankfurt am Main: Fischer, 1969);

Pauli Gerhardi Geistliche Andachten (1667): Samt den übrigen Liedern und den lateinischen Gedichten, edited by Friedhelm Kemp (Bern: Francke, 1975);

Karl Hesselbachers Paul Gerhardt, der Sänger fröhlichen Glaubens, edited by Siegfried Heinzelmann (Neuffen: Sonnenweg, 1980);

Paul Gerhardt, Geistliche Lieder, edited by Gerhard Rödding (Stuttgart: Reclam, 1991).

Editions in English: *Lyra Germanica: Hymns for the Sundays and Chief Festivals of the Christian Year,* translated by Catherine Winkworth (New York: Stanford, 1857; republished, Boston: Dutton, 1962);

Paul Gerhardt's Spiritual Songs, translated, with a biographical sketch, by John Kelly (London: Strahan, 1867);

Songs for the Household: Sacred Poetry, translated by Winkworth (New York: Worthington, 1882);

Lyra Gerhardti; or, A Selection of Paul Gerhardt's Spiritual Songs, translated by Bernhard Pick (Burlington, Iowa: German Literary Board, 1906);

"O Sacred Head, now wounded," translated by James W. Alexander, in *The Hymnal,* edited by Clarence Dickinson and Calvin Weiss Laufer (Philadelphia: Presbyterian Board of Christian Education, 1933), p. 151;

The German Lyric of the Baroque in English Translation, edited by George C. Schoolfield (Chapel Hill: University of North Carolina Press, 1961), pp. 110–115.

OTHER: Johann Crüger, *Praxis pietatis melica. Das ist: Übung der Gottseligkeit in christlichen und trostreichen Gesängen* (Berlin: Printed by Christoph Runge, 1648; enlarged, 1648; enlarged again, 1653; enlarged again, 1656; enlarged again, 1661) – includes poems by Gerhardt;

"Paul Gerhardt: Testament für seinen Sohn Paul Friedrich," in *Der Protestantismus des 17. Jahrhunderts,* edited by Winfrid Zeller (Bremen: Schünemann, 1962), pp. 285–287.

Paul Gerhardt, who wrote Lutheran hymns almost exclusively, may be the most widely known German poet of the seventeenth century. Many Germans today know by heart those of his texts that have survived, together with their melodies, the general decline of religious culture. Even many who disdain the rituals of faith regard Gerhardt's hymns as the essence of individual spirituality. His songs have helped to overcome the countless confessional, regional, and political differences that have haunted German history. For three hundred years they have inspired and consoled people – even fictional characters – at all stages of their lives. According to Ernst Kurt Exner, the poet Theodor Gottlieb von Hippel reported that his mother said of Gerhardt: "Er dichtefe während dem Kirchengeläute, er drehte sich beständig nach der ewigen Seligkeit" (He created his songs while the churchbells were ringing; he always pointed the way toward eternal salvation). For Hermann Hesse's mother, Gerhardt's hymns were the "tägliches manna ihrer Seele" (daily manna of her soul) that had done more good in this world than the works of Johann Wolfgang von Goethe, Friedrich Schiller, and William Shakespeare. When Hesse's Magister Ludi, Joseph Knecht, takes leave of the "pedagogical province" of Castalia, he sings a song by Gerhardt and then plays it on his recorder. Such instances support Curt von Faber du Faur's observation: "Some twenty of [Gerhardt's] songs have thus become the indestructible possession of the Evangelical portion of the German nation; every child has grown up with them, and they impress themselves on one's memory so well that they can never be forgotten." Since 1683 German immigrants to the United States have brought hymns by Gerhardt along as part of their cultural heritage; the *Evangelisches Gesangbuch* (Lutheran Hymnal), printed in Saint Louis in 1894, included twenty-six of them. Most admirers of Gerhardt today know little of the contradiction between the serene, elemental religiosity of his poems and the life of the rather dogmatic cleric who created them.

Gerhardt was born on 12 March 1607 in Gräfenhainichen, a small town in Saxony near Wittenberg, of which his father, Christian Gerhardt, a farmer and innkeeper, sometimes served as mayor. Paul was named after his grandfather, a town councillor. His mother, Dorothea, came from a family of Lutheran clergymen; her father, Caspar Starcke, superintendent in Eilenburg, was once suspended from his duties because he opposed the practice of exorcism in the Protestant church too zealously. Gerhardt's father died in 1619 and his mother in 1621; perhaps because of his early loss of his parents, his songs often compare God's special affection for the human soul to that of parents for their children. In the well-known evening hymn "Nun ruhen alle Wälder" (Now rest the woods again) he asks that Jesus command the angels to sing and protect him during the night as a hen guards her chicks. In childlike prayer, the author places "meine Lieben" (my loved ones) too under God's care. Another song advises: "Tu als sein Kind und lege dich / In deines Vaters Arme" (Be as his child and lie down / In your father's arms).

In 1622 Gerhardt was awarded a scholarship to the Fürstenschule (state academy) at Grimma. The school, an elite institution devoted mainly to training Lutheran pastors, was housed in a former monastery. The curriculum, in the orthodox Protestant spirit, demanded a high degree of self-discipline

of the students, who received a thorough training in the classical languages, philosophy, theology, and sacred music. After passing his examinations the young man went to Wittenberg in 1628 to study theology in preparation for a career as a pastor, as his parents had wished. Martin Luther himself had lived and had established the Protestant church in Wittenberg, where Gerhardt came under the influence of a faculty steeped in Lutheran orthodoxy and concerned especially with disputing Calvinist doctrines. It was there that he acquired an unswerving loyalty to the "Lutherisches Glaubens Bekenntnuß Formulam Concordiae" (Lutheran Formula of Doctrinal Concord) of 1577.

Augustus Buchner, a professor of rhetoric and poetics at Wittenberg, enthusiastically supported Martin Opitz's "reform" of German poetry in the spirit of the Renaissance. Gerhardt's poems consistently pursue specific public ends with artfully utilized means, attempting to reach the souls of the people by inspiring their quest for faith, in the spirit of Buchner's lecture of 1642, "Vom Amt und Zweck des Poeten" (On the Office and Purposes of the Poet). Like Buchner, he saw humanity as in even greater need of spiritual strength than of physical nurture.

Gerhardt remained in Wittenberg for about fifteen years. Scholars have speculated on why he studied theology for such an unusually long time and had not yet been ordained when he left the university at thirty-eight. The Thirty Years' War and attendant outbreaks of the plague almost certainly impeded his progress; many churches in the region were destroyed, and poverty was widespread.

Gerhardt left Saxony around 1643 for Berlin, then the capital of the province of Brandenburg. As in Wittenberg, he supported himself as a private tutor for the children of the prosperous middle class. To eke out his slender income he also wrote occasional poems and began to write hymns. He was evidently well liked and respected by the Lutheran laity and clergy of Berlin; although he was encouraged by his influential friends to seek a pastoral position, he did not do so. He served as a substitute preacher in various churches, but not until 1651 was he ordained as pastor of Mittenwalde, a small village near Berlin. On 11 February 1655 he married Anna Maria Berthold, daughter of the Berlin attorney Andreas Berthold, who had employed Gerhardt as a tutor. The couple had three sons and two daughters, but only one son, Paul Friedrich, would survive his parents. In 1657 Gerhardt accepted an offer to return to Berlin as third deacon of the Nikolaikirche (Church of Saint Nicholas). The city was then rapidly becoming a center of absolutist culture under the "Great Elector," Friedrich Wilhelm.

Two *Kantoren* (directors of church music) served at the Nikolaikirche during Gerhardt's tenure: Johann Crüger and his successor, Johann Georg Ebeling. Gerhardt's development as a poet would have been quite different or might not have occurred at all without their active encouragement and the musical settings they supplied for his texts. It is because of Crüger and Ebeling that so many of his hymns have been preserved, for Gerhardt himself was noted for his modesty. Eighteen hymns by Gerhardt, who had begun to write well before his ordination, appeared in Crüger's hymnal of 1648, *Praxis pietatis melica. Das ist: Übung der Gottseligkeit in christlichen und trostreichen Gesängen* (Piety Practiced in Uplifting Christian Songs). Gerhardt's productivity evidently increased dramatically with the onset of his pastoral duties, for the 1653 edition of Crüger's hymnal includes eighty-two texts bearing his signature, a number that increases only slightly in the editions of 1656 and 1661. Gerhardt also enjoyed the friendship of other influential citizens who encouraged and supported his literary efforts.

When the Thirty Years' War ended in 1648 Gerhardt wrote an anthem of thanksgiving, "Gott Lob! Nun ist erschollen" (Thank God! It Hath Resounded), appealing to Germany to live according to God's commandments. Details of the horrifying destruction of war, in the fashion of Opitz or Andreas Gryphius, dramatize the immediacy of the nation's losses – "ihr zerstörten Schlösser / Und Städte voller Schutt und Stein" (your ravaged castles / And cities full of rubble and stones) – and symbolize a spiritual brutalization that can only be healed through faith in the Lord, who has sent these trials to an erring world. Such passages speak for Gerhardt's awareness of the contemporary political situation and for his compassion and idealism.

Luther himself had founded the tradition of the Protestant *Kirchenlied* (church hymn), which he insisted should be central to Christian worship. Luther's own hymns established themes and structures that have remained stable to the present day. Centering on vivid metaphors from the Psalms, most famously in "Ein' feste Burg ist unser Gott" (A Mighty Fortress Is Our God, 1529), he used short, simple words to create strophes of great forcefulness that would convey the doctrines of the new faith to the congregation and instill in it solidarity and courage. Most of Gerhardt's songs follow the Lutheran traditions of the *Bekenntnislied* (song of affirmation of the faith) and *Frömmigkeitslied* (song of

piety). They are based on the Bible, and some are also inspired by mystical thought of the Middle Ages and by such works of the seventeenth century as the *Paradyss Gärtlein* (Little Garden of Paradise, 1612), by Johann Arndt. During the twenty-five years that he served the Protestant Church it was Gerhardt's primary goal, both as clergyman and as poet, to guide his flock in what he regarded as the true faith.

Because his poetry deals with universal themes and was written over a relatively short time span, some scholars contend that his work reveals no poetic development and reflects little of its author's real situation or how his thinking changed over the years. Gerhardt did, however, provide occasional glimpses into his life and into how his ideas evolved. In an ode celebrating the appearance of a devotional book in 1650 Gerhardt proudly distinguishes himself from secular writers, whom he derisively calls "Weltscribenten und Poeten" (worldly scribblers and poetasters); their usefulness is limited to times when nothing troubles us. The ideals of Plato, Homer, and Virgil are inadequate in the face of the world's tribulations and of death: when we are beset by misery and evil, only the radiance of the Bible can penetrate the darkness. Gerhardt rejected whatever he thought unessential to the life of the soul and its journey toward grace.

While he clearly hearkened back to the formal traditions of Luther's Kirchenlieder, Gerhardt created a uniquely personal form of the hymn that reflected the religious and aesthetic values of his own age. Thanks probably to Buchner's influence, Gerhardt's hymns generally fulfill the criteria for prosody and clarity of expression set forth by Opitz in his *Buch von der deutschen Poeterey* (Book of German Poetry, 1624). Gerhardt's hallmark, however, is the sense of an intensely personal encounter with the essence of the divine that his hymns, in their simple directness, impart to those who sing them and to their listeners. This quality is evident in the best known of his earliest hymns, "O Haupt voll Blut und Wunden" (O Sacred Head! Now Wounded), which appeared in the 1653 edition of Crüger's *Praxis pietatis melica* under the title "An das leydende Angesicht Jesu Christi" (On the Suffering Countenance of Jesus Christ), with music by Ebeling. Here Gerhardt essentially created anew, in the German poetic language of his day, Bernard of Clairvaux's Latin hymn *Salve caput cruentatum*. Through the repetition of the greeting and by the emphatic use of contrasts, Gerhardt dramatizes the believer's shock, on confronting the suffering of the crucified Christ, at the paradox of the Lord's eternal divinity and the brutality that his temporal humanity must suffer:

1. O Haupt voll Blut und Wunden,
Voll Schmerz und voller Hohn,
O Haupt, zum Spott gebunden
Mit einer Dornenkron!
   O Haupt, sonst schön gezieret
Mit höchster Ehr und Zier,
Jetzt aber hoch schimpfieret,
Gegrüßet seist du mir!

2. Du edles Angesichte,
Davor sonst schrickt und scheut
Das große Weltgewichte,
Wie bist du so bespeit,
   Wie bist du so erbleichet,
Wer hat dein Augenlicht,
Dem sonst kein Licht nicht gleichet,
So schändlich zugericht?

(1. O sacred Head, now wounded,
With grief and shame weigh'd down;
Now scornfully surrounded
With thorns thy only crown:
O sacred Head, what glory,
What bliss till now was thine!
Yet though despised and gory,
I joy to call thee mine.

2. O noblest brow and dearest,
In other days the world
All fear'd when thou appearedst;
What shame on thee is hurl'd!
How art thou pale with anguish,
With sore abuse and scorn;
How does that vision languish,
Which once was bright as morn?)

[translation by James W. Alexander]

The believer must accept responsibility and guilt for the Lord's sacrifice but also the solace in the face of death and the faith in salvation that proceed from it. In recasting this venerable Catholic hymn Gerhardt brings to the *Kirchenlied* an intensity of personal devotional feeling that is relatively new to the traditional Protestant form. Although Gerhardt's theological views surely did not tend in that direction, the hymn appears to prefigure the advent of Pietism and its more individual forms of worship within the Lutheran faith.

    Many of Gerhardt's 134 surviving hymns are related to the feast days of the ecclesiastical year. Their subjects include Christian life and worship, the solace of the Cross, praise of the Lord and thanksgiving, and death and eternity. Like the Psalms, on which many of them are based, Ger-

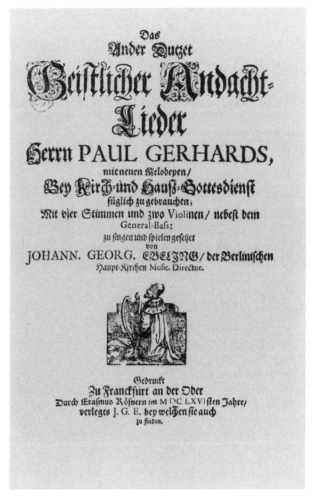

Title page for the second dozen hymns in Johann Georg Ebeling's collection of 120 hymns by Gerhardt

hardt's hymns are personal, immediate expressions of an *Ich* (I) addressing itself to God, who, for all of his power, is accessible as *Du* (Thou); indeed, sixteen of them begin with the word *Ich*. Christ is addressed as "Jesu, allerliebster Bruder" (Jesus, beloved brother), "meine Liebe" (my beloved), and "Herzensros'" (rose of the heart), often in a spirit of fervent, mystical adoration that is not usually associated with the austerity of Lutheran religious practices.

    The beauty of nature as an expression of God's power and grace is a theme from the Psalter that struck a responsive chord in Gerhardt. "Geh aus mein Herz und suche Freud'" (Go out my heart and seek joy; translated as "Go out in this dear summertide") exemplifies the way he sees the natural world: as a delight for the senses and an allegory of divine benevolence. In the hymn's first half Gerhardt points out "Narzissus und die Tulipan, Die ziehen sich viel schöner an Als Salomonis Seide" (narcissus and tulips clothed more richly than the silks of Solomon). He describes the bustling, thriving activity of summer, in which the *Ich* is a crucial participant, establishing the link between the physical world and its metaphysical significance:

7. Der Weizen wächset mit Gewalt,
Darüber jauchzet Jung und Alt
Und rühmt die große Güte
    Des, der so überflüssig labt
Und mit so manchem Gut begabt
Das menschliche Gemüte.

8. Ich selbsten kann und mag nicht ruhn;
Des großen Gottes großes Tun
Erweckt mir alle Sinnen:
    Ich singe mit, wenn alles singt,
Und lasse, was dem Höchsten klingt,
Aus meinem Herzen rinnen.

(7. The wheat grows large with all its might,
And does both young and old delight:
They sing the bounteousness
Of Him Who soothes so generously
And does such countless property
Upon man's spirit press.

8. Now I can neither rest, nor will:
Great God's great manufactures thrill
Awake my every sense.
I sing along, when all does sing,
And let what shall to Heaven ring
From out my heart commence.)

[translation by George C. Schoolfield]

Like Luther, Gerhardt believed that although people may legitimately take pleasure in the beauty of God's universe, their capacity to understand it is limited. In "Du bist ein Mensch, das weißt du wohl" (You are human, and you know that well) he denies the humanists' optimism regarding the human ability to perceive nature accurately. He argues that human plans and deeds cannot change or accomplish anything in the world and that it is wrong to trust the senses and the reason:

Du traust und glaubest weiter nicht,
Als was dein Augen spüren;
    Was du beginnst, da soll allein
Dein Kopf dein Licht und Meister sein,
Was der nicht auserkoren,
Das hältst du als verloren.

(You only trust and then believe
What your own eyes have seen,
    Whate'er you do, your head alone
Must be your lord and light.
You judge as lost and wasted,

Things it does not command.)

Rather than continue in such self-deception we should trust God, who cares for us far better than we are capable of doing for ourselves.

Gerhardt's congregation and his superiors thought highly of him, but political and religious events in Brandenburg led to drastic changes in his life. The Great Elector's grandfather Johann Sigismund, a devout Lutheran, had converted to Calvinism in 1613 to strengthen the claims of the Hohenzollern dynasty to territories in western Germany, while his wife, like practically all of his subjects, continued to adhere to Lutheranism. Because the ruler's official faith differed from that of his subjects, the government tolerated a degree of religious pluralism that was exceptional in Germany: Huguenots, Catholics, Jews, and members of other faiths that were suppressed fiercely elsewhere could worship freely in Brandenburg. Lutherans and Calvinists, however, often despised each other's faiths more than they did Catholicism, particularly in those areas where they competed directly. In Brandenburg, Lutheran pastors attacked the doctrines of the Reformed church, to which the Great Elector owed allegiance, and the Calvinists answered in kind. As the Calvinist minority, residing mainly in Berlin, was prosperous and influential, Friedrich Wilhelm commanded Lutheran pastors in Berlin to refrain from criticizing his faith from their pulpits. In 1662 and again in 1664 they were required, on pain of dismissal from office, to sign an agreement not to express their opinions of other denominations in public.

Although Gerhardt had not played a leading role in the controversy and had even participated in councils meant to reconcile the two churches, he refused to sign the agreement. He did not want to promise to refrain from acts that he had never committed; also, as only the Lutheran clergy had to sign the agreement, Gerhardt felt that they were being unfairly singled out. Following a hearing on 6 February 1666 the authorities suspended him from office. He was not banished, however, and continued to receive his salary. On 25 July he wrote to the countess of Lippe, declaring that only his conscience mattered to him and expressing surprise that the elector was still waiting for his signature without taking further steps. Gerhardt's humility and the stoicism of his faith made possible his proud defiance:

Ist es meines Gottes Wille, das ich ihm noch in dieser
Wellt wieder alls ein offentlicher Prediger dienen soll,

will ich Ihm zu Ehren das wenige, was noch übrig ist
von meinem Leben, gern auffopfern. Will er aber nicht,
so will ich ihn dennoch in meiner Einsamkeit seeg[n]en
und preysen, loben und dancken, so lange sich mein
Mund reget unnd meine Augen offen stehen.

(If it is my God's will that I serve him again in this world
as a preacher, I will gladly sacrifice the remaining years
of my life in his honor. If, however, he does not want
this, I will nevertheless bless, praise, and thank him in
my solitude as long as my mouth can speak and my eyes
are open.)

As Gerhardt was popular and had well-situated friends, petitions soon began to arrive protesting his innocence, about which even the Calvinists agreed, and pleading that he be reinstated. The Berlin city fathers and Gerhardt's congregation also supported him. It finally became clear that the political price of insisting that Gerhardt formally agree to obey the Edict of Toleration was too great. The elector reinstated him in January 1667, granting to Gerhardt alone exemption from signing the agreement but expecting his tacit obedience to its provisions. Gerhardt, however, had hardened his stance, and he refused to take up his duties as a preacher because he could not reconcile acknowledging Calvinism as a Christian denomination with his sworn allegiance to the Lutheran Formula of Doctrinal Concord of 1577. The process of replacing him was delayed as long as possible in the hope that he would change his mind, but finally, on 15 August 1668, Gerhardt's pastorship officially came to an end.

Although he appears not to have actively sought another position, Gerhardt soon accepted an invitation from the city of Lübben, in the Spreewald region of the Saxon province of Lausitz, to serve as *Archidiakonus* (main pastor) there. Gerhardt's wife had died on 5 March 1668, following a long illness; his widowed sister-in-law and his son accompanied him to Lübben, where he delivered his first sermon on 6 June 1669. He looked back on the past as the "kleine berlinische Leiden" (little crucifixion in Berlin). Gerhardt wrote no more Kirchenlieder; the last of his hymns appear to date from 1667. Ebeling published practically all of the hymns in that year under the title *Pauli Gerhardi Geistliche Andachten bestehend in hundert und zwantzig Liedern* (Paul Gerhardt's Spiritual Devotions in 120 Hymns). Other than some funeral poems, no other poetry of his was printed during his lifetime.

Gerhardt died on 27 May 1676. In his will he had instructed his son to study theology and to lead an honorable and devout life, but Paul Friedrich

Gerhardt became a pauper who had to sell his father's valuable library of some 1,150 volumes. While looking for a position at Zerbst, he gave the local pastor, Johann Heinrich Feustking, his father's copy of an edition of the hymns, with the poet's handwritten corrections and changes. He died in Berlin in 1716.

In his celebrated biographical work about German writers, *De poetis Germanicis* (On German Poets, 1695), Erdmann Neumeister wrote that Gerhardt was a "Poëta vere Christianus, dulcis, perspicuus; cujus *Hymni* perplures, pii omnes ac infucati neutiquam, Ecclesiæ nostræ oppido sunt familiares" (true Christian poet, pleasing and clear. He has written many church hymns, all pious, not at all artificial, and familiar to our congregations). Gerhardt is still widely appreciated as a "true Christian poet"; modern English hymnals include his hymns in translation. He is buried in Lübben before the altar of the church where he preached and that bears his name today. In 1907 a monument in his honor was erected in front of the church. Paul Gerhardt's most lasting memorial, however, is to be found in his contributions to the religious and musical life of the German people.

Bibliographies:

Rudolf Eckart, *Paul Gerhardt-Bibliographie: Stimmen und Schriften über Paul Gerhardt* (Pritzwalk: Tiencken, 1908);

Gerhard Dünnhaupt, *Personalbibliographien zu den Drucken des Barock,* volume 9, part 3 (Stuttgart: Hiersemann, 1991), pp. 1589–1598.

References:

L. L. Albertsen, "Die Krise in der Pflege des barocken Kirchenliedes: Zum Schicksal der Lieder Paul Gerhardts in den deutschen und dänischen Gesangbüchern des 18. Jahrhunderts," *Daphnis*, 8, no. 1 (1979): 145–167;

J. S. Andrews, *A Study of German Hymns in Current English Hymnals* (Bern & Frankfurt am Main: Lang, 1981);

Elke Axmacher, "Paul Gerhardt als lutherischer Theologe," in *450 Jahre evangelische Theologie in Berlin,* edited by Gerhard Besier and Christof Gestrich (Göttingen: Vandenhoeck & Ruprecht, 1989), pp. 79–104;

Johann Friedrich Bachmann, *Zur Geschichte der Berliner Gesangbücher: Ein hymnologischer Beitrag* (Hildesheim & New York: Olms, 1970);

Brigitte Eva Bennedik, "Paul Gerhardts Morgenlieder in englischen und amerikanischen

Übersetzungen," dissertation, University of Southern California, 1974;

William Dallmann, *Paul Gerhardt: His Life and His Hymns* (Saint Louis: Concordia, 1921);

Rudolf Eckart, *Paul Gerhardt: Urkunden und Aktenstücke zu seinem Leben und Kämpfen* (Glückstadt, 1907);

Ernst Kurt Exner, *Paul Gerhardt: Der deutsche Kirchensänger* (Berlin: Union, 1954);

Curt von Faber du Faur, "Paul Gerhardt," in his *German Baroque Literature* (New Haven: Yale University Press, 1958), pp. 126–127;

Gerald Gillespie, *German Baroque Poetry* (New York: Twayne, 1971), pp. 131–135;

Heinz Hoffmann, ed., *Paul Gerhardt: Dichter-Theologe-Seelsorger. 1607–1676. Beiträge der Wittenberger Paul-Gerhardt-Tage 1976* (Berlin: Evangelische Verlagsanstalt, 1978);

Hans-Georg Kemper, *Deutsche Lyrik der frühen Neuzeit,* volume 2: *Konfessionalismus* (Tübingen: Niemeyer, 1987);

Kemper, "Paul Gerhardt," in *Literatur-Lexikon: Autoren und Werke deutscher Sprache,* volume 4, edited by Walter Killy (Munich: Bertelsmann, 1989), pp. 125–127;

Hans-Henrik Krummacher, "Paul Gerhardt," in *Deutsche Dichter des 17. Jahrhunderts: Ihr Leben und Werk,* edited by Harald Steinhagen and Benno von Wiese (Berlin: Schmidt, 1984), pp. 270–288;

Volker Michels, Paul Rathgeber, and Eugen Würzbach, "Hermann Hesse: 1877–1962," *Marbacher Magazin,* special issue, 54 (1990): 34;

J. V. Moore Jr., "Historical and Stylistic Aspects of Paul Gerhardt's German Songs," dissertation, Princeton University, 1964;

Gerhard Rödding, *Paul Gerhardt* (Gütersloh: Mohn, 1981);

Waltraut Ingeborg Sauer-Geppert, *Sprache und Frömmigkeit im deutschen Kirchenlied* (Kassel: Stauda, 1984);

Wolfgang Trillhaas, "Paul Gerhardt: 1607–1676," in *Die Großen Deutschen,* volume 1, edited by Hermann Heimpel, Theodor Heuss, and Benno Reifenberg (Berlin: Propyläen, 1956), pp. 533–546;

Winfried Zeller, "Zur Textüberlieferung der Lieder Paul Gerhardts," *Jahrbuch für Liturgik und Hymnologie,* 19 (1979): 225–228.

Papers:

Manuscripts for Paul Gerhardt's funeral sermons are in the Deutsche Staatsbibliothek, Berlin, and in the Berliner Stadtbibliothek.

Georg Greflinger
(1620? – 1677)

Günter Berghaus
University of Bristol

BOOKS: *Weihnacht-Gedancken: Mit angehengtem Newen Jahres wuntsch* (Dresden: Printed by Wolfgang Seyffert, 1639);

Querela Germaniae, anonymous (Liegnitz, 1640);

Des jetzigen Deutschlandes erbärmliche Beschaffenheit. Anno 1643 (Hamburg, 1643);

Hochzeit-Gedichte (N.p., 1643);

Das klagende Deutschland (N.p., 1644);

Ferrando-Dorinde. Zweyer hochverliebtgewesenen Personen erbärmliches Ende (Frankfurt am Main: Eduard Schleich, 1644);

Zwey Sapphische Lieder, von der Geburt und von dem Leyden unsers getrewen Heylandes Jesu Christi (Frankfurt am Main: Published by Eduard Schleich, printed by Matthias Kempfer, 1644); first poem republished as *Sapphische Ode von der Geburt Christi* (Hamburg, 1651);

Seladons Beständtige Liebe (Frankfurt am Main: Eduard Schleich, 1644);

Deutscher Epigrammatum erstes Hundert (Danzig, 1645);

Ethica Complementoria; Complementier-Büchlein, anonymous (Hamburg: Heinrich Werner, 1645); enlarged as *Complementier-Büchlein, darin eine richtige Art abgebildet wird, wie man so wol mit hohen als niedrigen Persohnen, auch bey Gesellschafften vnd Frawen-Zimmer hoffzierlich reden vnd vmb gehen sol* (Hamburg: Johann Naumann, 1647);

Der Teutsche Krieg poetisch auff das kurtzeste beschrieben. Erster Theil (N.p., 1647); enlarged as *Die grausam-blutige Tragoedia vom Deutschlande ist eine Erzehlung deß Deutschen Krieges, von 1616 biß 1648* (Hamburg, circa 1650); enlarged as *Der Deutschen Dreyßig-Jähriger Krjeg, poetisch erzählet* (N.p., 1657);

Geistliche Liederlein über die jährlichen Evangelien (Hamburg, 1648);

Cochleatio Novissima. Das ist, Waare Abbildung der heut zu Tag zu viel vblicher Kunst der Löfflerey, attributed to Greflinger (Liebstadt: Printed by Lambert Remeler [fictitious place of publication and printer], 1648);

Ihrer Königl. Mayestät von Engeland Carls, Klag- oder Sterblied, anonymous (Hamburg, 1649);

Caroli Secundi Regis Magnae Britanniae Dancklied, als jhn Gott von seiner Feindlichen Vnterhanen Hand in Franckreich brachte durch hülffe einer Adelichen Frawen (N.p., 1651);

Gesprächlied zwischen dem König von Engeland und Cromweln (Hamburg, 1651);

Diarium Britannicum. Das ist: Kurtze und unpartheyische Erzählung derer Dinge, welche sich von Anno 1637. biß auff den 1. Octobr. 1651. in den dreyen Königreichen Engeland, Schott- und Jrrland zugetragen haben (Hamburg, 1651);

Seladons Weltliche Ljeder. Nechst einem Anhang Schimpff- vnd Ernsthaffter Gedichte (Frankfurt am Main: Published by Caspar Wächtler, printed by Matthias Kempfer, 1651);

Der zwölff gekröhnten Häupter von dem Hause Stuart unglückselige Herrschafft, jn kurtzem aus glaubwürdigen Historien Schreibern zusammen getragen (Hamburg?, 1652);

Kurtze Erzehlung aller vornehmsten Händel, welche sich Von Anno 1618. biß den 1. Feb. 1653. jm Römischen Reiche. Von Anno 1637. biß den Decemb. 1651. jn Engel- Schott- und Jrrland. Von Anno 1652. biß den 16. Maij. 1653. zwischen Engeland und Holland zugetragen haben (Hamburg, 1653); enlarged as *Kurtze Anzeigungen der vornehmsten Kriegs-Händel und anderer denckwürdigsten Sachen die sich von Anno 1650. biß 1658. im Römischen Reiche. Von Anno 1655. biß 1658. zwischen den Schweden, Pohlen, Moßcowittern und derer allijrten. Von Anno 1657. biß 1658. zwischen den Schweden und Dehnen begeben haben* (Hamburg: Georg Greflinger, 1658); enlarged as *Unparteyischer Anweiser was vor denckwürdigste Sachen von Anno 1650. biß 1659. im Römischen Reiche. Von Anno 1655. biß 1659. zwischen dem Schweden, Pohlen, Moßcowittern und derer allijrten. Und von Anno 1657. biß 1658. zwischen den Nordischen Königen vorgefallen seyn. Zu guter Erinnerung gestället* (Hamburg: Georg Greflinger, 1659); enlarged

121

as *Anzeiger der denckwürdigsten Krieges- und anderer Händel zu unseren Zeiten jm Römischen Reiche und dessen angrentzenden Ländern, von 1618. biß Septemb. 1660. jm Königreiche Pohlen auch dessen angrentzenden Ländern, von 1655. biß Septembr. 1660. und jm Königreiche Dennemarck von 1657. biß August. 1660. beschehen unpartheyisch ausgegeben D* (Hamburg: Georg Greflinger, 1660);

Poetische Rosen vnd Dörner, Hülsen vnd Körner (Hamburg, 1655);

Freude: Uber die Englische Freude (N.p., 1660);

Eines Deutschen gewesenes Leid und anwesende Freud über jhrer Königlichen Majestät von groß Britannien &c. Caroli Secundi Erlittenen Hohn und jetzige Kron (Hamburg, 1660);

Papiren Feyer-Werck, nach der Europaeischen Tragi-Comoedia, absonderlich aber nach dem Nordischen Leid in Freud verwandeltem Spiel gesehen im grossen Wunder Jahr 1660. angestecket an der Elbe (Copenhagen: Lamprecht, 1660);

Celadonische Musa jnhaltende Hundert Oden vnd etlich Hundert Epigrammata (Hamburg, 1663);

Zeit-Büchlein vom itzigem Türcken-Kriege wider das Königreich Vngarn, Siebenbürgen und die Kayserliche Erb-Länder. Kürtzlich, was von Monat zu Monat darin passiret ist (Hamburg, 1663); enlarged as *Zeit-Büchlein erst- und ander Theil. vom jetzigen Türcken-Krieg, wider das Königreich Ungarn, Siebenbürgen und die Käyserliche Erb-Länder* (Hamburg, 1664);

Des Nordischen Mercurii Wegweiser aus der Stadt Hamburg nach den äusersten grossen Städten von Deutschland (Hamburg: Georg Greflinger, 1671); enlarged as *Des Nordischen Mercurij verbesserter Weg-Weiser, von zehen Haupt-Reisen aus der Stadt Hamburg* (Hamburg: Georg Greflinger, 1674).

Edition: *Der Deutschen Dreyßig-Jähriger Krieg 1657,* edited by Peter Michael Ehrle (Munich: Fink, 1983).

OTHER: Benedictus Arias Montanus, *David Virtvosus. Das ist: Deß Frommen und Tapfferen Königs und Propheten Davids Ankufft, Leben und Ende, in schönen Kupfferstichen abgebildet, von Ioh. Theodoro de Bry, p.m. vnd mit zierlichen Versen erklaret,* includes poems by Greflinger (Frankfurt am Main: Johann Ammon, 1644);

Jean Jacques Boissard, *Wahre Abbildungen der Türckischen Kayser und Persischen Fürsten, so wol auch anderer Helden und Heldinnen von dem Osman, biß auf den andern Mahomet,* includes poems by

Greflinger (Frankfurt am Main: Johann Ammon, 1648).

TRANSLATIONS: Pierre Corneille, *Die Sinnreiche Tragi-Comoedia genannt Cid, ist ein Streit der Ehre und Liebe* (Hamburg: Printed by George Pape, published by Johann Naumann, 1650);

Antonio Mira de Amescua, *Verwirrter Hof oder König Carl* (Hamburg: Printed by Jakob Rebenlein, 1652);

Johann Ulrich Strauß, *Distichorum Centuria prima et secunda cum Versione Germanica* (Hamburg: Printed by Jakob Rebenlein, 1654);

Pieter van Ængelen, *Der verständige Gärtner uber die zwölff Monaten des Jahres. Jst eine Unterweisung, Bäume- Kräuter- und Blumen-Gärten auf das beste zu bepflantzen und zubesaamen* (Hamburg, 1655);

Schatz über Schatz. Das ist: Was ihr alle lang verlanget habt. nähmlich das Mittel bald reich zu werden (Hamburg: Printed by Jakob Rebenlein, 1655);

Cesare Ripa, *Zwo Hundert Außbildungen von Tugenden, Lastern, Menschlichen Begierden, Künsten, Lehren und vielen andern Arten: Aus der Iconologia oder Bilder-Sprache deß Hochberühmten Caesaris Ripa von Perusien* (Hamburg: Printed by Michael Pfeiffer, published by Johann Naumann, 1659);

Paul Scarron, *Von der unnötigen Vorsorge vor Kluges Frauenvolck* (Hamburg: Johann Naumann, 1660);

Scarron, *Der unschuldige Ehebruch* (Hamburg: Printed by Christoph Demler, published by Johann Naumann, 1662);

Nicolas de Bonnefons, *Der Frantzösische Baum- und Stauden-Gärtner* (Hamburg, 1663);

Bonnefons, *Der Frantzösische Küchen-Gärtner* (Hamburg, 1664);

Bonnefons, *Der Frantzösische Becker* (Frankfurt am Main, 1665);

Bonnefons, *Der Frantzösische Confitirier, welcher handelt: Von der Manier, die Früchte in ihrer natürlichen Art zu erhalten* (Hamburg, 1665);

Bonnefons, *Der Frantzösische Koch* (Hannover: Thomas Heinrich Hauenstein, 1665);

Des Hamburgischen, Ao. 1603. in Niedersächsischer Sprache verfasseten, Stadt-Recesses Hochteutsche Übersetzung (Hamburg, 1667);

Julius Wilhelm Zincgref, *Emblematum ethico-politicorum Centuria* (Heidelberg: Printed by Abraham Ludwig Walter, published by Clemens Ammon, 1681).

George Greflinger's significance as a poet is based on his ability to bridge the gap between *Volks-*

lied (popular song) and *Kunstdichtung* (literary poetry). He drew from the rich tradition of South German folk songs and poetry written for social occasions, and he purified their often clumsy and irregular formal conventions in accord with Martin Opitz's reform program. Greflinger sought to elevate and refine the popular traditions of poetry without succumbing to the artificiality and mannerism that characterized much of North German poetry. His poems express an exuberant zest for life and an effervescent cheerfulness. In a war-stricken era he described the sunny side of existence, the mirth and merriment of taverns and festivities, the light-hearted and frivolous pursuits of the younger generation. Greflinger was clearly a fun-loving, humorous man, but his cheerful disposition did not prevent him from writing some subtle and sensitive love poems. Most of them have an autobiographical basis, but some belong to the Petrarchan tradition and portray fictitious amorous experiences. He also wrote some satiric poetry that describes, in a witty and humorous fashion, the all-too-human faults and foibles of his contemporaries. Although the quality of Greflinger's poetry cannot compete with the works of the best and foremost authors of the German baroque, he made an important contribution to the poetic literature of the period and has few competitors in the genre he chose as his favorite medium of expression.

Besides his significance as a poet, Greflinger must be regarded a journalist of historical importance. He progressed from the *historisches Volkslied,* a kind of journalism in song form performed by professional itinerant singers, to *Nachrichtenschreiberei* (the compilation and translation of news items), to the composition of extensive chronicles of major historical upheavals of his time. Finally, he published his own newspaper and printed historiographical writings by other authors.

Greflinger was born around 1620 in Neunburg vorm Wald, a small town in the Palatinate some thirty miles north of Regensburg. Growing up on a small farm owned by his father, he worked as a cowherd and shepherd. While still a youth he lost his family and possessions in the turmoil of the Thirty Years' War. He studied at the Protestant gymnasium in Regensburg before registering at Wittenberg University on 10 June 1635 as "Georgius Greblingerus, Neoburgo Palatin, non iuravit propter aetatem" (Georg Greblinger from Neuburg in the Palatinate, not sworn in because of his age). His literary interests were fostered by Augustus Buchner, a leading professor of poetry and rhetoric, and he became a close friend of August

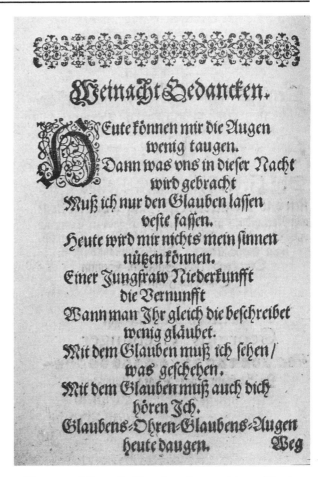

First page of Georg Greflinger's earliest surviving publication

Augspurger, another pupil of Buchner's. Through Augspurger's father Greflinger established contacts with high-ranking civil servants at the court of Saxony. Buchner's patron, Christian Reichbrot, procured for Greflinger some work as a scribe or clerk in Dresden. In 1639 Greflinger moved to Silesia, where he had found new patrons in Duke Georg Rudolf of Liegnitz and Reichschancellor Otto Freiherr von Nostitz. In August 1639 he was still calling himself "Georgius Greblinger Neoburgo Palatinus Phil. Studiosus" (Georg Greblinger from Neuburg in the Palatinate, Student of Philosophy), but it is unlikely that he was still pursuing any regular studies at a university. In 1640 he was in Vienna, probably on business for the duke of Liegnitz. He spent most of the years 1640 to 1643 in Danzig, East Prussia (today Gdansk, Poland).

Greflinger's earliest surviving publication is a collection of seven poems titled *Weihnacht-Gedancken: Mit angehengtem Newen Jahres wuntsch* (Christmas Thoughts: With Appended New Year's Wish, 1639). In the preface Greflinger justifies the plainness of his poetry, "welche zwar in Reymen, aber ohne alle hoch trabende Wort vnnd schönen Farben verfasset" (which is written in rhyme, but avoids all pompous words and colorful ornamentation), by referring to his modest origins, comparing himself to the shepherds visiting Christ's birthplace. Although the poems are religious, they have a political ring. By underlining Jesus' role as Prince of Peace, Greflinger expresses his desire for a speedy end to the war that had been raging in Germany for more than twenty years.

The same irenic quality can be found in his next work, the epic poem *Querela Germaniae* (German Troubles, 1640). The ninety-four verses deplore the ravished state of war-stricken Germany and mourn the afflictions and deprivations the population has to suffer. The "German Troubles" are also the theme of his next work, another epic poem: *Des jetzigen Deutschlandes erbärmliche Beschaffenheit* (The Present Miserable Condition of Germany, 1643). Its 172 verses express the same mood and political concerns as his previous publication and his *Das klagende Deutschland* (Lamenting Germany, 1644).

From this early period to the last year of his life Greflinger wrote nearly four hundred occasional poems, most of them mourning deaths or celebrating marriages. These poems give a clear indication of his social connections, which consisted mainly of members of the lower gentry and the patriciate, and of his travels to Leipzig, Dresden, Vienna, Thorn, and Danzig. Most occasional poems were written on commission, and these works must have offered Greflinger a welcome source of income. None of his early publications, however, whether religious, historical, or occasional poetry, can have earned him more than a few thalers. In one of his later poems he remembered that in those days he could not live off his poetry and that "weil du entmittelt lebest, Du sehr offt von ihr entkamst / Und den Krieg zur Nahrung nahmst" (because you lived without private means, you often had to flee poetry and earn a living from war), and he hoped that "vielleicht erlange ich durch den Degen, was ich durch die Feder und Küssen niemals erwerben können" (perhaps I shall achieve through the sword what I could never win through my pen or kisses). But it is unclear whether he joined the army. It has been suggested that the "living from war" did not take the form of service pay but was earned by reporting on the battles in newspapers, pamphlets, and broadsheets. This suggestion is given plausibility by the extensive historical knowledge Greflinger displayed in his later chronicles of the Thirty Years' War, the English Civil War, and the Nordic War. It

is also possible that he worked as a Zeitungssänger (singer who reported on current events through the medium of the "rhymed newspaper"). These singers traveled around the country, setting up booths, tables, or benches in the marketplaces of the towns; there they sang or recited their texts and offered them in printed form to those who could read.

In Danzig, Greflinger probably eked out a poor existence as a clerk in a government office or a scribe in a merchant firm; he may also have worked for a newspaper. Whatever his employment may have been, it did not prevent him from pursuing his poetic interests. In his early phase he vacillated between spiritual and historical-political poetry; as his next publications indicate, he also produced a sizable body of Gesellschaftslieder (songs sung at social gatherings and festivities). Many of the melodies were composed by Greflinger; others were set to existing popular tunes. In the seventeenth century the Gesellschaftslied was gradually being replaced by the more-sophisticated Kunstlied (refined compositions for skilled and, often, professional singers), and Greflinger was one of the last great representatives of the Gesellschaftslied. As a country boy who had received only a patchy education, he lacked the classical learning required of an academic poet; he was, however, able to turn this lack of sophistication into his real strength. His low social standing meant that he lived in close contact with the masses, and he was familiar with their folk songs. But he had also received some higher education and had learned the rules of academic poetry. His contacts with the artistic circles of Saxony, Königsberg (today Kaliningrad, Russia), and Danzig brought him up to date with the new poetic developments in Germany, especially the reforms of Opitz. Although Greflinger was strongly influenced by these new trends in baroque poetry, he never became a slavish imitator of any of the great poets of his time; Opitz, for example, clearly was an important model for him, but he never copied Opitz's style. He followed the established patterns and remained more or less faithful to his models, but the variations he offers on well-known themes and topics have an energy and freshness that distinguishes them from the works of the pure epigones of the period.

These characteristics are particularly evident in *Seladons Beständtige Liebe* (Seladon's Constant Love, 1644), comprising some forty poems written between 1639 and 1643; his pseudonym is variously spelled *Seladon* and *Celadon*. Most of the poems have a strongly autobiographical character, and the first part is a rare example for the period of highly personal love poetry. These poems express authentic feelings for a real person, not a Petrarchan allegory of love. The Elisa to whom the poems are written was the daughter of respectable Danzig burghers who were apparently not too pleased about her liaison with a poor peasant's son from Regensburg, and Greflinger's unsteady lifestyle and pleasure-seeking character would not have improved his chances of receiving her parents' consent to the match. Greflinger acknowledges in the poems his delight in "Löffeley" (flirting) and "Sünd- vnd Buhlen Spiel" (sinful love games). But now, having found his beloved Elisa, he has been converted: "Gemeine Dierne suchen, Gassaten-gehen, Fluchen, versauffen Geld vnd Blut was alles köstlich gut" (visiting common whores, night-reveling, swearing, and squandering money and blood have been a great pleasure), but now he wants to quit his old habits. He feels pure love for his Elisa and wants to lead her into the haven of marriage.

The poems provide a great deal of personal information about Greflinger. He describes himself as "eines schlechten Mannes Sohn, / Bey dem kein Reichthumb anzutreffen" (the son of a humble man, / in whose possession no riches can be found) and as "ein Bawer vom Geblüthe" (a peasant by extraction). He often makes reference to his dark complexion and his black hair. This "schwartzer Celadon" (black Celadon) is not an emasculated beauty but a sturdy, healthy man:

> Was ich hab' ist junges Leben,
> Frisches Hertze, freyer Muht,
> Sinne, die nach Ehren streben,
> Bin darbey ein ehrlich Blut:
> Was ich kan, kan Brod erwerben,
> Läßt mich leichtlich nicht verderben.

> (My only possessions are youth,
> A fresh heart, candor,
> Ambition.
> I'm an honest man:
> What I have learned can earn me a living
> And will not easily let me starve.)

In another verse he enlarges on this comment:

> Ich weiß mehr vom Felder pflügen,
> Wie man säet, wie man bricht.
> Was mein Vatter hat getrieben
> Ist auch noch bey mir geblieben.

> (I know how to plow a field,
> How to sow and till the soil.
> What my father practiced

I still know how to do.)

He excuses his lack of education by citing his poverty, which was caused by the war:

> Ich hab' etwas schlecht studirt,
> Weil mir niemals Mittel waren,
> Mars hat all mein Haab entführt

> (I have studied rather poorly,
> Because I never had the means;
> Mars carried off all my property.)

He says that he has not learned any foreign languages and knows nothing of warfare, but these claims might be false modesty: "Viel zu prahlen, viel zu lügen, / Viel zu buhlen weiß ich nicht" (I do not know how to boast a lot, lie a lot, / Or flirt a lot).

In the last poem of *Seladons Beständtige Liebe* the poet is forced by the war to leave his fatherland to preserve life and limb. He wants to return to Danzig on the Baltic shore, where he can lead a more peaceful existence. But, as the second part of the collection, "Seladons Wanckende Liebe" (Seladon's Fickle Love), reveals, his girl has been married off to a rich merchant. His dreams of his goddess are shattered, and he is totally demoralized. To cure his sorrow, he reverts to his old lifestyle:

> Buhlen, Buhlen ist mein Sinn,
> Heute die, die ander morgen,
> Das ist eine Lust vor mich

> (Flirting, flirting is on my mind.
> Today the one, tomorrow another,
> That's how I find my pleasure.)

The rest of the collection consists of Anacreontic verses on his new lovers and his freewheeling life in the taverns. The last section of the book, "Schertz und Ernsthaffte Gedichte" (Joke and Serious Poems) is made up of aphorisms and epigrams on various themes.

The collection was published in Frankfurt am Main, where Greflinger had gone in 1643 – probably in an attempt to secure a position in the publishing or newspaper business. He made valuable contacts there: *Seladons Beständtige Liebe* was published by his friend Eduard Schleich and introduced by the journalist Johann Georg Schleder; the frontispiece was engraved by Sebastian Furck. Johann Naumann, who would publish many of Greflinger's later works in Hamburg, was another acquaintance he made in Frankfurt. In the epilogue to the volume Greflinger remembers their wine-drenched evenings, and the later collection *Seladons Weltliche Lie-der* (Seladon's Worldly Songs, 1651) includes a poem describing how these "Musicanten vnd Poeten, Mahler, Setzer, Kupfferstecher" (musicians and poets, painters, typesetters, engravers) sat together talking, singing, and dancing and how they "recht vertreulich lebten" (lived cordially together).

Greflinger's other publications during his Frankfurt stay were the small volume *Zwey Sapphische Lieder, von der Geburt und von dem Leyden unsers getrewen Heylandes Jesu Christi* (Two Sapphic Odes on the Birth and on the Life of Our True Savior Jesus Christ, 1644) and an odd drama that might have been conceived as an opera libretto, *Ferrando-Dorinde* (1644). Both were published by Schleich, while Johann Ammon in nearby Hanau printed a set of forty poems by Greflinger commenting on the engravings in a 1644 German translation of Benedictus Arias Montanus's *David, virtutis exercitatissimae probatum Deo spectaculum* (The Sorely Afflicted David, 1597).

Returning to Danzig, in 1645 Greflinger published a collection of ninety-eight epigrams revealing his mastery of a genre of which he had already presented specimens in *Seladons Beständtige Liebe*. A paean of 492 alexandrines, "Das blühende Dantzig" (Flowering Danzig), completed in 1646, remained unpublished.

Greflinger's poetic production during his second stay in Danzig was slim. His new patron, Councillor Gregor Cammermann, offered him free board and lodging, but otherwise Greflinger found "daß in dieser Preussner Erden Wenig Glücke vor mich sey" (that this Prussian soil offers little luck for me). He was unable to secure a permanent position and was forced to make a living from his pen. It is not known whether he continued his journalistic activities or simply worked again as a scribe. Most of his publications during his second sojourn in Danzig were written purely for financial gain. One of them was his most popular work, *Ethica Complementoria; Complementier-Büchlein* (A Manual of Good Manners and Polite Conversation, 1645), which ran through no fewer than twenty editions during the author's lifetime. It teaches "wie man recht Maße vnd Weise im Scherzen zu reden und anzuhören halten solle" (the proper way to tell and listen to jokes) and "wie man im complementiren bei Hofe Collegial-Stimmen, Geselschafften, Frauen und Jungfrauen sich gebürlich verhalten musse" (how to converse and behave at court, at official functions, at social occasions, and the proper form of conduct with women and young ladies). Interspersed with the text are aphorisms, poems, songs, and *Leberreime*

(hepatical rhymes – a kind of limerick recited at banquets). Later editions of the book included two parts written by Heinrich Schaeve and Andreas Klette, and a further section of twenty-four rather coarse, if not obscene, poems titled "G. Greflingers N.P. Reimen auff confectscheiben" (The Notary Public Georg Greflinger's Tidbit Verses).

Greflinger is also believed to have written *Cochleatio Novissima* (The Latest Art of Flirting, 1648), a brief treatise on the art of flirting and how to court a young lady. But for stylistic reasons this attribution is extremely doubtful. Similarly, he probably had nothing to do with "Der unterrichtete Student, oder: Academischer Discours zwischen zweyen Freunden Seladon und Damon" (The Educated Student; or, Academic Discourse between Two Friends, Seladon and Damon), which was published in Johann Balthasar Schupp's *Zugab Doct: Ioh: Balth: Schuppii Schrifften* (Supplement to Dr. Johann Balthasar Schupp's Writings, 1667).

Greflinger left Danzig in 1646. Probably in the same year he settled in Hamburg, where he lived for the rest of his life. His first work after moving there was a set of Latin and German poems to accompany a new edition of Jean Jacques Boissard's engravings of figures from the Ottoman Empire, *Wahre Abbildungen der Türckischen Kayser vnd Persischen Fürsten* (True Portraits of the Turkish Emperors and Persian Princes, 1648), originally published in 1596. The book was published by Ammon in Frankfurt. Another set of poems, designed to be recited or sung by children, was published in Hamburg as *Geistliche Liederlein über die jährlichen Evangelien* (Short Hymns on the Yearly Gospels, 1648).

Greflinger's appointment in 1648 as notarius publicus caesareus (imperial notary public) at long last conferred on him an honorable middle-class status, but the income from the office was insufficient for his needs. His financial difficulties increased when he got married around 1650 and had to support a family – in a poem of 1653 he speaks of three others who are living with him. To increase his income he compiled and edited news items for Martin Schumacher's *Wöchentliche Zeitung* and the Thurn und Taxis family's *Europäische Zeitung*. His work as a journalist provided him with the most up-to-date information on the political events in Europe. From 1647 to 1657 he published, in successively enlarged installments, a poetic narrative of the Thirty Years' War, which in its final version runs to 5,030 alexandrines divided into twelve books. An annalistic prose treatment of the same material was published in 1653 as *Kurtze Erzehlung aller vornehmsten Händel* (Brief Report on German Affairs). Subsequent edi-

Title page for one of Greflinger's several works dealing with the Stuart kings of England

tions of this work were considerably enlarged with accounts of the English Civil War, the English-Dutch War of 1652–1653, the Swedish-Polish War of 1655–1656, the Swedish-Danish War of 1657–1658, and the Nordic War of 1658–1660.

More than any other German city, Hamburg was involved in the English Civil War. It supplied weapons to Royalists and Puritans, maintained diplomatic relations with king and Parliament, and offered exile to both parties. Greflinger dealt with the English events not only in his prose chronicle of the various European wars but also in a series of *Zeitungslieder:* an elegy on the death of Charles I (1649), Charles II's song of gratitude after the Battle of Worcester (1651), a dialogue between Charles II and Oliver Cromwell (1651), five epigrams on Charles I and England (1655), a paean on Charles II's entry into London (1660), and an ode on the restoration of the House of Stuart (1660).

A work of historical significance was *Die Sinnreiche Tragi-Comoedia genannt Cid* (The Ingenious Tragicomedy Titled Cid, 1650), Greflinger's translation of Pierre Corneille's *Le Cid* (1636). It is the first German translation of a work by Corneille and

a remarkable attempt at introducing the achievements of French neoclassical drama to the German stage. In a 1651 poem Greflinger says that he could not speak French, Italian, English, or Spanish, but this claim was clearly false. One may also doubt that the *Cid* was written only, as the preface claims, as an "Ubung [um] mier hierdurch die Sprache bekant [zu machen]" (an exercise [to] acquaint myself with the [French] language). It is much more readable and performable than Johann Christoph Gottsched's translation. Greflinger's word formation, although operating on a different stylistic level, captures the meaning of Corneille's text and makes the speeches sound German without too much coaxing. The text is, however, as Greflinger points out, only a shadow of Corneille's masterpiece and captures "mehr aber den Verstand als die Worte" (the meaning more than the words). A paraphrase rather than a literal translation, it takes considerable liberties with Corneille's sophisticated range of expression. The original's elegance of style is largely lost, and the courtly tone of conversation is often rendered in an idiom that belongs to the lower strata of society. But Greflinger made a skillful attempt at translating Corneille's alexandrines, and he remained quite close to French metric and prosodic patterns. On the whole, the work compares favorably with other translations of the period.

Another adaptation of a foreign drama, *Verwirrter Hof oder König Carl* (The Confused Court; or, King Charles, 1652), is a prose version of a Spanish play, *El palacio confuso* (1634), which Greflinger read in the 1647 Dutch translation by Leonard de Fuyter. In the Dutch edition the text is ascribed to Lope de Vega, but the real author was Antonio Mira de Amescua. The theme of the play is quite typical of the period: a person stands in as a double for the king, creating confusion at court. But what must have attracted Greflinger to the work was its political topicality: it deals with the conflict between the king and the estates; the absolutist tendencies of the early modern state versus the privileges of the old aristocracy; the rivalry between old and new nobility; and the question of who is more qualified to hold state offices, the professional, bourgeois civil servant or the privileged member of the aristocracy.

The next original work by Greflinger, and his second important collection of poems, was *Seladons Weltliche Lieder;* it was published in 1651 on the occasion of a visit to Frankfurt, where he met his friend and fellow journalist Schleder again. In the preface Greflinger speaks of himself with his usual modesty as "nur ein Liebhaber der Poeterey vnd kein Poet" (only a lover of poetry, not a poet). He says that he publishes these songs and poems only because friends have asked him to do so and because they are covering the printing costs. As to his artistic credo, he says:

> Belangend die Art zu schreiben, so kehre ich mich an das newe nicht groß, weil sich die meisten nit daran kehren vnd vor auß meine Oberländer, wir sind so von den Alten, und nicht *à la modo* Teutschen. Was ich aber für thunlich erachte, dem folge ich sehr gerne. Allem neuen nach zu ahnen, dienet nicht, weil ich es noch ohne Grund vnd sehr wetterwendisch sehe.

> (Concerning the art of writing, I do not care a great deal about the modern fashion. Others do not either, especially my South Germans, who, like me, belong to the old-fashioned and not the fashionable Germans. I like to abide by what I regard as expedient. Imitating everything that is new is, in my view, pointless, unsound, and capricious.)

The volume comprises four dozen songs, printed with their melodies; 191 epigrams; and twelve occasional poems. In contrast to *Seladons Beständtige Liebe,* most of the songs and poems in this collection are Übungs-Stücke (exercises) in the current poetic genres, not expressions of Greflinger's personal feelings – for example, "Hylas wil kein Weib nicht haben" (Hylas Will Have No Wife) puts forth a series of arguments against marriage, only to be followed by a "Wider-Ruff" (Recantation) that presents arguments against uncommitted lovemaking. The only exceptions are a couple of poems dealing with Flora's (that is, Elisa's) unfaithfulness, and they are to some extent neutralized by other poems dealing with the inconstancy of women in general. Favorite topics of the other poems are the conventional "Venus Sachen" (love matters), feasting, drinking, and dancing. Some of them had already been published in *Seladons Beständtige Liebe,* but they have been polished and rewritten. The love poems include many references to the Petrarchan and Anacreontic traditions, but they do not depict an imaginary pastoral world. Although he calls his protagonists Hylas, Dorinde, Phyllis, and Amynthas, they are realistic characters from an actual, recognizable world that Greflinger has observed and seeks to capture in a heightened poetic fashion.

In 1654 Greflinger was crowned poet laureate; the *carmen gratulatorium* (congratulatory song) on the event was reprinted in Greflinger's third major collection of poems, *Poetische Rosen und Dörner, Hülsen und Körner* (Poetic Roses and Thorns, Husks and Grains, 1655). The volume includes fifty-three songs, 240 epigrams, and a few highly personal poems that offer some information about his life in Hamburg. Despite his highly reputable position as *Notarius,* he says, his financial situation has not markedly improved. He describes his lifestyle as modest, but he appears to be happy with his lot. He mistrusts his fellow citizens who pretend to be Croesuses but probably have more debts than he has. He derives great satisfaction from his marriage and from seeing his daughters grow up. He does not begrudge others the fortunes they have inherited from their parents:

> Aber viel durch Müh erwerben,
> Acht' ich auch nicht gar gering. . . .
> Es gereichet mehr zu Ehren,
> Nichts gewesen seyn und dann
> Sich mit seinen Jahren mehren. . . .
> Was ich hab', hat GOttes Gnade,
> Und mein Schweiß mir zugelenckt,
> Was ich hab ist keines Schade,
> Niemand hat mir was geschenckt.

> (But I don't consider it a mean thing
> To acquire riches through one's hard work. . . .
> It is more honorable

To have been a nobody and
To have grown in prosperity over the years. . . .
What I have is due to God's grace
And my own sweat and toil.
What I own has not been to the detriment or harm of
    someone else.
No one gave me anything.)

To improve his financial position, Greflinger began to translate books that were not, like the *Cid,* the *Palacio confuso,* or his friend Johann Ulrich Strauß's *Distichorum Centuria prima et secunda* (First and Second Collection of One Hundred Distichs, 1654), works of artistic merit, but treatises on rather mundane topics. The first was a publication appropriate to his situation: an anonymous French treatise on accounting and how to become rich quickly, *Schatz über Schatz* (Treasury on Wealth, 1655). It was followed by translations of a popular Dutch handbook on gardening, Pieter van Ængelen's *Der verständige Gärtner* (The Knowledgeable Gardener, 1655); Cesare Ripa's *Iconologia* (1659); two short novels by Paul Scarron, *Von der unnötigen Vorsorge vor Kluges Frauenvolck* (Of Taking Unnecessary Precautions against Intelligent Womenfolk, 1660) and *Der unschuldige Ehebruch* (The Innocent Adultery, 1662); and several immensely popular handbooks by Nicolas de Bonnefons, *Der Frantzösische Baum- und Stauden-Gärtner* (The French Tree and Bush Gardener, 1663), *Der Frantzösische Küchen-Gärtner* (The French Vegetable Gardener, 1664), *Der Frantzösische Becker* (The French Baker, 1665), *Der Frantzösische Confitirier* (The French Confectioner, 1665), and *Der Frantzösische Koch* (The French Cook, 1665). For the Hamburg city council he translated the city's statutes and treaties from Low Saxon into High German (1667).

In 1663 Greflinger – who by then had been admitted into Johann Rist's literary society, the Elbschwanenorden (Order of Elbe Swans), founded in 1660 – published the last and definitive edition of his poetry, *Celadonische Musa* (Celadonic Muse), which included, with a few exceptions, only poems and epigrams that had already appeared in his earlier collections. A year later he started his own newspaper, the *Nordischer Mercurius,* which continued until well after his death; it was edited by his son Friedrich Conrad Greflinger until 1698.

In 1664 Greflinger was granted the citizenship of the Free City of Hamburg and could buy a house in the Große Neumarkt. The poor, orphaned peasant from South Germany had achieved what he could hardly have expected in his youth: he had become a respected man of solid middle-class status. His toil had been rewarded, but it had aged him pre-

maturely. In a poem of 1654 he had mentioned his gray hair, and in 1665, though he was only in his forties, he described himself as an elderly man. But retiring from his office was out of the question: the status he had achieved carried no financial rewards. In 1676, the year before his death, he was still so poor that he could not afford to offer the newly elected mayor the customary gift; a poem had to do. His last occasional poems indicate that his health was rapidly declining after 1675. But he never lost his sense of humor. On his deathbed he could still write verses such as:

Ich alter krancker Mann!
Mir bitet mein Herr Artzt kein Römrichen nicht an!
Verbitet mir dazu das Kühl-Bier von der Weser.
Ich fasse bald den Muth und lasse mir was holen!
Was Krafft kan endlich mehr vor alte Leuty seyn,
Bey aller Artzeney, als ein recht edler Wein?

(I'm an old and sick man!
My doctor does not offer me a glass of hock!
And forbids me the cooled beer from the Weser.
But soon I'll take courage and have some brought up
    to my bed!
What has a better effect on old folks,
Among all the medicines in the world, than a fine and noble
    wine?)

Greflinger died in 1677; the exact date is not known.

Bibliographies:
Johann Moller, *Cymbria Literata* (Copenhagen: Kisel, 1744), pp. 245–246;

Hans Schröder, *Lexikon der hamburgischen Schriftsteller* (Hamburg: Perthes-Besser & Mauke, 1854), pp. 579–582;

Karl Goedecke, *Grundriß zur Geschichte der deutschen Literatur aus den Quellen,* volume 3 (Dresden: Ehlermann, 1887), pp. 87–90;

Walter Raschke, *Der Danziger Dichterkreis im 17. Jahrhunderts* (Rostock: Wintersberg, 1921);

Elger Blühm, "Neues über Greflinger," *Euphorion,* 58, no. 1 (1964): 74–97;

Franz Heiduck, "Georg Greflinger: Neue Daten zu Leben und Werk," *Daphnis: Zeitschrift für Mittlere Deutsche Literatur,* 9, no. 1–2 (1980): 191–197;

Gerhard Dünnhaupt, *Personalbibliographien zu den Drucken des Barock,* volume 9, part 3 (Stuttgart: Hiersemann, 1991), pp. 1680–1751.

References:
Günter Berghaus, "Georg Greflinger als Journalist und historisch-politischer Schriftsteller,"

Wolfenbütteler Barock-Nachrichten, 12 (1985): 1–14;

Johannes Bolte, "Verdeutschungen von J. Cats' Werken," *Tijdschrift voor Nederlandsche taal- en letterkunde,* 16 (1897): 245–251;

Bolte, "Zu Georg Greflinger," *Anzeiger für deutsches Alterthum,* 13 (1887): 103–114;

Russel Weldon Godwin, "Greflinger and van Heemskerck: A Comparative Exegesis of the Earliest German and Dutch Translations of Corneille's 'Le Cid,'" dissertation, Tulane University, 1974;

Otto Friedrich Gruppe, *Leben und Werke deutscher Dichter,* volume 1 (Leipzig: Brandstetter, 1872), pp. 264–311, 680–688, 740–744;

Lutz Mackensen, "Die Entdeckung des Insul Pines: Zu Georg Greflinger und seinem 'Nordischen Mercurius,'" *Mitteilungen aus der deutschen Presseforschung zu Bremen,* 1 (1960): 7–47;

L. Neubaur, "Georg Greflinger: Eine Nachlese," *Altpreußische Monatsschrift,* new series 27 (1890): 476–503;

Wolfgang von Oettingen, *Über Georg Greflinger von Regensburg als Dichter, Historiker und Übersetzer* (Strasbourg: Trübner, 1882);

Klaus Reichelt, *Barockdrama und Absolutismus* (Frankfurt am Main: Lang, 1982), pp. 284–297;

Claudia Sedlarz, "*Der Beitrag Georg Greflingers zur Rezeption von Ripas "Iconologia" in Deutschland,*" dissertation, University of Munich, 1989;

Theo Stemmler, ed., *Schöne Frauen – Schöne Männer: Literarische Schönheitsbeschreibungen,* (Tübingen: Narr, 1988), 199–246;

C. Walther, "Georg Greflingers Hamburgisches Reisehandbuch und Beschreibung von Hamburg im Jahre 1674," *Zeitschrift des Vereins für Hamburgische Geschichte,* 9 (1894): 122–149;

Walther, "Rezension zu Wolfgang von Oettingen, *Über Georg Greflinger,*" *Anzeiger für deutsches Alterthum,* 10 (1884): 73–127;

Theodor Weever, "Bredero's liedboek en de liederen van Georg Greflinger," in *Album Prof. Dr. Frank Bau,* volume 2 (Antwerp: Standart-Boeckhandel, 1948), pp. 347–360;

Jutta Weisz, *Das deutsche Epigramm des 17. Jahrhunderts* (Stuttgart: Metzler, 1979).

Papers:

The manuscripts for Georg Greflinger's *Gedancken von der Geburt Christi aufgesetzt von Georg Greblinger aus Regenspurg anno 1645* and *Das blühende Dantzig aufgesetzt von Georg Greflinger aus Regenspurg anno 1646* are in the Biblioteka Gdanska Polskiej Akademii Nauk, Gdansk.

Andreas Gryphius

(2 October 1616 – 16 July 1664)

Blake Lee Spahr
University of California at Berkeley

BOOKS: *Herodis Furiae, et Rachelis lachrymae* (Glogau: Wigand Funck, 1634);

Dei Vindicis Impetus et Herodis Interitus (Danzig: Georg Rhete II, 1635);

Parnassus . . . virtute . . . domini G. Schönborneri a Schönborn . . . renovatus (Danzig: Georg Rhete II, 1636);

Sonnete (Lissa: Wigand Funck, 1637);

Fewrige Freystadt (Lissa: Wigand Funck, 1637);

Brunnen Discurs bey dem hochkläglichen Leichbegängnuß, des WolEdlen, Gestrengen Hoch vnd großachtbaren Herrn George Schönborners (Danzig, 1638?);

Son- undt Freyrtags-Sonnete (Leiden: Bonaventura & Abraham Elzevier, 1639);

Sonnete: Das erste Buch (Leiden, 1643);

Oden: Das erste Buch (Leiden, 1643);

Epigrammata: Das erste Buch (Leiden: Frans Heger, 1643);

Epigrammatum Liber I (Leiden, 1643);

Olivetum Libri tres (Florence, 1646; revised edition, Lissa: Daniel Vetter, 1648);

Teutsche Reim-Gedichte Darein enthalten I. Ein Fürsten-Mörderisches Trawer-Spiel, genant. Leo Armenius. II. Zwey Bücher seiner Oden. III. Drey Bücher der Sonnetten denen zum Schluß die Geistvolle Opitianische Gedancken von der Ewigkeit hinbey gesetzet seyn (Frankfurt am Main: Johann Hüttner, 1650);

Thränen über das Leiden Jesu Christi (N.p., 1652);

Deutscher Gedichte, Erster Theil, 10 volumes (Breslau: Johann Lischke, 1657) – comprises volume 1, *Leo Armenius, oder Fürsten-Mord: Trauerspiel;* volume 2, *Catharina von Georgien. Oder Bewehrte Beständigkeit: Trauerspiel;* volume 3, *Ermordete Majestät. Oder Carolus Stuardus König von Großbrittannien: Trauer-Spiel;* volume 4, Nicolaus Caussinus, *Beständige Mutter, oder Die Heilige Felicitas. Aus dem Lateinischen Nicolai Causini übersetztes Trauer-Spiel,* translated and adapted by Gryphius; volume 5, *Cardenio vnd Celinde, oder Unglücklich Verliebete: Trauer-Spiel;* volume 6, *Majuma, Freuden-Spiel. Auff dem Schauplatz Gesangsweise vorgestellet;* volume 7,

Andreas Gryphius; engraving by Philipp Kilian

Kirchhoffs-Gedancken; volume 8, *Oden;* volume 9, *Thränen über das Leiden Jesu Christi. Oder seiner Oden, Das Vierdte Buch;* volume 10, *Sonette;*

Absurda Comica. Oder Herr Peter Squentz, Schimpff-Spiel (Breslau: Veit Jacob Trescher, 1658);

Freuden und Trauer-Spiele auch Oden und Sonnette samt Herr Peter Squentz Schimpff-Spiel (Breslau: Johann Lischke & Veit Jacob Trescher, 1658);

Großmüttiger Rechts-Gelehrter, oder Sterbender Aemilius Paulus Papinianus (Breslau: Georg Baumann's heirs, 1659);

Letztes Ehren-Gedächtnüß der Hoch-Edelgebohrnen Hoch-Tugend-Zucht und Ehrenreichen Jungfrawen

Jungfr. Marianen von Popschitz aus dem hause Crantz auff Gröditz v.d.g. welche den Tag vor Himmelfahrt, des Erlösers der Welt jn dem XV. Tag des Mey Monats, des M D CLX. Jahres seeligst die Welt gesegnet (Steinau an der Oder: Printed by Johann Kuntze, 1660);

Verlibtes Gespenste, Gesang-Spiel (Breslau: Georg Baumann's heirs, 1660); enlarged as *Verlibtes Gespenste, Gesang-Spil. Die gelibte Dornrose, Schertz-Spill* (Breslau: Jesaias Fellgiebel, 1661);

Mumiae Wratislavienses (Breslau: Veit Jacob Trescher, 1662);

Freuden vnd Trauer-Spiele, auch Oden vnd Sonette (Breslau: Veit Jacob Trescher, 1663);

Epigrammata oder Bey-Schriften (Jena: Veit Jacob Trescher, 1663);

Horribilicribrifax Teutsch (Breslau: Veit Jacob Trescher, 1663);

Dissertationes Funebres, oder Leich-Abdanckungen, bey vnterschiedlichen hoch- und ansehnlichen Leich-Begängnüssen gehalten. Auch nebenst seinem letzten Ehren-Gadächtnüß und Lebens-Lauff (Breslau: Veit Jacob Trescher, 1666);

Teutsche Gedichte, edited by Christian Gryphius (Breslau: Jesaias Fellgiebel's heirs, 1698).

Editions and Collections: *Andreas Gryphius: Werke,* 3 volumes, edited by Hermann Palm, Bibliothek des literarischen Vereins Stuttgart, volumes 138, 162, 171 (Tübingen: Hiersemann, 1878–1884); republished as *Andreas Gryphius: Werke in drei Bänden mit Ergänzungsband,* 4 volumes, edited by Friedrich-Wilhelm Wentzlaff-Eggebert (Darmstadt: Wissenschaftliche Buchgesellschaft, 1961);

Cardenio und Celinde, edited by Hugh Powell (Leicester, U.K.: Leicester University Press, 1961);

Carolus Stuardus, edited by Powell (Leicester, U.K.: Leicester University Press, 1963);

Verliebtes Gespenst; Die Geliebte Dornrose, edited by Eberhard Mannack, Komedia: Deutsche Lustspiele vom Barock bis zur Gegenwart, no. 4 (Berlin: De Gruyter, 1963);

Andreas Gryphius: Gesamtausgabe der deutschsprachigen Werke, 12 volumes published, edited by Powell, Marian Szyrocki, Karl-Heinz Habersetzer, and others (Tübingen: Niemeyer, 1963–);

Leo Armenius: Trauerspiel, edited by P. Rusterholz, Reclams Universal-Bibliothek, no. 7960 (Stuttgart: Reclam, 1971);

Horribilicribrifax Teutsch: Scherzspiel, edited by Gerhard Dünnhaupt, Reclams Universal-Bibliothek, no. 688 [2] (Stuttgart: Reclam, 1976);

Absurda Comica. Oder Herr Peter Squentz, edited by Dünnhaupt and Habersetzer, Reclams Universal-Bibliothek, no. 7982 (Stuttgart: Reclam, 1983);

Gebroeders. Die Gibeoniter. Die Rache zu Gibeon, edited by Egbert Krispyn, Nachdrucke deutscher Literatur des 17. Jahrhunderts, volume 28 (Bern: Peter Lang, 1987).

OTHER: *Glogauisches Fürstenthumbs Landes Privilegia aus denn Originalen an tag gegeben,* edited by Gryphius (Lissa: Wigand Funck, 1653);

Andreæ Gryphii Ubersetzte Lob-Gesänge, oder Kirchen-Lieder, translated by Gryphius (Breslau: Georg Baumann's heirs, 1660);

Thomas Corneille, *Der Schwermende Schäfer Lysis,* translated by Gryphius (Brieg: Christoff Tschorn, 1661);

Girolamo Razzi, *Seugamme oder Untreues Haußgesinde. Lust-Spiel,* adapted by Gryphius (Jena: Veit Jacob Trescher, 1663);

Sir Richard Baker, *Frag-Stück und Betrachtungen über das Gebet des Herren,* translated by Gryphius (Leipzig: Veit Jacob Trescher, 1663);

Josua Stegmann, *Himmel Steigente HertzensSeüfftzer ubersehen und mit newen Reimen gezieret,* edited by Gryphius (Breslau: Veit Jacob Trescher, 1665).

Andreas Gryphius was the greatest lyric poet, as well as the greatest dramatist, of seventeenth-century Germany. In lyric poetry his voice is the voice of the century. He gives unforgettable utterance to the horrors of the Thirty Years' War, during which he grew up; to the fears of the plague, which raged throughout Germany during his lifetime; and to the personal uncertainty of a tortured soul held fast by the fetters of a strict Protestant faith while witnessing the miracles of the new scientific discoveries in which he participated. On the other hand, his dramas are not dramatic but are based on the rhetorical principles that dominated the form of the baroque drama. At the same time, he is a trailblazer, one of the first in his country to compose stage productions in the vernacular that are playable and can still be appreciated today in spite of their often ponderous language and lack of dramatic qualities. In his own day his dramatic prowess far outweighed, in the public eye, his reputation as a lyric poet; in fact, he was hailed as the greatest dramatist in the history of his country, as the "German Sophocles." His tragedies provided ample opportunity for his natural penchant for staid, dignified (today one might say bombastic)

Title page, frontispiece, and two illustrations from a funeral oration by Gryphius, published in 1660

language, while his comedies, though rather unsophisticated, are amusing. He is one of the few baroque poets whose reputation did not suffer oblivion in the ensuing period. Although he is no longer on a pedestal, even a dusty one, his image has been paid that obscure respect afforded venerable but rarely read pioneers. This situation persisted until the middle of the nineteenth century, when the literary historian Georg Gervinus characterized him as the high point of German literature of the seventeenth century. From that time on, scholarly interest has grown.

Gryphius's life is a catalogue of misfortune punctuated by intervals of patronage, accomplishment, and recognition. He was born on 2 October 1616 to the fifty-six-year-old Lutheran archdeacon of Glogau in Silesia, Paul Gryphius, and his third wife, Anna, née Erhard, who was thirty-two years younger than her husband. (Both 29 September and 11 October are listed in the secondary literature as the birth date of the poet. The first of these erroneous dates stems from a sonnet in which Gryphius moved his birthday forward three days, presumably so that it might coincide with the feast of the archangel Michael; the second may be attributed to a misreading of the Roman numeral II.) During this time Silesia was a hotbed of religious strife, and Glogau was particularly affected. Nominally in the hands of the Roman Catholics, who were supported by the emperor, the town was populated by a majority of Lutherans, and there were constant altercations between the two camps. As archdeacon, Gryphius's father must have played a leading role in the disturbances.

On 5 January 1621 Paul Gryphius died unexpectedly. Twenty years later the poet said in a sonnet that the cause of death had been poison administered by a false friend, but it has been assumed that this was poetic hyperbole to intimate that the staunch old Lutheran archdeacon had been betrayed by a supposed ally and had been so perturbed that he died of a heart attack. The circumstances might bear out this theory: Friedrich V von der Pfalz (of the Palatinate), the so-called Winter King, on his retreat after his defeat in the decisive Battle of the White Mountain, spent the night of 4 January 1621 in Glogau. The next day the king, a Calvinist, stripped the Lutheran church of its silver treasures and continued his march. One may well imagine that the archdeacon might have been driven to death's door by this action, although his tombstone claims that the cause of death was "catharrho, proh! suffocativo extinctus" (a pulmonary disorder resulting from a cold).

Two months after his father's death Gryphius entered the school in Glogau; a year later Gryphius's mother married one of the teachers there, Michael Eder. In 1622 some eight thousand mercenaries passed through the city, while others were quartered in and about the area. The military atrocities that were normal for this period added to the financial ills of the city, which was only slowly recovering from a fire that had destroyed much of it in 1616. In 1628 Gryphius's mother died of tuberculosis. That year a dispute over the repossession of the Lutheran church by the Catholics caused the city to be occupied by the infamous Lichtensteiner dragoons, who forcefully converted some six thousand Protestants and drove the rest, including Gryphius's stepfather, to take refuge across the Polish border.

The Catholics demanded that all boys under the age of fifteen and all girls under the age of thirteen remain in the city, along with any inheritance due them. Gryphius was able to join his stepfather a few months later in Driebitz. Since the town lacked an adequate school, Eder tutored Gryphius at home. In 1629 Eder married the eighteen-year-old Maria Rissmann, daughter of a prominent judge. She bore him six children, but all died or were born dead. She seems to have been drawn ever closer to Gryphius, who was only a little more than four years younger than she. It is possibly through her love of music and literature that Gryphius gained his inclination to the arts, while his erudition certainly had its roots in the teaching of Eder.

In 1631 Gryphius traveled to Görlitz, where he hoped to enter the gymnasium, but, perhaps because of the threat of nearby troop movements, he retreated to Rückersdorf, where his elder brother, Paul, was pastor. For unknown reasons he soon returned to Glogau, where another tremendous fire broke out and reduced the city to a mere sixty houses. On the heels of the fire came the plague, which claimed fifty victims a day. Gryphius fled to his brother's house, where he spent the summer immersed in Latin studies.

At this time Eder acquired the position of pastor in the Polish town of Fraustadt, and Gryphius enrolled in the school there in 1632. Fraustadt and neighboring Lissa offered a haven for Silesian Protestants driven from their homes by the Catholics, who were becoming ever more powerful. Gryphius rapidly acquired a reputation as a brilliant student, a powerful and convincing orator, and an actor, winning a competition for a principal role in a Latin drama.

In 1634 his first published work appeared: *Herodis Furiae, et Rachelis lachrymae* (Herod's Rage and Rachel's Tears), the first part of an epic on the birth and passion of Christ. The second part, *Dei Vindicis Impetus et Herodis Interitus* (The Attack of God the Avenger and the Death of Herod), was published in Danzig (today Gdansk, Poland) the following year. Part 1, begun in 1633, shows the influence of Gryphius's Latin schooling. It is almost a cento, borrowing extensively from other authors – especially Virgil, from whom whole sentences are taken. In staid yet vivid Latin hexameters it tells of the bloodbath when Herod slaughtered the innocent children at the birth of Christ. That in the year of the poem's composition the plague carried off more than eighteen thousand innocent inhabitants of Breslau (today Wrocław, Poland) may have influenced Gryphius. The work opens in hell, where the news of Christ's birth has been announced. The devils confer among themselves, and Beelzebub claims that Herod is the antithesis of the Savior. The slaughter takes place, and the piece ends with Herod and the forces of hell triumphant. A magnificent litany, the lament of Rachel over her lost children, concludes part 1.

Gryphius created in his first work a prototype that would follow him throughout his career. His favorite genre is the martyr drama, which combines the Stoic and Christian attitudes and in which the constancy of the victim is opposed to the supreme evil of the tyrant, the passive resistance of the hero to the active malevolence of the persecutor. Herod is the baroque tyrant par excellence, a personification of evil into whom hell itself has entered. If the first part of the epic shows this villain in triumph, then the second must portray his downfall. Borrowing from the Jewish historian Josephus Flavius, Gryphius gives a picture of the dying Herod, a depiction that has been characterized as the most lurid of this period. Herod lies in bed, his head dripping with pus and blood, his decaying flesh melting away from his bones, exposing his vitals, as he fondles the severed head of his murdered son, Hyrcan, whom he mocks by summoning him to take revenge for his murder by devouring his father's flowing intestines.

What is remarkable in this early work is not Gryphius's mastery of Latin – which is, however, amply demonstrated – but his use of the language to a vivid dramatic end and his portrayal of one of the most impressive baroque villains of the age. His technique has been formed. He uses the baroque antithesis as a schematic device for descriptions, portrayal, and structure. His rhetorical flow of language is evident in the litany of Rachel, and all of the baroque devices, so typical of the age, are em-

ployed with consummate skill by the sixteen-year-old poet.

In May 1634 Gryphius entered the academic high school in Danzig, a trade center that was one of the richest and most significant cities in Europe. He supported himself by tutoring. *Parnassus . . . renovatus* (Parnassus Renewed), a rather pedestrian Latin panegyric to the political scientist Georg Schönborner, whom Gryphius had probably met while visiting his brother, Paul, in Freistadt, appeared in 1636.

After a severe illness, the nature of which has not been determined, Gryphius returned to Fraustadt in 1636. On the way he apparently fell from the stagecoach and was disabled for a time; but, presumably in August of the same year, he went on to Schönborner's estate near Freistadt, where he had been summoned as tutor to Schönborner's sons. Apparently the rich and influential Schönborner regarded Gryphius almost as an adopted son. He shared his extensive library with Gryphius and involved him in frequent discussions of political theory. On the appearance of Gryphius's *Sonnete* (Sonnets) in 1637 Schönborner, exercising his rights as Kaiserlicher Pfalzgraf (imperial count palatine), conferred on his protégé the title of master of philosophy, which implied the *venia legendi* (right to lecture at a university), and had his fourteen-year-old daughter, Elisabeth, crown the young man as poet laureate. Gryphius was undoubtedly in love with Elisabeth, and she is probably the "Eugenia" to whom he addressed several love poems. (The Greek etymology of this covert designation yields, in German, *schöngeboren* [born beautiful].) It is possible that this love affair was what motivated her father, visualizing a future match between his daughter and his favorite, to raise Gryphius to the ranks of the nobility – a distinction of which Gryphius never made use. During this period a bitter blow for the young poet was the death of his stepmother, for whom he seems to have had greater affection than for his real mother. His poem in her memory rings with sincerity.

The *Sonnete,* generally known as the *Lissaer Sonettbuch* (Lissa Sonnet Book), is a collection of thirty-one poems that includes some of Gryphius's best-known sonnets. He would revise and polish the poems through later editions; most of the changes seem to have been dictated by the new fashion of qualitative meter and by the observance of the strict prescriptive rules that had been introduced by the young poet and theoretician Martin Opitz, whose influential *Buch von der Deutschen Poeterey* (Book of German Poetry, 1624) was to become Gryphius's manual for the writing of verse throughout his life.

Twenty-nine of the sonnets are repeated in succeeding editions, and there are few changes for the better. Among the best known of the poems is "Vanitas, Vanitatum . . . ," dealing with the ills of the war and the transitoriness of human existence, a favorite theme that is also evident in "Menschliches Elende" (Human Misery) and "Trawrklage des verwüsteten Deutschlandes" (Lament of Devastated Germany). There are eulogies of friends, patrons, teachers, and relatives, as well as epigrammatic castigations of probable real-life subjects. The collection demonstrates, both in language and form, the consummate skill of the poet.

Shortly after the appearance of the volume fire destroyed virtually the entire city of Freistadt. Gryphius commemorated the event in a long poem, *Fewrige Freystadt* (Fiery Freistadt), which appeared as a pamphlet in 1637. In the same year his patron, yielding to a short illness, died in his arms. Gryphius wrote a moving funeral sermon, the *Brunnen Discurs* (Discourse at the Fountain), which was published the following year.

Accompanied by Schönborner's two sons, Gryphius went to Leiden to study law. The University of Leiden was one of the most illustrious in Europe: René Descartes was lecturing in philosophy, as was Justus Lipsius, who was renowned also for his studies in classical philology. Gryphius struck up a close acquaintance with the humanists Daniel Heinsius and Claudius Salmasius (Claude de Saumaise) and associated with his countryman Christian Hoffmann von Hoffmannswaldau, one of the celebrated poets of the century, a lifelong friend whom he had first met in Danzig. He also came into contact with various members of the ruling house of the Palatinate, a connection that was to stand him in good stead in the future. His acquaintance with the works of the leading Dutch dramatists, Joost von den Vondel, Pieter Hooft, and Gerbrand Bredero, was to be important for his later dramatic production. Gryphius's studies ranged from law, through philosophy, rhetoric, and medicine, to mathematics, while the lectures he gave, possibly as private tutorials, cover the fields of astronomy, geography, metaphysics, physiognomy, trigonometry, and even chiromancy. But he also experienced an illness so severe that the doctors gave him up for lost.

In 1639 Gryphius published *Son- undt Freyrtags-Sonnete* (Sonnets for Sundays and Holidays), a collection of one hundred sonnets: one or more for each Sunday of the church year – sixty-five in all – and one for each of the thirty-five church holidays. This second sizable collection of poems, although highly rhetorical in style, demonstrates the skill and facility Gryphius had acquired in the writing of verse. Bound by the rigid sonnet form and restricted to the religious themes of the pericopes, the poems nonetheless flow freely and show little or no sign of constraint.

In 1643 the earlier sonnet book, thoroughly revised and increased by nineteen sonnets, was republished; two of the former sonnets were omitted. Some of the revisions show a distinct improvement, while other poems are polished at the expense of their freshness. Gryphius contributed to the development of the ode by employing the Pindaric form for religious purposes; previously it had been almost exclusively used for encomiums. A collection of one hundred German epigrams and one of sixty-eight Latin epigrams also appeared in 1643. The epigrams are undoubtedly the most inferior of all Gryphius's verses. The petty and often vindictive use to which they are put gives evidence of a spitefulness that was all too common in the age.

During Gryphius's stay in Leiden the Netherlands' greatest dramatist, Vondel, wrote *De Gebroeders* (The Brothers); it premiered in 1641. Gryphius translated the work into German as *Die sieben Brüder, oder Die Gibeoniter* (The Seven Brothers; or, The Gibeonites). He probably did so toward the end of his stay in Leiden, for his mastery of Dutch is quite impressive; but, like many of Gryphius's works, the translation was not published until many years later – in this case, in a posthumous edition of 1698. Gryphius may well have been present at the premiere of Vondel's play, for he adds stage directions that seem to have been derived from an actual production. The source of the play is the biblical account in 2 Sam. 21:1–14 of David's revenge on Saul's children for Saul's treatment of the Gibeonites. Gryphius has tried to remain as close to the Dutch original as possible, and there are many examples of a too-literal rendition. There are also, however, instances where he has added descriptive adjectives or expanded the sentence structure; a prologue and an epilogue have also been added. (Christian Gryphius, the poet's son, mentioned that his father had, at some unspecified date, completed an original drama, *Die Gibeoniter,* as far as the fifth act.)

Two more translations may have been completed in Leiden, although they were both published much later. In 1634 Gryphius acquired a collection of Latin dramas by the Jesuit Nicolaus Caussinus, father confessor to Louis XII. In this collection is the story of the martyr Saint Felicity, a tale filled with the most grisly descriptions of tortures and dismemberment, a reflection of which would later appear in Gryphius's *Catharina von Georgien. Oder Bewehrte Beständigkeit* (Catharine of Georgia; or, Constancy Maintained, 1657). The poet translated the drama from Latin under the title *Beständige Mutter, oder Die Heilige Felicitas* (The Constant Mother; or, Saint Felicity). Scholars differ greatly in assigning a date to this composition; in any case, it did not appear until 1657, and it was produced by students eight times in the following year in Breslau. While Gryphius's translation of Vondel's work was faithful to the original, this translation strays far enough from its source to be termed a re-creation. There is not really an alteration in substance, but there is certainly a change of emphasis and a stylization. The rather cool and staid humanist Latin yields to the exaggerated, dynamic style of the German baroque.

The other translation is of the Italian comedy *La Balia* (The Nursemaid), by the Florentine Renaissance writer Girolamo Razzi. Although the translation would appear only in the collected edition of 1663, Gryphius mentions that he had begun it in his early youth. *Seugamme oder Untreues Hausgesinde* (The Wet Nurse; or, Unfaithful Servants) is a completely faithful translation into German prose. The plot is complex, including a supposed incest that turns out to be a spoof. The many devices of the commedia dell'arte are all present, culminating in a happy ending consisting of a series of marriages. Gryphius prefixes the translation with a stodgy prologue in which he claims that the immorality of the times reminded him of this *comédie des mœurs,* but this statement seems to be an attempt to justify translating a work containing such libertinage rather than an explanation of his motivation for doing so. The play affords convincing evidence that Gryphius, in addition to French, Dutch, and Latin, was also adept in Italian.

The poet remained in Leiden until June 1644, when he departed for the tour of France and Italy that was part of the education of all well-brought-up young noblemen of the day. As to the source of his finances for the journey, one may assume that he was a paid traveling companion to Wilhelm Schlegel, son of a well-to-do Pomeranian merchant, and four young noblemen who had become his friends as well as his charges. Details of his trip are sparse. He was in Paris in July, where he visited the legal authority Hugo Grotius and where he was particularly interested in the extensive library of the late Cardinal Richelieu. From Paris he traveled via Angers to Marseilles and then to Florence, where he viewed the art collection of the grand duke; in 1646 he arrived in Rome, where he met the well-known Jesuit writer and scholar Athanasius Kircher. He probably came into closer contact with the commedia dell'arte and the Italian opera, evidence of both of which is to be found in his works.

His return led through Florence, Bologna, and Ferrara to Venice, where he presented his second Latin epic, *Olivetum* (The Mount of Olives, 1646), to the republic of Venice. The first edition was printed in Florence; a second, slightly revised, followed in 1648. It, too, was dedicated to Venice but also to the prince elector of Brandenburg, Friedrich Wilhelm, and to his cousin the Countess Palatine Elisabeth, daughter of the Winter King. There is doubt about the date of its composition, but the earliest date that has been suggested, 1637, is almost certainly incorrect.

While still dependent on classical style, *Olivetum* shows considerable differences from the earlier Herod epic. If Gryphius painted a prototypical villain in Herod, here he creates Herod's opposite in the prototypical martyr figure of Christ. No longer the biblical passive sufferer, Gryphius's Christ is a baroque hero, beset by all possible goads to a betrayal of his mission. Hunger, thirst, sickness, care, even desire and lust assail him until the Angel of Divine Love rescues him from his temptations. Abstractions are personified; Treachery and Greed speak to Judas; Peter becomes a larger-than-life braggart as he boasts of his loyalty to his master. On the cross Jesus assumes the form of a favorite image of the baroque age, a *Wundchristus* (wounded Christ) covered with blood, sweat, and wounds oozing pus, as he faces the hour of his Passion. Some of Gryphius's most powerful poetic effects are evident in these graphic descriptions.

How long Gryphius remained in Italy is not known. On his return through Germany he took up residence in Strasbourg, where he was in contact with some of the most celebrated scholars at the university. There, too, he completed his first and, in the opinion of many, his best drama, *Leo Armenius, oder Fürsten-Mord* (Leo Arminius; or, Regicide). He left the manuscript for this play, along with expanded versions of his other youthful works (with the exception of the Latin epics), in the hands of a Strasbourg publisher, who, because of financial difficulties, did not produce the edition. The works came into the hands of a Frankfurt publisher, Johann Hüttner, who published them in 1650, without Gryphius's knowledge, along with works of other poets as *Teutsche Reim-Gedichte* (German Rhymed Poems).

Gryphius's tragedies differ vastly from the modern concept of the drama and, hence, are often criticized on the basis of false criteria. Derivative from Seneca but immediately dependent on the Dutch theater, they reflect a Stoic attitude within a Christian framework. There is no real concept of the dramatic, of creating suspense, or even of tragic guilt. The Christian parameter permits only martyrdom or the violation of God's social, political, or religious order as causes of tragedy, and the Christian virtue of constancy coupled with Stoic acceptance of the world are the heroic qualities most highly valued. Historical events may be interpreted but not altered in a substantive way. Thus, the dramatist's only chore is to present the facts about his subject in a manner worthy of that subject. Since tragedy is limited to the higher social order, members of the royalty or the high nobility are featured as both heroes and villains, and the language and style must be of an elevated nature, rhetorical, and replete with gnomic sentiments. There is often little action – in fact, much of the action takes place between the acts – while the dialogue consists of long monologues, sometimes merely relating the historical background or delineating the state of mind of the character, but always composed of noble – or, equally, ignoble – sentiments that can be quoted out of context. Gryphius borrowed from Dutch drama the concept of the *Reyen,* a combination of the classical chorus with a moralizing summation of the events depicted. These *Reyen,* which usually appear after each act, may be in the form of a recitative chorus or a short sketch.

The impetus for *Leo Armenius* may well have come from the work of a Jesuit author, Joseph Simon, who treated the same material in his drama *Leo Armenus seu Impietas punita* (Leo Armenus; or, Impiety Punished); the play had been performed in Rome during the spring of 1646, a time when Gryphius was probably in the city. It is the story of a Byzantine emperor who, having acquired the rule from the former emperor by an army coup, was deposed and assassinated by his general, Michael Balbus; the original source was the account by the Byzantine historians Johannes Zonaras and Georgios Cedrenus. By a daring analogy of the emperor Leo to Christ, Gryphius provides powerful support for the divine right of kings, or at least of those kings who acquired their power lawfully. Gryphius's patron, Schönborner, had taught that tyrants who came to their rule by lawful means could be deposed or resisted only by such means, whereas those who had usurped the power could be removed by force. In Gryphius's play the former emperor is represented as having abdicated the throne on hearing that Leo had been chosen by the army to assume the imperial power; thus, Leo could be considered the rightful emperor. Gryphius sets the play on Christmas Eve and calls attention to the symbolism of Leo, the lion, as an icon of Christ; moreover, he has Leo murdered before the high altar while clinging to the true cross. Running somewhat athwart this analogy is the justification for Leo's actions: the pretender, Michael Balbus, has been taken prisoner and condemned to death. But in view of the holy festival, Leo's wife begs Leo to postpone the execution. Leo yields to sentiment, which he places before his duty as emperor, thus violating his role as governing power ordained by God: the ruler is the sword of God, destined to carry out the execution as part of the divine order. The postponement gives Michael Balbus the opportunity to escape from prison and organize a conspiracy that results in Leo's death. It is suggested that Leo's wife is merely the tool of the priests, thus injecting into the play the concept of the church as a political power – perhaps a blow of the Protestant Gryphius against the Roman Catholic Church, whose power he had felt, and was to feel again, in his native Silesia.

In spite of the highly rhetorical style and long declamatory passages the play is successful as a drama and closely corresponds to the modern notion of high tragedy. The striking scene in the church, which occurs offstage but is vividly reported; a soothsayer, with his eerie magic charms, who is consulted by the conspirators and who delivers an ambiguous prediction; and the final scene, in which Leo's wife (reminiscent of Ophelia in William Shakespeare's *Hamlet* [circa 1600–1601]) delivers a declamation of fantasy that may be either insanity or prophetic clairvoyance – all make for good drama in the modern sense. The message of the work is clearly expressed in the prophecy of the soothsayer that Michael Balbus will possess what the emperor now possesses – that is, his crown – and the certainty of his forthcoming death: the emperor is dead; long live the emperor, who will also die. History is a circle: the good fortune of today turns to death on the morrow, but the successor will suffer the same fate; the glories of this world are transient. These are baroque clichés, but Gryphius illustrates them most effectively.

Gryphius departed Strasbourg in May 1647 for Leiden, whence he returned via ship to the North German port of Stettin, arriving in his home country on 25 July after an absence of nine years. In Stettin he stayed at the home of his friend and traveling companion Schlegel and worked on his second drama, *Catharina von Georgien,* which he probably completed before his departure in November for Frauenstadt. It did not appear in print until 1657.

Catharina von Georgien has its origin in an event that transpired during Gryphius's lifetime. In 1624 the queen of Armenian Georgia was killed by the shah of Persia after being held prisoner for several years. Gryphius was so impressed with her unwavering constancy that he composed this "martyr drama" to narrate the last day of her life. Gryphius depicts the shah as madly in love with Catharina and determined to make her his wife. He swears that she will be "free" by the evening either by becoming his wife and espousing his religion or by suffering torture and death. She rejoices at this opportunity of gaining immortal life via martyrdom. Her tortures are described in gruesome detail, and in the final scenes her severed head is brought in to be kissed by the Russian emissary who had been sent to procure her release. The shah, meanwhile, is tortured by remorse and by the prophecy that he will have to live through war and disgrace, a hell on earth, whereas she will go to her eternal reward.

The play, aside from the sensationalism of the tortures reported and the ghastly spectacle of the severed head, is a tedious recitation of historic events rather than a representation of any semblance of dramatic action. Act 3 opens on a long monologue, more than three hundred lines of alexandrine verse that provide all the details of the historical background – most of which are already known from an equally tedious recitation in the first act. As a martyr drama, the play's weakness lies in the fact that Catharina really has no choice: she cannot give in to the shah, for she would thereby become an object of scorn in the eyes of her son and her people and yet would gain nothing thereby; the shah could give her nothing that she does not have already, and she realizes that she would, at best, become just another of his concubines. And the betrayal of her religion, her country, and the memory of her husband, who had been killed by the Persians, would be unthinkable. But by the death sentence, she gains eternal life. Martyrdom is only conferred by free choice, and in Catharina's case there is no alternative to her decision.

Gryphius arrived in Fraustadt to find his stepfather, Eder, in bad health and worse financial condition. But the poet's fame and influential connections were widespread by this time. He received calls to the University of Frankfurt an der Oder and the University of Heidelberg as professor of mathematics; the Swedish ambassador to Holland had promised him a professorship at the University of Uppsala, as well. He refused all of these positions, probably because he already had the prospect of becoming Syndikus (syndic) – roughly, the legal ad-

Title page for the 1698 posthumous collection of Gryphius's poems, edited by his son Christian

viser and juristic representative of the landed nobility – in Glogau. As such, he would be the legal go-between for Silesian Protestants and imperial Catholics, a position demanding diplomacy and tact.

A year and a week after his return to Silesia he became engaged to Rosine Deutschländer, the daughter of a well-to-do merchant in Fraustadt. He married her in January 1649. They would have seven children, four of whom would die young. A son would live to the age of twenty-four, and a precocious daughter would fall prey to a strange malady that would rob her of speech and understanding. The eldest son, Christian, would become a poet and the editor of a posthumous edition of his father's works.

After his return to Germany, Gryphius had another period of productivity. His drama *Cardenio und Celinde* (1657) was written at this time, as well as his tragedy about the recently executed English king, *Ermordete Majestät. Oder Carolus Stuardus König von Großbrittannien* (Murdered Majesty; or, Charles Stuart, King of Great Britain, 1657). He probably also completed in these few years two comedies, *Absurda Comica. Oder Herr Peter Squentz* (Absurd Comedy; or, Mr. Peter Squentz, 1658) and *Horribilicribrifax* (The Horrible Sieve-maker, 1663).

The impetus to the composition of *Cardenio und Celinde* had come during Gryphius's stay in Amsterdam, on his way back to Germany, in the summer of 1647: a nocturnal walk with friends through a graveyard inspired him to tell a ghost story that he claimed to have heard in Italy as a true occurrence, and his narration made such an impression on his friends that they demanded that he commit it to written form just as he had related it. A few years later he acceded to their request but converted the material into a "tragedy" – even though the participants, as he notes, are too low in social status for so exalted an art form and the language is scarcely more elevated than that of real life. Actually, it is not a tragedy but a ghost story recast in declamatory form. The source was a *novela* from a 1624 Spanish collection by Juan Pérez de Montalván. A young Spanish nobleman studying at the University of Bologna falls in love with the beautiful Olympia, who returns his love. His fiery temperament, which leads him into frequent swordplay, robs him of his love, who becomes betrothed to the opportunistic Lysander. Out of despair Cardenio takes up with a "kept woman," Celinde, murders her lover, and plots to kill his rival. But finally God's order is realized: Olympia and Lysander are married, while the title figures retire to an improbable cloistered life. Most of the action takes place before the play begins; only the murder plot, which never materializes, is depicted onstage. And the ending, in which the unworthy Lysander gains the hand of Olympia, a less than ideal heroine, is decidedly unsatisfactory. A macabre scene in which Celinde, at the behest of a sorceress, attempts to cut out the heart of her dead lover, who is partially decayed in the grave, and another in which Cardenio, about to embrace Olympia, sees her turn into a skeleton pointing a deadly arrow at his heart, impart a ghostly atmosphere to the play. The poet's attempt to remain faithful to his source was no doubt responsible for at least some of the work's defects.

The beheading of Charles I of England in 1649 was an event of world-shaking proportions in the absolutist Hapsburg empire – especially for Gryphius, who had been schooled by his mentor, Schönborner, in the divine right of kings. He must have set to work immediately on hearing the news, for *Ermordete Majestät* was certainly finished in 1650. For unknown reasons he withheld it from publication, complaining in 1652 that the work, which he had wanted to keep to himself, had somehow come into the hands even of royalty. Only in 1657, in his collected works, did he release the drama, but he revised it drastically for the next edition of the collected works in 1663. It is not clear whether this revision was a result of additional information that reached him in the interim, or whether artistic considerations were the motivating forces.

The earlier version is a somewhat tedious recitation of the facts as Gryphius knew them. Charles is ready to die and is presented as a true martyr, for he rejects willingly all attempts to rescue him. Oliver Cromwell, on the other hand, is weak and wavering, whereas Gen. Thomas Fairfax is depicted as a staunch defender of the king. There is a hint of a conspiracy to save the king, but it comes to nothing. Religion, personified, appears in a chorus to bemoan the crimes committed in her name. After many declarations of the sad state of affairs, Charles is executed onstage while a chorus of the spirits of murdered English kings calls out for revenge. The ponderous mass of continuous recitation gives a sermonlike quality to the piece.

In the second version a plot to save the king, directed by Fairfax's wife, produces some dramatic interest. There is an entirely new first act, and the former second and third acts are combined. Fairfax is transformed into a weak, vacillating personality, while Cromwell becomes the staunch opponent, and this change is accomplished simply by exchanging their lines. The plot to save the king is somewhat reminiscent of *Leo Armenius,* in that the wife is the power behind the machinations. A new character, the mad regicide Poleh, is introduced. The new version has led some to believe that Gryphius was presenting Charles as an analogue to Christ, Fairfax to Pontius Pilate, and Poleh to Judas. The drama can be read as overt political support for divine right, in spite of the opposition in Silesia to Hapsburg Catholicism.

In *Absurda Comica* Peter Squentz is Peter Quince, from the play-within-the-play of Shakespeare's *A Midsummer Night's Dream* (circa 1595–1596), although it is fairly certain that Gryphius did not know Shakespeare's work. The original was probably a farce by Daniel Schwenter, a professor at the University of Altdorf, to whom Gryphius accords the credit, although Schwenter's play, if it existed, is lost. This circumstance has led to controversy concerning the real authorship of the piece, but the extant version is certainly the work of, or a drastic reworking by, Gryphius. Using the spectacle of ignorant village artisans producing Ovid's *Pyramus and Thisbe*, Gryphius satirizes the traditional productions of such popular comedies as those of Hans Sachs. The refined noble audience is duly amused at the slapstick production. The work has remained the most popular comedy of the German baroque and has been frequently produced.

The title character of *Horribilicribrifax* is so called for his propensity of making his opponents look like sieves when he duels with them. It is not surprising that Gryphius should take up the theme of the braggart soldier back from the wars, for Germany must have been full of them. The ultimate source was the *Miles Gloriosus* of Plautus, but the theme was not new to Germany. Around 1594 Heinrich Julius, Duke of Brunswick, had produced a typical example in *Vincentius Ladislaus*, but Gryphius was undoubtedly more directly influenced by the figure of Capitano Spavento of the commedia dell'arte. He doubles the figure of the braggart by presenting a foil to him in the person of Daradiridatumtarides, differentiating between them only by having the one lard his language with Italian, the other with French phrases, both distorted and mispronounced. An extremely complicated plot involves such other stock figures as the schoolmaster who constantly cites Latin and Greek phrases and an old crone whose linguistic stock-in-trade is folkloristic phrases and popular nonsense. In fact, the main source of the humor is a continual give-and-take dependent on characters misunderstanding one another's learned or foreign phrases. A series of marriages ties up the strands of the various subplots. There are strong indications that the play never reached its final form, for it is full of contradictions, including variant forms of the names of some of the characters. It consists of five acts and was included in the collected works in 1663.

In 1650 appeared the collection of Gryphius's works that he had left in Strasbourg but that had been handed over to Hüttner in Frankfurt am Main. In the same year he assumed his office as syndic for the Glogau estates. Not much is known of the final years of his life. In 1653 he published a collection of legal papers, *Glogauisches Fürstenthumbs Landes Privilegia aus den Originalen* (The Rights and Privileges of the Landed Aristocracy in the Principality of Glogau, from the Original Version). They are in Latin, German, and Czech. Also in 1653 he wrote

Majuma, Freuden-Spiel, a mini-operetta to which the music has been lost. It was in honor of the coronation of Ferdinand IV as king and was probably produced in June of that year. It uses a rather hackneyed mythological setting to encomiastic ends. The most that can be said of it is that it is typical of such frilly occasional pieces.

Fleeing from a new onslaught of the plague, Gryphius and his family took refuge at the estate of his former patron, Schönborner. The first part of his collected works appeared in 1657; it was completed in 1658 by an edition that was identical except for the title page and the inclusion of *Absurda Comica*. In the 1657 edition appears a short rumination on death and the vanities of human existence, "Kirchhoffs-Gedancken" (Cemetery Thoughts), which contains some of the most drastic and macabre descriptions of decaying corpses to be found in Gryphius's writings. A small collection of translated Latin hymns and a tripartite cantata also appeared in 1657. Possibly around this time was conceived "Weicher-Stein" (Smooth Stone – the name of a rock formation), in which Gryphius and his friends J. C. von Gersdorff and J. C. von Schönborner, the son of his patron, each contributed a commemoration of an afternoon picnic's entertainment; it would be included in his *Epigrammata oder Bey-Schriften* (Epigrams; or, Annotations, 1663).

The greatest event of the 1650s for Gryphius was undoubtedly the composition of his tragedy *Großmüttiger Rechts-Gelehrter, oder Sterbender Aemilius Paulus Papinianus* (The Courageous Jurist; or, The Death of Paulus Papinianus, 1659). Written between 1657 and 1659, it tells in compressed form the story of the emperor Caracalla, who murders his half-brother Geta, then attempts to gain legal justification of the murder via the testimony of the great legal scholar Paulus Papinianus. The latter refuses to compromise his principles and chooses death for himself and his family rather than accede to the wishes of the emperor. The play is, in the opinion of some, a secularized martyr drama in which morality rather than religion motivates the choice of death. But Gryphius seems to have fused a Lutheran attitude with a Stoic morality, both of which he presents within the framework of the martyr. A problem is that, by deliberately going to his death, Papinianus deprives the corrupt empire of his staunch, righteous voice. There are several subplots, such as the possible revenge of the empress Julia for the murder of her son, and the evil plans of the counselor Laetus, who has cast his envious eye on the imperial throne. Papinianus is offered several ways out of his dilemma – joining the empress to seize the throne, or taking over the military in a coup d'etat, or simply acquiescing passively in the emperor's request to condone the murder. Since the sixteenth century this case had been a quandary for legal thinkers, an object lesson of the end justifying the means. As a stage production, its lurid horrors surpass even those of *Catharina von Georgien:* the heart is torn from the living body of Laetus and trodden underfoot by the raging empress; Papinianus holds up the severed head of his son; on his own beheading, his wife kisses the hands and head of her husband and of her son before collapsing on the truncated corpse of her husband.

The work is generally recognized as the most mature of Gryphius's dramas. The language as well as the actions of the personalities are not so tightly contained within a rhetorical straitjacket as in his earlier plays. And the philosophical problem may well reflect Gryphius's own situation as syndic, representing the Protestant estates yet owing at least passive obedience to the Catholic emperor. Judging from its reception, it was also the most popular of Gryphius's tragedies: in 1660 it was produced seven times on the stage of the Elisabeth Gymnasium in Breslau.

Gryphius had become a well-known and respected figure, not only in the political sphere as an important functionary of the estates and in literary circles as a poet and dramatist of the greatest fame, but also as a man of erudition in the most widely divergent areas. In 1658 the city of Breslau came into the possession of three Egyptian mummies, two of them well preserved and one fragmented. Gryphius was called on to take part in their dissection. In 1662 he published a detailed description of the dissection under the title *Mumiae Wratislavienses* (Breslau Mummies).

In 1660 Gryphius wrote a *Lust- und Gesangspiel* (comic operetta) titled *Piastus,* concerning the dynastic origin of the dukes of Brieg, Liegnitz, and Wohlau. The occasion was probably the pregnancy of Duchess Luise, wife of Duke Christian of Wohlau, who was hoping to produce an heir to the line of Silesian Piast rulers, the last descendants of the first Polish royal dynasty; the duchies would fall prey to Bohemia if a male heir were not born. (The son, Georg Wilhelm, would die at fifteen, ending the line.) It is an active little piece, featuring fireworks, a wild Tartar dance, a comic interchange, and a final dance to which provisions for an additional ballet are appended. It was only published in the posthumous edition of 1698.

An occasional piece, written for the marriage celebration of Duke Georg III of Liegnitz and Brieg and the Countess Palatine, Elisabeth Maria Charlotte, was perhaps Gryphius's most accomplished comedy, which has been considered worthy even of a Gotthold Ephraim Lessing: the double playlet *Verlibtes Gespenste, Gesang-Spiel* (The Amorous Ghost: Operetta) and *Die gelibte Dornrose, Schertz-Spill* (Beloved Dornrose: Farce). The first edition appeared in 1660 and included only *Verlibtes Gespenste;* in 1661 both playlets were published together. The operetta, while in no sense a translation or even a reworking, nonetheless shows the influence of the French writer Philippe Quinault's *Le Fantôme amoureux* (The Amorous Ghost, 1658). Gryphius's playlets are interwoven, the acts alternating between the works, a traditional technique perhaps originating in the necessity to provide time for changes of scenery and costume. While there is no attempt at contrived parallelism, the juxtaposition of the individual acts, as well as that of the two plays as a whole, creates a skillful mirror image. The operetta presents a kind of daisy-chain series of love affairs, with each character loving someone who loves someone else. The title is derived from a climactic scene in which the principal lover, playing dead, is conjured "back to life" by the tears of his beloved. The language is that of the alexandrine line in elevated discourse; the framework is classical mythology interspersed with Christian references; and the personnel are of a high social order. On the other hand, *Die gelibte Dornrose* is in many ways a parody of the operetta. The poetic line has yielded to prose, the elevated speech becomes dialect, and the aristocracy has changed places with the peasantry. Within this framework there is a Romeo-and-Juliet plot, with the lovers separated by the feuding of their guardians. Only when the heroine's lover saves her from being raped by a crude bumpkin is the way paved for a happy ending. Both plays are graceful and light. Either could stand on its own as an individual work, but the combination of the two is a mark of genius.

The play *Der Schwermende Schäfer Lysis* (The Rapturous Shepherd Lysis, 1661) is a translation of *Le Berger extravagant* (The Extravagant Shepherd, 1639), by Thomas Corneille, who in his day shared at least equal fame with his brother Pierre. It was a commissioned occasional piece for the first birthday of the last duke of the Piast dynasty, Georg Wilhelm. Gryphius adheres closely to the original text but moves the locale to his homeland. Originally intended as a satire of the pastoral mode, the French original is sufficiently exaggerated to make it difficult to differentiate between intended satire and "normal" affectation.

It was part of the devotional exercises of many poets during the seventeenth century to compose works of meditation from a religious standpoint. In 1663 Gryphius translated, probably from a Dutch translation of the original English, a large collection of the religious writings of Sir Richard Baker. In 1665 he reworked *Himmel steigente HertzensSeüfftzer* (Sighs from the Heart Ascending to Heaven, 1626), by the theologian Josua Stegmann. Throughout his life Gryphius was invited or commissioned to write and deliver funeral orations on the deaths of prominent patrons or acquaintances. These works were published as individual editions and collected as *Dissertationes Funebres, oder Leich-Abdanckungen* (Funeral Dissertations; or, Funeral Orations, 1666). Typically an allegorical theme is developed via emblematic iconography, and many of the images are also to be found in Gryphius's dramas. Recent scholarship has established the importance of these lugubrious works for the development of his prose style and for the understanding of his imagery.

In 1662, in a somewhat belated recognition of his stature as a writer, Gryphius was accepted into the most celebrated literary society in Germany, the Fruchtbringende Gesellschaft (Fruit-bringing Society). The sobriquet accorded to him, after the practice of the society, attests to the respect in which he was held: he was called "der Unsterbliche" (the Immortal). He is, indeed, one of the few baroque poets whose fame persisted through the succeeding eras of literary criticism. On 16 July 1664, while attending a session of the landed estates in his capacity as syndic, he suffered a fatal heart attack. He is remembered as Germany's greatest poet of the seventeenth century.

Bibliographies:

Victor Manheimer, *Die Lyrik des Andreas Gryphius: Studien und Materialien* (Berlin: Weidmann, 1904);

M. Johannes Theodor Leubscher, "Andreas Gryphius," *Text + Kritik,* 7/8 (March 1980): 112–128;

Gerhard Dünnhaupt, *Personalbibliographien zu den Drucken des Barock,* volume 3 (Stuttgart: Hiersemann, 1991), pp. 1855–1883.

Biographies:

Marian Szyrocki, *Der junge Gryphius,* Neue Beiträge zur Literaturwissenschaft, volume 9 (Berlin: Rütten & Loening, 1959);

Szyrocki, *Andreas Gryphius: Sein Leben und Werk* (Tübingen: Niemeyer, 1964);

Baltzer Siegmund von Stosch, "Danck- und Denck-Seule des Andreae Gryphii (1665)," *Text + Kritik,* 7/8 (March 1980): 2–11;

Christian Stieff, "Andreae Gryphii Lebens-Lauf," *Text + Kritik,* 7/8 (March 1980): 24–31;

Conrad Wiedemann, "Andreas Gryphius," in *Deutsche Dichter des 17. Jahrhunderts: Ihr Leben und Werk,* edited by Harald Steinhagen and Benno von Wiese (Berlin: Erich Schmidt, 1984), pp. 435–472;

Eberhard Mannack, *Andreas Gryphius,* Sammlung Metzler, volume 76 (Stuttgart: Metzler, 1986).

References:

Judith P. Aikin, "The Audience within the Play: Clues to Intended Audience Reaction in German Baroque Tragedies and Comedies," *Daphnis,* 13, no. 1–2 (1984): 187–201;

Aikin, "The Comedies of Andreas Gryphius and the Two Traditions of European Comedy," *Germanic Review,* 63 (Summer 1988): 114–120;

J. R. Alexander, "A Possible Historical Source for the Figure of Poleh in Andreas Gryphius's *Carolus Stuardus,*" *Daphnis,* 3, no. 2 (1974): 203–207;

Günter Berghaus, *Die Quellen zu Andreas Gryphius' Trauerspiel "Carolus Stuardus": Studien zur Entstehung eines historisch-politischen Märtyrerdramas der Barockzeit,* Studien zur deutschen Literatur, no. 79 (Tübingen: Niemeyer, 1983);

Werner Eggers, *Wirklichkeit und Wahrheit im Trauerspiel von Andreas Gryphius,* Probleme der Dichtung, volume 9 (Heidelberg: Winter, 1967);

Willi Flemming, *Andreas Gryphius: Eine Monographie* (Stuttgart: Kohlhammer, 1965);

Flemming, *Andreas Gryphius und die Bühne* (Halle: Niemeyer, 1921);

Gerhard Fricke, *Die Bildlichkeit in der Dichtung des Andreas Gryphius: Materialien und Studien zum Formproblem des deutschen Literaturbarock* (Darmstadt: Wissenschaftlich Buchgesellschaft, 1967);

Maria Fürstenwald, *Andreas Gryphius. Dissertationes Funebres: Studien zur Didaktik der Leichabdankungen,* Abhandlungen zur Kunst-, Musik- und Literaturwissenschaft, volume 46 (Bonn: Bouvier, 1967);

Herbert Heckmann, *Elemente des barocken Trauerspiels: Am Beispiel des "Papinian" von Andreas Gryphius* (Darmstadt: Gentner, 1959);

Gerd Hillen, *Andreas Gryphius: Cardenio und Celinde,* De Proprietatibus litterarum: Series Practica, no. 45 (The Hague: Mouton, 1971);

Dietrich Walter Jöns, *Das "Sinnen-Bild": Studien zur allegorischen Bildlichkeit bei Andreas Gryphius* (Stuttgart: Metzler, 1966);

Gerhard Kaiser, ed., *Die Dramen des Andreas Gryphius: Eine Sammlung von Einzelinterpretationen* (Stuttgart: Metzler, 1968);

Hans-Henrik Krummacher, "Andreas Gryphius und Johann Arndt: Zum Verständnis der 'Sonn- und Feiertagssonette,' " in *Formenwandel: Festschrift für Paul Böckmann* (Hamburg, 1964);

Krummacher, *Der junge Gryphius und die Tradition: Studien zu den Perikopensonetten und Passionsliedern* (Munich: Fink, 1976);

W. Kühlmann, "Der Fall Papinian: Ein Konfliktmodell absolutistischer Politik im akademischen Schriftum des 16. und 17. Jhs.," *Daphnis*, 11, no. 1-2 (1982): 223-252;

Henri Plard, "Gryphiana," *Text + Kritik*, 7/8 (February 1965): 37-53;

Plard, "Gryphius und noch immer kein Ende," *Etudes germaniques* (January–March 1973): 61-85; (April–June 1973): 185-204;

Plard, "De Heiligheid van de Koninklijke Macht in de Tragedie van Andreas Gryphius," *Tijdschrift van de Vrije Universiteit van Brussel*, 2 (1960): 202-229;

Plard, "Sur la jeunesse d'Andreas Gryphius," *Etudes germaniques* (January–March 1962): 34-40;

Hugh Powell, "Andreas Gryphius and the 'New Philosophy,' " *German Life and Letters*, new series 5 (July 1952): 275-278;

Powell, "Observations on the Erudition of Andreas Gryphius," *Orbis Litterarum*, 25, no. 1-2 (1970): 115-125;

Powell, "Probleme der Gryphius-Forschung," *Germanisch-romanische Monatschrift*, new series 7 (1957): 328-343;

Sibylle Rusterholz, *Rostra, Sarg und Predigtstuhl: Studien zur Form und Funktion der Totenrede bei Andreas Gryphius*, Studien zur Germanistik, Anglistik und Komparatistik, no. 16 (Bonn: Bouvier, 1974);

Marvin S. Schindler, *The Sonnets of Andreas Gryphius: Use of the Poetic Word in the Seventeenth Century* (Gainesville: University of Florida Press, 1971);

Hans-Jürgen Schings, *Die patristische und stoische Tradition bei Andreas Gryphius: Untersuchungen zu den Dissertationes funebres und Trauerspielen* (Cologne: Böhlau, 1966);

Albrecht Schöne, *Emblematik und Drama im Zeitalter des Barock* (Munich: Beck, 1964);

Blake Lee Spahr, "Gryphius and the Holy Ghost," "Cardenio und Celinde," "Herod and Christ: Gryphius' Latin Epics," in his *Problems and Perspectives: A Collection of Essays on German Baroque Literature* (Frankfurt am Main: Peter Lang, 1981), 111-122, 131-150, 151-159;

Janifer Gerl Stackhouse, *The Constructive Art of Gryphius' Historical Tragedies*, Berner Beiträge zur Barockgermanistik, no. 6 (Bern: Peter Lang, 1986);

Stackhouse, "The Mysterious Regicide in Gryphius' Stuart Drama: Who is Poleh?," *Modern Language Notes*, 89 (1974): 797-811;

Harald Steinhagen, *Wirklichkeit und Handeln im barocken Drama: Historisch-ästhetische Studien zum Trauerspiel des Andreas Gryphius*, Studien zur deutschen Literatur, no. 51 (Tübingen: Niemeyer, 1977);

Adolf Strutz, *Andreas Gryphius: Die Weltanschauung eines deutschen Barockdichters*, Wege zur Dichtung, 11 (Zurich: Münster-Presse, 1931);

Elida Maria Szarota, *Geschichte, Politik und Gesellschaft im Drama des 17. Jahrhunderts* (Bern: Francke, 1976);

Szarota, *Künstler, Grübler und Rebellen: Studien zum europäischen Märtyrerdrama des 17. Jahrhunderts* (Bern: Francke, 1967);

Erich Trunz, "Andreas Gryphius: Über die Geburt Jesu," "Tränen des Vaterlandes," "Es ist alles eitel," in *Die deutsche Lyrik: Form und Geschichte*, edited by Benno von Wiese (Düsseldorf: Bagel, 1957), pp. 139-151;

Wilhelm Vosskamp, *Untersuchungen zur Zeit- und Geschichts-auffassung im 17. Jahrhundert bei Gryphius und Lohenstein*, Literatur und Wirklichkeit, no. 1 (Bonn: Bouvier, 1967);

Mara R. Wade, *The German Baroque Pastoral "Singspiel,"* Berner Beiträge zur Barockgermanistik, no. 7 (Bern: Peter Lang, 1990);

F. Meyer von Waldeck, "Der Peter Squenz von Andreas Gryphius, eine Verspottung von Hans Sachs," *Vierteljahrsschrift für Litteraturgeschichte*, 1 (1888): 195-212;

Friedrich-Wilhelm Wentzlaff-Eggebert, *Dichtung und Sprache des jungen Gryphius* (Berlin: De Gruyter, 1966);

Günther Weydt, "Sonettkunst des Barocks: Zum Problem der Umarbeitung bei Andreas Gryphius," *Jahrbuch der deutschen Schillergesellschaft*, 9 (1965): 1-32;

Louis G. Wysocki, *Andreas Gryphius et la tragédie allemande au xviie siècle* (Paris: Bouillon, 1893).

Georg Philipp Harsdörffer

(1 November 1607 – 16 September 1658)

Peter Hess
University of Texas at Austin

SELECTED BOOKS: *Memoria Viri prosapiâ, Virtute atq; eruditione Nobilissimi, Christophori Füreri ab Haymendorf et Wolckersdorf, &c.* (Nuremberg: Printed by Johann Andreas Endter, 1639);

Vollständiges Trincir-Büchlein, anonymous (Nuremberg: Johann Christoph Lochner the Elder, 1640);

Germania Deplorata sive Relatio, qua Pragmatica Momenta Belli Pacisqve Expendvntvr (Nuremberg: Wolfgang Endter, 1641);

Gallia Deplorata sive Relatio de Luctuoso Bello, quod Rex Christianissimus contra Vicinos Populos Molitur (Nuremberg: Wolfgang Endter, 1641);

Frawen-Zimmer Gespräch-Spiel, 2 volumes (Nuremberg: Wolfgang Endter, 1641, 1642); revised and enlarged as *Frauenzimmer Gesprechspiele, so bey Ehr- und Tugendliebenden Gesellschaften, mit nutzlicher Ergetzlichkeit, beliebet und geübet werden mögen*, 8 volumes (Nuremberg: Wolfgang Endter, 1643–1649, 1657);

Aulæa Romana Contra Peristromata tvrcica Expansa: Sive Dissertatio Emblematica, Concordiae Christianae Omen Repraesentans (Nuremberg: Wolfgang Endter, 1642);

Pegnesisches Schaefergedicht, in den Berinorgischen Gefilden, angestimmet von Strefon und Clajvs, by Harsdörffer and Johann Klaj (Nuremberg: Wolfgang Endter, 1644);

Ehrengedichte der Kunstlöbblichen Druckerey des Erbaren und Wolvornehmenden Herrn Wolfgang Endters in Nürnberg, by Harsdörffer and Klaj (Nuremberg, n.d. [circa 1644–1646]);

Der Pegnitz Hirten Frülings Freude, Herrn M. Andre Jahnens [und] Jungfer Marien Simons Myrtenfeste gewidmet, den vj. des Blumen Monats, by Harsdörffer, Klaj, and Sigmund von Birken (Nuremberg, 1645);

Lustgedicht zu hochzeitlichem Ehrenbegängniß Herrn D. Johann Röders, und Jungfer Maria Rosina Schmidin, auf der siebenröhrigen Schilffpfeifen Pans wolmeinend spielet von den Pegnitzhirten by Hars-

Georg Philipp Harsdörffer (engraving by Jakob Sandrart, after a drawing by Georg Strauch)

dörffer, Klaj, and Birken (Nuremberg: Wolfgang Endter, 1645);

Stechbüchlein: Das ist, Hertzensschertze, in welchen der Tugenden und Untugenden Abbildungen, zu wahrer Selbst Erkantnis mit erfreulichem Nutzen außzuwehlen, as Fabianum Athyrum (Nuremberg: Wolfgang Endter, 1645); enlarged as *Das erneurte Stamm- und Stechbüchlein* (Nuremberg: Printed by Christoph Gerhard, published by Paul Fürst, 1654);

Specimen Philologiæ Germanicæ, Continens Disquisitiones XII. de Linguae nostrae vernaculae Historia, Methodo, et Dignitate (Nuremberg: Wolfgang Endter, 1646);

Porticus Serenissimo atque Celsissimo Principi, ac Domino, Domino Augusto, Brunswicensium atque Luneburgensium Duci potentissimo, Principum eruditissimo, Patricii Noric. et ejusdem Dicasterii Assessoris (Nuremberg: Printed by Wolfgang Endter, 1647);

Poetischer Trichter, die Teutsche Dicht- und Reimkunst, ohne Behuf der lateinischen Sprache, in VI. Stunden einzugiessen, anonymous (Nuremberg: Printed by Wolfgang Endter, 1647; enlarged, 1650);

Poetischen Trichters zweyter Theil (Nuremberg: Wolfgang Endter, 1648);

Icones Mortis Sexaginta imaginibus, totidemque inscriptionibus insignitae, versibus quoque Latinis et novis Germanicis illustratae, by Harsdörffer, Georgius Aemilius, and Caspar Schmidt (Nuremberg: Printed by Johann Christoph Lochner, published by Paul Fürst, 1648);

Hertzbewegliche Sonntagsandachten: Das ist, Bild- Lieder- und Bet-Büchlein, aus den Sprüchen der H. Schrifft, nach den Evangeli- und Festtexten verfasset, 2 volumes (Nuremberg: Wolfgang Endter, 1649, 1652);

Der Grosse SchauPlatz jämmerlicher Mordgeschichte, 4 volumes (Hamburg: Johann Naumann, 1649–1650);

Der Große Schau-Platz Lust und Lehrreicher Geschichte, anonymous (Nuremberg, 1650; enlarged edition, Frankfurt am Main: Printed by Caspar Rötel, published by Johann Naumann in Hamburg, 1651);

Nathan und Jotham: Das ist Geistliche und Weltliche Lehrgedichte, 2 volumes (Nuremberg: Michael Endter, 1650, 1651);

Göttliche Liebesflamme: Das ist, Christliche Andachten, Gebet, und Seufftzer, by Harsdörffer and Johann Michael Dilherr (Nuremberg, 1651);

Fortpflantzung der Hochlöblichen Fruchtbringenden Geselschaft: Das ist, Kurtze Erzehlung alles dessen, was sich bey Erwehlung und Antrettung hochbesagter Geselschaft Oberhauptes, deß Höchteursten und Wehrtesten Schmackhaften, begeben und zugegragen. Samt etlichen Glückwunschungen, und einer Lobrede deß Geschmackes, anonymous (Nuremberg: Printed by Michael Endter, 1651);

Delitiæ Mathematicæ et Physicæ: Der Mathematischen und Philosophischen Erquickstunden Zweyter Theil (Nuremberg: Jeremias Dümler, 1651);

Prob und Lob der Teutschen Wolredenheit. Das ist: deß Poetischen Trichters Dritter Theil (Nuremberg: Printed by Wolfgang Endter the Elder, 1653);

Delitiæ Philosophicæ et Mathematicæ: Der Philosophischen und Mathematischen Erquickstunden, Dritter Theil (Nuremberg: Published by Wolfgang & Johann Andreas Endter, 1653);

Jm Meyen, soll man Freyen. Das ist, Morgen-Lust vnd Schertzgedichte . . . bey dem Hochzeitlichen Ehren- vnd Freuden-Fest, deß . . . Hrn. Joh. Jac. Dimpfels . . . May-Monats im Jahr M. DC. LIIII. Vberschickt vnd eingehändiget, von hohen Personen; grossen Gönnern, vnd guten Freunden, by Harsdörffer, Veit Ludwig von Seckendorf, Daniel Richter, and others (Regensburg, 1654);

Der Geschichtspiegel: Vorweisend hundert denckwürdige Begebenheiten, mit seltnen Sinnbildern, nutzlichen Lehren, zierlichen Gleichnissen, und nachsinnigen Fragen aus der Sitten-Lehre und der Naturkündigung, benebens XXV. Aufgaben von der Spiegelkunst, an das Leicht gesetzt, durch ein Mitglied der hochlöblichen Fruchtbringenden Gesellschafft (Nuremberg: Wolfgang Endter the Younger & Johann Andreas Endter, 1654);

Geographische Spielkarten. Nach den IV Theilen der Welt Kunstrichtig außgebildet (Nuremberg, 1655);

Ars Apophthegmatica, das ist: Kunstquellen denckwürdiger Lehrsprüche und ergötzlicher Hofreden, 2 volumes (Nuremberg: Wolfgang Endter the Younger & Johann Andreas Endter, 1655, 1656);

Der Teutsche Secretarius: Das ist: Allen Cantzley-Studir- und Schreibstuben nützliches und fast nohtwendiges Formular- und Titularbuch, 2 volumes (Nuremberg: Wolfgang Endter the elder, 1655, 1659);

Historische Spielkarten (Nuremberg, 1656);

Die Hohe Schul Geist- und Sinnreicher Gedancken, in CCCC. Anmuhtungen, aus dem Buch Gottes und der Natur vorgestellt, durch Dorotheum Elevtherum Melethepilum. Mit Anfügung Salomonis Tugend-Regiments- und Hauslehre (Nuremberg: Wolfgang Endter the Younger & Johann Andreas Endter, 1656);

Das Astronomische Kartenspiel: Das ist: Kunstrichtige Abbildung aller Gestirne am Himmel, ober und unter der Erden, zu Behuf der lehrgierigen Jugend gleich den Geographischen und Historischen Spiel-Karten verfasset (Nuremberg: Wolfgang & Johann Andreas Endter, 1656);

Arcus Triumphalis in honorem Invictissimi Romanor. Imperatoris Leopoldi semper Augusti, Germaniae, Hungariae, Bohemiae, Dalmatiae, Croatiae, Sclavoniae, Regis, Archi Ducis Austriae, Ducis Burgundiae, Brabantiae, Stiriae, Carinthiae, Car-

niolae, Luxembergi, Wirtembergae, Superioris & Inferioris Silesiae Principis Sueviae, &c. A S.P.Q. Noribergensi humili cultu Adornatus. Anno Clementiae Divinae, anonymous (Nuremberg: Wolfgang Endter the Younger & Johann Andreas Endter, 1658);

Drey-ständige Sonn- und Festtag-Emblemata, oder Sinnebilder (Nuremberg: Johann Andreas Endter & the heirs of Wolfgang Endter the Younger, 1669).

Editions and Collections: *Auserlesene Gedichte von G. P. Harsdörffer, Johann Klaj, Sigmund von Birken, Andern Scultetus, J. G. Schottel, Adam Olearius und Johann Scheffler,* edited by Wilheim Müller (Leipzig: Brockhaus, 1826);

Das deutsche evangelische Kirchenlied des 17. Jahrhunderts, edited by Albert Friedrich Wilhelm Fischer and W. Tümpel, volume 5 (Gütersloh: C. Bertelsmann, 1911; reprinted, Hildesheim: Olms, 1964), pp. 1–31;

Vom Theatrum oder Schawplatz, edited by Heinrich Stümcke (Berlin: Elsner, 1914);

Poetischer Trichter, edited by Reginald Marguier (Berlin: Die Rabenpresse, 1939);

Christliche Welt- und Zeitbetrachtungen: 12 Monatslieder (Munich: Kösel, 1961);

Jämmerliche Mordgeschichten: Ausgewählte novellistische Prosa, edited by Hubert Gersch (Neuwied: Luchterhand, 1964);

Das Schauspiel teutscher Sprichwörter (Berlin: Gerhardt, 1964);

Die Pegnitz Schäfer: Georg Philipp Harsdörffer, Johann Klaj, Sigmund von Birken: Gedichte, edited by Gerhard Rühm (Berlin: Gerhardt, 1964);

Pegnesisches Schaefergedicht, by Harsdörffer and Klaj, edited by Klaus Garber (Tübingen: Niemeyer, 1966);

Das Geistliche Waldgedicht oder Freudenspiel genant Seelewjg (Tübingen: Niemeyer, 1968);

Frauenzimmer Gesprechspiele, 8 volumes, edited by Irmgard Böttcher (Tübingen: Niemeyer, 1968–1969);

Pegnesisches Schaefergedicht, by Harsdörffer and Klaj, edited by Dietmar Pfister (Nuremberg: Glock & Lutz, 1969);

Poetischer Trichter, 3 volumes (Darmstadt: Wissenschaftliche Buchgesellschaft, 1969);

Poetischer Trichter, 3 volumes (Hildesheim: Olms, 1971);

Vollständiges Trincir-Büchlein (Hildesheim: Olms, 1971);

Der große Schau-Platz jämerlicher Mordgeschichte (Hildesheim & New York: Olms, 1975);

Der große Schau-Platz lust und lehrreicher Geshichte (Hildesheim & New York: Olms, 1978);

Ars Apophthegmatica, edited by Georg Braungart (Frankfurt am Main: Keip, 1990);

Nathan und Jotham: Das ist Geistliche und Weltliche Lehrgedichte, 2 volumes, edited by Guillaume van Gemeret (Frankfurt am Main: Keip, 1991).

OTHER: Johann Klaj, *Herodes der Kindermörder,* epilogue by Harsdörffer (Nuremberg: Wolfgang Endter, 1645); reprinted in Klaj's *Redeoratorien,* edited by Conrad Wiedemann (Tübingen: Niemeyer, 1965);

Klaj, *Der Leidende Christus,* epilogue by Harsdörffer (Nuremberg: Wolfgang Endter, 1645);

Giovanni Francesco Biondi, *Eromena,* part 1, translated by Johann Wilhelm von Stubenberg, introduction by Harsdörffer (Nuremberg: Michael Endter, 1650);

Franz Ritter, *Speculum Solis, das ist: Sonnen-Spiegel, oder kunstständiger, leichter und grundrichtiger Bericht von den SonnenUhren, und was denselbigen angehöret, vormals durch M. Franciscum Rittern von Nürnberg in zweyen Theilen beschrieben, nunmehr aber mit dem dritten Theil, allerhand neuer Erfindungen vermehret und mit nothwendigen Kupferstücken gezieret. Durch einen Liebhaber deß Studii Mathematici,* edited by Harsdörffer (Nuremberg: Printed by Heinrich Pillenhofer, 1652);

Philipp Uffenbach, *De Quadratura Circuli Mechanici, das ist Ein neüer, kurtzer, hochnützlicher und leichter mechanischer Bericht von der Vierung oder Quadratur deß Circkels, wie man solche Kunstrichtig zu Wercke bringen soll,* edited by Harsdörffer (Nuremberg: Printed by Heinrich Pillenhofer, published by Paul Fürst, 1653);

"Schutzschrift für Die Teutsche Spracharbeit," in *Bilder aus dem deutschen Leben des 17. Jahrhunderts,* edited by Richard Hodermann (Paderborn: Schöningh, 1890), pp. 43–76.

TRANSLATIONS: Anonymous, *Peristromata Turcica, sive Dissertatio Emblematica, Praesentem Europae Statum Ingeniosis Coloribus Repraesentans,* translated by Harsdörffer (Nuremberg: Wolfgang Endter the Elder, 1641);

Jean Desmarets de Saint-Sorlin, *Japeta. Das ist Ein Heldengedicht, gesungen jn dem Holsteinischen Parnasso durch die Musam Calliope* (Nuremberg, 1643);

Jorge de Montemayor, *Diana,* translated by Harsdörffer and Hanns Ludwig von Kuffstein

(Nuremberg: Michael Endter, 1646; reprinted, Darmstadt: Wissenschaftliche Buchgesellschaft, 1970);

Anonymous, *Sophista, sive Logica et Pseudopolitica* (Nuremberg: Wolfgang Endter, 1647);

Pierre Fortin, *Catechisme Royal: Der Königliche Catechismus* (Nuremberg: Endter, 1648);

Jean Pierre Camus, *Heraclitus und Democritus: Das ist C. Fröliche und Traurige Geschichte,* 2 volumes (Nuremberg: Michael Endter, 1652, 1653);

Camus and Joseph Hall, *Pentagone Historique H. von Belley, historisches Fünffeck, auf jeder Seiten mit einer denckwürdigen Begebenheit gezieret: Diesem sind angefüget H. Joseph Halls Kennezeichen der Tugenden und Laster gedolmetscht durch ein Mitglied der hohlöblichen Fruchtbringenden Gesellschaft* (Frankfurt am Main: Published by Johann Naumann, 1652);

Luigi Novarino and Paul de Barry, *Göttliche Liebes-Lust, das ist: Die verborgenen Wolthaten Gottes, zu Erweckung himmlischer Liebe entdecket, von Aloysio Novarino. Diesem sind angefügt: H. Pauli de Barry Heilige Meinungen oder Verträge mit Gott. Zu nützlicher Ergötzligkeit in die hochdeutsche Sprache überbracht durch ein Mitglied der hochlöblichen Fruchtbringenden Gesellschafft,* 2 volumes (Hamburg: Published by Johann Naumann, 1653);

Luigi Cornaro, *Der Mässigkeit Wolleben, und Der Trunckenheit Selbstmord* (Ulm: Published by Georg Wildeisen, 1653);

William Ames, *Von dem Recht deß Gewissens, und Desselben begebenden Fällen. Jn 5. Büchern verfasset* (Nuremberg: Published by Wolfgang Endter the Younger & Johann Andreas Endter, 1654);

Eustache du Refuge, *Kluger Hofmann* (Frankfurt am Main & Hamburg: Published by Johann Naumann, 1655);

Mercurius Historicus: Der historische Mercurius. Das ist: Hundert neue und denckwürdige Erzehlungen, theils trauriger, theils frölicher Geschichte: aus Parival, Sarpeto, Astolvi Balvacensi und etlich andern wenig bekanten Scribenten, gedolmetscht und mit nützlichen Lehren und Sprüchen der H. Schrifft beleuchtet: Mit Anfügung eines umbständigen Discursus von der Höflichkeit, durch Octavium Chiliadem (Hamburg: Printed by Michael Pfeiffer, published by Johann Naumann, 1657).

Georg Philipp Harsdörffer, one of the most prolific and influential poets, theoreticians, and translators in seventeenth-century Germany, was the founder and leader of the so-called Nuremberg Poet's Circle, known for its playful and onomatopoeic early mannerist style. A polymath, he used many fiction and nonfiction genres to write about every topic that would be of interest to a general educated audience of that century: poetics, literature, the arts, religion, mathematics, natural sciences, manners, everyday culture, and civilization. He was well read in all major European literatures – Neo-Latin, French, Italian, Spanish, Dutch, and English – and used an enormous amount of material from these literatures, both in his own poetic works and in his translations and adaptations, thus becoming one of the most important transmitters of Romance literatures in Germany.

The Harsdörffer family is known to have resided in Nuremberg since the late fourteenth century; it became eligible for the city council around 1450. The family acquired a country estate in Fischbach, outside of Nuremberg, in 1537. On this estate Harsdörffer was born on 1 November 1607 to Philipp Harsdörffer, a wealthy patrician, and Lucretia Harsdörffer, née Scheurl von Defersdorf; he was baptized at the Saint Sebald church. After a private education at home, under the supervision of his parents, on 20 March 1623 he began his studies in law, philosophy, and philology at the nearby University of Altdorf, together with his friend Christoph Fürer von Haimendorf. One of the most influential teachers at Altdorf was Daniel Schwenter, whose *Deliciæ Physico-Mathematicae* (Physical and Mathematical Delights, 1636) would later be completed by Harsdörffer; there is no evidence, however, that Harsdörffer had any contact with Schwenter during his time at the university.

On 10 July 1626 Harsdörffer and Fürer von Haimendorf moved to the University of Strasbourg to study under Matthias Bernegger. Bernegger's eclectic approach to knowledge, his polyhistorical tendencies, and his use of dialogue for didactic purposes had a profound impact on Harsdörffer. Moreover, Bernegger's opinion that citizens may use force against the emperor under certain circumstances reinforced Harsdörffer's anti-imperial leanings.

From 1627 to 1632 Harsdörffer and Fürer von Haimendorf traveled and studied in France, the Netherlands, England, Switzerland, and Italy. It is assumed that Harsdörffer acquired his profound knowledge of Romance literatures and proficiency in French, Italian, Spanish, and English during this period. In spite of their extensive studies, neither man earned an academic degree, as academics could not be seated in the Nuremberg city council.

Harsdörffer's father died on 25 December 1631, leading Harsdörffer to return to Nuremberg in early 1632. In March 1633 he served as an aid to Johann Jacob Tetzel in a diplomatic mission to keep the free imperial city of Nuremberg out of the Thirty Years' War. On his return Harsdörffer was appointed as assessor to Nuremberg's *Untergericht* (lower court). After 1633 Harsdörffer would only leave Nuremberg for short cures in health spas. On 9 June 1634 he married Susanne Fürer von Haimendorf. Of their five sons and three daughters only Carl Gottlieb, born in 1637, and Johann Sigmund, born in 1639, would survive him. After the death of his wife in 1646, his widowed sister, Lukretia, would take charge of his household until his own death.

Harsdörffer was appointed assessor to the highest civilian court of justice in Nuremberg, the Stadtgericht, on 15 April 1637. The high court consisted of the judge, two associate judges with law degrees, and six jurors representing the patriciate. The duties of the assessor were to do legal research, to organize the files for the court, and to prepare all documentation needed by the jurors. Although Harsdörffer would remain in this position for eighteen years, there is virtually no trace of his court activities in his writings. His affinity for moral instruction, however, can perhaps be seen as a reaction to the abundant evidence of moral weakness he encountered in his work at the court.

Given his privileged birth, Harsdörffer's public career was modest. Furthermore, he seems to have had no part in the management of his family's extensive estate, and he repeatedly complained about financial difficulties. Writing became Harsdörffer's main occupation rather than a pastime, as was more typical for an author of his social status. Therefore, he cannot serve as an example of the ideal baroque symbiosis between politics and poetry envisioned by late-Humanist poets such as Martin Opitz.

Aside from two occasional poems, published in 1637 and 1639, the *Vollstädiges Trincir-Büchlein* (Complete Handbook on Serving Food, 1640) was Harsdörffer's first publication. The richly illustrated book on ceremonial aspects of banquets offers an eclectic mix, a pattern typical of many of his later works. On a pragmatic level it instructs the reader in how to lay a table, how to use knife and fork, how to carve various foods and present them on a platter, and which types of food are available during which seasons. Harsdörffer also discusses the social norms observed in formal dinners and dinner entertainments, such as after-dinner plays, and he gives detailed accounts of some historical state dinners. Finally, he answers questions on food and health, on eating habits, and on table manners. The book is adorned with inserted poems, such as the al-

legorical "Der Götter Blumenmahl" (The Gods' Flower Feast).

Harsdörffer's best-known and most influential work was *Frawen-Zimmer Gespräch-Spiel* (Playful Colloquies for the Ladies). Two volumes appeared in 1641 and 1642; in 1643 Harsdörffer published a completely revised edition of the first volume, increasing the number of fictional participants from four to six and introducing the hallmark transverse octavo format. Volumes three to seven appeared in the new format at yearly intervals from 1643 to 1647; the final volume, delayed by a shortage of paper at the end of the war, was published in 1649. The second volume was revised and put into the transverse octavo format in 1657.

The colloquies represent an anthropological treasure trove. In three hundred conversation games, three men and three women discuss virtually every topic that would interest a seventeenth-century reader. Harsdörffer quotes 849 sources, representing all major European languages and cultures. The conversation games, with their strict rules, are playful in the sense of the rhetorical concept of play (*ludus*): they allow for the discussion of problems and the testing of strategies without consequences. The practice of rhetorical skills often leads to mannerist experimentation with language and forms; the goal is *decorum,* the acquisition of the ability to use language in a way that is appropriate for the conversation partner and the topic under discussion. The games thus prepare the participants — and, by implication, the reader — for real-life situations.

The colloquy form is of Italian origin but can be traced back to the dialogues of Greek antiquity. The dialogue was considered the most effective mode of instruction, and Harsdörffer clearly sought to educate through play. He most likely studied Italian models — particularly Balthasar Castiglione's *Il libro del cortegiano* (The Book of the Courtier, 1528) — during his stay in Siena. Harsdörffer's work, in turn, greatly influenced *Rosen-mând* (1651), by Philipp von Zesen; *Monatsgespräche* (Monthly Colloquies, 1663), by Johann Rist and Erasmus Francisci; and *Pegnesische Gesprächspiel-Gesellschaft* (Colloquy Society on the Pegnitz, 1665), by Sigmund von Birken.

Harsdörffer's colloquies take a multitude of forms: debates, riddles, guessing games, charades, spelling bees, role plays, skits, moralistic treatises, and even entire stage plays. In the final volume he gives a classification of the material presented in the colloquies: the three general topics under discussion are human activities and social reality, including arts, crafts, hunting, dancing, and heraldics; histori-

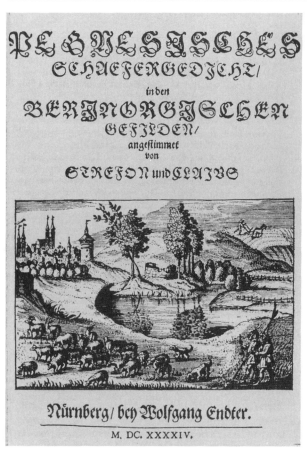

Title page for an eclogue written by Harsdörffer and Johann Klaj for a double wedding in Nuremberg

cal narrations and fictional allegories; and the physical world, including colors, numbers, astronomy, the elements, and gardening. His didactic goals are to give the reader a better understanding of the world, to discuss contemporary issues, and to help the reader achieve success in dealing with social and professional issues. The colloquies' yearly appearance can be considered an early form of journal or magazine.

The setting for the colloquies is an idyllic and comfortable country estate. The host is an elderly nobleman with courtly experience; a middle-aged soldier contributes reason and practical experience; and an erudite young student provides book knowledge. All three males are worldly, widely traveled, and well read. It is noteworthy that the student, the only participant not of noble birth, is the one who brings in new ideas and is the main source of inspiration and stimulation for the group. Harsdörffer typically speaks through him: erudition allows members of the bourgeoisie to compete with the lower nobility and, at the same time, guarantees acceptance into the

ranks of the nobility for the fictional student, as it did for Harsdörffer himself.

The women are less distinguished. An elderly, presumably married woman plays the role of facilitator and provider of moral guidance; the other two are young, impressionable, unmarried, and in need of male tutelage. Throughout the colloquies Harsdörffer presents an education program for women. In his view it is perfectly appropriate for women to display intellectual curiosity; they are just as intelligent as men and have the same ability to reason. Yet he does not support formal education for women: women can only be educated in their homes, which puts men firmly in control of their education, as they are in the colloquies. The games are dominated by the male participants, and the women typically are assigned the easier tasks or losing viewpoints, reflecting their inferior rhetorical skills and educational levels. This model for women's education reflects the context of the Lutheran Reform, which shifted the emphasis from visual religious imagery to the printed word. A basic education was essential to ensure proper religious instruction and a dignified spiritual life for women.

Harsdörffer hoped to acquire visibility through the colloquies. The preface to the first volume addresses the Fruchtbringende Gesellschaft (Fruit-bringing Society), the most important German language society, and the dedicatory poem is directed to Prince Ludwig of Anhalt-Köthen, who founded the society in 1617. The response to Harsdörffer's implicit request for membership was prompt: he entered as number 368 in 1642 under the name Der Spielende (The Playful One), no doubt in reference to his colloquies. Harsdörffer became one of the most active members of the society: he introduced more than fifty new members and identified himself as a member on the title pages of virtually all of his publications. This acceptance also brought him membership in Zesen's Deutschgesinnte Genossenschaft (German-minded Association) and started him on a varied poetic career.

In 1643 appeared *Japeta,* Harsdörffer's translation of *Europe, Comédie héroique* (1643), by Jean Desmarets de Saint-Sorlin. The five-act play of intrigues, written in alexandrines in the style of French classicism, focuses on the new order favoring the French in the middle of the war. Japeta is an allegorical figure who stands for Europe; other figures represent various European monarchs. The work is an explicitly political gesture, like his appeal to the Fruchtbringende Gesellschaft.

But by 1644 Harsdörffer was turning in a new direction: pastoral literature. This new interest may have been due to the influence of Johann Klaj, who arrived in Nuremberg in late 1643 or early 1644; he had studied in Wittenberg with Augustus Buchner, the earliest supporter of dactylic verse, which had been rejected by Opitz in his poetry reform. Harsdörffer's first bucolic work was "Das Geistliche Waldgedicht, oder Freudenspiel genannt Seelewig, Gesangsweis auf Italianische Art gesetzet" (The Spiritual Sylvan Poem; or, Comedy Called Seelewig, Set to Music in the Italian Manner), which was first published in 1644 as an appendix to volume four of the *Frawen-Zimmer Gespräch-Spiel*. The earliest German singspiel still in existence, it draws heavily on Jesuit pastoral allegory and is based on an anonymous German prose play of 1637 that, in turn, is a translation from the Italian. The music was composed by Sigmund Theophil Staden. Its only known performance took place in Wolfenbüttel on 10 April 1654, on the occasion of the seventy-fifth birthday of Duke August, and was sponsored by Duchess Sophie Elisabeth.

Later in 1644 Harsdörffer and Klaj collaborated on *Pegnesisches Schaefergedicht* (Shepherd Poem of the Pegnitz) for a double wedding on 16 October involving three prominent Nuremberg families; the two authors appear to have contributed equally to the work. The poem is an eclogue patterned after Opitz's *Schäfferey von der Nimfen Hercinie* (Shepherd Poem of Hercinie the Nymph, 1630). In a prose narrative frame two shepherds, Strefon and Klajus, wander through a pastoral grove that resembles the surroundings of Nuremberg and are led by an allegorical figure to an elaborate temple commemorating the three families involved in the wedding. Leaving the temple, the shepherds engage in a singing contest on love, marriage, and fertility. Prominent stylistic features, prototypical for the Nuremberg poetic style, are the extensive use of dactylic verse, the imitation of the sounds of nature through onomatopoeia, the heavily metaphoric language, and mannerist tendencies.

Nuremberg's own language society, the Pegnesischer Blumenorden (Order of Flowers on the Pegnitz), was founded in late 1644 under Harsdörffer's leadership. Only fourteen members, including one woman, were admitted, most of them in the first two years. In contrast to the courtly model of the Fruchtbringende Gesellschaft, this urban society was exclusively supported by the learned bourgeoisie. The members, who were similar in background, education, and interests, chose emblematic flower insignia – wildflowers were used rather than exotic domesticated ones, reflecting the bourgeois orientation of the society – and wore silk armbands. The

society names of the original members, such as Strefon (or Strephon) for Harsdörffer, were taken from Sir Philip Sydney's *Arcadia* (1590), which had appeared in a German translation in 1629. The society's motto was "mit Nutzen erfreulich" (enjoyable while beneficial), its emblem the panpipe. The most important local members were Klaj, Birken, and Johann Hellwig; Johann Rist and Justus Georg Schottelius were important corresponding members. Johann Michael Dilherr, who became pastor at Saint Sebald in 1646, greatly influenced the spiritual direction of the group, although he never formally became a member. Since there are no references to the society in the minutes of the city council before 1672, one must assume that it was of a private rather than a corporate character. Meetings typically took place outside Nuremberg, in the bucolic landscape described in the *Pegnesisches Schaefergedicht*. Poetic texts were read or composed, and intellectual and literary topics were discussed. In Harsdörffer's time the Pegnesischer Blumenorden enabled the poets to create a sense of community. Since only two new members were admitted after 1646, the level of activity must have dropped off after that date. Under the leadership of Birken, who revived the society in 1662 after a four-year interregnum, the membership rapidly expanded; at that time the Pegnesischer Blumenorden evolved into a more traditional language society.

The society advocated standardization and "purification" of the German language. In his introduction to volume five of *Frawen-Zimmer Gespräch-Spiele* Harsdörffer developed a generic ideal for members of such an organization, excluding enemies of virtue and of the heroic German language: a model member shall pray devoutly, study industriously, be of a happy disposition, be kind to everyone, learn from the knowing, teach the ignorant, and act ethically; he or she shall not offend anyone, speak ill of anyone, or get involved in other people's business. Harsdörffer's emblem book *Stechbüchlein* (Little Book of Engravings, 1645) includes fifty emblems in the shape of a heart, conveying the aesthetic and moral ideas of the society.

The pastoral motif of the *Pegnesisches Schaefergedicht* reappears in Harsdörffer's translation of Jorge de Montemayor's 1559 novel *Diana* (1646). A translation by Hanns Ludwig von Kuffstein had been published in 1619; Harsdörffer edited Kuffstein's translation, particularly the inserted poems, and republished the work in 1646, adding his own translation of a supplemental third part by Gil Polo (1564). In his programmatic introduction to *Diana* Harsdörffer responds to the traditional argument that fiction is morally questionable because it seduces the reader into identifying with immoral events. In his view, invented stories are much more effective as teaching tools because the didactic potential of true stories is limited by the restrictions of actual events; in fiction, by contrast, the author has great latitude to arrange a story to fit its moral intent. Even the depiction of sensual love is justifiable, because it can be shown to be virtuous; for example, there are explicit love stories in the Bible.

Harsdörffer was also fighting other intellectual battles of his day. Since the publication of *Deutscher Sprachlehre Entwurf* (Outline of a Course in the German Language), by Christian Gueintz, and of *Teutsche Sprachkunst* (German Grammar), by Schottelius, both in 1641, two competing linguistic theories had been debated in the Fruchtbringende Gesellschaft. Gueintz sought to base grammatical and orthographic norms on the language of Martin Luther and of the Meissen region, while Schottelius grounded his theories on what he saw as the organic inner logic of language, manifesting itself in inherently monosyllabic *Stammwörter* (root words). He viewed German as a *Hauptsprache* (major language) and tried to prove its relationship to Hebrew and, ultimately, to the "Adamic" language. Through its monosyllabic roots, he claimed, German retains an essential connection between the word and what it represents; thus, he argues, it reflects nature and is uniquely suited for philosophical discourse. By its presumed closeness to Hebrew – and, thus, to the Cabala – the German language, he claims, has maintained its ability to express the secrets of nature. This concept of language leads to the numerological speculation, letter and word games, onomatopoeia, and heavy use of metaphors seen in the writings of Schottelius's followers, such as the Nuremberg circle.

Prince Ludwig of Anhalt-Köthen, the founder and leader of the Fruchtbringende Gesellschaft, supported Gueintz, while Harsdörffer's *Specimen Philologiæ Germanicæ* (A Model for a German Study of Words, 1646) argued in favor of Schottelius's views. Yet by including a panegyric (also published separately in an enlarged version in 1647 under the title *Porticus Serenissimo atque Celsissimo Principi, ac Domino, Domino Augusto*) to Duke August of Wolfenbüttel, a prominent member of the Fruchtbringende Gesellschaft, and by mentioning him on the title page, Harsdörffer rendered it virtually impossible for other members of the society to attack his views.

Harsdörffer's systematic framework strongly resembles Schottelius's. In *Specimen Philologiæ Germanicæ* – which, ironically, is written in Latin to reach the learned public in all of Europe – Harsdörffer declares the end of the monopoly of Latin. He advocates the use of the vernacular in arts and sciences, the development of German dictionaries, and the translation of the works of all major authors into German. In a lengthy chapter that constitutes the first extensive survey of German literature of the seventeenth century, he assesses the writings of forty-one contemporary poets. His intention is to bring into evidence the accomplishments of German poetry, to prove that German writers are not inferior to those writing in Latin, and to create a canon of exemplary German poets.

These deliberations culminated in Harsdörffer's main theoretical work, which systematically develops his poetological views: *Poetischer Trichter, die Teutsche Dicht- und Reimkunst, ohne Behuf der lateinischen Sprache, in VI. Stunden einzugiessen* (The Poet's Funnel: The Art of German Poetry and Prosody, to be Poured in Six Hours without Help of the Latin Language), published in three volumes in 1647, 1648, and 1653. *Poetischer Trichter* is Harsdörffer's best-known – and possibly least-understood – work. The funnel metaphor had been used by Wilhelm Schickart in *Der hebraische Trichter* (The Hebrew Funnel, 1629), and Harsdörffer may have used it to assure commercial success for his own book. In his introduction Harsdörffer dismisses the notion, which might seem to be implied by the title, that the art of poetry can be learned in six easy lessons.

Volume one addresses a general educated reader who needs to acquire the skill to write occasional poetry. Its six chapters deal with poetry in general, poetic invention (*inventio*), the poetic properties of the German language, qualities and types of rhymes, and appropriate poetic language. Harsdörffer's discussion of prosody incorporates the innovations by Opitz, Buchner, Zesen, and Schottelius. The appendix to volume one includes a discussion of orthography and punctuation, as well as the "Fünffacher Denckring der teutschen Sprache" (Fivefold Ring for Thinking in the German Language). The ring exemplifies an adaptation of cabalist thought based on the ideas of the medieval Catalan mystic Ramon Llull (also known as Raymond Lully) and promulgated in the seventeenth century by Athanasius Kircher. The ring consists of five rotatable concentric disks and an indicator that are held together in the center by a staple. The first and smallest disk lists forty-eight prefixes, the fifth twenty-four suffixes. The three center disks are used to form combinations of all accurate monosyllabic German word roots: they contain 60 initial letters or consonant clusters, 12 stem vowels or diphthongs, and 120 consonants or consonant clusters to conclude the word root. In Harsdörffer's view, the ring is the basic tool needed to compile a German dictionary that would include poetic words not in everyday usage. It would also help the poet to find rhyming words: for this purpose disks three and four, containing the stem vowel and the following consonant cluster to make the rhyme, are fixed, while the second disk is rotated until a fitting word is found; in the case of disyllabic words, disk five may be fixed as well. The ring captures the entire German language in its simplicity and variety and reflects the language's presumed capacity to represent nature.

In volume two, published in 1648, Harsdörffer added another six hourly lessons, discussing various literary genres and the sources of poetic invention. An appendix lists more than twenty-five hundred German root words. Volume three, published in 1653 under the title *Prob und Lob der Teutschen Wolredenheit* (Testimony and Praise of the Art of German Eloquence), discusses the properties of German poetic language in one hundred paragraphs. The second part, "Bestehend in poetischen Beschreibungen, verblümten Reden und Kunstzierlichen Ausbildungen" (Consisting of Poetic Descriptions, Flowery Orations, and Ornate Formulations), provides the user with extensive poetic definitions of 539 terms in alphabetical order, covering such diverse words and concepts as *Aal* (eel), *Abend* (evening), *Aberglaub* (superstition), *Acker* (arable field), *Adel* (nobility), and *angenehm* (pleasant); its objective is not to give encyclopedic definitions but to assemble a collection of expressions, idioms, phrases, metaphors, analogies, figures of speech, similes, and comparisons. Harsdörffer also indicates how each term may be represented visually in emblems. In many entries the allegorical meaning of a term is explained; for example, "Der Staub hat die Deutung der Nichtigkeit und Verachtung" (Dust has the meaning of vanity and contempt). Under each subject heading the poet can find a wealth of circumlocutions that can be used to provide adornment for poetry written for special occasions. The book is a poetics meant to help amateur writers produce "polished" poetry.

The aspiring poet, Harsdörffer says, needs to master the rules of poetics, to study the canon of exemplary poets from Catullus and Horace to Pierre de Ronsard and Opitz, and to practice by imitating the works of such poets and translating their poems into German. Even the most industrious student, however, will never become a poet unless he possesses talent and *natura* (natural disposition), particularly a good *ingenium* (imagination). *Iudicium* (good judgment) is part of this natural gift: a poet needs to be able to assess the cohesiveness, stylistic uniformity, and inner logic of a text and to consider its communicative context and *consilium* (social implications). But talent alone will not bear fruit unless it is complemented by *furor poeticus* (divine inspiration), which can be received only by poets who possess virtue and faith. An inspired poet, therefore, is by definition also a *vir bonus* (ethical person) who will not use poetry or fiction to deceive or seduce his reader.

Still following the humanist rhetorical model, Harsdörffer describes the phases of text production. In the first phase, *inventio* (poetic invention), the poet collects ideas and formulations regarding the subject matter. Traditional topical categories help him find and organize his material. Harsdörffer prefers four topoi: word, qualities of the object, circumstances, and comparison. In the second step, *dispositio,* the writer decides on the use of genre, structures his argumentation, and organizes the material. The third step, *elocutio,* is the actual formulation of the text; here Harsdörffer discusses language in general, poetic language, poetic style, and rhetorical tropes and figures. The poetic style chosen needs to be in agreement both with the subject matter (*aptum*) and with the intended audience (*decorum*).

Nuremberg had engaged in a policy of strict neutrality to stay out of the Thirty Years' War and maintain its independence. The predominantly Lutheran city was torn between support for the Protestant coalition led by the Swedish, and the French and loyalty to the Catholic emperor, who was the guarantor of its status as a free city. The citizens had not been allowed publicly to take sides in the conflict, and the city council had censored all statements that might damage the city. At the same time, religious tolerance and neutrality turned Nuremberg into a haven for political and religious refugees such as Klaj and Birken. Even during the peace negotiations in Münster and Osnabrück in the fall of 1648, the military situation in Franconia remained tense.

In early November Harsdörffer published a *Lobgesang* (panegyric) to the Swedish general Carl Gustav Wrangel, who had set up camp in the vicinity of Nuremberg. Harsdörffer apparently believed that the work had been approved by the censor, but the city council immediately confiscated all copies of the text and questioned Harsdörffer and the printer, Heinrich Pillenhofer, between 8 November and 10 November. Harsdörffer was jailed during this time and was released after being reprimanded by the council. This incident may explain why Harsdörffer remained silent during the peace celebrations in Nuremberg during the following two years, while his colleagues Klaj and Birken contributed occasional poems, speeches, broadsheets, and longer works.

The year 1649 brought a significant reorientation in Harsdörffer's writings and began the most productive period of his career. He concluded *Frawen-Zimmer Gespräch-Spiele* and turned his attention to devotional literature and collections of prose stories and novellas with a clear didactic agenda. While *Frawen-Zimmer Gespräch-Spiele* had relied on argumentation, his stories seek to affect readers' behavior by evoking their interest in often sensational factual and fictional events.

Devotional literature figures much more prominently in Harsdörffer's poetics and in his creative output than is generally acknowledged in literary histories. One example is his *Hertzbewegliche Sonntagsandachten* (Heart-moving Sunday Meditations, 1649, 1652). Each *Andachtsgemähl* (devotional emblem) is dedicated to a specific day in the church calendar and consists of a quote from the Bible, an emblematic representation, annotations, a didactic or allegorical devotional poem expanding on the quotation and the emblem, a topical poem or hymn, and a prayer. Each of the two volumes comprises seventy-six such reflections, one dedicated to each Sunday or holiday in the church year.

Harsdörffer published six highly successful multivolume collections of stories and novellas; most of the works were adapted from French, Spanish, or Italian sources. The first and best-known collection is *Der Grosse SchauPlatz jämmerlicher Mordgeschichte* (Grand Theater of Lamentable Murders, 1649–1650), eight parts in four volumes, each comprising fifty stories. Harsdörffer's most successful work, it went through at least eight editions, the last in 1713. The first two parts are based on *L'Amphithéâtre sanglant* (1630), by Jean Pierre Camus, the bishop of Belley; the stories in the other six parts are drawn from other contemporary sources. Harsdörffer's collections were used, in turn, as sources by other German writers, including Hans Jacob Christoph von Grimmelshausen.

Each story begins with a short enigmatic or paradoxical title, such as "Der Liebs- und Todeskampf" (The Fight for Love and Death) or "Die blinde Verzweiffelung" (Blind Despair). The characters are not kings and princes but common people. Each story is reduced to a didactic formula that is summarized in a short poem. The simplicity in content and style enables the reader to comprehend the message without much reflection.

The stories are intended to instill fear and horror in the reader, and the effect is amplified by a remarkably detached narrative perspective: even the most gruesome details are told in a straightforward manner. "Das Gespenst" (The Ghost), for instance, is the story of an old butcher who kills his wife so that he can marry a younger woman: "Er lässet einen Sarg machen, weil damals die Pest regierte, und zerspaltet dem schlaffenden Mütterlein das Haubt, mit seinem Schlachtbeil, mit welchem er die Rinder zu schlachten pflegte, legte sie in den Sarg, mit vorgeben, sie were eiligst an der Pest gestorben" (He had a coffin made because the area was afflicted by the plague. He split the skull of the old woman with the ax he used to slaughter the cattle and put her into a coffin, pretending that she had suddenly died of the plague). He marries the young woman, but his wife's ghost brings him to justice.

Harsdörffer followed his first collection with a two-volume companion anthology of two hundred stories, *Der Große Schau-Platz Lust und Lehrreicher Geschichte* (Grand Theater of Delightful and Edifying Stories, 1650); its sources include Camus, Miguel de Cervantes, and many other French, Spanish, and Italian writers. Again, the stories focus on the private lives of ordinary persons. In the dedication Harsdörffer calls the world the most beautiful book, thus evoking the common Neoplatonic and pansophist topos of the "book of nature." Human circumstances and actions, he says, constitute the most beautiful chapter in this book.

Contrary to what the title implies, many stories in the collection deal with human weaknesses and vices. The fifth story is typical: the Spanish nobleman Alfrede rapes the virgin Ilirta with the help of his friend Heinrichmond. Since each accuses the other of being the chief culprit, the governor forces the two to roll the dice. The winner, Heinrichmond, has to marry Ilirta; Alfrede is decapitated, and his possessions form the bride's dowry. As in *Der Grosse SchauPlatz jämmerlicher Mordgeschichte,* the transgressors find their due punishment and order is reinstated.

In both collections the reader frequently encounters moral lessons that do not follow logically from the narrative. "Das gefährliche Vertrauen" (Dangerous Trust) tells of a young man's romantic adventure with an anonymous noble lady. The story does not focus on the immorality of the sexual relationship but on how the young man was deceived by blindly trusting a servant. Such mismatches of story and moral may be explained by

Harsdörffer's combining narrative elements from various sources.

The two-volume collection *Nathan und Jotham: Das ist Geistliche und Weltliche Lehrgedichte* (Nathan and Jotham: That is, Spiritual and Secular Didactic Poems, 1650, 1651) is named after two narrators of parables in the Old Testament; it consists of six hundred parables, allegorical stories, and didactic prose poems, each followed by an interpretation. Harsdörffer again used many sources, most notably the writings of Joseph Hall, to offer parables on a wide range of topics. The collection concludes with an appendix, titled "Simson," that comprises one hundred riddles on related topics.

Schwenter's *Deliciæ Physico-Mathematicæ,* a collection of 663 tasks, problems, experiments, and games from all fields of science and philosophy of nature, had appeared in 1636; Schwenter had died a few months before the work's publication. Harsdörffer continued the work in two more volumes, under slightly varied titles, in 1651 and 1653. Each volume comprises five hundred entries, drawn from a multitude of sources. Harsdörffer used Schwenter's unsystematic division into sixteen scientific disciplines, which, in turn, was based on *Récréation mathématique* (Mathematical Recreation, 1624), by the French Jesuit Jean Levrechon: the seven liberal arts are complemented by mechanical and alchemical arts. For Harsdörffer, natural science provides insight into divine creation; Harsdörffer's interest was not in scientific truth but in using science for moral-didactic purposes. Like Schwenter, Harsdörffer was only vaguely familiar with the leading scientific theories of the time.

On 8 May 1651 Duke Wilhelm IV of Saxe Weimar was inaugurated as head of the Fruchtbringende Gesellschaft, succeeding Ludwig of Anhalt-Köthen, who had died the previous year. Although Harsdörffer presumably was not present at the ceremonies in Weimar, he chronicled the events in *Fortpflantzung der Hochlöblichen Fruchtbringenden Geselschaft: Das ist, Kurtze Erzehlung alles dessen, was sich bey Erwehlung und Antrettung hochbesagter Geselschaft Oberhauptes, deß Höchteursten und Wehrtesten Schmackhaften, begeben und zugegragen* (Continuation of the Highly Revered Fruit-bringing Society: That Is, a Brief Narration of All That Occurred during the Selection and Inauguration of the Cherished and Inestimable Tasteful One, the Head of the Above-Mentioned Society, 1651). Each member presents a distich extending good wishes that contains a reference to the duke's society name. In his acceptance speech Wilhelm addresses each member

with a similar distich, making a reference to the member's society name. Other texts deal with the transfer of the seal and the files from Köthen to Weimar. Harsdörffer added his own treatise, "Lobrede deß Geschmackes" (Praise of Good Taste), which doubled the size of the volume. Harsdörffer said in a letter that the book otherwise would have been too slim to honor such an important person and to commemorate such a significant event.

In the following two years Harsdörffer published two additional collections of stories that are similar to the *Große Schau-Platz* anthologies. The first was the two-volume *Heraclitus und Democritus: Das ist C. Fröliche und Traurige Geschichte* (Heraclitus and Democritus: That is, One Hundred Happy and Sad Stories, 1652, 1653). Each volume consists of a hundred stories, mostly adapted from Camus's works. Each story has a moral introduction, typically referring to biblical teachings; the main narrative illustrates the point, which is reinforced by a concluding quote from the Bible. The other collection, published in 1652, is an adaptation of Camus's *La pentagone historique* (1631) and of Hall's *Characters of Vertues and Vices* (1608).

From 1652 to 1654 Harsdörffer published five adaptations of nonfiction works. Two are mathematical: Franz Ritter's *Speculum Solis, das ist: Sonnen-Spiegel* (Mirror of the Sun, 1652), first published in 1607, and Philipp Uffenbach's *De Quadratura Circuli Mechanici* (The Mechanical Squaring of the Circle, 1653), first published in 1619. The others are of a devotional and moralizing nature: *Göttliche Liebes-Lust* (Delights of Divine Love, 1653), which comprises translations of Luigi Novarino's *Deliciae divini amoris* (1641) and Paul de Barry's *Sanctae intentiones* (1646); *Der Mässigkeit Wolleben, und Der Trunckenheit Selbstmord* (The Benefits of Moderation and Suicidal Inebriation, 1653), a translation of Luigi Cornaro's *Trattao de la vita sobria* (Treatise on the Sober Life, 1558); and *Von dem Recht deß Gewissens, und Desselben begebenden Fällen* (Of Conscience and Its Foundation, 1654), a translation of William Ames's *De Conscientia et ejus jure* (1630).

In 1654 Harsdörffer brought out another collection of short stories: *Der Geschichtspiegel: Vorweisend hundert denckwürdige Begebenheiten* (The Mirror of Stories: Containing One Hundred Memorable Incidents, 1654). Each story begins with a motto illustrated by an emblem. In "Die Eheliche Liebe" (Marital Love), for example, the first paragraph explains the emblem that follows and includes the motto "Gleich und gleich macht freudenreich" (equal and equal brings about joy). The story is about a soldier whose wife loves him so much that she accompanies him into battle. She is captured, and he dies in the attempt to free her. She then throws herself into the battle so that she can die with him, but she miraculously survives. The lengthy commentary on the tale is introduced by the question: "Ob der Mann, oder das Weib mehr zu der Liebe geneiget seye?" (Whether man or woman is more predisposed to love?); Harsdörffer determines that men and women are equally loving and faithful. In a play on words, he concludes that in marriage the "Kuß-Jahr" (kissing year) – the first blissful year – is followed by many "Buß-Jahre" (years of repentance). The geometrical and optical properties of the mirror that serves as the metaphor for the collection are explained in the appendix.

On 17 April 1655 Harsdörffer was elected to the forty-two-member city council. It is unclear why he was chosen at the relatively advanced age of forty-eight, after having spent more than twenty years in public life; it has been suggested that his earlier reprimands by the council hindered the advancement of his political career. After 1655 his literary production slowed considerably, possibly because his new duties did not allow as much time for writing. During the last three years of his life an increased concern for political and courtly issues is noticeable in his works. A typical representative of the urban patriciate, he aspired to imitate the attitudes and lifestyles of the nobility. The honest German bourgeois is to be introduced into the world of courtly sophistication by means of the literary text, although without the moral corruption that often accompanies courtly life. Such is the function of *Kluger Hofmann* (Prudent Courtier, 1655), Harsdörffer's translation of *Traicté de la Cour* (Treatise on the Court, 1616), by Eustache du Refuge. The new learned, considerate, bourgeois "courtier" who is devoted to God, prince, and virtue is the ideal servant of the absolutist state. The prudent courtier is a bourgeois who uses his well-rounded education for social advancement.

The acquisition of a courtly conversational style is one of the main purposes of the two-volume *Ars Apothegmatica, das ist: Kunstquellen denckwürdiger Lehrsprüche und Ergötzlicher Hofreden* (The Art of Apothegms; That Is: Sources of the Art of Memorable Maxims and of Delightful Speeches at Court, 1655). The genre of the apothegm first appeared in antiquity and was revived in the Renaissance. Harsdörffer's models were collections by Desiderius Erasmus (1532) and Julius Wilhelm Zincgref (1626). His apothegms have a bipartite structure that reflects his didactic interest: a brief historical narration is followed by its interpretation in a pointed maxim. Harsdörffer's six thousand apothegms range from simple didactic sentences, proverbs, and witticisms to short humorous anecdotes. The collection reintroduces the playfulness of some of his earlier works; its intent is not just education but also enjoyment. Two examples illustrate the range of the apothegms. "Galgen" (Gallows) tells the briefest of anecdotes: "Es fragte ein Soldat einen Bettler für dem Thor einer Reichsstadt: Warumb ist der Galgen so leer? Der Bettler sagte: Die Dieb sind alle in den Krieg gezogen" (A soldier asked a beggar in front of the gates of an imperial city: Why is the gallows so empty? The beggar replied: The thieves all went to war). "Heuraten" (Marrying) is of the proverb type: "Wilt du ein gutes Jahr haben, so heurate dich: wilt du zwey gute Jahre haben, so heurate nicht" (If you want to have a good year get married. If you want to have two good years don't get married). In these finely honed short pieces Harsdörffer implicitly devised the ideal of gallant conversation that dominated the later seventeenth century.

Both volumes are preceded by extensive poetological introductions where Harsdörffer lists the sources of poetic invention. He instructs the reader in how to use the apothegms as source material for his or her own poetic invention. Harsdörffer says that he employed ten categories from the canon of rhetorical topoi to organize his apothegms: didactic maxims; the sound, composition, etymology, and motivation of words; dual meanings; the natural organization of things; causes and appropriate consequences; inappropriate and exaggerated acts and consequences; similes and parables; opposites; obscure questions and answers; and stories. In the collection itself, this organizing principle is hardly discernible; the wide array of information defies any attempt to categorize it.

The acquisition of a written, rather than oral, communication style that is both sophisticated and effective is the purpose of *Der Teutsche Secretarius* (The German Secretary, 1655, 1659). It is a handbook for public officials and for private individuals who deal with business, government, and personal correspondence. It is both a letter writer's handbook and a directory of aristocratic titles that systematically teaches the correct forms of address and the choice of appropriate language. At the same time, it is a textbook of jargon for political, official, business, social, and amatory exchanges and, thus, a mirror of the social order of the time. The list of honorary titles of all noble persons, from the Hertzog von Amalffi to the Herr von Zintzendorff, and of all chancellors at the important courts is followed by instructions on how to structure and formulate letters for all imaginable occasions. Each section consists of a brief introduction and a large number of sample letters. The appendix lists fifty standard formulations for requests and responses.

Though works with political and courtly overtones dominated the last three years of his life, Harsdörffer also returned to earlier interests. He published a last volume of devotional literature, which includes thoughts gathered from various sources under four hundred alphabetically organized subject headings: *Die Hohe Schul Geist- und Sinnreicher Gedancken, in CCCC. Anmuhtungen, aus dem Buch Gottes und der Natur vorgestellt* (The High School of Spiritual and Discerning Thoughts, Presented in 400 Meditations from the Books of God and of Nature, 1656). His last major work, *Mercurius Historicus* (The Historical Mercury), which repeats the model of his earlier story collections, appeared in 1657. The playful motif of *Frawen-Zimmer Gespräch-Spiele,* finally, is echoed in four or five sets of geographical and astronomical playing cards that Harsdörffer designed and produced between 1655 and 1658. Only one of them survives, *Das Astronomische Kartenspiel* (The Astronomical Card Game, 1656), which includes an instruction booklet.

In 1657 Harsdörffer was appointed *Rugherr* (magistrate at the craftsmen's court). The court, which consisted of five members of the city council, prosecuted criminal and moral offenses. Harsdörffer died on 16 September 1658 and was buried on 22 September in the Johannisfriedhof (Saint John's Cemetery).

After his death Harsdörffer's poetry and poetics remained influential, particularly among mannerist writers, until the early eighteenth century. Andreas Georg Widmann's *Vitae curriculum Georg. Philipp. Harsdorferi* (The Life and Works of Georg Philipp Harsdörffer), a public lecture at the University of Altdorf on 7 May 1707, practically marks the end of the influence of his works. The replacement of late baroque mannerism by the early Enlightenment ideal of a simple and clear style brought a quick end to Harsdörffer's influence.

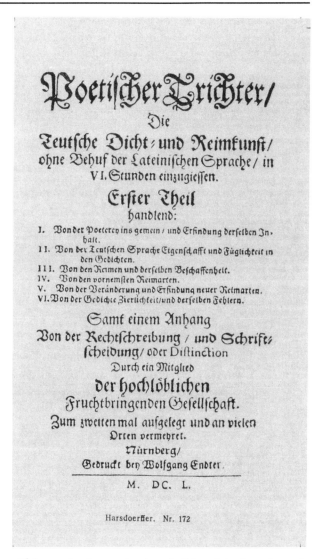

Title page for the second, enlarged edition of the first volume of Harsdörffer's principal theoretical work on the art of poetry

vergleichende Litteraturgeschichte und Renaissance-Litteratur, new series 4 (1891): 100–103;

Carl August Hugo Burkhardt, "Aus dem Briefwechsel Georg Philipp Harsdörffers zur Geschichte der Fruchtbringenden Gesellschaft 1647–1658," in his *Altes und Neues aus dem Pegnesischen Blumenorden,* volume 3 (Nuremberg: Schrag, 1897), pp. 23–140;

Herbert Blume, "Harsdörffers 'Porticus' für Herzog August d.J.: Zu bisher unbekannten bzw. unbeachteten Briefen Harsdörffers," *Wolfenbütteler Beiträge,* 1 (1972): 88–101.

Bibliographies:

Heinz Zirnbauer, "Bibliographie der Werke Georg Philipp Harsdörffers," *Philobiblon,* 5 (March 1961): 12–49;

Letters:

Der Fruchtbringenden Gesellschaft ältester Ertzschrein: Briefe, Devisen und anderweitige Schriftstücke, edited by Gottlieb Krause (Leipzig: Dyk, 1855; reprinted, Hildesheim & New York: Olms, 1973);

Josef Ettlinger, "Briefwechsel zwischen Hofmanswaldau und Harsdörffer," *Zeitschrift für*

Gerhard Dünnhaupt, *Personalbibliographien zu den Drucken des Barock,* volume 9, part 3 (Stuttgart: Hiersemann, 1991), pp. 1969–2031.

Biographies:

Johann Michael Dilherr, *Der Menschen Stand in Göttes Hand* (Nuremberg: Wolfgang Endter, 1658);

Veit Georg von Holtzschuher, *Memoria eruditae nobilitatis viri magnifici, nobilissimi, perstrenui, amplissimi ac prudentissimi Dn. Georgii Philippi Harsdörfferi* (Altdorf: Georg Hagen, 1659);

Andreas Georg Widmann, *Vitae curriculum Georg. Philipp. Harsdorferi* (Altdorf: Daniel Meyer, 1707);

Johann Gabriel Doppelmayr, *Historische Nachricht von den Nürnbergischen Mathematicis und Künstlern* (Nuremberg: Monath, 1730);

Johannes Herdegen, *Historische Nachricht von deß Löblichen Hirten- und Blumen-Ordens an der Pegnitz Anfang und Fortgang* (Nuremberg: Christoph Riegel, 1744);

Irmgard Böttcher, "Der Nürnberger Georg Philipp Harsdörffer," in *Deutsche Dichter des 17. Jahrhunderts: ihr Leben und Werk,* edited by Harald Steinhagen and Benno von Wiese (Berlin: Schmidt, 1984), pp. 289–346.

References:

Judith P. Aikin, "Narcissus and Echo: A Mythological Subtext in Harsdörffer's Operatic Allegory 'Seelewig' (1644)," *Music and Letters,* 72 (August 1991): 359–371;

Italo Michele Battafarano, "Harsdörffers 'Frauenzimmer Gesprächspiele': Frühneuzeitliche Zeichen- und (Sinn-) Bildsprachen in Italien und Deutschland," in *Die Sprache der Zeichen und Bilder: Rhetorik und nonverbale Kommunikation in der frühen Neuzeit,* edited by Volker Kapp (Marburg: Hitzeroth, 1990), pp. 77–89;

Battafarano, "Zwischen Bagagli und Loredano: Harsdörffers Vorstellung der accademie letterarie italiane," in his *Res publica litteraria: Die Institutionen der Gelehrsamkeit in der frühen Neuzeit* (Wiesbaden: Harrassowitz, 1987), pp. 35–53;

Battafarano, ed., *Georg Philipp Harsdörffer: Ein deutscher Dichter und europäischer Gelehrter* (Bern: Peter Lang, 1991);

Theodor Bischoff and August Schmidt, eds., *Festschrift zur 250jährigen Jubelfeier des Pegnesischen Blumenordens* (Nuremberg: Schrag, 1894);

Gerd Dethlefs, "Die Nürnberger Dichterschule und die Friedensmedaille 1648/50," *Wolfenbütteler Barock-Nachrichten,* 16 (May 1989): 1–18;

Leonard Forster, "Harsdörffer's Canon of German Baroque Authors," in *Erfahrung und Überlieferung: Festschrift for C. P. Magill,* edited by H. Siefken and A. Robinson (Cardiff: University of Wales Press, 1974), pp. 32–41;

Guillaume van Gemert, "Cervantes' Novelle El licenciado Vidriera in Deutschland: Frühe Belege für ihre Verbreitung," *Wolfenbütteler Barock-Nachrichten,* 15 (December 1988): 85–89;

Gerald Gillespie, "Humanistic Aspects of the Early Opera Libretto after the Italian Fashion," *Chloe,* 9 (1990): 109–131;

Karl Helmer, "Lehrende Wissenschaft: Zur Grundlegung einer Pädagogik bei Georg Philipp Harsdörffer (1607–1658)," *Pädagogische Rundschau,* 34 (1980): 333–344;

Helmer, *Weltordnung und Bildung: Versuch einer Kosmologischen Grundlegung barocken Erziehungsdenkens bei Georg Philipp Harsdörffer* (Frankfurt am Main & Bern: Peter Lang, 1982);

Peter Hess, "Imitatio-Begriff und Übersetzungstheorie bei Georg Philipp Harsdörffer," *Daphnis,* 21, no. 1 (1992): 9–26;

Hess, *Poetik ohne Trichter: Harsdörffers "Deutsche Dicht- und Reimkunst"* (Stuttgart: Heinz, 1986);

Gerhard Hoffmeister, *Die spanische Diana in Deutschland: Vergleichende Untersuchungen zu Stilwandel und Weltbild des Schäferromans im 17. Jahrhundert* (Berlin: Erich Schmidt, 1972);

Steven R. Huff, "The Early German Libretto: Some Reconsiderations Based on Harsdörffer's 'Seelewig,'" *Music and Letters,* 69 (July 1988): 345–355;

Ferdinand van Ingen, "Georg Philipp Harsdörffer und die Pegnitz-Schäfer Johann Klaj und Sigmund von Birken," in his *Deutsche Dichter* (Stuttgart: Reclam, 1988), pp. 449–463;

Dietrich Jöns, "Literaten in Nürnberg und ihr Verhältnis zum Stadtregiment in den Jahren 1643–1650 nach den Zeugnissen der Ratsverlässe," in *Stadt – Schule – Universität – Buchwesen und die deutsche Literatur im 17. Jahrhundert,* edited by Albrecht Schöne (Munich: Beck, 1976), pp. 84–98;

Wolfgang Kayser, *Die Klangmalerei bei Harsdörffer: Ein Beitrag zur Geschichte der Literatur, Poetik und Sprachgeschichte der Barockzeit* (Göttingen: Vandenhoek & Ruprecht, 1932);

Peter Keller, *Die Oper Seelewig von Sigmund Theophil Staden und Georg Philipp Harsdörffer* (Bern: Haupt, 1977);

Günter Kieslich, "Auf dem Wege zur Zeitschrift: Georg Philipp Harsdörffers 'Frauenzimmer

Gesprechsspiele' (1641–1649)," *Publizistik,* 10 (1965): 515–525;

Kenneth G. Knight, "G. P. Harsdörffer's Frauenzimmergesprächsspiele," *German Life and Letters,* 13 (1959–1960): 116–125;

Albert Krapp, *Die ästhetischen Tendenzen Harsdörffers* (Berlin: Ebering, 1903);

Jean-Daniel Krebs, "Deutsche Barocknovelle zwischen Morallehre und Information: Georg Philipp Harsdörffer und Theophraste Renaudot," *Modern Language Notes,* 103 (April 1988): 478–503;

Krebs, *Georg Philipp Harsdörffer (1607–1658): Poétique et Poésie,* 2 volumes (Bern & Frankfurt am Main: Lang, 1983);

Krebs, "Journalismus und Novelle," *Wolfenbütteler Barock-Nachrichten,* 14 (July 1987): 6–8;

Krebs, "Kuriose Trinkgedichte," *Wolfenbütteler Barock-Nachrichten,* 16 (May 1989): 19–25;

Krebs, "Quand les Allemands apprenaient à trancher," *Etudes Germaniques,* 41 (January–March 1986): 8–23;

Krebs, "Von der Schelde zur Pegnitz oder von den 'Emblemata Sacra' zum Lehrgedicht," *Simpliciana,* 6/7 (1985): 185–203;

Joy A. Large, "'Der Sterne Würkung': Harsdörffer's Astrological Chariots," *Simpliciana,* 4/5 (1983): 27–47;

Joseph Leighton, "Die Wolfenbütteler Aufführung von Harsdörffers und Stadens 'Seelewig' im Jahre 1654," *Wolfenbütteler Beiträge,* 3 (1978): 115–128;

Eberhard Mannack, "'Realistische' und metaphorische Darstellung im 'Pegnesischen Schäfergedicht,'" *Jahrbuch der deutschen Schillergesellschaft,* 17 (1973): 154–165;

Volker Meid, "Barocknovellen?: Zu Harsdörffers moralischen Geschichten," *Euphorion,* 62, no. 1 (1968): 72–76;

Dieter Merzbacher, "Der Abendmahlstreit zwischen dem Vielgekrönten und dem Spielenden, geschlichtet vom Unveränderlichen: Georg Philipp Harsdörffers Lehrgedicht 'Vom H. Abendmahl Christi' in einer Anhalter Akte aus dem Jahre 1651," *Daphnis,* 22, no. 2/3 (1993): 347–392;

Georg Adolf Narciss, *Studien zu den Frauenzimmergesprächspielen Georg Philipp Harsdörffers (1607–1658): Ein Beitrag zur deutschen Literaturgeschichte des 17. Jahrhunderts* (Leipzig: Eichblatt, 1928);

Jean Baptiste Neveux, "Un 'parfait Secrétaire' du XVIIe siècle: 'Der Teutsche Secretarius'

(1655)," *Etudes Germaniques,* 19 (October–December 1964): 511–520;

Jane Ogden Newman, *Pastoral Conventions: Poetry, Language, and Thought in Seventeenth-Century Nuremberg* (Baltimore & London: Johns Hopkins University Press, 1990);

John Roger Paas, "Poeta incarceratus: Georg Philipp Harsdörffers Zensur-Prozeß 1648," *Germanisch-romanische Monatsschrift,* supplement, 1 (1979): 155–164;

Oliver Pfefferkorn, *Georg Philipp Harsdörffer: Studien zur Textdifferenzierung unter besonderer Berücksichtigung seines Erbauungsschrifttums* (Stuttgart: Heinz, 1991);

Pfefferkorn, "Luthersprachliche Einflüsse auf Harsdörffers 'Geistreiche Betrachtungen nach den Sieben Bitten in dem heiligen Gebete Vater unser,'" in *Beiträge zur Sprachwirkung Martin Luthers im 17./18. Jahrhundert,* edited by Manfred Lemmer (Halle: Martin-Luther-Universität Halle-Wittenberg, 1978), pp. 110–123;

Pfefferkorn, "Soziolinguistische Probleme der Textdifferenzierung bei Georg Philipp Harsdöffer," in *Zu Stellenwert und Bewältigung soziolinguistischer Fragestellungen in aktuellen germanistischen sprachhistorischen Forschungen: Beiträge zum wissenschaftlichen Kolloquium Rostock 30. 11. und 1. 12. 1987,* edited by Gisela Brandt and Irmtraud Rösler (Berlin: Akademie der Wissenschaften der DDR, Zentralinistitut für Sprachwissenschaft, 1988), pp. 113–119;

Pfefferkorn, "Texttraditionen in den Erbauungsschriften Georg Philipp Harsdörffers," in *Neue Fragen der Linguistik: Akten des 25. Linguistischen Kolloquiums, Paderborn 1990, I: Bestand und Entwicklung; II: Innovation und Anwendung,* 2 volumes, edited by Elisabeth Feldbusch, Reiner Pogarell, and others (Tübingen: Niemeyer, 1991), I: 197–202;

Hans Gerd Rötzer, "Die Rezeption der 'Novelas ejemplares' bei Harsdörffer," *Chloe,* 9 (1990): 365–383;

Rötzer, "Variationen der Pikareske: Cervantes und Harsdörffer," in *Il picaro nella cultura Europea,* edited by Italo Michele Battafarano and Pietro Taravacci (Gardolo di Trento: Reverdito, 1989), pp. 223–242;

Harold Eugene Samuel, *The Cantata in Nuremberg during the 17th Century* (Ann Arbor: UMI Research Press, 1982);

Ferdinand Josef Schneider, *Japeta (1643), ein Beitrag zur Geschichte des französischen Klassizismus in Deutschland* (Stuttgart: Metzler, 1927);

Manfred Edwin Schubert, "Historisch-kritische Neuausgabe von Georg Philipp Harsdörffers Poetischem Trichter, Teil 1," dissertation, Stanford University, 1965;

Christoph E. Schweitzer, "Harsdörffer and Don Quixote," *Philological Quarterly,* 37 (January 1958): 87–97;

Bernhard Siegert, "Netzwerke der Regionalität: Harsdörffers 'Teutscher Secretarius' und die Schicklichkeit der Briefe im 17. Jahrhundert," *Modern Language Notes,* 105 (April 1990): 536–562;

Franz Günter Sieveke, "Topik im Dienst poetischer Erfindung: Zum Verhältnis rhetorischer Konstanten und ihrer funktionsbedingten Auswahl oder Erweiterung (Omeis – Richter – Harsdörffer)," *Jahrbuch für Internationale Germanistik,* 8/2 (1976): 17–48;

Blake Lee Spahr, *The Archives of the Pegnesischer Blumenorden: A Survey and Reference Guide* (Berkeley & Los Angeles: University of California Press, 1960);

Elizabeth Ann Spence, "Music as a Means to an End: An Inquiry in the Musical Content of the Works of Georg Philipp Harsdörffer," dissertation, University of British Columbia, 1983;

Winfried Theiß, "Nur die Narren und Halsstarrigen die Rechtsgelehrte ernehren: Zur Soziologie der Figuren und Normen in G. Ph. Harsdörffers 'Schauplatz'-Anthologien von 1650," in *Literatur und Volk im 17. Jahrhundert: Probleme populärer Kultur in Deutschland, II,* edited by Wolfgang Bruckner, Peter Blickle, and Dieter Breuer (Wiesbaden: Harrassowitz, 1985), pp. 899–916;

Julius Tittmann, *Die Nürnberger Dichterschule: Harsdörfer, Klaj, Birken* (Göttingen: Dieterich, 1847; reprinted, Wiesbaden: Sandig, 1965);

Mara R. Wade, "The Earliest Extant German Opera and Its Antecedent," *Daphnis,* 14, no. 3 (1985): 559–578;

Wade, *The German Baroque Pastoral Singspiel* (Bern: Peter Lang, 1990);

Helmut Waibler, "Ein Autor von Lehrkartenspielen," *Anzeiger des Germanischen Nationalmuseums* (1975): 90–114;

Helen Watanabe-O'Kelly, "The Equestrian Ballet in Seventeenth-Century Europe: Origin, Description, Development," *German Life and Letters,* 36 (April 1983): 198–212;

Karin A. Wurst, "Die Frau als Mitspielerin und Leserin in Georg Philipp Harsdörffers 'Frauenzimmer Gesprächspielen,'" *Daphnis,* 21, no. 4 (1992): 615–639;

Rosmarie Zeller, *Spiel und Konversation im Barock: Untersuchungen zu Harsdörffers 'Gespraächspielen'* (Berlin & New York: De Gruyter, 1974).

Papers:
Papers of the Harsdörffer family are in the Stadtarchiv Nuremberg and in the family archive in Fischbach. Materials on the Pegnesischer Blumenorden are in the Germanisches Nationalmuseum in Nuremberg.

Heinrich Julius of Brunswick

(15 October 1564 – 20 July 1613)

Barton W. Browning
Pennsylvania State University

BOOKS: *Tragica Comoedia Hibeldeha von der Susanna, wie dieselbe von zweyen Alten, ehebruchs halber, fälschlich beklaget, auch vnschüldig verurtheilet, aber entlich durch sonderliche Schickung Gottes des Allmechtigen von Daniele errettet, vnd die beiden Alten zum Tode verdammet worden* (Wolfenbüttel, 1593);

Tragica Comoedia Hidbelepihala von der Susanna, wie dieselbe fälschlich von zweyen Alten des ehebruchs beklaget, auch vnschüldig verurtheilet, aber entlich durch Schickung Gottes des Allmechtigen von Daniele errettet, vnd die beiden Alten zum Tode verdampt worden (Wolfenbüttel, 1593);

Tragoedia Hibeldeha. von einem Buler vnd Bulerin, wie derselben Hurerey vnd Vnzucht, ob sie wol ein Zeitlang verborgen gewesen, gleichwol entlich an den Tag kommen, vnd von Gott grewlich gestraffet worden sey (Wolfenbüttel, 1593);

Comoedia Hidbelepihal von einem Weibe, wie dasselbige jhre Hurerey für jhrem Eheman verborgen (Wolfenbüttel, 1593);

Comoedia Hidbelahe von einem Wirthe, wie derselbige von dreyen Wandergesellen drey Mahl vmb die Bezahlung betrogen sey worden (Wolfenbüttel, 1593);

Tragoedia. Hiehadbel. von einem vngeratenen Sohn, welcher vnmenschliche vnd vnerhörte Mordthaten begangen, auch endlich neben seinen mit Consorten ein erbaermlich schrecklich vnd grewlich Ende genommen hat (Wolfenbüttel, 1594);

Tragedia Hibaldeha von einer Ehebrecherin, wie die jren Man drey Mahl betreucht, aber zu letzt ein schrecklich Ende genommen habe (Wolfenbüttel, 1594);

Tragica Comoedia, Hibaldeha von einem Wirthe oder Gastgeber (Wolfenbüttel, 1594);

Comoedia Hibaldeha von einem Edelman, welcher einem Abt drey Fragen auffgegeben (Wolfenbüttel, 1594);

Comoedia Hibelepihal von Vincentio Ladislao Sacrapa von Mantua Kempffern zu Rosz vnd Fuesz, weiland des edlen vnd ehrenuesten, auch manhafften vnnd streitbaren Barbarossae Bellicosi von Mantua, Rittern zu

Heinrich Julius of Brunswick; engraving by Lucas Kilian after a portrait by Hans von Aachen

Malta ehelichen nachgelassenen Sohn (Wolfenbüttel, 1594);

Illustre Examen Auctoris Illustrissimi (Helmstedt, 1608);

Wahrhafftiger vnd Summarischer Bericht, wegen der im verschienen 1610. Jahrs, nicht erfolgter Abdankung des Passawischen Kriegsvolks (Prague, 1611);

Gründlicher vnd wahrhafftiger Bericht, wegen der zwischen der Röm. Keys. Mayt. Herrn Rudolpho dem Andern, etc. vnd der Kön. Wr. zu Vngern, Herrn Matthiae,

etc. getroffener Vergleichung (Helmstedt: Jacob
Lucius, 1611).

Editions: *Die Schauspiele des Herzogs Heinrich Julius
von Braunschweig nach alten Drucken und Handschriften,* edited by Wilhelm Ludwig Holland,
Bibliothek des Literarischen Vereins in Stuttgart, volume 36 (Stuttgart, 1855; reprinted,
Amsterdam: Rodopi, 1967);

*Die Schauspiele des Herzogs Heinrich Julius von
Braunschweig,* edited by Julius Tittmann (Leip-
zig: Brockhaus, 1880; reprinted, Nendeln,
Liechtenstein: Kraus, 1974);

"Von einem Buler und Bulerin," edited by Willi
Flemming, in his *Das Schauspiel der Wander-
bühne,* second edition (Hildesheim: Olms,
1965), pp. 277–324;

Vincentius Ladislaus, edited by Flemming, in his *Die
deutsche Barockkomödie,* second edition (Hildesheim: Olms, 1965), pp. 59–108;

Von einem Weibe – Von Vincentio Ladislao: Komödien, edited by Manfred Brauneck (Stuttgart: Reclam,
1967).

In many respects Heinrich Julius, Duke of
Brunswick, epitomized the role of a late-Renaissance
German prince. A patron of the arts known for his
support of the painter Hans von Aachen and the
composer Michael Praetorius, Heinrich Julius was
himself a talented amateur who dabbled in literature, music, and painting. A determined, ambitious,
and often unprincipled ruler, he was a formidable
legal scholar, a resolute friend, and an implacable
foe. Literary historians know him best for the
eleven dramas he composed in the early 1590s, the
period during which his Wolfenbüttel court led the
rest of Germany in hosting the newly arrived English comedians; the duke's literary efforts clearly
reflect the influence of these foreign actors. The
final years of his life also made him somewhat of a
celebrity on the central European political stage. Between 1607 and his death in 1613 he was to rise to
the uppermost levels at Rudolf II's imperial court at
Prague. In the process he became the emperor's
confidant, conscience, and friend. During these last
years he played a major role in attempting to steady
the course of the Holy Roman Empire of the German Nation in the troubled times preceding the outbreak of the Thirty Years' War.

Born on 15 October 1564 at Schloß Hessen to
Duke Julius of Brunswick and Duchess Hedwig of
Brandenburg, Heinrich Julius entered a world
fraught with familial strife. His paternal grandfather, Heinrich the Younger, was a bitter opponent
of Martin Luther and the Protestant movement.

Heinrich the Younger's own son Julius, Heinrich
Julius's father, occupied a prominent position
among these apostates. When Heinrich appeared
one day at his grandson's cradle with a drawn dag-
ger, there were well-founded fears for the child's
safety. Instead, the old duke's encounter with his infant grandson apparently softened his heart enough
to allow the breach with his own son to be patched
over, if not healed entirely. While father and son
reached no formal accommodation, Heinrich the
Younger came to terms with Julius's succession, and
he began to use his leverage and cunning to ensure
that Brunswick's future ruler, his grandson Heinrich Julius, should be well provided for.

Exerting his influence on the bishopric of
Halberstadt, Heinrich arranged in 1566 to have his
infant grandson initiated as bishop postulate of
Halberstadt. This title meant that Heinrich Julius
would assume the full rights and responsibilities of
bishop on reaching his legal majority. While two-
year-old bishops were hardly common for the time,
the arrangement seems not to have been unique.
Additionally, the Halberstadt Cathedral chapter's
possible opposition was assuaged by an assurance –
subsequently abrogated – that Heinrich Julius
would be reared in the Catholic faith.

Duke Julius viewed the proper education of
his son as a major duty. Ever methodical, he requested the advice of the well-known theologian
Jakob Andreä. Andreä's plan called for the constant
instruction of the boy under the supervision either
of Heinrich von der Luhe, his tutor, or Joachim
Aretsche, his preceptor. Additionally, he received
regular instruction on the organ and engaged in
daily physical activities, including lessons in riding
and fencing.

Heinrich Julius seems to have been an intellectually gifted student. At the age of ten he was required to participate in public theological disputations at the Gandersheim Pedagogium, the institution that would evolve into Helmstedt University.
Predictably enough, his arguments on those occasions inspired the admiration of all those in attendance. The young prince became aware of the
darker side of his future role as ruler in 1575, when
he presided over the sentencing phase of a trial for
conspiracy against the ducal throne. Heinrich Julius
rejected all pleas for clemency, pronounced the conspirators guilty, and condemned seven major figures to various forms of painful death.

In 1576 Heinrich Julius received a new tutor,
Curd von Schwicheldt, and a new preceptor, the jurist Heinrich Grünfeld. His expanded course of
study included, above all, the Bible and religious in-

struction, followed by Latin, French, history, ethics, and customs. In addition to Cicero's *De officiis,* Schwicheldt recommended the works of Julius Caesar, Sallust, Livy, Terence, and Plautus. This education was specifically aimed at giving Heinrich Julius the knowledge and skills necessary for a ruler; that theological study played a predominant role in the young duke's education reflects the extent to which religion and political power were inextricably intertwined in late-sixteenth-century Germany.

In 1576 Heinrich Julius received another major office. Helmstedt University, founded in that year by Duke Julius, was soon to grow into the second largest university in northern Germany. While Julius took care to staff his fledgling institution with a faculty of high quality, there was to be no question as to where the ultimate power lay. Thus, on his twelfth birthday Heinrich Julius presented a lengthy Latin address before the initial meeting of the learned heads of the Helmstedt faculty as he rose to accept the office of *rector perpetuus.*

There was still the problem of the religious split in the bishopric of Halberstadt and Heinrich Julius's status as bishop postulate. After protracted but futile negotiations with Rome, Julius arrived at a face-saving solution with the help of imperial intervention: the forms would be observed even if the spirit was not. In 1578 the emperor declared the fourteen-year-old Heinrich Julius to be of age, and on 7 December of that year, having taken the first vows of priesthood, he was anointed as the Catholic bishop of Halberstadt. Even though Julius arranged an ostentatiously Protestant service on their return to Wolfenbüttel, this apparent capitulation to the wishes of the Roman church irreparably damaged relations with many of Julius's zealously Protestant subjects. Exercising his rights as bishop, Heinrich Julius took possession of the palace at Gröningen and established his own court there, albeit still under the immediate supervision of his tutors and the distant but watchful attention of his father in Wolfenbüttel.

Heinrich Julius continued to make excellent progress in his formal studies, showing a special gift for legal questions – a passion for the law remained a lifelong preoccupation; but not all of his energies went into such serious matters. The elder duke's anxieties about the conduct of his progeny appear to have had some justification. While Julius labored to solidify his financial base and expand his territories through the acquisition of Brunswick-Celle, the young bishop of Halberstadt labored to convert his palace in Gröningen into a late-Renaissance pleasure dome. Heinrich Julius's attempts at establish-ing a lavish existence in Gröningen foreshadowed his later extravagant expenditures for art and entertainment as reigning duke.

In 1582 he received a further appointment as bishop of Minden, a post he held until 1585. On 19 September of that year he married Dorothea, the daughter of August, Elector of Saxony. Dorothea not only represented a good political union but also held the promise of tempering the high spirits that had led to Heinrich Julius's youthful escapades. The marriage began a brief but relatively happy period during which Heinrich Julius fathered his first child. The birth of Dorothea Hedwig in 1587 was, however, dearly bought: Dorothea died in childbirth. Ever the planner, Duke Julius took it upon himself to distract his son from his grief by appointing him head of the ducal court. This role well fitted the passion for legal questions that Heinrich Julius had evidenced since his youth. The ducal court gave him first-hand acquaintance with both the major issues and the petty squabbles of the realm that was one day to be his. The legal proceedings depicted in his plays may reflect his experience with Brunswick-Wolfenbüttel's judicial apparatus.

With his father's death in 1589 Heinrich Julius stepped into the role for which his training had prepared him. In the next twenty-four years he put his personal stamp on the House of Brunswick, raising it to a status and power in central Europe that began to recall the glory his line had enjoyed in the High Middle Ages under his illustrious ancestor Heinrich der Löwe (the Lion). In short order he moved to reform court regulations so as to tighten an already austere budget. In the religious sphere, Halberstadt soon felt the effect of his new power as he proceeded with the reformation of his bishopric. In a final blow to his grandfather's agreements with the church, he compelled all remaining Catholic officials to convert to Protestantism if they wished to retain their posts.

While Heinrich Julius acquired some contemporary notoriety as a burner of witches – the Wolfenbüttel execution grounds were described as a small forest of charred stakes – recent findings indicate that his reputation far surpassed the actual number of executions. Executions for necromancy fell off to almost nothing after the first three years of his rule, but in the initial phases of his reign the number of witches executed in one year was as high as 18. Still, of the 114 men and women accused of witchcraft in Wolfenbüttel between 1590 and 1620, fewer than half were put to death, and at least 39 were released without penalty.

Heinrich Julius's mother, Duchess Hedwig, after her death on 21 October 1621; woodcut attributed to Elias Holwein

Heinrich Julius's first year on the ducal throne had another dark side. Whereas Duke Julius had allowed Jews to live and work in his lands with few restrictions, Heinrich Julius, for reasons that are unclear, immediately took a hard line: a 1589 ducal edict banned Jews from living in the principalities under Heinrich Julius's control. Jewish residents were given only a brief time to dispose of their possessions and quit the dukedom; nonresident Jews were neither to be admitted nor even allowed the right to travel through the territory. The duke's decisive action occasioned positive comment from church officials; more than two decades later funeral orations held in Heinrich Julius's honor would still recall the banning of the Jews as a major accomplishment of his regime. After many Jewish residents managed to ignore or evade the original edict, a second and more stringent proclamation was issued in 1591; but by 1594 Jews were again allowed to enter the dukedom on a temporary basis. From that point on, the situation of the Jews seems to have improved. Whether he needed external resources to support his shaky financial position or

whether he was acting out of humane considerations, Heinrich Julius made both broad and specific exceptions to his own regulations.

One of Duke Julius's last tasks had been to oversee the negotiations in 1589 for his son's second marriage. The chosen bride was Princess Elizabeth, sister of King Christian IV of Denmark. This union was well calculated to expand the prestige and influence of the House of Brunswick: Denmark was a well-established royal house with connections throughout Europe, and the impending marriage of Elizabeth's sister Anna to King James VI of Scotland, who would become James I of England, linked Heinrich Julius to the next ruler of Europe's leading power.

In the spring of 1590 Heinrich Julius and a wedding party of almost two hundred set out from Wolfenbüttel for the journey to Denmark, where the marriage was to take place in April. According to a contemporary chronicle, Heinrich Julius disguised himself as a jewelry merchant and approached the Danish castle alone. When his bride-to-be expressed an interest in his wares, the masquerading duke informed her that they could be had at the price of sharing his bed. Outraged, the princess had the putative jeweler thrown into the dungeon, where he languished until his courtiers arrived to reveal the joke. While apocryphal, this tale underlines Heinrich Julius's reputation for a love of disguise and deception; it also points toward an interest in the theatrical that was to become manifest two years later when some of the earliest English traveling players to visit German soil found their way to his Wolfenbüttel court.

Wolfenbüttel court records for July 1592 describe a group of acrobats from England who gave a musical presentation and acted a comedy. These notes represent the first unambiguous documentation of a dramatic production by English actors at a German court. The activity of English actors in Wolfenbüttel would expand in the next century. Thomas Sackville, the leader of subsequent troupes, and the dancer and acrobat John Bradstreet would ultimately obtain regular court appointments and would serve in Wolfenbüttel long after the conclusion of their theatrical careers. Of the two, Sackville exceeded Bradstreet in prominence and recognition. He usually played a clown character named Jan Bouset; so well known was Sackville in this role that the name Jan Bouset — or such variations as John Bouset, Johan Bouset, Johann Buschet, Jan Posset, Johann Boset, and so on — became a generic designation for the clown figure in the plays of both Heinrich Julius and Jakob Ayrer.

The occurrence of the first certified contact between Heinrich Julius's court and the English players shortly before the flowering of the duke's literary productivity provides a basis for the assumption that English dramatic style influenced Heinrich Julius in the composition of his plays. Furthermore, the records of this contact constitute grounds for arguing that Heinrich Julius's Wolfenbüttel court was the site of the first permanent stage in Germany. How Heinrich Julius came to host these traveling players remains undetermined, but the Danish connection seems a likely starting point. While neither Danish court records nor the Wolfenbüttel correspondence mention dramatic performances at his wedding festivities, Heinrich Julius would have had ample opportunity in Denmark to learn from his future brother-in-law James VI about the startlingly new entertainments the English players could provide.

One year after the first recorded appearance of the English actors in Wolfenbüttel, Heinrich Julius began publishing his own dramatic efforts. All of them are in prose, a marked departure from the era's usual versified plays. Ten plays appeared in print in 1593–1594; two of them are separate versions of the same play, *Susanna* (1593), his only biblical drama. While all of these plays appeared without authorial attribution, each of their title pages carried a variation of the initials *HIEBALDEHA* – Heinricus Iulius Brunsvicensis Et Lunaeburgensis Dux Episcopus HAlberstadensis – a designation that appeared on official documents and portraits of Heinrich Julius as well. An additional play, *Der Fleischhawer* (The Butcher), remained in manuscript form (it was published in Wilhelm Ludwig Holland's edition of Heinrich Julius's plays in 1855). After this burst of authorial activity in 1593–1594 Heinrich Julius never published another play. A likely explanation is that the decade's growing political, legal, and military pressures left him little opportunity to pursue his literary interests. While all the printed dramas appeared during the span of two years, the precise time and sequence of their composition remain uncertain.

The plays fall into three rough categories. The two *Susanna* dramas, *Comoedia Hidbelepihal von einem Weibe, wie dasselbige ihre Hurerey für ihrem Eheman verborgen* (Comedy . . . about a Woman Who Hid Her Fornication from Her Husband, 1593), *Tragoedia Hibeldeha. von einem Buler und Bulerin, wie derselben Hurerey und Unzucht, ob sie wol ein Zeitlang verborgen gewesen, gleichwol entlich an den Tag kommen, und von Gott grewlich gestraffet worden sey* (Tragedy . . . about a Lover and a Mistress Who Concealed Their Forni-

cation and Unchasteness for a Time, Nevertheless, It Came to Light and Was Horribly Punished by God, 1593), and *Tragedia Hibaldeha von einer Ehebrecherin, wie die ihren Man drey Mahl betreucht, aber zu letzt ein schrecklich Ende genommen habe* (Tragedy . . . about an Adultress Who Deceives Her Husband Three Times and Comes to a Dreadful End, 1594) all deal with the domestic sphere. *Der Fleischhawer, Comoedia Hidbelahe von einem Wirthe, wie derselbige von dreyen Wandergesellen drey Mahl umb die Bezahlung betrogen sey worden* (Comedy . . . about an Innkeeper Who Was Swindled out of His Payment Three Times by Traveling Apprentices, 1593), *Tragica Comoedia, Hibaldeha von einem Wirthe oder Gastgeber* (Tragicomedy about an Innkeeper or Publican, 1594), and *Comoedia Hibaldeha von einem Edelman, welcher einem Abt drey Fragen auffgegeben* (Comedy . . . about a Nobleman Who Asks an Abbot Three Questions, 1594) look at abuses of position in the trades and in society. *Tragoedia. Hiehadbel. von einem ungeratenen Sohn, welcher unmenschliche und unerhörte Mordthaten begangen, auch endlich neben seinen mit Consorten ein erbaermlich schrecklich und grewlich Ende genommen hat* (Tragedy . . . about a Wayward Son, Who Committed Inhuman and Shocking Murders and Finally Came to a Miserable, Frightful, and Horrible End with His Accomplices, 1593) and *Comoedia Hibelepihal von Vincentio Ladislao Sacrapa von Mantua Kempffern zu Rosz und Fuesz, weiland des edlen und ehrenuesten, auch manhafften unnd streitbaren Barbarossae Bellicosi von Mantua, Rittern zu Malta ehelichen nachgelassenen Sohn* (Comedy . . . about Vincentius Ladislaus Sacrapa of Mantua, Fighter on Horse and on Foot, the Surviving Legitimate Son of the Late Noble and Most Honored, also Manly and Valiant Barbarossa Bellicosi of Mantua, Knight of Malta, 1594) move to the realm of the court and its tragic and comic intrigues.

The longer of the two versions of *Susanna* is presumably Heinrich Julius's earliest play, and it is one of his best. This five-act recapitulation of the popular biblical detective tale ranges through a spectrum of human experience. Its scope embraces the clown's blasphemous but witty dialect exchanges, the high pathos of Susanna, and the laments of her small children. Justice prevails when Daniel brings divinely sanctioned retribution for the judges' sins and repays them for their many examples of low cunning. As the prologues of both versions promise, these plays provide both instruction and comfort while at the same time leavening the action with a healthy mixture of humor. The epilogue's moralizing notwithstanding, Heinrich Julius knew quite well the necessity of mixing entertainment with instruction even in a biblically inspired work.

Von einem Weibe stands out among Heinrich Julius's domestic dramas and ranks with *Vincentius Ladislaus* as one of his best comedies. With a small cast of characters and a rapidly moving plot, *Von einem Weibe* is a light and entertaining sketch featuring the amorous intrigues of the merry adultress Meretrix; her husband, Thomas Mercator, stumbles harmlessly through his role as a cuckold who effectively wills his own deception. Supporting the action and reflecting on his master's ineptitude, the clown Johan Bouset provides classic bits of visual and verbal comedy and, as the knowing fool, offers a direct link to the audience with his comments *ad spectatores*. For its basic plot *Von einem Weibe* depends heavily on Hans Wilhelm Kirchhof's 1563 tale of a one-eyed knight who, returning unexpectedly from the war against the Turks, nearly surprises his wife in bed with her young lover. Swiftly hiding her paramour, the wife claims to have dreamed that her husband's vision had been restored. Covering his good eye with a cloth, she pretends to test his sight while her young nobleman escapes from behind the door, leaving their crime undetected. Mercator capsules himself off from unpleasant reality, while Meretrix manipulates the situation to her own ends. Bouset, Mercator's neighbor Adrian, and the barber warn against the abuse of the marriage bonds, furnishing the moral compass that ensures the audience's proper perception of the play. On the whole, *Von einem Weibe* plays lightly with the question of adultery; little actual harm is done, and the worst critique is a mild shake of the head at human foolishness. The protagonists of Heinrich Julius's remaining domestic dramas, however, do not have it so easy.

Aside from the bodies littering the stage at its conclusion, *Von einem Buler und Bulerin* has little justification for its label as a tragedy; this drama of adultery and punishment presents an example of divine retribution rather than a tragic conflict. Having glimpsed Dina, the young wife of the sixty-year-old Joseph, during a church service, Pamphilus tries desperately to locate her dwelling. Aided by the devil figure Satyrus, he gains Dina's address and finds that their attraction is mutual. After an interlude of music and dance, they consummate their affair. Almost trapped by the return of the drunkard husband, Joseph, the lovers manage to arrange a second meeting. When the city's night watchmen interrupt their revelry, a fight ensues in which Pamphilus and a watchman are killed. Distraught with grief and remorse, Dina kills herself, and

Satyrus arrives to claim the dead souls. An epilogue recapitulates the story's moral and issues a further warning to any who might be contemplating similar damnable behavior.

Von einer Ehebrecherin also bears the label *tragedy;* but while extremely well written, it reveals a lack of genre sense comparable to that of *Von einem Buler und Bulerin*. Only in the last pages of the text does *Von einer Ehebrecherin* turn "tragic": Scortum takes her husband's madness to heart, despairs at her hopelessly fallen moral state, and commits suicide amid bitter self-accusations. Until that point, however, the play is a clever domestic farce. Heinrich Julius's source for *Von einer Ehebrecherin,* Michael Lindener's 1559 tale of a goldsmith and a poor student, supplied the basic comic elements, but *Von einer Ehebrecherin* is far richer. Determined to prove that his wife, Scortum, is an adulteress, the merchant Gallichoraea bribes the traveling student Pamphilius to seduce her; he does not reveal his relationship to her. Scortum entertains Pamphilus on three occasions, each time outwitting her husband as he arrives prepared to catch them in the act. As in *Von einem Weibe,* the wife employs an ambiguous catchphrase to warn her lover to escape while she distracts her husband's attention. In the initial encounter she leads Gallichoraea in the wrong direction; the second time she covers his head with a cloth; on the third occasion Gallichoraea threatens to burn the entire house, whereupon she begs him first to save a large basket of linens in which, of course, Pamphilus has hidden. Gallichoraea's frustration grows with each defeat as the student reports to him on his successes. The clown Johan Bouset acts as a warning voice throughout, repeatedly blurting out the truth that his master, Gallichoraea, is desperately trying to conceal: that he is a cuckold and that his status is to a great extent self-inflicted. Finally driven to madness, Gallichoraea cavorts wildly about the stage reveling in his shame until Bouset entices him into a lunatic's cage. The play then takes a vicious turn as Bouset directly accuses Scortum of being a whore. In an otherwise unmotivated shift she plunges into a suicidal depression and, with the help of attendant devils, kills herself.

Three of Heinrich Julius's dramas dealing with the abuse of mercantile and social advantages — *Der Fleischhawer, Von einem Wirthe,* and *Von einem Wirthe oder Gastgeber* — indicate the trade of their protagonists in their titles; the fourth, *Von einem Edelman,* contrasts representatives of three social and vocational classes: the poor but pious charcoal burner, the self-righteous abbot, and the rapaciously greedy nobleman. All four dramas criticize the economic and spiritual abuses their protagonists inflict on a defenseless public. On the whole, their dramatic quality is much inferior to that of the domestic dramas.

Critics agree that *Der Fleischhawer* is both the earliest and weakest of this set. Heinrich Julius must have recognized its inadequacies, because he never allowed it to be published. As opposed to the dramas of domestic conflict, *Der Fleischhawer* apparently has neither a borrowed anecdote nor a published tale as its basis. The play's minimal action depends on the sort of insider's knowledge reflected in the Wolfenbüttel court's edicts on butchers or in Heinrich Julius's own exposure to the butcher's trade. (His opponents delighted in claiming that butchery was one of the duke's favorite pastimes.) Matz the butcher announces at the outset his intent to deceive his customers. He lists a catalogue of tricks of the trade that he proceeds to put into play. Combining his professional knavery with well-placed bribes to the market master and the magistrate, he ensures himself of official protection. Matz cheats and bullies his customers with impunity until the clown, appearing here under the name Johan Conget, entices him into making a crooked sale to the market master himself. Deprived of official protection and banned from practicing his livelihood, Matz enters a dull-witted pact with the devil and turns to large-scale thievery. He is caught, tried, and sentenced to hang. As in *Susanna,* the court scene with its legalisms and formulaic speeches undoubtedly recalls Heinrich Julius's experience in presiding over the ducal court. As a clear warning to corrupt authorities, he has the market master and the magistrate experience devastating guilt and perish in disgrace. At the play's conclusion the pastor who has accompanied Matz to the gallows delivers an epilogue warning tradesmen and officials against abusing their positions.

Von einem Wirthe marks a significant advance over the crude dramatic structure of *Der Fleischhawer.* Three young apprentices, Adrian, Thomas, and Johan, arrange three successive skirmishes with a greedy innkeeper and his servant. In each episode one of the tricksters comes up with a new device to avoid paying the innkeeper his due; in all three cases their guile and linguistic cunning allow them to emerge victorious over the avaricious but stupid innkeeper. Each of the three encounters is accompanied by an ever taller set of tales, which the innkeeper blithely accepts, and ends with the luckless innkeeper berating his hapless servant, Jan Bouset, whose haggles with three different pairs of trades-

Duchess Elizabeth, formerly Princess Elizabeth of Denmark, whom Heinrich Julius married in 1590

people provide a comic prelude to each of the three innkeeper/apprentices scenes. This compositional balance makes *Von einem Wirthe* one of Heinrich Julius's most tightly constructed plays. Its literary qualities, however, still leave much to be desired. In the final encounter the apprentices trick Bouset into participating in a game of blindman's buff; the person he catches will be responsible for their bill. After some merry stage play involving a lusty paddling of the blindfolded Bouset, they rush off as Bouset seizes his newly arrived master. Caught in his servant's arms, the luckless innkeeper is thus obligated to pay the apprentices' bill.

In its detailed exposition of its central character's illicit stratagems, *Von einem Wirthe oder Gastgeber* returns to the technical insider's depiction that characterized *Der Fleischhawer.* The nameless publican gives Bouset extensive instructions and an illustrated example of how to give short weight while measuring grain. This innkeeper's satisfaction with his lot stems in no small part from knowing that others must toil in the sweat of their brow while he can eat well, go to bed early, and arise to find money waiting for him. If his guests attempt to protest his drastically inflated bills, he holds their horses and luggage hostage until they pay. Not content with changing the numeral *V* into an *X* on his bills and, thus, doubling his fees, the innkeeper charges twenty to thirty times more than is justified by the services delivered. A Bavarian traveler denounces him and his ilk in a tirade that recalls Desiderius Erasmus's scornful critique of German inns: the service is surly and slow, the tablecloths filthy, the bread moldy, the plates unwashed, the food inedible; the wine, for which premium prices are charged, is sour and so heavily adulterated that the guest's stomach suffers for days afterward. As the Swabian peasant Conrad argues, innkeepers are far worse than thieves: one can defend oneself against thieves or pursue them with the law, but innkeepers have their guests totally at their mercy.

In *Von einem Wirthe oder Gastgeber* the devil appears, curiously enough, as the only one able to punish the innkeeper's villainy. Throughout the play the innkeeper has repeatedly tempted fate by inviting the devil to take him if his charges are false. This conventionally empty oath remains unredeemed until the final scenes, when the innkeeper incautiously attempts to overcharge the devil himself. Throwing off their disguises, the devil and his helpers drag the innkeeper from the stage and beat him mercilessly. Bouset warns pregnant women in the audience to avert their eyes as the innkeeper returns. Ripped, bruised, and barely able to speak, the innkeeper drags himself onto the stage to deliver a serious epilogue in which he warns other innkeepers against the practices he himself had exemplified. Thus, the devil's physical torments bring about the conversion that public opinion and citizen pressure had not been able to obtain.

The title of *Comoedia Hibaldeha von einem Edelman, welcher einem Abt drey Fragen auffgegeben* is misleading in several ways. First, the play has little to do with its titular noble protagonist; second, though the final scenes provide a broadly comic solution to the riddles posed earlier, the play itself focuses on a serious condemnation of loose-living nobility and, even more, on the abbot's abuse of his privileged position; third, the riddling contest arises only in the last two acts. For the first two acts the play's dominant figure, a charcoal burner, overshadows all other characters; then he disappears entirely. The play thus divides into an initial serious section in which both the nobleman and the abbot are confronted with the charcoal burner's simple virtue, and a second, primarily humorous, section then centering on Johan Bouset's solutions to the nobleman's seemingly impossible questions. Johan's Latin denunciation of all monks, which Heinrich Julius took verbatim from Kirchhof's *Wendunmuth*

(1563–1603), seems strangely out of character for a conventional clown. Here, however, Johan's words constitute a polemical epilogue that emphasizes the play's strong anticlerical message. The weak-spirited nobleman proves himself a corrupt ruler; the greedy and hypocritical cleric sends up empty, hypocritical prayers; only the saintly charcoal burner can withstand closer ethical scrutiny. As opposed to the witty interjections and merry pranks of his comic predecessors, Johan Bouset's wit serves here to pound home the play's social criticism.

Von einem ungeratenen Sohn takes place in a courtly setting. While the title recalls the parable of the prodigal son, the play contains little of the biblical themes of filial transgression and remorse and paternal forgiveness. In a plot that consists primarily of an appalling sequence of horrid deeds, Heinrich Julius assembles a catalogue of murders and atrocities exceeding the mayhem of the bloodiest English tragedies. Violent death, in a multiplicity of forms, dominates the play from beginning to end; with a thoroughness that may reflect some of Heinrich Julius's personal intensity, the drama proceeds through waves of murder and mayhem until the villainous Nero, the play's main figure, stands alone on the stage trying in vain to find a means to kill himself. During the course of six acts Nero brings about the deaths of his father, Duke Severus; his mother, Patientia; his brother, Probus; his brother's wife, Pudica; the child in her womb, his nephew Innocens; and his own bastard son, Infans. In a brief scene that amounts to little more than a throwaway he also causes the execution of three of his father's counselors. In addition to the deaths arranged by Nero, two of his evil counselors kill each other in a senseless duel, and a third poisons himself in remorse over his role in Pudica's death. Garrulus, who has acted as Nero's spy and confidant, avoids death but cuts out his tongue as self-punishment for his own malefactions.

The methods of execution exhibited in the play include poisoning, stabbing, clubbing, strangling, and, finally, decapitation. A bit of cannibalism rounds out the roster of Nero's heinous offenses against the laws of God and humanity. This horrific compilation seems unrelated to the world of Heinrich Julius's mild Reformation farces or even to the unhappy domestic struggles that he chose to label tragedies. Tellingly, it is also his only play that does not feature a clown. Critics have long speculated that the source of this particularly gory tale lies in the English theatrical tradition that Sackville had brought with him from his native shores. *Von einem ungeratenen Sohn* leaps from one outrage to another with only the thinnest connecting material; in this respect it is faithful to the English actors' tradition of playing only a sequence of striking scenes. Nonetheless, even the bloodiest Elizabethan theatrical spectacle would have been hard pressed to match the gore shed in this striking departure from the duke's conventional style.

Vincentius Ladislaus is the Heinrich Julius's most widely acclaimed work and the one most closely identified with him; this identification, however, fails to take into account the play's anomalous position within his dramatic production. First, it contains more than a hint of Italian roots, as opposed to the English traditions that inform the other dramas; the braggart soldier – the stock figure Scaramuccio from the commedia dell'arte – may well lie behind the Mantua soldier Vincentius's boastful preening. Second, the clown's role has split into two separate parts: Johann Bouset, who serves primarily as a foil to Vincentius's outrageous tales, and Vicentius himself. Third, there are no dialect roles, an essential part of the characterization of the lower classes in his other dramas.

Such reservations aside, the relative fame of *Vincentius Ladislaus* has much to do with subsequent developments in literary history: it anticipates and satirizes dramatic styles and conventions that would become dominant in the following century. The drama breaks with Reformation comedy traditions in that it rises beyond the conventional sphere of village stereotypes and domestic quarrels. In terms of its social scope, *Vincentius Ladislaus* takes in the world of the court as well as that of the inn. Vincentius's attempts at assuming patrician mores anticipate the exaggerated affectations that would be attributed to the pretentious soldiery in the coming century. In a specifically literary sense, Vincentius seems the typological forebear of the dual protagonists of Andreas Gryphius's *Horribilicribrifax* (The Horrible Sieve-maker, 1663), the bombastic braggart Daradirdatumtarides and his redoubtable and equally boastful opponent Horribilicribrifax. These figures, along with such comic notables as William Shakespeare's Falstaff, have their origin in Plautus's Miles Gloriosus, the archetypal blustering soldier. In Vincentius's case, however, Heinrich Julius has added further traits calculated to undermine his protagonist's claims to a higher social status. Vincentius claims to be not only a formidable fighter and adventurer but also a master of courtly skills. The elaborate honorifics that he demands from his servants each time they address him epitomize his pretensions: noble, honorable, manly warrior on foot and on horseback, experienced and renowned in martial affairs and in other praiseworthy liberal arts, strict lord and master. Little does he seem to recognize that his martial experiences do not fit into to what he terms the other liberal arts, and his ineptitude in fencing, dancing, and music further reveal the discrepancy between his putative sophistication and his comic insufficiencies. Much to the delight of his court, the duke leads Vincentius on, encouraging him to ever greater lies while allowing him to reveal his manifold shortcomings. In a final display of overreaching, Vincentius declares his love for one of the ladies in waiting; when he tries to get into her bed he tumbles instead into a tub of water, to the general laughter of the court.

In addition to his interest in the drama, Heinrich Julius in the early 1590s was a patron of other arts. Musically trained, albeit not to the degree of expertise possessed by his fellow regent and occasional rival Moritz von Hessen, Heinrich Julius distinguished himself through his willingness to expend significant sums of money for court musicians. The English lutenist John Dowland claimed that the duke offered to match the amount offered by any prince in Europe if Dowland would join his court in Wolfenbüttel. Although Dowland declined the offer, Heinrich Julius scored a major coup in attracting the young composer Michael Praetorius to his court. With the acquisition of Praetorius, Heinrich Julius transformed Wolfenbüttel from an adequate but undistinguished musical center into an important focus of late-Renaissance German composition. In addition to his many commissions to local Wolfenbüttel painters, Heinrich Julius's most direct connection with the visual arts came through his acquaintance with the painter Hans von Aachen. Their encounters deepened into a friendship that saw Aachen hosting Heinrich Julius as a guest in his house in Prague and culminated in a 1611 directive whereby Aachen received a monthly sum of forty florins from Heinrich Julius's salary at the imperial court.

Heinrich Julius also left his mark on his territories as a patron of architecture. An inscription in the Schöne Kirche (Beautiful Church) in Gröningen credits Heinrich Julius himself with the structure's basic design. His early studies in the art of building and fortification also proved useful as he greatly expanded Wolfenbüttel's defensive capabilities and gave his architect, Paul Franke, commissions for two major projects: the Juleum Novum, an elaborately decorative building for Helmstedt University, begun in 1594; and the Marienkirche (Saint Mary's Church), begun in 1604 in Wolfenbüttel. In addi-

Heinrich Julius, age thirty-nine; woodcut attributed to Holwein

tion to its architectural distinction, the latter structure is significant both as the second-largest church ever built by the House of Brunswick – only the Brunswick Cathedral is larger – and also as the first major ecclesiastical structure of the Protestant Reformation.

A little-known aspect of Heinrich Julius's activities as patron is his role in the expansion of the ducal library. While Wolfenbüttel's renowned Herzog August Bibliothek would come into full flower only later, the acquisitions of Heinrich Julius and his father provided a significant basis for the collection that exists today. While most of his additions to the library were legal works, according to the 1613–1614 library catalogue he left behind a collection of forty-three hundred volumes, several of which stemmed either wholly or in part from his own pen.

Throughout the 1590s Heinrich Julius continued to expand his territory and influence, often employing legal maneuvers of somewhat questionable validity; many of his gains had to be returned after his death. Leading the way in these acquisitions was Heinrich Julius's chancellor Johann Jagemann, a dedicated champion of Roman law. Disallowing claims made under the dukedom's older Saxon law,

Heinrich Julius and Jagemann imposed Roman law on the realm, much to the dismay and disadvantage of the older landed classes.

Heinrich Julius's first – and relatively late – venture into military affairs came about as a side effect of his position as director of the Lower Saxon Imperial Circle. Formed in 1512, the ten imperial circles had responsibility for regional defense, as well as for defense of the empire as a whole. These loose confederations elected their own directors and, by concentrating on regional matters, served as a stabilizing factor within an empire stressed by religious strife. As the director of his circle, Heinrich Julius began in 1598 to raise troops and money to withstand the ever-growing threat posed by the army of the Spanish general Francisco de Mendoza. While Heinrich Julius gained experience in the arming and provisioning of troops, the affair was a costly adventure that brought him neither the success nor the recognition he might have anticipated. His military ventures in the next few years would prove far more expensive but, unfortunately for both his dukedom and the fate of the empire, equally unsuccessful.

The city of Brunswick was an abiding irritant in the dukedom's body politic; it had opposed

Heinrich Julius at each turn from the beginning of his rule. Refusing to pay homage to him and rejecting its designation as Heinrich Julius's *Erb- und Landstadt* (hereditary possession), Brunswick constantly struggled to establish its independence from ducal rule. In 1600 Heinrich Julius accused the city of outright rebellion. Brunswick fought back with appeals to the imperial court, which failed to decide the issue. Heinrich Julius thereupon pressed his case on both the legal and the political fronts. During a 1602 visit to Prague he promised to supply Emperor Rudolf II with three thousand soldiers for the campaign against the Turks in Hungary. Not surprisingly, imperial favor began to tilt toward Heinrich Julius's cause. By the fall of 1605 Heinrich Julius had assembled an army of around sixteen thousand men, many of them veterans of the fighting in Hungary. On 16 October, in an almost theatrical plot filled with deceit, deception, and military cunning, he sent a party of soldiers disguised as civilians through the city's gates, where they quickly overpowered the unsuspecting citizen guards. Even though its defenses had been breached, the city succeeded – albeit just barely – in fighting off Heinrich Julius's bid for absolute control.

Wounded both militarily and in his pride, Heinrich Julius laid siege to the city in an unorthodox but highly effective fashion. Establishing a base downstream from the city, the duke's men dammed up the Oker River and sent its waters flooding back into the streets of Brunswick. With no flowing stream, the mills could no longer grind, and the rising water drove people into upper stories or out of their houses altogether. Hunger and discomfort might have forced the city to accept the duke's conditions, had not the dam broken in early December. Supported by his brother-in-law, King Christian IV of Denmark, Heinrich Julius kept up pressure on the city and on 30 January 1606 agreed to an armistice that led to an exchange of prisoners. Brunswick, however, had no intention of surrendering. Instead, it used the respite to gain the support of other Hanseatic cities, which sent a contingent of troops under Heinrich Quadt to the city's rescue.

Seeing imperial pressure as a better means to overcome Brunswick than direct military power, Heinrich Julius made a shift in the focus of his campaign that was to take him repeatedly to the imperial court in Prague. From this new orientation would follow not only his astonishing rise in the emperor's favor but also his relative neglect of pressing obligations at home. In the late summer of 1609 Heinrich Julius made a final trip to Prague, where, as it proved, he was to stay for the remaining four years of his life. He soon gained the respect and confidence of the aging and capricious Emperor Rudolf II. Whereas Heinrich Julius had a reputation as an angry and vengeful opponent in the Brunswick struggle, in Prague he served as an emissary of reason, calming outraged opponents, suggesting new compromises, and working tirelessly to bring about amicable resolutions.

Two major undertakings stand out among Heinrich Julius's many activities at the imperial court: the forging of a compromise between Rudolf and his brother Matthias and the dismissal of the Passau troops. Neither was ultimately successful, but both attempts reflect Heinrich Julius's dedicated striving to prevent the fragile edifice of imperial power from plunging into chaos and disarray. In the first case, the brothers' mutual detestation proved too strong for the pacifying attempts of the Brunswick duke, and the hard-won compromise soon fell into ruin. The second situation was related to the first: seeing Archduke Leopold's troops in Passau as a threat, Matthias made their disbanding one of the conditions for any further reconciliation between himself and Rudolf. Once again, Heinrich Julius took upon himself a thankless task by trying to convince the troops to lay down their arms. Repeatedly undercut by Rudolf's vacillation, he finally admitted defeat. The result was that the troops pillaged through Austria and occupied a large section of Prague until Matthias drove them out in March 1611. In *Ein Bruderzwist in Habsburg* (1872; translated as *Family Strife in Hapsburg,* 1940) the Austrian dramatist Franz Grillparzer commemorated Rudolf's struggle with his brother, depicting Heinrich Julius's role as a well-meant but futile effort to avoid the impending religious war that would consume the next three decades. Grillparzer, who did detailed historical studies in preparing his play, paid special tribute to Heinrich Julius as one of the few admirable players in the personal and political conflicts of the day.

In July 1611 Emperor Rudolf II named Heinrich Julius *Obersthofmeister* (high steward), the highest official position at court next to the emperorship itself, and shortly thereafter made him *Kayserlich römischer Mayestät Geheimen Raths bestalter oberster Direktor* (director of the imperial privy council). That a Protestant should hold these preeminent appointive offices at a Catholic court testifies to the high regard in which Heinrich Julius was held in imperial circles. Rudolf even seems to have considered marrying one of Heinrich Julius's daughters, but his death on 20 January 1612 put an end to any such plans. The newly crowned Emperor Matthias re-

tained him on the privy council – another indication of the esteem the Brunswick duke enjoyed
among almost all segments of the imperial court.

In the summer of 1613 Heinrich Julius fell seriously ill after a long drinking bout with Count
Wilhelm Slawata. In a letter to his wife he reported
that he had been overcome by a high fever. Refusing medication and relying on his strong constitu-
tion and on God, on 20 July 1613 Heinrich Julius
died to the accompaniment of fervent prayers. The
fact that Heinrich Julius's host was a leader of the
Catholic faction at court – Slawata was later to gain
fame as one of the principal victims of the Prague
Defenestration – led to speculation that poison
might have led to the duke's relatively early death,
but nothing was ever proved.

During his tenure at the imperial court
Heinrich Julius had obtained enough power to provide a potential Protestant counterbalance to the
growing strength of narrowly Catholic interests.
Yet, even if he had lived longer, the ever-increasing
enmity between Catholic and Protestant factions
and the lack of an effective imperial policy would
probably have outweighed even his best efforts at
compromise. While later students of imperial politics have given Heinrich Julius high marks for his
work in Rudolf's service, his long absence from
home and the resulting decline of his dukedom gave
rise to strong domestic criticism. Given a successor
of Heinrich Julius's own scope and daring, or even
a methodical, business-oriented ruler in the mold of
Julius, the dukedom might have recovered. Such
was not to be the case. Heinrich Julius's son
Friedrich Ulrich assumed the throne at age twenty-
two and never gained full control. Heinrich Julius's
second son, Christian – known as *Der Tolle* (The
Madman) – shared his father's dashing spirits, but
he fell in the Thirty Years' War and, thus, was not
available to assume control of the dukedom when
Friedrich Ulrich died in 1634. Heinrich Julius's
other three sons – he had a total of five sons and six
daughters – also preceded Friedrich Ulrich in
death. With the end of the so-called Middle House
of Brunswick the ducal throne of Brunswick-
Wolfenbüttel passed to a member of a collateral
line, the distinguished prince and collector August,
whose name graces the great Wolfenbüttel library
Heinrich Julius had helped to found.

Biographies:

Richard Friedenthal, "Herzog Heinrich Julius von
    Braunschweig (1564–1613) als Dramatiker: 1.
    Sein Leben, mit besonderer Berücksichtigung

seines geistigen Werdegangs," dissertation,
    University of Munich, 1922;

Hilda Lietzmann, *Herzog Heinrich Julius zu
    Braunschweig und Lüneberg (1564–1613):
    Persönlichkeit und Wirken für Kaiser und Reich,*
    Quellen und Forschungen zur Braunschweig-
    ischen Geschichte, volume 30 (Langenhagen:
    Selbstverlag des Braunschweigischen
    Geschichtsvereins, 1993).

References:

Eduard Bodemann, "Herzog Julius von Braunsch-
    weig: Kulturbild deutschen Fürstenlebens und
    deutscher Fürstenerziehung im 16. Jahr-
    hundert," *Zeitschrift für deutsche Kulturgeschichte,*
    new series 4 (1875): 193–239, 311–348;

Barton W. Browning, "Dramatic Activities and the
    Advent of the English Players at the Court of
    Heinrich Julius von Braunschweig," in *Opitz
    und seine Welt: Festschrift für George Schultz-
    Behrend,* edited by Barbara Becker-Cantarino
    and Jörg-Ulrich Fechner (Amsterdam:
    Rodopi, 1990), pp. 125–139;

Browning, "The Manuscript Version of Heinrich
    Julius von Braunschweig's *Von einem un-
    geratenen Sohn,*" in *Barocker Lust-Spiegel: Fest-
    schrift for Blake Lee Spahr,* edited by Martin
    Bircher and others (Amsterdam: Rodopi,
    1984), pp. 175–185;

Fritz Brüggemann, *Versuch einer Zeitfolge der Dramen
    des Herzogs Heinrich Julius von Braunschweig aus
    den Jahren 1590 bis 1594* (Aachen: Aachener
    Verlags- und Druckerei-Gesellschaft, 1926);

Harald Burger, "Heinrich Julius von Braunschweig:
    Vicentius Ladislaus. Zu einer Kontroverse der
    Literaturkritik," *Literaturwissenschaftliches Jahr-
    buch der Görres Gesellschaft,* new series 9 (1968):
    65–82;

Paul F. Casey, "The Fool in the Dramas of Heinrich
    Julius von Braunschweig," *Colloquia Germanica,*
    10, no. 2 (1976–1977): 121–127;

Christian Emmrich, "Das dramatische Werk des
    Herzogs Heinrich Julius von Braunschweig,"
    dissertation, Jena University, 1964;

M. B. Evans, "Elizabethan Ghosts and Herzog
    Heinrich Julius of Braunschweig," *Journal of
    English and Germanic Philology,* 22, no. 2 (1923):
    195–216;

Evans, "Traditions of the Elizabethan Stage in Ger-
    many," *Philological Quarterly,* 2 (1923): 310–
    314;

Willibald Gurlitt, *Michael Praetorius (Cruezenbergen-
    sis): Sein Leben und seine Werke* (Leipzig: Breit-
    kopf & Härtel, 1915);

A. H. J. Knight, "Duke Heinrich Julius of Brunswick's Comedy *Vincentius Ladislaus*," *Modern Language Review,* 34 (January 1939): 50-61;

Knight, *Heinrich Julius Duke of Brunswick* (Oxford: Blackwell, 1948);

Knight, "The Tragi-Comedies of Duke Heinrich Julius von Braunschweig," *Modern Language Review,* 41 (April 1946): 164-176;

Wilhelm Pfützenreuter, *Heinrich Julius von Braunschweig und der norddeutsche Späthumanismus* (Dülmen in Westfalen: Laumann, 1936);

Richard E. Schade, "*Todsündendidaktik:* On Its Function in Representational and Literary Art (Hans Sachs, Heinrich Julius, Grimmelshausen)," *Daphnis,* 15, nos. 2-3 (1986): 551-584;

Schade, "*Vincentius Ladislaus* (1594): The Function of the Miles-Gloriosus Satire," in his *Studies in Early German Comedy 1500-1650* (Columbia, S.C.: Camden House, 1988), pp. 123-146;

Ingrid Werner, *Zwischen Mittelalter und Neuzeit: Heinrich Julius von Braunschweig als Dramatiker der Übergangszeit* (Frankfurt am Main: Peter Lang, 1976);

Paul Zimmermann, "Englische Komödianten am Hofe zu Wolfenbüttel," *Braunschweigisches Magazin,* 8 (1902): 37-45, 53-57.

Papers:

The main depositories of Heinrich Julius of Brunswick's papers are the Herzog August Bibliothek Wolfenbüttel; the Niedersächsisches Staatsarchiv, Wolfenbüttel; and the Niedersächsisches Hauptstaatsarchiv, Hannover.

Johann Hellwig
(Montano)
(29 July 1609 – 4 June 1674)

Max Reinhart
University of Georgia

BOOKS: Ἀλφάβητον ἰατρικόν hoc est Brevis Totius Medicinae Hippocraticae in paucas Tabellas redactae delineatio (Nuremberg: Wolfgang Endter, 1631);

Die Nymphe Noris in Zweyen Tagzeiten vorgestellet (Nuremberg: Jeremias Dümler, 1650);

Prodromus Apologeticus Super Relatione Medica, de Eminentissimi ac Illusstrissimi Cardinalis de Wartenberg morbo & obitu, ad Danielem Geygerum, Philosoph. Medic. Chirurgum (Nuremberg, 1662);

Observationes Physico-Medicae, posthumae, in lucem editae, edited by Luca Schröck (Augsburg: Printed by Jacob Koppmayer, published by Gottlieb Göbel, 1680).

Edition: *Johann Hellwig's "Die Nymphe Noris," (1650): A Critical Edition,* edited by Max Reinhart (Columbia, S.C.: Camden House, 1993).

OTHER: "Lobgedicht an den Spielenden," in volume 5 of *Frauenzimmer Gesprechspiele, so bey Ehr- und Tugendliebenden Gesellschaften, mit nutzlicher Ergetzlichkeit, beliebet und geübet werden mögen,* by Georg Philipp Harsdörffer (Nuremberg: Wolfgang Endter, 1645); reprinted, edited by Irmgard Böttcher (Tübingen: Niemeyer, 1969), pp. 46–52;

"Etliche Hirtengedichte," in volume 6 of *Frauenzimmer Gesprechspiele, so bey Ehr- und Tugendliebenden Gesellschaften, mit nutzlicher Ergetzlichkeit, beliebet und geübet werden mögen,* by Harsdörffer (Nuremberg: Wolfgang Endter, 1646); reprinted, edited by Böttcher (Tübingen: Niemeyer, 1969), pp. 36–42;

"Schauplatz der Vollkommenheit," in volume 7 of *Frauenzimmer Gesprechspiele, so bey Ehr- und Tugendliebenden Gesellschaften, mit nutzlicher Ergetzlichkeit, beliebet und geübet werden mögen,* by Harsdörffer (Nuremberg: Wolfgang Endter, 1647); reprinted, edited by Böttcher (Tübingen: Niemeyer, 1969), pp. 17–33;

Johann Hellwig in 1655; engraving by Jacob Sandrart after a painting by Georg Christoph Eimart the Younger

Francesco Pona, *Ormund Das ist, Lieb- und HeldenGedicht, in welchem des Hoflebens Sitten, Gefahren und seltene begebenheiten eigentlich ab- und ausgebildet werden,* translated by Hellwig (Frankfurt am Main: Johann David Zunner, 1648; revised, 1666);

Wilibald Pirkheimer, *Beschreibung des Flekkens Neuhofes,* translated by Hellwig (N.p., 1648);

Boethius, *Christlich vernünftiges Bedenken,* translated by Hellwig (Nuremberg: Christoph Gerhard, 1660).

Noting in 1741 the obscurity into which a translation by Johann Hellwig had fallen, Johann Christoph Gottsched acidly observed "daß die Seltenheit eines Buches öfter ein Zeichen eines schlechten, als eines sonderbaren Werthes sey" (that the obscurity of a book is more often an indication of meager than of unique worth). With this remark Hellwig was reduced to little more than a footnote in literary history until his rehabilitation in the late twentieth century. Although he lacked the genius of his mentors Georg Philipp Harsdörffer, Johann Klaj, and Sigmund von Birken, he possessed acute skills of invention and was one of the most active members of the Nuremberg literary society Löblicher Hirten- und Blumenorden an der Pegnitz (Honorable Order of Shepherds and Flowers on the Pegnitz), usually called the Pegnesischer Blumenorden. He was a prolific composer of occasional verse; he made noteworthy contributions to the genre of pattern poetry; he was active as a translator; and he was a master of *Schäferey* (prose eclogue) and significantly developed its potential as a vehicle for social commentary. During his lifetime he was less widely known as a poet than as a medical scholar, as one of Nuremberg's preeminent physicians, and, later, as personal physician to Franz Wihelm von Wartenberg, bishop of Regensburg. Hellwig receives mention in biographical encyclopedias of medicine as late as the third edition of August Hirsch's *Biographisches Lexikon der hervorragenden Ärzte aller Zeiten und Völker* (Biographical Lexicon of the Foremost Physicians of All Times and Nations, 1962).

The second of seven children of Christoph and Maria Hellwig née Mörl, Johann Hellwig was born in Nuremberg on 29 July 1609. His father was a wealthy merchant and one of the directors of the city market. As well-to-do merchants, the Hellwigs were corporately bound with lawyers, physicians, apothecaries, academicians, and other professionals in the second estate, *die Ehrbare* (honorable citizens), and enjoyed all legal and social privileges save those reserved for the patrician first estate. All non-patricians, regardless of wealth or learning, were barred from the city's innermost governing body, the Small Council; the two to three hundred honorable families constituted most of the Greater Council, whose function was essentially that of ratifying the decisions of the Small Council. Christoph Hellwig served in the Greater Council from 1621 until his death in 1634.

In 1621 Johann Hellwig was sent to school in Erfurt. He became ill after three years and returned to his hometown to finish his secondary education at the Aegidianum. Like other cities in Germany that had implemented educational reforms since the Reformation, Nuremberg made ethical and religious principles the cornerstone of its schools, with emphasis on New Testament Greek, Scripture, the Lutheran catechism, and theology. But in the early seventeenth century a new feature was added: a pleasurable approach to learning that emphasized practice and question-and-answer drills. It is difficult not to assume a causal relationship between the methodology of their early education and the playful, experimental character of the work of the poets of the Pegnesischer Blumenorden.

Like many of Nuremberg's young men being groomed for the professions, in 1627 Hellwig began his university education at Altdorf. Located in an idyllic rural setting southeast of Nuremberg, Altdorf was home to one of Germany's most progressive universities, particularly in the fields of natural science, medicine, and law. The empirical view that dominated scientific theory at Altdorf derived from the Aristotelian principles of its founder, Philipp Melanchthon, which were systematized by Nicolaus Taurellus in the late sixteenth century. The pastoral works of Hellwig and his colleagues in the 1640s resonate with the positive, inquisitive attitude toward nature fostered during their years at Altdorf. Under his adviser Georg Noessler, Hellwig distinguished himself as a student and was awarded the *stipendium aureum* (golden stipend) in 1631 for his Ἀλφάβητον ἰατικόν (Physician's Lexicon), a tabular summation of Hippocratic principles, which he dedicated to Nuremberg's city fathers.

After concluding his studies at Altdorf in 1631, Hellwig set out on a *peregrinatio academica* (academic tour) that would keep him abroad for three years. His itinerary included some of Europe's most prestigious centers of medical learning: Strasbourg for five months; Montpellier for two years; and Padua, where he heard lectures by the renowned physicians Benedictus Sylvaticus, Fortunatus Licetus, Johannis Veslingius, Jacobus Thomasinus, Johannis Rhodius, and his mentor, Julius Sala, and received his doctorate in medicine in August 1634. His father's death in September brought him home at a moment when his medical services were desperately needed to help combat the plague that was ravaging Nuremberg. He was received in late 1634 into the Collegium Medicum, then under the presidency of Johann Jacob Tetzel, whom Hellwig would celebrate in *Die Nymphe Noris in Zweyen Tagzeiten vorgestel-*

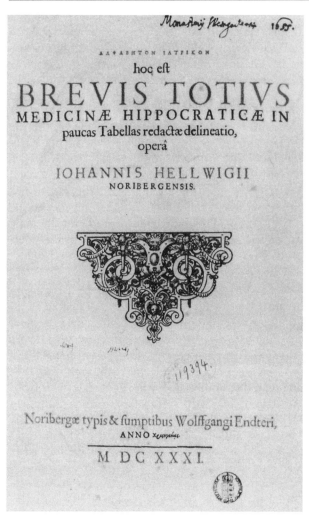

Title page for Hellwig's summary of Hippocratic principles, his first published work (National Library of Medicine)

let (The Nymph Noris Presented in Two Days' Time, 1650) as one of the city's outstanding citizens.

In October 1635 Hellwig married Helena Schlüsselfelder, fourteen years older than he and the daughter of the patrician Senator Carl Schlüsselfelder; the union was childless. By his marriage Hellwig became related to the patrician Kolers; they, in turn, were related to the Kresses and other patricians with whom Hellwig enjoyed friendships. In 1648, in the dedication poem in his translation of Wilibald Pirkheimer's *Beschreibung des Flekkens Neuhofes* (Description of the Place Neu[n]hof), Hellwig would recall pleasant evenings spent with the Kolers and the Jenisches: "Ich, die ringste Zucht der Musen, hab auch oftmals mich ergetzt, / Mich mit Eurer hohen Gunste, diesen Orts, zur Quell gesetzt, / Mit Gesprech' und külem Trunck' in die Nacht den Tag gestekket, / Nachmals vor dem blassen Mond

nach der leichten Dek gestrekket / Bis ich sänftlich ausgeruhet" (I, least child of the Muses, have often taken my pleasure / By your gracious kindness, in this place, sitting beside the fountain, / In conversation and with a refreshing drink watching day turn into night, / until, stretched out under my airy blanket beneath a pale moon, / I gently drifted off to sleep). This close association with the patrician estate is basic to much of Hellwig's literary work. In *Die Nymphe Noris* and the unpublished "Sacrarium Bonae Memoriae Noribergensium" (Shrine to the Good Memory of Nuremberg Citizens) together more than three hundred Nuremberg families of high birth are commemorated in verse. The rich genealogical detail in these works provides strong evidence that Hellwig had privileged access to the archives of many of the families. Helena died in June 1641; in September 1643 Hellwig married Euphrosyna Koch, daughter of the prominent merchant Jacob Koch. Two sons and four daughters were born to the couple, of whom two girls preceded their father in death.

Like almost all seventeenth-century German poets, Hellwig had no literary career in the modern sense. The period during which he regularly published was brief but intense and corresponded to the first flowering of the Pegnesischer Blumenorden, from its inception in late 1644 until the peace celebrations at the end of the Thirty Years' War began to diminish in 1650. He was accepted into the society in 1645 under the name Montano, at about the same time as Sigmund Betulius (later von Birken), Samuel Hund, Johann Sechst, Christoph Arnold, Johann Georg Volkamer, and Friedrich Lochner.

Hellwig's first original contribution as a member of the society was a bucolic piece dedicated to Harsdörffer in volume five (1645) of the latter's *Frauenzimmer Gesprechspiele* (Playful Colloquies for the Ladies). As the shepherd Montano he is inspired by the nymph Noris to compose a poem in praise of "Strephon" (Harsdörffer). The seven-page piece is a gem of writing in the Nuremberg bucolic style, a miniature version of the prose eclogue genre created by Opitz in 1630 in his *Schäfferei von der Nimfen Hercinie* (Idyll of the Nymph Hercinie) and adopted as the quintessential Nuremberg form by Harsdörffer and Klaj in their *Pegnesisches Schäfergedicht* (Pegnitzian Idyll, 1644). Obviously, Hellwig had by this time studied Harsdörffer and Klaj's work and its sequel, Birken's *Fortsetzung der Pegnitz-Schäferey* (Continuation of the Pegnitz Idyll, 1645). The major features of those works are present: a verse introduction; a nature walk; a visit with a spring nymph; the transmission of privileged knowledge from the nymph to the poet; the commissioning of a task; heraldic descriptions and panegyric; and a concluding nature walk.

Hellwig expanded these elements to produce a full-scale prose eclogue, *Die Nymphe Noris;* begun in late 1645, it was published in 1650. It is not easy to place *Die Nymphe Noris* into a genre. On the one hand, it is obviously a prose eclogue; but it also belongs to the praise-of-city tradition of Sigismund Meisterlin, Conrad Celtis, and Eobanus Hessus. Hellwig announces his intention to describe "nicht allein desselben [seines lieben Vatterlandes] von Gott reichgesegnet Landsart ... sondern auch zugleich dessen hochrühmliche Regimentsform, benebenst denen Adelichen Geschlechten, denkwürdigsten Begebenheiten, und namhaftesten Gebäuen" (not only [his beloved fatherland's] divinely blessed countryside ... but also its celebrated government, its noble families, its greatest historical events and most noteworthy edifices). The commemorations of more than 150 families are interspersed with allusions to local history and culture. No other prose eclogue of the seventeenth century is so unremittingly positive in tone; an atmosphere of ideal harmony prevails in "Neronsburg" (Hellwig's allegorical name for Nuremberg). But as in Virgil's *Eclogues,* behind the serene Arcadian landscape a real world of social and political turmoil is palpable. Neronsburg and Nuremberg, in short, are not the same, and Hellwig means to remind readers of the distance that separates claims of nobility from true nobility. His exploitation of the critical potential of German prose eclogue represents a step beyond his predecessors and remains unmatched in the seventeenth century.

Probably under way by the late 1640s was a work that likewise draws heavily on genealogy and the poetic rites of commemoration, "Sacrarium Bonae Memoriae Noribergensium," a catalogue of verse commemorating notable Nurembergers who had died in other cities. Never printed, "Sacrarium Bonae Memoriae Noribergensium" differs from *Die Nymphe Noris* in that it offers no narrative; it shares with *Die Nymphe Noris* the fascination with memory and the art of encapsulating the enduring qualities of lives well lived.

Hellwig's occasional poems include many thematic and formal types: aphorism, debate, dedication, epicedium (mourning poem), epithalamium, genethliacon (poem celebrating a birth), hunting, motto, prayer, and utopia. Their common denominator is the question of what qualities constitute the truly good life; the answer is *vera nobilitas* (true nobility), which reduces human distinctions to basics

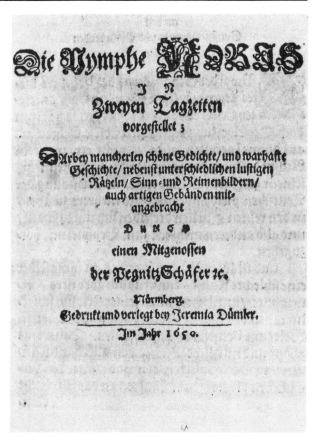

Title page for the prose eclogue in which Hellwig presents an idealized version of Nuremberg

and effectively relegates inherited privilege to nonessential status. Besides his many separately published poems, two of Hellwig's larger works consist in great part of verses addressed to specific individuals, families, or things, for a specific occasion. It would, therefore, not be far-fetched to argue that "Sacrarium Bonae Memoriae Noribergensium," and somewhat less so *Die Nymphe Noris,* are occasional poems in large format.

Hellwig was an especially accomplished writer of pattern poetry (now known as concrete poetry), in which the lines of a poem are typographically arranged to create a visual representation of the object described by the text. A poem to Strephon in *Die Nymphe Noris,* for example, depicts the triple-turreted tower of the Harsdörffer escutcheon as the text extols Strephon's station in both the mundane and the heavenly realms, thereby interpreting the attribute of loftiness in the tower. Besides his own compositions, Hellwig promoted the work of others in the genre. In *Die Nymphe Noris* he collects twelve pattern poems by himself and his fellow Pegnitz Shepherds and a statement on the subject by Harsdörffer.

First page of a 1655 letter from Hellwig to Athanasius Kircher (Pontifica Università Gregoriana)

Several months after undertaking work on *Die Nymphe Noris* Hellwig began to translate *L'Ormondo* (1635), by Francesco Pona. One of a host of German translations of Italian court novels to appear during the 1640s and 1650s, *Ormund* (1648) is an adventure story brimming with knightly romanticism; its complicated plot is based loosely on historical conflicts between England and Scotland. Hellwig stresses its usefulness for the education of a prince in his dedication to the fourteen-year-old Anton Ulrich, son of Duke Ernst August of Brunswick-Lüneburg.

Probably commissioned by the owners of the Neunhof estate – which can still be visited in the outer quarter north of Nuremberg – *Beschreibung des Flekkens Neuhofes* is a translation of selections from the humanist Pirkheimer's Latin description of the property. Some of Hellwig's finest work can be found in this unforced imitation of the original's simple bucolic style, which is marred only insofar as it fails to match Pirkheimer's economy. For example, Pirkheimer's "Praecipue tamen Philomela canora querelas repetit solitas, ac Itim suum voce deflet suaviplora" is rendered by Hellwig as "Und sonderlich die singende Nachtigal wiederhohlet zum öftern ihre gewöhnliche Klage, indeme sie mit ihrer holdklingenden Kehle, ihren lieben Freund betrauret" (Especially the singing nightingale repeats over and over her usual complaint as she grieves, with her sweetly echoing voice, for her dear friend).

In 1649 Hellwig was called to Regensburg to become personal physician to Bishop Wartenberg. Away from Nuremberg and the encouragement of Harsdörffer and the others, he seems to have lost his poetic direction and motivation; he depended heavily for his literary ideas on the city's history and culture, even its problems. Aside from some occasional poems, his main undertaking after leaving Nuremberg was *Christlich vernünftiges Bedenken* (Christian Rational Reflection, 1660), a translation of Boethius's *De Consolatione Philosophiae* (On the Consolation of Philosophy, circa 524); it was prompted by the death in September 1658 of Harsdörffer, who had recommended in 1643 that the work be translated into modern German. (Hellwig had actually initiated the translation in the mid 1640s.) Another – and, by modern standards, a better – translation was published seven years later by Christian Knorr von Rosenroth and Franciscus van Helmont; in the introduction Knorr von Rosenroth calls Hellwig's version "unverständlich" (unintelligible). Hellwig's translation then passed into obscurity; it was rediscovered in the eighteenth century, though Hellwig was not identified as the

translator until 1805. In the seventh volume (1741) of *Beyträge zur Critischen Historie der Deutschen Sprache, Poesie und Beredsamkeit* (Studies in the Critical History of German Language, Poetry, and Oratory, 1732–1744) Gottsched compared the two translations; in a blatantly skewed analysis based on his own new stylistic principles he attributed the earlier work to a member of the Fruchtbringende Gesellschaft (Fruit-bringing Society), Germany's first literary society, and concluded that it fully deserved to be forgotten.

Hellwig may, at least, have found comfort in Boethius's message of stoic resolve and inner calm in face of adversity. He was still grieving for his friend and mentor Harsdörffer when the sudden death in late 1661 of Wartenberg, who by then was a cardinal, robbed him of an employer who had become a close friend. Worst of all, a rival, Dr. Daniel Geyger, immediately began to circulate a letter challenging the conclusions of Hellwig's autopsy of the cardinal. Hellwig responded with *Prodromus Apologeticus Super Relatione Medica* (Defense of the Autopsy, 1662), in which he explained his procedures in detail and attempted to show that Geyger's criticism had been motivated by envy and spite. Geyger thereupon sued Hellwig for libel; how the controversy ended is not known.

During the final decade of his life Hellwig was at work on a collection of medical observations, but he was able to finish only about half of it before he died on 4 June 1674. He was buried on 8 June in Saint Peter's Cemetery in Regensburg. His former Nuremberg colleague Johann Georg Volkamer gathered Hellwig's notes and encouraged Dr. Luca Schröck to complete the work, which was published in 1680 under the title *Observationes Physico-Medicae, posthumae.*

Even before Gottsched's vilification, Hellwig was considered a minor poet; he does not deserve to be forgotten, however. His pattern poetry and idylls, in particular, merit attention. Furthermore, reappraisal of Hellwig's work has added to scholarly understanding of the Pegnesischer Blumenorden. Its agenda was broader and more ambitious than the textbooks suggest, involving a social mission as well as a strictly literary one, and it would appear that the second tier of poets behind Harsdörffer, Klaj, and Birken played a substantially greater role in that mission than was previously thought.

Bibliography:

Max Reinhart, *Johann Hellwig: A Descriptive Bibliography* (Columbia, S.C.: Camden House, 1993).

Biographies:

Johann Antonida Linden and Georg Abraham Mercklin, *De scriptis medicis libri duo* (Nuremberg: Wolfgang Moritz Endter, 1686), pp. 601–602;

Paul Freher, "Johannes Helwigius," in his *Theatrum virorum eruditione clarorum* (Nuremberg: Johann Hoffmann, 1688), pp. 1414b–1415a;

Johann Herdegen, "Montano," in his *Historische Nachricht von deß löblichen Hirten-und Blumen-Ordens an der Pegnitz Anfang und Fortgang* (Nuremberg: Riegel, 1744), pp. 242–245;

Georg Andreas Will, "Helwig (Johann)," in his *Nürnbergisches Gelehrtenlexikon* (Nuremberg & Altdorf: Schüpfel, 1756), pp. 86–88;

August Hirsch, *Biographisches Lexikon der hervorragenden Ärzte aller Zeiten und Völker*, third edition, volume 3 (Munich: Urban & Schwarzenberg, 1962), p. 149;

Max Reinhart, "Life and Works," in his *Johann Hellwig: A Descriptive Bibliography* (Columbia, S.C.: Camden House, 1993), pp. 1–20.

References:

Jeremy Adler, "Pastoral Typography: Sigmund von Birken and the 'Picture-Rhymes' of Johann Helwig," *Visible Language*, 20 (Winter 1986): 121–135;

Adler and Ernst Ulrich, *Text als Figur: Visuelle Poesie von der Antike bis zur Moderne*, second edition (Weinheim: VCH, 1988), pp. 75a, 145b, 152, 165a;

Peter M. Daly, *Literature in the Light of the Emblem: Structural Parallels between the Emblem and Literature in the Sixteenth and Seventeenth Centuries* (Toronto: University of Toronto Press, 1979), pp. 127–132;

Johann Christoph Gottsched, "Severini Boethii Christlich vernünftiges Bedenken," in *Beyträge zur Critischen Historie der Deutschen Sprache, Poesie und Beredsamkeit*, volume 7, edited by Gottsched (Leipzig: Breitkopf, 1741; reprinted, Hildesheim: Olms, 1970), pp. 491–501;

Dick Higgins, *Pattern Poetry: Guide to an Unknown Literature* (Albany: State University of New York Press, 1987), pp. 76–77;

Gottfried Kirchner, *Fortuna in Dichtung und Emblematik des Barock: Tradition und Bedeutungswandel eines Motivs* (Stuttgart: Metzler, 1970);

Jane Ogden Newman, *Pastoral Conventions: Poetry, Language, and Thought in Seventeenth-Century Nuremberg* (Baltimore & London: Johns Hopkins University Press, 1990), pp. 228–232;

Max Reinhart, "*De Consolatione Philosophiae* in Seventeenth-Century Germany: Translation and Reception," *Daphnis*, 21 (1992): 65–94;

Reinhart, "Historical, Poetic and Ideal Representation," *Daphnis*, 19, no. 1 (1990): 41–66;

Reinhart, "Poets and Politics," *Daphnis*, 20, no. 1 (1991): 199–229;

Werner Schultheiß, "Woher stammt die Bezeichnung 'Noris'?," *Mitteilungen des Vereins für Geschichte der Stadt Nürnberg*, 52 (1963/1964): 551–553;

Julius Tittmann, *Die Nürnberger Dichterschule: Harsdörffer, Klaj, Birken* (Wiesbaden: Sändig, 1965), pp. 67–68;

Harry Vredeveld, "Zur Herkunft des Wortes 'Noris'," *Mitteilungen des Vereins für Geschichte der Stadt Nürnberg*, 71 (1984): 208–211;

Robert C. Warnock and Roland Folter, "The German Pattern Poem: A Study in Mannerism of the Seventeenth Century," in *Festschrift für Detlev W. Schumann zum 70. Geburtstag*, edited by Albert R. Schmitt (Munich: Delp, 1970), pp. 40–73.

Papers:

Johann Hellwig's papers are scattered among various libraries; principal repositories are the Germanisches National Museum (Archiv des Pegnesischen Blumenordens), Nuremberg; and the Universitätsbibliothek, Erlangen. The manuscript "Sacrarium Bonae Memoriae Noribergensium" is in the Österreichische Nationalbibliothek, Vienna.

Anna Ovena Hoyers

(1584 – 27 November 1655)

Barbara Becker-Cantarino
Ohio State University

BOOKS: *Gespräch eines Kindes mit seiner Mutter, von dem Wege zu wahrer Gottseligkeit* (N.p., 1628);

Das Buch Ruth. Jn Teutsche Reimen gestellet vnd ans Liecht gebracht (Stockholm: Heinrich Keyser, 1634);

Ein Schreiben über Meer gesand an die Gemeine in Engelland auß einer alten Frawen handt, die ungenandt, Gott ist bekandt. Anno 1649., anonymous (N.p., 1649);

Geistliche und Weltliche Poemata (Amsterdam: Ludwig Elzevier, 1650).

Edition: *Geistliche und Weltliche Poemata (1650)*, edited, with a biographical afterword, by Barbara Becker-Cantarino (Tübingen: Niemeyer, 1986).

OTHER: Enea Silvio Piccolomini, *Süßbittere Freude; oder Eine wahrhafftige Historie von zwey liebhabenden Personen, unter verdeckten Namen Eurylai und Lucretiae, durch Æneam Sylvium Lateinisch beschrieben, durch Nicolaum von Weil, Stadtschreibern, verdeutscht, ietz aber in Deutsche Reimen gestellt*, German paraphrase by Hoyers (Schleswig, 1617).

Anna Ovena Hoyers was one of the few German women in the early seventeenth century whose writings appeared in print. Because of her religious fervor and her association with Anabaptists, she has gone down in literary history as a "Schwärmerin" (religious zealot). Yet even a superficial examination of Hoyers's *Geistliche und Weltliche Poemata* (Religious and Secular Poetry, 1650), a collection of her most representative poetry, shows the one-sidedness of such a judgment: Hoyers's verses reflect her deep religiosity, her love for her children, and her independence and self-determination in religious and secular matters, as well as her contempt for bookish learning and for the hypocrisy of the Lutheran orthodoxy. Her poetry attests to her unorthodox thinking and lifestyle.

Anna Owens was born in 1584 (the exact date is unknown) in Koldenbüttel in the Eiderstedt region, on the west coast of what was then the duchy of Schleswig-Holstein-Gottorf, to Hans Owens, a wealthy and educated landowner who died in the year of her birth, and Wennecke Owens, née Hunnens. Her mother came from a wealthy, fiercely independent, upper-class family in the lucrative dairy business. Orphaned at an early age, Owens was raised by an uncle. She did not receive formal theological instruction – it was unthinkable for girls to attend Latin schools or universities; at best, they had catechism lessons in which they learned to read and write. She read devotional works as well as spiritual and secular literature and may have learned Latin at this time; she knew enough of the language to use it rather cleverly in a few of her poems.

Provided, as her parents' sole heiress, with a large dowry of more than a hundred thousand marks, Owens was barely fifteen years old when she married Hermann Hoyers, the *Staller* (governor) of Eiderstedt, Everschop, and Utholm; his family, one of the most prominent in the area, was related to the royal household of Denmark. They lived at his estate, Hoyersworth, just outside the town of Tönning, and at his castle in Tönning. The couple had nine children, six of whom would live to adulthood.

For several decades the Lutheran clergy in Schleswig had bitterly opposed the Mennonites and the Jorites, Anabaptist groups that were emigrating from the Netherlands and making converts. The governors – Anna's husband and his father before him – evicted them and confiscated their property. As the governor's wife, Hoyers never openly raised any religious questions or concerns.

Widowed in 1622, Hoyers found herself responsible for the management of her husband's dairy business and extensive landholdings, which had incurred large debts. Years of litigation followed, during which she tried to preserve her inheritance and maintain the properties. In 1623 Duke Friedrich III of Schleswig-Holstein granted the Ana-

Anna Ovena Hoyers

baptists a refuge, later named Friedrichstadt, because they were important in the agricultural industry and were major taxpayers. But the religious disputes continued, and Hoyers was soon in the midst of the controversies. In addition to the works of Martin Luther and his translation of the Bible, she read the writings of the unorthodox religious thinkers Johann Arndt, Kaspar Schwenckfeld von Ossig, Valentin Weigel, and David Joris. She also read devotional and religious tracts of the Reformers and Anabaptists, attended their services, and invited the controversial physician Nicolaus Teting to her estate. Teting, who had studied medicine and alchemy in Leiden and had been chased out of Flensburg by the Lutheran clergy because of his religious views, held church services in his patroness's home and formed there a *Gemeinde* (community) of seekers after "true Christianity."

In 1623 Friedrich III ordered an investigation of Teting's activities, and Teting moved to Husum. Hoyers followed him with her children. In 1624 Teting was banished from Husum and moved to Hamburg. Hoyers remained in Husum but seems to have made several trips to Hamburg; she was certainly there in 1628, when the plague was rampant. Hoyers survived it while apparently also caring for the family of her oldest daughter, who was married and living in Hamburg.

Anna Ovena Hoyers — the form of her name that appears on the title pages of her works — had begun to write religious hymns and other spiritual verses in the 1620s. Many of the poems have satiric political passages as a consequence of her confrontations with the clergy, who attacked her from their pulpits. In 1625 she wrote a biting satire, "Schreiben an die Herrn Titultrager von Hohen-Schulen" (Letter to Titleholders from Universities), against two Lutheran ministers from Flensburg, reminding them that she had never received consolation from their church and that they had no authority over her. She also attacked their bookish learning: "Die glärten sind (wie Luther sagt) / Die verkehrten" (The learned are [as Luther says] / Hypocrites).

The best known of her satiric works is her Low German "De Denische Dörp-Pape" (The Danish Country Parson, 1630), in which she chastises the drunkenness, pugnacity, and foolishness of the country parson and the narrow-minded and petty thinking of the town clergy. Her anticlerical diatribe reflects her disappointment in the established church.

Hoyers's didactic poem *Gespräch eines Kindes mit seiner Mutter, von dem Wege zu wahrer Gottseligkeit* (Conversation of a Child with His Mother about the Path to True Devotion, 1628) is not a dogmatic treatise but a piece of practical religious instruction in dialogue form. The mother teaches that earthly life begins with sin; the recognition of sin is followed by repentance and reacceptance into Christ's grace, after which one may live in the imitation of Christ and attain eternal salvation. The frontispiece of the first edition of the work reflects its content. It shows the mother in a simple dress; her son stands nearby with his hand on his heart, the seat of faith. On the table are the Old and New Testaments, and a lute hangs on the wall; these objects point to the idea that both words and music serve as media for religious instruction. On the floor an open book lies near Mercury's staff, suggesting that the present work should serve the boy as a guide for his soul's journey. In the background the soul, clothed in armor, holds a shield embossed with a cross – the shield of faith – in his left hand and a raised sword in his right and wards off Death and the Devil, who aim arrows at him. The warrior-soul shines in the heavenly light of Truth, and it has just emerged from the body of a naked man, the "old Adam," which lies on the ground. While two angels with palm branches and a laurel wreath descend from heaven, to the right a female figure, Religio, offers the chalice of communion to the reborn soul; under her feet she crushes crowns and hats, the symbols of secular and spiritual authority.

In the seventeenth century there was, as yet, no distinction between church hymns and spiritual songs; hymns were sung in the home during private worship and tended to reflect the personal beliefs of the writers. Hoyers's hymns follow this pattern, which she considered to be thoroughly Lutheran. The Lutheran clergy thought otherwise, however, and branded her a sectarian. Hoyers created her own melodies for her hymns or cited those of well-known church hymns or secular songs.

Hoyers had a special liking for acrostics, chronograms, and anagrams. Letter-crosses often serve as mottoes to introduce longer works; they also frame her hymns, highlight themes in her poems, and close poems by concisely summarizing the meaning of the preceding verses. Frequently an anagram or

cryptonym of her own name will appear in the refrain of a stanza. This use of her name is not meant to call attention to her as an individual; on the contrary, she means to show that she has become an integral part of God's universe, in which she is hidden and secure. Her verses are a religious confession in poetic form: "Ich werd getrieben, muß es sagen / Habs ehe geschrieben, wills mehr wagen / Sollt es auch kosten kopff und kragen" (I am driven, I must profess / I've earlier written about it, will wager again / even if it costs my life).

In occasional verses that have survived only in manuscript form, Hoyers tells of her travels to Hamburg; about a trip to Denmark with her children to flee invading troops during the Thirty Years' War; and about the great Nordstrand flood of 1634, during which she sat for three days with her children in the loft at her estate at Tönning, waiting for the waters to recede. In these events she sees God's power and a sign of God's coming.

In the mid 1630s – the exact year cannot be ascertained – Hoyers had to sell her properties and leave Schleswig-Holstein under pressure from her creditors and the orthodox clergy. She immigrated to Sweden with all of her children except her married oldest daughter. Hoyers lived for about ten years in the fishing village of Västerwik, supporting herself and her family by running a dairy farm. In the 1640s she moved to Stockholm, where, through the patronage of Maria Eleonora, Queen Christina's mother, she received a small piece of property in 1649.

In 1650 a collection of her verses, *Geistliche und Weltliche Poemata,* was published in Amsterdam, the printing center of northern Europe and a place where controversial political and religious works could appear. The collection was condemned as heretical in her homeland of Schleswig-Holstein in 1651; sale of the book was forbidden, and copies were confiscated and burned. Hoyers died on 27 November 1655.

Bibliography:

Anna Ovena Hoyers, *Geistiche und Weltliche Poemata,* edited by Barbara Becker-Cantarino (Tübingen: Niemeyer, 1986), pp. *99–*112.

Biography:

Dieter Lohmeier, "Anna Ovena Hoyers," in *Schleswig-Holsteinisches Biographisches Lexikon,* volume 3 (Neumünster: Wachholtz, 1973), pp. 155–159.

References:

Barbara Becker-Cantarino, "Low German as a Literary Language in Schleswig-Holstein in the Seventeenth Century: A Poem by Anna Ovena Hoyers," in *Languages and Cultures: Studies in Honor of Edgar C. Polomé,* edited by Mohammed Ali Jazayeri and Werner Winter (Berlin, New York & Amsterdam: De Gruyter, 1988), pp. 63–72;

Becker-Cantarino, "Die Stockholmer Liederhandschrift der Anna Ovena Hoyers," in *Barocker Lust-Spiegel: Festschrift für Blake Lee Spahr,* edited by Martin Bircher (Amsterdam: Rodopi, 1984), pp. 329–344;

Johanna Fries, "Die deutsche Kirchenlieddichtung in Schleswig-Holstein im 17. Jahrhundert," dissertation, University of Kiel, 1964;

Boy Hinrichs, "Anna Ovena Hoyers und ihre beiden Sturmflutlieder von 1634," *Nordfriesisches Jahrbuch,* new series 21 (1985): 195–221;

Cornelia Niekus Moore, "Anna Hoyers 'Posaunenschall': Hymns of an Empire at War and a Kingdom to Come," *Daphnis: Zeitschrift für Mittlere Deutsche Literatur,* 13, no. 1–2 (1984): 343–362;

Moore, "'Mein Kindt, nimm diß in acht.' Anna Hoyers 'Gespräch eines Kindes mit seiner Mutter von dem Wege zu wahren Gottseligkeit' als Beispiel der Erbauungsliteratur für die Jugend im 17. Jahrhundert," *Pietismus und Neuzeit,* 6 (1980): 164–185;

Adah Blanche Roe, *Anna Owena Hoyers: A Poetess of the Seventeenth Century,* Bryn Mawr College Monographs, no. 19 (Bryn Mawr, Pa.: Bryn Mawr College, 1915);

Hans Joachim Schoeps, "Anna Ovena Hoyers (1584–1655) und ihre ungedruckten schwedischen Gedichte," *Euphorion,* 46, no. 2 (1951): 233–267;

Paul Schütze, "Anna Ovena Hoyers und ihre niederdeutsche Satire 'De Denische Dörp-Pape,'" *Zeitschrift der Gesellschaft für die Herzogtümer Schleswig, Holstein und Lauenburg,* 15 (1885): 245–299.

Papers:

The Royal Library, Stockholm, acquired in 1854 a manuscript (catalogue number V.Y. Vu. 76) that was probably written by Anna Ovena Hoyers's oldest son, Caspar, around the time of her death. The manuscript includes fourteen poems that were published in *Geistliche und Weltliche Poemata* and other hymns and religious poems occasioned by specific events; some of the latter have been published in articles by Barbara Becker-Cantarino, Boy Hinrichs, and Hans Joachim Schoeps. The manuscript includes two short samples of Hoyers's handwriting.

Athanasius Kircher

(2 May 1602 – 27 November 1680)

Joscelyn Godwin
Colgate University

BOOKS: *Ars Magnesia. Hoc est Disqvisitio Bipartita-empeirica seu experimentalis, Physico-mathematica de Natvra, Viribvs, et Prodigiosis Effectibvs Magnetis* (Würzburg: Printed by Elias Michael Zinck, 1631);

Primitiae Gnomonicae Catoptricae Hoc Est Horologiographiae Novae Specvlaris (Avignon: Printed by J. Piot, 1635);

Prodromvs Coptvs sive Ægyptiacvs (Rome: Printed by the Sacred Congregation for the Propagation of the Faith, 1636);

Specvla Melitensis Encyclica, Hoc est, Syntagma Novvm Instrvmentorvm Physico-Mathematicorvm, as Salvatore Imbroll (Naples: Printed by Secundino Roncaglioli, 1638);

Magnes siue De Arte Magnetica Opvs Tripartitvm (Rome: Printed by Lodovico Grignani, published by Hermann Scheus, 1641; corrected edition, Cologne: Jodocus Kalckhoven, 1643; enlarged edition, Rome: Printed by Vitale Mascardi, published by Blasius Deversin & Zanobio Masotti, 1654);

Lingva Aegyptiaca Restitvta Opvs Tripartitvm (Rome: Printed by Lodovico Grignani, published by Hermann Scheus, 1643);

Ars Magna Lvcis et Vmbrae in decem Libros digesta (Rome: Printed by Lodovico Grignani, published by Hermann Scheus, 1646; revised edition, Amsterdam: Printed by Johannes Jansson van Waesberge & Eliseus Weyerstraten's heirs, 1671);

Mvsvrgia Vniversalis sive Ars Magna Consoni et Dissoni in X. Libros Digesta (Rome: Printed by Francesco Corbelletti's heirs & Lodovico Grignani, 1650); excerpts translated into German by A. Hirsch as *Philosophischer Extract und Auszug aus der Musurgia universalis* (Schwäbisch-Hall, 1662); excerpts translated by J. Godwin in his *Music, Mysticism and Magic* (London: Routledge & Kegan Paul, 1986), pp. 153–161, and in his *Harmony of the Spheres* (Rochester, Vt.: Inner Traditions International, 1993), pp. 263–285;

Athanasius Kircher in 1664; engraving by an unidentified artist

Obeliscvs Pamphilivs (Rome: Printed by Lodovico Grignani, 1650);

Oedipus Aegyptiacvs. Hoc est Vniuersalis Hieroglyphicae Veterum Doctrinae temporum iniuria abolitae Instavratio, 3 volumes (Rome: Printed by Vitale Mascardi, 1652–1654);

Itinerarivm Exstaticvm qvo Mvndi Opificivm . . . explorata (Rome: Printed by Vitale Mascardi, 1656);

Iter Exstaticvm II. (Rome: Printed by Vitale Mascardi, 1657);

Scrvtinivm Physico-medicvm Contagiosae Luis, quae Pestis dicitur (Rome: Printed by Vitale Mascardi, 1658); translated anonymously into German as *Natürliche und medicinalische Durchgründung der leidigen ansteckenden Sucht* (Augsburg, 1680);

Diatribe. De prodigiosis Crucibus, quae tam supra vestes hominum, quam res alias, non pridem post vltimum incendium Vesuuij Montis Neapoli comparuerunt (Rome: Printed by Vitale Mascardi, sold by Blasius Deversin, 1661);

Polygraphia Nova et Vniversalis ex Combinatoria Arte Detecta (Rome: Printed by L. Varesi, 1663);

Mundus Subterraneus, in XII Libros digestus (Amsterdam: Printed by Johannes Jansson van Waesberge & Eliseus Weyerstraten, 1665);

Historia Evstachio-Mariana qua Admiranda D. Eustachij, Sociorumque Vita ex varijs Authoribus collecta (Rome: Printed by L. Varesi, 1665);

Arithmologia sive De abditis Numerorum mysterijs qua Origo, Antiquitas & fabrica Numerorum exponitur (Rome: Printed by L. Varesi, 1665);

Kurtzer Bericht von dem Cometen und dessen Lauff welcher gestalt derselbe den 4/14 Decembris des vorigen 1664 Jahrs in Rom gesehen, und daselbst von gemeltem Dato an, biß auf den 20/30 desselben Monats observiret werden können (N.p., 1665); Latin version published as *Jter Cometae anni 1664 a 14. Decemb. vsque ad 30 Romae observatum* (N.p., 1665);

Obelisci Aegyptiaci nuper inter Isaei Romani rudera Effossi Interpretatio Hieroglyphica (Rome: Printed by L. Varesi, 1666);

China Monumentis qva Sacris quà Profanis, nec non variis Naturæ & Artis Spectaculis, Aliarumque rerum memorabilium Argumentis Illustrata (Amsterdam: Printed by Johannes Jansson van Waesberge & Eliseus Weyerstraten, 1667); translated by Charles D. van Thuyl as *China Illustrata* (Muskogee, Okla.: Indian University Press, 1988);

Magneticvm Naturæ Regnvm sive Disceptatio Physiologica (Rome: Printed by Ignatio di Lazaris, 1667);

Ars Magni Sciendi, in XII Libros Digesta (Amsterdam: Printed by Johannes Jansson van Waesberge & Eliseus Weyerstraten's widow, 1669);

Latium. Id Est, Nova et Parallela Latii tum Veteris tum Novi Descriptio (Amsterdam: Printed by Johannes Jansson van Waesberge & Eliseus Weyerstraten's heirs, 1671);

Principis Christiani Archetypon Politicum sive Sapientia Regnatrix (Amsterdam: Printed by Johannes Jansson van Waesberge, 1672);

Phonurgia Nova sive Conjugium Mechanico-physicum Artis & Natvrae Paranympha Phonosophia Concinnatum (Kempten: Rudolph Dreherr, 1673); trans-

lated by Agatho Carione (pseudonym for Tobias Nisslen) as *Neue Hall- und Thonkunst* (Nördlingen, 1684);

Arca Noë, in Tres Libros Digesta (Amsterdam: Printed by Johann Jansson van Waesberge, 1675);

Sphinx Mystagoga, sive Diatribe Hieroglyphica (Amsterdam: Johann Jansson van Waesberge, 1676);

Romani Collegii Societatis Jesu Musaeum Celeberrimum, by Kircher and Giorgio di Sepi (Amsterdam: Printed by Johann Jansson van Waesberge, 1678);

Turris Babel, sive Archontolia qua Primo Priscorum post diluvium hominum vita (Amsterdam: Printed by Johann Jansson van Waesberge, 1679);

Tariffa Kircheriana Id Est Inventvm Avcthoris Novvm Expeditâ, & mirâ arte combinatâ methodo, vniuersalem Geometriae, & Arithmeticae Practicae Summam continens, anonymous (Rome: Niccolò Angelo Tinassio, 1679);

Physiologia Kircheriana Experimentalis, qua Summa Argumentorum Multitudine & Varietate Naturalium rerum scientia per experimenta Physica, Mathematica, Medica, Chymica, Musica, Magnetica, Mechanica comprobatur atque stabilitur, edited by Johann Stephan Kestler (Amsterdam: Printed by Johann Jansson van Waesberge, 1680).

Editions: *Selbstbiographie des Pfarrer Athanasius Kircher,* translated by N. Seng (Fulda, 1901);

Phonurgia Nova, Monuments of Music II, no. 44 (New York: Broude, 1966);

China monumentis (Frankfurt am Main: Minerva, 1966);

Musurgia Universalis, edited by Ulf Scharlau (Hildesheim & New York: Olms, 1970).

Athanasius Kircher has a fair claim to have been the most learned German-born writer of his century: his works on Egyptology, music, optics, geology, linguistics, and comparative religion are all definitive for their time. But history has not been kind to him for several reasons. First, he wrote only in Latin, while other scholars were turning to the vernacular. Second, the breadth of his interests makes it almost impossible to appreciate his work as a whole. Third, his adherence to Christian Hermetism rooted his thought in a set of assumptions that the learned world was discarding; among these assumptions were the descent and ascent of the soul, the doctrine of correspondences, and the existence of occult powers. Yet, while his work was a tardy monument to the Renaissance ideal of universal knowledge, its celebration of nature opened new fields of study that heralded the age of secular science.

Kircher says in his autobiography (published in Ambrosius Langenmantel's selection of his letters, 1684; translated into German, 1901) that he began life at three o'clock in the morning on the Feast of Saint Athanasius, 2 May 1602. (Elsewhere he gives the year as 1601.) He was born in Geisa, near Fulda, an island of Catholicism in the generally Protestant region of Hesse-Darmstadt, to Johann Kircher, who taught theology at the Benedictine monastery in nearby Heiligenstadt, and Anna Kircher, née Gansek. Johann Kircher sent Athanasius, the last of his nine children, to the Jesuit school in Fulda.

Kircher's childhood was full of adventurous incidents. At least four times he escaped an early death: from being caught in a millrace; from falling under the feet of racing horses; from getting lost in a forest; and from gangrene contracted while skating. As he relates these misfortunes with all the relish of favorite tales, Kircher says that his deliverances were nothing short of miraculous. Even in his youth he felt favored by God and marked out for some special destiny.

After failing in his first application to the Jesuit college in Mainz, he was admitted as a novice to the college at Paderborn in 1618. Out of modesty he concealed his intelligence and was regarded as rather dull. By 1620 his novitiate was completed and his first vows taken, but the onset of the Thirty Years' War interrupted his education. The advance of the fiercely anti-Jesuit Duke Christian of Brunswick prompted him and two companions to flee in January 1622. They struggled for three days through deep snow, penniless and begging for their food, until a Catholic nobleman took them in. After a week at the Jesuit college at Münster they were advised to continue to Cologne. Passing through Düsseldorf, they came to the frozen Rhine. When they were halfway across, a piece of ice broke loose, and Kircher was carried away on it. His companions expected never to see him again, but he swam through the freezing water to the bank and walked for three hours to the Jesuit college in Neuss.

In 1623 Kircher completed his course in Scholastic philosophy in Cologne and was sent to Koblenz to study humanities and teach Greek at the Jesuit school. Abandoning his pretense of mediocrity, he aroused so much jealousy that he was transferred to the college at Heiligenstadt, where his father had once taught. The journey was a dangerous one through Protestant territory; but Kircher obstinately refused to wear a disguise, saying that he would rather die in the robes of his order than travel undisturbed in worldly dress. He nearly suffered exactly that fate: he was ambushed by Protestant soldiers, who, after stripping and beating him, prepared to hang him from the nearest tree. But his calm demeanor so moved one of the men that he persuaded his comrades to spare the young Jesuit's life and even return his property.

In Heiligenstadt, Kircher taught mathematics, Hebrew, and Syrian. In 1625, when delegates of the archbishop-elector of Mainz, Kurfürst Swickard, visited the college, Kircher arranged an astonishing entertainment of moving scenery and fireworks. Some onlookers feared that it was done by black magic until he explained how it worked. As a result, he was summoned to the archbishop's court at Aschaffenburg to construct more such curiosities and to draw up a survey of the principality.

On the archbishop-elector's death in 1626, Kircher moved from Aschaffenburg to Mainz, where he studied theology. While there he acquired a telescope, through which he observed the then unexplained phenomenon of sunspots. In 1628 he entered his tertianship (spiritual preparation for the ministry) at Speyer. A new world of humanistic learning opened for him at this time when, in a book on the Sistine Obelisk, he first saw pictures of Egyptian hieroglyphs; he could not yet pursue this interest, however, as after his ordination as priest he was sent to teach at Würzburg. A manuscript notebook from this period shows that Kircher had some skill in drawing and mechanical design, suggesting that he played a large part in the many illustrations of his later works. In 1630 he petitioned to go as a missionary to China but was refused. In Würzburg, Kircher published his first book, *Ars Magnesia* (The Magnetic Art, 1631). The first part of the work describes magnetic phenomena and experiments, largely based on William Gilbert's *De magnete* (1600). Kircher's explanation of magnetism, unlike Gilbert's mechanistic one, is that things have an innate appetite or inclination toward their own good. In the second part he discusses the deviations of compass needles and the use of magnets in medicine, entertains the possibility of creating perpetual motion by using magnets, and describes magnetic tricks and toys. Thus, his first work announces his characteristic blend of mathematics and experimental science with Hermetic philosophy and a delight in natural and artificial wonders.

In October 1631 the Swedish army entered the region, and the Würzburg college was hastily disbanded. Kircher fled to Mainz with his lifelong disciple, Caspar Schott, leaving behind all his manuscripts. Since there was no future in Germany for a promising young Jesuit scholar, Kircher's superiors

Frontispiece for Kircher's encyclopedic study of magnetism. The double-headed eagle is the symbol of the Hapsburg emperor, to whom the book is dedicated.

Kircher's linguistic research was interrupted in 1633 when he was summoned to Vienna to succeed Johannes Kepler, who had died in 1630, as mathematician to the Hapsburg court. While he obediently set out on the long journey, Peiresc wrote protesting letters to Pope Urban VIII and the pope's nephew, Francesco Cardinal Barberini. Since Germany was still at war, Kircher traveled by the southern route, sailing from Avignon to Marseilles and thence to Genoa. A series of storms brought him unintentionally to Civitavecchia, the main port for Rome. Unable to resist the opportunity to see the Eternal City, he made the forty-mile hike there and discovered to his amazement that he was expected. Peiresc's petition had succeeded, and Kircher was appointed to the Roman College, the hub of the whole Jesuit order, as professor of mathematics, with a special commission to study hieroglyphs. This institution was to be his home until his death.

Kircher made only one further journey. In 1636 Friedrich, landgrave of Hesse-Darmstadt, was converted to Catholicism largely through Kircher's efforts, received into the church with great solemnity in Rome, and made a cardinal. Wishing to travel in Italy, he chose Kircher as his confessor and companion. Kircher took every opportunity to explore new areas of natural science. In Syracuse he tried to ascertain whether Archimedes could have destroyed the Roman fleet with a burning mirror in 212 B.C. Since the landgrave was an enthusiast for the Order of the Knights of Saint John, the party sailed to Malta. It was there, presumably, that Kircher invented the rotating astronomical device described in *Specula Melitensis Encyclica* (Circular Maltese Mirror, 1638). On the way home, in March 1638, he saw the eruptions of Etna and Stromboli and the destruction of the island of Saint Euphemia by a volcano. When they reached Naples, Vesuvius was threatening to erupt too. The insatiable Kircher climbed the volcano and had himself lowered into the crater to observe the process more closely.

Back in Rome, Kircher resumed his teaching duties. Mathematics and science were important components in the education of Jesuit missionaries because technology was useful in impressing the "heathen" with a view to converting them; the missionaries, in turn, sent back reports from every corner of the globe. Receiving these reports from Chile, Peru, Brazil, Mexico, Tunisia, Aleppo, Esfahan, Agra, Surat, Goa, Manila, Guam, and from all of Europe, Kircher was at the center of the world's most efficient and best-educated scientific

allowed him to go to France, where he passed through Lyon on his way to Avignon to teach mathematics, philosophy, and oriental languages. For the Avignon college he designed an elaborate clock, described in his *Primitiae Gnomonicae Catoptricae* (First Fruits of the Reflective Sundial, 1635). More important, he entered a new, cosmopolitan world of learning, thanks to Nicolaus Claude Fabri de Peiresc, member of the parliament at Aix and a wealthy collector and patron of scholarship. Through Peiresc, Kircher met Pierre Gassendi and started a correspondence with Marin Mersenne, men of universal learning and wide connections. Peiresc invited Kircher to decipher his collection of Ethiopian, Arabic, and Coptic manuscripts, resulting in the foundational work of all Coptic studies, *Prodromus Coptus* (Introduction to Coptic, 1636). The book includes the first Coptic grammar, for which a special typeface was made, and argues correctly that Coptic bears a relationship to the language of ancient Egypt.

network. He was the first to hear of any new discovery and was always eager to share it with the world.

Permanently excused from his teaching duties in 1641, Kircher began to publish his major works, producing a didactic encyclopedia on a different scientific or antiquarian subject every three or four years. First he returned to magnetism with *Magnes* (The Magnet, 1641). One object of the work was to eliminate the magnetic argument for the Copernican theory, with which Kircher himself had flirted in his Avignon period but which, after Galileo's condemnation, was anathema. Otherwise, *Magnes* develops the same themes as Kircher's earlier work on the subject, especially the Hermetic idea of universal attraction and repulsion. This notion is manifested in Kircher's plans for a sunflower clock, which would turn to face the sun, as well as in the music of the tarantella, which was believed to dislodge the poison of the tarantula from the bloodstream. At its highest, the same magnetic force attracts the human soul to God.

Lingua Aegyptiaca Restituta (The Egyptian Language Restored, 1643) is another expansion of an earlier work. He uses the information from the traveler Pietro della Valle to compile a vocabulary of Coptic, Latin, and Arabic in parallel columns. This book, which would help Jean-François Champollion decipher the Rosetta Stone nearly two hundred years later, includes material on Egyptian chronology, weights and measures, fauna, flora, place names, and philosophical terms. In recognition of the Hapsburgs' ambition to restore a theocratic empire like that of the Egyptians, the book is dedicated to the emperor Ferdinand III as "Rex Trismegistus" (Thrice-greatest King).

Ars Magna Lucis et Umbrae (The Great Art of Light and Shadow, 1646) overlaps with *Magnes* in several places. It treats eclipses, comets, astrological influences, phosphorescence, color, optics, timekeeping, and sundials. It includes the first printed picture of Saturn, showing it as flanked by two ellipses (which were how the rings appeared in Kircher's telescope), and the first illustration of a magic lantern.

Musurgia Universalis (Universal Music-Making, 1650) does for sound what *Ars Magna Lucis* did for light. Coming at the crucial juncture of the Renaissance and baroque styles, it announces the "doctrine of the affections" that underlies the latter. Unlike the Italian academies, whose admiration of ancient Greek music had given birth to opera, Kircher's ideal was the music of the ancient Hebrews, and King David, rather than Orpheus or Pythagoras, was his model of the supreme musician.

Musurgia begins with an exhaustive treatment of ancient music and mathematical tuning theory, then describes all the musical genres and instruments current in Kircher's day. Natural magic is never far away as he explains acoustical marvels, megaphones, eavesdropping devices, talking statues, and aeolian harps. Always practical, he gives directions for the construction of a composing machine and offers a respectable example of his own composition in three parts. About fifteen hundred copies of the book were printed; three hundred were given to Jesuits coming to Rome for the election of a new superior-general, thus ensuring its wide dispersion.

Kircher was committed to the free exchange of information, irrespective of nationality or religion. Thus, he sent a copy of *Musurgia* to August the Younger, Duke of Brunswick-Lüneburg. This gift led to a long correspondence and friendship with the Protestant ruler and bibliophile, who was the founder of the Herzog-August-Bibliothek (Duke August Library) in Wolfenbüttel. But Kircher never succeeded in his gentle efforts to convert Duke August to Catholicism.

His growing reputation as a linguist made Kircher the obvious person to consult when Pope Innocent X decided to reerect a fallen obelisk and restore its inscription. In *Obeliscus Pamphilius* (The Pamphilian Obelisk, 1650) Kircher sets out his principles for interpreting the Egyptian hieroglyphs. Ironically, he already knew their language – Coptic – but did not understand their connection with it. Instead, he read the hieroglyphs as a purely symbolic writing, mainly used for statements of the Hermetic philosophy that he attributed to ancient Egypt.

This field of research came to fruition in Kircher's longest book, *Oedipus Aegyptiacus* (The Egyptian Oedipus, 1652–1654), in which he assembles all that was known about the history and geography of Egypt. Its printing was facilitated by a gift of three thousand scudi from Ferdinand III. In seeking the meaning of the hieroglyphs, Kircher plumbed the sources of the "ancient theology" as understood in the Renaissance: the Book of Enoch; the writings attributed to Zoroaster, Orpheus, Hermes Trismegistus, Pythagoras, Plato, and Proclus; the Greek myths; the Chaldaean Oracles; and the Hebrew Cabala. He had no doubt that there was authentic sacred wisdom in the "heathen" nations – especially in Egypt, the cradle of arts and sciences after the Flood and the place where both Moses and Jesus had been educated. Kircher's lack of attention to the proof, by the Protestant philologist Isaac Casaubon, that the writings ascribed to Hermes Trismegistus dated from the early centuries of the Christian era makes him almost the last in the chain of Christian Hermetists that had begun with Marsilio Ficino and Giovanni Pico della Mirandola in fifteenth-century Florence. At the same time, through extending his study of ancient religion to include the new discoveries in India, China, Japan, and the Americas, he was the first to cultivate the discipline of comparative religion.

Kircher's *Itinerarium Exstaticum* (Ecstatic Journey, 1656) had its origin in a dream, following a sublime performance by three lutists. The author, as "Theodidactus" (Taught by God), is led by the angel Cosmiel on a journey through the regions of the moon, sun, and planets. While he makes use of Galileo's observations, Kircher's cosmology is geocentric: Jesuit policy favored the scheme of Tycho Brahe, who believed that the planets go around the sun, which in turn goes around the earth. Kircher says that the heavenly bodies – which are not, as in Aristotle's teaching, composed of a different element from those found on earth – send down influences in accordance with their traditional astrological characters. Saturn's influence is evil but necessary to the general economy, in the same way that reptiles and decay have their place on earth. The planets are uninhabited, but each one, and every star, has its own intelligence or angel. Everything in the universe is created for the sake of humanity, and humanity for God.

The second volume of the work, *Iter Exstaticum II.* (1657), takes Theodidactus on a voyage in the opposite direction, beneath the surface of the earth. Here he learns from another angel, Hydriel, that the seas are sucked in at the North Pole and spewed out at the South Pole, and he makes a terrifying journey from one pole to the other. Cosmiel returns to teach him about the circulation of fire in the bowels of the earth. There is much discussion of how creatures are generated from the seeds enclosed in the earth, the growth of birds and fish, and the nature of whales. Kircher was among the first to suggest that mountains are produced by natural movements in the earth's crust.

One of the consequences of the Thirty Years' War was a resurgence of the bubonic plague, which broke out in Rome in 1656. In *Scrutinium Physicomedicum Contagiosae Luis* (Physio-Medical Investigation of the Contagion of the Plague, 1658) Kircher explains the epidemic as a visitation from God to test human beings' faith. On a more practical level, Kircher examined the blood of victims under a microscope and saw "animalcules." Scholars disagree as to whether his equipment would have allowed him to see the actual plague bacilli, or whether he

was seeing larger bacteria. But he is still to be credited with the theory that disease may be caused by germs, rather than by imbalance of the humors, deviltry, and so forth. At the same time, however, he recommended wearing a dead toad around one's neck as a magnet to attract poisonous vapors away from the wearer.

Another phenomenon that the seemingly omniscient Kircher was invited to explain was the appearance of cross-shaped markings on the garments of those exposed to the fall of volcanic ash from Mount Vesuvius. In *Diatribe. De prodigiosis Crucibus* (Discourse on the Remarkable Crosses, 1661) he rejects any cause more mysterious than the pattern of the weaving of the garments. Kircher's linguistic interests next led to *Polygraphia Nova et Universalis* (New and Universal Polygraphy, 1663). In a typically Jesuit combination, it includes both material for a universal language and a treatise on secret writing and cryptography.

In the summer of 1661 Kircher signed a contract with the Amsterdam publisher Johann Jansson van Waesberge. The first of his many works to emerge from Jansson van Waesberge's efficient press was *Mundus Subterraneus* (The Subterranean World, 1665), which expands on the themes of *Iter Exstaticum II.* while appealing to a wider public through lavish illustrations. It also develops Kircher's earlier theories of volcanism and of the generation of animals and plants. Convinced that even frogs and mice can arise through spontaneous generation, Kircher explains that the Creator has infused in the *massa chaotica* (chaotic mass) of the earth a *panspermia rerum* or *semen universale* (universal seed of things) endowed with *vis radiativa* (radiating energy). This substance is the source of all bodily existence, growing, as circumstances permit, into all manner of creatures. Other themes in *Mundus Subterraneus* on which Kircher's opinions are of historical interest are the tides, alchemy, petrefaction, and palingenesis. The work is less a scientific treatise than a pageant or spectacle whose underlying intention is to display the wonders of creation, and hence to induce love and respect for the Creator. At the same time, it opened up many new areas to popular interest and scientific discussion.

By this time Kircher was a celebrated figure. His portrait, engraved in 1655 by Cornelius Bloemaert, was published as the frontispiece to *Mundus Subterraneus.* Visitors to Rome sought interviews with him, or at least entry to the museum that he was assembling in the Jesuit college. This collection had begun with the donation of Peiresc's Egyptian manuscripts and grew as objects arrived from the

Frontispiece, designed by J. Paul Schor, for Kircher's
treatise on music

various Jesuit missions, including natural freaks and enigmas such as stones with designs imprinted on them (another result, Kircher thought, of the "universal seeds"). Kircher added ingenious machines of his own design, based on tricks of magnetism and optics. The museum was raided for souvenirs after his death and fell into decay. After the confiscation of Jesuit property in 1870 the remaining contents were dispersed to various Italian museums.

For recreation Kircher explored the countryside around Rome. In 1661, while searching for antiquities near Marino, he found the ruins of an old sanctuary built by the emperor Constantine at the site where Saint Eustace had seen a vision of Christ between the horns of a stag. Kircher arranged for its restoration as a place of pilgrimage, and it became his favorite retreat. This episode is described in *Historia Eustachio-Mariana* (History of Eustace and Marino, 1665).

Arithmologia (Arithmology, 1665) is a treatise on number, especially on its cabalistic and magical

uses. Kircher did not believe in magic in the usual sense of supernatural operations, but his Hermetic worldview, based on the correspondence of all levels of being, did allow for influences to travel from higher to lower levels, such as from the planets to plants and the human body. The exploitation of these correspondences and the harnessing of the occult or hidden forces in matter is *natural* magic, which shades imperceptibly into technology. At the summit of the Hermetic chain of being is the mind of God, in which number is the archetype of archetypes.

The unearthing of a broken obelisk near the former Temple of Isis, and the decision of Pope Alexander VII to reerect it, led to *Obelisci Aegyptiaci* (1666). The side facing the ground was not visible, but Kircher, after studying and translating the other three sides, successfully predicted in the book the hieroglyphs that would be found on it.

Reports from Jesuit missionaries in the Far East enabled Kircher to compile *China Monumentis . . .*

Illustrata (China Illustrated with Monuments, 1667; translated as *China Illustrata,* 1988), one of his least original works but in many ways the most important historically, as it was the foundation of oriental studies. It included new documents on oriental geography, geology, botany, zoology, religion, and language, including the first picture of the Potala in Lhasa, Tibet; the first Chinese vocabulary; and the first reproduction of the Sanskrit alphabet and treatment of the grammar of the language. Kircher's attitude to oriental religions was, in general, that they derived from the deviant stream started by Noah's son Ham, who had revived antediluvian magic and idolatry.

A short third book on magnetism, *Magneticum Naturæ Regnum* (The Magnetic Kingdom of Nature, 1667), comprises Kircher's last thoughts on sympathies and antipathies in the animal, vegetable, and mineral realms. It was probably the new phenomena from the East, such as the Indian snake-stone that reputedly cured snakebite, that prompted him to write on the subject once again. His main efforts during the mid 1660s went into the composition of *Ars Magni Sciendi* (The Great Art of Knowledge, 1669), his most ambitious attempt to lay a foundation for all possible knowledge. He appears to have known nothing of Francis Bacon's *Novum Organum* (New Organon, 1620), in which the experimental method is advocated as a way of finding out things unknown rather than, as Kircher used it, as a way of confirming a worldview that was already fixed. He ignored René Descartes's *Discours de la méthode* (Discourse on Method, 1637), which recommended acquiring knowledge by starting from a standpoint of feigned ignorance or skepticism. There was no skepticism about Kircher, who assumed that since everything in the universe was connected, it was all knowable if only one had a framework into which to fit it. The framework, in his case, was a blend of Aristotelian and Thomistic logic with the categories of the fourteenth-century Catalonian mystic Ramon Llull (Raymond Lully). Kircher develops a symbolic language for syllogistic and other statements, based on his own expansion of Llull's categories.

Kircher's wanderings in the countryside gave rise to *Latium* (1671), a topography of the region around Rome illustrated with imaginative reconstructions of the ancient Roman villas, as well as with drawings of the modern palaces in which he was a welcome guest. A longer work on a similar subject, "Iter Hetruscum" (Etruscan Journey), remained unpublished. *Principis Christiani Archetypon Politicum* (Political Archetype of a Christian Prince, 1672) is a study of the idea of monarchy, illustrated

with emblems. It is an atypical work for Kircher, produced for his aristocratic patrons.

Kircher's *Phonurgia Nova* (New Acoustics, 1673) is the first book devoted exclusively to acoustics. It describes the propagation and amplification of sound through devices such as the speaking trumpet. *Arca Noë* (Noah's Ark, 1675) and *Turris Babel* (The Tower of Babel, 1679) form a pair, designed (surely at the behest of the publisher, Jansson van Waesberge) as an attractively illustrated compendium of prehistory. *Arca Noë* is dedicated to the twelve-year-old Charles II of Spain and reads like a fairy tale as Kircher descries and classifies all known animals, including mythical ones. In *Turris Babel* he continues the story to show how the world was repopulated after the Flood and how the original single language and religion of humanity split into their present multiplicity. His descriptions and illustrations of the Tower of Babel and the Seven Wonders of the Ancient World belong within the Jesuit traditions of mystical architecture and the "Art of Memory" (a mnemonic device wherein imagined buildings are used to organize and store images).

Kircher returned once more to Egyptology in *Sphinx Mystagoga* (The Sphinx, Teacher of the Mysteries, 1676), in which he interprets the hieroglyphs on some mummy cases recently brought to Europe. The book includes a lengthy discourse on ancient beliefs in metempsychosis and reincarnation. Kircher's last work, befitting one who had begun his career as a mathematics professor, was *Tariffa Kircheriana* (Kircherian Table, 1679), treating the squaring of the circle, trigonometry, and musical proportion. It was published with a comprehensive set of multiplication tables (necessary in prelogarithmic days) furnished by the Bologna mathematics professor Benedetto Benedetti.

In Kircher's final year of life Jansson van Waesberge published a digest of experiments drawn from his many works. *Physiologia Kircheriana Experimentalis* (Kircher's Experimental Physiology, 1680) was compiled by Johann Stephan Kestler and shows what a good editor could have made of Kircher's other works, which are often so prolix and all-encompassing as to be unreadable. Suffering the ailments of old age, Kircher had by this time withdrawn from public life and was giving himself increasingly to spiritual exercises. He died on the same day as his friend, the sculptor Gian Bernini: 27 November 1680.

In *Universale Bildung im Barock* (Universal Education in the Baroque Period, 1981) John E. Fletcher has traced Kircher's connections to other German literary figures. In the spring of 1646

Kircher guided Andreas Gryphius around Rome. Another Silesian poet, Hans Assmann von Abschatz, also knew Kircher in Rome. Johannes Scheffler, the "Angelus Silesius" (Silesian Angel), knew of Kircher through his fellow mystic Abraham von Franckenberg, who was one of Kircher's correspondents. Other correspondents included the poet Georg Philipp Harsdörffer and the philosopher Gottfried Wilhelm von Leibniz. Kircher's work was used by the novelists Johann Jakob Christoffel von Grimmelshausen, Philipp von Zesen, Daniel Casper von Lohenstein, and Johannes Rist. Among later figures, Gotthold Ephraim Lessing was a sympathetic and Johann Gottfried Herder an unsympathetic reader of Kircher. Johann Wolfgang von Goethe enjoyed *Ars Magna Lucis* and wrote a couplet inspired by *Mundus Subterraneus:* "Je mehr man kennt, je mehr man weiß, / Erkennt man, alles dreht im Kreis" (The more one learns, the more one knows / One realizes that everything turns in a circle). Thus, there is a tenuous but real link between Kircher's universal learning and *Naturphilosophie* and concepts of German Romanticism.

Letters:

Fasciculus epistolarum Adm. R. P. Athanasii Kircheri, edited by Ambrosius Langenmantel (Augsburg: Printed by Simon Utzschneider, 1684) – includes Kircher's autobiography, *Vita a semet ipso conscripta;*

Corpus epistolarum Athanasii Kircheri, edited by O. Hein and H. Kastl (Wiesbaden & Rome: Edizioni del Mondo, 1976).

Bibliographies:

Carl Sommervogel, *Bibliothèque de la Compagnie de Jésus,* volume 4 (Brussels & Paris: Schepens & Picard, 1893), pp. 1046–1077;

Gerhard Dünnhaupt, *Personalbibliographien zu den Drucken des Barock,* volume 9, part 3 (Stuttgart: Hiersemann, 1991), pp. 994–1016.

References:

L. R. C. Agnew, ed., *Athanasius Kircher, 1602–1689. An Exhibition* (Kansas City: Clendening Medical Library, 1958);

C. Allen, "The Predecessors of Champollion," *Proceedings of the American Philosophical Society,* 104 (1960): 527–547;

Don Cameron Allen, *Mysteriously Meant: The Rediscovery of Pagan Symbolism and Allegorical Interpretation in the Renaissance* (Baltimore: Johns Hopkins University Press, 1970), pp. 120–133;

José Alfredo Bach, "Athanasius Kircher and His Method: A Study in the Relations of the Arts and Sciences in the Seventeenth Century," dissertation, University of Oklahoma, 1985;

Martha Baldwin, "Athanasius Kircher and the Magnetic Philosophy," dissertation, University of Chicago, 1987;

Jurgis Baltrusaïtis, *La Quête d'Isis: Essai sur la légende d'un mythe. Introduction à l'égyptomanie* (Paris: Perrin, 1967);

W. Beinert, "Die Mentorella," *Korrespondenzblatt für die Alumnen des Collegium Germanicum et Hungaricum* (May 1960): 35–50;

Maristella Casciato, Maria Grazia Ianniello, and Maria Vitale, eds., *Enciclopedismo in Roma Barocca* (Venice: Marsilio Editori, 1986);

Giovanni Cipriani, *Gli obelischi egizi: Politica e cultura nella Roma barocca* (Florence: Olschki, 1993);

A. E. Covington, "The Partial Acceptance of the Copernican Theory by Athanasius Kircher," *Journal of the Royal Astronomical Society of Canada,* 67 (1973): 311–317;

John E. Fletcher, "Astronomy in the Life and Works of Athanasius Kircher," *Isis,* 61 (Spring 1970): 52–67;

Fletcher, "Athanasius Kircherus Restituendus: The Bibliographic Basis of Biographic Research for a 17th Century Figure," *Australian Academic and Research Libraries,* 3 (December 1972): 187–203;

Fletcher, "Claude Fabri de Peiresc and the Other French Correspondents of Athanasius Kircher (1602–1680)," *Australian Journal of French Studies,* 3 (September–December 1972): 250–273;

Fletcher, "G. P. Harsdörffer, Nürnberg, und Athanasius Kircher," *Mitteilungen des Vereins für Geschichte der Stadt Nürnberg,* 59 (1971): 203–210;

Fletcher, "Medical Men in the Correspondence of Athanasius Kircher," *Janus,* 56 (1969): 259–277;

Fletcher, ed., *Athanasius Kircher und seine Beziehungen zum gelehrten Europa seiner Zeit* (Wiesbaden: Harrassowitz, 1988);

Fletcher and Ulf Scharlau, eds., *Universale Bildung im Barock: Der Gelehrte Athanasius Kircher* (Rastatt: Selbstverlag der Stadt Rastatt, 1981);

Paul Friedländer, "Athanasius Kircher und Leibniz: Ein Beitrag zur Geschichte der Polyhistorie im XVII. Jahrhundert," *Atti della Pontificia Accademia Romana di Archeologia,* 13 (1937): 229–247;

Joscelyn Godwin, *Athanasius Kircher: A Renaissance Man and the Quest for Lost Knowledge* (London: Thames & Hudson, 1979);

Sylvia Goodman, "Explorations of a Baroque Motif: The Plague in Selected Seventeenth-Century English and German Literature," dissertation, University of Maryland, 1981;

Joseph Gutmann, *Athanasius Kircher (1602–1680) und das Schöpfungs- und Entwicklungsproblem* (Fulda: Parzeller, 1938);

Erik Iversen, *The Myth of Egypt and Its Hieroglyphs in European Tradition* (Copenhagen: Gad, 1961);

Iversen, *Obelisks in Exile I: The Obelisks of Rome* (Copenhagen: Gad, 1968);

Marilyn J. Norcini, "From Kircher to Kodachrome: A History of Lantern Slide Projection," thesis, New York College at Oneonta, 1975;

Dino Pastine, *La nascita dell'idolatria. L'oriente religioso di Athanasius Kircher* (Florence: La Nuova Italia, 1978);

P. Conor Reilly, S.J., *Athanasius Kircher S.J., Master of a Hundred Arts (1602–1680)* (Wiesbaden & Rome: Edizioni del Mondo, 1974);

Valerio Rivosecchi, *Esotismo in Roma barocca: Studi sul Padre Kircher* (Rome: Bulzoni, 1982);

Luis Robledo, "Poesía y música de la Tarántula," *Poesía,* 5–6 (1979–1980): 223–232;

Ulf Scharlau, *Athanasius Kircher, 1601–1680, als Musikschriftsteller: Ein Beitrag zur Musikanschauung des Barock* (Marburg: Görich & Weiershäuser, 1969);

Baleslaw Szczesniak, "Athanasius Kircher's *China Illustrata,*" *Osiris,* 10 (1952): 385–411;

René Taylor, "Hermetism and Mystical Architecture in the Society of Jesus," in *Baroque Art: The Jesuit Contribution,* edited by R. Wittkower and I. B. Jaffe (New York: Fordham University Press, 1972), pp. 63–97;

Lynne Thorndike, *A History of Magic and Experimental Science,* volume 7 (New York: Macmillan, 1958), pp. 567–589;

Harry Beal Torrey, "Athanasius Kircher and the Progress of Medicine," *Osiris,* 5 (1938): 246–275;

W. A. Wagenaar, "The True Inventor of the Magic Lantern: Kircher, Walgenstein or Huygens?," *Janus,* 66 (1979): 193–207;

Frances A. Yates, *Giordano Bruno and the Hermetic Tradition* (London: Routledge & Kegan Paul, 1964), pp. 416–421.

Papers:

Athanasius Kircher's correspondence is in the Pontificia Università Gregoriana, Rome, Mss. 555–568. Manuscripts for some of his published works are in the Biblioteca Nazionale Centrale Vittorio Emanuele, Rome. Unpublished manuscripts and letters are in the Biblioteca Vaticana, Vatican City; the Biblioteca Angelica, Rome; the Biblioteca Nazionale Centrale, Rome; the Lancisiana, Rome; the Archivio Dora-Pamphilii, Rome; the Biblioteca Nazionale, Naples; the Biblioteca Nazionale, Florence; the Biblioteca Palatina, Parma; the Badische Landesbibliothek, Karlsruhe; the Herzog-August-Bibliothek Wolfenbüttel; the Oesterreichische Nationalbibliothek, Vienna; and the Bibliothèque Nationale, Paris.

Johann Klaj

(1616 – 16 February 1656)

Max Reinhart
University of Georgia

SELECTED BOOKS: *Aufferstehung Jesv Christi jn ietzo neuübliche hochteutsche Reimarten verfasset, und in Nürnberg bey hochansehnlicher Volkreicher Versammlung abgehandelt* (Nuremberg: Wolfgang Endter, 1644);

Höllen- und Himmelfahrt Jesu Chrjstj, nebenst darauf erfolgter sichtbarer Außgiessung Gottes deß Heiligen Geistes. Jn jetzo Kunstübliche Hochteutsche Reimarten verfasset, und in Nürnberg bey Hochansehnlicher Volkreichster Versammlung abgehandelt (Nuremberg: Wolfgang Endter, 1644);

Pegnesisches Schaefergedicht, in den Berjnorgjschen Gefjlden, angestimmet von Strephon und Clajvs, by Klaj and Georg Philipp Harsdörffer (Nuremberg: Wolfgang Endter, 1644);

Weyhnacht-Liedt der Heiligen Geburt Christi zu ehren gesungen (Nuremberg, 1644);

Lobrede der Teutschen Poeterey, abgefasset und in Nürnberg einer Hochansehnlich-Volkreichen Versamlung vorgetragen (Nuremberg: Wolfgang Endter, 1645);

Herodes der Kindermörder, nach Art eines Trauerspiels ausgebildet und in Nürnberg einer Teutschliebenden Gemeine vorgestellet (Nuremberg: Wolfgang Endter, 1645);

Der leidende Christvs, jn einem Trauerspiele vorgestellet (Nuremberg: Wolfgang Endter, 1645);

Der Pegnitz Hirten FrülingsFreude, by Klaj, Harsdörffer, and Sigmund von Birken (Nuremberg, 1645);

Fortsetzung der Pegnitz-Schäferey, behandlend, unter vielen andern rein-neuen freymuhtigen Lust-Gedichten und Reimarten derer von Anfang des Teutschen Krieges verstorbenen tugend-berühmtesten Helden Lob-Gedächtnisse; abgefasset und besungen durch Floridan und Klajus, die Pegnitz-Schäfer. Mit Beystimmung jhrer andern Weidegenossen, by Klaj and Birken (Nuremberg: Wolfgang Endter, 1645);

Lustgedicht zu hochzeitlichem Ehrenbegängniß Herrn D. Johann Röders, und Jungfer Maria Rosina Schmidin, auf der siebenröhrigen Schilffpfeiffen Pans, by Klaj, Birken, Harsdörffer, and others (Nuremberg: Wolfgang Endter, 1645);

Des Süßspielenden Strephons Namens-feyer feyret unsre Pegnitz Schäferleyer den 1. Des Rosenmonats, by Klaj, Johann Hellwig, F. Lochner, J. Sechst, and J. G. Volkamer (Nuremberg, 1645);

AndachtsLieder (Nuremberg: Johann Friedrich Sartorius, 1646);

Pegnesisches Schäfergedicht, in den Nördgauer Gefilden, angestimmet von Filanthon und Floridan, by Klaj, Birken, and Anton Burmeister (Nuremberg, 1648);

Das gantze Leben Jesu Christi mit schönen Kupffern abgebildet, neuen Reimarten und Biblischen Sprüchen außgezieret (Nuremberg: Paul Fürst, 1648);

WeihnachtGedichte (Nuremberg: Jeremias Dümler, 1648);

Schwedisches Fried- und Freudenmahl, zu Nürnberg den 25. des Herbstmonats, im Heiljahr 1649. gehalten, in jetzo neu-üblichen Hochteutschen Reimarten besungen (Nuremberg: Jeremias Dümler, 1649);

Springendes Fried- vnd Freudenlied, denen Lobwürdigsten Tapffern vnd Weltberühmten Kriegs- vnd Sieges-Helden, zu Vnsterblichen Ehrenruhm und Lobgedächtnuß auffgesetzet vnd Bey dem jn Nürnberg auff dem Rahthauß-Saal den 25. Septemb. 1649. einmüthig angestellten hochvertreulichen Fried- vnd Freudenmahl zu frölicher Auffmunterung überreichet, as Victorinum Friedenhold (Nuremberg, 1649);

Engel- und Drachen-Streit (Nuremberg: Jeremias Dümler, 1649);

Wahrhaffter Verlauff, was sich bey geschlossenem und unterschriebenen Frieden zu Nürnberg auf der Burg begeben Den 16/26 Junii, im Jahr 1650 (Nuremberg: Jeremias Dümler, 1650);

Freudengedichte der seligmachenden Geburt Jesu Christi, zu Ehren gesungen (Nuremberg: Jeremias Dümler, 1650);

Trauerrede über das Leiden seines Erlösers (Nuremberg: Wolfgang Endter, 1650);

Geburtstag deß Friedens, oder rein Reimteutsche Vorbildung, wie der großmächtigste Kriegs- und Siegs-Fürst Mars auß dem längstbedrängten und höchstbezwängten Teutschland, seinen Abzug genommen, mit Trummeln, Pfeiffen, Trompeten, Heerpaucken, Musqueten- und Stücken-Salven begleitet, hingegen die mit vielmalhunderttausend feurigen Seuftzen gewünschte und nunmehrerbetene goldgüldene Jrene mit Zincken, Posaunen, Flöten, Geigen, Dulcinen, Orgeln, Anziehungen der Glocken, Feyertägen, Freudenmalen, Feuerwercken, Geldaußtheilungen und andern Danckschuldigkeiten begierigst eingeholet und angenommen worden (Nuremberg: Wolfgang Endter, 1650);

Jrene, das ist, Vollständige Außbildung deß zu Nürnberg geschlossenen Friedens 1650 (Nuremberg: Wolfgang Endter the Elder, 1651).

Collections and editions: *Hoch- und Spätbarock,* edited by Herbert Cysarz (Leipzig: Reclam, 1937);

Die Pegnitz Schäfer Georg Philipp Harsdörffer, Johann Klaj, Sigmund von Birken: Gedichte, edited by Gerhard Rühm (Berlin: Gerhardt, 1964);

Redeoratorien und "Lobrede der Teutschen Poeterey," edited by Conrad Wiedemann (Tübingen: Niemeyer, 1965);

Friedensdichtungen und kleinere poetische Schriften, edited by Wiedemann (Tübingen: Niemeyer, 1968);

Deutsche Barock-Lyrik, edited by Herbert Cysarz, second edition (Stuttgart: Reclam, 1968), pp. 36–41, 122–125;

Die Pegnitz-Schäfer: Nürnberger Barockdichtung, edited by Eberhard Mannack (Stuttgart, 1968).

Editions in English: "Bright shimmering silver," in *Selections of German Poetry from the Beginnings to 1720,* translated by Charles G. Loomis (Berkeley, Cal., 1958), p. 42;

"Oh golden life, awaken," "The Soldiers of Lucifer Sing," and "Stroll-Joy," in *The German Lyric of the Baroque in English Translation,* translated by George Schoolfield (Chapel Hill: University of North Carolina Press, 1961), pp. 194–197;

"Stroll-Joy," "Oh golden life, awaken," in *German Poetry from the Beginnings to 1750,* translated by Schoolfield, edited by Ingrid Walsøe-Engel (New York: Continuum, 1992), pp. 228–231.

OTHER: August Buchner, *Joas Der heiligen Geburt Christi zu Ehren gesungen,* translated by Klaj (Wittenberg: Johann Hake, 1642);

"Das allgemeine Weltliecht, die Goldbestrahlte Sonne," in *Frauenzimmer Gesprechspiele,* volume 5, by Georg Philipp Harsdörffer (Nuremberg: Wolfgang Endter, 1645);

"Die Ziegeunerische Kunstgöttinnen," in *Frauenzimmer Gesprechspiele,* volume 6, by Harsdörffer (Nuremberg: Wolfgang Endter, 1646);

"Der Hof ist eine Gedultschuele," in *Ormund,* by Francesco Pona, translated by Johann Hellwig (Frankfurt am Main: David Zunner, 1648), leaves 1v–3v;

Harold Jantz, "A Recovered Work by Johann Klaj," in *Barocker Lust-Spiegel,* edited by Martin Bircher, Jörg-Ulrich Fechner, and Gerd Hillen (Amsterdam: Rodopi, 1984), pp. 101–114.

SELECTED PERIODICAL PUBLICATION – UNCOLLECTED: Lamar Elmore, "Klaj's Last Known Work," *Modern Language Notes,* 93 (April 1978): 361–373.

Johann Klaj was one of the earliest representatives of German baroque mannerism and one of seventeenth-century Nuremberg's most gifted poets – perhaps *the* most gifted. Cofounder of the important poetic society Löblicher Hirten- und Blumenorden an der Pegnitz (Eminent Order of Shepherds and Flowers on the Pegnitz), generally known as the Pegnesischer Blumenorden (Flower Order on the Pegnitz), he played a leading role in restoring a level of literary quality unknown in Nuremberg since its golden age of Konrad Celtis, Eobanus Hessus, and Philipp Melanchthon. Klaj achieved greatness as the master of two forms in particular: *Friedensdichtung* (irenic verse) and *Redeoratorium* (declamatory oratorio). His irenic verse was a vehicle for celebrating the end of the Thirty Years' War; declamatory oratorio was a virtuosic performance genre of which Klaj himself was the creator and sole practitioner. In these two genres the musicality of his language is matched by few writers of the German baroque, and it is, therefore, difficult to place him within conventional stylistic categories. Klaj may have lacked the universal genius of his older colleague, Georg Philipp Harsdörffer; but as a forgotten contemporary astutely observed in 1645, "Herr Harsdorff trefflich spielet / Herr Klaj den Himmel fühlet" (Harsdöffer is playful, spry, / But heaven stirs in Klaj).

The son of Diederich Klaj, a well-to-do cloth maker in Meissen in Saxony, Klaj is presumed to have been born in 1616. He probably attended the local school, which emphasized religion, Latin, and Greek. Allusions in some of his later works leave little doubt that he began university studies in Leipzig around 1633; but in 1634, possibly owing to the intensity with which war was being waged around the city, he transferred to the more congenial environment of Wittenberg and took up the study of theology. Among his professors were such noted scholars as Paul Roeber, Johann Huelsemann, and Jakob Martini. Roeber and Martini befriended the young theologian; the latter was an especially articulate spokesman for theological and political tolerance. Klaj's irenic poetry of 1649–1650 bears elegant witness to the lasting quality of Martini's influence.

Biographers have commented on the notoriously unambitious nature of Klaj's life in Wittenberg, where he was a kind of "professional student," failing to complete a master's degree in ten years. It could be said, however, that his lack of professional resolve ended happily for German literature, for he came to possess the vision of a German nation at last stirred from its cultural slumber by an elite society of new poets. He would express this vision in *Pegnesisches Schaefergedicht* (Pegnitzian Idyll, 1644):

Entzwischen tröstet mich, daß so viel neue Feben
Erhalten meine Sprach' und Wolkenan erheben;
　　Was neulich Opitzgeist beginnet auß dem Grund,
　　Ist ruchtbar und am Tag auß vieler Teutschen
　　Mund.

(But how it doth console that new Apollos rise,
Attending to my language, exhalting to the skies.
What one man, Opitz, caused to spring from
　　German ground
Now's heard from every mouth the entire realm around.)

The person most responsible for Klaj's turn to poetry was the eminent philologist August Buchner, professor of poetry and rhetoric at Wittenberg and one of the century's outstanding literary theoreticians. An ardent advocate of the poetic reforms of Martin Opitz, he himself made important formal and stylistic contributions to the same cause, most notably in his *Kurzer Weg-Weiser der Teutschen Tichtkunst* (Brief Guide to the Art of German Poetry), which was not published until 1663 but circulated in manuscript as early as 1638. The *Weg-Weiser* was innovative in its recommendation of dactylic verse and its doctrine of natural imitation. With the dactyl a new metrical idiom became accessible to German that eluded the strict Opitzian principle of alternation; it would become a hallmark of the so-called Nuremberg manner. Buchner sought in his imitational theory to transform poetry into a kind of speaking portrait, a concept that is useful in appreciating both the style and the content of Klaj's declamatory oratorios. Buchner's influence was disseminated throughout Germany by a generation of loyal students, among them Christian Queintz, Andreas Buchholtz, Paul Gerhardt, Justus Georg

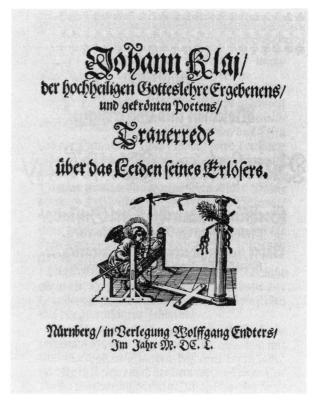

Title page for a Passover sermon by Klaj

Schottelius, and Philipp von Zesen. Klaj brought Buchner's ideas to Nuremberg, where they found their most fruitful reception among the experimental poets of the Pegnesischer Blumenorden.

Klaj's profound and lifelong indebtedness to Buchner was apparent as early as 1642, when his first publication appeared: *Joas,* a German translation of Buchner's celebration of the nativity. *Joas* has been largely overlooked, but it includes many seeds that grow to maturity in Klaj's later works. These seminal elements include his fascination with the birth, suffering, and death of Jesus; with landscape; and, especially, with war and peace.

Little is known about the personal life of Klaj, who was, despite his recitations of the declamatory oratorios, retiring and socially awkward. Legend has it that he arrived in Nuremberg in early 1644 as a penurious exile who found his savior in Harsdörffer. While this picture contains a kernel of truth, it probably derives from the fanciful opening scene of *Pegnesisches Schaefergedicht,* composed by the two men some six to eight months after Klaj's arrival. A reenactment of Virgil's first eclogue, it shows an exiled Clajus (corresponding to Virgil's Meliboeus) being welcomed by the shepherd Strephon (Harsdörffer, corresponding to Virgil's

Tityrus). The legend also diminishes the role played in Klaj's career by Johann Michael Dilherr, the former professor of history and rhetoric at the University of Jena who had recently been called to Nuremberg as pastor of Saint Sebald's church. Dilherr arranged Klaj's initial public performances of his works and facilitated – perhaps with Harsdörffer's assistance – their subsequent publication by the prestigious house of Wolfgang Endter. Both Dilherr and Harsdörffer actively supported Klaj's personal and professional development in Nuremberg; Harsdörffer seems to have acted as his literary adviser, while Dilherr functioned as a kind of promotion manager for his socially helpless protégé.

Architecture in Nuremberg had been enjoying a renaissance since about the second decade of the century; in music, the latest methods of composition and performance flourished in the hands of Johann Herbst, Sigmund Theophil Staden, and Johann Kindermann. Poetry, on the other hand, had been in decline since the passing of the great neo-Latin writers. The mastersinger tradition continued, but pedantically, with no practitioner of the measure of Hans Sachs to elevate it to the level of art. Only the patrician polymath Harsdörffer understood how to bring about the needed reform of poetry. By the time Klaj arrived in Nuremberg, Harsdörffer, a member of the distinguished, mostly aristocratic, Weimar poetic group, the Fruchtbringende Gesellschaft (Fruit-bringing Society), founded in 1617 by Prince Ludwig von Anhalt-Köthen, was widely known and respected in Germany. Harsdörffer's reform efforts took two main forms. On the one hand, the Pegnesischer Blumenorden would further the Weimar ideals of linguistic purity and an elite poetic academy. On the other hand, he realized that poetic reform was of a piece with cultural reform and could be accomplished only through the education of those responsible for the administration of the home – women. His *Frauenzimmer Gesprechspiele* (Playful Colloquies for the Ladies, 1641–1657) had been appearing in annual volumes since 1641. He hoped thereby to introduce to Nuremberg's upper middle class the best in European manners and thought. But Harsdörffer lacked both time and talent to inspire, by himself, a true revival of poetry in Nuremberg. A poetic genius was needed.

On 23 April 1644, Easter Sunday, a remarkable event took place that boded well for the future: a public recitation in the new auditorium of the Saint Egidian Academy by a young theologian from the north, Johann Klaj, of a most unusual work,

Aufferstehung Jesu Christi (Resurrection of Jesus Christ). Attended by a near-capacity audience, the event put Nuremberg back on the literary map. The first part of *Aufferstehung Jesu Christi* begins near dawn of the third day after the crucifixion and deals with the events of Easter morning; the second part portrays the risen Christ's appearances to his disciples; the third part is a victor's song. A single speaker declaims the entire work, save for the orchestrated choruses. Monologues and reportage overwhelm dialogue; there are no stage directions; the poet, in alexandrine (six-foot iambic) recitatives, frequently addresses the audience, moralizing and instructing. The familiar paschal events, the liturgy, and the Jesuit love-of-Jesus tradition in Mary Magdalen's lament show the declamatory oratorio's kinship with the mystery play; by contrast, Klaj's often idiosyncratic rendering of the Bible sometimes startles in its remoteness from all tradition.

Declamatory oratorio is not drama; neither is it epic, notwithstanding the presence of epic elements; nor do its many lyric passages constitute it a lyrical genre. Some critics believe that an early form of Italian oratorio provided Klaj's model, arguing that Harsdörffer became acquainted with it during his travels in Italy in 1629–1630; Klaj is silent on the subject of his inspiration. He conceived of the genre as an experiment in the use of meter for expressing emotion: dactyls for joy, trochees for pain, and so on. A revealing annotation to the published version of *Aufferstehung Jesu Christi* (the notes exceed the body of the work in length) speaks to the relationship between meter and personality in one of the work's most complex characters: "Maria Magdalena führet allerhand Arten der Verse, weil sie als betrübtes Weibesbild bald in diese, bald in jene Gedanken gerät" (Mary Magdalen speaks in a variety of meters since, as an emotionally distraught character, she is torn between conflicting thoughts). Buchner might have called this practice verbal portraiture.

For the Ascension festival on 15 June 1644 Klaj recited, to an audience that overflowed the large hall in the Augustinian monastery, the second of his oratorios, *Höllen- und Himmelfahrt Jesu Christi* (Descent into Hell and Ascension of Jesus Christ). The work begins with a horrifying glance into the pits of hell; the opposing forces of the Archangel Michael and Lucifer are assembled, using the technical language of contemporary warfare; and Lucifer's forces are crushed. The second part depicts Christ's Ascension: there are elaborate personifications of Christian virtues, a procession to the Mount of Olives, and eschatological maneuvers

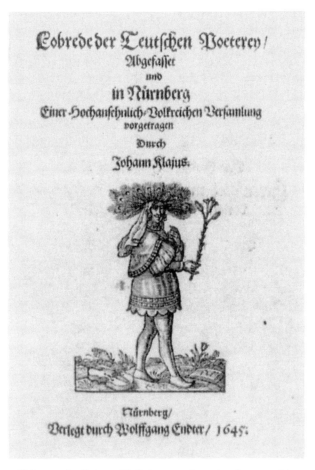

*Title page for Johann Klaj's lecture advocating the composition
of poetry in German*

among the stars by the legion of angels; finally, Christ ascends to the right hand of the Father amid a chorus of angel voices. The printed version of the work concludes with an unrelated review of the miracle of Pentecost and a hymn in dactyls. Its annotations run to thirty pages, longer than the oratorio proper.

Klaj's financial success did not improve in direct proportion to his celebrity. Although both *Aufferstehung Jesu Christi* and *Höllen- und Himmelfahrt Jesu Christi* were dedicated to the city fathers, and although Klaj's dire straits were no secret, pecuniary assistance was not forthcoming. (The painter Albrecht Dürer had complained of Nuremberg's niggardliness to its artists.) Appeals by Harsdörffer and Dilherr did little to loosen purse strings, and Klaj was kept waiting until November to receive an honorarium for his first two public recitations; when it came, it amounted to a mere six florins. Klaj had to support himself in these years as a private tutor.

In October 1644 Harsdörffer and Klaj collaborated in the founding of the Pegnesischer Blumen-

orden, a *Sprachgesellschaft* (literally, language society; more accurately, literary academy). The Fruchtbringende Gesellschaft in Weimar had aligned itself with courtly society and sought its members almost exclusively from noble and patrician circles. Conversely, the Nuremberg poets came, with few exceptions, from the midde ranks of society and pursued social advancement by way of higher education. All seventeenth-century German literary societies aimed to promote an uncontaminated vernacular both in poetry and in civil life; far more than comparable institutions, however, the Pegnesischer Blumenorden is noted for its predilection for play and experimentation. *Klangmalerei* (sound painting) is the concept most commonly associated with the society: through unusual combinations of meter and other devices the Nuremberg poets attempted to imitate the mysteries of the universe, in keeping with the doctrine of "the language of nature" to which they subscribed. The excitement generated by Klaj's public recitations helped create a general readiness for a literary reawakening. Also, the influence of Opitz, which elsewhere in Germany was beginning by this time to have a conservative, even retarding effect on the development of poetry, remained minimal in Nuremberg because of Harsdörffer's preference for foreign – especially Italian and Spanish – models and to the infusion, through Klaj, of liberal Buchnerian principles.

Klaj and Harsdörffer wrote *Pegnesisches Schaefergedicht* for a patrician double wedding in October 1644. The work is prosimetric in form – that is, it alternates passages in prose and verse; the genre is, accordingly, known as *Prosaekloge* (prose eclogue), a term that further reflects the two pastoral traditions from which it arose: the Virgilian eclogue and the southern European pastoral novel. The prose eclogue is typically structured in three parts: an extended middle section devoted to the praise of the patron or other dignitaries is surrounded by lengthy and loquacious descriptions of nature walks. Opitz had provided the model in 1630 with his *Schäfferey von der Nymphen Hercinie* (Idyll of the Nymph Hercinie). The genre flourished in Germany, especially in Nuremberg, during the seventeenth century. It was popular especially because of the spacious, leisurely sections in which matters of poetological, biographical, and social interest could be discussed at length.

The *Pegnesisches Schaefergedicht* begins with the arrival of the exiled shepherd Klajus in Neronsburg (Nuremberg). Klajus's praise of the city – a barely concealed appeal for recognition – describes Nuremberg as a trans-Alpine Rome. The shepherd-poets walk around the outskirts of Nuremberg, poetically transforming everything along the way, be it nature or technology (such as the mills for which Nuremberg was known). As in Virgil's eclogues, a friendly competition develops between Klajus and Strephon. The latter's playfulness unites with the former's musical imagination to create a work of the highest order of inventiveness and charm. In the end their productions are judged by Fama (fame), who determines that both men are worthy of the prize. A year later, in *Fortsetzung der Pegnitz-Schäferey* (Continuation of the Pegnitz Idyll), Klaj and Sigmund Betulius (later von Birken) depicted the poetry contest as the inauguration of the Pegnesischer Blumenorden.

Eleven days after the double wedding Klaj delivered a well-attended public lecture on the value of German as a poetic language. *Lobrede der Teutschen Poeterey* (In Praise of German Poetry, 1645) gives historical, aesthetic, cultural, and political reasons for composing poetry in German. Klaj defers to the authority not of Opitz but of Buchner, a small her-

esy that won him severe criticism from certain quarters. Parting company with many of his contemporaries who argued for the eminence of German solely or principally from its antiquity, Klaj admits that this "Wunderkräfftige, Wortmächtige und Qwelreiche Sprache" (language of immense power, mighty in expression, arising from ancient fountains) remains, even after the great Martin Luther, a flawed instrument in need of perfecting. Against the backdrop of the war and its political and moral devastation of Germany, and standing in opposition to the prevailing voices of doom, Klaj's speech is a patriotic call for the nation's educational and cultural renewal.

Klaj's productivity continued unabated through 1645 with two more declamatory oratorios, both of them reworkings of neo-Latin dramas by well-known Dutch poets. *Herodes der Kindermörder* (Herod the Infanticide), a work in a tragic vein, was presented, probably in Saint Sebald's Church, on 12 January. It is based on *Herodes infanticida* (1632), by Daniel Heinsius. Klaj remodels the original, a lengthy Senecan tragedy written for a sophisticated audience, into a recitation requiring only an hour and a half, including instrumental choruses, for a popular audience. Any action not directly related to Herod is scrapped. A high point is a dream monologue by Herod, following his decision to have the children murdered. Tossing in bed in a pestilent fever, Herod is visited in a nightmare by his wife, Mariamne, whom he had put to death. The ensuing lines, with their stumbling rhythms and irregular lengths, portray the king's horror:

> Ach! mein liebes Ehgemahl
>   Wilstu mich umarmen?
> Ach! ihr Geister aus der Qwal
>   Ubet doch erbarmen.
> Lauter Ungemach,
> Uberfält mich, Ach, Ach, Ach, Ach!
>
> (Alas, my dearest wedded mate,
>   Art thou come to hold me?
> Alas, thou ghosts of hate
>   In mercy do enfold me.
> Miserable distress
> Befalls me, Alas, Alas, Alas, Alas!)

One of Klaj's most unusual works, *Herodes der Kindermörder* was criticized into the eighteenth century as a failed attempt at tragedy. Writing in 1741 in a staunchly antibaroque journal, Johann Elias Schlegel, while granting Klaj's talent, derided his techniques: the play, he said, has no unity of place, action, or character. In short, he accused Klaj of failing to abide by Aristotelian rules. This misun-

Frontispieces for Klaj's two collections of poems published in celebration of the treaty ending the Thirty Years' War

derstanding of declamatory oratorio prevailed well into the mid twentieth century, when Conrad Wiedemann's groundbreaking studies on the subject at last applied more-judicious standards of appreciation.

On the following Palm Sunday, Klaj presented his fourth declamatory oratorio, *Der leidende Christus, in einem Trauerspiele vorgestellet* (Suffering Christ, Presented in a Tragedy), a work based on the celebrated tragedy *Christus Patiens* (1608), by Hugo Grotius. As in his adaptation of the Heinsius tragedy, Klaj pares speeches to an essential few and intensifies imagistic and acoustic effects. With his decision to employ vocal choruses along with instrumental ones in *Der leidende Christus,* declamatory oratorio began to approach the dimensions of the *Gesamtkunstwerk* (total work of art). On its title page, the published version of *Der leidende Christus* introduces its author as a poet laureate: Klaj had been bestowed with the laurel on 25 March by the count palatine, Georg Achatius Heher. This honor did nothing to improve Klaj's material condition; by the mid 1640s the poetic coronation was becoming so common in the realm as to be all but meaningless. About a month after his coronation, on the recommendation of Harsdörffer, he was inducted into Hamburg's *Deutschgesinnte Genossenschaft* (German-

ophile Society), under the presidency of his old Wittenberg friend Zesen.

During his first year in Nuremberg, Klaj had been uncommonly active and successful – he had produced four major works and a spate of shorter ones, including occasional poems in both Latin and German, and had had his efforts crowned with the imperial laurel. His slowdown after the spring of 1645 is, therefore, surprising. In a letter to Birken on 4 July 1646 Harsdörffer sadly speaks of Klaj as a "quondam noster" (formerly our colleague), describing him as having become phlegmatic and melancholy. Dilherr also seems to have put distance between himself and his former protégé. With the loss of his important friends went his publishing privileges with Endter, and until matters were eventually ironed out the few works he did produce were printed by lesser houses. Among these works are the five beautiful lyric poems in *AndachtsLieder* (Devotional Songs, 1646), one of which, "Kriegs Trost" (Consolation in Time of War), offers a moving portrait of war-torn Germany and concludes on a strong note of faith.

In May 1647, apparently on the recommendation of Dilherr, Klaj was appointed to a well-endowed teaching post at Saint Sebald's Latin School, and not long thereafter he received Nuremberg citizenship. On 25 September 1648 he married Maria Elisabeth Rhumelius, the daughter of the respected physician Johann Conrad Rhumelius. Johann Hellwig and Johann Georg Volkamer, early members of the Pegnesischer Blumenorden, had introduced Klaj to his future bride; Hellwig was an old friend of her father from their student days at Altdorf University.

Klaj returned to his art as suddenly as he had abandoned it, initiating a period of creativity that was uninterrupted until he left Nuremberg two years later. During the remainder of 1648 he published two sets of poems, *Das gantze Leben Jesu Christi mit schönen Kupffern abgebildet* (The Complete Life of Jesus, Portrayed in Handsome Copper Engravings) and, in December, the tender *WeihnachtGedichte* (Christmas Poems); the poems on the Christmas season are some of Klaj's loveliest lyrics.

No other event so stirred Klaj to action as the end of the war. The Peace of Westphalia was signed in Münster and Osnabrück in mid October 1648. Nuremberg was selected as the location for the working out of the final details among the imperial, Swedish, and French parties, and the city spared no expense in preparing suitably lavish celebrations. Nuremberg, which had taken little previous notice of its small band of poets, called their talents into public service. For one brief, shining moment in Nuremberg's history, intelligentsia and power embraced; the result was the high point of the Nuremberg literary baroque. Harsdörffer advised on the overall design of certain festivities; Birken gave speeches, wrote plays, and functioned on behalf of the Catholic-imperial delegation; the Protestant Klaj wrote mainly, though not exclusively, for the Swedish faction. His *Schwedisches Fried- und Freudenmahl* (Swedish Banquet of Peace and Joy, 1649) is a description in verse of the magnificent festival banquet held on 25 September 1649 in the great hall of the courthouse; it had been arranged by Count Palatine Karl Gustav, to whom Klaj dedicates the poem, to celebrate the completion of the Interim Treaty. The banquet was captured for posterity in the painting by Joachim Sandrart that now hangs in the courthouse.

The declamatory oratorio *Engel- und Drachen-Streit* (Battle of the Angels and the Beast, 1649), also dedicated to Karl Gustav, must have appeared about this time. This four-act oratorio is the epic story of Lucifer's original glory, overweening pride, and fall. Klaj begins with the Creation, which he relates in stately alexandrine verse, before turning to a variety of metrical forms and verse lengths suitable to the respective speakers and occasions. The high point is reached in the third act as the great battle between the forces of the former Lucifer, now Satan, and the Archangel Michael is recited by an all-seeing poet. Onomatopoeia, echo, and rapid alternation of iambs and dactyls and of long and short lines combine to make this one of Klaj's most sensually riveting episodes.

Klaj's final and most mature declamatory oratorio appeared in 1650, with music by Staden. Dedicated to the great Swedish general Carol Gustav Wrangel, *Freudengedichte der seligmachenden Geburt Jesu Christi* (Poetic Celebration of the Blessed Birth of Jesus Christ) is Klaj's only work in this genre that lacks a scholarly apparatus. Klaj returns to one of his favorite themes, the Nativity, but in an expanded design that encompasses the realms of heaven and earth. Instrumental and vocal music, allegory, ballet, and poetry combine in this exuberant production to achieve Klaj's fullest realization of Gesamtkunstwerk.

At the end of March 1650 Klaj delivered a lengthy and impassioned Passover sermon, complete with choral interludes, that was published, with annotations, the same year as *Trauerrede über das Leiden seines Erlösers* (Lamentation on the Suffering of His Savior). It demonstrates an immediacy of experience that is deeply touching. The reader-listener is invited to view the paschal events as though from the foot of a stage: "Schaue nochmaln, liebe Seele. . . . Hier, hier auf Golgatha ist die grüne Bühne, auf welcher das Schauspiel der Welt, der Engel und der Menschen fürgestellet wird" (Look again, Dear Soul. . . . Here, right here at Golgotha, is the verdant stage upon which the theater of the world, of angels, and of men is played). But Klaj's often excruciatingly empathetic identification with the suffering Savior provides an example of how close a German baroque author could approach *Erlebnisdichtung* (experiential poetry), an accomplishment that would not be commonly acknowledged among German poets for another century.

In 1649–1650, in addition to his greatest declamatory oratorios, Klaj finished two large collections of irenic poetry; these poems show Klaj at the height of his powers. *Irene, das ist, Vollständige Außbildung deß zu Nürnberg geschlossenen Friedens 1650* (Irene; or, Complete Depiction of the Peace Treaty Concluded in Nuremberg in 1650), though not published until 1651, was probably completed first. Its centerpiece is *Schwedisches Fried- und Freudenmahl*, which had been published separately in 1649. The grandeur of the occasion is well matched by Klaj's poem. Like his late declamatory oratorios, *Irene* is a total work of art, complete with choral sections and a variety of speakers; lavish use is made of word painting. The goddess of peace, Irene, is greeted in long panegyrical strophes; city dignitaries – a chancellor, a senator, a burgher – each has his moment to apostrophize her; the various dinner courses (fish, fowl, wild game, fruits and vegetables, wines) are indulgently described. Klaj employs a leitmotivic, rondolike format, in which the leading topic of peace is repeatedly interrupted and ornamented by *Begleitverse* (accompanying verse) – for example, a depiction of emerging spring, a reenactment of a struggle between Mars and Irene, a prayerful lament by personified Germania.

Geburtstag deß Friedens (The Birthday of Peace, 1650) celebrates the final signing of the peace treaty. Many of the mythological and allegorical figures introduced in *Irene* return here, and, again as in *Irene,* epic narration of historic events is accompanied by involved lyrical sections that serve as commentaries on those events. The disconnected format of the collection has offered compilers of literary anthologies easy pickings, and many readers of modern German literature may be unaware that familiar poems are selected from either *Geburtstag deß Friedens* or *Irene.* The well-known allegory of the fireworks, "Castell deß Unfriedens" (Castle of Discord), and the masterful "Vorzug deß Frülings" (The Entrance of Spring), for example, are both found in *Geburtstag deß Friedens.*

As a result of Dilherr's mediation, Klaj was made pastor of Kitzingen in January of the new year. He remained in the post until his death. These years were marred by controversies with his congregation over both great and small issues, ranging from his salary to his conciliation with the bishop of Würzburg, Johann Philipp von Schönborn – the latter a horrifying situation in the minds of his staunchly Protestant congregants, who expected from their pastor bold defiance of the Catholic Church. He produced virtually no poetry in those six years; in a Latin letter of 1654 to Johann Heinrich Calisius, Klaj ceremoniously and willingly yields the torch of poetry to attend more fully to the duties of his pastoral office. It would appear that Klaj had exhausted himself with his last great outpouring of 1649–1650 and that he was resigned, without regret, to that fact. He died on 16 February 1656.

The antibaroque wave that swept Germany in the first half of the eighteenth century carried many great writers to an early and undeserved fate of silence. In 1704 the president of the Pegnesischer Blumenorden itself, Magnus Daniel Omeis, set the fatal tone that would be picked up and sung at a

higher pitch by Johann Christoph Gottsched and others of the early Enlightenment when he included Klaj among the poets who had "durch gezwungene Red- Fügungs- und Wort-Versetzungen in den Versen zimliche Freiheit genommen" (rather strained the limits of poetic license in their habit of forcing words and thoughts into unnatural patterns). Thus, Klaj was accused and dismissed, along with those poets of the late baroque whose often fustian rhetoric may have deserved the condemnation, of the unforgivable vice of *Schwulst* (bombast). At this point Klaj was essentially stripped of citizenship within orthodox literary history. In the 1930s Herbert Cysarz attempted to revive Klaj's reputation by claiming that he was the greatest of all baroque poets, but exaggeration did little to restore Klaj to his rightful position. That task remained for Wiedemann, who reprinted Klaj's oeuvre in the 1960s so that readers could judge it for themselves. Wiedemann's thorough exploration of Klaj's richly nuanced language led to a new appreciation of Klaj as, above all, an avant-garde poet who pushed the limits of form and expression to a level even his experimentally minded colleagues of the Pegnesischer Blumenorden were incapable of following.

Bibliographies:

Erdmann Neumeister, *Specimen Dissertationis Historico-Criticae de Poëtis Germanicis hujus seculi praecipuis,* second edition (Leipzig? 1706), pp. 60–61;

Karl Heinrich Jördens, *Lexikon deutscher Dichter und Prosaisten,* volume 1 (Leipzig: Weidmann, 1806), pp. 306–309;

Karl Goedeke, *Grundriß zur Geschichte der deutschen Dichtung aus den Quellen,* volume 3, second edition (Dresden: Ehlermann, 1887), pp. 111–112;

Curt von Faber du Faur, *German Baroque Literature,* 2 volumes (New Haven: Yale University Press, 1958, 1969), I: nos. 517–526; II: nos. 523a–526e;

Blake Lee Spahr, "Johann Klaj (1616-1656)," in his *The Archives of the Pegnesischer Blumenorden: A Survey and Reference Guide* (Berkeley & Los Angeles: University of California Press, 1960), pp. 15–17;

Harold Jantz, *German Baroque Literature: A Descriptive Catalogue of the Collection of Harold Jantz and a Guide to the Collection on Microfilm,* volume 1 (New Haven: Research Publications, 1974), nos. 1492 and 1493;

Gerhard Dünnhaupt, *Personalbibliographien zu den Drucken des Barock,* volume 9, part 4 (Stuttgart: Hiersemann, 1991), pp. 2351–2372.

Biographies:

Johann Herdegen, "Clajus," in his *Historische Nachricht von deß löblichen Hirten- und Blumen-Ordens an der Pegnitz Anfang und Fortgang* (Nuremberg: Riegel, 1744), pp. 234–238;

Bartholomäus Dietwar, *Leben eines evangelischen Pfarrers im früheren markgräflichen Amte Kitzingen von 1592–1670,* edited by Volkmar Wirth (Kitzingen: Stahel, 1887);

Albin Franz, *Johann Klaj: Ein Beitrag zur deutschen Literaturgeschichte des 17. Jahrhunderts* (Marburg: Elwert, 1908; New York: Johnson Reprint, 1968).

References:

Theodor Bischoff, "Georg Philipp Harsdörffer: Ein Zeitbild aus dem 17. Jahrhundert," in *Festschrift zur 250jährigen Jubelfeier des Pegnesischen Blumenordens* (Nuremberg: Schrag, 1894), pp. 197–208, 219–235;

Hans P. Braendlin, "Individuation und Vierzahl im *Pegnesischen Schäfergedicht* von Harsdörffer und Klaj," in *Europäische Tradition und deutscher Literaturbarock: Internationale Beiträge zum Problem von Überlieferung und Umgestaltung,* edited by Gerhart Hoffmeister (Bern & Munich: Francke, 1973), pp. 329–349;

Thomas Bürger, "'Und giebet auch den Kleinesten das leben': zu zwei handschriftlichen Gedichten Johann Klajs," *Wolfenbütteler Barock-Nachrichten,* 11, no. 1 (1984): 1–5;

Rüdiger Campe, "Homonymie von expressio und elocutio im poetischen Ausdruck (Johann Klaj)," in his *Affekt und Ausdruck: Zur Umwandlung der literarischen Rede im 17. und 18. Jahrhundert* (Tübingen: Niemeyer, 1990), pp. 259–263;

Klaus Conermann, "Der Poet und die Maschine: Zum Verhältnis von Literatur und Technik in der Renaissance und Barock," in *Teilnahme und Spiegelung,* edited by Beda Allemann and Erwin Koppen (Berlin & New York: De Gruyter, 1975), pp. 173–192;

Herbert Cysarz, "Der große und fröhliche Meister Johann Klaj (1616–1656)," *Der Ackermann aus Böhmen,* 4 (1936): 361–366;

Cysarz, "Interpretation des Eingangsgedichtes zum *Leidenden Christus,*" in *Gedicht und Gedanke,* edited by H. O. Bürger (Halle: Niemeyer 1942), pp. 72–88;

Lamar Elmore, "Klaj and His Poetry of Peace," dissertation, Johns Hopkins University, 1975;

Vereni Fässler, "Johann Klaj: Das lichte Getümmel," in his *Hell-Dunkel in der barocken Dichtung* (Bern & Frankfurt am Main: Herbert Lang, 1971), pp. 27–46;

Willi Flemming, *Oratorium – Festspiel* (Leipzig: Reclam, 1933), pp. 7–26;

Klaus Garber, "Vergil und das *Pegnesische Schäfergedicht:* Zum historischen Gehalt pastoraler Dichtung," in *Deutsche Barockliteratur und europäische Kultur,* edited by Martin Bircher and Eberhard Mannack (Hamburg: Hauswedell, 1977), pp. 168–203;

Georg Gottfried Gervinus, *Geschichte der deutschen Dichtung,* volume 3, fourth edition (Leipzig: Engelmann, 1853), pp. 281–289, 412–414;

Johann Christoph Gottsched, *Nöthiger Vorrath zur Geschichte der deutschen Dramatischen Dichtkunst,* part 1 (Leipzig: Teubner, 1757), pp. 197–199, 204, 213;

Robert R. Heitner, "Johann Klaj's Popularizations of Neo-Latin Drama," *Daphnis,* 6, no. 3 (1977): 313–325;

Ferdinand van Ingen, "Dichterverständnis, Heldensprache, städtisches Leben: Johann Klajs *Lobrede der Teutschen Poeterey,*" in *Opitz und seine Welt,* edited by Barbara Becker-Cantarino and Jörg-Ulrich Fechner (Amsterdam & Atlanta: Rodopi, 1990), pp. 251–266;

Ingen, "Johann Klaj ca. 1616–1656," in *Deutsche Schriftsteller im Porträt: Das Zeitalter des Barock,* edited by Martin Bircher (Munich: Beck, 1979), pp. 100–101;

Gerhard Kaiser, "Mancherlei Lust: Ein Gedicht von Johann Klaj," *Neue Deutsche Hefte,* 28, no. 3 (1981): 513–516;

Jean-Daniel Krebs, "Interpretation eines Barockgedichts: Johann Klaj: 'Hellgläntzendes Silber . . . ,' " *Nouveaux cahiers d'allemand,* 4 (1986): 171–183;

Eberhard Mannack, "'Realistische' und metaphorische Darstellung im *Pegnesischen Schäfergedicht,*" *Jahrbuch der deutschen Schillergesellschaft,* 17 (1973): 154–165;

Bruno Markwardt, *Barock und Frühaufklärung,* volume 1 of his *Geschichte der deutschen Poetik,* second enlarged edition (Berlin: De Gruyter, 1958), pp. 92–97;

Heinrich Meyer, *Der deutsche Schäferroman des 17. Jahrhunderts* (Hannover-Döhren: Hirschheydt, 1978), pp. 28–29;

Daniel Georg Morhof, *Unterricht von der Teutschen Sprache und Poesie* (Kiel: Reumann, 1682), pp. 433–434;

Richard Newald, *Die deutsche Literatur vom Späthumanismus zur Empfindsamkeit 1570–1750*, volume 5 of *Geschichte der deutschen Literatur von den Anfängen bis zur Gegenwart*, second edition, edited by Helmut de Boor and Richard Newald (Munich: Beck, 1957), pp. 217–220;

Magnus Daniel Omeis, *Gründliche Anleitung zur Teutschen accuraten Reim- und Dicht-Kunst* (Altdorf: Meyer, 1704), pp. 52–53;

David L. Paisey, "Einige Bemerkungen aus Gelegenheitsgedichten über Wolfgang Endter den Älteren und sein Nürnberger Unternehmen sowie ein Lobgedicht auf den Buchhandel von Johann Klaj," *Archiv für Geschichte des Buchwesens*, 15 (1975): cols. 1293–1296;

Ewa Pietrzak, "Das lyrische Werk von Johann Klaj," in *Kindlers Neues Literatur Lexikon*, volume 9, edited by Rudolf Radler (Munich: Kindler, 1990), pp. 452–454;

Hans Recknagel, "Johann Klaj 1616–1656," in *Fränkische Klassiker*, edited by Wolfgang Buhl (Nuremberg: Nürnberger Presse, 1971), pp. 316–324;

Recknagel, "'. . . Johann Klaj, der Heiligen Schrift beflissener, und gekrönter Poet': Ein Kapitel barocker Literatursoziologie," *Mitteilungen des Vereins für Geschichte der Stadt Nürnberg*, 53 (1965): 386–396;

Ernst Rohmer, "Johann Klaj in Kitzingen: Bohemien oder Pastor orthodoxus," in *Pegnesischer Blumenorden in Nürnberg: Festschrift zum 350jährigen Jubiläum*, edited by Werner Kügel (Nuremberg: Tümmel, 1994), pp. 7–15;

Johann Elias Schlegel, "Herodes der Kindermörder," *Beyträge zur Critischen Historie der Deutschen Sprache und Beredsamkeit*, 7, no. 27 (1741): 355–378;

Justus Georg Schottel, *Ausführliche Arbeit von der deutschen Hauptsprache*, volume 2 (Tübingen: Niemeyer, 1967), p. 1203;

Malve K. Slocum, "Natur und Mensch in barocker Schäferdichtung: Am Beispiel eines Gedichtes von Johann Klaj," *Colloquia Germanica*, 7, no. 1 (1973): 50–54;

Marian Szyrocki, "Johann Klaj," in her *Die deutsche Literatur des Barok: Eine Einführung*, second edition (Reinbek bei Hamburg: Rowohlt, 1970), pp. 165–166;

Julius Tittmann, *Die Nürnberger Dichterschule* (Wiesbaden: Sändig, 1965), pp. 63–65, 83–92, 127–132, 161–178;

Conrad Wiedemann, "Druiden, Barden, Witdoden: Zu einem Identifikationsmodell barocken Dichtertums," in *Sprachgesellschaften, Sozietäten, Dichtergruppen*, edited by Martin Bircher and Ferdinand van Ingen (Hamburg: Hauswedell, 1978), pp. 131–149;

Wiedemann, "Engel, Geist und Feuer: Zum Dichterselbstverständnis bei Johann Klaj, Catharina von Greiffenberg und Quirinus Kühlmann," in *Festschrift für Heinz Otto Bürger*, edited by Wiedemann and Reinhold Grimm (Berlin: Schmidt, 1968), pp. 85–109;

Wiedemann, *Johann Klaj und seine Redeoratorien: Untersuchungen zur Dichtung eines deutschen Barockmanieristen* (Nuremberg: Carl, 1966).

Papers:

Johann Klaj's papers are in the Archiv des Pegnesischen Blumenordens in the Germanisches Nationalmuseum, Nuremberg.

Hans Ludwig von Kuffstein

(11 June 1582 – 27 September 1656)

Gerhart Hoffmeister
University of California, Santa Barbara

TRANSLATIONS: Jorge de Montemayor and Alonso Pérez, *Die schöne verliebte Diana, auß Hispanischer Sprach verteutscht* (Linz: Printed by Johann Blanck, 1619); enlarged as *Erster vnnd anderer Theil der newen verteutschten Schäfferey von der schönen verliebten Diana vnd dem vergessenen Syreno, darinnen viel schöner Historien, von mancherley liebhabenden, Adels- vnnd Vnadelspersohnen, sambt dero Beschreibung deß Tempels der Göttin Dianae, vnd deß Pallasts, so wol auch der Gesellschaft der weisen Frawen Felicia, sehr lustig vnnd kurtzweilig zu lesen. Auß Spanischer Spraach in Hochteutsch gebracht* (Linz: Printed by Johann Blancken, 1619);

Diego de San Pedro, *Ein schön Gedicht, genandt, Das Gefängnüß der Lieb. Darinnen eingebracht wird die Trawrige vnd doch sehr schöne Historia, von einem Ritter, genandt Constante, vnd der Königlichen Tochter Rigorosa. Auß Spanischer Spraach inn Hochdeutsch gebracht* (Oels: Printed by Johann Bössemesser, 1624); republished as *Carcell de Amor. Oder Gefängnüß der Lieb* (Leipzig: Michael Wachsmann, 1625);

Lucius Annaeus Seneca, *Der Christliche Seneca Das ist: Christliche Tugenden, auß denen Episteln L. Annaei Senecae gezogen . . . in teutsche Sprache versetzet* (Frankfurt am Main: Georg Müller, 1670).

Edition: *Gefängnüß der Lieb oder Carcell de Amor. Faksimiledruck der Ausgabe von 1625,* edited by Gerhart Hoffmeister with a bibliography of Kuffstein's works, Nachdrucke deutscher Literatur des 17. Jahrhunderts, no. 7 (Bern & Frankfurt am Main: Herbert Lang, 1976).

The translator and poet Hans Ludwig von Kuffstein played an important role as an intermediary between the courtly literature of Golden Age Spain (circa 1500–1680) and the early baroque writers who had fallen behind cultural and literary developments in western Europe in the wake of the Reformation and who, around 1600, attempted to lay a new foundation for German literature. Building on the Spanish tradition flourishing at the Hapsburg Court in Vienna, Kuffstein contributed significantly to the so-called *Linzer Humanismus* (Linz Humanism), Protestant literature in Upper Austria by writers such as Katharina Regina von Greiffenberg and Johann Wilhelm von Stubenberg. Of equal significance were Kuffstein's contributions as a diplomat who tried to settle differences among the emperor, the Protestant estates, and the peasants during the Thirty Years' War.

Kuffstein was born on 11 June 1582 in Linz, Upper Austria. Under his father, Johann Georg Kuffstein III, the Kuffsteins started their rise from the landed nobility of lower rank to high nobility employed by the court in Vienna. Hans Ludwig was the youngest surviving son among thirteen children from his father's marriage to his second wife, Anna von Kirchberg. At the age of eight he accompanied two of his older brothers to the University of Prague; from 1594 to 1597 he attended the University of Jena. He then went on a *Kavalierstour* (gentleman's tour) to some northern Italian universities, including Padua in 1600 and Bologna and Siena in 1601, and perhaps to Spain in 1603. It was on this trip that he learned Italian and Spanish. In 1607 he married Maria Grabnerin. She bore him fifteen children, none of whom survived for more than a few months.

In August 1611 Kuffstein began translating *Los siete libros de la Diana* (The Seven Books of the Diana, 1559) by Jorge de Montemayor and its continuation by Alonso Pérez (1564). The original was the most popular pastoral novel before 1600 in western Europe and was the only one Miguel de Cervantes had exempted from burning in *Don Quixote* (1605, 1615). Sireno, distraught over the marriage of his beloved Diana, visits the enchantress Felicia in the company of several other unhappy lovers to drink from her magic potion of oblivion. The novel was important for its elegant style, its ethic of chaste courtly love, and its analysis of other varieties of love. It is one of the first modern novels successfully to blend prose passages with interspersed poems.

Kuffstein's translation came out in 1619 as *Die schöne verliebte Diana* (The Beautiful Enamored Diana) and was enlarged the same year as *Erster unnd anderer Theil der newen verteutschten Schäfferey von der schönen verliebten Diana* (First and Second Part of the Newly Translated Pastoral of the Beautiful and Enamored Diana). It ushered in a new era of courtly writing according to French, Spanish, and Italian standards. The tradition of courtly writing had largely been lost in German letters by the mid thirteenth century.

Comparing Montemayor and Pérez's original with Kuffstein's rendition shows how the early baroque tried to introduce decorum into the crudities rampant among the late-medieval gentry and lower class. Dedicating his work to the duchess of Austria, Kuffstein strove to keep coarse German out of princely chambers by changing even Montemayor's innocent erotic and bucolic descriptions into courtly language. Rustic greetings among shepherds become noble forms of address; shepherdesses are transformed into noble ladies; bucolic scenes, with cows licking their calves, turn into courtly settings. Greeting and farewell ceremonies give Kuffstein an opportunity to transform elliptic Renaissance diction into more-elaborate baroque phrases and gestures: a Spanish embrace is transformed into a stately walk toward the other person, and prostrating oneself with gratitude is transformed into kneeling; Kuffstein does, however, adopt the Spanish custom of kissing the lady's hand. Instead of letting them sleep together, he separates male and female shepherds at nightfall. Nosebleeding replaces answering the call of nature, and handwashing replaces bathing. In part 2, by Pérez, a pair of lovers has been sleeping together for a month, but the translator keeps them conversing in a respectable parlor scene.

Martin Opitz is usually considered the father of the school of Petrarchism in German literature, that is, of those poets who followed Petrarch and his immediate Italian disciples in the composition of lovers' plaints. But by translating the love songs in *Los siete libros de la Diana* Kuffstein preceded Opitz in disseminating the tradition of the angelic yet cruel lady who enchains her lovers. In addition, by translating the included "Historia del Abencerraje y de la hermosa Xarifa" (Story of the Abencerraje and the Beautiful Jarifa) he introduced the first Moorish tale to German letters. Kuffstein's translation remained popular until the 1690s; Georg Philipp Harsdörffer incorporated it into his own expanded version, *Diana*, in 1646.

While Kuffstein was translating *Los siete libros de la Diana,* he was also laying the foundations of his diplomatic career. Between 1614 and 1616 he was a delegate to the Convention of the Protestant Estates in Lower Austria. After the outbreak of the Thirty Years' War in Bohemia in 1618, the estates entrusted him repeatedly with diplomatic missions to Upper Austria, to the Prince's Diet in Nuremberg in 1619, and, the same year, to the newly enthroned Emperor Ferdinand II in Vienna, to try to forestall hostilities among the quarreling factions in Austria. When, in his absence, radical elements took control of the estates, Kuffstein, although a moderate himself, was expelled from Vienna. He returned on his own to pay homage to Ferdinand in July 1620; thus, he did not participate in the Battle at White Mountain of November 1620, with its disastrous outcome for the Protestant rebels under the leadership of the elector Frederick of the Palatinate. By 1620 Kuffstein had become *Rat* (councillor) to the Lower Austrian government. His wife died on 8 January 1623; on 27 November of the same year he married a Protestant, Susanna Eleonora von Stubenberg, with whom he may have had another twenty-four children, since his last son's epitaph attests to thirty-nine in all.

During the early 1620s Kuffstein translated a second major novel of Golden Age Spanish literature, Diego de San Pedro's sentimental *Cárcel de Amor* (Prison of Love, 1492), as *Ein schön Gedicht, genandt, Das Gefängnüß der Lieb* (A Beautiful Poem Called The Prison of Love, 1624). In *Cárcel de Amor* Leriano, Princess Laureola's lover, is taken to a "prison of love"; the narrator is a go-between who carries letters back and forth between the two. Kuffstein renames the lovers Constante and Rigorosa, and he makes so many other changes and interpolates so much additional material that the German version is double the length of the elliptic Spanish original. Most of his insertions reinforce the courtly aspects of the work. To converse elegantly with a lady is shown to be a high point in a gentleman's career because ladies ennoble men, raise the level of virtue, and cultivate chivalry in high society. Kuffstein is interested in love as a social phenomenon, and he discusses two key questions: first, how a lady is to distinguish between true love and the false pretenses of sweet-talking deceivers; second, whether unrequited or mutual love is preferable. In regard to the latter question Kuffstein, reworking the mystical love passages in Diego's work, opts for mutual love, thus adapting the courtly tradition in the Spanish novel to the requirements of his native Austria. That his adaptation underwent eight editions between 1624 and 1675 gives an indi-

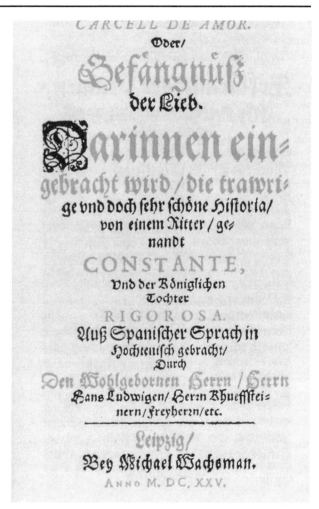

Frontispiece and title page for Hans Ludwig von Kuffstein's translation of Diego de San Pedro's novel of courtly love

cation of its popularity; around the middle of the century *Das Gefängnüß der Lieb* was among the favorite reading materials for courtly ladies, along with *Die schöne verliebte Diana* and the German translation (1569–1595) of *Amadís de Gaula* (circa 1508). A group of itinerant actors created a stage version with a happy ending, *Liebes-Gefängnüs Traur-Freuden-Spiel* (Love's Prison: A Tragicomedy, 1678), a prose play that blended the crude tradition of the comedians with operatic effects and the elevated style of Kuffstein's version.

In 1627 Kuffstein and his wife converted to Catholicism, to the amazement of his friends and foes alike. His motives were not solely opportunistic, as his former friends proclaimed, but also involved religious conviction; the step, however, made it possible for him to keep his family estate, whereas many of his Protestant acquaintances were forced into exile by the victorious imperial faction; also, it allowed him to rise in the civil service. In

1628 he was sent on an imperial mission to Sultan Murad IV in Turkey. In a handwritten report to the emperor, "Relation von der verrichten Türckischen Absandtung" (Report on the Completed Mission to Turkey, 1628), Kuffstein explains the purposes of this venture: to strengthen the peace agreement of Szöny (1627), which had been concluded between the emperor and the sultan because Ferdinand II needed a free hand to deal with the Protestant uprising; to regain some strongholds the Turks had occupied in the border region; and to collect information about the sultan's power and plans.

Kuffstein and his retinue of 180 set out down the Danube in eleven ships, then transferred to 250 horses and 72 wagons for the nine-month journey to Constantinople (today Istanbul) and back. The mission was not a great diplomatic success, but Kuffstein's report to the emperor is a valuable document of one of the rare encounters between Westerners and the Orient in the seventeenth century.

Moreover, Kuffstein returned with ten large oil paintings and eleven gouaches of some of the colorful meetings, painted by an unknown member of the mission; the paintings are now in the museum in Perchtoldsdorf, Austria.

The mission was one reason for Kuffstein's appointment as governor of Upper Austria in Linz in 1630. In this capacity he was responsible for the accommodation of imperial visitors as well as for the welfare of high-ranking Protestants taken prisoner in the Thirty Years' War. To his credit, he always tried to promote peaceful solutions – not always successfully, however, because he had to use force repeatedly between 1632 and 1648 to keep rebelling peasants in check. He was made Reichsgraf (imperial count) in 1634.

In his spare time Kuffstein continued to translate, as several manuscripts in the University Library of Budapest attest: "Seneca Christianus" (circa 1634), a translation of Seneca's *Epistolae morales ad Lucilium* (Letters to Lucilius on Moral Questions, circa 62 A.D.); a fragmentary translation of Luis de Granada's *Guía de peccadores* (Guide for Sinners, 1556–1557), a book of Dominican sermons about mortification of the senses, charity, and the fulfillment of one's duties; and two books of Juan Gonzalez de Mendoza's *Historia de las cosas mas notables . . . del gran Reyno de la China* (History of the Most Noteworthy Things . . . in the Great Empire of China, 1585). "Seneca Christianus" was published posthumously in 1670 as *Der Christliche Seneca Das ist: Christliche Tugenden, auß denen Episteln L. Annaei Senecae gezogen* (The Christian Seneca; That Is, Christian Virtues, Drawn from the Letters of L. Annaeus Seneca). Kuffstein's manuscript translation of Giovanni Boccaccio's *Fiammetta* (written 1344–1346), to which he refers in his preface to *Die schöne verliebte Diana,* appears to be lost. Kuffstein died in Linz on 27 September 1656.

Bibliography:

Gerhard Dünnhaupt, *Personalbibliographien zu den Drucken des Barock,* volume 9, part 4 (Stuttgart: Hiersemann, 1991), pp. 2429-2434.

Biography:

Karl Graf Kuefstein, *Studien zur Familiengeschichte,* part 3 (Vienna & Leipzig: Braumüller, 1915).

References:

Martin Bircher, "'Der christliche Seneca': Eine unbekannte Übersetzung von Georg Adam [*sic*] von Kuefstein," *Wolfenbütteler Barock-Nachrichten,* 10, no. 1-2 (1983): 475-478;

Bircher, *Johann Wilhelm von Stubenberg (1619–1663) und sein Freundeskreis* (Berlin: Erich Schmidt, 1968);

György Hölvenyi, "Nochmals: 'Der christliche Seneca.' Ein Fund wichtiger Kuefstein-Handschriften in Budapest," *Wolfenbütteler Barock-Nachrichten,* 12, no. 1 (1985): 25-26;

Gerhart Hoffmeister, "Antipetrarkismus im deutschen Schäferroman des 17. Jahrhunderts," *Daphnis,* 1 (1972): 128-141;

Hoffmeister, "Courtly Decorum: Kuffstein and the Spanish Diana," *Comparative Literature Studies,* 8 (1971): 214-223;

Hoffmeister, *Deutsche und europäische Barockliteratur,* Sammlung Metzler, 234 (Stuttgart: Metzler, 1987);

Hoffmeister, "Diego de San Pedro und H. L. von Kuffstein: über eine frühbarocke Bearbeitung der spanischen Liebesgeschichte *Carcel de amor,*" *Arcadia,* 6, no. 2 (1971): 139-150;

Hoffmeister, "The European Novel in 17th Century Germany," in *German Baroque Literature: The European Perspective,* edited by Hoffmeister (New York: Ungar, 1983), pp. 295-315;

Hoffmeister, "Kuffstein und die Komödianten," *Daphnis,* 13 (1984): 217-228;

Hoffmeister, "Profiles of Pastoral Protagonists, 1504-1754. Derivations and Social Implications," in *From the Greeks to the Greens,* edited by Reinhold Grimm (Madison: University of Wisconsin Press, 1989), pp. 18-33;

Hoffmeister, *Die spanische Diana in Deutschland: Vergleichende Untersuchungen zu Stilwandel und Weltbild des Schäferromans im 17. Jahrhundert* (Berlin: Erich Schmidt, 1972);

Werner Richter, *Liebeskampf 1630 und Schaubühne 1670,* Palaestra 78 (Berlin: Mayer & Müller, 1910);

Karl Teply, *Die kaiserliche Großbotschaft an Sultan Murad IV. 1628: Des Freiherrn H. L. von Kuefsteins Fahrt zur Hohen Pforte* (Vienna: Schendl, n.d. [1986?]);

Madelaine Welsersheimb, "H. L. von Kuefstein (1582-1656)," dissertation, University of Vienna, 1970;

Adam Wolf, *Geschichtliche Bilder aus Österreich* (Vienna: Braumüller, 1878).

Papers:

Manuscripts for Hans Ludwig von Kuffstein's translations are in the University Library of Budapest; manuscript reports about his mission to Turkey are in the Haus-, Hof- und Staatsarchiv, Vienna, and in the Oberösterreichisches Landesarchiv, Linz.

Johann Lauremberg

(26 February 1590 – 28 February 1658)

Mara R. Wade

University of Illinois at Urbana-Champaign

BOOKS: *Pompejus Magnus. Tragoedia* (Ratzeburg, 1610);

Προκλου Διαδοχου. Σφαιρα. *Procli Diadochi Sphaera* (Rostock: Christoph Reusner, 1611);

Κυπισ Πλεουσα. *seu Venus navigans, Epithalamium Petri Laurembergii, medici hamburgensis* (Paris: Typis Regiis, 1614); enlarged as Κυπισ Πλεουσα. *seu Venus navigans. Tempe Thessalica. Tuscia, Seu Medicaeorum Encomium. Ad Constantinvm Oeslervm Medicum celeberrimum* (Rostock: Printed by Joachim Fueß, 1618);

Panegyricus Fortissimo Heroi, Divo Ulrico Duci Megapolitano, Principi Vestutae Gentis Henetae, Comiti Suerinensi, Terrarum Rostochij & Stargardiae Dynastae, Publicè dictus (Rostock: Printed by Joachim Fueß, 1621);

Organum analogicum, seu Instrumentum proportionum, quo universa arithmetica & geometria compendiosè demonstrantur & usui accomodantur (Rostock: Printed by Joachim Fueß, 1621); translated by Christian Jacobi as *Clavis Instrumentalis Laurembergica. Das ist, Allerley nöthige, lustige vnd nützliche Operationen, auff dem analogischen Arithmetico-Geometrischen proportional Instrument, D. Johannis Laurembergii* (Leipzig: Elias Rehefeld & Johann Große, 1625);

Antiquarivs: In qvo Præter Antiqva et Obsoleta Verba ac voces minùs vsitatas, dicendi formulae insolentes, plurimi ritus Pop Rom. ac Graecis peculiares exponuntur & enodantur. Opvs ex Plurimis Latinæ Lingvæ Auctoribus multo labore concinnatum, & iuxta alphabeticam seriem digestum, quod cuiuis prolixi commentarij loco esse potest. Adiecta est in Fine Vetvstiorvm vocum ex glossariis aliquot collecta farrago (Lyon: Printed by Jean Anard, 1622);

Logarithmvs, sev Canon Nvmerorvm, Sinvvm ac Tangentivm Novvs: Cuius adminiculo operationes Arithmeticae & Geometricae per solam additionem & subtractionem perficiuntur (Leiden: Jacob Marcus, 1628);

Lusus et Recreationies ex fundamentis Arithmeticis depromptae (Copenhagen: Printed by Melchior Martzan, 1634);

Zwo Comoedjen, Darinnen fürgestellet I. Wie Aquilo, der Regent Mitternächtigen Länder, die Edle Princessin Orithyjam heimführet: II. Wie die Harpyiæ von zweyen Septentrionalischen Helden verjaget; vnd König Phinéus entlediget wird. Bey dem Hochfürstlichen Beylager des Durchleuchtigsten, Hochgebohrnen Fürsten vnd Herrn, Herrn Christian des V. zu Dennemarck, Norwegen, der Wenden vnd Gothen erwehlten Printzen, etc. vnd der Durchleuchtigen, Hochgebohrnen Fürstin vnd Fräwleins, Frewl: Magdalenen Sibyllen, Gebohrnen Hertzogin zu Sachsen, Gülich, Cleve vnd Berge, etc. Praesentiret vnd gehalten zu Copenhagen, den 7. vnd 12. Octob. Anno 1634., anonymous (Copenhagen: Jürgen Jürgensen Holst, 1635);

Satyra, quä rerum bonarum abusus, & vitia quaedam nostri seli [sic] *perstringuntur* (N.p., 1636);

Gromaticæ Libri Tres. I. De Jugeratione. II. De Podismo. III. De Centuriatione (Copenhagen: Melchior Martzan, 1639);

Ocium Soranum, sive Epigrammata, Continentia varias Historias, & res scitu jucundas, ex Graecis Latinisque Scriptoribus depromptas, & exercitationibus Arithmeticis accommodatas (Copenhagen: Printed by Melchior Martzan, published by Joachim Moltke, 1640);

Arithmetica, Peculiaribus observationibus, & Exemplis Historicis illustrata. Itidem Algebrae principia (Sorø: Heinrich Cruse, 1643);

Georgio Rosencrantzio, Oligeri Fil. Viro Antiquâ Nobilitate, Priscâ Fide, Patriâ Eruditorum, maximè insigni, Regiae & Equestris Academiae Soronæ Præsidi nuper constituto, Felicem & diuturnam gubernationem apprecatus, fine fuco (Sorø: Printed by Peter Jansson, 1647);

Schäfftige Martha, Dat ys Eentfoldige Beschriving Wo ydt mit dem Honnichsöten Fryen, vör- vnd by der Köst thogeydt. Jn de Fedder gefahtet vnd vpgedrücket

210

Dörch Jeckel van Achtern, Herr vp Lik (N.p., circa 1650);

Veer Schertz Gedichte I. Van der Minschen jtzigem Wandel und Maneeren. II. Van Almodischer Kleder-Dracht. III. Von vormengder Sprake, und Titeln. IV. Van Poësie und Rymgedichten. Jn Nedderdüdisch gerymet dörch Hans Willmsen L. Rost (N.p., 1652); translated by Constantin Christian Dedekind as *Vier Schertz-Gedichte* (N.p. [Dresden: Melchior Berg?], 1654);

Dn. Falconi Giøe de Hvidkild, cum Prebeno Brahe in Engelsholm filiam Susannam nupt. daret, acclamat academia Sorana (Sorø, 1653);

Ad. Perillustrem. Magnificum. et. Generosum. Heroa. dn. Georgium. Rosencarantzium. Hæreditarium. in. Kjelgaard. &c. Supremum. Nuper. Ærarii. Regii. Præfectum. Nunc. Vero. Regiæ. Atqve. Bqvestris. Soranæ. Academiæ. Præsidem. cum. ad. Suscipiendam. Provinciam. Hafnia. Anno. M. DC. LIII. Iduum. Novemb. Proficisceretur. Votiva. Acclamatio. Jacobii. Henrici. Paulli. Sim. F., anonymous (Copenhagen: Printed by Melchior Martzan, 1653);

Musicalisch Schawspiel, darinnen vorgestellet werden die Geschichte Arions. Dem Durchleuchtigstem [*sic*] *Großmächtigstem Fürsten und Herrn, Herrn Friderich dem Drtitten, König in Denmarck, Norwegen, &c.: Auch der Durchleuchtigsten Hochgebohrnen Fürstinn und Frawen, Frawen Sophia Amalia, Königinn in Denmarck, Norwegen, &c.: Zur Glückwündschung über die Hüldigung des Durchleuchtigsten Printzen Hertzog Christian, &c. Vnterthänigst praesentirt,* anonymous (Copenhagen: Printed by Peter Morsing, 1655);

Serenissimo, Potentissimoq; Principi ac Domino, Dn. Friderico III. Regi Daniae, Norvegiae, &c. Cum Serenissimo Principi ac Domino, Dn. Christiano, ab universis Daniae Ordinibus Homagium praestaretur, submisse & humiliter Gratulatur Regia & Equestris Academia Sorana (Copenhagen: Printed by Peter Morsing, 1655);

Illustribus ac Generosißimis Sponsis, Hugoni Lützovio & Idæ Rosencrantziæ, Conjugium felix diuturnum, foecumdum. comprecor J.L. (Sorø: Printed by Georg Hantsch, 1656);

Daphnorini querimonia (N.p., 1657);

Illustrissimum, Magnificum, Generosissimum Heroa, Dn. Christianum Thomæum Sehestedium, Dominum Stougardii, Cancellarium Regium, Regni Senatorem, Equitem Auratum, &c. An. M D CLVII. die V. Aug. Vita Mortali Egressum, Conservatorem et Patronum Suum Desideratissimum, Exsevali honore proseqvitur Lugens Moerensq: Regia & equestris Ac- *ademia Sorana,* anonymous (Sorø: Printed by Georg Hantsch, 1657);

Græcia Antiqua, edited by Samuel Pufendorf (Amsterdam: Johannes Jansson, 1660).

Editions: *Niederdeutsche Scherzgedichte,* edited by Johann Martin Lappenberg, Bibliothek des Litterarischen Vereins in Stuttgart, volume 58 (Stuttgart: Bibliothek des Litterarischen Vereins, 1861);

Scherzgedichte in handschriftlicher Fassung, edited by E. Schröder, Drucke des Vereins für niederdeutsche Sprachforschung, volume 5 (Norden & Leipzig: Scholtau, 1909);

A Description of Ancient Greece (Amsterdam: Hakkert, 1969).

Johann Lauremberg was a poet, a dramatist, and a satirist in both German and Latin. He was also a medical doctor, a professor of poetics, a professor of mathematics who published several textbooks and introduced logarithms into Denmark, a professor of fortifications, a cartographer, a geographer, and a scholar of ancient Greek language and culture. A renowned teacher, he helped to set educational policies and curricula not only at his home institution of Sorø but also at other schools in Denmark (as attested, for example, by a letter of advice to Hans Mikkelsen Ravn [Johann Michaelis Corvinus], rector at the school in Slagelse). He was also the author of occasional lyrics in Latin, German, French, and Danish in recognition of births, deaths, weddings, new employment, awarding of university degrees, and publications by friends. Lauremberg can be regarded as the court poet of Denmark during the later reign of Christian IV and the early reign of Frederik III, monarchs for whom he composed dramas for court performance. He also spoke on many occasions of public import as the official voice of the Danish Royal Academy in Sorø. He traveled widely as a young man and met and corresponded with important learned persons in Europe. Although his erudite study of classical Greece was not published until after his death, the existence of several illuminated manuscript versions attest to a widespread knowledge of his philological and topographical studies in his own time.

Lauremberg was born on 26 February 1590 to Wilhelm Lauremberg, a professor of medicine and mathematics at the University of Rostock, and Johanna Lauremberg, née Longueil. While studying at his father's institution from 1608 to 1612, Lauremberg published his first drama, the four-act Latin tragedy *Pompeius Magnus* (Pompeius the Great, 1610), the only known extant copy of which is in

Title page for Johann Lauremberg's collection of satires in Low German

the library of Schwerin. This work was followed the next year by a mathematical text on spheres, in parallel Greek and Latin, that was subsequently reprinted for use at the academy in Sorø. After leaving Rostock with a master's degree he traveled and studied in Holland, England, and France, receiving a doctorate in medicine in Rheims around 1616. During Lauremberg's sojourn in France his older brother Peter married, and Lauremberg published in Paris a nuptial poem in Greek and Latin, Κυπισ Πλεουσα. *seu Venus navigans* (1614). He also visited Rome and Florence. Lauremberg was called back to Rostock in 1618 to become professor of Latin poetics.

For the marriage in 1618 of Constantin Oesler, Lauremberg supplemented his *Venus navigans* with two additional Latin poems, "Tempe" and "Tuscia." On 23 May 1620 Lauremberg himself was married: his bride was Maria Lillie, daughter of Sebastian Lillie, a Hamburg merchant, and the wedding took place at the Trinitatis Church in Hamburg. The marriage produced at least two children: a son, Sebastian, born in 1626, who would become a professor of mathematics in Denmark; and a daughter, Elizabeth, whose date of birth is not known but who would marry in 1652.

Lauremberg's next significant publication, in 1621, was a Latin panegyric to Ulrik, Duke of Mecklenburg, which, according to the title page, was publicly declaimed by the author. What moved him to give such a speech nearly twenty years after the duke's death is not clear. A resident of Mecklenburg, Lauremberg may simply have wanted to honor its beloved duke. But there may have been other motivations, such as the hope of attracting the attention of the Danish royal house: Ulrik's daughter, Sophie, was the dowager queen of Denmark, and her son Christian IV was the king. Products of

Lauremberg's tenure as professor in Rostock were a Latin mathematical treatise, *Organum analogicum* (1621), which was republished in German translation in 1625, and *Antiquarius* (1622), a dictionary of obsolete Latin words and phrases.

Letters in the Royal Library in Copenhagen attest to a correspondence between Lauremberg and the Danish nobleman Holger Rosencrantz, who had provided the impetus for establishing a royal academy at Sorø at a meeting in 1620 of the *Rigsräd* (Council of the Realm) in Odense. The academy was not intended to compete with the University of Copenhagen but to make long study tours unnecessary by offering young Danish noblemen an excellent education in such courtly accomplishments as foreign languages, fencing, riding and tournaments, politics, mathematics, and fortifications in preparation for their careers as government officials. Even the younger sons of Christian IV – Dukes Frederik and Ulrik (later Count Waldemar) and Hans Christian and Ulrik Christian Gyldenløve – would be educated there. The academy was a prestigious institution, and Rosencrantz was able to attract learned men from all over northern Europe, among them Lauremberg, to teach there.

Although Lauremberg's study of classical Greece was not published until after his death – appearing in Samuel Pufendorf's Latin translation, *Graecia Antiqua,* in 1660 – the work existed long before. Several exquisite bound manuscripts of the work, which is dedicated to Rosencrantz, are preserved in the Royal Library, Copenhagen, and are worthy of a modern edition in the original Greek. Most versions consist of two parts: the Greek text with its illustrations, and a separate volume of thirty-one maps depicting important classical cities and other sites. Some of the volumes are hand-colored; one set is executed in gold leaf. Lauremberg always employed Greek verse in his occasional poetry commemorating Rosencrantz, and his few extant entries in *Stammbücher* (albums) of his pupils are invariably in Greek. In letters to Rosencrantz from 1622 he mentions the topographical part of the work and the maps that illustrate it and suggests a similar project to map Denmark. The idea may have led to Lauremberg's receiving the call to teach mathematics and engineering (that is, fortifications) at Sorø in 1623. Lauremberg published several mathematical texts on the subjects he was required to teach at Sorø, including surveying. With his *Logarithmus* (1628) he introduced logarithms into Denmark.

A royal missive of 11 April 1631 indicates that Lauremberg was to begin a mathematical mapping of Denmark, for which he traveled throughout Zeeland and Jutland and began surveying Zeeland and neighboring islands. In the late 1630s he negotiated with an engraver for the production of plates from his approximately 150 maps; the project was never published, however, and in 1645 Lauremberg was rebuked by the king. Two years later the project was taken from him and assigned to the cartographer Johann Mejer. Only fragments of most of Lauremberg's maps are known today: the philologist and historian Ole Worm published a detailed section of the map of the Ringsted area in his voluminous work on runes (1643), and modern scholarship indicates that the maps published in Amsterdam by Johannes Jansson and Johannes Blaeu (1644–1662) are based on Lauremberg's cartographical studies. Extant in its entirety is Lauremberg's map of his homeland, *Meklenburg Ducatus* (The Duchy of Mecklenburg), published by Jansson in his *Novus atlas absolutissimus* in 1658. A critical study of the relationship of seventeenth-century maps of Denmark to Lauremberg's studies is a desideratum.

Also in the 1630s Lauremberg made his debut as a poet of court drama. His *Zwo Comoedien, Darinnen fürgestellet I. Wie Aquilo, der Regent Mitternächtigen Länder, die Edle Princessin Orithyiam heimführet: II. Wie die Harpyiæ von zweyen, Septentrionalischen Helden verjaget; und König Phineus entlediget wird* (Two Comedies, in Which Is Depicted 1. How Aquilo, Ruler of the Midnight Lands, Brought Home as a Wife the Noble Princess Orithyia, and 2. How the Harpies Were Dispersed by Two Septentrionic Heroes and King Phineus Was Freed, 1635) were commissioned for the spectacular wedding celebrations of the Danish prince-elect Christian and the Saxon electoral princess Magdalena Sibylle in Copenhagen in October 1634. The occasion is known in Danish history as *de store bilager* (the Great Wedding); since representatives of all the major parties involved in the Thirty Years' War attended, the wedding provided the occasion for a European summit meeting. Lauremberg's two comedies, which formed the central entertainments in the festivities, treat the myth from Ovid's *Metamorphoses* of the rape of Orithyia by the North Wind, Boreas, here called by his Latin name, Aquilo; it is an allegorical bridal quest for the heir to the Danish crown in which Aquilo and Orithyia represent Prince-Elect Christian and Magdalena Sibylle. The second work portrays the offspring of the union of Aquilo and Orithyia, the Northern heroes Calais and Zetes, as members of Jason's Argonauts. The focus of the play is not the capture of the Golden

Fleece but the battle of Calais and Zetes against the Harpies, who plague King Phineus as part of his punishment for prideful behavior. Having defeated the foul creatures and banished them from the repentant Phineus's realm, the sons of Aquilo and Orithyia are led to a banquet celebrating their victory. The two four-act plays were intended to be performed in tandem as an allegory of the Danish-Saxon match; they are also connected with political developments during the Thirty Years' War, projecting in the figures of Calais and Zetes a future role for Denmark as the mediator of European peace. Not only did Lauremberg write these allegories of Danish national myth; court records indicate that he was also responsible for overseeing the stage designs.

Although they are in prose, Lauremberg's comedies are important milestones in the development of German opera. The royal kapellmeister Heinrich Schütz set to music the strophic *Lieder* (songs) inserted into Lauremberg's plays; one of these, a hunting song, is by Martin Opitz. The plays are remarkable for their comic scenes, not all of them relegated to the interludes, in Low German. The rustic exchanges between Chim and Matz and between Drewes and Cheel are similar to the dialect-comedy scenes in plays by other German baroque poets such as Johann Rist and Andreas Gryphius. Other comic scenes, between the servant maid Amaryllis and the cavalier student Blax, derive from the commedia dell'arte and the Italian comic tradition.

Lauremberg's *Satyra* (Satires, 1636), in Latin hexameters, could well have been based on his noble students at Sorø: here he parodies "French" ways and the far greater interest of noble youth in courtly accomplishments such as fencing than in intellectual pursuits. Much like the comedy of manners that occurs between Blax and Amaryllis in the wedding comedies and that provides the focus in his Latin satires, Lauremberg's Low German satires in *Veer Schertz Gedichte I. Van der Minschen itzigem Wandel und Maneeren. II. Van Almodischer Kleder-Dracht. III. Von vormengder Sprake, und Titeln. IV. Van Poësie und Rymgedichten. In Nedderdüdisch gerymet dörch Hans Willmsen L. Rost* (Four Satires: 1. About Humanity's Present-day Ways and Manners. 2. About Fashionable Attire. 3. About Mixing Languages and Titles. 4. About Poesie and Verse. Rhymed in Low German by Hans Willmsen L. Rost [Johann Wilhelm's son L(auremberg of) Rost[ock], 1652) poke fun at contemporary foibles in alexandrine verse. *Veer Schertz Gedichte* became an immediate best-seller and was published eighteen times in the next hundred years; the work is an achievement in Lauremberg's native dialect that was not equaled until Low German was revived as a literary language in the nineteenth century. Constantin Christian Dedekind's translation of the work into standard German, published in Dresden in 1654, may have been prompted by the widowed Magdalena Sibylle's return to Saxony in 1652 for her second marriage.

Lauremberg was able to produce competent poetry, in several languages, for virtually every type of occasion. For the wedding and the funeral (1647) of Prince-Elect Christian he wrote French verse; for the publication of Søren Terkelsen's *Astree SiungeKor* (1648) and the wedding of a Danish nobleman (1656) he wrote in Danish — his only poems in that language that are known to be extant. For the publication of a musical treatise by the Copenhagen organist Lorentz Achröder he wrote in German; for formal occasions at the Sorø academy he wrote exclusively in Latin; and for the funeral of his friend and mentor Rosencrantz in 1642 he wrote in Greek, with Latin paraphrases. Lauremberg's poetry is adept, graceful, and rhetorically sound, in each case demonstrating a thorough command of the language. A study has yet to be undertaken of Lauremberg's occasional verse, much of which, in all likelihood, has yet to be identified. Most certainly there is early poetry from his travels and his years in Rostock that is still to be uncovered.

Lauremberg's *Musicalisch Schawspiel, darinnen vorgestellet werden die Geschichte Arions* (Musical Drama in Which Is Depicted the Story of Arion) was performed in August 1655 for the swearing of the oath of allegiance to Prince Christian, the son of King Frederik III (the second son of Christian IV, who had succeeded his father in 1648) and Queen Sophia Amalia. The work tells the story of the poet-musician Arion, who is cast overboard and left to drown. A dolphin, hearing Arion's beautiful music, appears and carries the singer to shore on its back. Again, the myth is a thinly veiled allegory of the Danish monarchy. *Musicalisch Schawspiel* is divided into six sections, each with an *Oda* (ode) and a chorus. The strophic "odes" are of particular interest for the history of opera in the German language because they show for the first time the asymmetrical madrigal verse necessary to the development of true recitative. The Danish kapellmeister at the time was the composer Caspar Förster, who worked in the tradition of Venetian opera and was certainly capable of setting the text to music as an opera, but there is no extant music for the work. A manuscript version from 1653 that was originally intended as a ballet for the baptism of Prince Jørgen is in the Royal

Library, Copenhagen; it concludes with a rustic dance for a short, fat peasant and a tall, thin serving girl, thus providing a continuation of Lauremberg's dialect satire. *Musicalisch Schawspiel* was Lauremberg's last major work before his death on 28 February 1658. He is buried in the church at Sorø.

No complete evaluation of Lauremberg's work has been undertaken since Johannes Classen's study of 1841. Beginning with Ludvig Daae in 1884, scholarship has focused primarily on the author's satires, which are today available only in the edition by Johann Martin Lappenberg (1861). As the author of court dramas and occasional poetry, Lauremberg remains largely unknown. A scholarly assessment of his study of classical Greece would not only establish his reputation as one of the foremost scholars of antique Greece in the seventeenth century but would also further illuminate his methods and plans for mapping Denmark. Moreover, his abiding interest in classical antiquity helped to shape the national myth of the Danish monarchy as the Baltic empire. One of the main projects for German literary research of the twenty-first century should be the liberation of Lauremberg from scholarship of the nineteenth century.

Bibliography:

Gerhard Dünnhaupt, *Personalbibliographien zu den Drucken des Barock,* volume 9, part 4 (Stuttgart: Hiersemann, 1991), pp. 2512–2530.

References:

Johannes Bolte, "Lauremberg's handschriftlicher Nachlaß," *Jahrbuch für Niederdeutsche Sprachforschung,* 13 (1887): 42–54;

Johannes Classen, *Über das Leben und die Schriften des Dichters Johann Lauremberg* (Lübeck: G. C. Schmidt's Sons, 1841);

Ludvig Daae, *Om humanisten og satirikeren Lauremberg* (Christiania: Gundersen, 1884);

H. Jellinghaus, "Zwei plattdeutsche Possen von Johann Lauremberg," *Jahrbuch für Niederdeutsche Sprachforschung,* 11 (1885): 145–150;

Klaus Peter, *Der Humor in den niederdeutschen Dichtungen Johann Laurembergs: Seine Struktur und Funktion,* Mitteldeutsche Forschungen, volume 47 (Cologne: Böhlau, 1967);

Erik Sønderholm, "Johann Lauremberg som dansk digter," *Danske Studier* (1966): 47–58;

Mara R. Wade, "Heinrich Schütz and 'det store Bilager' in Copenhagen (1634)," *Schütz-Jahrbuch,* 11 (1989): 32–52;

Helen Wichert-Fife, "Johann Lauremberg, Son of the Folk," *Germanic Review,* 30 (February 1955): 27–39.

Papers:

Johann Lauremberg's manuscripts are in the Royal Library, Copenhagen.

Friedrich von Logau

(January 1605 – 24 or 25 July 1655)

Peter Hess

University of Texas at Austin

BOOKS: *FreudenGesang über von Löblicher Peregrination Glücklicher Wiederkunft der Durchlauchten Hochgeborenen Fürsten und Herren, H. Georgens und H. Ludwiges Gebrüder vnd Hertzoge in Schlesien zur Liegnitz vnd Brieg, unser Genädigen Landes Fürsten vnnd Herren* (Brieg: Augustin Gründer, 1635);

Erstes Hundert Teutscher Reimen-Sprüche Salomons von Golaw (Breslau: David Müller's heirs, 1638);

Anna Sophia oder Unterschiedene Getichte zu Ehren der Durchl. Hochgebor. Fürstin und Frauen, Frauen Anna Sophia, Geb. von Meckelburg, Vermählten Hertzoginn in Schlesien zur Liegnitz und Brieg, Fürstinn zu Wenden, Gräfinn zu Schwerin, der Lande Rostock und Stargart Frauen geschrieben von einem Gehorsamen Unterthan (Brieg: Christoph Tschorn, 1652);

Salomons von Golaw Deutscher Sinn-Getichte Drey Tausend (Breslau: Published by Caspar Kloßmann, printed in the Baumann printing office by Gottfried Gründer, 1654).

Editions and Collections: *S. v. G. Auferweckte Gedichte, denen hinzugefüget Unterschiedene bißher ungedruckte Poetische Gedancken Heroischen Geistern gewiedmet, nebst einem nöthigen Register* (Frankfurt am Main & Stettin: Published by Johann Adam Plener, 1702);

Friedrichs von Logau Sinngedichte: Zwölf Bücher. Mit Anmerkungen über die Sprache des Dichters, edited by Karl Wilhelm Ramler and Gotthold Ephraim Lessing (Leipzig: Weidmann, 1759);

Auszug des Besten aus Logau, Wernicke und Gryphius (Heilbronn, 1823);

Auserlesene Gedichte von Friedrich von Logau und Hans Assmann von Abschatz, edited by Wilhelm Müller (Leipzig: Brockhaus, 1824);

Friedrich von Logau und sein Zeitalter, geschildert in einer Auswahl von dessen Sinngedichten (Frankfurt am Main: Lizius, 1849);

Sinngedichte von Friedrich von Logau, edited, with a biography of Logau, by Gustav Eitner (Leipzig: Brockhaus, 1870);

Friedrichs von Logaus sämmtliche Sinngedichte, edited by Eitner (Tübingen: Litterarischer Verein, 1872; reprinted, Hildesheim & New York: Olms, 1974);

Sinngedichte, edited by Karl Simrock (Stuttgart: Meyer & Zeller, 1874);

Friedrich von Logau's Sinngedichte, edited by L. H. Fischer (Leipzig: Reclam, 1875);

Paul Fleming, Friedrich von Logau und Adam Olearius, edited by Hermann Oesterley (Berlin & Stuttgart: Spemann, 1885);

Logaubüchlein, edited by Otto Erich Hartleben (Munich: Langen, 1904);

Sinngedichte und Epigramme, edited by Pfarrer Todt (Halle: Hendel, 1905);

Deutsche Sprüche, edited by Reinhard Piper (Munich: Piper, 1916);

Die Fruchtschale Friedrich von Logau's, edited by Wilhelm Müller-Rüdersdorf (Görlitz: Verlagsanstalt Görlitzer Nachrichten und Anzeiger, 1921);

Die tapfere Wahrheit: Sinngedichte von Friedrich von Logau (Munich: Hyperion, 1921);

Selections of German Poetry from the Beginning to 1720, edited by Charles Grant Loomis (Berkeley, 1958);

Der gepfefferte Logau: Eine Auswahl gezielter Sinngedichte, edited by W. F. Karlos (Munich: Schöndorn, 1969);

Die tapfere Wahrheit: Sinngedichte, edited by Werner Schubert (Leipzig: Insel, 1978);

Sinngedichte, edited by Ernst-Peter Wieckenberg (Stuttgart: Reclam, 1984);

Sinngedichte, edited by Werner Schmitz (Zurich: Haffmanns, 1989);

Reimensprüche und andere Werke in Einzeldrucken, edited, with a biography of Logau, by Ulrich Seelbach (Tübingen: Niemeyer, 1992).

OTHER: "Was fühl ich doch vor Streit? wie wider-
    wertig sollen . . . ," in *Leichenpredigt auf Prof.
    Dr. Caspar Odontius,* by Georg König (Altdorf,
    1626), leaves C2ᵛ–D2;
"Abdanckung, bey letzter Einsenckung der Seligen
    Fr. Reydeburgin," in *Leichenpredigt auf Emeren-
    tia von Reydeburg, geb. von Nimptsch,* by Henning
    Schöer (Liegnitz: Zacharias Schneider, 1651),
    leaves A1ʳ–B2ᵛ.

Friedrich von Logau is known for a single
book, published in 1654, comprising texts of one
genre, the epigram. Yet, unlike most German baroque authors, Logau was never completely forgotten: in the eighteenth century Gotthold Ephraim
Lessing and Karl Wilhelm Ramler republished the
book, and Gottfried Keller based his novella cycle
Das Sinngedicht (The Epigram, 1880–1881) on Logau's works. His epigrams have been published in
many anthologies and remain popular today.

Logau's family had belonged to the Silesian
nobility since the thirteenth century; several of his
ancestors and descendants were poets. In the seventeenth century two lines of the family are in evidence: the Olbersdorf line acquired the title of
Freiherr (baron) in 1604; Logau belonged to the unti-
tled Altendorf line. He was born on the family estate at Brockut, near Nimptsch in the duchy of
Brieg, in January 1605, probably between 17 and 23
January. He was the only child of Georg von Logau
zu Altendorf auf Brockut and Anna, née von Reydeburg auf Dobergast. His father died before Logau
was a year old; his mother later married a man
named von Hohberg.

On 13 October 1614 Logau entered the gymnasium in Brieg, where he was instructed in all the
subjects of the traditional educational canon: grammar, logic, rhetoric, mathematics, philosophy, history, and law. He was admitted to the *Prima* (senior
class) on 26 March 1618. The rector, Melchior
Laubanus, directed his students to keep journals, in
which they collected sentences, proverbs, and short
poetry; they also had to keep notebooks with lists of
rhetorical *loci communes* (topics), poetic phrases, and
grammatical observations. Logau participated in
school plays and in disputations; he also performed
as a reciter and orator on various occasions.

It is unclear why Logau remained in the highest class for seven years. Possible explanations are
frequent school closings because of the Thirty
Years' War and the plague – Logau was not in attendance from late 1620 until 6 December 1622 –
and his financial situation, which did not yet permit
his attendance at a university. On 8 July 1623

Logau was elected to the *judicium scholasticum* (student government), which arbitrated conflicts among
students, evaluated student performances at decla-
mations and disputations, and imposed disciplinary
measures on students. There is no evidence that
Logau served as a page at the Brieg court during his
school years, as claimed by some biographers. He
left the school on 26 June 1625.

Logau and a friend from the Brieg gymnasium, Valentin Gerhard, registered at the University of Altdorf, near Nuremberg, on 6 July 1625.
After a relatively short period of obligatory general
studies – he appears to have gotten credit for his extensive schooling at Brieg – Logau was admitted as
a law student at the end of 1626; he remained in Altdorf until the end of 1627. One year of law school
was apparently enough for a young man of noble
birth to secure high administrative posts in government, no matter what was required of bourgeois
courtiers.

During his studies in Altdorf he and some
other Silesian students lived at the house of Johann
Caspar Odontius, a professor of mathematics. On
the occasion of Odontius's death on 17 July 1626,
Logau wrote his first extant poem, an epicedium
(mourning poem) in 228 alexandrines that was published in the printed version of the funeral sermon
by the theology professor Georg König.

Logau was also involved in student pranks.
On 24 August 1626 the students who lived in the
house of Odontius's widow attacked a couple of students who lived with Professor Georg Queck and
then continued to throw rocks at the Queck house;
the intervention of several professors ended the incident. As one of the minor participants, Logau was
reprimanded. In 1627 he was disciplined for dueling
and for damaging a cemetery wall.

There is no information on Logau's where-
abouts from 11 December 1627, the last date he can
be placed in Altdorf, until 1 July 1631, when he borrowed a thousand talers in Brieg from his maternal
uncle, Heinrich von Reydeburg, against the ten-
thousand-taler interest he had held in the Brockut
estate since 1615. The loan presumably was used to
start a household: Logau married Magdalena von
Gruttschreiber in 1631. The couple had one daughter, Anna. Since his uncle died in 1632 – Logau inherited his library – Logau never had to repay the
loan.

When Logau came into possession of the
Brockut estate around 1633, it was run down and
burdened by debt. Between 1634 and 1637 the estate could not be inhabited and cultivated because
of intense fighting in the area, and Logau and his

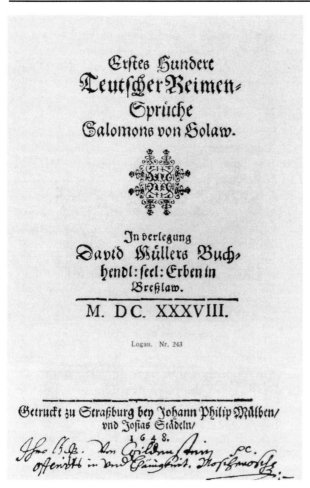

Title page for Friedrich von Logau's first collection of epigrams, published under his pseudonym

family lived in Brieg. In 1637 the Logaus took up residence at Brockut, but they were back in Brieg by 1641 because of renewed fighting in the area.

In 1635 Georg and Ludwig, the two young dukes of Liegnitz and Brieg, returned to Brieg after a five-year educational journey. To mark the occasion Logau wrote *FreudenGesang über von Löblicher Peregrination Glücklicher Wiederkunft der Durchlauchten Hochgeborenen Fürsten und Herren, H. Georgens und H. Ludwiges* (Joyous Song about the Happy Return of the Illustrious and Honorable Princes and Lords, Duke Georg and Duke Ludwig, from their Laudable Journey).

In 1638 Logau published his first collection of epigrams: *Erstes Hundert Teutscher Reimen-Sprüche Salomons von Golaw* (First Hundred German Sententious Verses by Salomon von Golaw). The first name of his pseudonym is a reference to the three books of Solomon in the Old Testament; the last name is an anagram for Logau. The book actually comprises two hundred epigrams: the second hun-

dred appear in part 2, which is bound together with the first part in a single volume. The epigrams of this early collection lack the satiric bite of some of his later ones and are more directly based on literary models such as Martial and John Owen. Logau's wife died in the summer of 1641; in 1643 he married Helena von Knobelsdorf, the daughter of the *fürstlich briegischer Hofmarschall* (Court Marshal of the Prince of Brieg), Balthasar von Knobelsdorf. They had four children: Balthasar Friedrich, born in 1645; Dorothea Magdalena, born circa 1647; Anna Helena, born in 1649; and Eleonora Sophia, born in 1653.

Logau's growing family was probably supported by official appointments rather than by income from the estate at Brockut. The duchy of Liegnitz and Brieg had been governed jointly by the brothers Georg III, Ludwig IV, and Christian since the death of their father on 24 December 1639, although each of them kept a separate court. Duke Ludwig gave Logau the position of *fürstlicher Rat* (princely councillor) on 29 September 1644. Most of his responsibilities seem to have been of a diplomatic or ceremonial nature, such as representing the duke at weddings, giving speeches, and delivering presents on the duke's behalf. His annual salary was a modest 306 talers plus a free apartment, a small keg of beer weekly, and a modest amount of wood and hay. It is not clear how extensive his duties were or whether the position was a full-time one. Logau kept the Brockut estate after his appointment; although he never returned there to live, its farming operations provided him with a small amount of much-needed additional income. Still, it appears that Logau was unable to make ends meet: in 1649 he took out a loan of four hundred talers against the estate.

In the summer of 1648 he accompanied Ludwig on a trip to Strelitz, where the duke asked for the hand of Anna Sophia von Mecklenburg-Güstrow. In Strelitz they were met by Christian Ernst Knoch, a representative of Prince Ludwig of Anhalt-Köthen, the founder and head of Germany's most important language society, the Fruchtbringende Gesellschaft (Fruit-bringing Society). The prince had instructed Knoch to invite Duke Ludwig and his two escorts, Logau and Caspar von Hohberg, to become members of the society. This unexpected honor filled Logau with pride; many of his epigrams praise the society and its founder. Logau, however, seems to have been unhappy with his society name, Der Verkleinernde (The Diminishing One), and his emblematic plant, the golden saxifrage, a common and undistinguished herb that was believed to reduce the swelling of the spleen. Nevertheless, his admittance to the society must have been a source of motivation for Logau: by the end of 1648 he had only written nine hundred epigrams, roughly a quarter of his total poetic production; the remainder would be written in only six years.

The only known prose text by Logau is "Abdanckung, bey letzter Einsenckung der Seligen Fr. Reydeburgin" (Funerary Oration at the Interment of the Deceased Mrs. Reydeburg), given on 28 June 1651 and printed in the published version of the funeral sermon by Henning Schröer. The oration includes several poems.

Logau dedicated his second collection of fifty epigrams, which appeared in 1652, to the wife of Duke Ludwig: *Anna Sophia oder Unterschiedene Getichte zu Ehren der Durchl. Hochgebor. Fürstin und Frauen, Frauen Anna Sophia, Geb. von Meckelburg, Vermähleten Hertzogin in Schlesien zur Liegnitz und Brieg* (Anna Sophia; or, Various Poems in Honor of the Illustrious and Honorable Princess and Lady, Lady Anna Sophia, née von Mecklenburg, Married Duchess in Silesia at Liegnitz and Brieg). The dedication may have been in honor of her twenty-fourth birthday on 29 November 1652; there is no other apparent occasion for it. Most of the poems are panegyrics to the beauty and virtue of the duchess.

On 14 January 1653 Duke Georg Rudolf of Liegnitz died without a direct heir, and the duchy passed to his nephews, Dukes Georg, Ludwig, and Christian. Logau was in charge of the funeral, which was held on 14 May 1653. By that time Logau apparently had become Duke Ludwig's senior adviser in both court and state affairs.

In April 1654 the collection of epigrams appeared on which his literary reputation rests: *Salomons von Golaw Deutscher Sinn-Getichte Drey Tausend* (Three Thousand German Epigrams by Salomon von Golaw). It is divided into three groups of one thousand poems each; the second thousand is followed by a supplement of 201 poems and the third by two supplements of 102 and 257 poems, respectively. The collection therefore comprises a total of 3,560 epigrams. All but six of the poems from the 1638 collection are included, most of them in edited versions; also, the mostly Latin titles of the earlier collection are translated into German. Many of the poems refer to specific events that can be dated exactly, as Gustav Eitner shows in the appendix to his edition of 1872. It can thus be assumed that all of the poems, with the exception of those from the 1638 collection, are arranged in chronological order.

Logau's definition of the epigram is largely based on Julius Caesar Scaliger's *Poetices libri septem* (The Seven Books of Poetics, 1561) and on Martin Opitz's *Buch von der Deutschen Poeterey* (Book of German Poetry, 1624). Scaliger differentiated between the *epigramma simplex* (mellow simple epigram), on the one hand, and the *epigramma compositum* (satiric composite epigram), with its often unexpected and pointed ending, on the other. In his introduction Logau expresses his preference for the satiric type. To his longest epigram – 196 verses – he adds an apologetic marginal note: "Epigramma est brevis Satyra; Satyra, est longum Epigramma" (The epigram is a short satire; the satire is a long epigram). Scaliger and Opitz attribute two essential qualities to the epigram: *brevitas* (brevity) and *argutia* (pointedness), the latter of which is ensured by an *acumen* (unexpected and witty turn). The proper length for an epigram cannot be prescribed in absolute terms; it depends on the complexity of the topic. But the formulation must always be succinct. Brevity and succinctness serve a third feature of the baroque epigram: didactic intent. In Logau's epigrams, moral instruction is given by praising the good example or by satirizing the bad. Many of his epigrams show genuine concern for the effect on the reader:

> An die Leser.
> Leser, wie gefall ich dir?
> Leser, wie gefellst du mir?
>
> (To my readers.
> Reader, how do you like me?
> Reader, how do I like you?)

Literary models have been identified for about sixteen hundred of his epigrams; the most important are Martial, Owen, and Euricius Cordus. In addition, Logau was influenced by the writings of Georg Rudolph Weckherlin, Paul Fleming, Andreas Tscherning, Andreas Gryphius, and Valentin Löber, who translated Owen's Latin epigrams into German in 1653. Logau also used collections of proverbs by Johannes Agricola and Sebastian Franck, as well as collections of apothegms by Julius Wilhelm Zincgref. His main sources for poetic ideas and formulations were *Der Teutschen Weissheit* (The German Wisdom, 1605), by Friedrich Petri; *Sphinx-theologica-philosophica* (1621), by Johann Heidfeld; and *Florilegium politicum* (1630), by Christoph Lehmann.

Despite his reliance on conventional norms and sources, Logau varied his verse and metric forms greatly. The alexandrine does not prevail, as it did in most of his contemporaries' poetry. In fact,

Title page for the collection of epigrams on which Logau's literary reputation rests

Logau prefers trochaic verse with a bipartite structure that allows for an antithetical representation; the caesura is achieved through dropping an unstressed syllable in the center of the line, thus creating the opposition of two stressed syllables. His frequent use of monosyllabic words reinforces the sense of harshness and urgency rendered by the caesura. Dactylic verse is used occasionally. Pointed formulations dominate, even in his nonsatiric epigrams, and take many forms: coining of words, false etymologies, plays on words and sounds, anagrams, chronograms, apostrophes, alliteration, onomatopoeia, parallels, parenthesis, asyndeton, graphic metaphors, rhetorical questions, riddles, and playful interaction with the reader.

Poetic language is a recurring theme in Logau's epigrams. He supports the development of a German vernacular literary language; he rejects the argument that German is too rough and uncultivated for poetic discourse. In his view, German poetry needs to emancipate itself from its models in antiquity. Moreover, while he opposes the use of foreign words, he supports moderate use of dialect. He attributes particular significance to the sounds of words and to rhymes, hence his preference for alliteration and onomatopoeia. In Logau's handling of the genre, rhyme is often the carrier of the pointed ending of the epigram:

> Untreuer Krieg.
> Was sich reimt das schickt sich auch,
> Spricht der frische Landes-Brauch;
> Drumb so schickt sich liegen, triegen,
> Auch so fein zu vnserm kriegen.

> (Unfaithful War.
> What rhymes is also proper,
> Is a popular saying;

That is why lying and betraying
Fit so well to our warring.)

As Scaliger pointed out, there are as many possible types of epigrams as there are topics. The gnomic type (in Jutta Weisz's typology) is by far the most frequently used by Logau: it reflects on worldly and spiritual matters and is clearly didactic in intent. Close to 40 percent of Logau's epigrams are of this type. In these gnomic epigrams the bipartite structure is less apparent, and pointedness plays a less prominent role. They are reflective and often sententious; Logau calls them *Sinngedichte* (reflective poems), a term coined by Philipp von Zesen. The satiric epigram is less represented in Logau's work than commonly assumed, constituting about 20 percent of the total. Moreover, following Martial's precept, the invective in such satires is never directed against specific individuals but always against types such as greedy lawyers, corrupt judges, incompetent doctors, betrayed husbands, and vain women, who are given fictitious names. More than 20 percent of the epigrams are of the playful type, often with a satiric component. Surprisingly, given Logau's position at court, fewer than one hundred epigrams are panegyrical. Most of these address a noble person from Silesia on a specific occasion in that person's life. The remaining epigrams in the 1654 collection are mixed forms that cannot be placed in any of the four major categories.

Although many of Logau's epigrams contain autobiographical references, they do not necessarily provide reliable information about his life. He saw his poetry as a pastime, as *Nacht-Gedancken* (thoughts of the night) after a hard day's work. Some autobiographical references, such as the loss of some poems because of the war, the worries about financial matters voiced throughout the collection, or complaints about the pain of gout toward the end of his life seem quite credible. Others, however, such as the early poems on marital bliss and the later ones on marital strife, which have often been linked to his two marriages, have no proven biographical significance; they appear to be rooted in more-general topical concerns.

The topics and themes of Logau's epigrams are as varied as the life experiences of a seventeenth-century writer and courtier. Some common topics are war, soldiers, court, nobility, magistrates, taxes, the medical profession, clergy, religion, epitaphs (fictional and real), women, marriage, wine, language, poetry, issues in contemporary Germany and Silesia, and vices such as hypocrisy. While most of Logau's epigrams are not linked, there are a few cycles, such as the description of the nine virtues of a ruler or the sixty-nine epigrams based on pericopes for all Sundays and church holidays.

While many poems praise Duke Ludwig, his wife, and other rulers, about two hundred harshly criticize courtly life. The invective, however, is impersonal and does not mention names. Logau castigates such courtly vices as opportunism, careerism, egotism, hypocrisy, flattery, envy, treachery, deceit, denigration, and slander, all of which he sums up under the term *politisch* (political). Logau saw the political operator, who quickly became indispensable at the larger, absolutistic courts, as a master of gallant conversation, of deception, of ruthless social advancement, and of moral indifference. One might think that such criticism would have hurt Logau's status at the Brieg court, but the contrary was the case. The evolution of the gallant courtier was still in its infancy at Brieg; thus, his criticism of courtly life was neither intended nor perceived as criticism of the court. Its purpose was, rather, to warn the ruler of this emerging type of self-serving and smoothly operating courtier. Logau tried to convince the Silesian princes to continue their tradition of paternalistic rule; he rejected the trend toward absolutism, which relied heavily on bureaucrats of bourgeois origin with legal training and which accelerated the isolation of the ruler from the nobility. Logau implicitly held himself up as the model of the selfless, honest, and responsible noble-born servant:

> Ein Fürsten-Rath.
> Wer ist, der seinen Rath dem Herren redlich gibt?
> Der, den sein Fürst? Nein der, der seinen Fürsten liebt.
>
> (Advice for a prince.
> Who is it who gives honest advice to his prince?
> The one whom his prince [loves]? No, the one who loves his prince.)

But even Logau could not resist advancing his own interests, as his 1652 collection dedicated to Duchess Anna Sophia demonstrates.

Another recurrent theme in Logau's epigrams is praise of country life, partly motivated by his homesickness for the family estate at Brockut. The countryside is seen as an idyllic place where a person can lead a virtuous life away from court and city. The epigram "Das Dorf" (The Village) ends:

> O Feld, O werthes Feld, ich muß es nur bekennen,
> Die Höfe, sind die Höll; und Himmel du zu nennen.

(O pasture, o beloved pasture, I have to confess,
The courts are hell; and you are to be named heaven.)

Not surprisingly, nearly two hundred epigrams deal with the Thirty Years' War. In spite of the gravity of the topic, many are witty or playful, as this chronogram demonstrates

Das Jahr 1640.
GIeb, gIeb, O gIeb Vns FrIeD, O FrIeDe gIeb Vns, Gott!
FrIeD Is Vns Ia so nVtz aLs etWa LIebes Brot.

(The year 1640.
Give, give, o give us peace, o give peace to us, God!
Peace is as useful to us as dear bread.)

The single most important topic is religion; about five hundred, or one out of seven, epigrams are religious texts. Silesia at that time was threatened by the Counter Reformation, and Logau's anti-Catholic polemic is quite vocal. His anti-Calvinist views are more subdued, partly because of the widespread sympathies for Calvinism among the Silesian nobility. Logau generally expresses orthodox Lutheran views:

Dreyerley Glauben.
Der Babst, der wil durch thun: Calvin, wil durch verstehn,
In Himmel aber wil durch Glauben, Luther gehn.

(Three Faiths.
The pope wants to go to heaven through actions: Calvin through understanding,
But Luther through faith.)

Logau deals with questions of dogma polemically – not irenically, as has commonly been claimed. He condemns the Catholic belief in good works: salvation is achieved *sola fide* (through faith alone), which is *sola gratia* (a gift of God's grace). At the same time, he denounces the Calvinist doctrine of predestination in favor of the Lutheran idea that God's grace is universal as long as one does not reject the gift of faith. He also defends the Lutheran dogma of the actual presence of Christ's body and blood in the Holy Communion against the Calvinist view that Christ's presence is only symbolic. Logau, like Martin Luther, distinguishes between corporeal and spiritual being; only the spiritual aspect of the person is free.

The duchies of Liegnitz and Brieg were divided among Dukes Georg, Ludwig, and Christian by a drawing of lots on 3 June 1654. Ludwig received the duchy of Liegnitz, and Logau followed him there. To his previous duties were added the di-

rection of all court activities and the supervision of court personnel. His salary was increased by two hundred talers.

Logau died during the night of 24–25 July 1655. His apartment was so small that the viewing of the body had to be moved to a friend's residence. The funeral took place on 22 August in the Fürstliche Stiftskirche Sankt Johannis (Princely Collegiate Church of Saint John) in Liegnitz. His friend Wenzel Scherffer von Scherffenstein wrote the only funerary oration.

Bibliography:

Gerhard Dünnhaupt, *Personalbibliographien zu den Drucken des Barock,* volume 9, part 4 (Stuttgart: Hiersemann, 1991), pp. 2584–2588.

References:

Ruth Angress, *The Early German Epigram: A Study in Baroque Poetry* (Lexington: University Press of Kentucky, 1971);

Hans Dieter Becker, "Untersuchungen zum Epigramm Lessings," dissertation, University of Düsseldorf, 1977;

Wiltrud Brinkmann, "Logaus Epigramme als Gattungserscheinung," *Zeitschrift für deutsche Philologie,* 93, no. 4 (1974): 507–522;

Angelo George De Capua, "Eine Leichenrede Friedrichs von Logau," *Archiv für das Studium der neueren Sprachen und Literaturen,* 196 (1960): 147–152;

Walter Dietze, "Abriß einer Geschichte des deutschen Epigramms," in *Erbe und Gegenwart,* edited by Walter Dietze (Berlin & Weimar: Aufbau, 1972), pp. 247–391;

Adalbert Elschenbroich, "Friedrich von Logau," in *Deutsche Dichter des 17. Jahrhunderts: Ihr Leben und Werk,* edited by Harald Steinhagen and Benno von Wiese (Berlin: Schmidt, 1984), pp. 208–226;

Winfried Freund, *Die deutsche Verssatire im Zeitalter des Barock* (Düsseldorf: Bertelsmann, 1972);

Anna Hilda Fritzmann, *Friedrich von Logau: The Satirist* (Bern: Lang, 1983);

Paul Hempel, *Die Kunst Friedrichs von Logau* (Berlin: Mayer & Müller, 1917; New York: Johnson Reprint, 1967);

Peter Hess, *Epigramm* (Stuttgart: Metzler, 1989), pp. 84–93, 98–102;

Hess, "Poetologische Reflexionen in den Epigrammen von Friedrich von Logau: Versuch einer Rekonstruktion seiner Poetik," *Daphnis,* 13, no. 1–2 (1984): 299–318;

Walter Heuschkel, *Untersuchungen über Ramlers und Lessings Barbeitungen von Sinngedichten Logaus* (Jena: Kämpfe, 1901);

Ivar Larsson, *Grundzüge der Sprache Logaus* (Uppsala: Almqvist & Wiksells, 1904);

Richard Levy, *Martial und die deutsche Epigrammatik des siebzehnten Jahrhunderts* (Stuttgart: Levy & Müller, 1903);

Axel Lindqvist, "Die Motive und Tendenzen des deutschen Epigramms im 17. Jahrhundert: Einige Konturen," in *Das Epigramm: Zur Geschichte einer inschriftlichen Gattung,* edited by Gerhard Pfohl (Darmstadt: Wissenschaftliche Buchgesellschaft, 1969), pp. 287–351;

Heidrun Ludolf, *Kritik und Lob am Fürstenhof: Stilunterschiede in den Epigrammen Friedrich von Logaus* (Hildesheim: Olms, 1991);

Wilhelm Metzger, *Logaus Sprache: Versuch einer systematischen Darstellung des Laut- und Formenstandes in Logaus Sinngedichten* (München: Kastner & Callway, 1904);

Sidney H. Moore, "A Neglected Poet: Friedrich von Logau," *German Life and Letters,* new series 3 (January 1949): 13–19;

Günther C. Rimbach, "Das Epigramm und die Barockpoetik: Ansätze zu einer Wirkungsästhetik für das Zeitalter," *Jahrbuch der Deutschen Schillergesellschaft,* 14 (1970): 100–130;

Peter Schaeffer, "Humanism on Display: The Epistles Dedicatory of Georg von Logau," *Sixteenth-Century Journal,* 17 (Summer 1986): 215–223;

Ulrich Seelbach, "Die Autographen Friedrich von Logaus," *Daphnis,* 19, no. 2 (1990): 267–292;

Seelbach, "Unbekannte Gedichte Friedrich von Logaus in den Abdankungsreden des Christoph von Reydeburg," *Daphnis,* 20, no. 3–4 (1991): 531–546;

Erich Urban, *Owenus und die deutschen Epigrammatiker des XVII. Jahrhunderts* (Berlin: Felber, 1900);

Theodor Verweyen, "Friedrich von Logau," in *Deutsche Dichter,* edited by Gunter E. Grimm and Frank Rainer Max, volume 2 (Stuttgart: Reclam, 1988), pp. 163–173;

Verweyen, "Friedrich von Logau: Ein unbekanntes Gedicht und Hinweise zur Biographie des Autors," *Euphorion,* 83, no. 2 (1989): 246–260;

Jutta Weisz, *Das Epigramm in der deutschen Literatur des 17. Jahrhunderts* (Stuttgart: Metzler, 1979);

Ernst-Peter Wieckenberg, "Herrscherlob und Hofkritik bei Friedrich von Logau," in *Europäische Hofkultur im 16. und 17. Jahrhundert: Vorträge und Referate gehalten anläßlich des Kongresses des Wolfenbütteler Arbeitskreises für Renaissanceforschung und des Internationalen Arbeitskreises für Barockliteratur in der Herzog August Bibliothek Wolfenbüttel vom 4. bis 8. September 1979,* edited by August Buck, Georg Kauffmann, and others (Hamburg: Hauswedell, 1981), pp. 67–74;

Wieckenberg, "Logau – Moralist und Satiriker," in *Gedichte und Interpretationen,* volume 1, edited by Volker Meid (Stuttgart: Reclam, 1982), pp. 257–266.

Daniel Georg Morhof

(6 February 1639 – 30 July 1691)

Karl F. Otto Jr.
University of Pennsylvania

SELECTED BOOKS: *Quod bene vortat! Diatribe Juridica de Morbis et Eorum Remidiis* (Rostock: Printed by Joachim Reumann, 1658);

Epigrammatum et Jocorum Centuria Prima, popularibus dicata (Rostock, 1659);

De Ente Rationis Carmen Joculare (Rostock: Printed by Johann Keil, 1663);

Primitiae Parnassi Kiloniensis (Kiel: Joachim Reumann, 1666);

Miscellanea Poetica. Accedunt Epigrammata Selecta (Kiel: Printed by Joachim Reumann, 1666);

Venerum et Funerum Liber (Kiel: Printed by Joachim Reumann, 1667);

Veneres novae, sive Epithalamia recentiora (Kiel: Joachim Reumann, 1667);

Autoschediasmata poetica (Kiel: Joachim Reumann, 1668?);

Horae Subsecivae Poeticae (Kiel: Joachim Reumann, 1671);

Epigrammatum liber primus (Kiel: Joachim Reumann, 1671);

Epistola de scypho vitreo per certum humanae Vocis conum ruptô ad V. CL. Joahannem Danielem Maiorem (Kiel: Printed by Joachim Reumann, 1672); enlarged as *Stentor Υαλοκλασ́τησ sive de Scypho vitreo per centum humanae vocis sonum fracto ad V. CL. Dn. Johannem Danielem Majorem* (Kiel: Joachim Reumann, 1682);

De Metallorum transmutatione ad Virum Nobilissimum & Amplissimum Joelem Langelottum, Serenissimi Principis Cimbrici Archiatrum Celeberrimum Epistola (Amsterdam: Johann Jansson van Waesberge, 1673);

Unterricht von der Teutschen Sprache und Poesie, deren Uhrsprung, Fortgang und Lehrsätzen. Wobey auch von der reimenden Poeterey der Außländer mit mehren gehandelt wird (Kiel: Printed & published by Joachim Reumann, sold by Johann Sebastien Richel, 1682);

Teutsche Gedichte (Kiel: Joachim Reumann, 1682);

Otia Divina sive Carminum Sacrorum Liber (Kiel: Joachim Reumann, 1685);

Polyhistor sive De Notitia Auctorum et Rerum Commentarii. Quibus Præterea Varia ad Omnes Dis- ciplinas Consilia et Subsidia Proponuntur, 2 volumes (Lübeck: Peter Böckmann, 1688, 1692);

Vita, qua, Praeter alia, labores ejus Academici, et Scripta praecipué, tùm edenda; et affecta haec quidem partim, partim animo tantùm concepta, enumerantur: Quam item in Polyhistore edendo rationem secutus sit, indicatur. Accedunt Elogia à clarissimo quodam viro collecta; et Carmina, Maximam partem à Summis Viris Morhofiano honori consecrata, atque adeò Elogiorum ferè loco habenda (Kiel: Joachim Reumann, 1691);

Tractatus polyhistoricus de excerpendi ratione in quo varia collectionem tum in eloquentia tum in disciplina instituendi, consilia & subsidia proponuntur (Lübeck: Peter Böckmann, 1692);

Collegium Epistolicum, quod equidem, cum in vivis esset, studiis tantum privatis auditorum suorum destinavit, jam vero ob summum variumque quem adultis aeque ac junioribus in hoc scribendi genere praestare poste, usum publica luce donatum (Leipzig: Friedrich Lanckisch II's heirs, 1693); revised and enlarged as *De ratione Conscribendarum Libellus, quo de artis Epistolographicae scriptoribus tam veteribus quàm recentioribus censurae feruntur* (Lübeck: Peter Böckmann, 1694);

Commentatio de Disciplina Argutiarum (N.p., 1693); enlarged as *De Arguta Dictione Tractatus* (Lübeck: Peter Böckmann, 1705);

Opera Poetica, edited by Heinrich Muhle (Lübeck: Peter Böckmann, 1697);

Orationes et Programmata, edited by Caspar Daniel Morhof and Friedrich Morhof (Hamburg: Gottfried Liebernickel, 1698);

Dissertationes Academicæ et Epistolicæ, quibus rariora quaedam argumenta erudité tractantur, omnes: in unum Volumen collatae, et Consensu Filiorum editae, accessit Autoris Vita, quae tum Lectiones Ejus Academicas, tum Scripta edita et edenda; Elogia item ac Judicia Clarorum Virorum exhibet (Hamburg: Gottfried Liebernickel, 1699);

Delitiæ Oratoriæ Intimioris sive De Dilatione et Amplificatione Rhetorica Liber Studiosae Juventuti utilissimus

Daniel Georg Morhof; engraving by Christian Fritzsch

et a multis hactenus desideratus cum Indice Necessario (Lübeck: Peter Böckmann, 1701);

De Pvra Dictione Latina Liber, edited by Johann Lorenz Mosheim (Hannover: Nicolaus Förster & Sons, 1725);

De Legendis, Imitandis et Excerpendis Auctoribus, Libellus Posthumus, Quem in Supplementum Polyhistoris Morhofiani, ex Accurato Quodam Manuscripto Luci Nunc Primum Tradit, edited by Johann Peter Hohl (Hamburg: Brandt, 1731);

Epigrammatum Libri II (Kiel, n.d.).

OTHER: Robert Boyle, *Tractatus de cosmicis rerum qualitatibus,* edited by Morhof (Amsterdam: Johann Jansson van Wasberge / Hamburg: Gottfried Schultz, 1671);

Johann Lauremberg, *Satyra elegantissima,* edited by Morhof (Kiel: Joachim Reumann, 1684);

Titus Livius, *De Patavinitate Liviana Liber. Ubi de Urbanitate et Peregrinate Sermonis Latini Universè agitur,* edited, with an introduction, by Morhof (Kiel: Joachim Reumann, 1684);

Nicaise Bax, *Medulla Eloquentiae, et Figurae aliquot Rhetoricae,* edited, with a preface, by Morhof (Kiel: Joachim Reumann, 1685);

Antonio Maria, Conte de' Majoragio, *Philochrysus sive De Laudibus Auri Orationes duae,* edited by Morhof (Lübeck: Peter Böckmann, 1690);

Francis Quarles, *Enchiridion morale, Anglicè cura ipsius denuo editum,* edited by Morhof (Kiel: Joachim Reumann, 1691);

Johannes Dekens, S.J., *Observationes poeticae, exemplis illustratae,* edited, with a preface, by Morhof (Kiel: Joachim Reumann, 1691).

Although Daniel Georg Morhof is not considered one of the premier poets of the seventeenth century, his importance cannot be denied. He was a noted teacher of the literatures of the era; a precursor of modern-day librarians; a developer of educational institutions; and a polymath or polyhistor – that is, one who is knowledgeable in many fields and, thus, exemplifies in his person virtually the total knowledge available to his era. As a polymath,

Morhof was second in importance in his time only to the philosopher Gottfried Wilhelm Leibniz. Despite his role in educational and intellectual history, he is scarcely known in the English-speaking world.

Morhof was born on 6 February 1639 in Wismar, the son of a lawyer, Joachim Morhof, who was a notary and a secretary in the local courts, and Agnes Morhof, née Hintz. When Morhof was scarcely a year old, his mother died during the birth of a second child. As was typical during that time, he began his studies at home under the tutelage of his father. After attending school in Wismar he moved on to the gymnasium in Stettin in 1655, then, two years later, to the University of Rostock to study law. Among his law professors were Heinrich Rahn, under whose guidance Morhof wrote his first academic dissertation in 1658, and Heinrich Rudolph Redecker. Morhof immediately began to study other subjects as well, especially logic, history, and poetry. He studied Latin and German poetry with Johann Lauremberg and Andreas Tscherning, the Silesian disciple of Martin Opitz with whom Morhof had corresponded when the latter was in Stettin. Morhof's first publications – occasional poetry, such as poems of condolence – began to appear when he was eighteen.

Tscherning, who was professor of literature at the University of Rostock, died in September 1659. Joshua Cand, the court preacher in Schwerin, had brought an unpublished humorous poem Morhof had written, "Funus Ciconiae" (The Funeral of a Stork) to the attention of Gustav Adolf, Duke of Mecklenburg, who appointed professors at the university, and on 16 October 1660 Morhof, who had recently acquired a master's degree, was appointed as Tscherning's successor. He was granted a one-year leave to visit the Netherlands and England before assuming the post. In England, where he seems to have spent some time in the library at Oxford, he made the acquaintance of several leading scholars of the day and witnessed the coronation of King Charles II. On the way back to Rostock he earned a doctorate of law at the University of Franeker (Frisia) after speaking on *de jure silentio* (the law of silence) at the university chapel on 26 September 1661.

When the University of Kiel was founded in 1665 by Christian Albert, Duke of Holstein, Morhof accepted an invitation to become professor of rhetoric and literature there. As was customary at the time, he wrote a panegyric honoring the duke; he also wrote a description of the rituals to be followed at the awarding of degrees at the university. He seems to have been an extremely successful

teacher; not only German students but also foreign ones, especially the English, flocked to hear him.

Shortly after Morhof assumed his new position in Kiel, his collected poems appeared under the title *Miscellanea Poetica. Accedunt Epigrammata Selecta* (1666); the majority are in Latin, the language he generally used for his poetic works. The first part includes poems for his friends Tscherning and Adam Olearius; the second part consists mainly of Latin epigrams. Additional occasional poems appeared in a 1667 collection, *Venerum et Funerum Liber,* which consists mainly of Latin wedding poems (among them one for Olearius's daughter) and Latin poems of condolence (including one honoring Tscherning). A second selection of wedding poems, *Veneres novae,* also appeared in 1667; it is dedicated to August Friedrich, bishop of Lübeck.

In 1669 Morhof became rector of the University of Kiel; he would hold the position again in 1677, 1685, and 1690, each time for a year. Shortly after assuming the rectorship he took a second trip to Holland and England, on which he became acquainted with many of the leading scholars of Europe, including Joannes Georgius Grävius, Jacobus Gronovius, Nicolaas Heinsius, Robert Boyle, and Isaac Vos. In London he presented to the Royal Society an account of an experiment he had seen in Amsterdam, in which a Rhenish wineglass was broken by a human voice singing a note an octave above the tone the glass gave off when struck. The Royal Society was unable to replicate the experiment. Morhof was accepted into the society, but into the philosophical, not the scientific, section. On his way back to Germany he stopped in Amsterdam. On a visit to the Elzevier bookstore he was almost killed when a case of books fell on him. Resuming his journey home, he again escaped death when his ship was wrecked.

On 23 October 1671 he married Margareta Deging, the daughter of Caspar Deging, a member of the Lübeck city council. The couple had four sons, only two of whom would outlive their father. In 1672 Morhof published an account of the wineglass experiment, *Epistola de scypho vitreo per certum humanae Vocis conum ruptô ad V. CL. Joahannem Danielem Maiorem.* This publication brought him into contact with still other leading intellectuals of his day, including the Jesuit Athanasius Kircher. In 1673 he took on additional responsibilities as professor of history; in 1680 he became the university librarian when Samuel Rachel left the position.

Morhof's first important work appeared in 1682. *Unter[r]icht von der Teutschen Sprache und Poesie* (Lessons on German Language and Poetry) is divided into three parts: a historical grammar, a history of literature, and a system of poetics. The three parts do not make up a coherent whole; although the system of poetics seems to be based on the first two parts, the three parts seem to have been individually written.

To place German literature within an international context, Morhof precedes the discussion of German literary history with short characterizations of French, Italian, Spanish, English, and Dutch literature. He makes a few errors here: for example, he maintains that the Italians got all of their poetic examples from the French and that the *Ernsthafftigkeit* (seriousness) of the Spaniards means that they are scarcely able to write good poetry. He is particularly angered by the English, who, according to him, seem to think that the drama originated with them. He regards the Dutch as, in effect, the real Germans and High German as merely a dialect of Low German or Dutch.

Morhof divides the history of German literature into three periods: from ancient times to Charlemagne; from Charlemagne to Opitz; and contemporary literature. Although he has dredged up many details about early German literature, he does nothing to make it more understandable, since he seems not to have understood it himself. He recommends that libraries and archives be thoroughly searched to find early literary manuscripts, which should then all be published. The account of the second period begins with a discussion of the merits of Charlemagne for German culture. Much of the material on the first golden age of German literature is extracted from Melchior Goldast's commentaries; Morhof spends considerable time on the *Meistersänger* and discusses the Limburg Chronicle. As he approaches his own day the poets are simply listed, often with no regard to chronology. The dawn of German-language poetry arrives with Opitz, who is recognized primarily for his historical importance; Morhof praises Tscherning, Paul Fleming, and Christian Weise's satires. Sigmund von Birken, Johann Klaj, Georg Philipp Harsdörffer, and Christian Hoffmann von Hoffmannswaldau receive briefer mention. The section concludes with an enumeration of women writers, among whom he especially praises Sibylle Schwarz.

Morhof begins the section on poetics with a discussion of Scandinavian poetry, especially the Eddas and other early documents. Morhof was the first to praise this literature, which later became important for German poetry and research. On the question of whether German or Scandinavian poetry is older, he decides for German. The discussion closes with a brief description of the literature of Finland and Lapland. In his poetic theory Morhof is not interested in teaching others to write, as, for example, Harsdörffer was, but in describing various poetic forms and their historical development; therefore, this section is not filled with rules and prescriptions. Nature, he says, teaches people the art of rhyming. He devotes considerable space to the development of the novel; he claims that the modern novel originated in France, and he notes the role played by French women writers, especially Madeleine de Scudéry.

Unterricht von der Teutschen Sprache und Poesie is the most important work of literary research of the seventeenth century. It is the first attempt at a general history of modern literature, though, since Morhof was not a historian, the work is not really literary history but a compilation or enumeration. There are manifold errors, and he seems not to have mastered all the literature he discusses. Nevertheless, one can only admire the astonishing breadth of his knowledge, his eye for important works, and the connections he draws between language and literature, between literature and national characteristics, and between literary history and poetics.

The book was highly successful, although readers were often quicker to point to the errors than to see the merits of the work. Those literary historians who immediately followed Morhof, such as Albrecht Christian Rotth, Magnus Daniel Omeis, and Weise, scarcely mention him, even though they are clearly inferior to him, but Johann Gottfried Herder is quick to mention Morhof as *the* source for his own work.

Morhof 's wife died in June 1687. His second important work, *Polyhistor,* had its origin in his academic lectures, which, for the most part, were given without notes. The first two parts of the lengthy work appeared in one volume in 1688; the third was published posthumously in 1692. The introduction makes it clear that the work is a reaction against the increasing disregard for general education; both teachers and students, according to Morhof, are becoming specialized at too early a stage in their careers. Morhof's view is that of the medieval Scholastic approach to learning, according to which it is only after one has acquired a general acquaintance with the whole of human knowledge that one should begin to specialize in subjects such as theology, law, medicine, mathematics, or astronomy. The humanists were the first to undermine the Scholastic approach, in part because the increase in knowledge was making it more and more difficult to claim to know everything. But, Morhof says, no individual area of knowledge can be learned by itself, since all are branches of the same tree; one has to see all things in context and understand how they are connected to one another. Morhof was especially critical of pansophism, a method adopted by many universities that called for students to learn a mixture of three or four "practical" disciplines without regard for mathematics, rhetoric, poetics, history, or natural sciences. What sets Morhof apart from the leading pedagogical theorist of his era, Johann Amos Comenius, is his recommendation that every student become a polymath.

The three parts of the work are "Polyhistor litterarius," "Polyhistor philosophicus," and "Polyhistor practicus." The first part is divided into the subsections "Liber bibliothecarius," which played a role in the development of library science; "Liber methodicus," in which Morhof gives his ideas on teaching methods (among the educational theories he discusses are those of Comenius, Desiderius Erasmus, Philipp Melanchthon, Johann Sturm, and Johann Joachim Becher); "Liber paraskeuasticus," in which he talks about the widespread practice of collecting quotations and creating florilegia; "Liber grammaticus," which deals with the origins of language and writing, the invention of movable type by Johannes Gutenberg, the possibility of the existence of a first or oldest language, and the various European vernaculars; "Liber criticus"; "Liber oratorius"; and "Liber poeticus."

The second part, "Polyhistor philosophicus," is also subdivided into several sections. The first deals, in fifteen chapters, with the history of philosophy: the Pythagoreans; Socrates and his followers; the Stoics; the Epicureans; the Skeptics; the Platonists; Aristotle and the Peripatetics; the Greek, Arabic, and Latin explications of the works of Aristotle and his opponents; the Scholastics; the nominalists; the realists; René Descartes; Thomas Hobbes; Paracelsus; and Comenius. The second section discusses principles and general concepts of philosophy, as well as such qualities of matter as place and emptiness, time, and motion. The Copernican heliocentric view of the solar system is correct, he says, and the ecclesiastical opposition to it will eventually disappear; Giordano Bruno should never have lost his life over the issue. The notion that there are only four basic elements is incorrect, but a better theory has not yet been proposed. The third section deals with such topics as light, colors (Sir Isaac Newton's theory of color is mentioned), fire, cold, air, water, earth, meteors, earthquakes, minerals,

magnets, jewels, plants, and animals. The fourth major section of this part deals with the mathematical sciences, with logic, and with metaphysics. In each case Morhof's main aim is to tell the reader where to find books on the topic; he adds little information of his own. The third book, "Polyhistor practicus," deals with the four schools into which universities of the era were divided: philosophy (ethics, politics, economics, and history), theology, law, and medicine. In *Polyhistor* Morhof provides an example of that for which he says others should strive: to have at one's command the entire corpus of knowledge currently available, but to use one's judgment to decide which aspects of this knowledge are useful.

In 1691 Morhof undertook, against his doctor's advice, a trip to the spas in Pyrmont. The trip and the treatment he received seem to have been too much for him: on 30 July 1691, on the way home, he died while visiting his parents-in-law in Lübeck. He is buried in the cemetery of Saint Catherine's Church in that city.

Biographies:

A. Clarmundus [Johann Christoph Rüdiger], "Daniel Georg Morhof," in his *Vitae clarissimorum in re literaria virorum, das ist: Lebensbeschreibung etlicher hauptgelehrter Männer* (Wittenberg: Ludwig, 1708), pp. 195-252;

Marie Kern, *Daniel Georg Morhof* (Landau Palatinate: Vorderpfälzische Genossenschafts Druckerei, 1928);

Wilhelm Schmidt-Biggemann, "Daniel Georg Morhof," in *Deutsche Schriftsteller im Porträt: Das Zeitalter des Barock,* edited by Martin Bircher (Munich: Beck, 1979), pp. 116-117.

References:

Italo Michele Battafarano, "Vico und Morhof," in his *Von Andreae zu Vico* (Stuttgart: Heinz, 1979), pp. 171-198;

H. Bergholz, "Daniel Georg Morhof – Overlooked Precursor of Library Science," *Libri: International Library Review,* 14, no. 1 (1964): 44-50;

Thomas Birch, *The History of the Royal Society of London,* volume 2 (London: Millar, 1756-1757), pp. 450, 453;

Friedrich Blume, "A. Pflegers Kieler Universitätsoden," *Archiv für Musikforschung,* 8 (1943): 5-26;

Albertus Fecamp, *De D. G. Morhofio, Leibnitii in cognoscendis linguis et germanico sermone reformando præcursore* (Montpellier: Grollier, 1894);

R. Hodermann, *Universitätsvorlesungen in deutscher Sprache um die Wende des XVII. Jahrhunderts* (Friedrichsroda: Schmidt, 1891);

Knut Kiesant, "Zur Rezeption spätmittelalterlicher Literatur im 17. Jahrhundert," in his *Deutsche Literatur des Mittelalters,* volume 3 (Greifswald: Ernst-Moritz-Arndt-Universität, 1986), pp. 376–385;

Sigmund von Lempicki, *Geschichte der deutschen Literaturwissenschaft bis zum Ende des 18. Jahrhunderts,* second edition (Göttingen: Vandenhoeck & Ruprecht, 1968), pp. 150–173;

Dieter Lohmeier, "Das gotische Evangelium und die cimbrischen Heiden: Daniel Georg Morhof, Johan Daniel Major und der Gotizismus," *Lynchos* (1977–1978): 54–70;

Henning Ratjen, "Daniel Georg Morhof," *Jahrbücher für die Landeskunde der Herzogthümer Schleswig-Holstein und Lauenburg,* 1 (1858): 18–32;

Eugen Reichel, "Aus Daniel Georg Morhofs Schriften," *Zeitschrift für Deutsche Wortforschung,* 13, no. 3 (1911/1912): 188–212;

Karl-Ludwig Selig, "Los proverbios españoles de Daniel Georg Morhof," in *Estudios sobre el Siglo de Oro en homenaje a Raymond R. MacCurdy,* edited by Angel Gonzalez, Tamara Holzapfel, Alfred Rodriguez, and others (Albuquerque: University of New Mexico Press / Madrid: Catedra, 1983), pp. 327–332;

Richard Treitschke, "Über Daniel Morhof und seinen Unterricht von der deutschen Sprache und Poesie," *Literarhistorisches Taschenbuch,* 6 (1848): 439–460;

Friedrich L. C. Volbehr, *Beiträge zur Geschichte der Christian-Albrechts-Universität zu Kiel* (Kiel: Universitäts Buchhandlung, 1876);

Conrad Wiedemann, "Polyhistors Glück und Ende: Von Daniel Georg Morhof zum jungen Lessing," in *Festschrift Gottfried Weber: Zu seinem 70. Geburtstag überreicht von Frankfurter Kollegen und Schülern,* edited by Heinz Otto Burger and Klaus von See (Bad Homburg: Gehlen, 1967), pp. 215–235;

Roger Zuber, "Litterature et urbanité," in *Le Statut de la litterature: Malanges offerts a Paul Benichou,* edited by Marc Fumaroli (Geneva: Droz, 1982), pp. 87–96.

Johann Michael Moscherosch
(Philander von Sittewalt)
(7 March 1601 – 4 April 1669)

Sigmund J. Barber
Grinnell College

BOOKS: *Visiones de Don Quevedo. Wunderliche vnd Warhafftige Gesichte Philanders von Sittewalt. Jn welchen Aller Welt Wesen, Aller Mänschen Händel, mit jhren Natürlichen Farben, der Eitelkeit, Gewalts, Heucheley vnd Thorheit bekleidet: offentlich auff die Schauw geführet, als in einem Spiegel dargestellet, vnd von Männiglichen gesehen werden,* as Philander von Sittewald (Strasbourg: Printed by Johann Philipp Mülb, 1642); republished as *Wunderliche und warhafftige Gesichte Philanders von Sittewald, das ist Straff-Schrifften Hanß-Michael Moscherosch von Wilstädt* (Strasbourg: Johann Philipp Mülb & Josias Städel, 1650);

Anderer Theil der Gesichte Philanders von Sittewalt (Strasbourg: Johann Philipp Mülb, 1643); enlarged, 1643); enlarged as *Gesichte Philanders von Sittewald, das ist, Straff-Schrifften Hanß-Michael Moscheroschen von Wilstädt* (Strasbourg: Johann Philipp Mülb & Josias Städel, 1650);

Epigrammatum Ioh: Michaelis Moscherosch, Germani. Centuria Prima (Strasbourg: Johann Philipp Mülb, 1643; enlarged edition, Strasbourg: Johann Philipp Mülb & Josias Städel, 1649; enlarged, 1650); enlarged edition, edited by Ernst Bogislav Moscherosch (Frankfurt am Main: Published by Sebastian Röhner, printed by Daniel Fievet, 1665);

Insomnis Cura Parentum. Christliches Vermächtnuß. oder, Schuldige Vorsorg eines Treuen Vatters. bey jetzigen Hochbetrübtsten gefährlichsten Zeitten den seinigen zur letzten Nachricht hinderlassen (Strasbourg: Johann Philipp Mülb, 1643); enlarged as *Omnis Cura Parentum Christliches Vermächtnüß oder Schuldige Vorsorg eines getreuen Vaters bei jtzigen höchstbetrübeste gefährlichsten Zeiten den seinigen zur letzten Nachricht hinderlassen. Nebenst einem Tractätlein so erstlich in Englischer Sprach beschrieben, aber nunmehr ins Teutsche übergesetzt, vnd diesen Titul Testament So eine Mutter jhrem noch vngebornen Kind gemacht vnd hinterlassen* (Strasbourg, 1647);

Johann Michael Moscherosch; engraving by Peter Aubry

Méditation sur la Vie de Jésus Christ (Strasbourg: Johann Philipp Mülb, 1646);

Technologie Allemande et Françoise Das ist, Kunst-übliche Wort-Lehre. Teutsch und Frantzösisch, completed by Hans Caspar Herrmann (Strasbourg: Josias Städel, 1656);

Die Patientia von H. M. Moscherosch, Nach der Handschrift der Stadtbibliothek zu Hamburg zum erstenmal herausgegeben, edited by Parisier, Forschungen zur neueren Litteraturgeschichte, volume 2 (Munich: Franke & Hausshalter, 1897).

Editions: *Insomnis Cura Parentum,* 2 volumes, edited by Ludwig Pariser, Neudrucke deutscher Litteraturwerke des XVI. und XVII. Jahrhunderts, volumes 108, 109 (Halle: Niemeyer, 1893);

Visiones de Don Quevedo (Hildesheim: Olms, 1974).

OTHER: Francesco de Quevedo y Villegas, *Les Visiones de Don Francesco de Quevedo Villegas. Oder Wunderbahre Satÿrische gesichte verteuscht durch Philander von Sittewald,* translated by Moscherosch (Strasbourg: Printed & published by Johann Philipp Mülb, 1640);

Samuel Bernard, *Anleitung zu einem Adelichen Leben. Jn welcher abgebildet wird, waß Adelicher Jugend zu lesen, zu lernen, zu vben anständig vnd nöthig ist. Erstlich von Samuel Bernhardt jn Frantzösischer Sprach beschrieben. Hernach jns Wälsche vnd Deutsche vbergesetzt: vnd jetzo wiederumb zum Truck verschafft,* translated by Moscherosch (Strasbourg: Johann Philipp Mülb, 1645);

Philanders von Sittewald Holländische Sybille, jetzigen Zustand des Reichs, und dessen Friedens-Handlungen betreffend, auß der Holländischen in Hoch-Teutsche Sprache versetzt, translated by Moscherosch (N.p., 1647);

Jacob Wimpheling, *Tutschland Jacob Wympfflingers von Slettstatt, zu Ere der Statt Straßburg vnd des Rinstroms,* translated by Moscherosch (Strasbourg: Mülb, 1648);

Desiderius Erasmus, *Epistola: Imago Reipublicae Argentinensis,* edited by Moscherosch (Strasbourg: Mülb, 1649);

Wimpheling, *Cis Rhenum Germania. Recusa Post CXLVIII. annos,* edited by Moscherosch (Strasbourg: Johann Pickel, 1649);

Wimpheling, *Catalogus Episcoporum Argentinensium. ad sesquiseculum desideratus. Restituit cum Supplemento et Notis,* edited by Moscherosch (Strasbourg: Johann Andreae's heirs, 1651);

Georg Gumpelzhaimer, *L. A. Dissertatio De Politico. auctior prodit opera & studio,* edited by Moscherosch (Strasbourg: Published by Eberhard Zetzner, 1652);

Gumpelzhaimer, *Gymnasma de Exercitiis Academicorum,* edited by Moscherosch (Strasbourg: Published by Eberhard Zetzner, 1652).

Johann Michael Moscherosch is one of the most important representatives of German bourgeois culture in the seventeenth century. An erudite man, he was the most vocal and vehement critic of the dangers of foreign influence on German culture; no other writer of the period was filled with a comparable fervor. Moscherosch wove into his writing an extraordinary amount of autobiographical detail and presents to today's reader, as does hardly another writer of his era, his reflections on the political, social, and religious issues of one of the most devastating periods in German history: the Thirty Years' War. In carrying forth the tradition of the great satiric writers of the sixteenth century, Moscherosch inspired the travelogues and satiric writings of the latter part of the seventeenth century, such as the works of Johann Jakob Christoffel von Grimmelshausen. Although there has been increased scholarly attention to Moscherosch since the mid 1980s, proper assessment of his oeuvre is hampered by the lack of modern critical editions.

Moscherosch was born on 7 March 1601 in Willstätt, near Strasbourg, to Michael Moscherosch, a well-respected farmer and manager of the church property of the county of Hanau-Lichtenberg, and Veronika Moscherosch, née Beck. By the time Moscherosch was eleven the local schoolmaster could no longer fill the needs of the intellectually gifted child, who began to attend the Strasbourg Latin School. Moscherosch was a diligent student whose parents provided him with enough money to assemble a personal library of several hundred volumes. Moscherosch would continue to collect books for the rest of his life; the library he would bequeath to one of his sons would contain almost twenty-three hundred volumes. He was also one of the first people ever to subscribe to a newspaper, which, given the budget of a student, demonstrates a unique eagerness to be well informed.

In Strasbourg, where he received a traditional rigorous Humanistic education, Moscherosch came into contact with several teachers who would have a lasting influence on him. The first was Caspar Brülow, who awakened in Moscherosch a love for poetry; Moscherosch's patriotism and respect for the Germanic past also stemmed from his study under Brülow, with whom he developed a personal friendship. Johann Paul Crusius also formed a close relationship with Moscherosch because of their shared literary interests.

In 1619 Moscherosch began to keep a Schreibkalender (memorandum book), in which he made short notes on a daily basis. This somewhat laconic diary gives the reader insight into the years 1619 through 1622 and 1629 to 1630. The early entries deal mainly with school, events in the city, the weather, and other such mundane matters. But as the Thirty Years' War reached Alsace, descriptions of its ravages become the main focus. On 20 August 1620 Moscherosch writes: "bese Zeit, beß geschrey. werden wohl Christi weißagungen Erfüllet. herr Gott erbarme dich" (Bad times, bad clamor. Surely Christ's prophesies are being fulfilled. Lord have mercy). The remembrance of the peaceful prewar world and a yearning for tranquillity remained with him throughout the war years.

In 1621 Moscherosch graduated with honors, and with the elevation of the Strasbourg Latin School to the status of a university Moscherosch could continue his studies there. At this time he came under the tutelage of the well-known professor of history and rhetoric Matthias Bernegger. From Bernegger, Moscherosch learned to see history as a key to contemporary politics, a guide for practical activity. Bernegger's colleague Laurentius Walliser introduced Moscherosch to the writings of Aristotle, but Walliser's influence on Moscherosch was not so much in the academic as in the ethical sphere. Moscherosch saw in Walliser the embodiment of proper moral behavior, the merging of ethical theory and practice. The discrepancy between theory and practice became a fundamental concern for Moscherosch and the basis for his activity as a satirist.

In 1624 Moscherosch took the examination for the master's degree and emerged as the best of the twenty-one candidates. At this point he set out on the travels that were expected of students prior to embarking on specialized studies. During such a *tour à la mode* the student was to broaden his horizons by studying at other universities as well as gathering practical experience. Moscherosch first went to Geneva, where, having given up his earlier plan to become a theologian, he began to study law. In 1625 he went on to Paris. These travels would give him much material for his later writings.

In 1626 Moscherosch returned to Strasbourg, but the war and pestilence had taken their toll. Unable to count on the financial support of his family, he ended his formal education and found a position as Hofmeister (private tutor) to the sons of Count Johann Philipp II of Leiningen-Dagsburg at the Hartenburg, the count's castle in the Rhenish Palatinate. Moscherosch had a quick temper and was intolerant of behavior that did not conform to his strict standards, and, after serving for just under two years, he was discharged from his post in June 1628 for dealing too severely with the count's eldest son.

This first experience of life at court provided Moscherosch with the impetus for "Patientia, ein traurig Gespräch" (Patientia, a Melancholy Dialogue); the unfinished work, which consists of trochaic quatrains with German and Latin prose insertions, as well as dialogues and prayers, was not published until 1897. Moscherosch introduces "Patientia" as the "Hertzliches wehklagen eines von seinen heimlichen Feinden angefochtenen, geängstigten undt verfolgten Christen" (heartfelt lamentations of an anxious, persecuted Christian, attacked by his secret enemies). Moscherosch, as "der Geängstigte" (the anxious one), complains to a fictitious friend about his bitter and disappointing experiences at the Hartenburg and the intrigues he witnessed at the court: "was ich redete, das wardt auffgefangen, hien undt her getragen mit Lügen vermehret undt heftig verbösert. Sagt ich etwas zu dem, das wuste der andere, redete ich viel, da war ich ein schwäzer, redete ich wenig da war ich ein bloch, lachte ich da war ich ein Narr, sahe ich Ernstlich, da war ich ein *saturnus;* ia auch das ienige so mir zu thun befohlen worden, das war nicht recht, es war alles sorge undt noth ... was ist hie für ein schröckliches Leben, ia Leben ohne Leben, der todt were ia besser als ein Ewiges Leiden" (whatever I said was picked up, carried here and there, augmented by lies and made severely malicious. If I said something to one, the other knew about it; if I talked a lot, I was called a babbler; If I didn't say much, then I was a blockhead; if I laughed, I was a fool; if I looked serious, then I was a sourpuss; yes, even what I was directed to do was not right; it was all grief and sorrow ... what a miserable life it is here, actually life without life; death would be better than eternal suffering). This view of life at court as hellish would become a recurrent theme in Moscherosch's writings.

Some critics have seen the melancholy mood that pervades this work as an expression of Moscherosch's perennial anxiety and have presented the author as a weak man who suffered from deep inner conflicts. This view has some merit, for complaints about Moscherosch's disproportionate share of misfortune can be seen throughout his works. But his conservative view of a divinely ordained social order, a view shaped by his Lutheran piety, advocates an attitude of resigned acceptance — the express lesson of *Patientia*. One should also keep in mind that the early stages of the Thirty Years' War engendered debates among the educated in Strasbourg about theodicy and became a source of religious doubt. It was in this climate that *Patientia* was conceived.

In 1628 Moscherosch, though still unemployed, married Esther Ackerman. The following year his former teacher and good friend Crusius died; Moscherosch attested to the extent of Crusius's influence on him in a poem: "Nunc CRUSI cineres tuos saluto! Qui me plus oculis tuis amabas, / Te Ducem prius & Patrem vocabam" (Now Crusius I greet your ashes! You who loved me more than your eyes, / You I called my guide and even more – Father). Moscherosch applied to succeed Crusius as professor of poetry at the University of Strasbourg; he did not receive the appointment, but by August 1630 he had a position as Amtmann (land steward) for Count Peter Ernst of Kriechingen.

The next few years brought Moscherosch much sorrow. His and Esther's first child died shortly after birth; their second child also died; and in 1632, shortly after the birth of their son Ernst Ludwig, Esther herself died. In 1633 Moscherosch married Maria Barbara Paniel. From 1633 to 1635 Moscherosch experienced firsthand the ravages of war. Kriechingen lost one-third of its population, mainly due to the plague brought in by the troops. Willstätt was pillaged, and Moscherosch's parents had to flee to Strasbourg after losing most of their possessions. By November 1635 Count Peter Ernst was dead. The Moscheroches left Kriechingen; but Maria became ill along the way and died on 6 November, before the family reached Strasbourg.

Shortly after arriving in Strasbourg, Moscherosch was asked by Duke Ernst Bogislav of Croy-Arschot to become administrator of the duke's lands in Finstingen. In 1636 Moscherosch married Anna Maria Kilburger, a choice driven by pragmatic concerns: he needed a mother for his son, and she came from one of the most notable families in Finstingen and could be helpful to Moscherosch in establishing himself in society. They would be together for thirty-two years and have ten children.

In Finstingen, Moscherosch published *Les Visiones de Don Francesco de Qvevedo Villegas. Oder Wunderbahre Satÿrische gesichte* (The Visions of Don Francesco de Quevedo Villegas; or, Wonderful Satiric Visions, 1640), a free translation of *Sueños* (1627; translated as *Visions,* 1640), by the Spanish author Francisco de Quevedo y Villegas; actually, Moscherosch used a French adaptation by the Sieur de la Geneste (1633) as the basis for his own work. In 1642 Moscherosch published a second edition, *Visiones de Don Quevedo. Wunderliche und Warhafftige Gesichte Philanders von Sittewalt* (Visions of Don Quevedo; or, Wonderful and True Visions of Philander of Sittewalt) – Sittewalt is an anagram for Willstätt – but he had so heavily reworked the original chapters by Quevedo and had added so many of his own experiences to them that the work was no longer a translation but rather a loose adaptation of *Sueños.* Moscherosch also added four original new chapters (visions). He kept adding to the work until the complete edition appeared in two parts in 1650 – the original seven chapters in the first part and Moscherosch's own seven chapters in the second part. The many authorized editions, plus sev-

Title page for the first edition of Moscherosch's epigrams, published in 1643; enlarged editions appeared in 1649, 1650, and 1665.

eral pirated editions, attest to the immense popularity of the work, which is generally known as the *Gesichte.*

Moscherosch gives his *Gesichte* a unity that is absent in *Sueños* by setting the visions in the context of a travelogue that is held together by the experiences and comments of Philander. Through the travels of Philander, Moscherosch reveals the shortcomings of the society he sees. His satire is usually directed not at individuals but at groups, such as doctors, lawyers, students, the nobility, beggars, soldiers, and so forth. Rather than describing the vices he is criticizing, he creates portraits of typical representatives of those vices. Moscherosch also provides Philander with a guide, Expertus Robertus, a character who does not appear in either the Spanish or French model. Robertus probes beneath the superficial and misleading surfaces of events and interprets them for Philander; thus, he is a mouthpiece through whom Moscherosch can preach to the reader from within the text.

In the *Gesichte* one can see clearly Moscherosch's self-appointed role of moral teacher and reformer. For example, in the chapter "A la mode Kehrauss" (A Cleaning Out of the à la Mode) he declares that the Germans should cast off their French habits, language, and clothes since the French are "im Sauffen den redlichen Teutschen, in Unreinigkeit den hitzigen Italiänern, in Unbarmhertzigkeit den strengen Spaniern, in Gottslästern und verläugnen aller Welt weit überlegen. Und dannoch sind wir Teutsche ins gemein so Alber, dass wir solche Völcker, als wunder, in Kleidung und Wesen nachahmen und äffen; auch wann sie schon einen Rock mit schällen trügen" (far ahead of the upright Germans in boozing, the hot-blooded Italians in uncleanness, the stern Spaniards in harshness, and in blaspheming and disavowing they surpass the entire world. In spite of all this, we Germans are in general so foolish that we imitate and ape such people in dress and conduct as marvels, even if they already wore a coat with bells [that is, fool's clothing]). This denunciation of the affectation of dress, manners, and language that invaded Germany through the courts during the seventeenth century attests not so much to hatred on Moscherosch's part of all things foreign, as past critics claimed, as to love for Germany. Moscherosch repeatedly points to glorious examples of German history to show his degenerate contemporaries how far they have fallen and to encourage them to accomplish great things. He thinks that each culture should maintain its own values; for Moscherosch, the danger in foreign influence is its potential to make Germans contemptuous of their own heritage. Moscherosch, however, bases his idealization of old Germanic values on a wholly uncritical view of the past.

Next to "A la mode Kehrauss," "Soldatenleben" (A Soldier's Life) is the best-known and most accomplished chapter of the *Gesichte*. Using soldiers' idiom, Moscherosch vividly shows the devastating effects of the war and how it confounds human relations and values. For example, Philander compares the behavior of the soldiers to what he learned as a child in catechism:

Aber mein Gott, was wunderliche Theologiam, unnd H. Schrifft, was für einen Herr Gott müssen diese Leuthe haben? wie können sie Glück, Heyl unnd Segen haben? wie solte müglich sein, daß sie nicht mit Leib und Seel verdampt werden solten? indem sie die Gebott Gottes gerad umbkehren vnd freuentlich sagen:

Der ist des Teuffels, der barmhertzig ist.
Der ist des Teuffels, der nicht tödtet.
Der ist des Teuffels, der nicht alles nimpt.
Der ist des Teuffels, der nicht alles redet.
Der ist des Teuffels, der nicht fluchet, sauffet, huret.
Der ist des Teuffels, der bettet.
Der ist des Teuffels, der der frömbste ist.
Der ist des Teuffels, der in die Kirche gehet.
Der ist des Teuffels, der Allmosen gibt. etc.

Und wann sie einen mit grausamlicher Marter ermorden, noch Schertz vnd Vexier darauß machen, als ob es nur gespielet wäre, und sagen, sie haben einen schlaffen gelegt, nidergelegt, schlaffen gezündet, das Liecht außgelöscht, etc. Wem solte nicht ob diesen grewlichen Dingen grawen?

(But my Lord, what a peculiar theology and Holy Scriptures, and what kind of Lord God must these people have? How can they have good fortune, salvation, and God's blessing? How is it possible that they won't be damned in body and soul, since they turn God's commandments inside out and say impiously:

He who is merciful belongs to the devil.
He who does not kill belongs to the devil.
He who doesn't take everything belongs to the devil.
He who doesn't say everything belongs to the devil.
He who doesn't curse, booze, or go whoring belongs to the devil.
He who prays belongs to the devil.
He who is the most pious belongs to the devil.
He who goes to church belongs to the devil.
He who gives alms belongs to the devil, etc.

And when they murder someone with cruel torture, and even joke and tease about it as if it were only a game, and say that they have put someone to sleep, laid him down, kindled sleep, turned out the light, etc., who wouldn't shudder at the thought of such ghastly things?)

Few documents of the period have the force of "Soldatenleben." Grimmelshausen's *Der Abenteuerliche Simplicissimus Teutsch* (The Adventurous Simplicissimus German, 1669), the best-known novel based on the Thirty Years' War, was modeled on Moscherosch's work.

In 1641 Moscherosch was attacked by a troop of soldiers and marauders while he was working in fields that belonged to his wife's family outside the city. He escaped, but some of his hired hands and all of his livestock were killed. The constant threat of death plus the feeling of responsibility toward his family brought about by the birth of his daughter Ernestine Amely shortly after the attack prompted him to write *Insomnis Cura Parentum* (Sleepless Concern of Parents) in just one week; it would not appear in print, however, until 1643. Moscherosch shares his anxieties with the reader:

> Ich wündsche aber, wer dises Wercklein nach meinem Absehen recht lesen wolte, daß er sich fest einbilden könte; Als ob er wäre mit feindes Volck umb und umbgeben, könte keinen schritt oder tritt thun ohne Gefahr lebens, müste sorgen es stünde ein Bluthund hinder ihm unnd wolte ihn niderstossen. . . . Wann er sich dieses alles und noch mehreres fest einbilden könte, so wirde er unserer Noth, darin ich dieses schreibe, ein theil verstehen mögen. Dann alles Ellend zu erzehlen ist unmüglich.

> (I hope that he who wishes to read this little work according to my intentions can imagine clearly what it would be like if he were surrounded by enemies, couldn't venture one step without being in mortal danger, had to be concerned that some bloodthirsty person stood behind him and wished to strike him down. . . . If he could well imagine all this and much more, then he could somewhat understand the distress in which we find ourselves as I write this. For to tell all of the misery is impossible.)

The model for *Insomnis Cura Parentum* was the immensely popular *The Mother's Legacie to Her Unborne Childe* (1624), by Elizabeth Joceline. Moscherosch did not translate the English work but used it as an inspiration for his own testament to his wife and children. *Insomnis Cura Parentum,* which established Moscherosch's reputation as a pedagogical author, is a compendium of bourgeois conduct and ethical child rearing that allows the reader insight into everyday life in a middle-class household of the time. The work is dedicated to Johannis Schmidt, a Strasbourg theologian and church president who was a leader of a reform movement aimed at awakening Lutherans to an intensification of personal piety. Although *Insomnis Cura Parentum* has received little scholarly attention, Moscherosch's contemporaries considered it to be just as significant as the *Gesichte,* and it was reprinted many times.

In 1642 Moscherosch moved his family back to Strasbourg. In May of the following year he accepted the position of secretary to Friedrich R. Mockel, commander of the Swedish occupation force in the nearby citadel of Benfeld. During the same year *Insomnis Cura Parentum,* the second edition of *Gesichte,* and the first edition of his Latin epigrams all appeared in print. Moscherosch, who acknowledges John Owen and Matthäus Zuber as exemplary masters of the genre, saw the epigram as a shorter form of satire, and his epigrams take up the same themes as his longer writings. Consisting mostly of short, witty verses with didactic or moralistic content, epigrams were a significant part of his literary activity from his school years until 1649; a complete edition was published by his son Ernst Bogislav in 1665. The epigrams have been accorded the least amount of critical attention of any of Moscherosch's works.

In 1645 Moscherosch became Fiskal (administrator) in the Strasbourg police department; his main responsibility was writing and enforcing decrees to maintain the manners and morals of the citizens in regard to such matters as smoking, night roving, dueling, and student conduct. Also in 1645 Moscherosch was accepted as a member of the prestigious Fruchtbringende Gesellschaft (Fruit-bringing Society), whose goals were to preserve the purity of the German language and to uphold the nation's social and cultural values. Each member had a society nickname; Moscherosch was known as Der Träumende (The Dreamer), an allusion to the visions of Philander. Finally, in 1645 he translated Samuel Bernard's *Tableau des ateliers de jeune gentilhomme* (1607) as *Anleitung zu einem Adelichen Leben* (Instructions for a Noble Life), continuing the role of educator he had taken up with *Insomnis Cura Parentum.* The next year he wrote *Méditation sur la Vie de Jésus Christ* (Meditations on the Life of Jesus Christ).

The Thirty Years' War ended in 1648. As part of the peace treaty all of Alsace except the city of Strasbourg was ceded to France. The historical works Moscherosch subsequently translated or edited reflect his patriotic fervor for his native region and for Germany. For example, *Tutschland* (Germania, 1648), his translation of *Cis Rhenum Germania* (1501), by the Alsatian humanist Jacob Wimpheling, countered French claims to Alsace. In 1649 he brought out a new edition of the original Latin version of Wimpheling's work.

Although Moscherosch's satire in *Gesichte* was usually directed at groups, there were individuals who believed that they recognized themselves in the work; thus, he amassed many enemies. The students in Strasbourg, whom Moscherosch had antagonized with the many edicts he had directed at them, also let their opposition to him be known. Finally, the Lutheran reform initiatives, with which Moscherosch had allied himself with his dedication of *Insomnis Cura Parentum* to Schmidt, had also fallen into disfavor in Strasbourg. Thus, with public sentiment against him, Moscherosch was accused of adultery and forced to resign his post with the police department in January 1656.

The following month he became counselor to Count Friedrich Kasimir of Hanau-Lichtenberg, under whom he had served briefly in 1629. In December 1660, after the count learned of Moscherosch's dismissal in Strasbourg, Moscherosch was compelled to resign this post as well. His time in Hanau and the next several years were a period of decline for Moscherosch. He published nothing of any consequence in Hanau or afterward, as he traveled in search of employment so that he could support his family. In a letter of 11 December 1660 to Count Friedrich Kasimir he poignantly describes his situation: "Hir bin ich persona misera, accusata et quasi cum infamia relegata und muß anfangen bücher schreiben gegen die meß, daß ich mich erhalte . . ." (Here I am a wretched person, accused and virtually driven out in disgrace, and must begin writing books for the fair in order to survive). He could still count on the popular *Gesichte* to bring in some money, but in letters after 1660 he complained constantly about his family's meager lifestyle. Moscherosch wanted to return to Strasbourg, but his attempts to find a position there were unsuccessful. In 1669, on the way to Frankfurt, where his son Ernst Bogislav was a teacher, Moscherosch became ill; he died in Worms on 4 April.

Bibliographies:

Arthur Bechtold, *Kritisches Verzeichnis der Schriften Johann Michael Moscheroschs* (Munich: Stobbe, 1922);

Gerhard Dünnhaupt, *Personalbibliographien zu den Drucken des Barock,* volume 9, part 4 (Stuttgart: Hiersemann, 1991), pp. 2849–2886.

Biographies:

Stefan Grunwald, *A Biography of Johann Michael Moscherosch (1601–1669)* (Bern: Lang, 1969);

Walter E. Schäfer, *Johann Michael Moscherosch: Staatsmann. Satiriker und Pädagoge im Barockzeitalter* (Munich: Beck, 1982);

Schäfer and Wilhelm Kühlmann, *Frühbarocke Stadtkultur am Oberrhein: Studien zum literarischen Werdegang J. M. Moscheroschs (1601–1669)* (Berlin: Schmidt, 1983).

References:

Wolfgang Peter Ahrens, "Johann Michael Moscherosch's 'Gesichte': A Study of Structural Devices," dissertation, Ohio State University, 1969;

Ahrens, "Moscherosch auf der Hartenburg," *Zeitschrift für die Geschichte des Oberrheins,* new series 41 (1928): 387–414;

La Verne Carl Buckles, "Moscherosch and the Baroque Transition: Narrative Structure in

Three Sections of 'Philander von Sittewald,' " dissertation, University of Colorado, 1970;

Curt von Faber du Faur, "Johann Michael Moscherosch, der Geängstigte," *Euphorion,* 51, no. 3 (1957): 233–249;

Faber du Faur, "Philander, der Geängstigte, und der Expertus Robertus," *Monatshefte für deutschen Unterricht, deutsche Sprache und Literatur,* 39 (December 1947): 485–505;

Ursula von der Gönne, "Die Weiterführung der alsässischen Narrenliteratur des 16. Jahrhundert durch Johann Michael Moscheroschs Satire 'Wunderliche und Wahrhafftige Gesichte Philanders von Sittewald,' " dissertation, Ernst-Moritz-Arndt University, 1987;

Klaus Haberkamm, "Johann Michael Moscherosch," in *Deutsche Dichter des 17. Jahrhunderts: ihr Leben und Werk,* edited by Harald Steinhagen and Benno von Wiese (Berlin: Schmidt, 1984), pp. 185–207;

Haberkamm, "Zu Rezeptionsgeschichte Johann Michael Moscheroschs: Ein Zeugnis in August Stöbers 'Erwinia,' " *Simpliciana,* 8 (1986): 112–116;

Wolfgang Harms, "Johann Michael Moscherosch," in *Deutsche Dichter,* volume 2, edited by Gunter E. Grimm and Frank Rainer Max (Stuttgart: Reclam, 1988), pp. 156–162;

Karl Helmer, "Das Konzept moralischer Erziehung in der 'Insomnis Cura Parentum' von Hans Michael Moscherosch," *Pädagogische Rundschau,* 32 (1978): 353–366;

Brigitte Höft, "Johann Michael Moscheroschs Gesichte Philanders von Sittewalt," dissertation, University of Freiburg, 1964;

Kenneth Graham Knight, "Johann Michael Moscherosch – An Early Baroque Satirist's View of Life," *Modern Language Review,* 49 (January 1954): 29–45;

Johannes Koltermann, "Die Hanauer Zeit des Satirikers Moscherosch nach den bisherigen Darstellungen," *Hanauisches Magazin,* 11 (1932): 41–48;

Wilhelm Kühlmann, "Johann Michael Moscherosch in den Jahren 1648–1651: Die Briefe an Johann Valentin Andreae (Mit einer Aufstellung der bisher bekannten Korrespondenz Moscheroschs)," *Daphnis: Zeitschrift für Mittlere Deutsche Literatur,* 14, no. 2 (1985): 245–276;

Kühlmann, "Moscherosch und die Sprachgesellschaften des 17. Jahrhunderts. Aspekte des barocken Kulturpatriotismus," *Bibliothek und Wissenschaft,* 16 (1982): 68–84;

Horst Langer, " 'Ala mode'-Gebaren und 'altdeutsches Wesen' in J. M. Moscheroschs Satire 'Wunderliche und wahrhafftige Gesichte Philanders von Sittewalt,' " in his *Deutung und Wertung als Grundprobleme philologischer Arbeit* (Greifswald: Ernst-Moritz-Arndt-Universität, 1989), pp. 152–161;

Cornelia Moore, "H. M. Moscherosch als Autor für Erwachsene und als Autor für Kinder: Ein Vergleich der 'Gesichte Philanders von Sittewalt' (1640) mit 'Insomnis Cura Parentum' (1643)," in *Kinderliteratur – Literatur auch für Erwachsene?: Zum Verhältnis von Kinderliteratur und Erwachsenenliteratur,* edited by Dagmar Grenz (Munich: Fink, 1990), pp. 135–140;

Walter Ernst Schäfer, "Die Lyrik Johann Michael Moscheroschs," *Daphnis: Zeitschrift für Mittlere Deutsche Literatur,* 14, no. 2 (1985): 277–302;

Schäfer, "Zwischen Freier Reichsstadt und absolutistischem Hof: Lebensräume Moscheroschs," *Zeitschrift für die Geschichte des Oberrheins,* 130 (1982): 167–180;

Adolf Schmidt, "Die Bibliothek Moscheroschs," *Zeitschrift für Bücherfreunde,* 2 (1898/1899): 497–506;

Schmidt, "Die Bibliothek Moscheroschs und ihre Kataloge," *Zeitschrift für Bücherfreunde,* new series 12 (1920): 133–141;

Schmidt, "Moscheroschs Schreibkalender," *Jahrbuch für Geschichte, Sprache und Literatur Elsass-Lothringens,* 16 (1900): 139–190.

Papers:

The Landesbibliothek Darmstadt has Johann Michael Moscherosch's Schreibkalender and the catalogue of his books.

Georg Neumark

(16 March 1621 – 8 July 1681)

Andreas Herz
Herzog August Bibliothek

Translated by Susanne Reichelt

BOOKS: *Betrübt-Verliebter, doch entlich hocherfrewter Hürte Filamon wegen seiner Edlen Schäffer-Nymfen Belliflora, Das ist, Kurtze Liebesbeschreibung zweyer Hoch-Edlen Personen, auff derer bitte in ein Pastoral gebracht, vnd die darin stehende Lieder mit Melodeyen vnd Symfonien außgeziehrt* (Königsberg: Published by Peter Hendel, printed by Johann Reusner, 1648);

Keuscher Liebes-Spiegel, das ist, Ein bewegliches Schauspiel von der holdseligen Kalisten, vnd ihrem Treubeständigen Lysandern, laut der Historischen Beschreibung in gewisse Abhandlung und Auffzüge gebracht, mit Musikalischen Stücken und bildlichen Stellungen außgezieret (Thorn, 1649);

Der Hochbetrübt-verliebte Hürte Myrtillus wegen seiner Edlen und Holdseligen Schäferin Eufrosillen. Pastoral oder Schäfer-Gedichte, als . . . Herr Achatz Bork . . . mit der . . . Jungfern Eufrosinen . . . von Schlieben . . . den 14. Wintermonatstag, des 1649. Jahrs . . . Seinen Hochzeitlichen Ehrentag feyerlich begieng (Königsberg: Printed by Johann Reusner, 1649);

Vnverhoffte doch gewünschte Liebes-Geschicht, zwischen dem Hochedlen Schäfer Fljldor und siner Jvljenen. der gleich Hochedlen und Holdseligen Schäferin. Hürten-Lied . . . zu sonderbahren Ehren . . . dem . . . Herrn Abraham Josaphath von Kreytzen . . . Als derselbe mit der . . . Julian-Elisabethen . . . Rauschkens . . . den 13. Hornungs-Tag des 1650sten Jahres . . . sein Hochzeitliches Ehren-Fest hochfeyerlich begienge. Aufgesetzet vnd mit einer Musike aus geziehrt (Königsberg: Johann Reusner, 1650);

Die Sieben Weisen, auß Griechenland. Das ist Deroselben Historische Lebensbeschreibung auß alten Scribenten, sonderlich aber auß dem Diog: Laertio kurtz, Lateinisch und Teutsch verfasset, und dero vornehmste Lehrsprüche in lange trochaische Zwey-Verse versetzet, translated by Neumark (Thorn: Printed by Michael Karnall, 1650);

Georg Neumark

Poetisch- und Musikalisches Lustwäldchen (Hamburg: Printed by Michael Pfeiffer, published by Johann Naumann, 1652); enlarged as *Fortgepflantzer Musikalisch-Poetischer Lustwald* (Jena: Georg Sengenwald, 1657);

Poetisch Lobthonende Ehrenseule welche dem Durchleuchtigen Hochgebohrnen Fürsten und Herrn

238

Herrn Wilhelm Hertzogen zu Sachsen . . . Seinem gnädigen Fürsten und Herrn, in einem Kupferstiche abgebildet, mit Trochaischen Verschen beschrieben, und zu Bezeugung unterthänigster gehorsamster Dienstfertigkeit aufgerichtet (Mühlhausen: Printed by Johann Hüter, 1652);

Hertzoglicher Ehrentempel oder Poetische Lobschrift welche der Durchleuchtigen Hochgebornen Fürstinnen und Frauen Eleonoren-Dorotheen Hertzoginnen zu Sachsen . . . aufgerichtet, und der Unsterblichkeit einverleibet (Jena: Printed by Georg Sengenwald, 1652);

Poetische Leichrede von der Sterblichkeit welche den 19. May, den Tag vor der Fürstlichen Leichbeysetzung der Durchleuchtigen, Hochgebohrnen Fürstinn und Freulein Freulein Wilhelminen-Eleonoren, Hertzoginn zu Sachsen, Jülich, Cleve und Berg, Landgräfinn in Thüringen, Markgräfinn zu Meissen, Gräfin zu der Mark und Ravensberg, Freulein zu Ravenstein, unseres weyland gnädigen Freuleins in der Schloßkirchen nach gethaner Predigt bey Volkreicher Versammlung gehalten und abgelegt (Jena: Printed by Georg Sengenwald, 1653);

Davidischer Regentenspiegel, das ist, Muhtmaßliches und unvorgreifliches Nachsinnen, was der Königliche Prophet David bey Aufsetzung seines 101. Psalms vor Gedancken muß gehabt, und vor Gott ausgeschüttet haben. Jn teutsche Versche gebracht (Jena: Printed & published by Georg Sengenwald, 1655); enlarged as *Christlicher Potentaten Ehren-Krohne* (Weimar: Printed by Johann Andreas Müller, published by the author, sold by Matthäus Birckner in Jena, 1675);

Ecloge Filaret oder Glükkwunschende Reimzeilen, als der Durchleuchtige, Hochgeborne Fürst und Herr, Herr Wilhelm der Vierdte, Hertzog zu Sachsen . . . zum acht und funfzigsten mal seinen erfreulichen Hochfürstlichen Geburtstag den 11. April des 1656sten Jahrs begieng, aufgesetzet und in Unterthänigkeit überreicht von Dero Fürstlichen Gnaden Gehorsamen Diener, anonymous (Jena: Printed by Georg Sengenwald, 1656);

Ecloge Aretina; oder Lobschallendes Hürtengespräch, welches auf das Hochfürstliche Beylager der Durchleuchtigen, Hochgebohrnen Fürsten und Herrn, Herrn Moritzen Hertzog zu Sachsen . . . Und der gleichfalls Durchleuchtigen, Hochgebohrnen Fürstinn und Freulein, Freulein Dorotheen-Marien, Hertzoginnen zu Sachsen . . . Plichtschuldig aufgesetzet, und unterthänig überreichet hat (Jena: Printed by Georg Sengenwald, 1656);

Ecloge Filirenus. Welche dem Durchleuchtigen, Hochgebohrnen Fürsten und Herrn, Hn. Friederichen dem ältern, Hertzogen zu Sachsen . . . Als von dem

Allerhöchsten Gott, nach seinem allein weisen Raht und Willen, deroselben Fürstliche Gnaden im 17. Jahre ihres Alters den 18. Augustmonatstag itztlauffenden 1656sten Jahrs von dieser Welt durch ein seeliges Sterbstündlein abgefordert, und den 19. Wintermonatstag in sein Fürstliches Erbbegräbnüß und Ruhekämmerlein versetzet wurden. Aus unterthäniger Schuldigkeit und hertzlichem Mitleiden, eilends bey andern damals nohtwendigen Fürstlichen obliegenden Gerschäften, verfertiget, anonymous (Jena: Printed by Georg Sengenwald, 1656);

Kurtzer Jnhalt des Theatralischen Aufzugs oder Gesprächspiels, von der Lobschrift und Gemüths-Gaben des Durchleuchtigsten, Hochgebornen Fürsten und Herrns, Herr, Wilhelms des Vierdten, Hertzogs zu Sachsen (Weimar: Printed by Thomas Eyliker, 1659);

Glükkwünschendes Neujahrs-Gedichte (Weimar: Printed by Thomas Eyliker, 1660);

Gerechter Trutz jn Gottes Schutz oder Poetische Gedanken über den 71. Psalm Davids (Weimar: Printed by Thomas Eyliker, 1660);

Theatralische Vorstellung eines Weisen und zugleich Tapfern Regenten (Weimar: Printed by Thomas Eyliker, 1662);

Unterthänigste Anagrammatische Glükkwünschungs-Zeilen, als dem Durchleuchtigsten, Hochgebohrnen Fürsten und Herrn, Herrn Johann-Ernsten, Hertzogen zu Sachsen . . . wie auch der Durchleuchtigsten, Hochgebohrnen Fürstin und Frauen, Fr. Christianen-Elisabeth, Hertzogin zu Sachsen . . . jhr erstes Junges Herrlein, Herr Wilhelm-Ernst, jm 1662sten Jahre, den 19. Weinmonatstag des Abends zwischen 9. und 10. Uhr glükklich gebohren, und darauf den 20. zur heiligen Tauffe gebracht wurde. Eylfertigst aufgesetzet und unterthänigst überreicht (Weimar: Printed by Thomas Eyliker's widow, 1662);

Anagrammatischer Zuruf, als der Durchleuchtigste, Hochgebohrne Fürst und Herr, Herr Bernhard, Hertzog zu Sachsen . . . seine hertz-vielgeliebte Gemahlin, die auch Durchleuchtigste, Hochgebohrne Fürstin und Frau Frau Maria, Hertzogin zu Sachsen . . . jn Begleitung des gleichfals Durchleuchtigsten, Hochgebohrnen Fürsten und Herrn, Herrn Heinrich-Carols von Tremolie, Hertzogs von Tarante &c. aus Frankreich über Cassel heimhohlete, und den 3. Nov. 1662. mit obhochgemeldeter seiner hertzliebsten Gemahlin, in Weinmar seinen Einzug erfreulich hielte, unterthänigst überreicht (Weimar: Printed by Thomas Eyliker's widow, 1662);

Poetisch-Historischer Lustgarten (Frankfurt am Main: Published by Thomas Matthias Götze, 1666);

Poetische Tafeln, oder Gründliche Anweisung zur Teutschen Verskunst aus den vornehmsten Authorn in funfzehen

Tafeln zusammen gefasset (Jena: Johann Jacob Bauhofer, 1667);

Der Neu-Sprossende Teutsche Palmbaum. Oder Ausführlicher Bericht, von der Hochlöblichen Fruchtbringenden Gesellschaft (Nuremberg: Published by Johann Hoffmann, printed by Joachim Heinrich Schmidt in Weimar, 1669);

Klag- und gestalten Sachen nach Freuden-Lied (Weimar: Printed by Joachim Heinrich Schmidt, 1669);

Der Tugendgöttin Areteen Klaglied. Über das höchstbetraurliche, jedoch seeligste Absterben der Durchleuchtigsten Fürstin und Frauen, Frauen Anna, Verwittibten Hertzogin zu Schleswig/Holstein (Weimar: Printed by Joachim Heinrich Schmidt, 1669);

Als der ädle und hoch benahmte Himmlischgesinnte zu Breßlau, in den Durchleuchtigsten Palmorden, oder so genannte Hochlöbliche Fruchtbringende Gesellschaft, genädigst auf- und angenommen wurde, beehrte schuldigster massen dessen würdigen Eintrit, mit gegenwertigem glükkwünschendem Zuruffe, as Der Sprossende (Weimar: Printed by Joachim Heinrich Schmidt, 1670);

Das Sprossenden unterschiedliche, so wol zu gottseliger Andacht; als auch zu Christlichen Tugenden aufmunternde Lieder (Weimar: Published by the author, printed by Johann Andreas Müller, 1675);

Deß Christlichen Frauenzimmers Geistliche Perlen-Krohne (Nuremberg: Johann Hoffmann, 1675);

Thränendes Haus-Kreutz, oder gestallten Sachen nach, Klag- Lob- und Dank-Opfer (Weimar: Printed by Johann Andreas Müller, 1681).

Auserlesene Gedichte von Jacob Schwieger, Georg Neumark und Joachim Neander, edited by Karl Förster (Leipzig: Brockhaus, 1828);

Der Neu-Sprossende Teutsche Palmbaum, edited by Martin Bircher (Munich: Kösel, 1970);

Poetische Tafeln oder Gründliche Anweisung zur Teutschen Verskunst, edited by Joachim Dyck (Frankfurt am Main: Athenäum, 1971).

OTHER: Jacob Cats, *Verhochteutschte Sofonisbe, mit beygefügten historischen Erklährungen der eigenen Nahmen und etliche dunkelen Redensahrten,* adapted by Neumark (Danzig: Printed by Andreas Hünefeld, published by Ernst Müller, 1651);

Cats, *Verhochteutschte Kleopatra, mit beygefügten Kupferstükken, und kurtzen Historischen Erklährungen, der eigenen Nahmen und etlicher dunkelen Redensahrten,* translated by Neumark (Danzig: Printed by Andreas Hünefeld, published by Ernst Müller, 1651);

Cats, *Verhochdeutschte Fryne Bozene. Mit beygefügten kurtzen historischen Erklährungen, der eigenen Nahmen und etliche dunkelen Redensahrten,* translated by Neumark (Danzig: Printed by Andreas Hünefeld, published by the author, 1651);

Sieghafter Davjd. Das ist: Kurtze Poetische Beschreibung des wunderbaren Kampfes zwischen dem kleinen David und dem großen Riesen Goliath. Nach Anleitung Göttlicher Schrift, aus dem Lateinischen, in Teutsche Trochaische Versche verabfasset, mit Lehrsprüchen und Gleichnüssen vormehrt, und, auf Begehren eines vornehmen Mitgliedes der Hochlöbl: Fruchtbr: Gesellschaft, zum Drukk befördert, verse paraphrase by Neumark (Jena: Printed by Georg Sengenwald, 1653);

"Eclogue Florelle oder Lob- und Trost-schallendes Hirtengespräch beim Tode Eleonoren-Justinen Krausen," in *Leichenpredigt auf Eleonora Justina Krause* (Jena: Georg Sengenwald, 1655);

Tägliche Andachts-Opfer oder Hand-Buch, edited with contributions by Neumark (Nuremberg: Published by Johann Hoffmann, printed by Joachim Heinrich Schmied in Weimar, 1668); enlarged as *Des Sprossenden vermehrte Andachts-Opfer, oder Handbuch* (Nuremberg: Published by Johann Hoffmann, printed by Johann Andreas Müller in Weimar, 1677).

In his own time Georg Neumark was recognized for his versatile literary publications, but not long after his death his work paled into insignificance in the eyes of posterity. Today he is well known among experts as historian and *Erzschreinhalter* (head of the archives) of the Fruchtbringende Gesellschaft (Fruit-bringing Society) in the time of Duke Wilhelm IV of Saxe-Weimar and also as author of the baroque poetics *Poetische Tafeln, oder Gründliche Anweisung zur Teutschen Verskunst* (Poetic Tables; or, Thorough Instruction in the Art of German Verse, 1667). His name is still found in standard works on the history of music, in particular of hymns, although this genre forms only a small part of his work; and he is considered one of the most imaginative composers of continuo songs in baroque Germany. He was well acquainted with some of the best-known contemporary poets, and authors such as Sigmund von Birken, Johann Michael Dilherr, Georg Philipp Harsdörffer, Martin Kempe, Johann Michael Moscherosch, Johann Rist, Justus Georg Schottelius, Caspar Stieler, Johann Wilhelm von Stubenberg, Johann Peter Titz, and Andreas Tscherning wrote dedications for his works; Adam Olearius called him *Orfeus unsrer Zeiten* (Orpheus of our times). Nevertheless, contemporary critical opinions were based on Neumark's inordinate obsession for honor and titles and his plagiaristic behavior toward Kempe, the Königsberg (today Kaliningrad, Russia) poet and polyhistor. The eighteenth and nineteenth centuries had no interest in him; a hundred years after his death Neumark's elaborate baroque art of poetry had vanished into the darkness of history.

Neumark was born on 16 March 1621 to Michael Neumark, a clothmaker, and Martha Neumark, née Plattner, in Langensalza in Thüringia. In 1623 the family moved to the free imperial city of Mühlhausen (today Mulhouse, France), where Neumark received his early education. From 1630 to 1636 he attended the Hennebergisches Gymnasium in Schleusingen, and in 1640 he attended the Gymnasium Ernestinum in Gotha, which at that time was under the direction of Andreas Reyher, an educational reformer influenced by Wolfgang Ratke. In September 1640 he left Gotha to escape the turmoil of the Thirty Years' War, intending to go to Königsberg to study at the Albertina, the university there; but on the way he was robbed of all his belongings on the Gardelegener Heath. He journeyed to Magdeburg, to Lüneburg, to Winsen, and finally to Hamburg in a futile search for employment.

In Hamburg his first printed work, the pastoral *Filamon und Belliflora,* was published in 1640. Today no copies of this first edition can be found; a second edition, probably revised, would appear in 1648 in Königsberg. It is a bucolic piece of the most dainty, graceful prose with interspersed songs that are not always metrically correct. Of these songs, the "Loblied der Schäfer- und Poeterey" (Panegyric to Sheep Farm and Poetry) remains well-known and can be found in many anthologies of baroque lyrical poetry. The song begins in the morning: Filamon complains about Belliflora's hard-heartedness; Belliflora, who first rebuffs him, softens and becomes enraptured with him. In the evening they celebrate a pastoral wedding before the altar of Venus. The influence of Martin Opitz, Johann Klaj, and Paul Fleming can be clearly seen, and the name of the character Chasmindo is an anagram for Simon Dach.

Continuing his search for a suitable position, Neumark went to Kiel, where he became a tutor to the children of Stephan Hemmings, an *Amtsmann* (civil servant) of the duchy of Schleswig-Holstein-Gottorp. There, in the winter of 1640–1641 he wrote the song of consolation "Wer nur den lieben Gott läßt walten" (Whoever allows dear God to prevail), which can still be found in the *Evangelischen Kirchengesangsbuch* (Evangelical Hymnbook). The

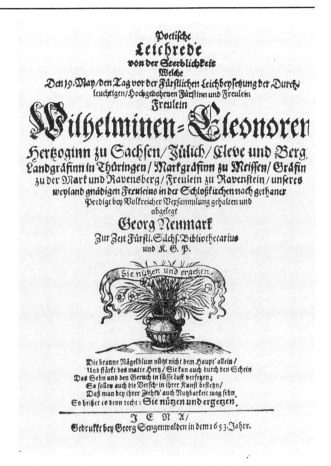

Title page for Neumark's verse eulogy for Duchess Wilhelmina Eleonora of Saxony

song was first published in 1657 in Neumark's *Fortgepflantzter Musikalisch-Poetischer Lustwald* (Propagated Musical-Poetic Pleasure Forest) with his own musical setting. Johann Sebastian Bach's cantata "Gott ist unsre Zuversicht" (God is Our Confidence, circa 1737) is an adaptation, both textually and musically, of Neumark's song. After three years as a tutor Neumark left Kiel and sailed from Travemünde via Danzig (today Gdansk, Poland) to Königsberg.

During the Thirty Years' War students from all parts of the Holy Roman Empire went to Königsberg because the city was largely unaffected by the war. On 21 June 1644 Neumark enrolled at the Albertina, which was celebrating the centennial of its founding. The festivities lasted from August until October, and one of the highlights was the drama *Sorbuisa,* also known as *Prussiarchus,* written for the occasion by Simon Dach, who held the chair in poetry. Neumark studied law for six years in Königsberg, earning his living as a tutor in the household of the royal Polish chamberlain, Lt. Col.

Christoph von Schlieben. In a fire at the home Neumark once more lost all his belongings. It seems likely that Neumark joined the Königsberg literary group that formed around Dach, Robert Roberthin, and Heinrich Albert and that also included Titz; the songs composed by the group had a strong influence on Neumark's early sacred and secular poems. It is known that Neumark, under the sponsorship of Titz, became a member of the Prussilschen Schäferey (Prussian Shepherds), which was founded in Königsberg in 1643; his society nickname was Thyrsis.

Completing his studies, in 1649 Neumark went to Thorn. His reading of contemporary works on poetry, rhetoric, and grammar led to his *Poetische Tafeln,* which is mainly a survey of what Titz had worked out in *Zwey Bücher von der Kunst Hochdeutsche Verse und Lieder zu machen* (Two Books on the Art of Writing High German Poems and Songs, 1642); Neumark's book is also indebted to Schottelius's *Teutsche Sprachkunst* (German Grammar, 1641). *Poetische Tafeln* was published in a small edition in Thorn in 1649, but no known copies of this edition exist; a second edition, with brilliant annotations and an introduction by Kempe, would be published in 1667. In Thorn, Neumark wrote *Keuscher Liebes-Spiegel* (Chaste Mirror of Love, 1649), a dramatization of Vital d'Audiguier's novel *Histoire trage-comique de nostre temps, sous les noms de Lysandre et de Caliste* (Tragicomic History of Our Times, under the Names of Lysander and Calista, 1622); Philipp von Zesen's translation of the novel as *Liebes-Beschreibung Lysanders und Kalisten* (Description of the Love of Lysander and Calista, 1644) presumably provided the basis for Neumark's dramatization, although he never mentions Zesen's work. While in Thorn, Neumark also wrote *Die Sieben Weisen aus Griechenland* (The Seven Wise Men of Greece, 1650). This Latin and German work tells in prose and verse about the lives of Solon, Thales, Chilon, Pittacos, Bias, Cleobulos, and Periander.

In 1650 Neumark moved to Danzig, where he wrote the three epic poems *Verhochteutschte Sofonisbe, Verhochdeutschte Kleopatra,* and *Verhochteutschte Fryne Bozene.* Published in 1651, they are relatively free translations into High German (*verhochteutscht*) of passages from *Trouringh* (1634), by the Dutch writer Jacob Cats. These poems, written in alexandrine verse, have been considered precursors of the great historical novels of the second half of the seventeenth century.

At the end of September 1651 Neumark was once again in Hamburg. On this occasion he made a short trip to Wedel to visit Rist. In the same year,

under the patronage of Duke Friedrich III of Schleswig-Holstein-Gottorp, he established contact with the court of Duke Wilhelm IV of Saxe-Weimar, who, as Der Schmackhafte (The Tasteful One), was one of the founding members and second head of the Fruchtbringende Gesellschaft. In 1652 Neumark was installed as the ducal librarian in Weimar, and a little later as ducal archivist. In gratitude Neumark wrote two panegyric for Duke Wilhelm and his wife, Eleanora Dorothea: *Poetisch Lobthonende Ehrenseule* (Poetic Praise-Sounding Monument) and *Hertzoglicher Ehrentempel oder Poetische Lobschrift* (Ducal Temple of Honor; or, Poetic Panegyric); both appeared in print in Mühlhausen in 1652. Under the sponsorship of Harsdörffer and Rist he was admitted into the Fruchtbringende Gesellschaft on 22 October 1653 with the society name Der Sprossende (The Proliferating One). That same year he published Sieghafter David (Victorious David), a "Kurtze Poetische Beschreibung" (short poetic description) of the battle of David and Goliath from 1 Samuel 17; according to the preface, it is a revision of "Carmen de pugna Davidis et Goliathi," a work by the son of an unnamed member of the Fruchtbringende Gesellschaft. Also in 1653 he was crowned imperial poet laureate. *Davidischer Regentenspiegel* (Mirror of the Regency of David, 1655), commissioned by Duke Wilhelm, is an extended verse paraphrase of the 101st Psalm, to which Neumark adds fifty-three dicta as a commentary. In 1655 Neumark married Anna Margaretha Werner, a merchant's daughter. The following year he was named Erzschreinhalter of the Fruchtbringende Gesellschaft.

Neumark wrote several Eclogen (eclogues) in mixed verses – *Florelle* (1655), *Filaret* (1656), *Aretina* (1656), and *Filirenus* (1656) – for festivities or sad occasions at the Weimar court. In his history of the Fruchtbringende Gesellschaft, titled *Der Neu-Sprossende Teutsche Palmbaum* (The Newly Sprouting German Palm Tree, 1669), Neumark says that he invented *Kettenverse* (chain verse) in his eclogues; he also treats this form of verse in *Poetische Tafeln.* He also wrote dramas and laudatory poems in his capacity as ducal poet for the usual occasions, such as birthdays, New Year's Day, visits to the court, and deaths.

In 1657 Neumark produced an enlarged edition of a work from his traveling and university years, *Poetisch- und Musikalisches Lustwäldchen* (Poetic and Musical Small Pleasure Forests, 1652), under the title *Fortgepflantzer Musikalisch-Poetischer Lustwald.* This edition includes nearly all of his early lyrics; most of the musical settings are by him. The first

Part of a page from Neumark's eulogy to Wilhelmina Eleonora, showing musical notation for one of the songs in the work

part comprises sacred songs, love songs, songs of friendship and sociability, wedding poems, mourning poems, and elegies – all of the baroque themes and motifs. The cycle of seven erotic poems about the *Schäferin* (shepherdess) Karitille – an autobiographical hint of a love affair he had during his first stay in Hamburg – can stand comparison with acknowledged models of the genre, such as Stieler's *Die geharnschte Venus* (The Armored Venus, 1660). The second part consists of sacred poems; the eclogues *Florelle, Filaret,* and *Aretina;* panegyrical poetry for the court; and occasional poems. All of the poems in this part have a bucolic motif. The third part includes religious and moral epigrams, along with a reprinting of *Die Sieben Weisen aus Griechenland.*

Neumark's allegorical festival play *Theatralischer Aufzug* (Theatrical Pageantry), was performed in honor of Duke Wilhelm's sixty-first birth-day in 1659; only an outline, published the same year, exists. In the play Mars and his retinue vie with the Muses, Pallas, and Apollo in praising Wilhelm as a man who is outstanding in warfare (a characterization that does not correspond to his unfortunate role during the Thirty Years' War) and in the arts, until an *Ehrenpforte* (triumphal arch) is solemnly unveiled, and a song of praise by Fama (Fame) closes the scene. This work is typical of Neumark's courtly-panegyrical "architectonic-lapidary" style, which keeps piling up poetic pillars, triumphal arches, and pyramids.

Neumark's collected narratives in verse and prose appeared in 1666 as *Poetisch-Historischer Lustgarten* (Poetic-Historical Pleasure Garden). It comprises *Sieghafter David;* "Die Verständige Abigail" (The Judicious Abigail), a paraphrase in verse modeled after *Sieghafter David;* "Die Erhöhete Fryne-Bozene" (The Exalted Fryne-Bozene); "Die

243

*Title page for Neumark's history of the
Fruchtbringende Gesellschaft*

plained in letters to Birken, Duke August of Saxe-Weißenfels became the new head of the Fruchtbringende Gesellschaft in 1667. Duke August's residence in Halle an der Saale became the society's headquarters, and his secretary, David Elias Heidenreich, succeeded Neumark as Erzschreinhalter of the society. In 1668 Neumark edited *Tägliche Andachts-Opfer* (Daily Prayer Offerings), a collection of prayers in prose and hymns, ten of them by his hand. An enlarged edition appeared in 1677.

Christlicher Potentaten Ehren-Krohne (Christian Potentate Crown of Honor) appeared in 1675. Its first part is a revised version of *Davidischer Regentenspiegel;* the second part is the pastoral dialogue "Der große Filaret" (The Great Filaret), a revised version of Neumark's *Theatralische Vorstellung eines weisen und zugleich Tapfern Regenten* (Theatrical Presentation of a Wise and also Valiant Regent, 1662). Both poems were written in honor of Duke Wilhelm, who is represented, in the characters of David and Filaret, as a prudent, righteous, and pious *Hausvater* (paterfamilias) and regent.

Neumark's late writings include the collections of sacred arias *Unterschiedliche Lieder* (Various Songs, 1675) and *Des christlichen Frauenzimmers geistliche Perlen-Krohne* (The Christian Lady's Spiritual Crown of Pearls, 1675), which include settings of texts by other authors, such as Dilherr and Johann Arndt, as well as prayers, didactic histories, and parables. In the foreword to *Unterschiedliche Lieder* Neumark complains about a roving singer who had added two stanzas to his well-known song "Wer nur den lieben Gott läßt walten"; even worse, she had claimed that the song was written by a parson from Mecklenburg. In 1679 Neumark was admitted into the Nuremberg literary society, the Löblicher Hirten- und Blumenorden an der Pegnitz (Honorable Order of Shepherds and Flowers on the Pegnitz River), under the name Thyrsis. He had first applied for membership in 1667; his admission had been delayed by Birken, who was gaining revenge for Neumark's ignoring Birken's 1656 petition to join the Fruchtbringende Gesellschaft. (Birken had finally joined the Fruchtbringende Gesellschaft in 1658 through the intervention of Stubenberg and Count Gottlieb von Windischgrätz.)

Almost blind in old age, Neumark dictated *Thränendes Haus-Kreutz* (Tearful Family Burden, 1681) to his children. A consolation poem about loneliness, illness, and the vexations of age ending in praise of and confidence in God, it also gives effusive thanks to the court in Weimar for continuing to pay his salary and allowing him to keep his title despite his unfitness for service. It was his last publi-

Verführerische Kleopatra" (The Seduced Cleopatra); "Die Unglükkliche Sophonisbe" (The Unhappy Sophonisbe); "Der Lieb-erfreute Filamon" (The Love-Gladdened Philamon); *Die Sieben Weisen aus Griechenland;* and fourteen epigrams. The revised edition of *Poetische Tafeln* was published in 1667: it is still a standard work on baroque poetry, along with the poetics of Birken, Martin Opitz, August Buchner, and Daniel Georg Morhof. Neumark never mentioned the considerable part in revising the edition that was played by Kempe; Kempe bitterly complained about this slight in several letters to Birken.

Duke Wilhelm had died in 1662; after wearisome negotiations, about which Neumark com-

cation and is filled with presentiment of death; the dedication is dated Weimar, 30 June 1681. Neumark died a week later, on 8 July.

Together with him and Duke August of Saxe-Weißenfels, who had died the year before, the Fruchtbringende Gesellschaft vanished. It had been the central reference point in Neumark's life and work. His inscription in the heraldry book of the Fruchtbringende Gesellschaft, which is in the Weimar State Archives, is dated 18 July 1653:

> Eben wie die braunen Nelken in der vollbeblühten Jugend,
> Nicht allein schön anzusehn, sondern sonst auch hoch an Tugend;
> Also wil ich laßen *Sprossen* meine muntre Tichterey,
> Daß es *Nützlich und Ergetzlich,* beydes Gott und Menschen sey.

> (Even as the brown cloves in their full-blooded youth
> Are not only beautiful to look at but also besides high in virtue,
> So will I allow my lively poetry to *proliferate,*
> That it might be *useful and delightful* to both God and human beings.)

Bibliographies:

Ilse Pyritz, *Bibliographie zur deutschen Literaturgeschichte des Barockzeitalters,* volume 2 (Bern: Francke, 1985), pp. 502–503;

Gerhard Dünnhaupt, *Personalbibliographien zu den Drucken des Barock,* volume 9, part 4 (Stuttgart: Hiersemann, 1991), pp. 2958–2978.

References:

Wolfgang Adam, *Poetische und kritische Wälder: Untersuchung en zu Geschichte und formen des Schriebens "bei Gelegenheit"* (Heidelberg: Winter, 1988), pp. 157–174;

F. W. Barthold, *Geschichte der Fruchtbringenden Gesellschaft* (Berlin: Duncker, 1848), pp. 277–295;

Martin Bircher, *Johann Wilhelm von Stubenberg (1619–1663) und sein Freundeskreis: Studien zur österreichischen Barockliteratur protestantischer Edelleute* (Berlin: De Gruyter, 1968);

Carl August Hugo Burkhardt, "Aus dem Briefwechsel Sigmund von Birkens und Georg Neumarks 1656–1669," *Euphorion,* 3 (1897): 12–55;

Albert Fischer and W. Tümpel, *Das deutsche evangelische Kirchenlied des siebzehnten Jahrhunderts,* volume 4 (Gütersloh, 1908), pp. 308–314;

Klaus Garber, *Der locus amoenus und der locus terribilis* (Cologne & Vienna: Böhlau, 1974);

Karl Goedeke, *Grundriß zur Geschichte der deutschen Dichtung: Aus den Quellen,* second revised edi-

tion, volume 3: *Vom dreißigjährigen bis zum siebenjährigen Kriege* (Dresden, 1887), pp. 74–77;

Hans Hattenhauer, "Beamtentum und Literatur im Barockzeitalter: Aus dem Leben Georg Neumarks," *Der Staat,* 20, no. 1 (1981): 31–53;

Johann Herdegen, *Historische Nachricht von deß löblichen Hirten- und Blumen-Ordens an der Pegnitz Anfang und Fortgang* (Nuremberg: Christoph Riegel, 1744), pp. 384–387;

August Friedrich Hoffmann von Fallersleben, "Wer nur den lieben Gott läßt walten!," *Weimarisches Jahrbuch für deutsche Sprache, Litteratur und Kunst,* 3 (1855): 177–184;

Franz Knauth, *Georg Neumark nach Leben und Dichten* (Langensalza: Beyer, 1881);

Eduard Emil Koch, *Geschichte des Kirchenlieds und Kirchengesangs mit besonderer Rücksicht auf Würtemberg,* volume 1: *Die Dichter und Sänger* (Stuttgart, 1847), pp. 166–167; volume 2: *Die Lieder und Weisen* (Stuttgart: Belser, 1847), pp. 293–299;

Helmut K. Krausse, "Religiöse Lyrik," in *Deutsche Literatur: Eine Sozialgeschichte,* edited by Horst Albert Glaser, volume 3: *Zwischen Gegenreformation und Frühaufklärung: Späthumanismus, Barock. 1572–1740,* edited by Harald Steinhagen (Reinbek bei Hamburg: Rowohlt, 1985), pp. 418–429;

Georg Kretschmer, "Georg Neumark, ein Weimarer Bibliothekar und Dichter des 17. Jahrhunderts," *Zentralblatt für das Bibliothekswesen,* 91, no. 2 (1977): 91–101;

Herman Kretzschmar, *Geschichte des neuen deutschen Liedes* (Hildesheim & Wiesbaden, 1966), pp. 110–113;

Siegfried Kross, *Geschichte des deutschen Liedes* (Darmstadt: Wissenschaftliche Buchgesellschaft, 1989), p. 48;

Joseph Leighton, "Deutsche Sonett-Theorie im 17. Jahrhundert," in *Europäische Tradition und deutscher Literaturbarock: Internationale Beiträge zum Problem von Überlieferung und Umgestaltung,* edited by Gerhart Hoffmeister (Bern & Munich: Francke, 1973), pp. 11–36;

Andreas Marti, "Wer nur den lieben Gott läßt walten – ein Rest modaler Melodiebildung?," *Jahrbuch für Liturgik und Hymnologie,* 31 (1987): 109–115;

Bernd Prätorius, "Georg Neumark," in *Literatur-Lexikon: Autoren und Werke deutscher Sprache,* edited by Walther Killy, volume 8 (Gütersloh: Bertelsmann, 1990), pp. 378–379;

Volker Sinemus, *Poetik und Rhetorik im frühmodernen deutschen Staat: Sozialgeschichtliche Bedingungen des Normenwandels im 17. Jahrhundert* (Göttingen: Vandenhoeck & Ruprecht, 1978), pp. 75, 222–227;

Blake Lee Spahr, *The Archives of the Pegnesischer Blumenorden: A Survey and Reference Guide* (Berkeley & Los Angeles: University of California Press, 1960), pp. 53–61;

Erich Trunz, "Die Entstehung von Georg Neumarks Lied 'Wer nur den lieben Gott läßt walten' in Kiel," *Nordelbingen: Beiträge zur Kunst- und Kulturgeschichte,* 51 (1982): 151–163;

Johann Kaspar Wetzel, *Historische Lebens-Beschreibung der berühmtesten Lieder-Dichter,* volume 2 (Herrnstadt: Samuel Roth-Scholtzen, 1724), pp. 220–225;

Carl von Winterfeld, *Der evangelische Kirchengesang und sein Verhältnis zur Kunst des Tonsatzes,* volume 2 (Leipzig: Breitkopf & Härtel, 1845; reprinted, Hildesheim: Olms, 1966), pp. 285–296.

Papers:

Thirty letters from Georg Neumark are in the Sigmund von Birken literary remains in the archive of the Pegnesischen Blumenordens in the German National Museum, Nuremberg; a letter to Duke August of Saxe-Weißenfels, dated 27 September 1667, is in the Biblioteka Jagiellonska, Kraków; several documents are in the Weimar State Archive; eight letters to Johann Ernst Gerhard are in the Forschungsbibliothek, Gotha; and a letter to Prince Friedrich of Anhalt-Harzgerode, dated Weimar, 10 May 1669, is in the State Archive, Magdeburg.

Adam Olearius

(15 August 1599 – 22 February 1671)

Renate Wilson
University of South Carolina

BOOKS: *Disputatio Metaphysica de Actu & Potentia, quam Deo, Actu purissimo, annuente, Permissu venerandae Facultatis Philosophicae, in florentißimâ Lipsiensi Academiâ* (Leipzig: Gregor Ritzsch, 1627);

Disputatio Ethica. De Summo Hominis Bono Practico, Quam Inclyti Collegii Philosophici in Illustri Academiâ Lipsiensi permissu Pro Loco (Leipzig: Gregor Ritzsch, 1629);

Kurtze Erinnerung vnd Bericht, von der grossen vnd erschrecklichen Sonnen-Finsterniß, so dieses 1630. Jahrs den letzten Maij bey vnm halb-weg 7. Vhr nach Mittag sich sehen lassen (Leipzig: Printed by Gregor Ritzsch, 1630);

Neues Astrolabium, auf viele und unterschiedliche elevationes poli gerichtet (Leipzig, 1632);

Sieges- vnd Triumffs-Fahne Gustavi Adolphi Magni, der Schweden, Gothen vnd Wenden Königs &c. Welcher in Meissen bey Lützen in der Schlacht als ein Heldt gestanden, vnd mitten im Siegen gefallen, den 6. Novembris Anno 1632. Zu dessen höchstlöblichen vnd vnsterblichen Gedächtnis auffgerichtet, as Ascanium Olivarium (Leipzig: Published by Andreas Oehlen, printed by Abraham Lamberg's heirs, 1633);

Lustige Historia, woher das Toback-Trincken kommt, etwas nach dem Niederländischen beschrieben, as Ascanium d'Oliva (Leipzig, 1633); republished as *Misocapnus. Rauch- und Schmauch-Fehder oder Toback-Feind. das ist, des allergelehrtesten Monarchen von Engel- Schott- und Jrrland Jacobi, Königsspiel, vom Mißbrauch des Tobacksauffens* (Leipzig, 1652);

Klage über die jetzige verkehrte Welt, as Corydon (N.p., 1641);

Grab- und Ehrengedächtniß des Edlen Oswald Belings, Fürstl. Holsteinischen Capitains (Schleswig: Jacob zur Glocken, 1646);

Offt begehrte Beschreibung der Newen Orientalischen Rejse, so durch Gelegenheit einer Holsteinischen Legation an den König in Persien geschehen (Schleswig: Jacob zur Glocken, 1647); translated by John Davies

Adam Olearius; painting by Jürgen Ovens (Statens Museum for Kunst, Copenhagen)

as *The Voyages and Travels of the Ambassadors sent by Frederick Duke of Holstein, to the Great Duke of Muscovy, and the King of Persia. Began in the year M.DC.XXXIII and finish'd in M.DC.XXXIX* (London: Thomas Dring & John Starkey, 1662); German version enlarged as *Vermehrte newe Beschreibung der Muscowitischen vnd Persischen Reyse so durch gelegenheit einer Holsteinischen Gesandschafft an den Russischen Zaar vnd König in Persien geschehen* (Schleswig: Printed by Johann Holwein, 1656); republished as *Außführliche Beschreibung der kundbaren Reyse nach Muscow und Persien, so durch gelegenheit einer Holsteinischen Gesandschafft von Gottorff auß an Michael Fedorowitz den grossen Zaar in Muscow, und Schach Sefi König in Persien*

247

geschehen (Schleswig: Printed by Johann Holwein, 1663);

*Gewunschter Todtergang. Der weiland viel ehr und
tugentreichen Gottliebenden Frauen Maria von
Sprekelsen, Geborne Müllerin des weiland . . . H.
Johan von Sprekelsen bey S. Katherinen Kirchen
treufleissigen Geschwornen hinterlassenen Wittiben*
(Hamburg: Michael Pfeiffer, 1649);

*Von Vnbeständigkeit der Weltlichen Dinge vnd Von
Herrligkeit vnd Lobe der Tugend. Jn einem
Fürstlichen Ballet auff dem HochFürstlichen Beylager
des Durchläuchtigen, Hochgebornen Fürsten vnd
Herrn Herrn Ludowigen, Landgraffen zu Hessen,
&c. mit der auch Durchläuchtigen, Hochgebornen
Fürstin vnd Fräwlein Fräwlein Maria Elisabeth,
geborne Hertzogin zu Schleßwig, Holstein, &c. Auff
der Fürstl. Residenz Gottorff vorgestellt, den 27.
Novemb. 1650,* anonymous (Schleswig, 1650);

*Compendium Fortificatorium, oder Kurtze Anleitung nach
heutiger Art Städte und Oerter zu befestigen, meist
nach Adam Freytags Architectura militari gerichtet*
(Schleswig: Johann Holwein the elder, 1660);

*Geistliche Sinnen-Bilder, mit Gottseligen Gedancken eines
rechtschaffenen Christen, durch welche die Frommen
getröstet, und die Gottlosen von jhrem bösen Leben
abgeschrecket und zu Gott bekehret werden können,*
anonymous (Hamburg: Published by Nicolaus
Pauschert: Printed by Johann Holwein in
Schleswig, 1662);

*Kurtzer Begriff einer Holsteinischen Chronic oder Summa-
rische Beschreibung der denckwürdigsten Geschichten,
so innerhalb von 200. und mehr Jahren, nemblich
von Anno 1448. biß 1662. in den NordLanden,
sonderlich in Holstein sich begeben,* anonymous
(Schleswig: Published by Johann Carstens,
1663);

*Historia von der Cleopatra, der überaus schönen wolbered-
samen aber unzüchtigen Königin in Ægypten. An
welcher die fürnehmsten Helden der Welt, als Julius
Caesar und Marcus Anthonius sich vernarret. Aus
vielen Historienschreibern zusammen getragen,* as
AdOnis (Schleswig: Printed by Johann Holwein, 1666);

*Gottorffische Kunst-Cammer, worinnen allerhand unge-
meine Sachen, so theils die Natur, theils künstliche
Hände hervor gebracht und bereitet* (Schleswig:
Printed by Johann Holwein, 1666);

*Der erfundene Weg zum rechten Paradieß, durch welchen
man einig und allein in den Himmel kommen kan.
Beschrieben durch ein Mitglied der Fruchtbringenden
Gesellschafft,* anonymous (Hamburg: Published
by Nicolaus Pauschert, printed by Johann
Holwein in Schleswig, 1666);

*Panegyricus Dictus Viro Generis nobilitate, ingenii acumine,
rarae Eruditionis spectabilitate, singulari rerum poli-
ticarum experientiâ, & Famae celebritate excel-
lentissimo, Dno. Johanni Wowerio, Serenissimi
Celsissimi Principis ac Domini Dni. Johannis Adolphi . . . olim Consiliario intimo, & Praefecto
Gottorpiensi dignissimo* (Kiel: Joachim Reumann,
1667);

Relation aus dem Gottorphischen Parnasse (N.p., 1668).

Editions: *Moskowitische Abenteuer,* edited by Edmund
Theodor Kauer (Berlin: Neufeld & Henius,
1927);

Die erste deutsche Expedition nach Persien (1635–1639),
edited by Hermann von Staden (Leipzig:
Brockhaus, 1927);

Muskowitische und persische Reise, edited by Eberhard
Meißner (Darmstadt: Progress-Verlag, 1959);

*Vermehrte newe Beschreibung der Muscowitischen und Per-
sischen Reyse so durch gelegenheit einer Holsteinischen
Gesandschafft an den Russischen Zaar vnd König in
Persien geschehen,* edited by Dieter Lohmeier
(Tübingen: Niemeyer, 1971);

*Moskowitische und Persische Reise: Die Holsteinische
Gesandtschaft beim Schah 1633–1639,* edited by
Detlef Haberland (Stuttgart & Vienna: Thiene-
mann, 1986).

Edition in English: *The Travels of Olearius in Seventeenth-
Century Russia,* translated by Samuel H. Baron
(Stanford: Stanford University Press, 1967).

OTHER: *D. Paul Flemings Poetischer Gedichten so nach
seinem Tode haben sollen herauß gegeben werden,
Prodromus,* edited by Olearius (Hamburg: Published by Tobias Gundermann, 1641);

D. Paul Flemings Teutsche Poemata (Lübeck: Published
by Laurentz Jauch, 1646); republished as
Geist- und Weltliche Poemata (Jena: Printed by
Georg Sengenwald, 1651);

Virgil, *Oswald Belings Verdeutschete Waldlieder, oder 10.
Hirten Gespräche des allerfürtrefflichsten Lateinisch:
Poeten virg. Marons, jn Deutsche Verse übersetzet,*
edited by Olearius (Hamburg: Published by
Johann Naumann, printed in Schleswig by
Jacob zur Glocken, 1649);

Sa'dī, *Persianischer Rosenthal. Jn welchem viel lustige
Historien, scharffsinnige Reden und nützliche Regeln.
Vor 400. Jahren von einem Sinnreichen Poeten
Schich Saadi in Persischer Sprach beschrieben. Jetzo
aber von Adamo Olerio, mit zuziehung eines alten
Persianers Namens Hakwirdi übersetzet,* translated
by Olearius (Hamburg: Published by Johann
Naumann, 1654);

Johann Albrecht von Mandelslo, *Des HochEdel-
gebornen Johan Albrechts von Mandelslo Morgenlän-*

dische Reyse-Beschreibung. Worinnen zugleich die Gelegenheit vnd heutiger Zustand etlicher fürnehmen Jndianischen Länder, Provincien, Städte vnd Jnsulen, sampt derer Einwohner Leben, Sitten, Glauben vnd Handthierung: wie auch die Beschaffenheit der Seefahrt über das Oceanische Meer, edited by Olearius (Hamburg: Published by Christian Guth, printed in Schleswig by Johann Holwein, 1658);

Cyprian, *Des alten KirchenLehrers vnd Märtyrers Cyprians Herrliche Gedancken vnd bewegliche Reden von der Sterbligkeit, so bey jtzigen gefährlichen Zeiten von frommen Christen wol zulesen, jtem ein Gebet desselben Verdeutschet,* translated by Olearius (Schleswig: Printed by Johan Holwein, 1659);

Cyprian, *Deß H. Vaters und Martyrers Cypriani geistreiche und sehr bewegliche Rede von dem grossen Gut der Christlichen Gedult von bekümmerten Hertzen in dieser trostlosen Welt tröstlich zu lesen,* translated by Olearius (Hamburg: Printed by Michael Pfeiffer, published by Johann Naumann, 1659);

HochFürstliche ansehnliche Leichbegängniß des Durchläuchtigsten Fürsten und Herrn, Herrn Friedrichs, Erben zu Norwegen, Hertzogen zu Schleßwig Holstein, Stormarn und der Dithmarschen, Graffen zu Oldenburg und Delmenhorst, &c. Welchen Gott der Herr den 10. Augusti 1659. aus diesem mühseligen Jammerthal durch einen sanfft und seligen Todt abgefodert, edited by Olearius (Schleswig: Printed by Johann Holwein, 1661);

Biblia. Das ist: Die gantze Schrifft Altes und Neues Testaments, translated by Martin Luther, edited by Olearius (Schleswig: Printed by Johann Holwein, 1664);

Das Schleßwigische und Holsteinische Kjrchen Buch, edited by Olearius (Schleswig: Printed by Johann Holwein, 1665);

Heinrich von Üchtritz, *Kurtze Reise Beschreibung,* edited by Olearius (Schleswig: Printed by Johann Holwein, 1666);

Jürgen Andersen and Volquard Iversen, *Orientalische Reise-Beschreibunge Jürgen Andersen aus Schleßwig der An. Christi 1644. außgezogen und 1650. wieder kommen. Und Volquard Jversen aus Holstein so An. 1655. außgezogen und 1668. wieder angelanget,* edited by Olearius (Schleswig: Printed by Johann Holwein, 1669).

Adam Olearius was dubbed by his contemporaries "der Holsteinische Plinius" (The Pliny of Holstein) and "der Gottorper Odysseus" (the Odysseus of Gottorf). These epithets capture the wide range of interests and achievements of this er-udite scholar who wrote the first scientific travel book in German and was one of the most accomplished translators of Persian poetry of his time.

Olearius was born Adam Ölschlegel in Aschersleben in Anhalt on 15 August 1599; he was the son of Adam Ölschlegel, a tailor, and Maria Ölschlegel, née Porst. After attending the Stephaneum gymnasium in Aschersleben, he went to the University of Leipzig in 1620 to study theology but switched to philosophy, mathematics, and the natural sciences, especially astronomy. Influenced by Philipp Müller, a professor with whom he maintained a cordial relationship long after the completion of his studies, he developed a special interest in mathematics and astronomy. He became a master of philosophy in 1627 with his disputation *De actu et potentia* (On Actuality and Potentiality). As was often the custom during this period, he began using the latinized form of his surname during his student years, signing his disputation "Olearius."

After taking his degree Olearius remained in Leipzig, earning a modest living as a teacher. In 1630 he became assistant director of the Nicolai School, where his duties included the teaching of Latin grammar and mathematics; but he was apparently not happy with the position and paid a substitute to teach handwriting, which was one of his responsibilities. He also took frequent leaves of absence for travel and other unspecified purposes. The position was poorly paid, and he had to augment his income by giving private lessons to students of the school. He applied unsuccessfully for a position at the Thomas School, where his income would have been considerably larger, because the teachers and students were paid to sing in church for funerals, weddings, and other occasions. He met Martin Opitz during the latter's visit to Leipzig in 1630, and Opitz recommended that Olearius improve his skill in versification by translating Virgil's Eclogues into German. Olearius attempted to follow Opitz's rules for versification in his long poem on the death of the Swedish king Gustav Adolph (1632), but the task of translating the Eclogues would fall many years later to a mathematics student of Olearius's, Oswald Beling, whose translation would be edited by Olearius after Beling's death and published as *Oswald Belings Verdeutschete Waldlieder* (Oswald Beling's Germanized Forest Songs) in 1649. Olearius published several scholarly tracts on scientific subjects, such as *Kurtze Erinnerung und Bericht, von der grossen und erschrecklichen Sonnen-Finsterniß* (Short Reminder and Report on the Great and Terrible Eclipse of the

*Engraved title page for the enlarged second edition of Olearius's
account of his journeys to Russia and Persia*

Sun, 1630) and *Neues Astrolabium* (New Astrolabe, 1632).

Olearius left secondary-school teaching in 1632, when he briefly joined a group of eight university instructors who supervised the academic progress of students to whom they rented rooms in the building in which they lived; their rental income was supplemented by the sale of beer to the students. As the newest member of the group, Olearius was responsible for selecting the students who would live in the building, collecting the rent, and making sure that the students returned to their rooms by curfew; he also received a smaller share of the proceeds.

Also during this period he became friends with Paul Fleming, with whom he shared a keen interest in poetry in the German language. Olearius seems to have been aware of the younger poet's superior gifts, and he helped further Fleming's career. Olearius was, to the extent of his abilities, Fleming's patron, audience, and critic; in a poem, Fleming called Olearius a "rechtgesinnter Richter" (rightly minded judge) of his works.

In 1633 Olearius was recruited by Philipp Crusius, an influential lawyer at the court of Holstein-Gottorf, on behalf of Friedrich III, one of the most learned rulers of his day, to join a mission to negotiate a new overland trade route from Persia through Russia to the Baltic by way of Gottorf, and from there to Western Europe. The court was heavily in debt, and Otto Brüggemann, a Hamburg merchant and adventurer, had led Friedrich to believe that Holstein-Gottorf could become a trade center for Western Europe, bringing great riches to the duchy. Olearius was to serve as secretary, and Fleming, whom Olearius had recommended to Crusius, as a *Hofjunker* (gentleman attendant). In addition to his duties as secretary, Olearius received special instructions from Friedrich to make a record of the history and geography of the places they visited.

Olearius himself constructed the astrolabe that he took on the journey.

The mission, under the leadership of Brüggemann and Crusius, left in November 1633 and traveled via Lübeck, Riga, Reval, and Novgorod, arriving in Moscow on 14 August 1634 after many hardships and tribulations. After long negotiations, Czar Michael Feodorovitch gave them permission to cross Russian territories en route to Persia. The members of the trade delegation fraternized with the Germans serving in the czar's court, from whom Olearius gained material for his description of conditions in Russia. Some members of the delegation, including Olearius, returned to Gottorf to prepare for the journey to Persia, while Fleming and others remained in Reval, an important trading city in Estonia with a sizable German population, to await their return with appropriate documents and additional personnel. In the spring of 1635 Olearius went on a diplomatic mission to Brussels. On the return trip he became seriously ill and had to be nursed at Brüggemann's house in Hamburg. During this time he wrote the poem *Lustige Historia, woher das Toback-Trincken kommt* (Merry Tale on the Origin of Drinking Tobacco, 1633), a humorous myth about the contemporary practice of consuming tobacco.

In spite of his weakened condition, Olearius joined the trade expedition when it departed on its second journey to Russia and Persia on 22 October 1635. On 8 November the legation's ship wrecked near the coast of Estonia; the party had to wait in Reval for three months for new letters of authorization to replace the ones lost in the wreck, delaying their arrival in Moscow until 29 March 1636. On 30 June the envoys departed for Persia on Russian boats, then boarded the *Friedrich,* constructed by shipbuilders who had been sent from Holstein. On 10 October the *Friedrich* sailed out onto the Caspian Sea, where the legation suffered another shipwreck. Brüggemann's erratic behavior and a shortage of funds caused the mood of the legation to grow increasingly despondent. The hardships they endured together drew Olearius, Fleming, Johann Albrecht von Mandelslo, Hartmann Gramann, and Hans Christoph von Üchtritz into a close friendship that Olearius would treasure many years later, when he was called upon to edit the works of Fleming, Mandelslo, and Heinrich von Üchtritz, a relative of Hans Christoph von Üchtritz's, after their deaths.

The legation reached Shemāchā, an important silk center, on 30 December 1636. During the three months the mission awaited an audience with the Persian shah Safi, Olearius began to learn the Per-

sian language and received a copy of the *Golestān*, the Persian poet Sa'dī's great poem, which Olearius would later translate into German. Persian scholars assisted him with astronomic coordinates of cities and maps of various regions of Persia, which helped him to draw his own remarkably accurate map of the country.

At the end of March 1637 the legation left for Ardabīl, reaching Isfahan, the capital of Persia, on 3 August. On 19 September Brüggemann assured the shah, in exchange for the exclusive right to import Persian raw silk to Europe, not only of Gottorf's financial and military assistance against the Turks but of the assistance of the German emperor and all other Christian rulers, as well. Such sweeping promises showed that Brüggemann had underestimated the Persians' political astuteness. He went even further by demanding that Persia remove all Dutch merchants from its territory. In addition to such political miscalculations, Brüggemann's unpredictable personal behavior did not meet with the approval of the Persians, and there were many occasions when the whole company feared for their lives.

On 21 December 1637 the legates started the return journey, which proved to be even more difficult than the journey to Persia had been. A few days later an envoy of the shah caught up with them and accompanied them on the rest of the journey; the Persians had evidently decided that Brüggemann's promises warranted further inquiry. The legation reached Moscow in January 1639 and left for Revel on 15 March, arriving on 13 April. Two days later Olearius left Revel; he returned to Gottorf ahead of the trade legation, which arrived on 1 August 1639, six years after first departing for Russia. The only results of the negotiations with the Russians and Persians were promises of further exchanges that were, however, never fulfilled. Some members of the Persian envoy's entourage decided to remain in Germany; among them was the envoy's secretary, Hakwirdi, and his son, both of whom were eventually baptized into the Christian religion. Hakwirdi stayed at Olearius's house until his death in 1650, further instructing Olearius in the Persian language and helping him with the translation of Sa'dī's *Golestān*. In December 1639 Brüggemann was arrested for exceeding his authority, especially regarding his offer of a military alliance with the shah; of acting behind the backs of the other envoys; of incorrect accounting; of moral indiscretions; and of many other offenses. He was found guilty and was executed on 5 May 1640. Although Crusius moved to Revel to conduct the negotiations, the attempt to

Pages from Olearius's Vermehrte Newe Beschreibung der Musowitischen und Persischen Reyse. *Olearius supervised the engraving of the illustrations, many of which were based on drawings he had made on the journeys.*

conclude a trade project with Persia failed. The project was abandoned in 1642.

Soon after his return from Russia and Persia, Olearius was named court mathematician at Holstein-Gottorf on the recommendation of his friend Johann Adolf Kielmann, an important minister at the court. (The czar had also offered him a position as court astronomer; but Olearius had wisely declined, as many Russians considered him a magician and astrologer.) Kielmann also encouraged Olearius to revise his journal of the trip to Persia for eventual publication. Olearius married Catharina Müller, the daughter of the prominent Revel merchant and senator Johann Müller, on 15 October 1640; they had three daughters and a son. Olearius made another trip to Russia for further negotiations with the czar in 1643. In Revel, Olearius prepared Fleming's poetry for publication; Fleming had died in 1640, shortly after completing the re-

quirements for his medical degree in Leiden. In April 1644 Olearius was given property near the castle of Gottorf, on which he built a home. His scientific pursuits during this period included the construction of a telescope and a microscope. His edition of Fleming's *Teutsche Poemata* (German Poems) appeared in 1646.

Olearius's *Offt begehrte Beschreibung der Newen Orientalischen Reise, so durch Gelegenheit einer Holsteinischen Legation an den König in Persien geschehen* (Often Desired Description of the Recent Oriental Journey That Occurred on the Occasion of a Holstein Legation to the King of Persia, 1647), which includes poems by Fleming commemorating cataclysmic events and describing natural phenomena, is considered the first scientific travel account in German. In his preface Olearius says that his intention is to serve the interests of both "Gelahrten und Ungelahrten" (informed and less-informed readers).

The informed reader is provided with an account of the journey and a firsthand description of the lands Olearius visited; by omitting generally known facts and concentrating on new and interesting information, Olearius appeals to the curiosity of a less-well-read but interested general public. The work was translated into French, Dutch, English, and Italian, but its greatest success was in Germany, where it benefited from the rising popularity of travel accounts and increasing interest in Russia, which was gradually emerging as a major European power. Most of the illustrations of cities were based on drawings Olearius had made on the journey; some portraits and other illustrations were contributed by two other members of the delegation. Olearius supervised the production of the engravings, which were often borrowed for inclusion in other books.

Olearius became court librarian in 1649, and much of his time in the next years was spent bringing order to the book collection. He added many treasures to the library, making it one of the richest in Northern Europe – second only to the library of Duke August of Wolfenbüttel – and attracting the many scholars whom Friedrich III generously permitted to use its resources. Its rich holdings of ancient and oriental manuscripts were known throughout Europe, and it also contained valuable works in Arabic, Turkish, and Persian. It is clear from the authors and works cited by Olearius in various writings that the library had an extensive collection of the travel literature of the period. In 1650 he supervised the construction of a church in Friedrichsberg in memory of Beling, whom Olearius had instructed in mathematical applications and military surveying and who had gained some literary note through his translation of Virgil.

In addition to his position as librarian, in 1650 Olearius was put in charge of the duke's *Kunstkammer* (art room), whose treasures included the natural history collection of the Dutch physician Bernhard ten Brocke (latinized as Paludanus), which the duke had purchased, as well as curios from the trade expedition to Russia and Persia. Olearius's catalogue, *Gottorffische Kunst-Cammer* (1666), including thirty-six engravings he produced himself, describes selected objects in the collection, which was one of the largest and most impressive in Europe. His descriptions are centered on the scientific value of the objects and display a thorough knowledge of the scientific literature of the period. As so many notable objects could not be included in his catalogue, Olearius

apparently hoped to publish a second volume, but his plans were never realized. A glossary of the Arabic, Turkish, and Persian languages was also never finished.

In 1651 Olearius became a member of the Fruchtbringende Gesellschaft (Fruit-bringing Society), a group devoted to the advancement of German language and literature. Each member had a special name; Olearius's was Der Vielbemühete (The One of Whom Much Is Required), pointing to his many responsibilities on behalf of his sovereign. Olearius's translation of Sa'dī's *Golestān* as *Persianischer Rosenthal* (Persian Rose Valley, 1654) is a monument in European knowledge of Persian culture. Selections from the work had been translated into German – often erroneously – in 1636 by Johann Friedrich Ochsenbach, who had followed a 1634 French translation by André du Ryer. Olearius's extensive knowledge of Persia enabled him to capture the spirit of the work and avoid the errors of previous translators.

The amazing success of his account of the trade mission to Russia and Persia inspired Olearius to enlarge the work. As he says in the introduction to the second edition, lack of time caused by other duties and personal misfortunes, not a shortage of material, had prevented a more comprehensive approach in the original edition. He also made changes in the structure of the narrative to make it more accessible to his readers. He began work on the enlarged edition in 1654, and it was published in 1656. The new edition is divided into six books: the first book describes the first journey to Moscow; the second details the journey of 1635; the third gives a description of Russia; the fourth recounts the journey to Isfahan; the fifth gives an enlarged description of Persia; and the sixth recounts the return trip. The second edition also includes Olearius's map of the course of the Volga, which was based on astronomical calculations he had made during the trip on the river and which he had once planned to publish separately. The second edition is enhanced by a bibliography of more than 160 titles and an index. Describing cultural and historic phenomena of the lands he visited, Olearius not only gives a detailed account of the journey itself but relates his experiences to ancient and recent writings on Russia and Persia. Stylistically, the second edition was improved by the elimination of many foreign words. Olearius sought to promote German as a means of literary expression in his account, which is considered a masterpiece of German baroque prose. Olearius's work was valued by such contemporaries as the novelist Hans Jacob Christoffel von Grimmelshausen, whose *Der abenteurliche Simplicissimus Teutsch* (The Adventurous Simplicissimus German, 1669) shows his familiarity with Olearius's book and the poet and dramatist Andreas Gryphius. Later, Johann Wolfgang von Goethe would make use of Olearius's travel account, as well as the translation of Sa'dī's *Golestān* in preparation for writing the poetic cycle *West-Östlicher Divan* (West-Eastern Divan, 1819). Olearius's work has received little attention among Anglo-American scholars of Russia, although Russian historians have praised it for its detail and clarity.

Adding to the renown of the duke's court, Olearius designed two gigantic astronomical models – one of the Copernican planetary system and the other of the earth and the heavens. He began work on the latter model, the so-called Gottorffer Globus, in 1654, and it was completed ten years later. The gigantic, planetarium-like movable sphere, representing all the known heavenly bodies, had room for ten people to sit on a bench it contained. It was much admired and attracted many visitors; it was sent to Saint Petersburg as a gift to Peter the Great in 1713. Olearius also designed a spacious building in the Persian style to house the Globus.

In 1658 Olearius revised Mandelslo's account of his journey to India and had it published as *Morgenländische Reyse-Beschreibung* (Description of an Eastern Journey). His editorial changes were similar to the ones he had done in revising his own travel account for its second edition: he rearranged text, divided the work into books and chapters, corrected the orthography, replaced foreign words with German ones, and added an index.

In 1658 the Gottorf court was drawn into the hostilities between Sweden and Denmark; an unfortunate consequence for Olearius was the looting of his home that year. Another blow was the death in 1659 of his patron and friend Friedrich III. Olearius edited the account of the funeral ceremony, *HochFürstliche ansehnliche Leichbegängniß des Durchläuchtigsten Fürsten und Herrn, Herrn Friederichs* (Exceedingly Regal Majestic Funeral Procession of His Royal Highness Our Sovereign Friedrich, 1661). Frederick was succeeded by Christian Albrecht, with whom Olearius maintained a cordial but restrained relationship. In 1660 the multifaceted Olearius published *Compendium Fortificatorium*, a work on military fortifications. His *Kurtzer Begriff einer Holsteinischen Chronic* (Short Concept of a Chronicle of Holstein, 1663) gives a history of events from 1448 until 1662. He edited Heinrich

von Üchtritz's *Kurtze Reise Beschreibung* (Brief Description of a Journey, 1665) and Jürgen Andersen and Volquard Iversen's *Orientalische Reise-Beschreibunge* (Descriptions of an Oriental Journey, 1669), adding important notes, dividing the works into books and chapters, and correcting the orthography. In his final years Olearius translated or edited several religious works at the request of Friedrich's widow, Maria Elisabeth.

Olearius died on 22 February 1671. The funeral ceremonies took place in the cathedral at Schleswig, and his epitaph is to be found there. Olearius is buried in the church that he built in Friedrichsberg.

Bibliography:

Gerhard Dünnhaupt, *Personalbibliographien zu den Drucken des Barock,* volume 9, part 4 (Stuttgart: Hiersemann, 1991).

References:

Ludwig Andresen and Walter Stephan, *Beiträge zur Geschichte der Gottorfer Hof- und Staatsverwaltung von 1544–1659,* 2 volumes (Kiel: Gesellschaft für Schleswig-Holsteinische Geschichte, 1928);

Hanno Beck, "Die Brücke Deutschland-Iran: Zur Geschichte der Verbindung zweier Kulturvölker," *Iranzamin,* 1 (March/April 1981): 60–67;

Barbara Becker-Cantarino, "Drei Briefautographen von Paul Fleming," *Wolfenbütteler Beiträge,* 4 (1981): 191–204;

Faramarz Behzad, *Adam Olearius' "Persianischer Rosenthal": Untersuchungen zur Übersetzung von Saadis "Golestan" im 17. Jahrhundert,* Palaestra, no. 258 (Göttingen: Vandenhoeck & Ruprecht, 1970);

Naime O. Bishr, "Das 'Persianische Rosenthal' von Adam Olearius und Sa'dīs 'Gulistan': Eine geistesgeschichtliche Untersuchung," dissertation, Rutgers University, 1974;

Steen Ove Christensen, "'Kurtzer Begriff einer holsteinischen Chronic' und die Kriegsereignisse . . . in der Regierungszeit Herzog Friedrich III," *Zeitschrift der Gesellschaft für Schleswig-Holsteinische Geschichte,* 109 (1984): 123–150;

Alfons Gabriel, *Die Erforschung Persiens: Die Entwicklung der abendländischen Kenntnis der Geographie Persiens* (Vienna: Holzhausen, 1952);

Aleksandr L'vovic Gol'dberg, "Adam Olearius 1603–1671," in *Wegbereiter der deutsch-slawischen*

Wechselseitigkeit, edited by Eduard Winter and Günther Jarosch (Berlin: Akademie-Verlag, 1983), pp. 7–15;

Fawzy D. Guirguis, "Bild und Funktion des Orients in Werken der deutschen Literatur des 17. und 18. Jahrhunderts," dissertation, Free University of Berlin, 1972;

Paul Habermann, "Adam Olearius, der 'Vielbemühete,'" in *Lebensbilder großer Stephaneer,* edited by Otto Ritzau (Aschersleben, 1930), pp. 13–30;

Lorenz Hein, "Adam Olearius und seine Begegnung mit der russisch-orthodoxen Kirche," *Kyrios,* 2 (1962): 1–17;

Uwe Liszkowski, "Adam Olearius' Beschreibung des Moskauer Reiches," in *Russen und Rußland aus deutscher Sicht 9.–17. Jahrhundert,* edited by Mechthild Keller (Munich: Fink, 1985), pp. 223–247;

N. Neuber, "Adam Olearius," *Archiv für die Geschichte der Naturwissenschaften,* 14/15 (1985): 723–728;

Anton Schiefner, "Über das Stammbuch von Adam Olearius," *Das Inland,* no. 44 (1851): 767–772;

Ernst Schlee, ed., *Gottorfer Kultur im Jahrhundert der Universitätsgründung: Ausstellungskatalog* (Flensburg: Wolff, 1965);

Karin Unsicker, *Weltliche Barockprosa in Schleswig-Holstein,* Kieler Studien zur deutschen Literaturgeschichte, no. 10 (Neumünster: Wachholtz, 1974);

H. H. Weil, "A Seventeenth-Century German Looks at Russia," *German Life and Letters,* 8 (1954–1955): 59–64.

Papers:

The largest collections of Adam Olearius's letters are at the Landesarchiv Schleswig-Holstein, Schloß Gottorf, and at the Universitätsbibliothek Kiel.

Martin Opitz

(23 December 1597 – 20 August 1639)

Barbara Becker-Cantarino
Ohio State University

SELECTED BOOKS: *Strenarum Libellus, Val. Sanftleben, Praetori et Rectori Patriae, consecratus* (Görlitz: Printed by Johann Rambau, 1616);

Aristarchus sive De Contemptu Linguae Teutonicae (Bethaniae: Printed by Johannes Dörfer, 1617);

Hipponax ad Asterien puellam formae et animi dotibus longè amabilissimam. Item Germanica quaedam ejusdem argumenti (Görlitz: Printed by Johann Rambau, 1618);

Zlatna, oder von Rhue des Gemütes (Liegnitz: Sebastian Koch, 1623);

Lob deß Feldtlebens (N.p., 1623);

Buch von der Deutschen Poeterey. Jn welchem alle jhre eigenschafft vnd zuegehör gründtlich erzehlet, vnd mit exempeln außgeführet wird (Breslau: Published by David Müller, printed by Augustin Gründer in Brieg, 1624); revised as *Prosodia Germanica oder gantz neu corrigirtes vnd verbessertes Buch von der Teutschen Poeterey, jn welchem alle jhre Eigenschafft vnd Zugehör gründlich erzehlet, vnd mit vielfeltigen Exempeln weder in vorheriger Edition zufinden außgeführt werden* (Breslau: David Müller, 1634);

Martini Opicii Teutsche Pöemata und Arjstarchvs wieder die verachtung Teutscher Sprach, Item Verteutschung Danielis Heinsij Lobgesangs Iesu Christi, vnd Hymni in Bachum sampt einem anhang mehr außerlesener geticht anderer Teutscher Pöeten. Der gleichen in dieser Sprach hiebeuor nicht auß kommen, edited by Julius Wilhelm Zincgref (Strasbourg: Eberhard Zetzner, 1624);

Lobgesang vber den Frewdenreichen Geburtstag vnseres Herrn vnd Heilandes Jesu Christi (Liegnitz: Sebastian Koch, 1624);

Martini Opitii Acht Bücher, Deutscher Poematum durch Jhn selber heraus gegeben, auch also vermehret vnnd übersehen, das die vorigen darmitte nicht zu uergleichen sind (Breslau: David Müller, 1625); enlarged as *Deütscher Poëmatum Erster Theil: Zum andern mal vermehrt vnd vbersehen herauß gegeben* (Breslau: David Müller, 1629);

Martin Opitz; painting by Stroble (Gdansk City Library)

Dafne. Auff deß Durchlauchtigen Hochgebornen Fürsten vnd Herrn, Herrn Georgen, Landtgrafen zu Hessen . . . vnd der Durchlauchtigen, Hochgebornen Fürstinn vnd Fräwlein, Fräwlein Sophien Eleonoren, Hertzogin zu Sachsen, music by Heinrich Schütz (Breslau: David Müller, 1627);

Jonas (Breslau: David Müller, 1628);

Die Episteln der Sontage vnd fürnehmsten Feste des gantzen Jahrs, auff die Weisen der Frantzösischen Psalmen in Lieder gefasset (Breslau: Published by David Müller, printed by Johann Albrecht Mintzel in Leipzig, 1628);

Vber das Leiden vnd Sterben vnseres Heilandes (Breslau: David Müller, 1628);

Lavdes Martis. Martini Opitii Poëma Germanicum. Ad Illustriß. Dn. Dn. Carolum Annibalem Burggravium Dohnensem (Breslau: David Müller, 1628);

Deütscher Poëmatum anderer Theil; zuevor nie besammen, theils auch noch nie herauß gegeben (Breslau: David Müller, 1629);

Vjelgvet (Breslau: Published by David Müller, printed by Augustin Gründer in Brieg, 1629);

Schäfferey von der Nimfen Hercinie (Breslau: Published by David Müller, printed in Brieg, 1630);

Silvarum Libri III. Epigrammatvm Liber Vnvs (Breslau: David Müller, 1631);

Vesvvivs. Poëma Germanicum (Breslau: David Müller, 1633);

TrostGedichte jn Widerwertigkeit deß Kriegs; Jn vier Bücher abgetheilt, vnd vor etzlichen Jahren von einem behandten Poëten anderwerts geschrieben, anonymous (Breslau: Published by David Müller, printed by Henning Köhler in Leipzig, 1633);

Judith (Breslau: Georg Baumann, 1635);

Lobgeticht an die Königliche Majestät zu Polen vnd Schweden (Thorn: Printed by Franz Schnellboltz, 1636);

Deutscher Poematum, 2 volumes (N.p., 1637);

Geistliche Poëmata, von jhm selbst anjetzo zusammen gelesen, verbessert vnd absonderlich herauß gegeben (Breslau: David Müller's heirs, 1638);

Weltliche Poëmata. Das Erste Theil. Zum vierdten mal vermehret vnd vbersehen herauß gegeben (Breslau: David Müller's heirs, 1638);

Opera Poetica. Das ist Geistliche und Weltliche Poemata. Vom Autore selbst zum letzten vbersehen vnd verbessert, 2 volumes (Amsterdam: Johannes Jansson, 1645–1646).

Collections and Editions: *Gesammelte Werke,* 3 volumes projected, 2 volumes published, edited by George Schulz-Behrend, Bibliothek des Literarischen Vereins Stuttgart, volumes 295–297 (Stuttgart: Hiersemann, 1968–   );

Schäfferey von der Nimfen Hercinie, edited by Karl F. Otto (Stuttgart: Reclam, 1969);

Gedichte: Eine Auswahl (Stuttgart: Reclam, 1970);

Jugendschriften vor 1619, edited by Jörg Ulrich Fechner (Stuttgart: Metzler, 1970);

Buch von der deutschen Poeterey (1624) (Stuttgart: Reclam, 1974);

Geistliche Poemata 1638, edited by Erich Trunz (Tübingen: Niemeyer, 1975);

Weltliche Poemata 1644, 2 volumes, edited by Trunz (Tübingen: Niemeyer, 1975).

OTHER: Sir Philip Sidney, *Arcadia der Gräfin von Pembrock: vom Herrn Grafen vnd Rittern Herrn Philippsen von Sidney jn Englischer Sprach* geschrieben, auß derselben Frantzösisch, vnd auß beyden erstlich Teutsch gegeben durch Valentinvm Theokritvm von Hirschberg: Jetzo allenthalben vffs new vbersehen vnd gebessert: die Gedichte aber vnd Reymen gantz anderst gemacht vnd vbersetzt,* translated by "Valentinus Theocritus von Hirschberg," revised by Opitz (Frankfurt am Main: Published by Matthäus Merian, printed by Wolfgang Hoffmann, 1638);

Incerti Poetae Tevtonici Rythmvs de Sancto Annone Colon. Archiepiscopo ante D. Avt Circiter annos conscriptus, edited by Opitz (Danzig: Printed by Andreas Hünefeldt, 1639);

François de Rosset, *Theatrum Tragicum oder Traurige Geschichten, mit vielen Alten vnd Newen warhafften Historien vermehret vnd mit fleiß Corigirt, Durch Martinum Zeillerum Styrum, die Fünffte Edition darinnen die Deutschen Reimen gantz anders gemacht,* revised by Opitz (Danzig: Andreas Hünefeldt, 1640).

TRANSLATIONS: Daniel Heinsius, *Lobgesang Jesu Christi des einigen vnd ewigen Sohnes Gottes* (Görlitz: Johann Rambau, 1621);

Heinsius, *Hymnus oder Lobgesang Bacchi, darinnen der gebrauch vnd mißbrauch des Weines beschrieben wird* (Liegnitz: Fürstliche Druckerei, 1622);

Lucius Annaeus Seneca, *Trojanerjnnen; Deutsch übersetzet, vnd mit leichter Außlegung erklert* (Wittenberg: Published by Zacharias Schürer, printed by August Boreck, 1625);

Die Klage-Lieder Jeremia; Poetisch gesetzt durch Martin Opitzen; sampt noch anderen seiner newen Gedichten (Görlitz: Johann Rambau, 1626);

John Barclay, *Argenis Deutsch gemacht* (Breslau: David Müller, 1626);

Salomons des Hebreischen Königes Hohes Liedt (Breslau: David Müller, 1627);

Hugo Grotius, *De Capta Rupella Carmen Heroicum* (Breslau: Printed by Georg Baumann, 1629);

Psalmus XCI. versibus Latinis ac Germanicis expressus (Breslau: Georg Baumann the Younger, 1629);

Antoine de Chandieu, *Von der Welt Eitelkeit. Auß dem Frantzösischen* (Breslau: David Müller, 1629);

Dionysius Cato, *Disticha de Moribvs ad Filium* (Breslau: Published by David Müller, printed by Georg Baumann, 1629);

Vber den CIIII. Psalm (Brieg: Printed by Augustin Gründer, 1630);

Julius Caesar Scaliger, *O Jesu. Unus e catellis sim.* (N.p., 1630);

Martin Becanus, *Becanvs Redivivvs, das ist, deß . . . Herrn Martini Becani der Societät Jesu Theologen S.*

*Handtbuch: Aller dieser Zeit in der Religion
Streitsachen in 5. Bücher abgetheilt* (Frankfurt am
Main: Johann Theobald Schönwetter, 1631);

Grotius, *Von der Warheit der Christlichen Religion auß
Holländischer Sprache Hochdeutsch gegeben*
(Breslau: David Müller, 1631);

A. M. de Mouchemberg, *Der Argenis Anderer Theyl*
(Breslau: David Müller, 1631);

Jean Puget de la Serre, *Die Süssen Todesgedancken. Auß
dem frantzösischen des von Serre* (Breslau: David
Müller, 1632);

Guy du Faur, Seigneur de Pibrac, *Vidi Fabri Pibracii
in supremo senatu Parisiensi praesidis olim
Tetrasticha Gallica, Germanicis versibus expressa*
(Danzig: Printed by Andreas Hünefeld, 1634);

*Zehen Psalmen Davids aus dem eigentlichen Verstande der
Schrifft, auff anderer Psalmen vnd Gesänge
gewöhnliche Weisen gesetzt* (Breslau: David
Müller, 1634);

*Der Achte, Drey vndt zwanzigste, Vier vndt Neunzigste,
Hundert vier vndt zwanzigste Hundert vndt Acht
vndt zwanzigste Psalm, auff anderer Psalmen
gewöhnliche weisen gesetzt* (Breslau: Georg
Baumann the Younger, 1635); enlarged as
*Sechs Psalmen auff anderer gewöhnliche Weisen
gesetzt* (Breslau: Georg Baumann the Younger,
1635);

*Zwölf Psalmen Davids auff jhre eigene vndt anderer
gewönliche weisen gesetz* (Breslau: David Müller's
heirs, 1636);

Sophocles, *Des Griechischen Tragödienschreibers
Sophoclis Antjgone* (Danzig: Printed by Andreas
Hünefeldt, 1636);

Die Psalmen Davids nach den Frantzösischen Weisen gesetzt
(Danzig: Andreas Hünefeldt, 1637; enlarged,
1638).

Martin Opitz was the major German representative of late Renaissance poetry in northern Europe. He ushered in a new era in German literature,
the baroque, with his programmatic *Buch von der
Deutschen Poeterey* (Book of German Poetry, 1624),
which set new standards for poetry fashioned after
elegant Neo-Latin, French, Italian, and Dutch Renaissance models while breaking with the popular,
often vulgar literary production and irregular versification of his German predecessors. With the example of his own poetry he propagated a national,
humanistic literary program in his own country,
which had adopted his views by the time of his pre-
mature death in 1639 – making him, in the eyes of
later generations, the "father of German literature."
His life and literary production were deeply affected
by the religious wars of the seventeenth century and

by the rising power of absolutist princes; thus, his
biography is as much influenced by politics as it is
exemplary of a poet and a learned man of his age.

Opitz was born on 23 December 1597 in the
Silesian town of Bunzlau, which was then predominantly Lutheran but belonged to the Bohemian
crown and was subject to the Catholic Hapsburgs.
His father was a butcher; thus, Opitz lacked the
connections to learned and wealthy patrician circles
that were necessary for a university education and
study tours abroad. With his outstanding intelligence and phenomenal memory, however, Opitz
quickly entered the world of learning, and he would
later have a splendid career in aristocratic circles.
As a scholarship student he was able to attend the
prestigious Maria-Magdalena Latin School in
Breslau, where he enjoyed an excellent humanist
education; he wrote his first poems in Latin as a
pupil in Breslau, publishing a collection of some
thirty-one poems addressed to distinguished citizens
of Bunzlau in *Strenarum Libellus* (A Book of New
Year's Presents) in 1616. In 1617 he transferred,
with the help of the headmaster of Maria-Magdalena,
Caspar Dornau (to whom he had dedicated a fine
Latin elegy on the occasion of Dornau's recovery
from severe illness), to the exclusive academy at
Beuthen recently founded by Georg von Schönaich.
During his school years he met learned humanists
and became acquainted with Calvinist and irenic
notions of religious tolerance. In Beuthen he readied himself for university study; it was there that he
had the vision of creating a poetics of the German
language equal to those of the other European literatures.

The first documentation of his desire for reform was the Latin speech *Aristarchus sive De Contemptu Linguae Teutonicae* (Aristarchus; or, On the
Contempt for the German Language, 1617). While
writing in Latin himself, Opitz claims that the Latin
language is in decline and that the future belongs to
German. He intends, he says, to encourage the
growth of an elegant, artistic literature in the native
language of his country, similar to those France,
Italy, and England had produced in the sixteenth
century and even earlier. Opitz recounts the glories
of the German past in the manner of Tacitus; he laments the deterioration of German and the increasing use of foreign terms and phrases; but he praises
the older German tradition into which he places his
own poetic endeavors: a poem in alexandrine meter
addressed to his friend and classmate Tobias
Scultetus von Schwanenseh, epigrammatic verses, a
sonnet, translations of the French *vers commun,* and
several anagrams. Opitz would expand on this po-

etic program in a more systematic and specific fashion in his *Buch von der Deutschen Poeterey*.

After a short stay in Frankfurt an der Oder, Opitz moved in 1619 to Heidelberg, which was then predominantly Calvinist, to study at the university; he never earned a university degree. In Heidelberg he lived as a tutor in the home of Privy Councillor Georg Michael Lingelsheim, a noted humanist, and met a community of like-minded students and important humanist scholars, among them Janus Gruter, a philologist and librarian at the Palatina, the Heidelberg library. He visited Strasbourg and the circle of Matthias Bernegger. In Tübingen he met Julius Wilhelm Zincgref, who was to publish the first – and unauthorized – edition of Opitz's poetry in 1624.

The Thirty Years' War had broken out in 1618. With the invasion of the Palatinate by Spanish troops Opitz, like many other scholars and students, fled. He traveled to the Netherlands, where he visited the Dutch classicist and poet Daniel Heinsius in Leyden; he admired Heinsius's *Nederduytsche Poemata* (Dutch Poetry, 1616), part of which he had translated and which he used as a model for his German verse. He also met the noted philologists Justus Scaliger and Gerard Vossius. After a seven-month stay in Jylland, Denmark – where, under the influence of Dutch Calvinism and Neostoicism, he conceived his *TrostGedichte in Widerwertigkeit deß Kriegs* (Poem of Consolation in the Adversity of War, 1633) – he returned to Silesia in 1621. He did not obtain employment at the court of Duke Georg Rudolf of Liegnitz, in spite of his prolific production of occasional and scholarly writings for the court. Finally, on Georg Rudolf's recommendation he received a position as professor at the newly established Weißenburg Latin Academy in Transylvania, in the service of Prince Bethlen Gabor, the Calvinist prince of Transylvania, in the spring of 1622. He had little interest in teaching, deriving more satisfaction from writing occasional and religious poems; collecting Roman inscriptions as an amateur archeologist; and visiting a friend's country home in the small mining town of Zlatna, which he used as a setting for his first major didactic poem, *Zlatna, oder von Rhue des Gemütes* (Zlatna; or, Of Calmness of the Mind, 1623). Because of the approach of the war, lack of money, and oppressive living conditions, in August 1623 Opitz returned to Silesia, where he finished *Zlatna* for publication.

In accordance with his credo that poetics contains within it all other arts and learning, Opitz placed the *Lehrgedicht* (didactic or philosophical poem) above all others. His earliest didactic poem,

Title page for Opitz's book of poetics, which revolutionized German poetry

Lob des Feldtlebens (In Praise of Country Life, 1623), was written during his student years and is a reworking of Horace's second epode; it also draws heavily on Virgil's *Georgica*. Opitz does not attempt to be true to reality; he contrasts an idealized rural life with the inconstant life at court and in times of war. The theme of constancy is more fully developed in *Zlatna*, growing out of his experiences in Transylvania: the sight of the remains of Roman antiquity reminds him of the transitoriness of earthly splendor. In the five hundred verses of *Zlatna*, which are replete with learned annotations, he insists that not at the court nor in the cities but only in the country can the human being come to self-reflection. Not honor or property, but calmness of the mind is the most enduring value. Opitz's hymn of praise to country life, where peace and constancy might best be achieved, sounds like an early "back to nature" piece; but it is not an emotional, impassioned call, like Jean-Jacques Rousseau's some hundred years later. Rather, in the rural idyll he advocates the self-sufficient ideal of an education of the mind associated with Epicurus, Seneca, and the Stoics.

On his return from Transylvania, Opitz again tried unsuccessfully to obtain a position with Georg Rudolf in Liegnitz. In the following years he drifted between Liegnitz and Breslau without finding a regular job, living sometimes with friends and sometimes with his parents. Economic restraints, however, did not dampen his productivity as a poet and scholar. He finally experienced a breakthrough in 1624 with *Buch von der Deutschen Poeterey,* followed in 1625 by the first of his authorized collections of poetry, *Martini Opitii Acht Bücher, Deutscher Poematum* (Martin Opitz's Eight Books of German Poetry). Both works were direct reactions to the 1624 publication of *Martini Opicii Teutsche Pöemata und Aristarchus wieder die verachtung Teutscher Sprach, Item Verteutschung Danielis Heinsii Lobgesangs Iesu Christi, und Hymni in Bachum* (Martin Opitz's German Poems and Aristarchus against the Contempt for the German Language, Likewise His Translation of Daniel Heinsius's Song of Praise of Jesus Christ, and Hymn to Bacchus), which Opitz had prepared for publication when he was in Heidelberg in 1620 but was instead published by Zincgref in Strasbourg. These texts no longer conformed to Opitz's stylistic ideal, and he arranged for a republication of his own revising and regrouping of the texts. For Opitz, a literature in his mother tongue would necessarily incorporate the learned ideals of humanism. Thus, Opitz's work departed sharply from the nonlearned, popular, even vulgar literature written in the vernacular during the sixteenth century in Germany. While Latin had been the language of choice for the educated and the courtier, with the appearance of his work Opitz's contemporaries realized that the German language held the promise of attaining literary distinction on an international level.

The *Buch von der Deutschen Poeterey,* supposedly written in five days in 1624, did not provide much that was substantially new, but it continued and expanded the vision expressed in *Aristarchus* of a renovation of German language and literature. The work had much the same significance as Joachim du Bellay's *La Defence et Illustration de la Langue Francoyse* (1549) had for French Renaissance literature; in its attention to technical detail it resembles Pierre de Ronsard's *Abrégé de l'art poétique* (1565), a set of prescriptions for writing poems in the high Renaissance style. Opitz draws heavily on the ideals of the Renaissance poets, on Ronsard, Heinsius, Horace, Julius Caesar Scaliger, and Johann Wower. Yet his departures from his sources usher in an entirely differ-

ent poetic, one that gives ample play to the baroque taste for contrast and surprise, as well as recommending a conscious verbal ambiguity entirely different from Pléiade poetics (the classicist style of French poets led by Pierre de Ronsard), as Wilfried Barner has pointed out.

Although *Buch von der Deutschen Poeterey* is a brief treatise, its guiding principles are of epoch-making proportions. The first four chapters address overarching questions of poetry. Opitz gives his reasons for writing the work: he has been requested to do so by aristocratic circles, and he wishes to further the elegance of his native tongue. Poetry is a gift to the poet, who is born and not made; it is inextricably related to the divine. It is fundamentally edifying, a form of philosophy, and not merely pleasurable; the poet has to be wise and educated, and poetry should be terse and sententious. Opitz asserts the worth of poetry and of the poet and criticizes poetry's detractors and hack poets. In chapter 4 he gives poetic examples from the Germanic tradition; the remaining three chapters deal with the technicalities of a new German poetic literature soon to be established, with poetic themes and subject matter, with various types of poetry and drama, with the choice of a truly poetic language, and with rhyme and metrics. In conclusion, Opitz suggests translating from Greek and Latin as an excellent exercise and a form of spiritual communication with wise men of distant times. He asserts the importance of learning over earthly wealth: it is far better to know much and to own little than to own much and to know little. Opitz directed his literary program to aristocrats and scholars, hoping that it could be realized in a principality whose ruler was interested in supporting cultural efforts. Early in the era of absolutism such a cultural program could survive only if power and intellect joined in a coalition of princes and scholars. The integration of literature into courtly circles is implicit in such a symbiosis.

The idea of literary rivalry and a fervor for a German national literature also characterize *Buch von der Deutschen Poeterey.* If Latin ceased to be a gauge of education, then the German writer should at least be able to prove his learning through the choice of scholarly themes and mastery of his artistic craft. Talent and knowledge balance one another. Opitz promotes a synthesis of rhetorical training and humanist education with poetic talent and inspiration. No amount of theoretical instruction can compensate for a lack of familiarity with the classics. A mastery of Latin and a thorough knowledge of all important fields of learning are indispensable.

Opitz provides a legitimation of the poetic enterprise, an enterprise that seemed questionable to many of his contemporaries. He supplies a list of justifications for respecting writing as an occupation. He was able to draw from a well-established pool of arguments in responding to the question of the goals of writing. The highest end is education: literature serves as a governess of life, facilitating good manners, control of the emotions, and good behavior; it is a practical philosophy that delivers its maxims with the help of demonstration and example. Opitz refutes accusations commonly made against poets, such as their uselessness, immorality, bad manners, mass production, social denigration, lack of love for truth, and preference for classical mythology over the Christian tradition (the deities of antiquity were considered by many of Opitz's contemporaries to be "heathen gods" and thus unacceptable for a Christian literature). Opitz expresses the wish that individuals of high social rank would write, so that German literature would no longer lag behind those of France and Italy. With Opitz, writing attains the level of a science: it presupposes education, knowledge, and training on the part of the poet. Herein lies the core of his reform, as Gunter Grimm has asserted.

Opitz outlines two avenues for bestowing literature in the native language with the character of a science: one argument relates to its content, the other to its form. In regard to content, Opitz claims that since poetry contains all other arts and learning within it, the poet must be well versed in all subjects; in regard to form, he argues for rhetorically sophisticated poetry. Education, persuasion, and entertainment are the goals of poetry, which consists of the trinity *inventio* (selection of subject matter), *dispositio* (arrangement of the material, or plot), and *elocutio* (stylistic and linguistic embellishment). The distinction between rhetorical speech and poetry lies exclusively in the metric form of the latter: poetry is rhythmic and rhymed rhetorical speech. The educational and political motivation implicit in this argument emerges: a poetic work that could be produced with the same techniques as the well-established rhetorical speech would readily be accepted as scholarly. Knowledge of the subject and rhetorical training and competence form the basic requirements for the successful *poeta doctus* (learned poet).

Buch von der Deutschen Poeterey had its most tangible and lasting effects with its concise statement of innovative accent regulation, which clearly fixed the relationship between metric emphasis in poetry and natural word accent in the German language,

thereby ending a century of uncertainty and the practice – soon to be regarded as awkward and old-fashioned – of free verse alternation in *Knittelvers* (doggerel verse). According to Opitz, in contrast to Greek and Latin, where syllabic length determines the accent, for the German language the stressed syllable is the deciding factor in accent position. Thus, the poet must pay attention to the agreement of metric and lexical accent. Nevertheless, Opitz recognized only the strictly alternating meters, the iambic and trochaic. He was cautious as concerned all other verse feet, such as the dactyl, as they could only be forced artificially onto the German language. The ensuing popularity of the alexandrine hexameter – consisting of six iambic feet – attests to the validity and importance of his suggestions in setting the standard; along with the pentameter, or *vers commun*, the alexandrine became the most common verse of the German baroque.

For the first half of the seventeenth century Opitz's classicistic ideals of style – elegance, purity, clarity, harmony, and appropriateness – were universally accepted. Opitz was a purist; his demand that the poet should avoid dialect and foreign words was justifiable in view of the widespread language confusion of the time. On the other hand, he encouraged the development of new metaphors. Opitz defines the appropriateness of expression according to criteria of social standing and literary genre, ignoring the communicative situation in which the work is received. Literary genres are accorded specific positions in the stylistic hierarchy: comedies and pastorals use the *stilus levis* (lower speech); epics and tragedies, which involve gods, heroes, and kings, use the *stilus gravis* (stately and elevated language); all other literary forms are placed in the middle as *stilus medius*.

The immense success of Opitz's poetics has been interpreted by Volker Sinemus as "ästhetische Vorausprojektion eines absolutischen Zentralstaates" (aesthetic prediction of an absolutist central state), as Opitz fought for "sprachliche und formale Einheit und gegen regionale Sondersprachen" (linguistic and formal unity and against specific regional demands). Grimm says that he supported "ein hierarchisches Ordnungsbewußtsein" (a hierarchical concept of order) and that he practiced "das Prinzip strenger Gesetzeslenkung" (the principle of strict ruling by laws) in the area of poetry. The idea of an aesthetic anticipation of absolutism is appealing, as it conveys the notion of an analogy between political and poetic structures. It does not hold true, however, in regard to Opitz's stylistic recommendations, as the elegance propagated by Opitz is noth-

Title page for the first authorized collection of Opitz's poetry

reading of biblical and classical texts in Latin and Greek was followed by translation and then by student's own attempts at creative imitation. Thus, it is not surprising to find many poems that are translations, adaptations, or responses to other poetic texts, to classical authors such as Horace, Ovid, and the Greek Anthology (then recently discovered and immensely popular), and to then-modern authors of the Renaissance, from Petrarch to Ronsard and, especially, Heinsius.

As is the case with all baroque collections, book 1 opens with religious poems: poems on the birth and death of Christ, an adaptation of the 104th Psalm, and the especially impressive long philosophical poem "Auff den Anfang des 1621. Jahres" (On the Beginning of the Year 1621). His earlier didactic poems *Lob des Feldtlebens* and *Zlatna* are reprinted as book 2, together with his translation of Heinsius's hymn to Bacchus. Book 3 comprises a series of occasional poems arranged by the recipient's social status, beginning with Archduke Carl of Austria. Book 4 consists of wedding poems. The occasional poem is a major genre, second only to the religious poem in the new German poetry of the baroque era. As Heinsius carefully groups his poetry in the vernacular according to the importance of its subject matter in his collection *Nederduytsche Poemata,* so Opitz places his love poems in book 5, his verses on secular topics in book 6, sonnets in book 7, and epigrams in book 8 – after the religious and occasional poems. Opitz would expand the collection in later editions in 1629 and would ultimately separate it into separate volumes of *geistliche* (religious) and *weltliche* (secular) poems in 1638. The secular poems are Opitz's most innovative and interesting poetic creations.

Opitz's importance as a writer lies foremost in the area of lyric poetry. He was the first to introduce Petrarchan love poetry, in its entire width of expression of motive and metaphor, into German poetry. He created exemplary works in all forms, above all the pleasing Anacreontic song, the Pindaric ode, and the sonnet. Here, too, imitation develops into creation, as when Renaissance carpe diem (seize the day) verse surfaces in one of his best-known poems, "Ich empfinde fast ein Grauen / Daß ich Plato für und für / Bin gesessen über dir . . . " (I almost feel a shudder / That I, Plato, have spent so much / Time with you . . .). The poem is a reworking of an ode of Ronsard's and is first included in the *Buch von der Deutschen Poeterey* as an example of an ode that is to evoke *fröligkeit* (happiness). But it has some innovative features, surprising turns, and ornamental and almost bizarre epithets that are

ing less than the adoption of the Latin ideal of *elegantia* and remains squarely within the framework of the humanist educational tradition, as Wilhelm Kühlmann maintains.

Opitz's division of the poetic process into inventio, dispositio, and elocutio places his mother tongue into the ancient rhetorical tradition; Opitz's model could thus be incorporated effortlessly into the existing educational system. The concepts developed in the *Buch von der Deutschen Poeterey* made it possible for German poets to transfer everything they had learned in the Latin schools and at the universities about the production of Latin poems onto German literature. The conformity with the Latin educational tradition is also evident in his adoption of the canon of *praecepta* (rules) and *exempla* (poetic models). Opitz saw himself not as a rebel against the classical European heritage but as a traditionalist. It is this agreement with the internationally accepted norms of humanism that guaranteed scholars the leading role as the future poets of Germany.

That Opitz's own poetry is a conscious selection and imitation of models is evident in his *Acht Bücher, Deutscher Poematum.* It shows the poet's development and practice of his craft, according to the practice of rhetoric in the Latin schools, where the

characteristic of Opitz's early baroque poetry. Perhaps because of the multiple literary models that inspired him, Opitz's oeuvre is more varied than the entire literary production of either Paul Fleming or Andreas Gryphius, although both are ranked above Opitz in importance.

With Opitz, poetry takes on intellectual and cerebral qualities. In another well-known carpe diem poem, "Ach Liebste, laß uns eilen . . . " (Ah, dearest, let us haste . . .), he uses the familiar Petrarchan catalogue of earthly beauties that must fade – the coral lips, snowy hands, fair cheeks that must perish; throughout the songlike poem, and especially in the last stanza, he pursues the idea of vanity and love that may overcome life's transitoriness, ending with the paradoxical assertion and admonishment: "Wo du dich selber liebest, / So liebe mich, / Gieb mir, das, wann du giebest, / Verlier auch ich" (As you love yourself, / Love me too; / Give me, that when you give, / I lose to you). With its conceits and rhetorical figures, Opitz's love poetry is much less subjective than that of later generations; it is almost without emotions – a far cry from the *Erlebnislyrik* (experiential poetry) ushered in by the Sturm und Drang poets, above all by Johann Wolfgang von Goethe. Opitz's lyrics rarely attempt to express a mood or feeling; they are reflective and artfully construed. Poetry, for him, is a social art that follows intrinsic poetic laws. His poetry is created with the calm artistic knowledge of a master confident of his technical skills and artistry.

Stylistically, the majority of Opitz's poems are far from the ornateness and decorative exaggerations that became popular in the second half of the century; thus, Richard Alewyn emphasizes unobtrusiveness as a characteristic of Opitz's poetic language, since the typically baroque superabundance of stylistic figures is missing in Opitz. The stylistic ideal that lies behind his translations and his own poetry is the balance between *res* (things) and *verba* (words), the relevance and correctness of expression; for this reason Alewyn terms this early phase of German baroque literature "pre-Baroque classicism."

Accompanying a diplomatic delegation of Silesian noblemen to Vienna in 1625, Opitz was crowned poet laureate by Emperor Ferdinand. Also in 1625 he visited the humanist professor August Buchner at Wittenberg University. In 1626 the Protestant Opitz accepted the post of private secretary to the Catholic Count Karl Hannibal von Dohna. He was knighted in 1627, assuming the name "von Boberfeld." Hannibal von Dohna, the only Catholic among the Silesian nobles and a loyal follower of the emperor, became an active participant in the ruthless and bloody Counter-Reformation measures in Silesia. That Opitz took the position under these circumstances throws a somewhat questionable light on his character. He even translated, at Dohna's request, the Jesuit Martin Becanus's *Manuale Controversarium* (1623), one of the most militant of the anti-Protestant tracts that were used for forced conversions. When Opitz's translation, *Becanus Redivivus, das ist, deß . . . Herrn Martini Becani der Societät Jesu Theologen S. Handtbuch: Aller dieser Zeit in der Religion Streitsachen* (The Revised Becanus, That Is, the . . . Theologian Sir Martin Becanus of the Society of Jesus' Handbook of Religious Controversies) appeared in 1631, it did not bear Opitz's name.

In his philosophical poem *Vielguet* (1629), celebrating Prince Heinrich Wentzel of Münsterberg's estate of that name, Opitz turns to the question of what the "highest good" for the human being is: "Komm mit mir and den Orth der Vielguet ist und heißt / In unserm Schlesien dem jetzt nicht reichen Lande / Das dennoch Vielguet hat . . . " (Come with me to a place that is named and is Vielguet [a great good] / In our Silesia, now no longer wealthy / Which still has a great good . . .). He praises the estate as a place of peace in nature, in contrast to the marble palace of the court. In this didactic poem Opitz explores critically his contemporaries' common notion that striving for money and honor at court is valuable. He asserts that the domination exercised by the court is merely an external one, because each human being can evade the ruler's power over his or her free will. In contrast to Hans Jakob von Grimmelshausen, who criticizes courtly life from the point of view of the common people, Opitz speaks here as a scholar. In spite of his positions at various courts and his panegyrics for several princes, he insists on preserving his intellectual freedom. Opitz's praise of the retiring and industrious life in the country, where the soul can find all good and delight in itself and can find its savior, is a description of the stoic and Christian way of life that was a typical ideal of intellectuals of the seventeenth century – especially when experiencing the ravages of war.

Opitz's knowledge of foreign languages and his facility with the pen were high recommendations for Hannibal von Dohna; Opitz was also a man of the world who knew when to speak and when to be silent, and Hannibal von Dohna respected his diplomacy and discretion. His position afforded Opitz advancement, ennoblement, life in courtly circles,

Illustration from Opitz's translation of John Barclay's Argenis
depicting Poliarchus and the pirates

political importance, and travel – in Hannibal von Dohna's company or with diplomatic missions he visited the court at Dresden and Berlin in 1626, and Warsaw and Prague in 1627. In 1929 Prince Ludwig of Anhalt-Köthen, the head of the literary society Fruchtbringende Gesellschaft (Fruit-bringing Society), invited him to become a member when Opitz paid him a visit; Opitz's society name was *Der Gekrönte* (The Crowned One). In 1630 a diplomatic mission led him to Paris, where the irenian Hugo Grotius strengthened his attitude of religious tolerance. He translated Grotius's important work *Bewys van den waren godsdienst* (1622), which advocated peace and tolerance among the major religions, as *Von der Warheit der Christlichen Religion* (The Truth about the Christian Religion, 1631).

Throughout Opitz's life, translations played an important role in his literary production. His translations of Seneca's *The Trojan Women* (1625) and Sophocles' *Antigone* (1636), the German version of the neo-Latin novel *Argenis* (1626), by John Barclay, and his revision of an earlier German translation of the pastoral novel *Arcadia* (1629), by Sir Philip Sidney, are especially noteworthy. Opitz contributed to the popularity of the pastoral with his *Schäfferey von der Nimfen Hercinie* (Pastoral of the Nymph Hercinie, 1630), dedicated to Hans Ulrich von Schaffgotsch, on whose estate in Warmbrunn he had found refuge from the war. The first bucolic idyll in German literature, the work is set in the present and in Opitz's homeland in the Sudeten area; the friendly conversation and rural setting provide a stark contrast to the war that was raging in Germany. Opitz transformed the literary model into an original expression of his deeply patriotic feelings and his legitimation of the poet and artist. With the translation of Ottavio Rinuccini's *Dafne* (1627) he supplied the composer Heinrich Schütz with the first German opera libretto. He also translated and revised many Neo-Latin, Italian, French, and Dutch lyric poems in addition to paraphrasing passages from the Bible such as *Die Klage-Lieder Jeremia* (Jeremiah's Songs of Lamentation, 1626), *Salomons des Hebreischen Königs Hohes Liedt* (The Song of Songs of the Hebrew King Solomon, 1627), and the entire Psalter in 1637.

In 1632 the fortunes of war turned. As Swedish troops neared Breslau, Hannibal von Dohna was forced to flee to Bohemia, where he joined Gen. Albrecht Eusebius Wenzel von Wallenstein in his efforts to gather an army to continue the fight against the Protestants. He died in Prague in February 1633. Opitz had remained in Breslau; after Hannibal von Dohna's death he entered the service of the Protestant dukes of Brieg and Liegnitz, for whom he undertook diplomatic missions to the camp of the Protestant armies. There he met Christian IV of Denmark, the new leader of the Protestants after Gustav Adolph's death in November 1632, and his son Prince Ulrich of Holstein.

The great war was a major theme in Opitz's poetic works. He expressed himself on the subject of war in three long philosophical poems. In *Laudes Martis* (In Praise of Mars, 1628), dedicated to his patron Hannibal von Dohna, he presents an indirect criticism of war in a satiric treatment of Mars. On 1 February 1633 he completed his *Vesuvius. Poëma Germanicum* (Vesuvius: German Poem). Dedicated to Johann Christian von Brieg, whose service Opitz entered on 12 April 1633, *Vesuvius* compares the eruption of the volcano in 1631 to the much greater catastrophe of war, which is created by human beings themselves. Volcanic eruptions, comets, and earthquakes were considered prophetic messages from God; the eruption of Vesuvius points to the destruction of Germany in the Thirty Years' War. A central passage of the poem is the exhortation for peace. Opitz closes with a prayer for peace and religious tolerance: "Gib daß man überall die Freyheit höre melden" (Let freedom be announced everywhere).

His philosophical poem in four books, *TrostGedichte in Widerwertigkeit deß Krieges,* which he had begun in 1621 during his seven-month stay in Denmark but did not publish until 1633, is Opitz's major literary achievement. With an almost unre-

strained baroque pathos, Opitz describes the ravages of war and human suffering without – in spite of all the poem's vivid realism – falling into crude naturalism or horror propaganda. His choice of words, mythological comparisons, and metaphors point to the work's rhetorical foundation. Opitz reminds his contemporaries that the war is a result of their own sins, that their misery is a God-sent punishment. As a positive reaction, he hopes for moral renewal, for the preservation of people's inner religiosity: "Gut von sich selber thun das heißt Religion / Das ist Gott angenehm" (To do good from within is religion, / This is pleasing to God). These are uncommon words in the midst of the Thirty Years' War, words of a peace-loving humanist scholar who sees the real duty of the Christian Church in the active following of Christ, not in the violent conversion of dissidents. Opitz's call for tolerance and religious freedom is certainly not a sign of religious indifference; rather, it springs from the realization that shrewd power politics hides behind seemingly confessional arguments. Only when freedom is in question does Opitz see a justification for war: "Die güldne Freyheit nun lest kein Mann eher fahren / Als seine Seele selbst" (No man allows golden freedom to depart any more / Than his own soul). Opitz speaks out implicitly against the hegemonious striving of the Hapsburgs. Calls for tolerance, for the defense of national identity, and for resistance to Catholic imperialism join with moral admonishment and consolation and peak in the closing prayer that depicts the utopia of an eternal realm of peace.

TrostGedichte in Widerwertigkeit deß Krieges exhibits in its poetic structure a series of echoes of Heinsius, allowing for the speculation that *De contemptu mortis* (On Contempt for Death, 1621) served as an inspiration for Opitz's poem. It is not an imitation of the Heinsius text; rather there are important affinities to Heinsius's didactic poetry and its classical model, Virgil's *Georgica*. For instance, Opitz begins book 3 with a discussion of war and peace that steers toward the argument for the *bellum iustum* (just war) as God's war: "Wer Gottes wegen kriegt für den kriegt auch Gott wieder" (Whoever wages war for God, for him God likewise wages war); for this idea the Huguenots serve as an example. This passage leads to a patriotic section: "Wer kan sein Vaterland auch wüste sehen stehen . . ." (Who can tolerate that his fatherland is devastated . . .). The defense of the fatherland, the example of the Netherlands for Germany, the praise of the hero's death for the fatherland, and the poet's immortalization of heroic deeds are further themes in book 3, which closes with one last call to the nation: "O werthes

Opitz in 1630; engraving by Paulus Fürst, after an earlier engraving made by Jacob von der Heyde on the occasion of a visit by Opitz to Strasbourg

Kriegs in 1621, Opitz would have been able to adopt a political perspective similar to that of Heinsius; but at the time of the work's publication in 1633, it was no longer possible to do so. Thus, Opitz had to revise the work, especially the third book, before publishing it.

Opitz dedicated *TrostGedichte in Widerwertigkeit deß Kriegs* to Ulrich von Holstein, but on 22 August 1633, just a few days after the drafting of Opitz's dedication, Ulrich was shot in the back while leaving Wallenstein's camp, where his father had taken part in peace negotiations. In the text of the work Opitz does not mention Ulrich; he leaves out any direct reference to a living prince, addressing "our Germany" and the "honored nation." Opitz sees himself as *Praeceptor Germaniae,* as speaker for and educator of the nation, as negotiator for religious parties and princes. He often uses the first person plural, with generalizing observations such as: "Wir Menschen sind geborn einander zu entsetzen / Und keinen durch Gewalt gestatten zu verletzen" (We human beings are born to help one another, / And to allow none to harm through power). He intensifies the pathos with the collective appeal and the charge: "Laßt vns doch hertzhafft seyn" (Let us be brave). This insistence on ethical values and the existence of the nation are expressed with greater urgency in 1633 than a decade earlier and are shaped by the historical situation. Just as important and convincing is Opitz's insistence in 1633 – after the brutal recatholicizing of Silesia under Hannibal von Dohna, whom Opitz had served as secretary since 1626 – on the free exercise of religious convictions and freedom of religious thought.

The unusually long and urgent prayer that closes book 4 also seems to reflect the situation of 1633 far more than the secure refuge on Jutland and the much more promising situation of 1621 when Opitz began writing the work. In the concretization, urgency, and intellectual and spiritual profundity of the closing prayer Opitz shows his striking independence from *De contemptu mortis,* where Heinsius's closing prayer barely moves beyond such conventional comments as "salve ingens leti domitor" (welcome, great conqueror of death) or "leti immemores, venturo incumbimus aevo" (unmindful of death, we walk into the coming age). Heinsius had closed his poem professing his belief in the story of Salvation; Opitz, in closing book 4 of *TrostGedichte in Widerwertigkeit deß Kriegs,* once again recalls the precipitousness of war and death and attempts to establish what Garber calls "a utopia of peace, transposed into the beyond as a realm of eternal salvation of the pious" as a philosophic-political alternative.

Volck . . . Halte veste, wancke nicht, vollende deinen Lauff" (Oh great nation . . . hold fast, falter not, complete your course). With Opitz, the appeal to the nation and to the individual stands in the foreground; his examples are more immediate than the many mythological descriptions and references to the ancients that appear in Heinsius, with his Neo-Latin images that are often used formally and according to classical models. Heinsius had dealt with the same themes, but from the secure vantage point of a successfully fought war and with an eye toward a new, powerful alliance of the Netherlands with Calvinist Sweden. In 1633, on the other hand, Silesia was in a weak position, and Opitz's text reflects the different circumstances. His call for freedom is more urgent; references to and hopes for a concrete historical solution are lacking; there is no address to a prince, as there is in Heinsius. When he began writing *TrostGedichte in Widerwertigkeit deß*

A utopia of peace was badly needed; the situation had become desperate for the Protestants in 1634, after Saxony broke its alliance with Sweden and went over to the side of the emperor. In 1635 Silesia was forced to swear allegiance to the emperor, and Opitz fled to Danzig (today, Gdansk). In 1637 he attained the position of royal court historiographer with the Polish king Vladislav IV. He continued his diplomatic missions and rendered valuable services as informant and political adviser to several princes and generals. During those years he published many occasional poems, such as *Lobgeticht an die Königliche Majestät zu Polen und Schweden* (Poem of Praise to the Royal Majesty of Poland and Sweden, 1636), and he readied his poetic production for another edition, which appeared in two sizable volumes in 1638.

At the end of 1638 the plague broke out in Danzig. Opitz was infected, and he died on 20 August 1639. Shortly before his death he had ordered his political correspondence to be burned. His library and his unpublished works were auctioned off by his father.

In Opitz's purely formal art, understanding and clarity take the place of poetic individuality. With his rhetorical, rational poetic writings Opitz created the basis for the poetic practice of the German baroque without developing the typical baroque style. If there was a German-speaking Renaissance poet, it was Opitz; yet Opitz was a latecomer who was both progressive and retrospective. His stylistic ideas exerted their influence, above all, on the genre of occasional poetry, while lyrical and mystical poetry developed quite independently of him. In the second half of the century the reformer seemed somewhat antiquated; the feudal-courtly, highly ornamental style displaced rational clarity. One must agree with Alewyn that Opitz's greatest accomplishment was the implementation of his major ideas, the "nationalizing of humanist poetry through the invention of a German poetic literature."

Johann Christoph Gottsched sang Opitz's praises in his *Lob- und Gedächtnißrede auf den Vater der deutschen Dichtkunst, Martin Opitzen von Boberfeld* (Eulogy to the Father of German Poetry, Martin Opitz, 1739). Gottsched and Gottfried Wilhelm von Leibniz, opponents of ornamentation and champions of a classicist style, point to the "trefflichen" (splendid) Martin Opitz and his ideal of "angenehme Leichtflüßigkeit" (pleasant fluidity): for them he figures as the first modern "poet of good taste." Not until Sturm und Drang did the programmatic poets, with Johann Gottfried Herder and

Gottfried August Bürger in the front lines, successfully campaign against Opitz's dismissal of folk poetry; finally, the Romantics threw all learned artistic praxis overboard. Opitz's poetics no longer served as a model for poetic endeavors. Today his works are appreciated for their fine stylistic qualities, as well as for their pathbreaking impact on German literature of the baroque era.

Biography:

Marian Szyrocki, *Martin Opitz* (Munich: Beck, 1974).

References:

Richard Alewyn, *Vorbarocker Klassizismus und griechische Tragödie: Analyse der "Antigone"- Übersetzung des Martin Opitz* (Heidelberg: Winter, 1925);

Wilfried Barner, *Barockrhetorik: Untersuchungen zu ihren geschichtlichen Grundlagen* (Tübingen: Niemeyer, 1970);

Barbara Becker-Cantarino, "Satyra in nostri belli levitatem: Opitz' Lob des Kriegesgottes Martis," *Deutsche Vierteljahrsschrift für Literaturwissenschaft und Geistesgeschichte,* 48 (May 1974): 291–317;

Becker-Cantarino, ed., *Martin Opitz: Studien zu Werk und Person* (Amsterdam: Rodopi, 1982);

Becker-Cantarino and Jörg-Ulrich Fechner, eds., *Opitz und seine Welt: Festschrift für George Schulz-Behrend,* (Amsterdam & Atlanta: Rodopi, 1990);

William L. Cunningham, *Martin Opitz: Poems of Consolation in Adversities of War,* Abhandlungen zur Kunst-, Literatur- und Musikwissenschaft, no. 134 (Bonn: Bouvier, 1974);

Rudolf Drux, *Martin Opitz und sein poetisches Regelsystem,* Literatur und Wirklichkeit, no. 18 (Bonn: Bouvier, 1976);

Joachim Dyck, "Apologetic Argumentation in the Literary Theory of the German Baroque," *Journal of English and Germanic Philology,* 68 (January 1969): 197–211;

Curt von Faber du Faur, "Der *Aristarchus:* Eine Neuwertung," *PMLA,* 69 (June 1954): 566–590;

Leonard Forster, *The Icy Fire: Five Studies in European Petrarchism* (London: Cambridge University Press, 1969);

Klaus Garber, "Martin Opitz," in *Deutsche Dichter des 17. Jahrhunderts: Ihr Leben und Werk,* edited by Harald Steinhagen and Benno von Wiese (Berlin: Erich Schmidt, 1984), pp. 116–184;

Garber, *Martin Opitz – der "Vater der deutschen Dichtung": Eine kritische Studie zur Wissenschafts-*

geschichte der Germanistik (Stuttgart: Metzler, 1976);

Garber, "Martin Opitz' *Schäferei von der Nymphe Hercinie* als Ursprung der Prosaekloge und des Schäferromans in Deutschland," *Daphnis,* 11, no. 3 (1982): 547–603;

Janis Little Gellinek, "Further Dutch Sources Used by Martin Opitz," *Neophilologus,* 53 (April 1969): 157–175;

Gellinek, *Die weltliche Lyrik des Martin Opitz* (Bern & Munich: Francke, 1973);

Johann Christoph Gottsched, *Lob- und Gedächt-nißrede auf den Vater der deutschen Dichtkunst, Martin Opitzen von Boberfeld nachdem selbiger vor hundert Jahren in Danzig Todes verblichen, zur Erneuerung seines Andenkens im Jahre 1739 den 20 August auf der philosophischen Catheder zu Leipzig gehalten* (Leipzig: Breitkopf, 1739);

Gunter Grimm, *Literatur und Gelehrtentum* (Tübingen: Niemeyer, 1983);

Richard D. Hacken, *The Religious Thought of Martin Opitz,* Stuttgarter Arbeiten zur Germanistik, no. 18 (Stuttgart: Kümmerle, 1976);

Wilhelm Kühlmann, *Gelehrtenrepublik und Fürsten-staat: Entwicklung und Kritik des deutschen Späthumanismus in der Literatur des Barockzeitalters* (Tübingen: Niemeyer, 1982);

Jane O. Newman, "Et in Arcadia Ego: Pastoral Po-etics, or Imitation as Survival in Theocritus,

Virgil, and Opitz," *Deutsche Vierteljahrsschrift für Literaturwissenschaft und Geistesgeschichte,* 59 (De-cember 1985): 525–550;

Newman, "Marriages of Convenience: Patterns of Alliance in Heidelberg Politics and Opitz' Po-etics," *Modern Language Notes,* 100 (April 1985): 537–576;

George Schulz-Behrend, "On Editing Opitz," *Mod-ern Language Notes,* 77 (1962): 435–438;

Schulz-Behrend, "Opitz' *Zlatna,*" *Modern Language Notes,* 77 (1962): 398–410;

Wulf Segebrecht, *Das Gelegenheitsgedicht: Ein Beitrag zur Geschichte und Poetik der deutschen Lyrik* (Stutt-gart: Metzler, 1977);

Volker Sinemus, *Poetik und Rhetorik im frühmodernen deutschen Staat: Sozialgeschichtliche Bedingungen des Normenwandels im 17. Jahrhundert,* Palaestra, 269 (Göttingen: Vandenhoeck & Ruprecht, 1978);

Bernhard Ulmer, *Martin Opitz* (New York: Twayne, 1971).

Papers:

No autograph manuscripts of Martin Opitz exist, except for several letters. George Schulz-Behrend of the University of Texas, editor of the historical-critical edition of Opitz's oeuvre, has gathered the most complete collection of Opitiana.

Johann Rist

(8 March 1607 – 31 August 1667)

Jill Bepler
Herzog August Bibliothek

SELECTED BOOKS: *Irenaromachia Das ist Eine newe Tragico-comaedia von Fried und Krieg,* by Rist and Ernst Stapel (Hamburg: Printed by Jacob Rebenlein, 1630);

Musa Teutonica Das ist: Teutscher Poetischer Miscellaneen Erster Theil (Hamburg: Printed by Jacob Rebenlein, 1635);

Perseus Das ist: Eine newe Tragoedia, welche in Beschreibunge theils warhaffter Geschichten, theils lustiger vnd anmuthiger Gedichten, einen Sonnenklahren Welt-und Hoffspiegel jedermänniglichen praesentiret und vorstellet (Hamburg: Printed by Heinrich Werner, 1635);

Philosophischer Phoenix Das ist: Kurtze, jedoch Gründliche vnnd Sonnenklare Entdeckunge der waren vnd eigentlichen Matery deß Aller-Edelsten Steines der Weisen (Hamburg: Zacharias Hertel, 1638);

Poetischer Lust-Garte Das ist: Allerhand anmuthige Gedichte auch warhafftige Geschichte auß Alten und Newen beglaubten Geschichtschreibern, mit fleiß außerlesen und benebenst mancherley Elegien, Sonetten, Epigrammaten Oden, Graabschrifften, Hochzeit- Lob- Trawr- und Klaag-Gedichten, etc. (Hamburg: Printed by Jacob Rebenlein, published by Zacharias Hertel, 1638);

Nothwendige Rettung vnnd rechtmässige Vertheidigung des Philosophischen Phoenix (Hamburg, 1638 [i.e., 1640]);

Kriegs- und Friedens Spiegel. Das ist: Christliche, Teutsche vnd wolgemeinte Erinnerung an alle Kriegs- und Frieden liebende Menschen (Hamburg: Printed by Jacob Rebenlein, published by Zacharias Hertel, 1640);

Lob- Trawr- und Klag-Gedicht, vber gar zu frühzeitiges, jedoch seliges Absterben, des weiland Edlen, Großachtbaren und Hochgelahrten Herren Martin Opitzen (Hamburg: Printed by Jacob Rebenlein, published by Zacharias Hertel, 1640);

Himlischer Lieder mit sehr anmuhtigen, mehreren theils von Herrn Johann: Schopen gesetzten Melodeyen. Das erste Zehen (Lüneburg: Johann & Heinrich Stern, 1641);

Johann Rist; engraving by F. Steürhelt

Himlischer Triumph-Lieder, mit sehr anmuhtigen, von Herrn Johann: Schopen, dero hochlöblichen Stadt Hamburg Capellmeistern gesetzten Melodeyen. Das Ander Zehn (Lüneburg: Johann & Heinrich Stern, 1642);

Himlischer Lieder mit sehr anmuhtigen, von Herrn Johann: Schopen, dero hochlöblichen Stadt Hamburg

269

Capellmeistern gesetzten Melodeyen. Das Dritte Zehn (Lüneburg: Johann & Heinrich Stern, 1642);

Himlischer Lieder, mit sehr anmuhtigen, von Herrn Johann: Schopen wolgesetzen Melodeyen. Das Vierdte Zehn (Lüneburg: Johann & Heinrich Stern, 1642);

Himlischer Lieder mit sehr anmuhtigen, von dem weitberühmten, Herrn Johann: Schopen gesetzten Melodeyen. Das Fünffte und letzte Zehn (Lüneburg: Johann & Heinrich Stern, 1642);

Rettung der Edlen Teütschen Hauptsprache, wider alle deroselben muhtwillige Verderber und alamodesirende Auffschneider, jn unterschiedenen Briefen, allen dieser prächtigsten und vollenkommensten Sprache auffrichtigen teütschen Liebhabern für die Augen gestellet, as Baptistæ Armati, Vatis Thalosi (Hamburg: Heinrich Werner, 1642);

Des Daphnjs aus Cimbrien Galathee, edited by Theobald Grummer (Hamburg: Jacob Rebenlein, 1642);

Starker Schild Gottes wider die gifftige Mordpfeile falscher und verleümderischer Zungen (Hamburg: Heinrich Werner, 1644);

Holstejns erbärmliches Klag- und Jammer-Lied, das erste, jn hundert sätzen außgefärtiget und gesungen, as Friedelieb von Sanftleben (Hamburg: Heinrich Werner, 1644);

Poetischer Schauplatz, auff welchem allerhand Waaren Gute und Böse Kleine und Grosse Freude und Leid zeugende zu finden (Hamburg: Heinrich Werner, 1646);

Friedens-Posaune, mit welcher nach wieder erlangetem und bestätigtem güldenen Land-Friede die hochlöbliche Holsteinische Fürstenthüme und Länder dem allergühtigsten Gott zu ewigem Lobe, Preise und Ehren, der hohen Landesfürstlichen Obrigkeit zuer unterthänigsten stets schüldigen dancksagung, denen sämtlichen Einwohnern und Unterthanen zuer Ermahrung, warnung und auffmunterung Wolmeinentlich werden angeblasen jm Jahr nach Christus gebuhrt 1646. (Hamburg: Printed by Jacob Rebenlein, 1646);

Das Friedewünschende Teütschland jn Einem Schauspiele öffentlich vorgestellet und beschrieben durch einen Mitgenossen der Hochlöblichen Fruchtbringenden Gesellschaft, anonymous (N.p., 1647);

Allerunterthänigste Lobrede an die Allerdurchläuchtigste Unüberwindlichste Römische Kaiserliche Maiestätt, Herren Ferdinand den Dritten als Allerhöchstgedachte Kaiserl. Maiest. Jhn durch den Hochwolgebohrnen Grafen und Herren Herren Herman Tschernin, des Heiligen Römischen Reiches Graffen von Chudenitz, Herren auf Petersburg, Gissibel, Neüdek, Kost, Mildschowes, Sedschitz, *Schmidberg, Römischer Kaiserlicher Maiestätt Raht, würklichen Kämmerer Landrechts Beisitzer im Königreich Böheim, Obristen und Oratorem an die Ottomannische Porten & caet. Mit Adelichen Freiheiten, Schild, Helm und Wapen auch der Poetischen Lorberkrohn von dero Kaiserliche Hofe aus allergnädigst hatte verehren lassen* (Hamburg: Printed by Jacob Rebenlein, 1647);

Holstein vergiß es nicht Daß ist Kurtze, iedoch eigentliche Beschreibung des erschreklichen Ungewitters, Erdbebens und überaus grossen Sturmwindes, welcher jn der Fastnacht dieses 1648 Jahrs . . . entstanden und an vielen Ohrtern in Holstein, sonderlich aber am Elbestrom . . . den feuerbrennenden Zorn Gottes, uns armen Sündern klährlich hat vor die Augen gestellet (Hamburg: Printed by Michael Pfeiffer, published by Johann Naumann, 1648);

Der zu seinem allerheiligsten Leiden und Sterben hingeführter und an das Kreütz gehefteter Christu Jesus, jn wahrem Glauben und Hertzlicher Andacht gesungen (Hamburg: Printed by Jacob Rebenlein, 1648); enlarged as *Neue Hoch-heilige Paßions-Andachten jn Lehr- und Trostreichen Liedern* (Hamburg: Johann Naumann, 1664);

Hamburgisches Fried- und Freüdenfeür (Hamburg: Printed by Jacob Rebenlein, 1650);

Blutige Thränen, vber das erbärmliche Ableiben deß weiland Durchleuchtigsten Herrn H. Carels deß Ersten, Königs von Groß-Britannien, Franckreich vnd Jrrland, Beschützers deß Glaubens. Welcher am dreißigsten Tage deß Jenners deß 1649. Jahrs, zu Londen öffentlich ist enthauptet worden, as Tirsis dem Tamschäffer (N.p., 1650);

Des Edlen Dafnjs aus Cimbrien besungene Florabella, music by Peter Meier (Hamburg: Printed by Jacob Rebenlein, published by the author, 1651);

Sabbahtische Seelenlust, Daß ist: Lehr- Trost- Vermahnung- und Warnungsreiche Lieder über alle Sontägliche Evangelien deß gantzen Jahres, music by Thomas Selle (Lüneburg: Printed & published by Johann & Heinrich Stern, 1651);

Neüer Himlischer Lieder Sonderbahres Buch (Lüneburg: Johann & Heinrich Stern, 1651);

Neüer Teütscher Parnass, auff welchem befindlich Ehr' und Lehr, Schertz und Schmertz, Leid- und Freüden-Gewächse (Lüneburg: Johann & Heinrich Stern, 1652);

Das Friedejauchende [sic] *Teutschland* (Nuremberg: Wolfgang Endter the Younger & Johann Andreas Endter, 1653);

Unterthänigste Lobrede, an den Durchläuchtigen, Hochgebohrnen Fürsten und Herren H. Christian Ludowig, Hertzogen zu Braunschweig und Lüneberg

&c. als Seine Fürstliche Gnade Jhr HochFürstliches Beilager hielte (Hamburg: Printed by Jacob Rebenlein, 1653);

Die Triumphirende Liebe, umgeben mit den Sieghafften Tugenden. Jn einem Ballet auff dem Hochfürstlichen Beylager des . . . H. Christian Ludowigs Hertzogen zu Brunswig und Lüneburg gehalten mit der auch durchläuchtigen Fräulein Dorothea Hertzogin zu Schleßwig/Holstein . . . auff der Fürstlichen Residentz Zelle vorgestellet am 12. Tage des Weinmonats jm 1653. Jahre (Lüneburg: Johann & Heinrich Stern, 1653);

Frommer und Gottseliger Christen alltägliche Haußmusik, oder Musikalische Andachten (Lüneburg: Johann & Heinrich Stern, 1654);

Neüe Musikalische Fest-Andachten, Bestehende jn Lehr- Trost- Vermahnungs- und Warnungsreichen Liederen über Alle Evangelien und sonderbahre Texte (Lüneburg: Johann & Heinrich Stern, 1655);

Depositio Cornuti Typographici, das ist: Lust- oder Freuden-Spiel: Welches bey Annehmung und Bestättigung eines Jungen Gesellen, der die edle Kunst der Buchdrukkerei redlich hat außgelernet, ohne einige Ärgernisse kan fürgestellet, vermittelst, welches auch künfftiger Zeit, junge angehende Personen nach Verfliessung Jhrer Lehr-Jahre, zu Buchdrukker-Gesellen können ernennet, bestättiget, an- und auffgenommen werden (Lüneburg: Johann & Heinrich Stern, 1655);

Neüe Musikalische Katechismus Andachten, Bestehende jn Lehr- Trost- Vermanung- und Warnungs-reichen Liederen über den gantzen heiligen Katechismum (Lüneburg: Johann & Heinrich Stern, 1656);

Geistlicher Poetischer Schrifften Erster Theil (Lüneburg: Johann & Heinrich Stern, 1657);

Geistlicher Poetischer Schrifften Zweiter Theil (Lüneburg: Johann & Heinrich Stern, 1658);

Die verschmähete Eitelkeit und die verlangete Ewigkeit jn vier und zwantzig Erbaulichen Seelengesprächen, music by Heinrich Scheidemann (Lüneburg: Johann & Heinrich Stern, 1658);

Geistlicher Poetischer Schrifften Dritter Theil (Lüneburg: Johann & Heinrich Stern, 1659);

Neüe Musikalische Kreutz- Trost- Lob- und DankSchule, Worinn befindlich unterschiedliche Lehr- und Trostreiche Lieder, in macherlei Kreutz, Trübsahl und Wiederwärtigkeit hochnützlich zu gebrauchen (Lüneburg: Johann & Heinrich Stern, 1659);

Neues Musikalisches Seelenparadis, jn sich begreiffend die allerfürtrefflichste Sprüche der heiligen Schrifft, Alten Testaments, jn gantz Lehr- und Trostreichen Liederen und Hertzens Andachten (Lüneburg: Johann & Heinrich Stern, 1660);

Neues Musikalisches Seelenparadis, jn sich begreiffend die allerfürtreflichste Sprüche der heiligen Schrifft, Neuen Testaments, jn Lehr- und Trostreichen Liederen und Hertzens Andachten (Lüneburg: Johann & Heinrich Stern, 1662);

Das AllerEdelste Nass der gantzen Welt, vermittelst eines anmuhtigen und erbaulichen Gespräches, welches ist diser Ahrt die Erste, und zwahr Eine Jänners-Unterredung, as der Rüstigen (Hamburg: Johann Naumann, 1663);

Das AllerEdelste Leben der gantzen Welt, vermittelst eines anmuhtigen und erbaulichen Gespräches, welches ist diser Ahrt Die Ander, und zwahr Eine Hornungs-Unterredung (Hamburg: Johann Naumann, 1663);

Die AllerEdelste Tohrheit der gantzen Welt, vermittelst eines anmuhtigen und erbaulichen Gespräches, welches ist diser Ahrt Die Dritte, und zwahr Eine Märtzens-Unterredung (Hamburg: Johann Naumann, 1664);

Die AllerEdelste Belustigung Kunst- und Tugendliebende Gemühter, vermittelst eines anmuhtigen und erbaulichen Gespräches welches ist dieser Ahrt, Die Vierte, und zwahr Eine Aprilens-Unterredung (Hamburg: Johann Naumann, 1666);

Die alleredelste Erfindung der Gantzen Welt, vermittelst eines anmuhtigen und erbaulichen Gespräches, welches ist dieser Art, Die Fünffte, und zwar eine Mäyens-Vnterredungen (Frankfurt am Main: Johann Georg Schiele, 1667);

Die alleredelste Zeit-Verkürtzung der Gantzen Welt: Vermittelst eines anmutigen und erbaulichen Gespräches, welches ist dieser Art, die Sechste, und zwar eine Brachmonats-Unterredungen (Frankfurt am Main: Johann Georg Schiele, 1668);

Die verschmäheten Eitelkeit und der verlangeten Ewigkeit Ander Theil, jn vier und zwantzig erbaulichen Seelengesprächen, und eben so viel Lehr-reichen Liedern (Frankfurt am Main: Johann Georg Schiele, 1668).

Editions and Collections: *Auserlesene Gedichte von Johann Rist und Daniel Georg Morhof,* edited by Wilhelm Müller (Leipzig: Brockhaus, 1826);

Das Friedewünschende Teutschland und Das Friedejauchzende Teutschland, edited by Hans Michael Schletterer (Augsburg: Schlosser, 1864);

Dichtungen, edited by Karl Goedeke and Edmund Goetze (Leipzig: Brockhaus, 1885);

Depositio Cornuti, in *Die Gebrüder Stern und das Depositionsspiel,* edited by Karl Theodor Gaedertz (Lüneburg: Stern, 1886), n. pag.; translated by William Blades in *An Account of the German Morality-Play Depositio Cornuti*

Typographici (London: Trübner, 1885), pp. 19–55;

Das Friedwünschende Teutschland, edited by Heinrich Stümcke (Gotha: Perthes, 1915);

Irenaromachia, in *Oratorium – Festspiel,* edited by Willi Flemming (Leipzig: Reclam, 1933; reprinted, Hildesheim: Olms, 1965), pp. 141–208;

Sämtliche Werke, 6 volumes published, edited by Eberhard Mannack (Berlin: De Gruyter, 1967–   ) – comprises volume 1: *Irenaromachia, Perseus* (1967); volume 2: *Das Friedewünschende Teutschland, Das Friedejauchzende Teutschland* (1972); volume 4: *Das alleredelste Nass, Das alleredelste Leben* (1972); volume 5: *Die alleredelste Torheit, Die alleredelste Belustigung* (1974); *Die alleredelste Erfindung, Die alleredelste Zeitverkürtzung* (1976); *Philosophischer Phoenix, Rettung des Phoenix, Teutsche Hauptsprache, Adelicher Hausvatter* (1981);

Soren Terkelensen, *Astree Siunge-Choer: Forste Snees 1648. Die dänischen Lieder mit ihren deutschen Vorlagen von Gabriel Voigtländer und Johann Rist,* edited by Erik Sonderholm and others (Neumünster: Wachholtz, 1975);

Neüer Teütscher Parnass, auff welchem befindlich Ehr' und Lehr, Schertz und Schmertz, Leid- und Freüden-Gewächse (Hildesheim: Olms, 1978).

OTHER: Jacques Gautier, *Capitan Spavento oder Rodomontades Espagnolles Das ist: Spanische Auffschneidereyen, auß dem Frantzösischen in deutsche Verß gebracht,* translated by Rist (Hamburg: Printed by Heinrich Werner, published by Tobias Gundermann, 1635);

Torquato Tasso, *Der Adeliche Hausvatter,* adapted by Rist (Lüneburg: Johann & Heinrich Stern, 1650).

Johann Rist was one of the most prolific German baroque poets. His lasting contribution to German culture has, however, proved to be his sacred poems set to music, among the best known of which is "O Ewigkeit, du Donnerwort" (Oh eternity, you word like thunder). Although he spent nearly all of his life in the provincial region of his birth – Holstein in northern Germany – Rist achieved widespread fame. By careful self-advertising and the establishment of his own language society he gained a reputation as an arbiter of poetical norms, a north German Martin Opitz.

One of twelve children, Rist was born in Ottensen in Holstein on 8 March 1607 to Caspar Rist, a preacher and the supervisor of the lunatic asylum in Ottensen, and Margarethe Rist, née

Ringemuth. Rist received an excellent education at the Johanneum in Hamburg and the Gymnasium Illustre in Bremen. From 1626 to 1628 he studied theology in Rostock, where he heard lectures on medicine and science that prepared the ground for his later interest in the natural sciences. Among his teachers in Rostock were the professor of rhetoric Peter Lauremberg and the mathematician Joachim Jungius. Rist was forced to leave Rostock because of an outbreak of the plague and the conquest and occupation of Mecklenburg by the imperial general Albrecht Eusebius Wenzel von Wallenstein. He continued his studies in Rinteln and appears also to have studied in the Netherlands, although no detailed record of this phase in his life has survived.

Rist must have spent some time in Hamburg during this period, for in 1630 a play, *Irenaromachia,* by Ernst Stapel, was published; according to his own statements, Rist co-authored the play and helped to stage it in Hamburg with a group of student players. The play treats a theme that remained central to Rist's dramatic works, making a plea for pacifism and indicting the dissolute state of society as the reason for the scourge of war. War has been sent down on an unrepentant populace by the gods of Olympus, whose debate with various allegorical figures on the continuation or cessation of war forms the main plot of the play. The debate, interrupted by comic dialect interludes with military boasters and peasants, is concluded by Justitia (Justice) in favor of peace. The allegorical figure of peace, Irene, who leads Mars in chains from the stage, warns the audience that he will remain fettered only until human behavior once more warrants terrible punishment from above.

In 1633 Rist became a tutor in the household of the Sager family in Heide in Holstein. He continued his dramatic activities, writing a tragedy, *Perseus,* which was performed by his pupils and other lay actors in Heide in 1634 and printed in Hamburg a year later. In the preface to *Perseus* Rist claims that drama has an equal value for both performers and audience, thereby expressing the overtly didactic aims that were to infuse his writings in all genres. The play is a strange mixture of bloodthirsty political tragedy – in which tyranny is avenged by the ghosts of the dead, who drive the usurper Perseus and his helpmate to suicide – and coarse burlesque scenes. Rist excuses his departure from the rules of tragedy by introducing comic interludes, claiming that he is catering to the entertainment needs of the common people. A further product of his early years was his first collection of poetry, *Musa Teutonica* (1635). The occasional poetry and love po-

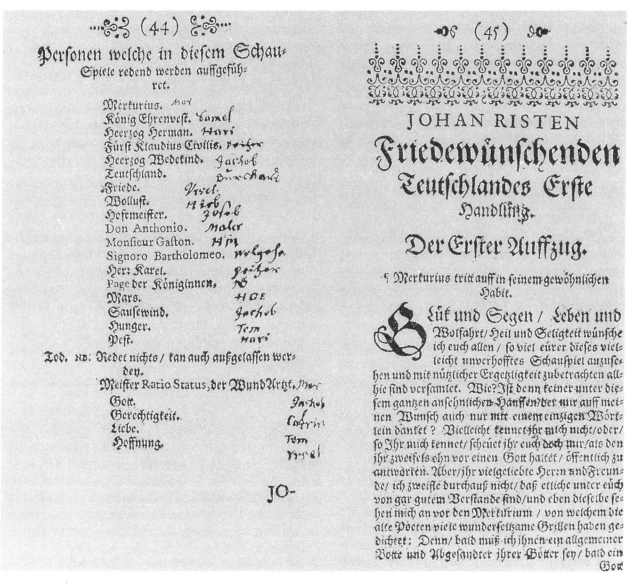

Two pages from a 1648 edition of Rist's allegorical pacifist drama. This copy belonged to the English actor Joris Joliphus (Yale University Library).

etry brought together in this volume are in strict accordance with Opitzian precepts. Also from this period is Rist's first translation from the French, a German verse rendering of Jacques Gautier's *Rodomontades Castellanas* (Castillian Braggarts, 1607) under the title *Capitan Spavento oder Rodomontades Espagnolles* (1635).

In 1635 Rist accepted the position of preacher in the market town of Wedel, on the outskirts of Hamburg, where he was to remain for the rest of his life. In this year he married Elisabeth Stapel, a sister of his co-author Ernst Stapel and of Peter Stapel, the governor of the region of Pinneberg, in which Wedel was located. They had five children, three of whom survived to adulthood. It has been suggested

that Rist's position in Wedel gave him a certain independence from church authority, with which he may well have come into conflict had he been preacher to a city parish. He was an orthodox Lutheran but expressed sympathy for the syncretistic ideas of his day, and his various poetical and theatrical activities could have provided the same grounds for criticism that brought his friend Johann Balthasar Schupp into bitter conflict with the church authorities in Hamburg. In Wedel, Rist lived a secluded but convivial existence centered on his house and garden, the scene of many social gatherings with his friends from the neighborhood and from Hamburg. His occasional poetry and the dedicatory poems prefacing his works bear witness to the scope of his personal and literary contacts. He built up a library, as well as a small laboratory with collections of natural objects and artifacts that allowed him to conduct experiments and indulge his interest in science. His *Philosophischer Phoenix* (Philosophical Phoenix, 1638) is concerned with alchemy and is a short justification of the search for the philosopher's stone. The work elicited criticism, to which Rist replied in *Nothwendige Rettung und rechtmässige Vertheidigung des Philosophischen Phoenix* (Necessary Rescue and Lawful Defense of the Philosophical Phoenix, 1640).

Throughout his life Rist kept up a steady production of occasional verse for his wide circle of friends and acquaintances; few other baroque German poets were so assiduous in publishing collections of their occasional poetry. These publications were one of his strategies for establishing himself as a literary authority, and he regularly demonstrated his impressive network of connections in this way. His anthology of poems *Poetischer Lust-Garte* (Poetical Pleasure Garden, 1638) is a mixture of mainly secular poems, epigrams, congratulatory and condolatory verses, and epic poetry describing events of local and national importance. His epic poem *Kriegs- und Friedens Spiegel* (Mirror of War and Peace, 1640) sets out the horrors of war in 1,440 lines of alexandrines, concentrating particularly on the Holstein landscape that Rist knew so well.

In 1641 Rist published the first volume of his *Himlischer Lieder* (Heavenly Songs), an anthology of hymns that was to be one of his most successful works. These songs, like all of his devotional poetry, were intended primarily for use in the home rather than as church music; he was an advocate of simple forms in verse and music that would enable the layperson to perform his songs. *Himlischer Lieder* includes the musical notations for some of the songs, which were set to music by the Hamburg violin virtuoso Johann Schop. Over the years Rist would collaborate with most of the minor northern German composers, paving the way for the later work of the Hamburg school of song.

The immediate success of *Himlischer Lieder* prompted Theobald Grummer to publish a collection of Rist's pastoral love poetry under the title *Des Daphnis aus Cimbrien Galathee* (Galathea by Daphne from Cimbria [Holstein], 1642). The poems are almost exclusively laments about love thwarted rather than enjoyed. It was, of course, highly inappropriate for a clergyman to publish love songs, and Grummer's preface and the conventional device by which he claims to have published the collection without the author's knowledge are meant as pro-

tection against an accusation of lasciviousness. *Des Daphnis aus Cimbrien Galathee* was a great success and established Rist as one of the most popular poets of the day. In 1642 he also published a satiric defense of the German language against foreign influences, *Rettung der Edlen Teütschen Hauptsprache* (Rescue of the Noble German Language), which takes the form of an exchange of letters between Pomposianus Windbrecher, a braggart soldier, and Liepholdt von Hasewitz, an à la mode suitor, on the one hand, and, on the other, the representatives of pure German language and morals Ernst Teutsch-Hertz and Adelheit von Ehrenberg.

The first years of Rist's literary productivity in Wedel were relatively unaffected by the Thirty Years' War. Toward the end of 1643, however, invading Swedish troops devastated his house and garden and stole or destroyed his collections of artifacts and books and the manuscripts for the dramas he had written and performed in his youth. The events of the following years, during which Rist was regularly forced to flee to Hamburg, are recorded in his epic poem *Holsteins Erbärmliches Klag- und Jammer-Lied* (Holstein's Pitiable Song of Lament and Woe, 1644).

After the death of Opitz in 1639 — lamented by Rist in a poem of more than six hundred alexandrines titled *Lob- Trawr- und Klag-Gedicht* (Poem of Praise, Mourning, and Woe, 1640) — Rist established himself as an authority in the German literary landscape. The dedicatory poems for his works show that he was in touch with the major literary figures of his day, and in the 1640s he received a series of titles reflecting his growing importance. In 1645 he was inducted into the Löblicher Hirten- und Blumenorden an der Pegnitz (Estimable Order of Shepherds and Flowers on the Pegnitz River), generally known as the Pegnesischer Blumenorden, the Nuremberg society of poets founded by Georg Philipp Harsdörffer. The members were given pastoral names; Rist was called "Daphnis aus Cimbrien," the pseudonym under which his poem *Galathee* had been published. In 1646 he was ennobled and crowned *poeta laureatus*. In the following year he published *Allerunterthänigste Lobrede* (Most Devoted Speech of Praise), an alexandrine poem of a thousand lines thanking Emperor Ferdinand III for the honors conferred on him. The volume includes many congratulatory poems from poets such as Sigmund von Birken, Johann Michael Moscherosch, and Andreas Tscherning. The scope of Rist's literary connections can also be seen in the dedicatory poems to his anthology of secular poetry, *Poetischer Schauplatz* (Stage of Poetry, 1646). This work includes an important preface in which Rist reflects on the state of German poetry, praising the efforts of the most important members of the Fruchtbringende Gesellschaft (Fruit-bringing Society) to raise the standard of German as a literary language. In 1647 Prince Ludwig of Anhalt-Köthen, head of the Fruchtbringende Gesellschaft, admitted Rist to its ranks as Der Rüstige (The Vigorous One). Clergymen were barred from membership in the society to avoid denominational strife; under Ludwig's leadership exceptions to this rule were made only for Rist and for the Stuttgart clergyman and utopian writer Johann Valentin Andreae.

In 1647 the progress of the peace negotiations in Münster made it clear that the Thirty Years' War was drawing to a close. At the request of a friend, the actor-manager Andreas Gartner, who had come to Hamburg with a group of itinerant student actors, Rist wrote his pacifist allegorical drama, *Das Friedewünschende Teütschland* (Germany Wishing for Peace, 1647), dedicating it to the Fruchtbringende Gesellschaft. The play is an indictment of the moral and political corruption that has brought war down on Germany as a divine punishment. The female allegorical figure of Germany is led astray by Lust, and various foreigners are sent to her by the god of war, Mars. Deluded by their promises of grandeur, she rejects her German ancestors and banishes Peace from her dominions, only to find herself a victim of those she had trusted. In the final act Peace intercedes with God and gains forgiveness for Germany. The main action of the play is interspersed with comic interludes showing the effect of war on the morals of the peasants and introducing the student-soldier Monsieur Sausewind.

All of Rist's works include prefaces in which he reflects on the purpose of his writing and on reader or audience response to it; the preface to *Das Friedewünschende Teütschland,* although mainly concerned with rebutting polemical accusations against Rist and his play, gives important insights into the problems of writing drama for performance in Rist's day. For instance, he justifies his use of prose, intermixed with musical interludes, rather than verse on the grounds that verse is difficult for actors to memorize and enunciate clearly. Rist's stage directions give clear instructions for the costumes of the various allegorical figures and the way in which the music is to be performed, as well as suggestions on how to overcome problems presented by a lack of actors or an inadequate stage. For example, the stage directions for an allegorical figure performing a song about the foreign influences that have led to Germany's ruin read:

Also bald darnach, wen die Kavallier sind hinweg gangen, muß einer mit etwas närrisch gemachten Kleideren, als einem Spanischen Wamse, Französischen Hosen, Polnischen oder Krabatischen Mützen und anderen dergleichen fremden Trachten angethan, herfürtreten, seltzam Geberde führen und folgendes Lied mit einem hönischen und offtverenderten Gesichte, bald als ein ernsthaffter Spanier, bald als ein leichtsinniger Franzose, bald als ein schmeichelhaffter Italianer und so fohrtan, nach dem eß der Jnnhalt gibt, fein langsahm singen und eine Spanische Kitarra oder Laute entweder selber dazu schlagen oder von einem anderen darinn spielen lassen, jedoch also, daß die wöhrter fein deütlich gesungen und von denen Zuhörern wol verstanden werden.

(Straight after, when the cavaliers have departed, someone must step forth wearing rather ridiculous clothes, such as a Spanish doublet, French trousers, a Polish or Croat cap and other foreign garb, making strange gestures and constantly changing his facial expression – from a sober Spaniard to a frivolous Frenchman, to a flattering Italian and so on as the content [of the song] requires – and sing very slowly, either having someone play a Spanish guitar or a lute or playing it himself, but in such a way that the words are sung very clearly and can be well understood by the audience.)

In February 1648 a storm devastated the region around Wedel, wrecking the roof and the organ of Rist's church. Rist wrote an epic poem on this event, *Holstein vergiß es nicht* (Holstein, Forget It Not, 1648), interpreting the storm as a sign of divine wrath and calling on his readers to repent. These moral failings and their punishment are also seen as having a causal connection with the death of the Danish king, Christian IV, which occurred in the same year. Also in 1648 Rist published *Der zu seinem allerheiligsten Leiden und Sterben hingeführter und an das Kreütz gehefteter Christu Jesus* (Jesus Christ Led to His Most Holy Suffering and Nailed to the Cross), a collection of devotional poetry set to music and providing starting points for meditation on Christ's Passion.

Rist produced a steady flow of occasional poetry, but his next major publication was *Der Adeliche Hausvatter* (The Father of a Noble Household, 1650), an adaptation of *Le père de famille* (The Family Father, 1632), J. Baudoin's French version of Torquato Tasso's dialogue *Il padre di famiglia* (1580). In preparing this translation Rist was conforming to the dictates of the Fruchtbringende Gesellschaft, which required its members to translate useful works so as to raise the general standard of German as a literary language. In keeping with the practice of his day, Rist's translation is far from literal. He provides a commentary on each chapter that is as

Title page for a collection of Rist's devotional poetry, with musical settings by Thomas Selle

long as, if not longer than, the chapter itself in which he explains the text to the German reader. The commentary draws on his own experience and seeks to bring the work up to date, and it includes open criticism of the contemporary German landed gentry.

Rist's growing importance as a local celebrity is shown by his being asked to provide the verses for a fireworks display in Hamburg to celebrate the conclusion of peace throughout Germany; he responded with *Hamburgisches Fried- und Freüdenfeür* (Hamburg's Fire of Peace and Joy, 1650). His popularity is also documented by the unauthorized publication of *Des Edlen Dafnis aus Cimbrien besungene Florabella* (Songs for the Noble Daphnis from Cimbria's Florabella, 1651), a collection of his pastoral poems set to music by the composer Peter Meier. In the same year Rist himself published *Sabbahtische Seelenlust* (Spiritual Pleasure for the Sab-

bath), a collection of his devotional poetry set to music by another Hamburg musician, Thomas Selle. This collection, like the *Himlischer Lieder,* provides songs that could be easily performed by lay musicians in the context of domestic devotional practice. *Neüer Himlischer Lieder Sonderbahres Buch* (A Special Book of New Heavenly Songs) appeared in the same year. In 1652 Rist published a compendium of his occasional poetry, *Neüer Teütscher Parnass* (The New German Parnassus), documenting his wide connections through poems addressed to the emperor, princes of the empire, nobles, and burghers. In the preface Rist says that the Parnassus of his title is a hill just outside Wedel with a splendid view over the Elbe, to which he retreats to write his poetry. He casts himself in the role of the hermit writing thousands of verses of songs and devotional poems and scorning worldly vanities in favor of rural simplicity: "hat Mir darauff nach verrichteter meiner Arbeit, manchesmal ein Stükke geräuchertes Spek und Trünklein Bier daselbst besser geschmekket, als wol manchen in den grossen Städten Wohnenden und bei Hofe lebenden fürnehmen Herren die allerköstlichste Speisen und anmuthigste Getränke" (often enough after completing my work a piece of smoked bacon and a drop of beer have tasted better to me there than the most delicious dishes and exquisite beverages would probably do to many fine gentlemen living in big cities and at court). Rist's preface also assesses the current state of German poetic practice. He pleads for poets to acquire a thorough grounding in German grammar and for an adherence to traditional meter. He also launches a fierce attack on those rhymesters who publish their unskilled verses, proffering his own collection as a model to be emulated by aspiring poets.

In 1653 Rist published two more works for the stage. His allegorical drama *Das Friedejauch[z]ende Deutschland* (Germany Shouting for Joy at the Peace) is a sequel to *Das Friedewünschende Teütschland.* In the main part of the play the allegorical figures Staatsmann (Statesman) and Frau Mißtrau (Madam Mistrust) embody the principles of Machiavellian statecraft. These principles, combined with the disastrous effects of war on the private and public morality of the various estates of the German body politic, have delayed the progress of peace, but all are eventually overcome by the positive Christian virtues that the figure of Germany embraces. In expansive interludes Rist introduces Low German comic scenes with peasant characters. The Sausewind character is expanded into a full-blown caricature of Philip von Zesen, Rist's former friend and main poetic rival. His other dramatic work of 1653 was *Die Triumphirende Liebe, umgeben mit den Sieghafften Tugenden* (Triumphant Love Surrounded by the Victorious Virtues), a libretto, published with illustrations, for a court ballet commissioned for the wedding of Christian Ludwig, Duke of Brunswick-Lüneburg, and Dorothea of Schleswig-Holstein. Eighteen short pieces danced by figures depicting vices and virtues were followed by a "grand ballet" in which the heroes of Roman history were danced by the ruling dukes of Brunswick themselves. Rist, who also wrote a eulogy on Duke Christian Ludwig, *Unterthänigste Lobrede* (Most Devoted Speech of Praise, 1653), was among the guests at the wedding in Celle. Rist's last dramatic work, *Depositio Cornuti Typographici* (The Deposition of the Horned Printer, 1655), is a reworking of a text by the Danzig typesetter Paulus de Vise that Rist undertook at the request of his friends and publishers, the brothers Johann and Heinrich Stern in Lüneburg. It was intended for performance at the initiation ceremony for new journeyman printers and is a curious example of the coarse and burlesque indignities of such rites, although the play purports to be a refined version of the original. The title refers to the horned cap that the apprentice wore during the ceremony, which was known as the deposition.

During the next decade Rist's literary production consisted almost exclusively of devotional works set to music. *Frommer und Gottseliger Christen alltägliche Haußmusik* (Devout and Saintly House Music for Every Day, 1654), poems with music by various Hamburg composers, was followed a year later by a supplement to *Sabbahtische Seelenlust* titled *Neüe Musikalische Fest-Andachten* (New Musical Feast Day Services, 1655) and the year after that by *Neüe Musikalische Katechismus Andachten* (New Musical Catechism Services, 1656). *Neüe Musikalische Kreutz-Trost- Lob- und DankSchule* (New Musical School of Suffering, Comfort, Praise and Thanks, 1659) was followed by the last works in the series, *Neues Musikalisches Seelenparadis* (New Musical Paradise of Souls, 1660, 1662).

From 1657 until 1660 Holstein was the main theater of war in a bitter conflict between the crowns of Sweden and Denmark. Rist's home in Wedel was plundered again, and in October 1658 he was forced to flee with his family to Hamburg. The losses he suffered were greater than those he had sustained during the Thirty Years' War. His wife fell ill shortly after their return to Wedel in 1659, and she died in 1662. The marriage of his only daughter left him without help in the running of his household, and in 1664 he married Anna

Hagedorn, the widow of a friend. The marriage was childless, and Rist is said not to have been happy in his choice. During the next few years his health declined, and he became something of a recluse, dedicating himself to his hobbies, his garden, and his parish.

Probably while he was in Hamburg in 1658 Rist founded his own language society, the Elbschwanenorden (Order of the Swans of the Elbe). The Elbschwanenorden was completely centered on Rist himself and did not long survive his death. There were about fifty members, among them such prominent northern German poets as Georg Greflinger, Balthasar Kindermann, Constantin Christian Dedekind, and Conrad von Hövelen. Like the other language societies the Elbschwanenorden used pseudonyms for its members; Rist was "Palatin," referring to the honor conferred on him by the emperor in 1654 when he was made *comes palatinus,* a rank that allowed its holder to crown poets, to issue patents of nobility, to legitimize children, and to perform other official acts that provided a significant source of income. The main forum for the society was provided by the prose works of Rist's final years, his monthly *Unterredungen* (Conversations). Like Harsdörffer's *Frauenzimmergesprechspiele* (Playful Colloquies for the Ladies, 1641–1657), these works furnish compendiums of all kinds of information in the guise of fictive conversations. They are a mine of data on Rist's life in Wedel and his opinions on all manner of subjects. Rist published six such works for the months January to June between 1663 and his death. They proved so popular that works for July to December were written by the Nuremberg polymath Erasmus Francisci. Each volume follows a standard pattern: the scene is Wedel, where members of the society are paying a visit to Palatin. The initial conversation usually revolves around the plants in Palatin's vicarage garden until Palatin suggests a topic for debate. Each of those present puts forward his views. After Palatin has given his judgment on their arguments, he presents his own case and thus resolves the matter, having both the final word and the deciding vote. The subjects debated in the volumes are what is the noblest liquid in the world, the noblest life, the noblest folly, the noblest entertainment, the noblest invention, and the noblest pastime. After a prolonged illness, Rist died at his home in Wedel on 31 August 1667.

Letters:

Der Fruchtbringenden Gesellschaft ältester Ertzschrein, edited by Gottlieb Krause (Leipzig: Dyk, 1855), pp. 403–410;

Briefe G. M. Lingelsheims, M. Berneggers und ihrer Freunde, edited by Alexander Reifferscheid (Heilbronn: Henninger, 1889).

References:

Leif Ludwig Albertsen, "Strophische Gedichte, die von einem Kollektiv gesungen werden. Das Zersingen, analysiert am Schicksal einiger Lieder Johann Rists," *Deutsche Vierteljahrsschrift,* 50 (April 1976): 84–102;

Gotthardt Frühsorge, "Die Gattung der 'Oeconomia' . . . Per Brahe – Johann Rist," in *Arte et Marte,* edited by Dieter Lohmeier and others (Neumünster: Wachholtz, 1978), pp. 85–107;

Karl Theodor Gaedertz, "Johann Rist als niederdeutscher Dramatiker," *Jahrbuch des Vereins für niederdeutsche Sprachforschung,* 7 (1881): 101–172;

Klaus Garber, "Pétrarchisme pastoral et bourgeoisie protestante: La poésie pastorale de J. Rist et J. Schwieger," in *Le genre pastoral en Europe du XVe au XVIIe siècle,* edited by Claude Longeon (Saint Etienne: Université de Saint Etienne, 1980), pp. 269–297;

Theodor Hansen, *Johann Rist und seine Zeit* (Halle: Waisenhaus, 1872; reprinted, Leipzig: Zentralantiquariat der DDR, 1973);

Alfred Jericke, *Johann Rists Monatsgespräche* (Berlin & Leipzig: De Gruyter, 1928);

Oskar Kern, *Johann Rist als weltlicher Lyriker* (Marburg: Elwert, 1919; New York: Johnson Reprint, 1968);

Dieter Lohmeier and Klaus Reichelt, "Johann Rist," in *Deutsche Dichter des 17. Jahrhunderts: Ihr Leben und Werk,* edited by Harald Steinhagen and Benno von Wiese (Berlin: Schmidt, 1984), pp. 347–364;

Donald Lee Madill, "Johann Rist as Hymnwriter: A Study of His Life and Works with Particular Emphasis on His 'Himlische Lieder' and 'Sonderbahres Buch,' " dissertation, University of Kansas, 1984;

Eberhard Mannack, "Grimmelshausens Rist-Lektüre und die Folgen: Jupiterepisoden und Friedensspiele," in *Barocker Lust-Spiegel: Studien zur Literatur des Barock. Festschrift für Blake Lee Spahr,* edited by Martin Bircher and others (Amsterdam: Rodopi, 1984), pp. 279–294;

Mannack, "Hamburg und der Elbschwanenorden," in his *Sprachgesellschaften, Sozietäten, Dichtergruppen* (Hamburg: Hauswedell, 1978), pp. 163–179;

Mannack, *Johann Rist, Gelehrter, Organisator und Poet des Barock* (Munich: Gesellschaft der Bibliophilen, 1988);

Mannack, "Johann Rists Perseus und das Drama des Barock," *Daphnis,* 1, no. 2 (1972): 141–149;

Rudolf Mews, "Rists Gesellschaftslyrik und ihre Beziehung zur zeitgenössischen Poetik," dissertation, Hamburg University, 1969;

Ulrich Moerke, *Die Anfänge der weltlichen Barocklyrik in Schleswig-Holstein. Hudemann, Rist, Lund* (Neumünster: Wachholtz, 1972);

Richard E. Schade, "Baroque Biography: Johann Rist's Self-Concept," *German Quarterly,* 51 (May 1978): 338–345;

Irmgard Scheitler, *Das geistliche Lied im deutschen Barock* (Berlin: Dunckler & Humblot, 1982);

Ingrid Schiewek, "Theater zwischen Tradition und Neubeginn: Die Zwischenspiele des Johann Rist," in *Studien zur deutschen Literatur im 17. Jahrhundert,* edited by Werner Lenk (Berlin: Aufbau, 1984), pp. 145–251;

Irmgard Clara Mecklenburg Taylor, "Untersuchungen zum Stil des Dramen Johann Rists," dissertation, Syracuse University, 1971;

Richard Hinton Thomas, *Poetry and Song in the German Baroque* (Oxford: Clarendon Press, 1963).

Papers:

Papers of Johann Rist are held by the Staatsbibliothek Berlin, the Staats- und Universitätsbibliothek Hamburg, the Bibliothek des Hansestadt Lübeck, and the Staatsarchiv Weimar.

Johann Scheffler
(Angelus Silesius)

(December 1624 – 9 July 1677)

Jeffrey L. Sammons
Yale University

BOOKS: *Bonus Consiliarius quantum potest Expressus in Andrea Langio* (Breslau: Printed by Georg Baumann, 1642);

Christliches Ehrengedächtniß des weiland WohlEdlen und Gestrengen Herren Herrn Abraham von Franckenberg auff Ludwigsdorff (Oels: Printed by Johann Seyffert, 1652);

Gründtliche Vrsachen und Motiven, warumb Er von dem Lutherthumb abgetretten, vnd sich zu der Catholischen Kirchen bekennet hat (Ingolstadt: Printed by Gregor Hänlin, 1653);

Geistreiche Sinn- vnd Schlussrime (Vienna: Johann Jacob Kürner the Elder, 1657); enlarged as *Cherubinischer Wandersmann oder Geist-Reiche Sinn- und Schluß-Reime zur Göttlichen beschauligkeit anleitende* (Glatz: Printed by Ignatz Constantin Schubart, 1675); selections translated by Paul Carus as *A Selection from the Rhymes of a German Mystic* (Chicago: Open Court, 1909);

Heilige Seelen-Lust oder Geistliche Hirten-Lieder, der in ihren Jesum verliebten Psyche, 2 volumes (Breslau: Printed by Gottfried Gründer at the Baumann printery, 1657); enlarged as *Heilige Seelen-Lust oder Geistliche Hirten-Lieder, der in jhren Jesum verliebten Psyche,* 1 volume (Breslau: Printed by Johann Christoph Factor at the Baumann printery, 1668);

Türcken-Schrifft von den Ursachen der Türckischen Uberziehung und der Zertretung des Volckes Gottes (N.p., 1664);

ChristenSchrifft, von dem herlichen Kennzeichen des Volckes Gottes vnd der wunderbahren Errettung der Christen, zu glücklicher Uberwindung des Türcken wiederumb an die Deutschen hochtröstlich zulesen (Neisse: Printed by Ignatz Constantin Schubart, 1664);

Kehr-Wisch zu abkehrung deß Ungeziefers mit welchem seine wolgemeinte Türkenschrifft Christianus Chemnitius Doctor, Professor, Pastor, Superintendens, und Decanus in Jehna, hat wollen verhasst machen. Zu rettung der Catholischen Wahrheit

Johann Scheffler; portrait by an unknown artist, painted after Scheffler's death (Bildarchiv Preußischer Kulturbesitz, Berlin)

nochmahls an die Deutschen. (Neisse: Printed by Ignatz Constantin Schubart, 1664);

Abdruk eines Sendschreibens D. Johannis Schefflers der Heil: Röm: Kirchen Pristers, die verläumbderische Schmähkarte betreffende, welche Johann Adam Schertzer, der Heil: Schrifft Licentiat (wie er sich schreibt) Türkenschrifft außgeworffen hat (Neisse: Printed by Ignatz Constantin Schubart, 1664);

Nachschrifft wegen Schertzers ungesaltzener Suppe die Oberhauptmannschaft des Römischen Bischoffs anbelangende (Neisse: Printed by Ignatz Constantin Schubart, 1664);

Und Scheffler redet noch! Das ist Johannis Schefflers Schutz-Rede für sich und seine Christen-Schrifft wieder seine schmähende Feinde Lic. Schertzern und D. Chemnitium (Neisse: Printed by Ignatz Constantin Schubart, 1664);

Triumph-Blatt über den überwundenen Chemnitium (Neisse: Printed by Ignatz Constantin Schubart, 1664);

SendSchreiben. An den Hochgelehrten Christianum Chemnitium (Neisse: Printed by Ignatz Constantin Schubart, 1664);

Verthädigte luthrische Wahrheit wieder den Unluthrischen Scherzter (Neisse: Printed by Ignatz Constantin Schubart, 1665);

Der Lutheraner und Calvinisten Abgott der Vernunfft entblösset dargestellt, sambt dem Bildnüß des wahren Gottes (Neisse: Printed by Ignatz Constantin Schubart, 1665);

Kommet her und sehet mit vernünfftigen Augen wie Joseph und die Heiligen bey den Catholischen geehret, und jhre Ehre verstanden werde (Neisse: Printed by Ignatz Constantin Schubart, 1665);

Send-Schreiben Christiani Bonamici An H. D. Schefflern . . . Betreffend Johann Adam Schertzers so viel als nichts (Neisse: Printed by Ignatz Constantin Schubart, 1665);

I. Zerblasung des Schertzerischen so viel als nichts, welches er wieder die Schutzrede der Christen-Schrifft herauß gegeben. II. Eigentliche Darstellung des dritten Elie und Propheten des Deutschlandes, des so vermeinten theuren mannes Lutheri, von Oleario abgezwungen (Neisse: Printed by Ignatz Constantin Schubart, 1665);

Gespräche mit dem Doctor Keinütz, fürnehmlich die ersten Luthrischen Prediger und Fürsten anbetreffende, allen und jeden Religions-genossen zur Nachricht der Wahrheit höchstnöthig zu lesen (Neisse: Printed by Ignatz Constantin Schubart, 1665);

M. Adam Beckers Auffschauers zu Züllichau Luthrischer Unbeweiß das ist Beweiß, daß die Lutheraner jhren Glauben gar nicht auß der Schrifft beweisen können. Von Johann Scheffler entgegen gesetzt der thörichten leeren Beckerischen Bundes- oder Wurmslade, in welcher kein Manna ist (Neisse: Printed by Ignatz Constantin Schubart, 1666);

Des Römischen Bapsts Oberhaubtmannschafft über die gantze allgemeine Kirche Christi (Neisse: Printed by Ignatz Constantin Schubart, 1666);

Gründtliche Außführung, daß die Lutheraner auff keine Weise noch Wege jhren Glauben in der Schrifft zu zeigen vermögen, und jhr Gott ein blosses Wahn-Bild oder Ding jhrer Vernunfft sey (Neisse: Printed by Ignatz Constantin Schubart, 1667);

D. Johann Adam Schertzers, der H. Schrifft und Ebreischen Sprache Professoris ordinarii, der Churfürstl. Stipendiaten Ephori, auch des grossen Fürsten Collegii Collegiati zu Leiptzig Abzugsblasung von dem wieder Herrn D. Scheffler geführten Streit; oder Bericht, wie dieser Streit zwischen beiden abgelauffen, und der Professor sich gegen D. Schefflers Luthrische Warheit und Oberhauptmannschafft des R. Bapsts verhalten habe (Neisse: Printed by Ignatz Constantin Schubart, 1668);

Antwort-Schreiben, eines catholisch Gewordenen, an einen Uncatholischen von der Communion unter einer Gestalt, anonymous (Dyherrnfurth an der Oder: Printed by Johann Theophil Kopydlansky, 1669);

Sendschreiben an alle Evangelische Universitäten, in welchem er seine Gewissens-Scrupel proponirt und zu erörtern bittet 1.) ob der in der Lutherischen Religion könne seelig werden, weil sie nicht die Catholische ist, in der allein secundum omnes Doctores die Seeligkeit zu hoffen? 2.) ob diejenige die Catholische sey, die so genennet wird, oder so es die nicht ist, welche es denn sey?, as Christianus Conscientiosus (Neisse: Printed by Ignatz Constantin Schubart, 1670);

Kurtze Erörterung der Frage, ob die Lutheraner in Schlesien der in Instrumenti pacis denen Augsburgischen Confessions-Verwandten verliehenen Religionsfreyheit, sich getrösten können, anonymous (Prague: Tuchscherer-Verlag, 1670);

Verthädigung des Send-Schreibens von der Communion unter einer Gestalt (Dyherrnfurth an der Oder, 1671);

Conscientiosus liberatus (Neisse: Printed by Ignatz Constantin Schubart, 1671);

Verthädigte Erörterung der Frage, ob die Lutheraner in Schlesien, der in Instrumento Pacis denen Augsburgischen Confessions-Verwandten verliehenen Religions-Freyheit sich getrösten können. Wieder das armseelige Patrocinium Valentini Alberti, anonymous (Neisse: Printed by Ignatz Constantin Schubart, 1671);

Paraenesis controversistica an die (sonderlich zu Leitzig) Studirende Luthrische Jugend und dritte Erweisung, daß die Lutheraner in Schlesien wie auch anderswerts nicht mehr Augsburgischer Confession seynd, und sie Valentinus Alberti zum andernmahl nicht dabey erhalten können, anonymous (Neisse: Printed by Ignatz Constantin Schubart, 1671);

Erweiß daß der größte Hauffe die rechte Kirche sey; und man sich kurtzumb zu der Catholischen Kirche, weil sie der gröste Hauffe ist, begeben müsse, wo man ewig seelig werden wil (Neisse: Printed by Ignatz Constantin Schubart, 1671);

J. E. Information-Schreiben wegen des Fegefeuers an E. V. (Neisse: Printed by Ignatz Constantin Schubart, 1672);

Zwey Sendschreiben D. Johannis Schefflers wegen der unsinnigen Lästerungen Ægidij Strauchs, Prädicanten zu Dantzig, die er in seinen Purim-Predigten wieder den Bapst und dessen Ablaßertheilung herauß-geschüttet hat (Neisse: Printed by Ignatz Constantin Schubart, 1673);

Prädicanten Beruff, oder Treuhertzige Ermahnung an die Prädicanten, ihren Beruff wol zuerwegen und in acht zunehmen (Neisse: Printed by Ignatz Constantin Schubart, 1673);

Beschirmung des Lichts der Catholischen Warheit wieder das so genandte hell-klare Licht der reinen Evangelischen Warheit . . . (Neisse: Printed by Ignatz Constantin Schubart, 1673);

Gerechtfertigter Gewissenszwang oder Erweiß, daß man die Ketzer zum wahren Glauben zwingen könne und solle, as Hierothei Boranowsky (Neisse: Printed by Ignatz Constantin Schubart, 1673);

Catholische Bekäntnüß aller strietigen Glaubens-artikel auß H. Schrifft, verthädigt durch Johann Schefflern wieder einen einbildischen Plauderer. Allen so wol Catholischen als Vncatholischen höchst nützlich zulesen (Neisse: Printed by Ignatz Constantin Schubart, 1674);

Schauführung des lästernden Höllenhundes, der sich Egidij Strauchs gewesene Information- Hauß- und Tischgenossen nennt (Neisse: Printed by Ignatz Constantin Schubart, 1674);

Concilium Tridentinum antè Tridentinum, Exquisitissimis orthodoxorum Patrum testimoniis in ipso fonte visis comprobatum (Neisse: Printed by Ignatz Constantin Schubart, 1675);

Vernünfftiger Gottesdienst durch augenscheinliche Zuschandenmachung deß so genandten "irräsonablen Abfalls von der evangelisch-lutherischen Religion zu der Bäptischen D. G." (Neisse: Printed by Ignatz Constantin Schubart, 1675);

Sinnliche Beschreibung der Vier Letzten Dinge, zu heilsamem Schröken und Auffmunterung aller Menschen in Druck gegeben (Schweidnitz: Printed by Gottfried Jon, 1675);

Simplicij Angeregte Vrsachen warumb Er nicht Catholisch werden könne, as Bonamicus (N.p., 1675);

Der Catholisch gewordene Bauer und Luthrische Doctor, anonymous (Glatz: Printed by Ignatz Constantin Schubart, 1675);

Alleiniges Himmelreich (Neisse: Printed by Ignatz Constantin Schubart, 1675);

Advocat wieder den sogenandten Peregrin Rechtsohn, as Bonamicus (Glatz: Printed by Ignatz Constantin Schubart, 1676);

Ecclesiologia oder Kirchen-Beschreibung. Bestehende jn Neun und dreyssig unterschiedenen außerlesenen Tractätlein von der Catholischen Kirche und dero wahren Glauben, wie auch von den Uncatholischen Gelachen und dero falschem Wahn (Neisse & Glatz: Printed by Ignatz Constantin Schubart, 1677).

Editions and Collections: *Sämtliche poetische Werke und eine Auswahl aus seinen Streitschriften,* 2 volumes, edited by Georg Ellinger (Berlin: Propyläen, 1923);

Sämtliche poetische Werke, 3 volumes, edited by Hans Ludwig Held (Munich: Hanser, 1952);

Cherubinischer Wandersmann: Kritische Ausgabe, edited by Louise Gnädinger (Stuttgart: Reclam, 1984).

Editions in English: *Selections from The Cherubinic Wanderer,* translated by J. E. Crawford Flitch (London: Allen & Unwin, 1932);

Alexandrines Translated from the "Cherubinischer Wandersmann" of Angelus Silesius 1657, translated by Julia Bilger (North Montpelier, Vt.: Driftwood Press, 1944);

The Cherubinic Wanderer: Selections, translated by Willard R. Trask (New York: Pantheon, 1953);

The Book of Angelus Silesius, translated by Frederick Franck (New York: Vintage, 1976);

The Cherubinic Wanderer, translated by Maria Shrady, edited by Josef Schmidt (New York & Toronto: Paulist Press, 1986).

OTHER: "Nun auf, o du mein Geist, du mußt nicht stille schweigen . . . ," in *Viri Clar. Dn. Chrysostomi Schultz* (Breslau: Georg Baumann, 1641);

"Wie ein Schiffmann, wenn er schneidet . . . ," in *Epicedia, in Obitum Dn. Joh. Blaufusii* (Brieg: Balthasar Klose, 1641);

"Jhr zartes Nymphenvolck am gelben Oderstrande . . . ," in *Viri supra eruditae laudis titulos, Dn. Christophori Coleri* (Breslau: Georg Baumann, 1642);

"Wie mögt Jhr Euch, mein Freund, um Euer Kind betrüben . . . ," in *Justa Amabilissimae Puellae, Anna Cathar. . . . Persoluta* (Oels: Johann Seyffert, 1652);

Deß unbeniembten Deutschen Gottliebs Gesellschaft der Liebe oder Geistliche Zugestellung der liebenden Seele zu Gott, edited by Scheffler (Neisse: Printed by Ignatz Constantin Schubart, 1666);

Anna Bijes, *Köstliche Evangelische Perle. Zu Vollkommener ausschmückung der Brautt Christi,* translated by Scheffler (Glatz: Printed by Ignatz Constantin Schubart, 1676).

Among the German religious poets of the seventeenth century Johann Scheffler, the "Angelus Silesius" (Silesian Angel or Messenger) is the best known to the world at large, though only for one of his works. There seem to be two main reasons for this situation. First, the mystical mode of expression in his major work is recognizable across cultures. Mystical discourse may seem, at first, somewhat exotic to those unfamiliar with it, but once its principles have been grasped it becomes intelligible in many forms and guises. Mysticism recurs throughout the Christian tradition, but there is also a Jewish mysticism that in many respects resembles it despite its different cultural origins; nor is it difficult to sense an affinity between the mystical verse of Angelus Silesius and the Japanese haiku of Zen Buddhism. Second, Scheffler's epigrammatic verse evidently presents a welcome challenge to translators. Surely the writing of no other German seventeenth-century poet has appeared in so many different English versions; it has also been translated quite successfully into French, as well as into Polish and Italian. At the same time, the programmatic imprecision of mystical expression gives a certain amount of leeway to the translator, who also has the option of choosing among Scheffler's hundreds of non-sequential couplets, retaining those that appear to yield and leaving out those that are resistant. It is true that the long alexandrine line, borrowed from French classicism to become the characteristic sound of German verse in the seventeenth century, has not had much fortune in English; it is most familiar as the closing line of the nine-line stanza that Edmund Spenser employed for *The Faerie Queen* (1589, 1596):

Fierce wárres and fáithfull lóues // shall móralize my sóng.

It is a six-beat line of twelve or thirteen syllables, regularly divided by a strong caesura placed usually, though not necessarily, after the third foot. Arranged in couplets, the alexandrine has obvious possibilities for antithesis, contradiction, and chiastic structure that are clearly attractive to dexterous versifiers.

Scheffler's father, Stanislaus, was a Protestant with a patent of minor Polish nobility who had been born in the Kraków area and had moved to Breslau (today Wroclaw) by 1619. It is not known how he earned his livelihood, but he was fairly prosperous. On 20 February 1624, at the age of sixty-two, he married the twenty-four-year-old Maria Hennemann. The marriage does not seem to have been a happy one; the record indicates that Stanislaus was a blustering, belligerent man. Johann Scheffler was born in December 1624 – presumably toward the end of the month, as he was baptized on Christmas Day. A second son, Christian, was feeble-minded. Stanislaus died in 1637 and his wife in 1639, so that Scheffler was an orphan at the age of fourteen.

Apart from the insecurity of his intimate environment, he was born into what have long been regarded as the worst times in modern German history before the twentieth century: the grim, grisly, and apparently interminable chaos of the Thirty Years' War, which was especially violent in Scheffler's native Silesia. The dimension of religious conflict, the ostensible though doubtless not the actual cause of the war, was also exceptionally pronounced in Silesia and continued long after the war's end, as the Counter Reformation re-Catholicized the land in a distinctly ungentle fashion. This process was the major determinant of the course of Scheffler's adult life.

The details of the boy's guardianship arrangement are not known, but he was given a good humanistic education at a highly reputed school, the Elisabeth Gymnasium in Breslau, where he came under the influence of Christoph Köler, a follower of Martin Opitz's poetic reform and Opitz's first biographer. Scheffler seems to have been an excellent pupil who participated in literary activities and wrote some occasional poetry, including an encomium on Köler that praises the German language for its potential for literary greatness. Scheffler left the school in 1643, attended the University of Strasbourg for one year, then transferred to the University of Leiden in the summer of 1644. His field of study was medicine, but he was exposed in the Netherlands to the most religiously tolerant environment in Europe, where not only Jews but also various Christian sectarians had found refuge. Some of these groups espoused a deinstitutionalized, personal religion of the heart, and Amsterdam was the publishing center of European mysticism. Later Scheffler would find himself constrained to downplay his exposure to pietistic and mystical communities in the Netherlands, but most scholars have concluded that he must have occupied himself with the mystical tradition to some extent during his two years there. He may also have been impressed and inspired by Andreas Gryphius's first book of sonnets, which had appeared in Leiden the year before Scheffler's arrival.

He left Leiden in the fall of 1646 and may have traveled for the year before he matriculated in September 1647 at the University of Padua, well known for its program in medicine. He received a combined M.D. and Ph.D. in July 1648. The only document of the next year is a letter that includes the phrase "mundus pulcherrimum nihil" (the world is a most beautiful naught), perhaps a sign of tension in his mind between an appreciation of the material beauty of the world and a religious conviction of the meaninglessness of that beauty.

The next few years were a period of elaborate spiritual upheaval. In June 1649 he was appointed court physician to Duke Sylvius Nimrod of Württemberg, the strictly and energetically orthodox Lutheran ruler of the principality of Oels in Silesia. Around 1650 Scheffler made the acquaintance of Abraham von Franckenberg, a nobleman who at an early age had transferred his property to his brother in order to live as an ascetic in his own castle. Franckenberg was a devotee of the visionary shoemaker Jakob Böhme, an edition of whose works he published in 1644. There can be little doubt that Franckenberg became Scheffler's mentor in mystical learning; he presented the young man with editions of works by major authors of the tradition, and on his death in June 1652 he left Scheffler his whole library of mystical and occult writings. Franckenberg apparently also acquainted Scheffler with manuscripts of works by contemporary mystical poets, including Johann Theodor von Tschesch, who wrote epigrams in Latin, and Daniel Czepko, whose unpublished alexandrine couplets in German, "Sexcenta monodisticha sapientium" (Six Hundred Epigrams of the Wise), were demonstrably the immediate model for Scheffler's.

Not long after Franckenberg's death Scheffler put together a volume of mystical prayers; but publication was forbidden, to his great bitterness, by the court chaplain of Oels, Christoph Freytag. Scheffler left Sylvius Nimrod's employ, and on 12 June 1653 he was converted to Roman Catholicism in Breslau. He took the name Johann Angelus, later adding Silesius to distinguish himself from a Lutheran theologian of the same name.

With his conversion Scheffler plunged himself into the public turmoil of the Counter Reformation. Quickly under attack, he published an apologia, Gründtliche Ursachen und Motiven, warumb Er von dem Lutherthumb abgetretten, und sich zu der Catholischen Kirchen bekennet hat (Fundamental Causes and Motives Why He Left Lutheranism and Professed the Catholic Church, 1653). He deals less with the theological issues than with the question of certainty, stressing the newness and arbitrariness of the Protestant doctrine, Martin Luther's tendency to contradict himself, and disunity within the Protestant camp. In

March 1654 he received from Emperor Ferdinand III the purely honorary title of royal imperial court physician; the connection of this honor to his conversion, if any, is not known. Around this time he caught the attention of Sebastian von Rostock, vicar general in Breslau and a ferociously aggressive champion of the Counter Reformation. Rostock, like the Lutheran chaplain Freytag, was a censor, and it was by his imprimatur that Scheffler's two first literary works were allowed to appear in 1657.

One of these came out at home in Breslau: Heilige Seelen-Lust oder Geistliche Hirten-Lieder, der in ihren Jesum verliebten Psyche (Holy Joy of the Soul; or, Spiritual Pastorals of Psyche Who Is in Love with Her Jesus, 1657), originally in two volumes totaling four books; a fifth book was added to the one-volume second edition in 1668. The other, perhaps owing to its riskier character, was published at a distance, in Vienna: Geistreiche Sinn- und Schlussrime (Ingenious Epigrams and Apothegms, 1657). The second edition of 1675, with a sixth book added, received the title by which the work has been known ever since: Cherubinischer Wandersmann oder Geist-Reiche Sinn- und Schluß-Reime zur Göttlichen beschauligkeit anleitende (Cherubinic Wanderer; or, Ingenious Epigrams and Apothegms Conducing to Divine Contemplation; selections translated as A Selection from the Rhymes of a German Mystic, 1909). This version includes 1,676 poems, most of them rhymed couplets, along with ten sonnets and some longer poems of from four to twenty-eight lines. Concerning the genesis of these two works nothing is known; they are customarily thought to have been written between 1651 and 1657, but all more-precise efforts at dating are speculative. It is not known which of the works is earlier, or whether they were written simultaneously. There is only Scheffler's claim that the first book of the Cherubinischer Wandersmann was composed in a four-day burst of inspiration. The dating question is frustrating because it makes it impossible to work out with assurance the relationship of the inner chronology of the works to the upheavals in Scheffler's life and convictions.

The two works are quite different from one another and lie in contrasting traditions of religious discourse. Scheffler signals the difference with the adjective cherubinic. In the traditional celestial order the cherubim are the angels of knowledge of God, the seraphim the angels of love service. Therefore, one might say that the Cherubinischer Wandersmann is a form of devotion as a mental exercise, while the seraphic Heilige Seelen-Lust nourishes devotion with emotion and sentiment. Both participate, though in different ways, in the European mystical tradition.

Much has been written about that tradition in connection with Scheffler because he was evidently erudite in it, though specifics are, again, largely a matter of speculation. Among the many relevant figures are Saint Bernard, Mechthild von Magdeburg, Saint Bonaventura, Meister Eckehart, Jan van Ruusbroec, Heinrich Suso, Johannes Tauler, Saint Bridget of Sweden, the anonymous author of the *Theologia Deutsch* (German Theology, before 1400), Nicholas of Cusa, and Saint Ignatius. It is known, from the researches of M. Hildburgis Gies, that Scheffler used a modern book, *Clavis pro theologia mystica* (Key to Mystical Theology, 1640), a kind of lexicon of mystical terms by the Jesuit Maximilian Sandaeus.

Mysticism is a complex and variegated phenomenon, but its fundamental idea is to empty the self of its worldly complicities so as to achieve, or recover, unity with God. Behind this idea, though not always explicitly, is a Neoplatonic doctrine according to which all creation, including humanity, is an emanation from God, inferior and degenerated in proportion to its distance from him. In some versions God is himself an emanation from a more abstract divine force, the Godhead. The religious soul yearns to reverse the process of creation, to rejoin with the Godhead. Because of this intensely individual relationship and quest, there is always a potential in mysticism for indifference to dogma and institutions, to rituals except in their symbolic dimension, and to priests as mediators, and thus it is recurrently vulnerable to charges of heresy; Freytag's refusal to allow Scheffler's book to be printed is an example of such an imputation. Scheffler was in a complicated situation because the writing of the *Cherubinischer Wandersmann* overlapped, one assumes, with his conversion to Catholicism. He was, therefore, much concerned in the preface to the work and elsewhere to assert his orthodoxy. The will to do so is evident in the text itself, which includes many verses of a doctrinally inoffensive sort, notably in books 3 and 4 and especially in the subsequently added book 6. But it is not difficult to find verses that are startling in their implications. For example, the yearned-for unity of the self and God is preempted by an assertion of their mutual dependence:

> Ich weiß daß ohne mich GOtt nicht ein Nu kan leben,
> Werd' ich zu nicht Er muß von Noth den Geist auffgeben.
> (I know that, without me, God cannot live a moment;

> Were I destroyed, he must needs give up the ghost.)

The concept of God can be negated:

> GOtt ist ein lauter nichts, Ihn rührt kein Nun noch Hier:
> Je mehr du nach Ihm greiffst, je mehr entwird Er dir.

> (God is naught but nothing, no now or here touches him;
> The more you grasp for him, the more he escapes you.)

The self must abolish itself to achieve unity:

> Mensch, wo du noch was bist, was weist, was liebst und hast;
> So bistu, glaube mir, nicht ledig deiner Last.

> (Man, if you still are something, know, love or hate something,
> Believe me, you are not free of your burden.)

Once this self-abolition is accomplished, however, the self and the Godhead become indistinguishable:

> Ich bin der Gottheit Faß in welchs sie sich ergeust,
> Sie ist mein tieffes Meer das mich in sich beschleust.

> (I am the cask of the Godhead into which it pours;
> It is my deep sea which encloses me in itself.)

Time dissolves into eternity:

> Wer in der Ewigkeit mehr lebt als einen Tag,
> Derselbe wird so Alt, als GOtt nicht werden mag.

> (Whoever lives in eternity more than one day,
> He becomes older than God would wish to be.)

Death itself is drawn into this unified condition:

> Ich sterb' und leb' auch nicht: GOtt selber stirbt in mir:
> Und was ich leben sol, lebt Er auch für und für.

> (I neither die nor live; God Himself dies in me:
> And what I should live, He lives also continually.)

The mystical use of language, employed, as in these examples, with incomparable dexterity, is a rhetoric designed to dismantle itself. Through such devices as shock, self-contradiction, apparent blasphemy, literalized metaphors, logical conundrums, the merging of assertion and denial, and words sequenced so that they rattle emptily, the definitions and distinctions of language are exhibited as hindrances to the return home of the soul and then are undermined and dissolved until, at the vanishing point of language, will and even thought are meant to vanish as well. The negative theology employs an antipoetry eloquently turned against itself, in the paradox of a language expressing the inexpressible by indirection.

Heilige Seelen-Lust lies in a different tradition, that of redirecting erotic feeling and its lyrical expression to the love of God. The model is obviously the biblical Song of Songs, but there is also a history of *Kontrafaktur,* the transformation of popular love lyrics into religious song. In Scheffler's case, not only love song and folk song but also a substantial amount of contemporary poetry can be shown to have fed into his work. The poems were published with music composed by Georg Joseph, and a few of them have lived on in both Protestant and Catholic hymnals. Unlike *Cherubinischer Wandersmann,* which rings changes on a single verse form, *Heilige Seelen-Lust* contains a wide variety of metrical and strophic forms; nowhere else is the breadth of Scheffler's poetic capabilities so evident. *Heilige Seelen-Lust* is also the more structured work. The first three books follow the liturgical year, from Advent through the birth of the Child, the Passion, the Resurrection and Ascension, to the Eucharist. Book 4, which was printed separately in the second volume of the first edition, recapitulates some of these themes and introduces figures who loved Jesus, such as Mary, John, and Mary Magdalene. Book 5, added in 1668, is vitiated by a need to remain within orthodox limits; the erotic element, in particular, is treated much more circumspectly.

The assumption that eroticism has been safely harnessed to religious purpose often releases a polymorphous androgyny that can be quite breathtaking in its liberation from conventional decorum. An example is the first three of the six stanzas of a much-discussed poem, "Die Psyche begehrt ein Bienelein auff den Wunden JEsu zu seyn" (Psyche Longs to Be a Little Bee on the Wounds of Jesus), that lies within a long metaphorical tradition:

> DU grüner Zweig, du edler Reiß,
> Du Honig-reiche Blüte,
> Du auffgethanes Paradeiß,
> Gezweig mir eine Bitte;
> Laß meine Seel ein Bienelein
> Auff deinen Rosen-Wunden seyn.

> Ich sehne mich nach ihrem Safft,
> Ich suche sie mit Schmertzen;
> Weil sie ertheilen Stärck' und Krafft
> Den abgematten Hertzen:
> Drumb laß mich doch ein Beinelein

Frontispiece for the first edition of the work that became, in its enlarged second edition, Scheffler's Cherubinischer Wandersmann

> Auff deinen Rosen-Wunden seyn.

> Ihr übertrefflicher Geruch
> Ist ein Geruch zum Leben;
> Vertreibt die Gifft, verjagt den Fluch,
> Und macht den Geist erheben:
> Drumb laß mich wie ein Beinelein
> Auff diesen Rosen-Wunden seyn.

> (You green branch, you noble shoot,
> You honey-rich blossom,
> You opened paradise,
> Grant me a boon.
> Let my soul be a little bee

On your rosy wounds.

I long for their juice,
I seek them with pain,
Because they confer strength and force
Upon the wearied heart.
Therefore let me be a little bee
On your rosy wounds.

Their exquisite fragrance
Is a fragrance for life,
Drives out the poison, chases away the curse
And makes the spirit rise.
Therefore let me be like a little bee
On these rosy wounds.)

The dangers in this mode, with its depth-psychological insouciance, lie near to hand – of sliding, on the one hand, into a kind of sweet-baby-Jesus kitsch, or, on the other, into self-indulgent perversity. The work was highly popular for a while but declined in interest after the middle of the eighteenth century. The poetry is not of a kind likely to have much appeal in the modern world, but it shows enough artistic virtuosity and lyrical lightness to make one wish that the remainder of Scheffler's life had been spent to better purpose than it was.

That purpose was Counter Reformation agitation and polemic. In 1660 he carried a cross with a crown of thorns on his head in an illegal procession, expressing in a memorandum his hope that he would be dishonored and scorned so as the more to imitate Christ. In May 1661 he was ordained a priest. In 1664 his mentor Rostock became prince-bishop of Breslau and appointed Scheffler his court marshal, an oddly worldly position in which he took little pleasure and from which he was able to extricate himself a couple of years later. By this time he had embarked on his polemical career, during which, according to his own account, he published fifty-five controversial pamphlets. Not all of these pamphlets have been located, but what has been preserved is quite enough for most people.

Probably the best that can be said for Scheffler's polemics is that they were fearless. He instigated controversies in a manner that not only enraged his enemies but sometimes made his allies shudder. A good example is the first extant pamphlet, *Türcken-Schrifft von den Ursachen der Türckischen Überziehung und der Zertretung des Volckes Gottes* (Turkish Pamphlet of the Causes of the Turkish Invasion and the Downtreading of the People of God, 1664), in which he draws on an Old Testament model to explain the Turkish advance in Eastern Europe as God's punishment for the Reformation. The Magdeburg city council, supported by several Catholic

bishops, demanded – without effect – that the emperor punish Scheffler for sedition; he was heating up the century-old religious strife at a time when the more thoughtful were attempting to cool it down. He proposed the abrogation of the legal rights of Silesian Protestants, defended the sovereignty of the pope, attacked the idolatry of reason and the negotiation of political solutions to sectarian conflict, insisted that salvation was possible only within the Catholic Church, and argued the perniciousness of tolerance in an extraordinary document, *Gerechtfertigter Gewissenszwang oder Erweiß, daß man die Ketzer zum wahren Glauben zwingen könne und solle* (Coercion of Conscience Justified; or, Proof that One Can and Should Force the Heretics to the True Faith, 1673).

Scheffler's polemics are notable neither for logic nor for theological subtlety. They are marked by slashing dogmatic assertions and the rich vocabulary of insult that was characteristic of this mode of discourse since Luther's time. These were no less the weapons of his enemies, especially of Christian Chemnitz and Johann Adam Schertzer, who tirelessly battled Scheffler for years. But Scheffler's literary advantages are evident in these exchanges. He is more lucid and resourceful. Sometimes he constructed dialogues in what he supposed to be a folksy tone, and these are not without touches of grim humor. In 1677 Scheffler collected and edited thirty-nine of his pamphlets in a large quarto, *Ecclesiologia oder Kirchen-Beschreibung. Bestehende in Neun und dreyssig unterschiedenen außerlesenen Tractätlein von der Catholischen Kirche und dero wahren Glauben, wie auch von den Uncatholischen Gelachen und dero falschem Wahn* (Ecclesiologia; or, Description of the Church, Consisting in Thirty-nine Various Selected Tractates about the Catholic Church and Its True Faith, as Well as about the Uncatholic Absurdities and Their False Delusion, 1677). Although it was republished in 1687 and in 1735, it was never influential.

Besides the expanded editions of *Heilige Seelen-Lust* in 1668 and *Cherubinischer Wandersmann* in 1675, Scheffler published two other works at the end of his life. One is a translation of a sixteenth-century mystical work thought to be by a Dutch nun, Anna Bijes: *Dye groote evangelische Perle* (Evangelical Pearl, 1539), which had been translated into Latin in 1545 as *Margarita Evangelica;* Scheffler's German translation is titled *Köstliche Evangelische Perle. Zu Vollkommener ausschmückung der Brautt Christi* (Precious Evangelical Pearl. For Perfect Ornamentation of the Bride of Christ, 1676). The other is a poem of 2,742 iambic lines, *Sinnliche Beschreibung der Vier Letzten Dinge, zu heilsamen Schröken und Auffmunterung aller Menschen* (Sensual Contemplation of the Four Last Things, for the Wholesome Terror and Encouragement of All People, 1675). The four last things are death, the Last Judgment, the eternal torments of the damned, and the eternal joys of the blessed. Scheffler meant "sensual contemplation" quite literally, as he seems to be condescending to a primitive imagination; the torments of the damned are dilated on for 576 lines of the most disgusting and sadistic images, while Paradise is a place of material pleasures and feudal luxuries. Few critics have ever been able to see this awful poem as anything other than a symptom of the deplorable turn Scheffler's career had taken. A Latin work he is supposed to have written about John the Evangelist has never been found.

Scheffler died on 9 July 1677, apparently of tuberculosis and the effects of his asceticism, in the Breslau church in which he had been living for some years. His eulogy, pronounced by a Jesuit named Daniel Schwartz, lauded Scheffler's angelic virtues, his selfless charity, and his activities as a physician but mentioned neither *Cherubinischer Wandersmann* nor *Ecclesiologia*. Scheffler's subsequent reputation rests entirely on the former work, which has intrigued many later writers from the Romantic to the modern period.

In the past, some of the commentary on Angelus Silesius has looked like a continuation of the controversies of his life: efforts were made to claim him for Catholicism, criticize him from a Protestant standpoint, or locate him in an extradenominational, often pantheistic context. A period of intense scholarly labor, mainly in the 1920s, superseded these disputes, establishing texts, wringing a biographical account out of the recalcitrant record, and researching the sources. In more-recent years there has been a reversion to the apologetic mode as Catholic partisans have defended his orthodoxy, rejected any pantheistic or otherwise heretical strand in his poetry, and repelled any secular consideration of his personality and motives. These exercises, though often learned, are not scholarly in the modern sense. What is still needed is a combination of a formally and aesthetically refined criticism with a social, historical, and psychological inquiry grounded outside the universe of discourse into which he was imprisoned by the pressures of his times and the weaknesses of his character.

Bibliography:

Gerhard Dünnhaupt, *Personalbibliographien zu den Drucken des Barock,* volume 9, part 5 (Stuttgart: Hiersemann, 1991), pp. 3527–3556.

Biography:

Georg Ellinger, *Angelus Silesius: Ein Lebensbild* (Breslau: Korn, 1927).

References:

Horst Althaus, *Johann Schefflers "Cherubinischer Wandersmann": Mystik und Dichtung* (Giessen: Schmitz, 1956);

Hildegard Aust, "Johannes Scheffler-Silesius," *Stimmen der Zeit,* 162 (1958): 258–270;

Jean Baruzi, *Création religieuse et pensée contemplative. I. La mystique paulienne et les données autobiographiques des épitres. II. Angelus Silesius* (Paris: Aubier, 1951);

János Bruckner, "Angelus Silesius und Nikolaus von Kues: Kusanisches im *Cherubinischen Wandersmann,*" *Euphorion,* 64, no. 2 (1970): 143–166;

Walter Dürig, "Johannes Scheffler als Streittheologe: Marginalien zu der gleichnamigen Veröffentlichung von Ernst Otto Reichert," *Archiv für schlesische Kirchengeschichte,* 28 (1970): 78–92;

Dürig, "Zum 300. Todestag des Angelus Silesius: Versuch einer Würdigung von Persönlichkeit und Werk," *Archiv für schlesische Kirchengeschichte,* 35 (1977): 115–140;

Edith Eilert, *Angelus Silesius als Streittheologe seiner Zeit* (Dresden: Dilkert, 1936);

M. Hildburgis Gies, *Eine lateinische Quelle zum "Cherubinischen Wandersmann" des Angelus Silesius: Untersuchung der Beziehungen zwischen der mystischen Dichtung Schefflers und der "Clavis pro theologia mystica" des Maximilian Sandaeus* (Breslau: Müller & Seiffert, 1929);

Louise Gnädinger, "Angelius Silesius," in *Deutsche Dichter des 17. Jahrhunderts: Ihr Leben und Werk,* edited by Harald Steinhagen and Benno von Wiese (Berlin: Schmidt, 1984), pp. 553–575;

Gnädinger, "Die Rosen-Sprüche des *Cherubinischen Wandersmann* als Beispiel für Johannes Schefflers geistliche Epigrammatik," in *Gedichte und Interpretationen,* volume 1: *Renaissance und Barock,* edited by Volker Meid (Stuttgart: Reclam, 1982), pp. 306–318;

Gnädinger, "Rosenwunden: Des Angelus Silesius 'Die Psyche begehrt ein Bienelein auff den Wunden JEsu zu seyn,'" in *Deutsche Barocklyrik: Gedichtinterpretationen von Spee bis Haller,* edited by Martin Bircher and Alois M. Haas (Bern & Munich: Francke, 1973), pp. 97–133;

Gnädinger, "Die spekulative Mystik im *Cherubinischen Wandersmann* des Johannes Angelus Silesius," *Studi Germanici,* 4 (February 1966): 29–59; (June 1966): 145–190;

Alois M. Haas, "Christus ist alles: Die Christusmystik des Johannes Scheffler," *Zeitwende,* 54 (1983): 65–87;

Hans-Georg Kemper, "Poesie als Sprachrohr mystischer Häresie (Angelus Silesius)," in his *Deutsche Lyrik der frühen Neuzeit,* volume 3: *Barock-Mystik* (Tübingen: Niemeyer, 1988), pp. 209–244;

Leszek Kolakowski, "Angelus Silesius: L'antinomie du panthéisme," in his *Chrétiens sans Eglise: La conscience religieuse et le lien confessionel au xviie siècle,* translated by Anna Posner (Paris: Gallimard, 1969), pp. 567–639;

K. Langosch, "Die 'Heilige Seelenlust' des Angelus Silesius und die mittellateinische Hymnik," *Zeitschrift für deutsches Altertum und Literatur,* 67 (1930): 155–168;

Jean Orcibal, "Les sources étrangères du 'Cherubinischer Wandersmann' (1657) d'après la bibliothèque d'Angelus Silesius," *Revue de la littérature comparée,* 18 (1938): 494–506;

Frederick Palmer, "Angelus Silesius: A Seventeenth-Century Mystic," *Harvard Theological Review,* 11 (1918): 171–202;

Grethe Wagner Petersen, "Zur Datierung und Deutung von Angelus Silesius: 'Cherubinischer Wandersmann,'" *Orbis Litterarum,* 3 (1945): 139–189;

Ernst Otto Reichert, *Johannes Scheffler als Streittheologe: Dargestellt an den konfessionspolemischen Traktaten der "Ecclesiologia"* (Gütersloh: Mohn, 1967);

Jeffrey L. Sammons, *Angelus Silesius* (New York: Twayne, 1967);

Renate Schäfer, "Die Negation als Ausdrucksform mit besonderer Berücksichtigung der Sprache des Angelus Silesius," dissertation, University of Bonn, 1959;

Irmgard Scheitler, "Angelus Silesius: 'Heilige Seelen-Lust.' Die Rezeption der 'Geistlichen Hirten-Lieder' vom 17. bis zum Anfang des 19. Jahrhunderts," in *Liturgie und Dichtung: Ein interdiziplinäres Kompendium,* volume 1, edited by H. Becker and R. Kaczynski (Sankt Ottilien: Eos Verlag Erzabtei Sankt Ottilien, 1983), pp. 711–753;

Franz-Josef Schweitzer, "Zeit und Ewigkeit bei Angelus Silesius," in *Grundfragen christlicher Mystik,* edited by Margot Schmidt and Dieter R. Bauer (Stuttgart-Bad Canstatt: Frommann-Holzboog, 1987), pp. 259–272;

Joachim H. Seyppel, "Freedom and the Mystical Union in *Der cherubinische Wandersmann,*" *Germanic Review,* 32 (February 1957): 93–112;

Peter Skrine, "Angelus Silesius; or, The Art of Being an Angel," *London Germanic Studies,* 1 (1980): 86–100;

Elisabeth Spörri, *Der cherubinische Wandersmann als Kunstwerk* (Horgen: Frei, 1947);

Friedrich-Wilhelm Wentzlaff-Eggebert, *Deutsche Mystik zwischen Mittelalter und Neuzeit: Einheit und Wandlung ihrer Erscheinungsformen,* third edition (Berlin: De Gruyter, 1969);

Benno von Wiese, "Die Antithetik in den Alexandrinern des Angelus Silesius," *Euphorion,* 29 (1928): 503–522.

Papers:

Johannes Scheffler's papers are in the State and University Library, Municipal Library, and the State and Municipal Archives, Wroclaw.

David Schirmer

(29 May 1623 – 1687)

Anthony J. Harper
University of Strathclyde

BOOKS: *Jesu Chrjstj Trjumph: So den Römischen vbertroffen, Denen Freybergern aber geholffen* (Freiberg: Printed by Georg Beuther, 1643);

David Schirmers Erstes [–Vierdtes] Rosen-Gepüsche (Halle: Printed by Melchior Oelschlegel's heirs, 1650; unauthorized edition, Leipzig: Printed by Johann Wittigau, 1653); enlarged as *David Schirmers Poetische Rosen-Gepüsche. Von Jhm selbsten aufs fleißigste übersehen, mit einem gantz neuen Buche vermehrt und in allem verbesserter heraus gegeben* (Dresden: Printed by Melchior Bergen, 1657);

Cartel des Ballets, von Paride und Helena, etc. welches der Durchlauchtigste . . . Herr Johann Georg, Hertzog zu Sachsen . . . dero beyderseits geliebten Herrn Brüdern . . . Herrn Christian vnd Herrn Moritzen . . . vnd denen beyderseits Hertzvielgeliebten Bräuten, Fräulein Christianen, vnd Fräulein Sophien Hedewig, Geschwisterten Hertzoginnen zu Schleßwig/Hollstein . . . vorstellete (Dresden: Printed by Christian & Melchior Bergen, 1650);

David Schirmers Sjngende Rosen oder Liebes- und Tugend-Lieder, music by Philipp Stolle (Dresden: Wolfgang Seyffert, 1654);

Entwurf derer Chur- und Hoch-Fürstlichen Ergetzlichkeiten (Dresden: Printed by Christian & Melchior Bergen, 1655);

David Schirmers Churf. Bibliothec. Verwundeter und wiedergeheileter Loewe. Drama (Dresden: Printed by Wolfgang Seyffert, 1658);

David Schirmers Churfürstlichen Sächsischen Bibliothecarii Poetische Rauten-Gepüsche in Sieben Büchern herausgegeben (Dresden: Published by Andreas Löffler, printed by Melchior Bergen, 1663).

Editions in English: Frank J. Warnke, trans., *European Metaphysical Poetry,* Elizabethan Club, Series 2 (New Haven: Yale University Press, 1961; second edition, 1974), pp. 194–203;

George C. Schoolfield, trans., *The German Lyric of the Baroque in English Translation,* University of North Carolina Studies in the Germanic Languages and Literatures, no. 29 (New York: AMC Press, 1966), pp. 264–267.

OTHER: Adam Krieger, *Neue Arien,* edited by Schirmer (Dresden: Wolffgang Seyffert, 1667).

TRANSLATIONS: Heinrich Freder, *Des Hochgelahrten Herrn Freders von Dantzig lustige Frage: Ob ein Mann sein Ehe-Weib zu schlagen berechtiget sey?* (Dresden: Bergen, 1652);

Johann Naeve, *Des Allerdurchleuchtigsten Römischen Keysers Ferdinands des Ersten Denckwürdiger Tafel-Reden* (Dresden: Printed by Melchior Bergen's heirs, 1673);

Nilus, *Des heiligen Märtyrers und Bischoffs Nili Güldene Sprüche* (Dresden: Printed by Johann Riedel, 1689);

Georg Arnold, *Georg Arnolds, Weyland Cantzlern des Bistthums Naumburg, Gründliche Beschreibung Lebens und Thaten des weyland Durchläuchtigsten Fürsten und Herrn, Herrn Moritzens* (Gießen & Frankfurt am Main: Published by Johann Reinhard Vulpius's widow & Eberhard Heinrich Lammers, 1719).

The generation of poets that was emerging at about the time of the deaths of Martin Opitz and Paul Fleming was able to exploit the results of the Opitzian verse reform and to write in German with a confidence that had been lacking a couple of decades earlier. David Schirmer was one of those poets whose writings span the central years of the seventeenth century. His love poetry, moral poetry, and occasional verse for the Saxon court demonstrate an elegance and fluency that he seems to have possessed from an early age. He is capable of handling the formality of the poem in alexandrines; although his sonnet cycle for "Marnia" is well known, and although he expressed himself in other short forms, such as the

Frontispiece for the enlarged edition of David Schirmer's first collection of poems

madrigal and the epigram, he was most prolific in the genre of the song.

Schirmer was born on 29 May 1623 in the village of Pappendorf, not far from Freiberg in Saxony; he was the second son of Magister David Schirmer, pastor of the local church, and Barbara Schirmer, née Wagner. Of their eleven children, three of the eight sons followed in their father's footsteps and became pastors, one of them in Pappendorf. Schirmer's love for his homeland would be expressed later in poems about the river Striegis. As a result of the separate peace concluded by the elector of Saxony with the German emperor in 1635, in the middle of the Thirty Years' War, Swedish troops made incursions into the province, and the hostilities disrupted Schirmer's schooling.

After education by private tutors at home, he spent some time at the gymnasium in Freiberg.

Around Easter 1640 Schirmer and his brother Melchior were sent to Halle to stay with their cousin Arnold Mengering while they attended the celebrated school of Christian Gueintz, an influential grammarian who was interested in poetics. Several important writers were educated there, including Philipp von Zesen, who had left the school in 1638. In 1641 David and his elder brother, Samuel, matriculated for the summer semester at the University of Leipzig. Leipzig was one of the most cosmopolitan towns of the time, with a strong musical tradition.

Schirmer's first dated poems stem from his time in Leipzig. In 1643 he returned to his old school in Halle to declaim his *Jesv Christi Triumph* (The Triumph of Jesus Christ), a celebration of the liberation of Freiberg from siege by Swedish forces that year – an event with personal significance for Schirmer, since his family had spent a winter of privation in the town. The highly rhetorical verse fitted the public nature of the performance. Other poems from this time fall into the pastoral tradition then in vogue in Germany and reveal the influence of Opitz and Fleming. In all these early works Schirmer expresses himself at much greater length than he would in his later poetry.

On 24 November 1645 Schirmer enrolled at the University of Wittenberg. Apart from its connections with Martin Luther, which attracted theology students, Wittenberg could boast the presence of the eminent professor of poetics Augustus Buchner, who had taught Zesen and other well-known poets. One important experience of the years at Wittenberg was his love for the girl he celebrates in his poetry as "Marnia," who must have died before his first collection was published in 1650. On 6 October 1647 he was chosen as the forty-first member of Zesen's Deutschgesinnte Genossenschaft (German-minded Guild), with the epithet "Der Beschirmende" (The Protecting One), a play on his name; his guild emblem was a laurel tree protecting a rose stem from lightning. On the occasion of a visit by the elector of Saxony, Johann Georg I, in the same year, Buchner had the elector greeted at table with one of Schirmer's songs.

Schirmer returned to Leipzig in the winter of 1648 and was soon preparing his first collection of poetry, *Erstes [-Vierdtes] Rosen-Gepüsche* (First [to Fourth] Rosebushes, 1650). The preface is dated 11 November 1649. In that year the elector turned to Buchner for advice in appointing a new court poet and master of ceremonies, and Buchner recommended Schirmer, who was invited to Dresden before the end of 1649.

Rosen-Gepüsche already shows the range of Schirmer's talents. Its four "Bushes" are divided by poetic genre. The first comprises love songs, serenades, and laments, mainly in the Petrarchan tradition and in a wide variety of meters and line lengths. Schirmer displays his virtuosity in songs with spectacular linguistic effects, such as "Sie Liebet Ihn" (She Loves Him) and "Seine tödliche Schmertzen an Rosomenen" (His Fatal Pains: To Rosomena). Most of the pastoral poems of the second "Bush" have geographical settings, often a Saxon river; they are variations on Opitz's "Coridon der gieng betrübet" (Coridon was walking, troubled, 1625). The sonnets of the third "Bush" are formed into a loose cycle about "Marnia," who dies in the course of the sequence. Although Schirmer uses models such as the Greek Anthology and Petrarch's sonnets to Laura, some of these poems may be rooted in personal experience. The style accords with the Petrarchan tradition and formally remains close to the sonnet schemes advocated by Opitz. The epigrams of the fourth "Bush" are dependent on classical and humanist sources. Although Schirmer's models are traditional ones, he has already evolved a light and decorative style that eschews heavy rhetoric and expresses passion with elegance. The popularity of his poetry is indicated by the appearance of a pirate edition in Leipzig in 1653.

By the time the collection appeared, Schirmer was at the Dresden court; he had no fixed salary but relied on favors from his prince. His responsibilities included the composition of occasional verse for birthdays and similar events and the production of festivities. One such occasion was the double marriage of Dukes Christian and Moritz on 19 November 1650, for which, on 2 December, Schirmer produced the *Ballet von dem Paride und Helena* (Ballet of Paris and Helen). In modern terms the work is a mixture of drama, opera, and ballet. The performance in the Riesensaal (Giant Room) lasted more than six hours and involved 105 roles and sixty-five actors and dancers. The composer is unknown, but the court musician Philipp Stolle played Mars in act 1 and Paris in act 3. Schirmer produced other, less extensive, ballets in later years.

Schirmer tried to leave Dresden in 1653 to resume his studies, prompting the elector's son, the future Johann Georg II, to retain him on a salary of 218 talers a year. With Stolle's help he set some of the poems in *Rosen-Gepüsche* to music; they appeared in 1654 as *Singende Rosen* (Singing Roses). The folio volume, of which only four copies are known to exist, comprises sixty-eight songs on love, manners, and nature; some criticize court life, with admonitions to courtiers and the prince about their duties. The variety of the texts, and Stolle's settings, make this Schirmer's most attractive collection.

In 1654 the court librarian, Christian Brehme, asked to be relieved of his post. On 21 November 1655 Schirmer was chosen as the new librarian; he was confirmed on 11 March 1656. This was a more substantial post, with a salary of one hundred gulden per annum; but underfunding meant that Schirmer, like his predecessor, was unable to carry through improvements in the structure of the building and in the cataloguing system. He also continued to serve as court poet until Georg Ferber from Zwickau was appointed to the post in 1663.

In 1657 Schirmer brought out an enlarged edition of *Rosen-Gepüsche* in two parts. The first part was a repetition of the 1650 volume; the second consisted of five new "Bushes." The first of these new "Bushes" is a miscellany of poems in alexandrines; the second consists of four elegies; the third comprises pastoral poems with geographical allusions; the fourth reprints most of the songs from the *Singende Rosen,* with the omission of those critical of court life (by this time Schirmer had more to lose); the final "Bush" includes epigrams, madrigals, and sonnets. Schirmer's strength lies in his songwriting: the restrained Petrarchism of love songs such as "Die Überschöne" (The Overbeautiful One) and the lively evocation of nature in "Über des Sommers Abend-Zeit an Sie" (On a Summer Evening: To Her) and "Über die liebliche Mayen-Lust an Sie" (On the Fair Pleasures of May: To Her) can stand beside the best poetry of the age.

In 1663 Schirmer produced a further collection, under the title *Poetische Rauten-Gepüsche* (Poetic Rue-Bushes) – an allusion to the Saxon emblem. The volume includes occasional verse for the electors and their families, the ballets and other entertainments written for the court, and other works from the years 1650 to 1663. The ballet-operas show a progressive change in Schirmer's role from poet to arranger. The occasional poetry for the events of court life, with its protestations of loyalty to the House of Saxony, tends not to be to the taste of the modern reader, but it fulfilled an important function in its time. Only rarely are there overt political comments, as in the 1655 poem commemorating the centenary of the Peace of Augsburg, in which traditional Protestant sentiments are expressed.

While serving at the court Schirmer also produced occasional poetry for bourgeois clients. His epicedia (funeral poems) and epithalamia are sometimes reminiscent of the pastoral poetry of his collections. For funeral poems for the upper bourgeoisie, as for the aristocracy, Schirmer often favors the formality of the Pindaric ode. He was also active as a translator and editor; for example, he edited the *Neue Arien* (New Arias) of the Leipzig songwriter Adam Krieger in 1667, one year after the latter's death.

In 1668 Schirmer married Anna Maria Leschke, the daughter of the master bookbinder of the court; she died two years later. Schirmer continued to produce occasional poetry from time to time, and he remained in his post as librarian until he was granted sick leave in 1682; he was dismissed, probably because of old age, in 1683. He died in poverty in Dresden in 1687; he was buried in the Sankt Johannis Churchyard on 12 August.

Bibliographies:

Karl Goedeke, *Grundriß zur Geschichte der deutschen Dichtung aus den Quellen,* second edition, volume 3 (Dresden: Ehlermann, 1887), pp. 69–71;

Erwin Kunath, "David Schirmer als Dichter und Bibliothekar," dissertation, University of Leipzig, 1922, pp. 8, 11–17;

Curt von Faber du Faur, *German Baroque Literature: A Catalogue of the Collection in the Yale University Library* (New Haven: Yale University Press, 1958), pp. 89–90;

Gerhard Dünnhaupt, *Personalbibliographien zu den Drucken des Barock,* volume 9, part 5 (Stuttgart: Hiersemann, 1991), pp. 3608–3638.

Biographies:

Reinhard Kade, "David Schirmer," *Neues Archiv für sächsische Geschichte,* 13, no. 1 (1892): 117–136;

Erwin Kunath, "David Schirmer als Dichter und Bibliothekar," dissertation, University of Leipzig, 1922.

References:

Anthony J. Harper, "David Schirmer," in *Deutsche Schriftsteller im Porträt: Das Zeitalter des Barock,* edited by Martin Bircher (Munich: Beck, 1979), pp. 152–153;

Harper, *David Schirmer – A Poet of the German Baroque,* Stuttgarter Arbeiten zur Germanistik, no. 32 (Stuttgart: Akademischer Verlag Hans-Dieter Heinz, 1977);

Harper, "In the Nürnberg manner? Reflections on a 17th Century Parody," *Neophilologus,* 58 (January 1974): pp. 52–65;

Harper, *Schriften zur Lyrik Leipzigs 1620–1670,* Stuttgarter Arbeiten zur Germanistik, no. 131 (Stuttgart: Akademischer Verlag Hans-Dieter Heinz, 1985), pp. 15–16, 34–38;

Arthur Kopp, "Eleonore, die Betrübte," *Euphorion,* 8 (1901): 264–274;

William F. Mainland, "An Example of 'Baroque' Elaboration," *Modern Language Review,* 41 (July 1946): 298–305;

Erdmann Neumeister, "Schirmer (David)," in *De Poetis Germanicis,* edited by F. Heiduk (Bern: Francke, 1978), pp. 94–95 (translation, pp. 234–236);

Emil Edmund Sattler, "David Schirmer: Metaphysical Poetry in the German Baroque," dissertation, University of Michigan, 1972;

Georg Witkowski, *Geschichte des literarischen Lebens in Leipzig,* Schriften der Königlichen Sächsischen Kommission für Geschichte, no. 17 (Leipzig & Berlin: Teubner, 1909), pp. 148–151.

Papers:

A letter from David Schirmer to Sigmund von Birken is in the Archives of the Pegnesischer Blumenorden, Nuremberg, catalogue number 4-11a.

Justus Georg Schottelius

(23 June 1612 – 25 October 1676)

Sara Smart
Exeter University

BOOKS: *Die hertzliche Anschawunge vnsers gecreutzigten Heylandes, sampt andächtigen Gedancken von Seinem Leyden für vns vnd seiner Liebe gegen Vns* (Brunswick: Balthasar Gruber, 1640);

Lamentatio Germaniae Exspirantis. Der numehr hinsterbenden Nymphen Germaniae elendeste Todesklage (Brunswick: Printed by Balthasar Gruber, 1640);

Teutsche Sprachkunst, darinn die Allerwortreichste, prächtigste, reinlichste, vollkommene, uhralte Hauptsprache der Teutschen auß jhren Gründen erhoben, dero Eigenschafften und Kunststücke völliglich entdeckt, und also in eine richtige Form der Kunst zum ersten mahle gebracht worden. Abgetheilet in drey Bücher (Brunswick: Printed by Balthasar Gruber, 1641; revised edition, Brunswick: Christoph Friedrich Zilliger, 1651);

Der Teutschen Sprache Einleitung, zu richtiger gewisheit und grundmeßigem vermügen der Teutschen Haubtsprache, samt beygefügten Erklärungen (Lübeck: Printed by Johann Meyer, published by Matthäus Dinckler in Lüneberg, 1643);

Dispvtatio Inavgvralis Invridica de Poenis, Ivxta Cvivscvnqve Delicti Meritvm Ivste Aestimandis (Helmstedt: Printed by Henning Müller, 1643);

Teutsche Vers- oder ReimKunst darin vnsere Teutsche MutterSprache, so viel dero süßeste Poesis betrift, in eine richtige Form der Kunst zum ersten mahle gebracht worden (Wolfenbüttel: Printed by Johann Bissmarck, published by the author, 1645; revised edition, Frankfurt am Main: Michael Cubach, 1656);

Fruchtbringender Lustgarte jn sich haltend die ersten fünf Abtheilungen, zu ergetzlichem Nutze ausgefertiget (Wolfenbüttel: Printed by Johann Bissmarck, published by Michael Cubach in Lüneberg, 1647);

Votiva acclamatio, pro firmâ & fidâ inter Christianos Pace, ad primum Monasterii & Osnabruggis 15. Octob. anni 1648. (Wolfenbüttel: Printed by Johann & Heinrich Stern, 1648);

Justus Georg Schottelius

Neu erfundenes FreudenSpiel genandt Friedens Sieg. Jn gegenwart vieler Chur- und Fürstlicher auch anderer Vornehmen Personen, in dem Fürstl. BurgSaal zu Braunsweig im Jahr 1642. von lauter kleinen Knaben vorgestellet (Wolfenbüttel: Conrad Buno, 1648);

Ausführliche Arbeit von der Teutschen HaubtSprache, Worin enthalten Gemelter dieser HaubtSprache Uhrankunft, Uhraltertuhm, Reinlichkeit, Eigenschaft, Vermögen, Unvergleichlichkeit, Grundrichtigkeit, zumahl die SprachKunst und VersKunst Teutsch und guten theils Lateinisch völlig mit eingebracht, wie nicht weniger die Verdoppelung, Ableitung, die Einleitung, Nahmwörter, Authores vom Teutschen

*Wesen und Teutscher Sprache, von der ver-
teutschung, jtem die Stammwörter der Teutschen
Sprache samt der Erklärung und derogleichen viel
merkwürdige Sachen. Abgetheilet jn Fünf Bücher*
(Brunswick: Christoph Friedrich Zilliger,
1663);

*Jesu Christi Nahmens-Ehr, worin alles auf den süssen Nah-
men Gottes und dessen Wort eingerichtet, mit vielen
Kupferstükken gezieret, und in gebundener und un-
gebundener Rede verfasset ist,* anonymous
(Wolfenbüttel: Published by Conrad Buno,
printed by Johann Bissmarck, 1666 [i.e.,
1667]);

*Eigentliche und sonderbare Vorstellung des Jüngsten Tages
und darin künfftig verhandenen Grossen und Letzten
Wunder-Gerichts Gottes: Wie es ordentlich nach
denen uns geoffenbarten Umständen, alsdan daher
gehen, endlich nach aus gesprochenem Uhrteile, die
Gottlosen samt den Teufelen zur Hölle, die Auser-
wehlten samt dem Herrn Jesu zu Himmel fahren auch
Himmel und Erde darauf samt den Elementen im
Feuer vergehen werden. Nachdenklich in Teutscher
Sprache beschrieben, mit nötigen Erklärungen und
schönen Kupfer-Stükken* (Brunswick: Christoph
Friedrich Zilliger, 1668; revised, 1674);

*Ethica: Die Sittenkunst oder Wollebenskunst, jn Teutscher
Sprache vernemlich beschrieben in dreyen Bücheren*
(Wolfenbüttel: Printed by Paul Weiß, 1669);

*De Singularibus quibusdam & antiquis in Germania Juri-
bus & Observatis. Kurtzer Tractat von vnterschied-
lichen Rechten in Teutschland, als zum Exempel das
Hagestoltzen-Recht* (Wolfenbüttel: Published by
Conrad Buno, printed by Johann Heinrich
Duncker in Brunswick, 1671);

*Sonderbare Vorstellung von der ewigen Seeligkeit jn
Teutscher Sprache nachdenklich beschrieben, samt
kurtzem Vorberichte von der Zeit und Ewigkeit. An
stat des andren Theils ist beigefügt eine Sterbekunst
oder sonderliche Erinnerung Gern, recht, bald und
frölig zusterben,* anonymous (Brunswick: Christoph Friedrich Zilliger, 1673);

*Horrendum Bellum Grammaticale Teutonum antiquissimo-
rum. Wunderbarer ausführlicher Bericht, Welcher gestalt vor länger als Zwey Tausend Jahren in dem
alten Teutschlande das Sprach-Regiment gründlich
verfasset gewesen,* anonymous (Brunswick,
1673);

*Sonderbare Vorstellung, wie es mit Leib und Seel des Men-
schen werde kurtz vor dem Tode, jn dem Tode, und
nach dem Tode bewandt seyn,* anonymous (Brunswick: Printed & published by Christoph
Friedrich Zilliger, 1674);

*Concordia seu Harmonia Quatuor Evangelistarum. Or-
dentliche zusammengefügte Vereinbarung der Vier*

*Heiligen Evangelisten. Auf sonderliche Art ver-
nehmlich und mit ungezwungenen deutlichen Reimen
oder Versen in Teutscher Sprache ausgefertiget,*
anonymous (Brunswick: Christoph Friedrich
Zilliger, 1675);

*Brevis et fundamentalis Manuductio ad Orthographiam &
Etymologiam in Lingua Germanica. Kurtze und
gründliche Anleitung zu der RechtSchreibung und zu
der WortForschung jn der Teutschen Sprache. Für
die Jugend in den Schulen, und sonst überall nützlich
und dienlich,* anonymous (Brunswick: Christoph Friedrich Zilliger, 1676);

*Grausame Beschreibung und Vorstellung der Hölle und der
höllischen Qwal, oder Des andern und ewigen Todes.
Jn Teutscher Sprache nachdenklich, und also vor die
Augen gelegt, daß einem gottlosen Menschen
gleichsam die höllischen Funken annoch in dieser Welt
ins Gewissen stieben, und Rück-Gedanken zur
Ewigkeit erwekken können,* anonymous (Wolfenbüttel: Conrad Buno's heirs, 1676).

Editions: *Friedens Sieg. Ein FreudenSpiel von Justus
Georg Schottelius,* edited by Friedrich Ernst
Koldewey, Neudrucke deutscher Literatur-
werke des XVI und XVII Jahrhunderts, no.
175 (Halle: Niemeyer, 1900);

*Lamentatio Germaniæ Exspirantis. Der numehr
hinsterbenden Nymphen Germaniæ elendeste Todesklage,* edited by Ernst Voss, *Journal of English
and Germanic Philology,* 7, no. 1 (1908): 1–31;

*Fruchtbringender Lustgarte in sich haltend die ersten fünf
Abtheilungen, zu ergetzlichem Nutze ausgefertiget,*
edited by Marianne Burkhard (Munich &
Bern: Francke, 1967);

Ausführliche Arbeit von der Teutschen HaubtSprache, ed-
ited by Wolfgang Hecht, Deutsche Neudrucke,
Reihe Barock, volumes 11 & 12 (Tübingen:
Niemeyer, 1967);

*Teutsche Vers- oder ReimKunst darin vnsere Teutsche
MutterSprache, so viel dero süßeste Poesis betrift, in
eine richtige Form der Kunst zum ersten mahle
gebracht worden* (Hildesheim: Olms, 1976);

Ethica die Sittenkunst oder Wollebenskunst, edited by
Jörg Jochen Berns (Bern & Munich: Francke,
1980);

*Der schreckliche Sprachkrieg: Horrendum Bellum
Grammaticale* (Leipzig: Reclam, 1991).

OTHER: Franz Julius von dem Knesebeck, *Dreistän-
dige Sinnbilder. Zu Fruchtbringendem Nutze, und
beliebender ergetzlichkeit, ausgefertiget durch den
Geheimen,* contributions by Schottelius (Brunswick: Buno, 1643);

Martin Zeiller, *Topographja vnd Eigentliche
Beschreibung der Vornembsten Stäte, Schlösser auch*

anderer Plätze vnd Örter in denen Herzogthümern Braunschweig vnd Lüneburg, vnd denen dazu gehörenden Grafschafften Herrschafften vnd Landen, edited by Schottelius (Frankfurt am Main: Matthaeus Merian's heirs, 1654).

The most eminent philologist of the German language in the seventeenth century, Justus Georg Schottelius strove to assert the supremacy of German over Latin. His grammar book was highly regarded at the time, and, while he wrote dramas and poetry, he is better known as the author of one of the most stimulating and influential poetics of the period. His achievement has to be seen within the context of the patriotic movement to promote both German culture and language; a manifestation of this movement was the establishment of the *Sprachgesellschaften* (language societies). The Thirty Years' War and the presence of foreign armies on German soil had intensified patriotic sentiments; according to Schottelius, the war had brought with it "eine eintringende Frömdgierigkeit" (a pernicious and pervasive tendency to emulate foreign fashions). This tendency had a particularly damaging effect on the German language, which he was determined to defend by proving its richness, unique quality, and potential. He was well established in the cultural scene of his day: apart from being engaged at the court of Brunswick-Wolfenbüttel, a major center of German culture, he was a prominent member of the Fruchtbringende Gesellschaft (Fruit-bringing Society) and was in contact with other patriots, scholars, and poets, among them Ludwig of Anhalt-Köthen, the head of the Fruchtbringende Gesellschaft; Sigmund von Birken; Georg Philipp Harsdörffer; the grammarian Christian Gueintz; Johann Rist; and Joachim Jungius. Schottelius's own scholarship, in accordance with contemporary practice, embraced a range of disciplines, including jurisprudence and philosophy. This universality explains the often remarkably vivid insight his oeuvre provides into the preoccupations and tensions of the period, into its psychology, and into the seventeenth-century perception of German culture and its heritage.

The son of a Lutheran pastor, Johannes Schottelius, and his second wife, Margarete, née Ilsen, Schottelius was born on 23 June 1612 in Einbeck. The families of both his parents were established and respected in Einbeck, which was a member of the Hanseatic League and was one of the more prosperous cities in northern Germany. His mother came from a family of successful merchants, and his father's background was academic; both grandfathers had been members of the city council.

Schottelius's emblem in the Fruchtbringende Gesellschaft

In 1617 or 1618 he began his education at the local school, where his father had formerly been deputy headmaster.

Schottelius first felt the direct impact of the Thirty Years' War in 1626, when his father died of the plague that swept Einbeck as a result of a massive influx of refugees. With the loss of the family's breadwinner, his mother hoped to settle her son in an apprenticeship, but in 1627 he left home to continue his studies at the Gymnasium Andreanum in Hildesheim. To support himself he worked as a tutor. In May 1628 he registered at the University of Helmstedt. In 1630 he moved to Hamburg. That city, whose fortifications made it uniquely secure against the ravages of the war, was home to two prestigious academic institutions: the Johanneum, a Latin school; and the Gymnasium Academicum. It is probable that Schottelius attended the former before beginning his studies at the latter. At the Gymnasium Academicum Schottelius encountered the philosopher Joachim Jungius, rector of the institute since 1627, whose progressive studies extended into the German language and were an inspiration to him.

In May 1635 Schottelius registered in the faculty of law at the University of Leiden, one of Europe's leading universities. Among his law professors were Petrus Cunaeus and Daniel Heinsius, both of whom were also renowned philologists. Heinsius was also well known as a poet who, in writing in his native tongue, set out to demonstrate that Dutch was a worthy vehicle of poetic expression. He profoundly influenced the patriotic Sprachgesellschaften in Germany, where he was admired as a liberator of the Germanic languages from Latin dominance. Such an environment allowed Schottelius to pursue his legal studies and simultaneously encouraged his concern with philology. In 1636 he declined an offer to become deputy headmaster at his former school in Einbeck and continued his studies, first in Leipzig and then in Wittenberg, where he may have registered in the winter of 1636. In 1638, when the Swedish army threatened Wittenberg, Schottelius fled to Brunswick.

There he became acquainted with the scholar and bibliophile Duke August of Brunswick-Wolfenbüttel, who was living in the city because his residence, Wolfenbüttel, was occupied by Catholic troops. Initially offered employment as preceptor to the duke's children, Schottelius would remain at the court of Brunswick-Wolfenbüttel until the end of his life. The unique access August allowed Schottelius to the ducal library, one of the largest libraries in Europe, facilitated his philological research. The duke also recognized Schottelius's ability as a lawyer. Thus began a period of extraordinary productivity and hard work, a virtue Schottelius actively endorsed: in the dedication to one of his first publications, the mystical poem *Die hertzliche Anschawunge unsers gecreutzigten Heylandes* (The Inmost Contemplation of Our Crucified Savior, 1640) he stresses the value of work both for the terrestrial and the celestial life. This character trait is symbolically endorsed on his coat of arms by an obelisk: an architectural structure built by careful labor.

Schottelius held his first post at court, as preceptor to the duke's children, from Easter 1638 to spring 1646; from Christmas 1645 he was assisted by Birken. Initially his pupils were August's daughters, the nine-year-old Sibylle Ursula and the six-year-old Clara Augusta, and his son, the five-year-old Anton Ulrich; in 1640 August's youngest son, Ferdinand Albrecht, then four years old, joined the

group. His charges also included the sons of nobles holding office at court, and he was responsible for the supervision of the young attendants who served the ducal children. The syllabus he devised for his noble pupils was in many ways similar to that offered at the Latin schools and included theology, ethics, rhetoric, grammar, logic, and geography. At the duke's behest Schottelius supervised his children's correspondence with Johann Valentin Andreae, pastor to the court of Stuttgart and a friend of August's; its purpose was to encourage their powers of articulation.

Another aspect of his pedagogy was the performance of plays, a practice that had developed in Protestant Germany under the auspices of Martin Luther and had become ubiquitous in the schools of the period. Jörg Jochen Berns credits Schottelius with lifting Protestant middle-class theater to a courtly level. In the foreword to the published version of his play *Friedens Sieg* (The Victory of Peace, 1648) he justifies the theater both as a moral institution whose vivid impact encourages virtuous behavior, and as a means of academic training, helping to improve the memory and sharpening the rational faculties; it also promotes skills essential to the courtier, such as clear enunciation and graceful deportment. Evidence suggests that this training was reserved for Schottelius's male pupils and that the young duchesses were excluded from performances.

Schottelius's best-known play, *Friedens Sieg,* was initially performed in 1642 to celebrate the Peace of Goslar, which ended August's involvement in the war; it was staged again in 1648 and 1649 — in the latter year in Berlin-Kölln. The three-act allegorical representation of the devastation caused by the war and the establishment of peace is significant in a variety of ways. Stylistically, the processional quality of the acts, involving the appearance of Fortuna, Mars, the Goddess of Peace, Iron Despair, and Green Hope, is evocative of courtly processions. The interludes, involving music, song, and dance, testify to Schottelius's collaboration with August's third wife, Sophie Elisabeth, a musician. Such a mixture of speech, music, song, and dance is typical of court theater. Ideologically, the casting of *Friedens Sieg,* with the young dukes, ages eight and five, taking the most important roles, endorses the absolutist order of society. The play also acts as a vehicle for Schottelius's patriotic and linguistic interests. Two heroes from the German past, Arminius (18 B.C.–A.D. 19) — the victor over the Romans — and King Heinrich I (876–936) are introduced into the play to offer a cure for the destruction and abasement of war-torn Germany. Their call for unity among German leaders is complemented by their criticism of the impurity of the German they hear spoken, with its abundance of foreign expressions. A connection is made between language and morality; abuse of language, it is argued, has led to moral depravity among Germans: "Auf die Enderung der Sprache folget eine Enderung der Sitten. Verenderte Sitten pflegen gemeiniglich das gemeine Leben also zu enderen, daß Unglükk und Untergang auf dem fusse daher folget" (A change in language is followed by a change in morals. Changed morals generally alter life in such a way that misfortune and disaster follow closely behind). This idea is fundamental to Schottelius's work as a philologist. The return to a pure German language, he believed, would engender a moral regeneration among Germans and thereby lead to Germany's restored independence and dignity. Schottelius's concerns as a patriot and philologist are reflected clearly in his insistence that his pupils perform plays in German. That he was successful in encouraging the employment of and respect for German is attested to by the achievements of Anton Ulrich, who wrote the libretti for German singspiele and was the author of major German courtly novels.

Three other examples of this type of play are known to have been written by Schottelius. In *Die Vorstellung des also genanten und vermeinten Gottes Pans* (The Presentation of the Supposed God Called Pan), performed in 1643 and 1646, five incidents from the life of Pan are depicted in overtly didactic fashion. Upholding the value of art and the virtue of hard work, the play reflects the century's preoccupation with order. *Theatralische neue Vorstellung von der Maria Magdalena* (The Theatrically New Presentation of Mary Magdalene, 1644), where the music, composed by Heinrich Schütz, seems to have been of greater importance than the spoken word, links Schottelius with Martin Opitz and August Buchner as a contributor to the development of German musical drama. *Die Gebuhrt unsers Heylandes* (The Birth of Our Savior), a nativity play, was performed in December 1645. These works, either in their entirety or in extract form, are included in Schottelius's *Fruchtbringender Lustgarte* (Fruitbearing Pleasure Garden, 1647), a collection of poems, many of a religious character, divided into five parts, each dedicated to one of August's children. Schottelius wrote no more works for the theater after his duties as preceptor ceased, which they did when his pupils passed an official examination involving academics from the University of Helmstedt and taken at the duke's insistence.

While working as preceptor, Schottelius was also engaged in his philological research. During

Frontispiece for Schottelius's 1647 collection of poems

the 1640s a series of publications appeared in rapid succession, suggesting that his ideas on grammar and poetic theory were already well developed before his employment at August's court. In championing the German language, these works expand ideas present in *Friedens Sieg*. The first, *Lamentatio Germaniae Exspirantis. Der numehr hinsterbenden Nymphen Germaniae elendeste Todesklage* (The Most Miserable Death Lament of the Dying Nymph Germania, 1640), is an allegorical poem in alexandrines in which the nymph Germania, a personification of Germany, articulates patriotic sentiments. Fundamental to the work is the contrast between Germany's glorious past, when Germania was a queen among nations and the head of Christendom, and her present condition as a blood-spattered beggar woman exuding the stench of war – an image complemented by graphic descriptions of the actual state of Germany. This contrast between the present and an idealized past enhances the propagandistic impact of the work. Germania bemoans the ubiquitous presence of marauding foreigners on German soil and castigates Germans for allowing themselves to be exploited by foreign powers, for aping foreign fashions, and, above all, for neglecting the German language. The link between such neglect and moral turpitude is stressed. The conclusion of the work, a paean to August celebrating, among other virtues, his concern for his mother tongue, testifies to his active support both of the patriotic movement – August had been a member of the Fruchtbringende Gesellschaft since 1634 – and of Schottelius's work. (Scholars have linked August's initial offer of employment to Schottelius, then an unknown student, to this mutuality of interest.)

Another theme sounded in *Lamentatio Germaniae Exspirantis* – that the dominance of Greek and Latin is nearing its end – receives amplification in Schottelius's next publication, his grammar book *Teutsche Sprachkunst* (The Art of the German Language, 1641). In the introduction he denounces as an absurdity the fact that German is not taught in German schools. He points to the time and energy devoted to learning Latin and Greek, when German is the language pupils will ultimately employ to earn their livings. Schottelius saw his *Teutsche Sprachkunst* as an authoritative fundament necessary both for the development of German as an academic language and to counter the prevalent view that it was a coarse language without structure and sophistication. This publication was followed by Schottelius's membership in the Fruchtbringende Gesellschaft in 1642 under the pseudonym Der Suchende (The Searcher). Although *Teutsche Sprachkunst* never won favor with Ludwig of Anhalt-Köthen, it was widely used in schools.

In 1643 appeared another lengthy allegorical poem in alexandrines, *Der Teutschen Sprache Einleitung* (An Introduction to the German Language), dedicated to Ludwig of Anhalt-Köthen. The introduction expresses the familiar contrast between the German past and present. In this instance Schottelius identifies bravery and military prowess as dominant characteristics of past generations of Germans, who guarded Germany against attack and thus secured the purity of the German tongue. This theme is developed in the poem, in which the personification of the German language stresses her inspirational quality; in the past her use has given rise to valor and struck fear in the past into Germany's enemies. She looks to contemporary knights of the pen to liberate her from her current degradation. In 1645 Schottelius's contribution to the theory of Ger-

man poetry, *Teutsche Vers- oder ReimKunst* (The Art of German Verse or Rhyme) was published. The significance of this work was great, in that it represented an attempt to liberate German poetics from classical tradition by producing a genuinely German poetic theory, conceived in accordance with the character of the German language. In recognition of his contribution to the language and as a poetologist, the Nuremberg poets made him the tenth member of the Pegnesischer Blumenorden (The Flower Order of the Pegnitz River) in 1646, giving him the pseudonym Fontano.

In the 1640s Schottelius also completed his legal studies, qualifying him for service in the duke's bureaucracy. August had appointed him a member of the Hofgericht (ducal court) in 1642; after the attainment of his doctorate of law in 1646 Schottelius became a member of the Hofrat (ducal council), with responsibility for the small territory of Dannenberg, as well as of the Konsistorium, the official body overseeing matters relating to the church and in charge of education. As a member of the Hofgericht, Konsistorium, and Hofrat he was involved in the three major chambers responsible for the government of Brunswick-Wolfenbüttel. In September 1646, a year after the duke had awarded him a canonry with a sinecure, Schottelius married Margarete Cleve; she died exactly a year later after giving birth to a daughter, Sophia Elisabeth. In 1649 he married Anna Maria Sobbe, the daughter of an Einbeck lawyer. Their son, Anton Albrecht, was born in 1651; his godparents included Dukes Anton Ulrich and Ferdinand Albrecht. In the same year an enlarged edition of *Teutsche Sprachkunst* appeared. In 1653 Schottelius was appointed *Kammerrat* (chamber councillor). An amended second edition of *Teutsche Vers- oder ReimKunst* was published in 1656. The years 1655 and 1656 saw the birth of a son, Andreas Joachim, and a daughter, Hedwig Elisabeth, both of whom died in early infancy. Another daughter, Juliane Marie, was born in 1657, followed two years later by a son, Christoph.

In 1663 Schottelius's *Ausführliche Arbeit von der Teutschen HaubtSprache* (A Thorough Study of the German Principal Language) was published. Based largely on his works of the 1640s, which appear here in their final and most authoritative form, *Ausführliche Arbeit von der Teutschen HaubtSprache* represents the culmination of Schottelius's career as a philologist. Its fifteen hundred pages are divided into five books: the first comprises ten *Lobreden* (eulogies) in praise of the German language; the second and third comprise *Teutsche Sprachkunst;* the fourth consists of *Vers- oder ReimKunst;* and the fifth

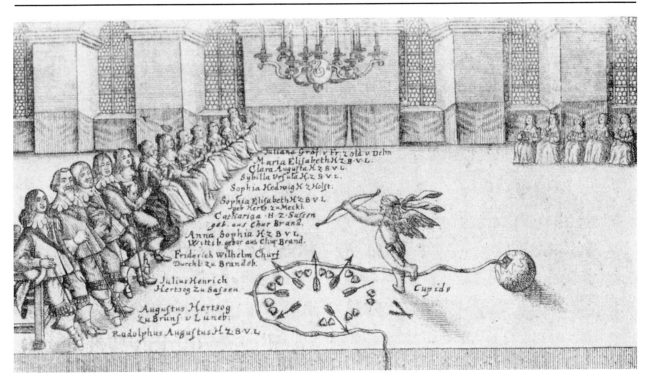

Cupid's dance: illustration from Schottelius's Friedens Sieg

is composed of seven essays or treatises. A key to understanding Schottelius's intention in publishing this work is given in the title by the term *Haubt-Sprache* (principal language). In the sixteenth and seventeenth centuries the term was applied to Hebrew, Greek, and Latin; that Schottelius boldly designated the German language a HaubtSprache is testimony to his aim to enhance the status of German at home and abroad and to assert its equality with those other languages.

To support his case he refutes the belief that German is a relatively new language. In accordance with seventeenth-century scholarship Schottelius holds that prior to Babel one universal language had existed, but with the building of the Tower and the resulting confusion sixty-nine languages emerged. One of these, Schottelius argues, was Ancient Celtic, which he identifies with Ancient German and which was brought to Europe by Ascenas, one of Noah's descendants. This language had been spoken in the areas known in his own time as Germany, France, Spain, England, Scotland, Norway, Lapland, Sweden, Denmark, Thrace, and Illyria. He goes on to prove that a form of German had been written and had acted as a vehicle of learning prior to the development of Greek and Latin. He also maintains that the ubiquity of Celtic or Ancient German in earlier times supports his contention that

Icelandic, Norwegian, Danish, Swedish, English, Scottish, Irish, and Welsh are dialects of German. The Germans were the chief Celtic tribe; thus, the original Celtic language can be detected in its purest form in German. This purity and the venerability of German manifest themselves in the immediacy of the relationship between *res* (thing) and *verbum* (word). As was the case with the original universal language, German, above all other post-Babel languages, conveys the essence of the object described: there is a natural correspondence between the German word and the object it denotes. He illustrates this point by reference to the onomatopoeic quality of the German language, an observation that particularly interested the Nuremberg poets.

This interest in origins and purity also informs his approach to grammar. To provide norms on which the development of German could be based, he focuses on what he regards as innate or inherent to the language. He regards it as his duty as a grammarian to reveal the *Grundrichtigkeit* (fundamental essence) of German. This Grundrichtigkeit is found in the *Stammwörter* (stem words), in which the original purity of the language is maintained. Schottelius believed that the number of Stammwörter served as a criterion by which a language could be judged, and German is particularly rich in them. These Stammwörter were present in the origins of the lan-

Frontispiece for Schottelius's massive study of the German language

tion, discussing a variety of forms of affixation and systems of compounding. (The word *Jahrhundert* [century] was, for example, initially coined by Schottelius.) This codification demonstrates, Schottelius argues, the wealth of expression inherent in the German language. As Berns and Kathrin Gützlaff have pointed out, his aim to reveal the potential within the German language was inextricably linked with a desire to increase its vocabulary.

If Schottelius's study of etymology constitutes the major significance of *Ausführliche Arbeit von der Teutschen HaubtSprache,* the work also embraces a vast range of other issues: problems of translation into German are discussed, German writers are assessed, and, complementary to the collection of Stammwörter, there is a collection of idiomatic expressions, which Schottelius also believed to be fundamental to the language. The comprehensiveness of Schottelius's approach has led critics to describe the *Ausführlich Arbeit von der Teutschen HaubtSprache* as the *summa philologica* of the period. This research provided the ideas and basis for Schottelius's two later philological publications, *Horrendum Bellum Grammaticale Teutonum antiquissimorum* (The Horrible Language War, 1673), an allegorical account of the history of the German language based on the tradition of grammar satire associated with Andrea Guarna, and *Brevis et fundamentalis Manuductio ad Orthographiam & Etymologiam in Lingua Germanica. Kurtze und gründliche Anleitung zu der RechtSchreibung und zu der WortForschung in der Teutschen Sprache* (A Short and Thorough Guide to German Spelling and Etymology, 1676).

In 1669 a work of a different type appeared. Schottelius's unique achievement in *Ethica Die Sittenkunst oder Wollebenskunst* (Ethics: The Art of Moral Behavior or Virtuous Living) was to produce a philosophy of ethics written in German, not Latin, which could be used in schools. It was entirely logical that Schottelius, convinced of the immediate connection between language and morality, should have written a work on ethics in his native tongue. All his skills as a philologist were required by the task, which demanded that he develop a whole new vocabulary to render German equivalents of the traditional Latin philosophical terminology. Through his *Ethica* Schottelius offered proof of two intimately related linguistic merits: in addition to showing the potential for articulation in German, he demonstrated the status of German as an academic language. By choosing to write in German he deliberately disqualified himself from involvement in current philosophical debate, which was conducted in Latin. Consonant with the practicality informing his

guage; while their number could not be increased, it could be reduced through abuse and carelessness. To counter such malpractice the tenth *Lobrede* includes a plan for a projected Stammwort dictionary, while book 5 presents a collection of about five thousand of these words. As the term *Stammwort* suggests, Schottelius viewed the language as a living organism: he also refers to the *Sprachbaum* (tree of language). Stammwörter, also referred to as *Würzeln* (root), provide the substance from which the language drew strength and could grow.

Schottelius was the first grammarian to produce a comprehensive system of word formation. The potential to add to or to compound Stammwörter was, according to Schottelius, innate to the German language and a reflection of patterns in Ancient German. *Ausführliche Arbeit von der Teutschen HaubtSprache* deals extensively with word forma-

Frontispiece and title page for Schottelius's final work, a vivid description of the torments of hell

endeavors to bring about the establishment of German in schools, Schottelius was concerned that his secularized moral philosophy should be of use to the young. Although dedicated to Anton Ulrich's eldest son, August Friedrich, the work was as much intended to encourage virtue in "der teutschen Jugend und sonst andern so vielen teutschliebenden Gemüthern" (German youth and other patriots) as in the young duke.

His characteristic patriotic concern is also evident in his extremely successful legal publication investigating past legal procedure, *De Singularibus quibusdam & antiquis in Germania Juribus & Observatis. Kurtzer Tractat von unterschiedlichen Rechten in Teutschland* (Short Treatise on Diverse Laws in Germany,

1671). It provides evidence of Schottelius's belief, shared by many of his contemporaries, in the existence of witches and the need to execute them. Otherwise, the final decade of his life is marked above all by the publication of religious works. Apart from attesting to his profoundly held Christian beliefs, this poetry reflects the context in which it was produced. The court was the focal point of diverse religious interests. There was close contact with the theological faculty at Helmstedt, one of the most eminent in Europe, where Georg Calixt, the prominent irenicist, was professor. August also had a mystical tendency, as can be seen in his admiration for Johann Arndt and his friendship with Andreae, both of whom were regarded with suspicion by the Lutheran orthodoxy. Andreae wanted August to be patron of his utopian societies; there is no indication that August accepted, nor is it known whether Schottelius's request to join such a society, the *Societas Christiani*, in 1644 was granted. That August was prepared to challenge orthodoxy is evident in his insistence that his own translation of the Gospels, and not that of the Lutheran Bible, be read in the churches in his principality. His example stimulated a tradition of religious writing both among his family – Anton Ulrich published two collections of religious verse – and his courtiers.

Schottelius's religious writings include *Jesu Christi Nahmens-Ehr* (In Honor of the Name of Jesus Christ, 1667); *Eigentliche und sonderbare Vorstellung des Jüngsten Tages* (The True and Mysterious Representation of the Day of Judgment, 1668); *Sonderbare Vorstellung von der ewigen Seeligkeit* (A Mysterious Representation of Eternal Bliss, 1673); *Sonderbare Vorstellung, wie es mit Leib und Seel des Menschen werde kurtz vor dem Tode, in dem Tode, und nach dem Tode bewandt seyn* (A Mysterious Representation of the State of the Human Body and Soul Shortly before Death, in Death and after Death, 1674); *Concordia seu Harmonia Quatuor Evangelistarum. Ordentliche zusammengefügte Vereinbarung der Vier Heiligen Evangelisten* (Corncordia; or, Harmony of the Four Gospels. A Properly Assembled Account of the Four Evangelists, 1675), in which he attempts to improve on the Lutheran Bible by intensifying its moral impact through vivid presentation; and *Grausame Beschreibung und Vorstellung der Hölle und der höllischen Qwal* (A Cruel Description and Representation of Hell and Its Torment, 1676). Colored by mysticism, some of these works, as their titles indicate, reveal a fascination with punishment and the horrors of hell. Schottelius's language is dramatically evocative; drawing on his own theories, he used onomatopoeia and produced richly imagistic compounds such as *AngstLust* (fear-pleasure) and *SorgenSucht* (griefmania). Once again, he develops the expressive potential of the German language. Schottelius died on 25 October 1676 and was laid to rest the following month in the Beatae Mariae Virginis Church in Wolfenbüttel.

Bibliographies:

Erdmann Neumeister, *De Poetis Germanicis,* edited by Franz Heiduk and Günter Merwald, reprint of the original edition of 1695 (Bern: Francke, 1978), pp. 466–468;

Hans Pyritz, *Bibliographie zur deutschen Literaturgeschichte des Barockzeitalters,* continued and ed-

ited by Ilse Pyritz, volume 2 (Bern & Munich: Francke, 1985), pp. 611–614;

Gerhard Dünnhaupt, *Personalbibliographien zu den Drucken des Barock,* volume 9, part 5 (Stuttgart: Hiersemann, 1991), pp. 3824–3846.

References:

Stjepan Barbaric, *Zur grammatischen Terminologie von Justus Georg Schottelius und Kaspar Stieler* (Bern, Frankfurt am Main & Las Vegas: Lang, 1981);

Jörg Jochen Berns, "Justus Georg Schottelius," in *Deutsche Dichter des 17. Jahrhunderts: Ihr Leben und Werk,* edited by Harald Steinhagen and Benno von Wiese (Berlin: Schmidt, 1984), pp. 415–434;

Berns, *Justus Georg Schottelius 1612–1676: Ein Teutscher Gelehrter am Wolfenbütteler Hof* (Wolfenbüttel: Ausstellungskataloge der Herzog August Biblothek, 18, 1976);

Berns, "Der Pegnitzschäfer Raabe: Kommentar zu sieben vergessenen Briefen," *Jahrbuch der Raabe-Gesellschaft* (1975): 16–32;

Berns, "Probleme der Erschließung und Edition des Schottelius-Briefwechsels," in *Briefe deutscher Barockautoren: Probleme ihrer Erfassung und Erschließung,* edited by Hans-Henrik Krummacher, Wolfenbütteler Arbeiten zur Barockforschung, no. 6 (Hamburg: Hauswedell, 1978), pp. 95–106;

Berns, " 'Theatralische neue Vorstellung von der Maria Magdalena' – Ein Zeugnis für die Zusammenarbeit von Justus Georg Schottelius und Heinrich Schütz," *Schütz Jahrbuch,* 2 (1980): 120–129;

Berns, "Trionfo-Theater am Hof von Braunschweig-Wolfenbüttel," *Daphnis: Zeitschrift für Mittlere Deutsche Literatur,* 10, no. 4 (1981): 663–711;

Berns, "Der weite Weg des Justus Georg Schottelius von Einbeck nach Wolfenbüttel: Eine Studie zu den Konstitutionsbedingungen eines deutschen Gelehrtenlebens im 17. Jahrhundert," *Einbecker Jahrbuch,* 30 (1974): 5–20;

Kathrin Gützlaff, "Simon Stevin und J. G. Schottelius – Spuren der deutsch-niederländischen Beziehungen im 17. Jahrhundert," in *Sprache in Vergangenheit und Gegenwart,* edited by Wolfgang Brandt and Rudolf Freudenberg (Marburg: Hitzeroth, 1988), pp. 91–108;

Gützlaff, "Der Weg zum Stammwort: Der Beitrag von Justus Georg Schottelius zur Entwicklung einer Wortbildungslehre des Deutschen," *Sprachwissenschaft,* 14, no. 1 (1989): 58–77;

Paul Hankamer, *Die Sprache: Ihr Begriff und ihre Deutung im 16. und 17. Jahrhundert* (Bonn: Cohen, 1927);

Josef Jansen, "Patriotismus und Nationalethos in den Flugschriften und Friedensspielen des Dreißigjährigen Krieges," dissertation, University of Cologne, 1964;

Wolfgang Kayser, *Die Klangmalerei bei Harsdörffer: Ein Beitrag zur Geschichte der Literatur, Poetik und Sprachtheorie der Barockzeit,* Palaestra, no. 179 (Leipzig: Mayer & Müller, 1932);

Wilfried Kürschner, "Zur Geschichte der Sprachkultur in Deutschland: Notizen zu Schottelius und Leibniz," in *Pragmantax: Akten des 20. Linguistischen Kolloquiums Braunschweig 1985,* edited by Arnim Burkhardt and Karl-Hermann Körner, Linguistische Arbeiten, no. 171 (Tübingen: Niemeyer, 1986), pp. 335–345;

Mary Elizabeth Lee, "Justus Georg Schottelius and Linguistic Theory," dissertation, University of Southern California, 1968;

Etienne Mazingue, *Anton Ulrich duc de Braunschweig-Wolfenbüttel (1633–1714): Un prince romancier au XVIIme siècle,* 2 volumes (Bern, Frankfurt am Main & Las Vegas: Lang, 1978);

Rudolf Meissner, "Eine Anmerkung zu Schottels *Horrendum bellum grammaticale,*" *Neophilologus,* 9 (1924): 258–263;

George T. Metcalf, "The Copyright patent in Schottelius' 'Ausführliche Arbeit' (1663): The blue pencil helps shape the Haubt-Sprache," in *Wege der Worte: Festschrift für Wolfgang Fleischhauer,* edited by Donald C. Riechel (Cologne & Vienna: Böhlau, 1978), pp. 11–26;

Metcalf, "Schottel and Historical Linguistics," *Germanic Review,* 28 (April 1953): 113–125;

Richard Moderhack, ed., *Braunschweigische Landesgeschichte im Überblick,* no. 23 (Brunswick: Selbstverlag des Braunschweigischen Geschichtsvereins, 1976);

William Mohr, "J. G. Schottelius' Spelling Rules Compared with the Practices of Some of His Printers," dissertation, Univeristy of Chicago, 1966;

Jörg Jochen Müller, "Ausführliche Arbeit Von der Teutschen HaubtSprache," in *Kindlers Literatur Lexikon,* supplementary volume (Zurich: Kindler, 1974), cols. 119–122;

Müller, "Fürstenerziehung im 17. Jahrhundert. Am Beispiel Herzog Anton Ulrichs von Braunschweig und Lüneburg," in *Stadt – Schule – Universität – Buchwesen und die deutsche Literatur im 17. Jahrhundert,* edited by Albrecht Schöne (Munich: Beck, 1976), pp. 243–260;

Gisela M. Neuhaus, *Justus Georg Schottelius: Die Stammwörter der Teutschen Sprache samt derselben Erklärung, und andere Stammwörter betreffende Anmerkungen: Eine Untersuchung zur frühneuhochdeutschen Lexikologie, Göppinger Arbeiten zur Germanistik,* 562 (Göppingen: Kümmerle, 1991);

Josef Plattner, "Zum Sprachbegriff von J. G. Schottel, aufgrund der 'Ausführlichen Arbeit Von der Teutschen HaubtSprache' von 1663," dissertation, University of Zurich, 1967;

Paul Raabe and Eckhard Schinkel, eds., *Sammler, Fürst, Gelehrter: Herzog August von Braunschweig-Lüneburg 1579–1666* (Wolfenbüttel: Ausstelungskataloge der Herzog August Bibliothek, 27, 1979);

Nikolaus Ritt, "The Dictionary of Justus Georg Schottelius or 'Generativism' in a 17th-Century Grammar!?," in *Meaning and Lexicography,* edited by Jerzy Tomaszczyk and Barbara Lewandowska-Tomaszczyk (Amsterdam & Philadelphia: Benjamins, 1990), pp. 57–72;

Monika Rössing-Hager, "Ansätze einer deutschen Sprachgeschichtsscheibung vom Humanismus bis in das 18. Jahrhundert," in *Sprachwissenschaft,* edited by W. Besch, O. Reichmann, and S. Sonderegger (Berlin & New York: De Gruyter, 1985), pp. 1564–1614;

Sara Smart, *Doppelte Freude der Musen: Court Festivities in Brunswick-Wolfenbüttel 1642–1700,* Wolfenbütteler Arbeiten zur Barockforschung, no. 19 (Wiesbaden: Harrassowitz, 1989);

Smart, "Justus Georg Schottelius and the Patriotic Movement," *Modern Language Review,* 84, no. 1 (1989): 83–98;

Blake Lee Spahr, *The Archives of the Pegnesischer Blumenorden: A Survey and Reference Guide* (Berkeley & Los Angeles: University of California Press, 1960);

Hiroyuki Takada, "J. G. Schottelius, die Analogie und der Sprachgebrauch: Versuch einer Periodisierung der Entwicklung des Sprachtheoretikers," *Zeitschrift für Germanistische Linguistik,* 13, no. 2 (1985): 129–153;

Paul Zimmermann, "Matthaeus Merians Topographie der Herzogtümer Braunschweig und Lüneburg," *Jahrbuch des Geschichtsvereins für das Herzogtum Braunschweig,* 1 (1902): 38–66.

Papers:

The majority of Justus Georg Schottelius's correspondence can be found in Wolfenbüttel in the Niedersächsisches Staatsarchiv and in the Herzog August Bibliothek.

Johann Balthasar Schupp

(March 1610 – 26 October 1661)

Jill Bepler
Herzog August Bibliothek

BOOKS: *Oratiuncula: In qua Proponvntvr verae & genuinae causae Respublicas corrumpentes* (Marburg: Printed by Nicolaus Hampel, 1632);

Hercules Togatus sive De Illustrissimo Celsissimoqve Heroe Domino Georgio II. Cattorum Landgravio, Comite in Cattimeleboco, Decis, Zigenhaina & Nidda, &c. Pacificatore pio & prudentissimo. Oratio, Effvsa Potivs qvam Elaborata (Marburg: Printed by Nicolaus Hampel, 1638);

Deucalion Christianus sive De Vero Natali Jesu Christi Controversia Chronologica (Marburg: Printed by Nicolaus Hampel, 1638);

Orator Ineptus Paucis Regulis Raptim Informatus (Marburg: Printed by Nicolaus Hampel, 1638);

Xenium sive De Usu et Praestantia Nihili. Dissertatio Philosophica (Marburg: Printed by Nicolaus Hampel, 1639);

De Opinione Dissertatio Praeliminaris (Marburg: Printed by Nicolaus Hampel, 1639);

Oratio de Felicitate Hujus Seculi XVII. ad tractandum proposita (Marburg: Printed by Caspar Chemlin, 1639);

Somnivm (Marburg: Printed by Nicolaus Hampel, 1640);

Quod Felix Faustumque Esse Jubeat Sacro Sancta Trinitas. Disputatio Theologica (Marburg: Printed by Nicolaus Hampel, 1641);

Eusebia Prodeambulans (Marburg: Printed by Caspar Chemlin, 1642);

Aurora (Marburg: Printed by Caspar Chemlin, 1642);

[Untitled collection of the Latin works] (Marburg: Caspar Chemlin, 1642);

PassionLieder è Museo (Marburg: Printed by Caspar Chemlin, 1643);

De Arte Ditescendi Dissertatio Prior ex Avellino ad Philosophos in Germania (N.p., 1648);

Gedenck daran, Hamburg. Oder eine Catechismus-Predigt, von dem dritten Gebot, am Freytag nach Mariae Heimsuchung jm Jahr 1656. in der Kirchen zu St. Jacob in Hamburg gehalten (Hamburg, 1656);

Salomo oder Vorbild eines guten Regenten aus den Eilff ersten Capituln des ersten Buchs der Königen entworfen, und andern Gottsführchtigen und sinnreichen Politicis auszuführen und zu elaboriren, as Antenor (Hamburg: Printed by Michael Pfeiffer, 1657);

Freund in der Noth (Hamburg: Printed by Christoph Demler, published by Zacharias Dose, 1657);

Der Rachgierige und unversöhnliche Lucidor, erinnert und ermahnt, as Antenor (Hamburg: Printed by Christoph Demler, published by Zacharias Dose, 1657);

Send-Schreiben, an einem vornehmen Cavallier. Betreffend die Schwedischen und Polnischen Waffen, &c. as Ambrosius Mellilambius (N.p., 1657);

Ein Holländisch Pratgen von dem vorigen Krieg zwischen den beyden Nordischen Königreichen gehalten, anonymous (N.p., 1657);

Publica invitatio ad adornandum memoriale Biblicum (Hamburg: Printed by Christoph Demler, 1657);

Sieben böse Geister, welche heutiges Tages Knechte und Mägde regieren und verführen. Zur Abschewung vorgestellet (Hamburg: Printed by Georg Pape, 1658);

Der Bücher-Dieb, gewarnet und ermahnet (N.p., 1658);

Relation aus dem Parnasso, welche bey jüngster Post Mercurius anbracht hat, as Antenor (Wolfenbüttel: Printed by Johann Bissmarck, 1658);

Calender (Wolfenbüttel: Printed by Johann Bissmarck, 1659);

Erste und Eylfertige Antwort auff M. Bernhard Schmitts Discurs de Reputatione Academicâ (Altona: Printed by Victor de Löwe, 1659);

Eylfertiges Sendschreiben an den Calenderschreiber zu Leipzig (Altona: Printed by Victor de Löwe, 1659);

Deutscher Lvcianvs (N.p., 1659);

Der geplagte Hiob. Das ist, Fürstellung des grossen Creutzträgers Hiobs, und der manchfaltigen, schmertzhafften und jammervollen Begegnissen, mit

Johann Balthasar Schupp; engraving by Philipp Kilian

denen Er auf die Gedultprob gesetzet worden, as An-
    tenor (Nuremberg: Endter, 1659);
Abgenöthigte Ehren-Rettung (Leipzig: Johann Bar-
    tholomäus Oehler, 1660);
*Corinna die Ehrbare und scheinheilige Hure. Beschrieben
    und andern zur Warnung vorgestellet,* as
    Ehrnhold, a priest in Gambrivia (Nineveh:
    Jonas Warner [fictitious place and publisher],
    1660);
*Die Krancken Wärterin, oder Eine Auslegung des Heiligen
    Vater unsers, wie man es mit armen einfältigen
    krancken Leuten beten kan* (Lübeck: Published by

Michael Volck, printed by Valentin Schmal-
    hertz's heirs, 1661);
*Einfältige Erklärung der Litaney, den Kindern, Knechten,
    Mägden, und andern einfältigen Leuten im Kirchspiel
    zu St. Jacob in Hamburg, zum Neuen Jahre
    mitgetheilet* (Lübeck: Published by Michael
    Volck, printed by Valentin Schmalhertz's
    heirs, 1661);
*Golgatha oder Eine kurtze Anleitung, wie ein krancker
    Mensch ihm die Sieben Wort, welche der Herr Jesus
    am Stamm des heiligen Creutzes gesprochen hat, auff
    seinem Todtbette solle zu Nutze machen,* anony-

mous (Lübeck: Published by Michael Volck, printed by Valentin Schmalhertz's heirs, 1661);

Doct: Joh: Balth: Schuppii Schrifften (Hanau, 1663);

Der Hauptmann von Capernaum, das ist: Ein Gottesfürchtiger Kriegs-Mann, as Philander (N.p̈., 1666);

Zugab. Doct: Joh: Balth: Schuppii Schrifften (Hanau, circa 1667);

Ninivitischer Buß-Spiegel, as Antenor (Frankfurt am Main: Balthasar Christoph Wust the Elder, 1668);

Der schändliche Sabbath-Schänder durch alle und jede Stände (Hamburg: Printed by Henning Brendeke, 1690).

Editions and Collections: *Der Freund in der Not,* edited by W. Braune (Halle: Niemeyer, 1878);

Der teutsche Lehrmeister − Vom Schulwesen, edited by Paul Stötzner (Leipzig: Richter, 1891);

Streitschriften, 2 volumes, edited by Carl Vogt (Halle: Niemeyer, 1910, 1911);

Corinna, edited by Vogt (Halle: Niemeyer, 1911);

Der Bücher-Dieb, edited by Reinhard Wittmann (Munich: Kraus, 1981).

OTHER: Christoph Helwig, *Theatrum Historicum et Chronologicum,* edited by Schupp (Marburg: Printed by Nicolaus Hampel, 1638);

Helwig, *Chronologia Universalis, ab Origine Mundi per Quatuor Monarchias ad Praesens tempus compendiosè deducta,* edited by Schupp (Marburg: Printed by Caspar Chemlin, 1639);

Consecratio Avellini, edited by Schupp (Marburg: Printed by Caspar Chemlin, 1640).

Johann Balthasar Schupp is best known as the author of popular works of moral satire whose wit and spontaneity of expression make him one of the more accessible German baroque authors for the modern reader. Schupp's literary career divides clearly into two phases: during the first half of his life he wrote exclusively in Latin for an academic public, in keeping with his main role as a university professor of rhetoric; after moving to Hamburg in 1649 to take up a post as a preacher he wrote mainly satiric and devotional tracts in the vernacular, aimed at the moral improvement of his readers. Schupp's works, especially his earlier Latin treatises, have yet to be adequately researched. The lack of a reliable modern scholarly edition has certainly contributed to his neglect.

Schupp was born and grew up in Giessen, a small town in the province of Hesse, not far from the free city of Frankfurt am Main and subject to the landgrave of Hesse-Darmstadt, an orthodox Lutheran. This was an area destined to be hit hard by the effects of the Thirty Years' War, a formative experience for Schupp, and by the fighting between the Lutheran landgraves in Darmstadt and the Calvinist landgraves in Kassel for supremacy in the territory of Hesse itself. The exact date of Schupp's birth is not known; his parents, Johann Eberhart Schupp, a city councillor in Giessen, and Anna Elisabeth, née Russ, had him baptized on 29 March 1610. A child of affluent parents belonging to the ruling elite of the town, Schupp received a good education at the *paedagogium illustre* of his hometown, a school renowned for its progressive educationalists. Men such as Konrad Dietrich, Kaspar Finck, and Schupp's future father-in-law, Christoph Helwig, had experimented there with the new teaching methods propagated by the radical educational reformer Wolfgang Ratke. Ratke's proposals for school reform promised an improvement of society as a whole, in which the introduction of the use of the vernacular would lead not only to linguistic but also to social and religious harmony.

In 1625 Schupp enrolled at the University of Marburg, where he studied philosophy under Rudolph Goclenius, professor of logic and ethics. Schupp was later to express bitter regret for the years he had been forced to waste on the useless study of Aristotelian logic, learning by rote obscure terminology that was of no practical use in later life. Many of his own Latin writings would call for a pragmatic approach to rhetoric and teaching.

Schupp's unease with the state of traditional German university teaching intensified during his travels. In 1628 he set off on his *peregrinatio academica,* journeying, he was later to claim, mainly on foot to the universities and academies of Poland, Livonia, Prussia, and Denmark. In Königsberg (today, Kaliningrad, Russia) Schupp studied rhetoric with Samuel Fuchs; at the Danish academy in Sorø he met the satiric poet Johann Lauremberg. It was Peter Lauremberg, the poet's brother and professor at the University of Rostock, however, who exerted the greatest influence over the young student from Marburg: it was probably he who first introduced Schupp to theories of mnemotechny − the art of memory − that would often be the subject of Schupp's own university lectures in Marburg. Although they mainly remained unpublished, these lectures, in which Schupp advocated the use of emblems and pictures to train the memory, would be a lasting influence on students such as Johann Buno and Johann Justus Winckelmann, who would go on to write standard works on the subject. In 1632 Schupp was awarded the degree of master of arts by the University of Rostock, after a disputation presided over by Peter Lauremberg, and returned to the University of Marburg.

In Marburg, Schupp began to study theology, and on 29 April 1632 he gave a public lecture on the causes of the evils afflicting most political states and the reasons for the superiority of Hesse in comparison to those states. This lecture, *Oratiuncula* (A Short Speech, 1632), was his first published work. He accepted a post at the university, where he gave courses on rhetoric, but the institution was soon forced to move to Giessen when the plague struck Marburg. By the spring of 1634 Hesse had become the scene of major battles, forcing the university to suspend teaching altogether.

Schupp became tutor to a young nobleman and was engaged to accompany him on his travels to the Netherlands. This second phase of traveling was of central importance to Schupp's later career. He studied rhetoric in Leiden under Marcus Zuerius Boxhorn and in Amsterdam under Gerardus Vossius and Kasper van Baerle, whose works on rhetoric, political emblems, and mnemotechny provided the sources for several of Schupp's later works. Schupp was impressed by the pragmatic approach to rhetoric taught at the Dutch universities, but he was also shocked by the petty feuds among academics. The political and economic life of the Netherlands, both as experienced firsthand and expounded on in the Leiden lectures of the national economist Claude de Saumaise, seemed to Schupp exemplary. It provided him with a model that he would often cite in his own political and satiric works.

In 1635 Schupp returned to Marburg, where he was given the chair of rhetoric and history. In the same year he married Anna Elisabeth Helwig, daughter of the Giessen schoolmaster Christoph Helwig. This family connection was of great significance for Schupp's literary career, for his wife brought her father's manuscripts and papers. Over the next years Schupp benefited greatly from working with his father-in-law's materials. He reedited and expanded Helwig's historical compendium, *Theatrum Historicum et Chronologicum* (1638; translated as *The Historical and Chronological Theater of Christopher Helvicus,* 1687), which had first been published in Giessen in 1609. Schupp was also engaged in a project to write a political history of the house of Hesse, but it was never realized.

Helwig had been at the forefront of the discussion of educational reform in Germany and of the introduction of the vernacular into teaching, and his papers led Schupp to formulate many of his own ideas on the subject. He became increasingly critical of the significance attached to the learning of Latin at the expense of other intellectual activities. His works abound with witty attacks on the subject; for example: "Wenn der Witz in der lateinischen Sprache bestehet, wäre es genug gewesen, wenn uns Christus die Lateinische Grammatic als daß er das Evangelium hinterlassen" (If wit consists of the Latin language, it would have been enough for Christ to bequeath us a Latin grammar and not the Scriptures). His publications over the next several years are a result of his experience of teaching rhetoric at the university. In various lectures he satirized the practice of debating on ridiculous topics. In 1638 he published one of his most popular Latin works, *Orator Ineptus* (The Clumsy Orator), which was already into its third edition by 1642 and was translated into German by Balthasar Kindermann in 1660. In 1639 Schupp took this biting satire on the barren nature of university teaching to extremes in a parodic public oration with the title *Xenium sive De Usu et Praestantia Nihili* (Xenium; or, On the Uses and Excellence of Nothing, 1639).

Schupp was a popular figure at the university, and a circle of students met regularly in his garden house on the outskirts of Marburg, which he christened Avellinum. Schupp never made any pretensions to poetical talents, but he encouraged the efforts of his students and acquainted them with the manuscript for August Buchner's handbook of vernacular poetry and with the poetical reforms introduced by Martin Opitz. The occasional poetry written by these students was published with a preface by Schupp in 1640 under the title *Consecratio Avellini* (Dedication to the Avellinum). In his Latin foreword Schupp advocates the use of the vernacular and praises German poetry. He was a great admirer of the translations of the early members of the prominent German language society Fruchtbringende Gesellschaft (Fruit-bringing Society) but was opposed to slavish adherence to the metrical norms dictated by Opitz's *Buch der deutschen Poeterey* (Book of German Poetry, 1624). Among contemporary writers Schupp singled out the work of the Nuremberg poet Georg Philipp Harsdörffer for unqualified praise; he was impressed by the didactic strength of Harsdörffer's conversational work *Frauenzimmer Gesprechspiele* (Playful Colloquies for the Ladies, 1641–1657). He was, however, opposed to the pastoral mode of poetry that characterized the work of the Nuremberg poets, rejecting it as alien to the "masculine" spirit of the German language.

Around 1641 Schupp resumed his theological studies and received the degree of licentiate in the same year, after a disputation supervised by his friend and later correspondent Meno Hanneken, the orthodox Lutheran professor of theology. As well as fulfilling his university duties, Schupp became one of the preachers at the Church of Saint Elisabeth in Marburg. During this period he composed the hymns that were first published in 1643 under the title *PassionLieder* (Songs of the Passion). In 1645 he was cited by the church elders for not adhering to the formula for prayers set down in the Hessian church order; it seems that Schupp had established an extra prayer and catechism circle for the poor and sick in his congregation that was attracting many who were not usual churchgoers and was arousing the jealousy of his fellow clergymen. It was a problem that would repeat itself later, as would Schupp's reaction, which was to ridicule his opponents and, far from submitting to the authority of his church superiors, to challenge them by appealing to a higher, secular authority, in this case the landgrave.

In December 1645 Schupp was awarded the degree of doctor of divinity, having obviously decided that his future lay in preaching. He had already demanded his release from the chair of rhetoric and history at the university — where, because of the plight into which the war had driven the country, his pay was hopelessly in arrears — and had hopes of finding a living in Schmalkalden or Frankfurt. The war put an end to the former plan, and for the latter he lacked influential friends. He reluctantly accepted the offer of a post as court preacher to Landgrave Johann II of Hesse in Braubach, although, as he wrote in a letter of 10 September 1645 to his patron Maximilian zum Jungen, "die Wahrheyt zu bekennen, hab ich nicht gern mit Fürsten und Herrn zu thun" (to confess the truth, I do not like to have dealings with princes and lords). His later works show that he maintained his opinion about the dangers of associating with the ruling classes; nevertheless, Schupp actively engaged in discussion of the political and economic problems of the tiny territory of Braubach, advising the landgrave on all manner of improvement schemes.

In 1648 Schupp published one of his last major works in Latin, *De Arte Ditescendi* (On the Art of Growing Rich), a utopian tract addressed to his former Avellinum students from his "exile" in Braubach, into which he incorporated some of his improvement schemes. Driven from their homes by the war, a group of artisans, farmers, and academics has gathered together on the banks of the Rhine.

Schupp discourses with them on the nature of true poverty and ironically depicts the advantages of beggary. In a dream he sees a boat approaching the banks of the river, carrying the English philosopher Sir Francis Bacon. Bacon claims to have just returned from a voyage to Peru, during which he has accidentally come across an island called New Atlantis, which he is now seeking to colonize. A debate ensues on the kind of people needed to found such a colony and the nature of the institutions to be established, giving Schupp an opportunity to expound on his educational theories. Various artisans and academics come forward to offer their advice and services to Bacon. John Barclay, the Scottish satirist, also appears, making a case for taking along experts in all fields of knowledge and technology so as to found a solid economy. In contrast to the utopian writings of Bacon himself or of Johann Valentin Andreae, Schupp's work is primarily concerned with pragmatic moral and economic questions, not with developing a vision of an ideal state. The tract ends abruptly, as do most of Schupp's works — the narrator is awakened by the crowing of a cock, which he angrily orders to be slaughtered — without resolving the question of the best way of achieving prosperity.

In 1648 Landgrave Johann sent Schupp as an emissary to the peace negotiations at Münster that were to mark the end of the Thirty Years' War. The Swedish chancellor Axel Oxenstierna asked Schupp to preach a sermon of thanksgiving at the conclusion of the negotiations, which was well received. Schupp used the time in Münster to apply to the city of Hamburg for the position of preacher at the church of Saint Jacob that had just become vacant. He was invited to preach before the church elders and was subsequently offered the position. An offer of a similar position in Augsburg reached him soon after he and his family had moved to Hamburg.

Schupp's wife died soon after their arrival in June 1650, leaving the widower with four young children. The funeral work published in her memory included a consolatory poem by Schupp's friend Johann Rist, preacher in Wedel, just outside Hamburg, and head of the language society Elbschwanenorden (Order of the Swans on the Elbe). In November 1651 Schupp married Sophia Eleonora Reinking, daughter of the former Danish chancellor in Schleswig-Holstein, Theodor Reinking. Again Schupp had made a significant choice of father-in-law. Reinking had retired from active politics and was living in Glückstadt, where he devoted himself to his studies and writing. Reinking's work

Biblische Policey (Biblical Statecraft, 1653) was much in keeping with Schupp's own writings, calling for political ethics based on Christian virtues rather than on Machiavellian principles.

In 1656 Schupp published one of his sermons, *Gedenck daran, Hamburg* (Think on This, Hamburg), in which he chastised his congregation for breaking the Sabbath. In contrast to the practice of many contemporary clergyman, Schupp did not publish other of his sermons, either individually or in collections, although his son would publish a posthumous collection with the title *Der schändliche Sabbath-Schänder* (The Shameful Sabbath-breaker, 1690). The literary works Schupp published in Hamburg in 1657 and 1658, however, brought him into conflict with church authority once more and involved him in controversies that would last until his death. In 1657 he was cited to appear before the church elders, headed by the senior minister Johann Müller, where he was accused on four charges: publishing theological works under a pseudonym, "Antenor," an action deemed unfitting for a clergyman; inventing apocryphal works such as a 151st Psalm; failing to submit his works to the censorship of the church senior; and, most important, of writing works in which fables, student pranks, satire, jokes, and ridiculous stories were to be found side by side with quotations from the Bible and holy matters. Schupp replied that he would comply with the first two objections but saw no reason to change the style of his writings, as his works were not religious but political. This response and Schupp's ill-concealed scorn for Müller set him at loggerheads with the authorities, who asked the theological faculties of Strasbourg and Wittenberg to pronounce on the case.

One of the works to which the authorities had objected was *Salomo oder Vorbild eines guten Regenten* (Solomon; or, The Model of a Good Ruler, 1657). Its explicit aim is to use the first eleven chapters of the Book of Solomon to demonstrate political virtues. In the dedicatory preface Schupp explains that the Bible, especially the Old Testament, contains "eine vollkomene Politic" (a complete politics), teaching just as much about statecraft as do the works of Tacitus and Niccolò Machiavelli. Although he takes his reader through the events at Solomon's court and the building of the Temple, Schupp uses these biblical texts to launch into moralizing anecdotes culled from his own reading, especially of his father-in-law Reinking's *Biblische Policey,* but mainly from his own experiences in Marburg,

Braubach, and Hamburg. It is not Solomon who is the central figure of the work, but Schupp himself.

The same is true of *Freund in der Noth* (A Friend in Need, 1657), which is addressed to Schupp's eldest son, Anton Meno, who is about to set off to a university. In the tradition of educational tracts in the guise of letters from parents to their children, Schupp warns his son against the inconstancy of friendship and the pitfalls of pride. He recommends hard work, honest recreation, and reliance on experience rather than academic knowledge: "Versichere dich, daß ich offt aus eines Kauffmanns, oder aus eine Schippers discurs, mehr gelernet hab, als hiebevor auf Universitäten aus grossen Büchern. Niemand kennet die Welt recht, als wer die Welt gesehen hat" (Be assured that I have often learned more from the discourse of a merchant or a ship's captain than previously in great tomes at universities. No one knows the world properly but those who have seen the world).

In defending himself against the Hamburg ministry, Schupp had claimed that his works were political, not theological. The clergymen had crisply replied that he should leave politics to the politicians. All of Schupp's writings try to correct concrete moral and social ills and are a direct result of contact with his own congregation at Saint Jacob's, a relatively poor Hamburg parish. Thus, his *Sieben böse Geister, welche heutiges Tages Knechte und Mägde regieren* (Seven Evil Spirits That Govern Today's Menservants and Maids, 1658) deals with the moral failings of domestic servants. Schupp's writings evince a great sympathy for the lower classes and a firm belief in their right to an education, an opinion he voices in the posthumously published tract *Ninivitischer Buß-Spiegel* (The Mirror of Repentance for Nineveh, 1668):

> Ist ein Handwercksmann kranck, oder macht sonsten in seiner Werckstadt Feyerabend, so kan er mit lesen die Zeit vertreiben, und sich in den Büchern belustigen. Wie offt geschiehet es, daß ein armer Bürger ihm das jenige, was er in seiner Jugend in der Schulen erlernet hat, zu nutz macht, und zu einem Burgermeister, zu einem Rathsherrn, oder in ein ander Ehrenampt erhoben wird? Die Weißheit deß Geringen bringt ihn offtsmahls zu Ehren, und setzt ihn bey den Fürsten.

> (When a craftsman is ill or leaves off work in his workshop, he can pass the time by reading or amusing himself with his books. How often is it the case that a poor citizen makes use of what he has learned in his youth at school and is raised to mayor or city councillor or some other position of honor? The wisdom of the lowliest of men often brings him honors and seats him next to princes.)

Schupp's defense of the vernacular also stems from this egalitarian educational impulse, setting him apart from the aesthetic and elitist concerns of most of the German language societies of his day.

The conflict with the Hamburg ministry escalated when Schupp was called to hear the replies from Wittenberg and Strasbourg and refused to appear until he had been given the chance to read the verdicts and prepare his case. As in Marburg, Schupp sought help from a political authority, asking the Hamburg senate to rule in his favor. The senate did negotiate a reconciliation between the parties, but thenceforth Schupp was prohibited from publishing in Hamburg.

In 1658 he published a short work, *Der Bücher-Dieb* (The Book Thief), in which he remonstrates with printers who pirated authors' works – marking an early plea for author's copyright. In the guise of a response to *Der Bücher-Dieb* called *Wider Antenors Bücher-Dieb* (Against Antenor's Book Thief, 1658), and using a pseudonym, "Butyrolambius," himself, Müller, Schupp's Hamburg adversary, began a series of bitter and personal polemical exchanges with Schupp that would dominate the latter's writing thereafter.

By this time, however, Schupp had gained the support of the great bibliophile Duke August in Wolfenbüttel. By recommending himself as a former correspondent of the duke's protégé, the utopian writer Andreae, Schupp entered into correspondence with August, whom he visited in 1658, paving the way for the publication of his next works, *Relation aus dem Parnasso* (Report from Parnassus, 1658) and *Calender* (Almanac, 1659), in Wolfenbüttel. Both of these polemical works are mainly concerned with justifying Schupp in his controversy with the Hamburg authorities. In *Relation aus dem Parnasso* news of Müller's attacks on Schupp has reached the ears of the gods, and Müller is duly ridiculed. *Calender* is ostensibly a satire on almanac writers inspired by a letter Schupp has received in which his son Anton Meno, now a student, announces his intention of earning money by writing almanacs. Within a few pages, however, attention is turned to replying to Müller's attacks on Schupp's integrity as a writer and preacher.

Schupp's moral tale *Corinna die Ehrbare und scheinheilige Hure* (Corinna the Honorable and Hypocritical Whore, 1660) was dedicated to the Wolfenbüttel prince Ferdinand Albrecht, with whom Schupp seems to have corresponded. Set in Hamburg, which Schupp calls Nineveh to denote his function as a preacher of penitence, the story recounts the fate of the young Corinna, who is cor-

rupted by her mother, Crobyle, and led into a life of prostitution while keeping up an outward show of godliness. Corinna repents when she is left destitute after the death of her mother. Her evil life has led her to contract syphilis, from which she dies attended only by the preacher Ehrenhold. Although it has been compared with Hans Jakob Christoffel von Grimmelshausen's picaresque novel *Trutz Simplex* (circa 1669), *Corinna* is primarily a moral tract in which the fictional framework provides Schupp, thinly disguised as Ehrenhold, a vehicle to inveigh against the sinful sexual and social mores of his readers, attacking such evils as of the widespread practice of wet-nursing, the custom of preaching hypocritical funeral sermons, and the superficial piety of female churchgoers. Only in the early part of the work do Corinna, Crobyle, and the aristocratic debaucher Holofernes come to life. Throughout his works Schupp repeatedly justifies addressing both the sins of his congregation and broader social and political concerns. In typical style he replies in *Corinna* to criticism that he neglected to preach against the heathens but concentrated on such subjects as wet-nursing:

> Ich solte wieder die Jüden und Papisten predigen. Allein was fragt der Teuffel darnach, ob ich wider die Jüden predge? Es begehrt kein Jüde aus Hamburg oder Altenau in die Kirche zukommen, wenn ich predige. Ich glaube auch nicht, daß einer unter meinen Zuhörern sey, der sich wolle beschneiden lassen und ein Jüde werden. Allein Hurer, Ehebrecher, Diebe, Betrieger, und dergleichen Gottloses Volck sehe ich immerdar vor mir, wenn ich predigen soll.

> (I am meant to preach against the Jews and Catholics. But what does the devil care if I preach against the Jews? No Jew from Hamburg or Altona wants to come to church when I preach. Nor do I believe that there is anyone in my congregation who wants to have himself circumcised and become a Jew. I only ever see whores, adulterers, thieves, frauds, and such godless folk in front of me when I am meant to preach.)

At no time do Schupp's texts achieve the narrative sophistication of his contemporary Grimmelshausen. But as a self-styled writer of "political" works with an explicit moral and didactic purpose akin to that of his sermons, Schupp had no ambition for such sophistication.

Schupp exhausted himself in his polemical battles against Müller in Hamburg and Bernhard Schmid in Leipzig, who had taken issue with Schupp's criticism of the state of German universities. He died on 26 October 1661. Peter Lambeck,

310

later librarian to the emperor in Vienna, held a funeral oration for Schupp.

Letters:

Briefe G. M. Lingelsheims, M. Berneggers und ihrer Freunde, edited by Alexander Reifferscheid (Heilbronn: Henninger, 1889);

W. Nebel, "Briefwechsel Johann Balthasar Schupps mit dem Landgrafen Johann von Hessen," *Mitteilungen des oberhessischen Geschichtsvereins,* 2 (1890): 49–94;

Otto Lerche, "J. B. Schupp an Herzog August d.J. von Braunschweig-Wolfenbüttel," *Euphorion,* supplement 8 (1909): 16–17.

Biographies:

Theodor Bischoff, *Johann Balthasar Schupp: Beiträge zu seiner Würdigung* (Nuremberg, 1890);

Wilhelm Diehl, "Neue Beiträge zur Geschichte von Johann Balthasar Schupp in der zweiten Periode seiner Marburger Professorentätigkeit," *Archiv für hessische Geschichte,* new series, 5 (1907): 225–326;

Carl Vogt, "Johann Balthasar Schupp," *Euphorion,* 16 (1909): 6–27, 245–320, 673–704; 17 (1910): 1–48, 254–287, 473–537; 18 (1911): 41–60, 321–367; 19 (1912): 476–482; 21 (1914): 103–128, 490–520; 22 (1915): 393–395;

Vogt, *Aus Johann Balthasar Schupps Marburger Tagen* (Giessen, 1910);

H. Schütz, "Zur Lebensgeschichte Johann Balthasar Schupps," *Archiv für hessische Geschichte,* new series, 19 (1936): 99–157.

References:

Guillaume van Gemert, "Johann Balthasar Schupp und der gemeine Mann," in *Literatur und Volk im 17. Jahrhundert,* edited by Wolfgang Brückner and others (Wiesbaden: Harrasowitz, 1985), pp. 259–271;

Klaus Schaller, "Johann Balthasar Schupp, Muttersprache und realistische Bildung," in *Stadt – Schule – Universität – Buchwesen,* edited by Albrecht Schöne (Munich: Beck, 1975), pp. 275–285;

Maike Schauer, *Johann Balthasar Schupp, Prediger in Hamburg 1649–1661* (Hamburg: Museum für Hamburgische Geschichte, 1973);

Paul Stötzner, *Beiträge zur Würdigung von Johann Balthasar Schupps "Lehrreiche Schriften"* (Leipzig: Richter, 1890);

Hildegard E. Wichert, *Johann Balthasar Schupp and the Baroque Satire in Germany* (New York: Columbia University Press, 1952).

Papers:

Johann Balthasar Schupp's papers are held by the Staatsarchiv Darmstadt, the Staats- und Universitätsbibliothek Hamburg, the Bibliothek des Hansestadt Lübeck, and the Staatsbibliothek Munich.

Sibylle Schwarz

(14 February 1621 – 31 July 1638)

Barbara Becker-Cantarino
Ohio State University

BOOK: *Sibyllen Schwarzin vohn Greiffswald aus Pommerm, Deutsche Poëtische Gedichte, nuhn zum ersten mahl, auß ihren eigenen Handschrifften herauß gegeben und verleget,* 2 volumes, edited by M. Samuel Gerlach (Danzig: Georg Rhete's widow, 1650).

Edition: *Deutsche poëtische Gedichte: Faksimiledruck nach der Ausgabe von 1650,* edited by Helmut W. Ziefle (Bern: Peter Lang, 1980).

During her short life, which was encompassed by the Thirty Years' War, Sibylle Schwarz wrote original and innovative verses. Her poetry follows the new models propagated by Martin Opitz, especially the new metrics of French and Dutch verse. Her poetic production is multifaceted; she wrote religious, occasional, and secular poetry, including sonnets on love and friendship with personal tones that were rare in poetry of the seventeenth century. She is one of the few women of her age – perhaps the first woman in German literature – who consciously referred to the female *I* and attempted to bring it into the literary-scholarly tradition.

Schwarz was born on 14 February 1621 into a Protestant, upper-class family in Greifswald, a university town in Pomerania, in northern Germany on the Baltic Sea. Her father, Christian Schwarz, was a lawyer, city councilman, and mayor from 1631 until his death in 1648; he had traveled to the Netherlands and to Spain in 1616 and later served in a diplomatic mission with the duke of Brandenburg. Her mother was Regina Schwarz, née Völschow, the daughter of a Greifswald law professor. Sibylle was the youngest of seven children; three brothers and two sisters would survive her. The oldest sister, Regine, was widowed in 1629, only six days after her wedding, and returned home; after their mother's death in 1630 she ran the

Sibylle Schwarz; engraving by Jacob Sandrart for the frontispiece for the second volume of her collected poems

household. After Regine remarried in 1631, care of the household went to Emerentia until her marriage on 31 July 1638 – the day of Sibylle's death. During all those years Schwarz assisted her father with his correspondence and acted as his private secretary.

Because of its maritime importance, Greifswald became the center for the imperial general Albrecht Eusebius Wenzel von Wallenstein's military activities against the Swedes. In November 1627 one thousand imperial troops were quartered there; the citizens had to house and feed the troops, pay them large sums of money, and endure their looting and atrocities. The troops burned down churches, a hospital, and several civic buildings to make room for fortifications, for which they used stones from existing houses and buildings; by 1629 more than half of the thousand houses in the town were vacant or destroyed. In 1631 the city was occupied by the Swedes, who were initially more disciplined; but after the Swedish king Gustav Adolph's death in November 1631 they became as demoralized as the other armies. Aristocratic officers were temporarily quartered in the Schwarz house, although members of the town council, their relatives, and professors of the University of Greifswald petitioned to be exempted from the quartering. Schwarz's father was often absent for months at a time on official duties for the city; after several years as privy councillor at the court in Stettin, he went to Stockholm as ambassador of the Pomeranian estates in 1633. While the poor were simply expelled from the city, the patrician families were able to escape temporarily to their country estates. The estate of Fretow offered a place of refuge for the Schwarz family for a few years; in 1637 they had to flee to Stralsund during the clash between the duke of Brandenburg, who had allied himself with the imperial side, and the Swedes. Fretow was plundered and burned down shortly thereafter. The war and the rather cultured and refined life of Greifswald's upper class and its university shaped the short life of Sibylle Schwarz.

Schwarz's father was acquainted with professors at the University of Greifswald and with many of its students, who came from wealthy, often noble families. This close connection to a center of humanist learning seems to have enabled Sibylle Schwarz to become familiar with literature and to write poetry. There is no evidence that she had any formal education; as was customary for bright women in patrician families in the seventeenth century, she probably received some private tutoring together with her brothers, perhaps instruction from her father and older brothers, and she probably taught herself through reading. She is supposed to have learned Latin and Dutch. Her first poetic attempts that can be dated are occasional poems: a wedding poem for friends of the family in December 1633 and a poem addressed to Ernst Bo-

rislaw of Croys, the reigning duke's nephew, who matriculated at the University of Greifswald on 2 September 1634. Though Schwarz was then only twelve or thirteen, her occasional poems soon made her poetic talents known to the citizens of Greifswald and to learned circles in northern Germany.

In 1637 she became acquainted with Samuel Gerlach, a magister of theology from Tübingen who in the 1630s worked as an army chaplain and private tutor in Mecklenburg and Lübeck. Gerlach became Schwarz's champion; he introduced her to the new models, especially the works of Opitz, and corresponded with her after he left Greifswald in 1638 to become court chaplain at Eutin. Little is known about the nature of the relationship between Schwarz and Gerlach; a few months after her death, he was married in Eutin. He later became a minister near Danzig, where, in 1650, he published her poems. This collection, *Deutsche Poëtische Gedichte* (German Poetic Writings), is the only contemporary edition of Schwarz's work. Besides the dedicatory poems customary in books of the time, the edition includes a few of Schwarz's letters to Gerlach; many occasional poems and verses in the style of the new poetry; a free adaptation of Ovid's *Daphne*; a mythological tragedy on the occasion of the destruction of the family's country seat by Swedish troops; the pastoral poem "Faunus"; and a cycle of love sonnets. Gerlach seems to have planned the publication for years; in letters dating from 1637 and 1638 Schwarz agreed to the publication of her poems, of which she sent handwritten copies; but she requested that her name be altered or withheld. The frontispiece of each of the two volumes is a portrait of Schwarz executed by the engraver Jacob Sandrart between 1644 and 1648. The edition served as a commemorative volume for the poet, and her family supported the printing financially.

Schwarz seems to have begun writing shortly after her mother's death. Her poetic production, which is fragmentary and uneven, includes some highly polished and accomplished verses in the new style. Schwarz speaks with pointed modesty about her literary poetry, referring to it in a letter to Gerlach of 18 March 1838 as "ungepfefferte Gedichte" (unseasoned poems) and "Ungeziefer" (bugs); but in a poem with the traditional topos "Wider den Neidt" (Against Envy) she defends her work against critics who attacked her for being a woman poet. Besides the usual arguments in support of poetry – poetry immortalizes, has a tradition that goes back to antiquity, is legitimized by the great Opitz – Schwarz refers to the feminine tradition: the muses are women; there is a Dutch woman poet, Anna Maria van Schurman; and she knows some fifty-eight woman poets altogether. She answers the criticism that her writing causes her to neglect her female duties:

> Sollt ich die Nadel hoch erheben
> Und über meine Poesey
> So muß ein kluger mir nach geben
> Daß alles endlich reisst entzwey;
> Wer kan so künstlich Garn auch drehen
> Das es nicht sollt in stücken gehen?

> (If I were to raise the needle high
> Above my poetry,
> Then a wise man will surely have to agree
> That everything in the end is torn asunder;
> Who is there who can twist yarn so artfully
> That it would not break into pieces?)

Further to defend her position as a woman poet, Schwarz translated the preface to Daniel Heinsius's *Spiegel van de doorluchtige Vrouwen* (Mirror of Eminent Women, 1606) as "Lob der Verständigen und Tugendsamen Frauen, verdeutscht auß dem Niederländischen" (In Praise of Wise and Virtuous Women, from the Dutch). It is a free rendition in the style of the translation exercises on which all contemporary authors trained.

Poetry meant everything to Schwarz; she uses the popular literary topos "Poëten gehn dem unadelichen Adel weit vor" (Poets are much more worthy than nobility) in a sonnet. In another sonnet, "Alß sie ein Poëtischer Geist triebe" (When Poetic Inspiration Came to Her), she writes confidently:

> . . . ich wil immer auch bei meinen Worten bleiben
> Und steigen mit dem Sinn des Himmels Leiter an
> Ein jeder sey bereit
> daß er mir folgen kann.

> (. . . I always want to stay with my words
> And with my mind ascend to heaven;
> Let all be ready
> To follow me.)

For the elevation that she finds in poetry, she gladly renounces superficial qualities. Her poetic model is Opitz, whom she admired as the great poet of her time. She asked Gerlach in a letter for new poems by Opitz, from whom she learned the metric rules of the new poetry and new verse forms such as the sonnet, which was then making its appearance in Germany. Besides Opitz she

refers only to August Buchner, Jacob Cats, and Heinsius's *Nederduytsche Poemata* (Dutch Poems, 1616), which her brother had given her and which had also served as a model for Opitz. Her penchant for mythological imagery is taken from the new poetry: mastery of ancient mythology belonged to the tools of the poet and attested to his learning. With Schwarz, however, this imagery often sounds stilted because her themes are usually not scholarly but personal. Such is the case in her short, lyrical pastoral poem "Daphne," based on the mythological female figure from Ovid's *Metamorphoses*. In the dramatic fragment *Susanna,* based on the biblical figure, Schwarz chooses a comparatively strong, independent, active female persona.

The war provided an important theme for, and lent a personal note to, Schwarz's poetry. In "Auff Ihren Abschied auß Greiffswald, Gesang" (On Her Taking Leave of Greifswald, a Song) she writes about how the demon of war had driven her away from Greifswald and destroyed the circle of her friends and family, and how Fretow no longer offered protection. Fretow was for her, she says, the place to "lesen, tichten, schreiben" (read, invent, write), an idyllic country place where she could live in leisure and the war could be forgotten. While these verses are influenced by idyllic pastoral poetry, such occasional poems often refer concretely to events of the time or to a personal experience. The war, she says, must be endured as God's punishment. Opitz had published similar alexandrine verses in 1633 in *TrostGedichte in Widerwärtigkeit des Krieges* (Poem of Consolation in the Adversity of War) and the didactic poem *Vesuvius. Poema Germanicum* (Vesuvius: German Poem), the first great war poems, which in motifs, form, and style would be models for the treatment of war themes in German baroque poetry.

The traditional humanist topic of friendship, applied to her own situation, is a theme of some of Schwarz's best poems. It is also a reflection of her friendship with Judith Tanck, a minister's daughter from Stralsund who had found refuge at Fretow and Greifswald after her father's death in 1633. Their close relationship ended abruptly on 29 May 1638, two months before Schwarz's death, when Tanck married the town syndic of Stralsund and moved there. Schwarz's friendship poems, addressed mostly to Judith, often refer to their relationship in subtle nuances; traditional friendship topoi and religious motifs are intermingled as in her sonnet "Wahre Freundschaft ist beständig" (True Friendship Endures):

drumb glaub ich
daß kein Ding so stark es immer sey
ohn Gottes Macht
den Band der Freundschaft reißt entzwey.

(thus I believe
that nothing, no matter how strong it may be,
except for God's will,
can break the bond of friendship.)

While the literary tradition offered topoi and examples, Schwarz found a personal, individual poetic style to describe her friendship with Judith.

Likewise, Schwarz transformed traditional love poetry, in which the active speaker is almost always a man. In an appendix of sixteen sonnets fashioned after Petrarchan models she plays with the themes and topoi of this love poetry and exhibits her formal skills in rewriting the poems. She does not distinguish between friendship and love except in the sonnet, in which the theme is clearly one of love. She transformed this poetic tradition without being concerned about critics or detractors who found it unsuitable for a woman to compose such verses. With this independence, perhaps even defiance, Sibylle Schwarz is exceptional for her time; comparable poetry by a woman in Germany, at any rate, is unknown.

Biography:

Christoph Hagen, *Himmlische Hochzeit-Predigt auf der Seligen und fröhlichen Heimfahrt der Jungfrauen Sibyllen Schwartzin Begräbnis 3. August 1638* (Greifswald, 1638).

References:

Barbara Becker-Cantarino, *Der lange Weg zur Mündigkeit: Frau und Literatur in Deutschland (1550–1800)* (Stuttgart: Metzler, 1987);

Susan Clark, "Sibylle Schwarz: Prodigy and Feminist," in *Women Writers of the Seventeenth Century,* edited by Katharina M. Wilson and Frank J. Warnke (Athens & London: University of Georgia Press, 1989), pp. 431–460;

Kurt Gassen, *Sibylle Schwarz: Eine pommersche Dichterin. 1621–1638* (Greifswald: Abel, 1921);

Franz Horn, "Erinnerung an Sibylle Schwarz," in his *Frauentaschenbuch auf das Jahr 1818* (Nuremberg, 1818), pp. 176–210;

George C. Schoolfield, *German Baroque Lyric,* University of North Carolina Studies in Germanic Languages and Literatures, no. 19 (Chapel Hill: University of North Carolina Press, 1961);

Robert Wöhler, "Sibylla Schwarz, die Pommersche Dichterin und ihre Zeit (1621–1638)," *Zeitschrift für Preußische Geschichte und Landeskunde,* 15 (1878): 70–89.

Friedrich Spee von Langenfeld

(25 February 1591 – 7 August 1635)

G. Richard Dimler
Fordham University

BOOKS: *Cautio Criminalis, seu De Processibus contra Sagas Liber. Ad Magistratvs Germaniae hoc tempore necessarius, Tum autem Consiliariis, & Confessariis Principum, Inquisitoribus, Judicibus, Advocatis, Confessariis Reorum, Concionatoribus, caeterisq. lectu utillissimus,* as Incertus Theologus Romanus (Rinteln: Printed by Peter Lucius, printer for the University of Rinteln, 1631);

Trutz-Nachtigall, oder Geistlichs-Poetisch Lvst-Waldlein, deßgleichen noch nie zuvor in Teutscher sprach gesehen (Cologne: Published by Johann Wilhelm Friessem, 1649);

Güldenes Tvgend-Bvch, das ist, Werck vnnd übung der dreyen Göttlichen Tugenden. des Glaubens, Hoffnung, vnd Liebe. Allen Gottliebenden, andächtigen, frommen Seelen; vnd sonderlich den Kloster- vnd anderen Geistlichen personen sehr nützlich zu gebrauchen (Cologne: Published by Johann Wilhelm Friessem, 1649).

Editions and Collections: *Trutz-Nachtigall, oder Geistlichs-Poetisch Lvst-Waldlein,* edited by Gustav Otto Arlt (Halle: Niemeyer, 1936);

Friedrich Spee Sämtliche Schriften: Historisch-kritische Ausgabe, 3 volumes, edited by Theo G. M. van Oorschot (volume 2, Munich: Kösel, 1968; volume 1, Bern: Francke, 1985; volume 3, Tübingen: Francke, 1992);

Cautio Criminalis, seu De Processibus contra Sagas Liber (Frankfurt am Main: Minerva, 1971);

Trutznachtigall, edited by G. Richard Dimler (Washington, D.C.: University Press of America, 1981);

"Mein ganze Seel dem Herrn Sing": 72 Gesänge durch das Kirchenjahr; mit 26 Liedern, edited by the Friedrich-Spee-Gesellschaft (Trier: Friedrich-Spee-Gesellschaft, 1991).

Friedrich Spee von Langenfeld is best known as a champion and defender of the rights of the accused in the witchcraft trials that took place throughout Germany in the seventeenth century; only since the 1980s has his stature as a major poet

Friedrich Spee von Langenfeld; painting by an unidentified artist (Dreikönigs-Gymnasium, Cologne)

and writer of the baroque been properly evaluated. Critical editions of his three major works have provided the essential components for this reassessment. He was the subject of major conferences and television documentaries celebrating the 350th anniversary of his death in 1985 and the 400th anniversary of his birth in 1991, and his preeminent position in seventeenth-century literary, moral, theological, and social history has been established. Spee's brilliance in the areas of literary theory — independently of Martin Opitz he espoused the use of natural verse and word accentuation and touted German as a literary language second to none — poetry, moral theology, ethics, and the composition of enduring *Kirchenlieder* (hymns) attest to his extraordinary versatility as theologian, spiritual writer, and poet.

Spee was born on 25 February 1591 in Kaiserswerth, a small town on the Rhine River not far from Düsseldorf. His father, Peter, was an administrative bailiff to the prince elector of Cologne during the latter part of the sixteenth century. Little is known of his mother, Mechtild Spee, née Dückers. Kaiserswerth during Spee's lifetime was principally known for its cathedral, built in honor of Bishop Suitberg, an Anglo-Saxon missionary active in Germany during the eighth century. Spee's appellation "von Langenfeld" derives from the name of his family's estate.

An ominous portent for Spee's later life was the murder in 1598 of the wife of the duke of Jülich-Cleve in Düsseldorf on suspicion of witchcraft; the witchcraft craze was beginning to sweep through Germany. Spee began attending the Jesuit school in Cologne, the Tricoronatum, in 1602; he transferred to the Montanum school, also in Cologne, in 1608 because of the plague. He was awarded an A.B. degree from the University of Cologne in 1609. On 21 September 1610 he entered the Society of Jesus and resided in the novitiate in Trier.

It was as a novice in Trier that he first came into contact with witchcraft trials, which had been taking place there since the late 1580s. Scholars believe that the trials arose because people were seeking a supernatural explanation for crop failures, plagues, and wars; Spee himself says that belief in witches stemmed from two sources: uncertainty and superstition, and envy and jealousy. Under torture, those accused as witches frequently confessed and implicated others; from 1583 to 1591, in the Trier area alone, several hundred persons had been burned at the stake. Even a famed professor of law at the University of Trier, Dietrich Flade, had been accused of witchcraft by a mentally deranged fifteen-year-old; he had confessed under torture and had been executed on 18 September 1589. The trials were still going on in Trier when Spee was there.

Belief in witchcraft had a long history. The church fathers saw paganism as the work of the devil; Saint Augustine believed that the old gods were demons and were involved in pacts with magicians. The medieval Scholastics constructed extended treatises on sorcery: Peter Lombard believed that sexual impotence was caused by the devil; Saint Thomas Aquinas believed in sorcery through satanic pacts, as well as in incubi and succubi. The Inquisition played a significant role in the rise of the witchcraft hysteria when sorcerers were included in condemnations in the latter part of the thirteenth century. Pope Innocent VIII charged two Dominicans, Heinrich Institoris and Jakob Sprenger, with searching out sorcerers and witches; their book, the *Malleus maleficarum* (Witches' Hammer, 1487) "vulgarized" Scholastic teaching with fantastic stories of witchery and laid down rules for the trials. Every means of torture was permitted to extract a confession from the accused. In Trier itself in 1589, the coadjutor bishop, Peter Binsfeld, published his *Tractatus de Confessionibus Maleficorum et Sagarum* (Treatise on the Confessions of Witches and Magicians), in which he defended the use of *Tormentum insomniae* (not permitting the accused any sleep) but did allow strangulation before the actual burning at the stake lest the condemned person blaspheme against God while being immolated.

When the plague broke out in Trier in 1612 the Jesuit novitiate was moved to Fulda, where Spee pronounced his first vows. After completing philosophical studies in Würzburg, he was awarded an M.A. in 1615. Once again he came into contact with the witchcraft trials: the case of Katherine Henot, a noblewoman who was burned at the stake, made an enormous impression on him. From 1615 to 1619 Spee was a teacher and catechist in Speyer, Worms, and Mainz; he then studied theology in Mainz from 1619 to 1623. In Speyer he first began writing catechetical hymns; he would eventually write some 126 of these works, many of which would appear in larger Catholic hymnals and in the Jesuit Cologne Psalter of 1636. To this day twenty-four of Spee's hymns are used in liturgical books throughout Germany. In 1617 he wrote from Worms to the Jesuit vicar general Mutius Vitelleschi of his willingness to go to India as a missionary in imitation of his boyhood hero, Saint Francis Xavier, but was ordered to concentrate on the needs of the church in Germany.

The witchcraft craze and hysteria had reached such a pitch that any physical deformity made someone suspect; the mere presence of a mole or birthmark was thought to be a sign of the devil's touch. The many witchcraft trials taking place in Worms, Würzburg, Trier, Speyer, and Cologne and the torture of innocent men, women, priests, the poor, the homeless, the disfigured, and the mentally deranged rankled Spee's sense of justice and charity. His interest in these unfortunates increased after his ordination to the priesthood in 1622 and while he was teaching logic, physics, and metaphysics in Paderborn from 1623 to 1626. Even though the local bishops and civil authorities not only condoned the trials but actively supported them, Spee, as priest con-

Frontispiece for Spee's posthumously published guide for the spiritual life

fessor, visited and comforted many of the victims and accompanied them to their executions. Legend has it that he accompanied more than three hundred women to their deaths during his lifetime; the philosopher Gottfried Wilhelm Leibniz says in a letter of 1697 that one such experience turned Spee's hair gray overnight.

Spee was attacked by unknown assailants – presumably Protestants – while riding on horseback to say mass on 29 April 1629 in Woltorf in northern Germany. He suffered gunshot wounds to the head and shoulder. Incredibly, he went on to the church and tried to preach, only to collapse in the pulpit as he began a sermon on the Good Shepherd. During

his convalescence in Falkenhagen and the Benedictine monastery in Corvey he begin to give final shape to *Trutz-Nachtigall* (Defiant Nightingale), which was published posthumously in 1649. *Trutz-Nachtigall* comprises fifty-two poems, including love songs between the spouse and Christ; songs of repentance and sorrow; songs on the birth, suffering, and resurrection of Christ; songs of praise; and a group of spiritual eclogues in imitation of Virgil and classical bucolic poetry. Although highly ornate by modern standards, these poems are considered masterpieces of early baroque religious verse. Most of them were probably written as early as 1620, while Spee was studying theology in Mainz.

Based on his firsthand knowledge of the trials, Spee wrote *Cautio Criminalis* (Precautions in Criminal Matters, 1631), a closely reasoned treatise condemning the trial procedures and tortures. The topics of the fifty-two theses include the rights of the accused, who should be considered innocent until proven guilty; the unjust methods used to produce confessions; and the absurdity of the idea of satanic pacts. Many of Spee's demands anticipate provisions of the United Nations' 1948 declaration of human rights. The publication of the *Cautio Criminalis,* against Spee's wishes, by the University of Rinteln press – at that time under the jurisdiction of the Benedictines of Corvey – would catapult Spee into a sea of troubles and swirling controversy within his own order and from civic and church leaders. His Jesuit rector in Paderborn and his fellow Jesuits denounced Spee, who was accused of fomenting disorder in his conversations with younger Jesuits and students. The local bishops were outraged; the coadjutor bishop of Paderborn, Johannes Pelcking, reported to the bishop of Osnabrück, Franz von Wartenberg, the appearance of this "pestilentissimus liber" (most nefarious book). Spee was transferred from Cologne, where the faculty had fled as a result of the Swedish troops threatening the Jesuits in Paderborn in 1631, to Trier in 1632 at his own request to escape the pressures from his fellow Jesuits. Only one other priest, Cornelius Loos, had had the courage to speak out against the trials; he had done so in 1591 and had been exiled, imprisoned, and forced to recant under the threat of torture.

When *Cautio Criminalis* appeared in a second edition in June 1632, much to the dismay of Vicar General Vitelleschi, who had seemed at first to be sympathetic to Spee, his situation within the order became even more critical. Only the finding of the local provincial and future vicar general, Goswin Nickel, that *Cautio Criminalis* had been published without Spee's knowledge or approval prevented his expulsion from the order; nevertheless, he was never admitted to final religious profession in the Society of Jesus.

It is remarkable that during this period of controversy Spee was able to produce another masterpiece, which, like *Trutz-Nachtigall,* would be published posthumously in 1649. *Güldenes Tugend-Buch* (Golden Book of Virtue) originated in Spee's work as spiritual adviser to secular nuns in the Cologne area in 1627–1628; he gathered these weekly conferences into a guide for the spiritual life based on growth in the theological virtues of faith, hope, and charity. Not surprisingly, *Güldenes Tugend-Buch* re-veals the strong influence of the *Spiritual Exercises* (1548) of Ignatius of Loyola, the founder of the Society of Jesus. Scholars and critics agree that this work is one of the greatest pieces of religious literature of the seventeenth century, and they are still evaluating its impact and message. Leibniz particularly admired its treatment of the distinction between two kinds of love: concupiscence and friendship; he was so taken by both *Güldenes Tugend-Buch* and *Cautio Criminalis* that he wrote a Latin elegy in praise of Spee.

During the great battle for Trier in 1634–1635 Spee acted as priest and confessor to the wounded and dying French invaders. In the process he contracted the plague; he died on 7 August 1635. It was not until 16 October 1980 that his remains were discovered in the crypt of the Jesuit church in Trier.

Bibliographies:
Gerhard Dünnhaupt, *Bibliographisches Handbuch der Barockliteratur,* volume 3 (Stuttgart: Hiersemann, 1981), pp. 1755–1757;
G. Richard Dimler, "Friedrich Spee von Langenfeld: Eine beschreibende Bibliographie. Part I: Ausgaben und Auflagen vor 1750," *Daphnis: Zeitschrift für Mittlere Deutsche Literatur,* 13, no. 4 (1984): 637–722;
Dimler, "Friedrich Spee von Langenfeld: Eine beschreibende Bibliographie. Part II: Forschungsliteratur," *Daphnis: Zeitschrift für Mittlere Deutsche Literatur,* 15, no. 4 (1986): 649–703;
Dünnhaupt, *Personalbibliographien zu den Drucken des Barock,* volume 9, part 5 (Stuttgart: Hiersemann, 1991), pp. 3928–3937.

Biographies:
Joachim-Friedrich Ritter, *Friedrich Spee von Langenfeld: 1591–1635. Ein Edelmann, Mahner und Dichter* (Trier: Spee, 1977);
Walter Rupp, *Friedrich von Spee: Dichter und Kämpfer gegen den Hexenwahn* (Mainz: Matthias-Grünewald, 1986);
Karl-Jürgen Miesen, *Friedrich Spee: Pater, Dichter, Hexen-Anwalt* (Düsseldorf: Froste, 1987);
Karl Keller, *Friedrich Spee von Langenfeld (1591–1635): Leben und Werk des Seelsorgers und Dichters* (Geldern: Keuck, 1990).

References:
Anton Arens, *Friedrich Spee von Langenfeld: Zur Wiederauffindung seines Grabes im Jahre 1980* (Trier: Spee, 1981);

Arens, ed., *Friedrich Spee im Licht der Wissenschaften: Beiträge und Untersuchungen,* Quellen und Abhandlungen zur mittelrheinischen Kirchengeschichte, volume 49 (Mainz: Selbstverlag der Gesellschaft für Mittelrheinische Kirchengeschichte, 1984);

Italo Michele Battafarano, ed., *Friedrich von Spee: Dichter, Theologe und Bekämpfer der Hexenprozesse* (Trent: Reverdito, 1988);

Robert M. Browning, "On the Numerical Composition of Friedrich Spee's 'Trutznachtigall,' " in *Festschrift Detlev W. Schumann zum 70. Geburtstag: Mit Beiträgen von Schülern, Freunden und Kollegen,* edited by Albert R. Schmitt (Munich: Dalp, 1970), pp. 28–39;

G. Richard Dimler, "The Arrow Motif in Friedrich Spee's *Trutznachtigall:* Function, Structure and Style," *Classical Folia: Studies in the Christian Perpetuation of the Classics,* 2 (1972): 279–288;

Dimler, "Death and Sacrament in Friedrich Spee's *Trutznachtigall:* Genesis and Function," *Daphnis: Zeitschrift für Mittlere Deutsche Literatur,* 4, no. 1 (1975): 42–50;

Dimler, *Friedrich Spee's Trutznachtigall,* German Studies in America, no. 13 (Bern & Frankfurt am Main: Lang, 1973);

Dimler, "The Genesis and Development of Friedrich Spee's Love-Imagery in the *Trutznachtigall,*" *Germanic Review,* 48 (March 1973): 87–98;

Dimler, "On the Structure and Composition of Friedrich Spee's *Trutznachtigall,*" *Modern Language Notes,* 89 (October 1974): 787–796;

Martina Eicheldinger, *Friedrich Spee – Seelsorger und poeta doctus: Die Tradition des Hohen Liedes und Einflüsse der ignatianischen Andacht in seinem Werk* (Tübingen: Niemeyer, 1991);

Gunther Franz, ed., *Friedrich Spee Dichter, Seelsorger, Bekämpfer des Hexenwahns Kaiserswerth 1591-*

Trier 1635: Katalog der Ausstellung der in Düsseldorf 1991, second revised edition (Trier: Paulinus, 1991);

Michael Härting, *Friedrich Spee – Die anonymen geistlichen Lieder vor 1623* (Berlin: Schmidt, 1979);

Eric Jacobsen, *Die Metamorphosen der Liebe und Friedrich Spees "Trutznachtigall,"* Studien zum Fortleben der Antike, no. 1 (Copenhagen: Munkegaard, 1954);

Hans Georg Kemper, "Friedrich von Spee," in *Deutsche Dichter des 17. Jahrhunderts: Ihr Leben und Werk,* edited by Harald Steinhagen and Benno von Wiese (Berlin: Schmidt, 1984), pp. 90–115;

Friedrich W. C. Lieder, "Friedrich Spee and the Théodicée of Leibniz," *Journal of English and Germanic Philology,* 11 (April 1912): 149–172; (July 1912): 329–354;

Valentin Probst, ed., *Friedrich Spee-Gedächtnis: Dokumentation anläßlich des 350. Todesjahres. Für die Friedrich-Spee-Gesellschaft Trier* (Trier: Friedrich-Spee-Gesellschaft, 1988);

Friedrich M. Rener, "Friedrich Spee's 'Arcadia' Revisited," *PMLA,* 89 (October 1974): 967–979;

Emmy Rosenfeld, *Friedrich Spee von Langenfeld: Eine Stimme in der Wüste* (Berlin: De Gruyter, 1958);

Rosenfeld, *Neue Studien zur Lyrik von Friedrich von Spee* (Mailand: Cisalpino, 1963);

Rosenfeld, "Theologischer Prozess: Die Rinteler Hexentrostschrift – ein Werk von Friedrich von Spee," *Deutsche Vierteljahrsschrift für Literaturwissenschaft und Geistesgeschichte,* 29 (1955): 37–56;

Hugo J. J. Zwetsloot, *Friedrich Spee und die Hexenprozesse: Die Stellung und Bedeutung der Cautio Criminalis in der Geschichte der Hexenverfolgungen* (Trier: Paulinus, 1954).

Philipp Jakob Spener

(13 January 1635 – 5 February 1705)

John Pustejovsky
Marquette University

SELECTED BOOKS: *Tabulae Progonologicae, quibus Plurimorum Regum Principium Comitum Dominorum . . . degunt Progenitores XXXII.* (Stuttgart: Johann Weyrich Rösslin, 1660);

Theatrum Nobilitatis Europeae, Tabulis Progonologicis Praecipuorum in Cultiori Christiano Orbe Magnatum et Illustrium Progenitores CXXIIX. LXIV aut XXII Justo Ordine Repraesentantibus Exornatum Studio, 4 volumes (Frankfurt am Main: Aegidius Vogel, 1668–1678);

Drei Christliche Predigten von Versuchungen (Frankfurt am Main: David Zunner, 1673); excerpt translated as "The Temptations of Satan (A Sermon on Matth. IV.3)," in *History and Repository of Pulpit Eloquence,* edited by Henry Clay Fish (New York, 1857);

Pia Desideria: Oder herzliches Verlangen nach gottgefälliger Besserung der wahren evangelischen Kirche samt einigen dahin abzweckenden einfältig christlichen Vorschlägen (Frankfurt am Main: David Zunner, 1675); translated by Theodore G. Tappert as *Pia Desideria* (Philadelphia: Fortress, 1964);

Einfältige Erklärung der Christlichen Lehr, nach der Ordnung deß kleinen Catechismi deß theueren Manns Gottes Lutheri (Frankfurt am Main: David Zunner, 1677);

Das geistliche Priesterthum aus göttlichem Wort kürzlich beschreiben und mit einstimmenden Zeugnüssen gottseelige Lehre bekräfftiget (Frankfurt am Main: David Zunner, 1677); translated by A. G. Voigt as *The Spiritual Priesthood* (Philadelphia: Lutheran Publication Committee, 1917);

Sendschreiben an einen Christeyffrigen außländischen Theologum, betreffende die falsche außgesprengte aufflagen, wegen seiner Lehre, und so genanter Collegiorum pietatis (Frankfurt am Main: David Zunner, 1677);

Sylloge Genealogico-Historica è Numero Praecipuorum familiarum (Frankfurt am Main: David Zunner, 1677);

Philipp Jakob Spener; mezzotint by E. Nessenthaler after a drawing by M. C. Steutner (Herzog August Bibliothek Wolfenbüttel)

Zwölff christliche Leichpredigten (Frankfurt am Main: David Zunner, 1677);

Abgenöthigte Erörterungen dreyer Lehr-Puncten (Merseburg: Kaspar Forberger, 1678);

Christliche Bußpredigten (Frankfurt am Main: David Zunner, 1678);

Deß thätigen Christentums Nothwendigkeit und Möglichkeit (Frankfurt am Main: David Zunner, 1680);

Die allgemeine Gottesgelehrtheit aller gläubigen Christen und rechtschaffenen Theologen (Frankfurt am Main: David Zunner, 1680);

Opus heraldicum, 2 volumes (Frankfurt am Main: Johann Dietrich Friedgen, 1680, 1690);

Tabulae Catecheticae, quibus 5 capita catechismi minoris . . . tractantur (Frankfurt am Main: Balthasar Wust the elder, 1683);

Christliche Aufmunterung zur Beständigkeit bei der reinen Lehr des Evangelii (Frankfurt am Main: David Zunner, 1684);

Die Evangelische Glaubens-Gerechtigkeit von Herrn D. Joh. Brevings vergeblichen Angriffen gerettet (Frankfurt am Main: David Zunner, 1684);

Der Klagen über das verdorbene Christenthum mißbrauch und rechter gebrauch, darinnen auch ob unsere Kirche die wahre Kirche oder Babel, und ob sich von deroselben zu trennen nöthig, gehandelt wird. Samt zweyen Anhängen (Frankfurt am Main: David Zunner, 1685);

Die lautere Milch des Evangelii (Frankfurt am Main: David Zunner, 1685);

Christliche Leichpredigten, 13 volumes (Frankfurt am Main: David Zunner, 1685–1707);

Ander Theil Christlicher Buß-Predigten (Frankfurt am Main: David Zunner, 1686);

Der innerliche und geistliche Friede (Frankfurt am Main: David Zunner, 1686);

Natur und Gnade, oder der Unterscheid der Wercke, so aus natürlichen Kräfften und aus den gnaden-Würkungen des H. Geistes herkommen (Frankfurt am Main, 1687);

Die Evangelische Glaubens-Lehre (Frankfurt am Main: David Zunner, 1688);

Kurze Katechismuspredigten (Frankfurt am Main: David Zunner, 1689);

Abgenötigte Rettung seiner reinen Lehre wider Dan. Hartnacci Beschuldigungen (Frankfurt am Main: David Zunner, 1690);

Erfordertes Theologisches Bedencken, über den von einigen des E. Hamburgischen Ministerii publicirten Neuen Religions-Eid (Plön: Thomas Schmitt, 1690);

Christliche Trau-Sermonen (Frankfurt am Main: David Zunner, 1691);

Die Freyheit der Gläubigen, von dem Ansehen der Menschen in Glaubens-Sachen (Frankfurt am Main: David Zunner, 1691);

Schriftlicher Kern evang. Andachten (Helmstedt, 1691);

Die evangelischen Lebenspflichten (Frankfurt am Main: David Zunner, 1692); excerpts translated by Peter Erb as "Meditations on the Suffering of Christ," "Resignation," "God-Pleasing Prayer," and "Christian Joy," in *Pietists: Selected Writings,* edited by Erb (New York: Paulist Press, 1983), pp. 76–96;

Sieg der Wahrheit und der Unschuld (Berlin: Schrey & Meyer, 1692);

Theologisches Bedencken über einige Puncten (N.p., 1692);

Die Seligkeit der Kinder Gottes (Frankfurt am Main: David Zunner, 1692);

Väterliches Vermahnungs-Schreiben, an seinen lieben Sohn in Leipzig (Leipzig: Johann Heinich, 1692);

Sprüche Heiliger Schrifft, welche von welt-leuten mehrmal zur hegung, und wider die so nothwendigkeit als möglichkeit des wahren innerlichen und thätigen Christenthums, mißbraucht zu werden pflegen, kürtzlich, aber gründlich gerettet (Frankfurt am Main: David Zunner, 1693);

Behauptung der Hoffnung künfftiger Besserer Zeiten (Frankfurt am Main: David Zunner, 1693);

Gründliche Beantwortung einer mit Lästerungen angefüllten Schrifft (Frankfurt am Main: David Zunner, 1693);

Das nötige und nützliche Lesen der Heiligen Schrifft (Leipzig: Johann Heinich's widow, 1695); excerpts translated by Erb as "The Necessary and Useful Reading of the Holy Scriptures," in *Pietists: Selected Writings,* edited by Erb (New York: Paulist Press, 1983), pp. 71–75;

Der Evangelische Glaubens-Trost (Frankfurt am Main: David Zunner, 1695);

Der hochwichtige Articul von der Wiedergeburt (Frankfurt am Main: David Zunner, 1696);

Rettung der gerechten Sache kunftiger Hoffnung besserer Zeiten (Frankfurt am Main: David Zunner, 1696);

Der wahre seligmachende Glaube (Frankfurt am Main: David Zunner, 1696);

Frommer Christen erfreuliche Himmels Lust, by Spener and others (N.p., 1696);

Christliche Verpflegung der Armen, als aus Churfürstl. gnädigster Verordnung das Gassen-Bettlen in den Churfl. Residentz-Städten abgeschaft, und zu liebreicherer Versorgung der Bedürfftigen Anstalt gemacht, auch dieselbe öffentlich der Gemeinde angezeiget worden . . . Sambt einem Anhang (Frankfurt am Main: Schrey & Hartmann, 1697);

Erklährung der Epistel an die Galater (Frankfurt am Main: David Zunner & Johann Adam Jung, 1697);

Wahrhaftige Erzählung dessen, was wegen des sogenannten Pietismi in Deutschland vor einiger Zeit vorgegangen (Frankfurt am Main: David Zunner, 1697);

Des Hocherleuchteten Apostels und Evangelisten Johannis Erste Epistel (Halle: Waisenhaus, 1699);

Erste Geistliche Schrifften, die vor dem in kleinem Format eintzeln heraus gegeben worden (Frankfurt am Main: David Zunner, 1699);

Das berühmte Bußgebet des H. Propheten Danielis, Cap. IX, 1–23 (Frankfurt am Main: David Zunner, 1700);

Briefe und Gutachten, gesammelt in den Theologischen Bedenken, 4 volumes (Halle: Waisenhaus, 1700–1702);

Das nötige und nützliche Lesen der Heiligen Schrifft, mit einigen dazu dienlichen Erinnerungen, in einer Vorrede über die Bibel vorgestellet. Und nun absonderlich gedruckt (Frankfurt am Main & Leipzig: Johann Heinich's widow, 1704);

Erklärung der Episteln an die Epheser und Colosser . . . wie auch einige . . . Pastoral-Predigten (Halle: Waisenhaus, 1706);

Predigten uber des seeligen Johann Arnds Geistreiche Bücher Vom Wahren Christenthum (Frankfurt am Main: David Zunner's sons, 1706);

Vertheidigung des Zeugnüsses von der Ewigen Gottheit unsers Herrn Jesu Christi, als des Eingebohrnen Sohns von Vater, von dem nun in Gott ruhenden . . . (Frankfurt am Main: David Zunner, 1706);

Die Evangelische Lebens-Pflichten in einem Jahrgang der Predigten bey den Sonn- und Fest-Täglichen ordentlichen Evangelien aus H. Göttlicher Schrifft . . . in der Furcht des Herrn vorgetragen (Frankfurt am Main: David Zunner, 1707);

Geistreiche Gesänge, welche Spener zu seiner Erweckung in dem Geist Christi gedichtet (Halle, 1708);

Consilia et Judicia Theologica Latina (Frankfurt am Main: David Zunner, 1709);

Christliche Passions-Predigten (Frankfurt am Main: David Zunner & Johann Adam Jung, 1709);

Letzte theologische Bedencken und andere brieffliche Antworten, edited by Karl Hildebrand von Canstein (Halle: Waisenhaus, 1711);

Drey Christliche Predigten von Versuchungen . . . (Frankfurt am Main: David Zunner, 1712);

Catechismus-Tabellen. Darinnen der gantze Catechismus D. Martin Luthers deutlich und gründlich erkläret . . . Aus dem Lateinischen ins Teutsche übersetzet, und mit einigen Einleitungs-Tabellen vermehret, edited by I. G. Pritio (Frankfurt am Main: David Zunner & Johann Adam Jung, 1717);

Lehrreiche Zuschrifft an seine Frau Tochter von denen nöthigen Pflichten einer jeden sonderlich aber einer Priester-Frau . . . Nebst einer Vorrede (Leipzig: Michael Blochberger, 1731);

Tugend-Spiegel christlicher Jungfrauen (Augsburg: David Raimund Mertz & Johann Jacob Mayer, 1737);

Bis anhero nur eintzeln gedruckt gewesene Kleine Geistliche Schriften, nunmehro in einige Bände zusammengetragen, und mit des seligen Mannes ausführlichen Lebens-Beschreibung, Historisch-Theologischen Einleitungen, auch nöthigen Vorreden und Registern, 2 volumes (Magdeburg & Leipzig: Christoph

Seidel's widow & Georg Ernst Scheidhauer, 1741, 1742).

Editions and Collections: *Memoirs of Ph. J. Spener,* revised by the Committee of Publication (Philadelphia: Sunday School Union, 1830);

Hauptschriften Philipp Jakob Speners, edited by Paul Grünberg, Bibliothek theologischer Klassiker, volume 21 (Gotha: Perthes, 1889);

Schriften, 7 volumes published, edited by Erich Beyreuther (Hildesheim: Olms, 1979–).

Editions in English: "The Spiritual Priesthood," translated by Peter Erp, in *Pietists: Selected Writings,* edited by Erb (New York: Paulist Press, 1983), pp. 50–64.

OTHER: "Christliches Gebet in gegenwärtiger Not und Gefahr der Kirchen zum Gebrauch gottseliger Haushaltungen," in *Zwei christliche Gebete* (Frankfurt am Main: David Zunner, 1694);

Balthasar Köpke, trans., *Dialogus de Templo Salomonis, das ist: Ein Geistliches Gespräch von der Heiligung und deroselben dreyen Stuffen . . . aus dem Fürbilde des Tempels Salomo, und dessen dreyen Vorhöffen . . . beschrieben . . . Aus dem Lateinischen in die deutsche Sprach übersetzt,* foreword by Spener (Neuruppin: Mahler, 1695).

Universally recognized as the "father of Pietism" and considered perhaps the single most important German religious figure since Martin Luther, Philipp Jakob Spener achieved this significance neither through theological genius nor an extraordinary personality. Rather he stands at the threshold of the age when, as F. Ernest Stoeffler puts it, "Reformed and Lutheran churches . . . lost touch with vital concerns of religion, concentrating their efforts on the attempt to answer questions which were no longer being asked"; and throughout a lifetime in the church he focused and fostered the impulses for reform that had been gathering for more than a century. But unlike others before him, Spener articulated his vision as a broad and coherent model of human life based on sincere Christian piety and intense self-reflection. In preaching, catechesis, and writing, he rooted his idea of reform in the experiences of a Christian life. Throughout his own life he defended this vision in learned theological argument, aligning it at every opportunity with Luther's writings. His loyalty to Luther's vision notwithstanding, having gained notoriety as the author of *Pia Desideria: Oder herzliches Verlangen nach gottgefälliger Besserung der wahren evangelischen Kirche samt einigen dahin abzweckenden einfältig christlichen Vorschlägen* (Pia

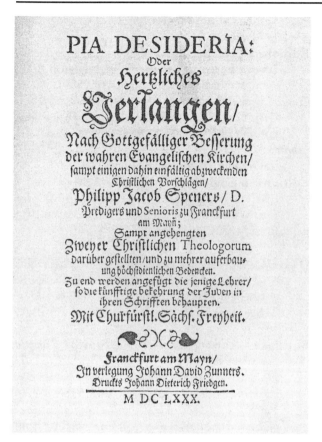

PIA DESIDERIA:
Oder
Hertzliches
Verlangen/
Nach Gottgefälliger Besserung
der wahren Evangelischen Kirchen/
sampt einigen dahin einfältig abzweckenden
Christlichen Vorschlägen/
Philipp Jacob Speners/ D.
Predigers und Senioris zu Franckfurt
am Mayn;
Sampt angehengten
Zweyer Christlichen Theologorum
Darüber gestellten/und zu mehrer auferbau-
ung höchstdienlichen Bedencken.
Zu end werden angefügt die jenige Lehrer/
so die künfftige bekehrung der Juden in
ihren Schrifften behaupten.
Mit Churfürstl.Sächß.Freyheit.

Franckfurt am Mayn/
In verlegung Johann David Zunners.
Druckts Johann Dieterich Friedgen.
M DC LXXX.

Title page for a 1680 edition of Spener's plan for the reform of the Lutheran Church

Desideria; or, Heartfelt Desire for a God-pleasing Reform of the True Evangelical Church, Together with Several Simple Christian Proposals Looking toward this End, 1675; translated 1964), Spener was for the rest of his life forced to clarify his own position between highly conservative Lutheran orthodoxy, on the one hand, and those whose vision of reformed Christianity was far more radical than his own, on the other. By placing his immense literary productivity in the service of his pastoral commitment, Spener became the seminal figure in the explosive, nondogmatic reappropriation of the tenets of Christian faith, its Scripture, and its view of history that was to occupy intellectuals and simple people alike in Europe and North America for the next century.

Spener was born on 13 January 1635 to the civil servant Johann Philip Spener and Agatha Spener, née Saltzmann, in the Alsatian town of Rappoltsweiler. He grew up in an atmosphere of ascetic Christianity and even in childhood devoted much time to inspirational reading. Johann Arndt's *Wahres Christentum* (True Christianity, 1606) and Lewis Bayly's *The Practice of Pietie* (1611), as well as works

of Emanuel Sonthomb and Daniel Dyke, were all well known to him. He seems to have been particularly impressed by the English authors' emphasis on the "blessed state" of true believers. Spener's biographer Paul Grünberg notes that this reading, together with the piety of his family, fostered in him both a serious disposition and an enthusiastic acknowledgment of the power of Christianity to engage individuals completely.

In 1651 he began studies at the University of Strasbourg, devoting himself initially to languages, philosophy, and history. He also cultivated interests in heraldry and genealogy. It was through these interests that he found access to noble circles, where he would move with ease throughout his life. His family had determined that he would pursue a career in the church, and Spener proved an ambitious student of theology. Among his teachers in Strasbourg, Johann Konrad Dannhauer was particularly influential. From him Spener heard criticisms of the abuses being tolerated in the Lutheran Church; he would later cite Dannhauer repeatedly in questions of ethics and dogma. From the end of his studies in 1659 until 1662 he traveled through southern Germany and Switzerland; in 1660, while in Geneva, he frequently attended the sermons of Jean de Labadie, the former Jesuit who had joined the Reformed Church. Even before his return from these travels Spener was offered a pastor's position in Strasbourg. Unsure of his ability to handle the burden of pastoral duties, he wavered until he was offered the position of *Freiprediger* (occasional preacher). This position permitted him to complete his doctoral studies; on 23 June 1664, the day he publicly defended his dissertation, he married Susanna Erhard, nine years his junior. (He had earlier expressed the desire to marry a widow, as he considered himself too serious to be able to please a younger woman.)

As it emerges in his sermons and later reminiscences, Spener's service in Strasbourg prefigures the issues that were to occupy him for the rest of his life. The most important of these issues was his conviction that all articles of faith should both reflect the doctrine on which they rest and foster the practice of that faith. Despite his enormous and lifelong devotion to theology, Spener always remained less interested in theological innovation for its own sake than in articulating the experiential nature of personal faith so as to make it the measure of all things, including doctrine.

In 1666, after several months of characteristic indecisiveness, Spener accepted the position of superintendent of the Lutheran ministry of Frankfurt am Main. In the prosperous inhabitants of this large commercial center Spener found much to criticize: excesses of luxury, laxness in sexual morality, and violation of Sunday observance by the conduct of commerce. In matters directly related to the church he found that the effects of preaching (insofar as it was not simply devoted to attacks on one's theological opponents) were negligible, owing to the laity's ignorance of even basic questions of faith. Catechesis, where it did exist, was most often in the hands of a poorly educated, unmotivated local schoolteacher, and the quality of instruction was lamentable. Equally lamentable was the fact that exclusion from Communion was the church's most common weapon against sinners. Spener pressed the Frankfurt magistrates to enforce a stricter observance of the Sabbath, especially by prohibiting trading on Sunday during the semiannual trade fairs. He prevailed on the local ministry to introduce confirmation, which had been only infrequently practiced. He himself undertook to reinvigorate the teaching of the catechism, making a practice of including the lesson in his Sunday sermon and testing children on their knowledge of the catechism.

In 1669 Spener observed in a sermon the small difference preaching alone seemed to be able to effect in these conditions. How useful it would be, he speculated, if, instead of spending Sunday in boisterous drinking, cardplaying, or revelry, small groups of Christians would gather to read edifying books or discuss a sermon; those to whom more has been given by God could instruct their weaker brethren. The following year a handful of respected laymen approached Spener with the wish to converse openly and freely on spiritual matters and to establish deeper friendships based on spiritual affinity. Spener discussed the request with his colleagues and found no opposition. The *collegium pietatis* began meeting twice weekly at Spener's house in the summer of 1670. The meetings opened with prayer, followed by a reading of the Sunday sermon or edifying literature. The group included women and men, separated by a partition; only the men were permitted to speak. Word of Spener's conventicle spread quickly through Frankfurt. As it was open to all without regard to class or status, and because many strangers regularly attended, the idea of fostering deeper spiritual friendships was soon abandoned. Beginning in 1675 only the Bible was read.

The reorganized conventicle represented a concrete step toward a practical reform group within the church. In the spring of 1675 Spener set a comprehensive argument for reform before the public. *Pia Desideria* first appeared as an introduction to a work by Arndt; by autumn 1675 it had been pub-

lished as a separate title. Spener commented in later years that *Pia Desideria* contained nearly all of the ideas that he sought to foster throughout his life. Its effectiveness, according to Stoeffler, lay in the fact that Spener had gone beyond his predecessors' and contemporaries' well-meaning but indiscriminate criticism of the church's condition and offered a plan of action. By the time of Spener's death in 1705, it had appeared in four editions as well as in a Latin translation.

The plan of *Pia Desideria* is straightforward: Spener offers a diagnosis, a prognosis, and a prescription. Its argumentation is elegantly simple. Two principal dangers face the evangelical church, he says. The first is the persecution of true doctrine at the hands of the Roman church; the second is the deplorable condition in which the evangelical church finds itself. In each of its three estates it reveals some profound defect. Civil authorities, where they do not choose simply to hold that they have nothing to do with anything but temporal matters, too often see their duty merely in protecting the purity of doctrine and stopping the influx of false religion. Some are guilty of an irresponsible "caesaropapism" and obstruct the work of godly men. Spener's assessment of the clergy is far stronger: just as one knows, when one sees a tree whose leaves are faded and withering, that there is something wrong with the roots, so when one sees that the people are undisciplined, one must realize that their priests are not holy. Spener identifies in them a worldly spirit, marked by worldly abuses: they seek advancement, move from parish to parish, and engage in all kinds of machinations. The apex of theology, to judge by their behavior, consists in disputation. Scandalous as these things are, an even greater scandal is caused when people get the notion that what they see in their preachers must be real Christianity. Grave offenses are also found among the laity: drunkenness, litigiousness, unscrupulous practices in business, and the unjustifiable inequalities between rich and poor. Spener laments the number of Christians who live a manifestly un-Christian life yet are firmly convinced that they will be saved by faith alone.

Spener's assessment is far-reaching and harsh. But far from concluding that the evangelical church has returned to Babel, Spener reminds his readers it was not enough for the Jews to leave their Babylonian exile; they were expected to restore the temple and its beautiful services. He encourages Christians to be thankful for being delivered from Rome but to correct the defects that still remain in their church. Spener's goal is not a church marked by the purity of its doctrine and its members' blameless conduct but a church marked by visible proofs of its saving faith. As proof that this goal is attainable, he refers to the example of the early Christian church. Were the modern church to become more like this model, it would rightfully anticipate the "better conditions" promised in Scripture. He urges Christians to let God work through them. It depends on all of us, he says, and even if we cannot bring about the conversion of the Jews or the fall of Babel-Rome, we can at least do as much as possible.

The book's third part offers six practical suggestions for improving the church. First, Spener calls for families to read Scripture at home or to gather for public readings. He also suggests a return to the church meetings described by Saint Paul: under the leadership of a minister, members of a congregation could read and discuss each verse to discover its meaning and whatever might be useful in it. Second, he urges the establishment and diligent exercise of the spiritual priesthood. In good works, but, more important, in a loving practice of exhorting, chastising, converting, and inspiring others, individuals will carry out the tasks originally given to all members of the church. Third, Christianity must be seen to consist not only in knowledge, but also in practice. Spener reminds his readers that love is the whole life of the person who has faith and declares that if one puts this love into practice, all that one desires will be accomplished. Fourth, he suggests that less energy be devoted to religious controversies. Errors in doctrine should be corrected, but the purpose of disputation should always be the conversion of one's opponents and the awakening of a holy obedience and gratitude to God. A fifth recommendation is for improvements in the education and spiritual formation of clergy. Intellectual training should be secondary to the formation of a genuine personal piety. The final recommendation is also directed at the clergy: preaching should not be an opportunity for demonstrating one's learning and rhetorical skill. Sermons should be prepared so that faith and its fruits will be awakened in one's listeners.

Models and sources for the *Pia Desideria* have been suggested, none convincingly. According to Johannes Wallmann, Spener caused the diagnosis and prescription to rest on the prognosis, the promise of better times. This point, which occupies only a few pages, has no known predecessor and makes the book unlike previous calls for church reform. Modest though it seems, its importance to Spener cannot be overstated. For without the certainty derived from the promise of better times, he admitted late in

his life, he would have been able to find no confidence in the word of God. In this hope of better times for the church, Spener turns away from the traditional expectation of an imminent Second Coming, an expectation expressed by Luther. The hope of better times for the church provides a temporal reprieve before the end, and therein lies the Christian's last chance. The Christian must sense the *Bewegung* (movement) of God in himself or herself and permit himself or herself to become God's instrument in history. This idea is altogether new in Protestant thought.

The literary impact of the *Pia Desideria* was enormous, not least because Spener's suggestions appeared to be of a practical nature and were set forth without rancor or contentiousness. Within four years Spener had received more than three hundred letters supporting his positions. Fellow theologians and ministers published similar calls for reform. Still, a year after the publication of the book, Spener commented that its success was more literary than real. He began to doubt that real reform could be furthered by civil authorities or brought about by the institutional church. Moreover, Spener could not control the uses others made of his writings or of the collegia pietatis. Try as he might to avoid giving false impressions of the nature of the conventicles, the gatherings became the subject of gossip and derision in Frankfurt. Women and young girls, it was rumored, were allowed to learn Greek and to preach; housewives supposedly neglected their family responsibilities to attend the meetings; men and women were said to dance naked before each other to demonstrate how fleshly desires had been mortified. Soon other conventicles were meeting, under the direction of figures far less cautious than Spener. Among these was one led by Johanna Eleonora von Merlau (later Petersen). On Spener's advice, she discontinued it, but she kept up her "work of edification" with young children. The number of conventicles in other German cities continued to grow. By contrast, Spener's actual ideas flourished in the small territorial principalities, where Spener moved easily among the nobility and where a ruler friendly to Pietist ideas could easily overrule a cautious or reactionary church ministry.

It gradually became apparent to others in the church that the "hope of better times" subordinated doctrine to a profound but entirely subjective experience of faith. Spener insisted on the primacy of such experience, asking how one who had had a personal experience of the working of God in time could be guilty of a fundamental error. The Frankfurt magistrates continued to receive complaints of

Frontispiece and title page for a posthumously published work by Spener

unauthorized preaching and heterodox teachings. Spener intervened to prevent the expulsion of Merlau in 1678, and he felt increasingly pressured to defend the ideas that had created such unusual activity.

In 1677 he did so in *Das geistliche Priesterthum* (translated as *The Spiritual Priesthood,* 1917), in which he explored a suggestion he had expressed in the *Pia Desideria.* While emphasizing that "spiritual priesthood" was not intended to encourage a separation from the church or a disdain for ordained ministers, Spener stresses that priesthood is common to all, as the gifts of the Spirit are common to all. Most significant is Spener's account of how the priesthood is initiated: by letting our souls and bodies be temples and abodes of God, by allowing our reason to be brought into captivity, by surrendering our will to the divine will, and by making a sacrifice of our spirits and souls in true repentance. Here can be found the criteria for "true obedience" that would be used by the Pietists both in self-observation and in assessment of the behavior of others. A second printing of *Das geistliche Priesterthum* was interdicted until the elector of Saxony intervened.

Spener's last years in Frankfurt were made difficult by his more-radical friends. The jurist Johann Jakob Schütz, one of the members of the original collegium, had since 1676 refused to take Communion, owing to the many "unworthy" people who also participated. Spener tolerated this behavior and maintained his friendship with Schütz even when the latter ceased to attend services altogether. He was forced to break with Schütz, however, when comments from Schütz's circle scandalized even Spener's orthodox beliefs. In *Der Klagen über das verdorbene Christenthum mißbrauch und rechter gebrauch* (The Abuse and Proper Use of the Complaints concerning Corrupted Christianity, 1685), he argued that those who clearly see the weaknesses of the church are obliged to remain within it and serve their brothers in humility. Sharing the sacraments with those who are unworthy does not, he says, corrupt one who is worthy. But the confrontation with the separatist wing brought about the end of the collegium pietatis in Frankfurt. In the end only Spener and theology students were permitted to speak.

In his last years in Frankfurt, as well as in Dresden, where he became chief court chaplain to the elector in 1686, Spener continued to examine the experiential aspects of faith. In a sermon on Christian joy published in 1692 he declares that the assurance of divine grace is accompanied by joy, which is felt in the soul itself. Often the joy passes quickly, like a lightning bolt. The fruit of joy is that it incites one to praise and honor of God in singing and makes one ready and eager to do good. Sadness, moreover, comes from unbelief. This association of minute psychological self-observation and spirituality was to become the norm in German Pietism and would prove tremendously influential on eighteenth-century thinkers.

Spener's move to Dresden did not bring him the opportunities for reform he had hoped to find there. The elector, whose excesses were well known, disliked him immediately, and Spener's influence on the court and the church was minimal. Having accepted this disappointment, he devoted himself to reforming catechism instruction and continued to write in support of his reforms. By 1691 he had freed himself from the uncomfortable position in Dresden and become provost of the church of Saint Nicholas in Berlin. There his official responsibilities were minimal, and he took up his literary activities with enormous vigor. He published many catechetical works and edited collections of his sermons. Equally important, he maintained contact with Pietist groups throughout Germany and abroad. By this time the Pietist cause was beginning to take advantage of the network of believers scattered throughout the country. In this "church within the church," the "brethren" responded by assisting in publishing enterprises and seeing to the appointment of their own in ministries and, especially, in the theological faculties of universities. Spener himself was able to effect the appointment of August Hermann Francke, Paul Anton, and Joachim J. Breithaupt to the faculty of the new University of Halle.

Spener had by this time become the "patron of Pietism," as Wallmann puts it. He saw the phenomenal growth of the Pietist institutions Francke established at Halle: the orphanage, the schools, the seminary, and the publishing house. Carl Hinrichs has described how the Prussian state encouraged Pietism to further its own political ends, but the reverse was also true. Thanks to Spener's "hope of better times," soldiers, civil servants, state authorities, and citizens could be seen as participating in the work of God through their service to the state.

Spener died on 5 February 1705. It is perhaps paradoxical that one whose literary output and influence were so enormous should be best known today as the author of the slender *Pia Desideria,* a work that is itself more often mentioned than read. Admittedly, many of his works were rooted in now-forgotten controversies of the time. Spener's significance, though, speaks much less in the works themselves than in the example of religious vocation he provided: of intellect, learning, and faith speaking on behalf of the individual's inner experience and of untiring efforts to reshape church, society, and institutions to conform to the truth of this inner experience.

Letters:

Litterarum a Spenero ad A. H. Franckium, edited by A. Tholuck (Halle: Universitätsprogramm, 1854);

Wenn du könntest glauben: Ausschnitte aus seinen Briefen, edited by Hans-Georg Feller (Stuttgart: Steinkopf, 1960);

Briefe aus der Frankfurter Zeit 1666–1686, edited by Johannes Wallmann (Tübingen: Mohr-Siebeck, 1992).

Biographies:

Konrad Gottfried Blanckenberg, *Das Leben der Gläubigen* (Frankfurt am Main, 1705), pp. 28–34;

Karl Hildebrand von Canstein, *Das Muster eines rechtschaffenen Lehrers oder ausführliche und erbauliche Lebensbeschreibung . . . D. Phil. Jakobs Speners* (Frankfurt am Main & Leipzig, 1729);

Paul Grünberg, *Philipp Jakob Spener,* 3 volumes (Göttingen: Vandenhoeck & Ruprecht, 1893–1906; reprinted, Hildesheim: Olms, 1988).

References:

Kurt Aland, "Philipp Jakob Spener und die Anfänge des Pietismus," *Pietismus und Neuzeit,* 4 (1979): 155–189;

Ernst Beyreuther, *Frömmigkeit und Theologie: Gesammelte Aufsätze zum Pietismus und zur Erweckungsbewegung* (Hildesheim: Olms, 1980);

Dietrich Blaufuß, *Pietismus-Forschungen: Zu Philipp Jakob Spener und zum spiritualistisch-radikalpietistischen Umfeld* (Frankfurt am Main: Peter Lang, 1986);

Peter C. Erb, *Pietists, Protestants and Mysticism: The Use of Late Medieval Spiritual Texts in the Work of Gottfried Arnold (1666–1714)* (Metuchen, N.J.: Scarecrow Press, 1989);

Mary Fulbrook, *Piety and Politics: Religion and the Rise of Absolutism in England, Württemberg and Prussia* (Cambridge: Cambridge University Press, 1983);

Martin Greschat, ed., *Zur neueren Pietismusforschung* (Darmstadt: Wissenschaftliche Buchgesellschaft, 1977);

Hans R. G. Günther, "Psychologie des deutschen Pietismus," *Deutsche Vierteljahrsschrift für Literaturwissenschaft und Geistesgeschichte,* 4, no. 1 (1926): 144–176;

Carl Hinrichs, *Preußentum und Pietismus: Der Pietismus in Brandenburg-Preußen als religiös-soziale Reformbewegung* (Göttingen: Vandenhoeck & Ruprecht, 1971);

Gerhard Kaiser, *Pietismus und Patriotismus im literarischen Deutschland: Ein Beitrag zum Problem der Säkularisation* (Wiesbaden: Steiner, 1961);

Friedrich Wilhelm Kantzenbach, *Orthodoxie und Pietismus* (Gütersloh: Mohn, 1966);

Hans-Georg Kemper, *Deutsche Lyrik der frühen Neuzeit,* volume 5.I: *Aufklärung und Pietismus* (Tübingen: Niemeyer, 1991);

Erhard Kunz, *Protestantische Eschatologie: Von der Reformation bis zur Aufklärung* (Freiburg: Herder, 1980);

August Langen, *Zum Wortschatz des deutschen Pietismus* (Tübingen: Niemeyer, 1968);

John Pustejovsky, "Iterating the Eschaton: Pietism and the New Myth of Sacred History," *Daphnis,* 19, no. 3 (1990): 471–491;

Martin Schmidt, *Der Pietismus als theologische Erscheinung* (Göttingen: Vandenhoeck & Ruprecht, 1984);

F. Ernest Stoeffler, *German Pietism during the Eighteenth Century* (Leiden: Brill, 1973);

Stoeffler, *The Rise of Evangelical Pietism* (Leiden: Brill, 1965);

Johannes Wallmann, *Philipp Jakob Spener und die Anfänge des Pietismus* (Tübingen: Mohr, 1970);

Wallmann, *Der Pietismus* (Göttingen: Vandenhoeck & Ruprecht, 1990).

Papers:
Philipp Jakob Spener's manuscripts and letters are held by libraries and archives in Augsburg, Berlin, Frankfurt am Main, Hamburg, Karlsruhe, Kempten, Kaliningrad, Leipzig, and Tübingen.

Caspar Stieler

(25 March 1632 – 24 June 1707)

Judith P. Aikin
University of Iowa

BOOKS: *De calido innato. Exercitatio onomatologica* (Erfurt: Paul Michael, 1649);

Die Geharnschte Venus oder Liebes-Lieder im Kriege gedichtet mit neuen Gesang-Weisen zu singen und zu spielen gesezzet nebenst ettlichen Sinnreden der Liebe Verfertiget und lustigen Gemüthern zu Gefallen heraus gegeben, as Filidor der Dorfferer (Hamburg: Printed by Michael Pfeiffer, published by Christian Guth, 1660);

Der Vermeinte Printz. Lustspiel, denen beyden Hochgräflichen Ehelich vertrauten als: Dem Hochgebohrnen Grafen und Herrn, Herren Albert Anthon, der vier Grafen des Reichs, Grafen zu Schwartzburg und Hohenstein, Herrn zu Arnstadt, Sondershausen, Leutenberg, Lohra und Clettenberg, &c. Wie auch, der gleichfalls Hochgebohrnen Gräfin und Freulein, Fr. Emilien Julianen, Gräfin und Freulein zu Barby und Mühlingen, etc. Auff deren Hochgr. Hochgr. Gn. Gn. Hochansehnlichen Grafl. Beylager, den siebenden Brachmonatst. 1665. Hochfeyerlich begangen, auff dem grossen Saale des Hochgräfl. Schlosses Heydeck in Rudolstadt, zu unterthänigen Ehren und gnädigen gefallen, treugehorsamst vorgestellet, anonymous (Rudolstadt: Caspar Freyschmidt, 1665);

Ernelinde MischSpiel bey dem Höchstverlangten und glücklichst angestelleten Beylagers Feste deß Hochgebornen Grafen und Herrn Herren Albert Anthon der vier Grafen des Reichs, Grafen zu Schwartzburg und Hohenstein, Herrn zu Arnstadt, Sondershausen, Leutenberg, Lohra und Clettenberg, &c. mit der auch Hochgebohrnen Gräfin und Fräulein, Fr. Emilien Julianen . . . So den 7ten Brachmonatstag in Rudolstadt mit Christ-Gräfl. Pracht hochfeyerlich begangen wurde jn dem grossen Saale deß Gräfl. Residentz Schlosses Heydeck unterthänig vorgestellt und auffgeführt, anonymous (Rudolstadt: Caspar Freyschmidt, 1665);

Die Wittekinden. Singe- und Freuden-Spiel. Von des Hochlöblichen Gräfflichen Schwartzburgischen Uhralten Hauses Auffnehmen, Fortwachsen und

Caspar Stieler; engraving by Cornelius Nikolaus Shurts after a drawing by Johann David Herlicus

Christenthum. Zu untertähnigen Ehren und gnädigen Gefallen dem Hochgebohrnen Grafen und Herrn Herrn Albert Anthonen der vier Grafen des Reichs, Grafen zu Schwartzburg und Hohenstein, Herrn zu Arnstadt, Sondershausen, Leutenberg, Lohra und Clettenberg, &c. als seine Hochgräfliche Gnaden das fünff- und zwantzigste Jahr ihres Alters mit Gesundheit und glücklichen Hochergehen antraten, auff dero Gräflichen Schlosse Heydeck vorgestellet den 2. Mertz. Im Jahr 1666, anonymous (Jena: Published by Johann Ludwig Neuenhahn, printed by Samuel Krebs, 1666);

Die erfreüete Unschuld. MischSpiel. Zu untertähniger [sic] *Glückwüntschender Freude, über den abermahls frölich erlebten Gebuhrts-Tag, der Hochgebohrnen*

Gräfin, und Freulein, Freulein Sophien Julianen, Gräfin zu Schwartzburg und Hohenstein, Herrn zu Arnstadt, Sondershausen, Leutenberg, Lohra und Clettenberg, &c. auf dem grossen Saale der Gräflichen Residentz Heydeck zu Rudelstadt [sic] gehorsamst vorgestellet, den dritten Tag des Mertzens, jm Jahr 1666., anonymous (Jena: Published by Johann Ludwig Neuenhahn, printed by Samuel Krebs, 1666);

Basilene. Lust-Spiel. Zu sonderbahren unterthänigen Ehren und Gnädigen gefallen dem Hochgeb. Graffen und Herrn, Herrn Albert Anthonen der vier Grafen des Reichs, Grafen zu Schwartzburg und Hohenstein, Herrn zu Arnstadt, Sondershausen, Leutenberg, Lohra und Clettenberg, &c. als seine Hochgräflichen Gnaden das 26. Jahr ihres Ruhmvollen Alters glücklich abgelegt und das 27. darauf fröhlich angetreten. Auf dero Gräfl. Residentz . . . Rudolstadt den 2. Mertz, anonymous (Rudolstadt: Printed by Caspar Freyschmidt, 1667);

Der betrogene Betrug: Lustspiel, anonymous (Rudolstadt: Printed by Caspar Freyschmidt, 1667);

Vortrab des Allzeitertigen Sekretariens. Das ist: Ein Versuch, wie allerhand Schreiben, höflich und geschicklich, jedoch kurz, und gleichsam mit flüchtiger Feder, abzufaßen. Denen Anfängern zum Behuf und vernünftiger Nachfolge heraus gegeben, und einem ausführlichern Werk, als wie zur Ausspähung vorgesändet, anonymous (Eisenach: Johann Günther Rörer, 1673);

Teutsche Sekretariat-Kunst, was sie sey, worvon sie handele, was darzu gehöre, welcher Gestalt zu derselben glück- und gründlich zugelangen, was Maßen ein Sekretarius beschaffen seyn solle, worinnen deßen Amt, Verrichtung, Gebühr und Schuldigkeit bestehe, auch was zur Schreibfertigkeit und rechtschaffener Briefstellung eigentlich und vornehmlich erfordert werde, as der Spahte, 2 volumes (Nuremberg: Published by Johann Hofmann, printed in Weimar by Joachim Heinrich Schmidt, 1673, 1674; enlarged edition, Jena: Johann Nisius, 1681; enlarged again, Nuremberg: Published by Johann Hoffmann's widow & Engelbert Streck, printed in Frankfurt am Main by Johann Philipp Andreä, 1705);

Der teutsche Advocat, oder Lehrschrift, anzeigend: Auf was Weyse ein rechtlicher Beystand in Teutschland, so wol vor Gericht, als auser demselben, Zunge und Feder, dem Rechten und Gerichtsbrauch gemäß, geschicklich, zierlich und gebührlich anwenden und führen solle . . . Allen neuangehenden Advokaten, Anwalden und Sachwaltern, ja auch Richtern und rechtlichen Partheyen nützlich, nöhtig, und gleichsam

unentbährlich, as der Spaht (Nuremberg: Published by Johann Hofmann, printed in Jena by Johann Nisius, 1678);

Der allzeitfertige Secretarius oder: Anweisung, auf was maasse ein ieder halbgelehrter bey Fürsten, Herrn, Gemeinden und in seinem Sonderleben, nach ieziger Art, einen guten, wolklingenden und hinlänglichen Brief schreiben und verfassen könne, anonymous (Nuremberg: Published by Johann Hofmann, printed in Jena by Johann Nisius, 1679);

Bellemperie: Trauerspiel, as der Spate (Jena: Printed by Johann Nisius, 1680);

Willmut, Lustspiel, as der Spate (Jena: Printed by Johann Nisius, 1680);

Auditeur oder KriegsSchulteiß, das ist: richtige und unbetrügliche Anweisung, Wasmassen ein General- und RegimentsAuditör ihr hochangelegenes richterliches Amt, so in Feldlägern, als Fest- und Besatzungen, wie nicht weniger in den Quartieren, auf Zügen und Rasttagen, denen Kriegsrechten und Gewohnheiten gemäß, klüglich, geschicklich, gewissenhaft und löblich verwalten und beobachten solle, as der Spate (Nuremberg: Johann Hofmann, 1683);

J. N. J. Jesus-Schall und Wiederhall, durch ein liebliches Echo von den trostreichen Sionsbergen Göttlichen Worts, aus den Felsritzen des ächzenden Turtelteubleins gleubiger Seelen herzsehnend zurückgesendet. Das ist: Jesus-Andachten, Lob und Preis, teils, durch inbrünstige Seufzer, teils anmutige Lieder, zu mehrer Entzündung der Gegenliebe und Vereinigung mit dem Geiste Jesu, vorgestellet und aufgezeichnet, as der Spate (Nuremberg: Johann Hofmann, 1684);

A. Z. Schattenriß der Welt, as der Spate (Nuremberg: Johann Hofmann, 1684);

Herzandächtiges Bet- Beicht- und Communion-Büchlein, worinnen nebst inbrünstigen Gebet und Seufzern, vor und nach der Beichte, auch Empfahung deß heiligen Abendmahls schöne neue Geistreiche hierzu dienliche Lieder zu befinden, as der Spate (Nuremberg: Johann Hofmann, 1686);

Relationes Curiosae oder Außerlesene Relationen von den denkwürdigsten . . . Sachen auß bewährten Autoribus aufgesucht, as der Spahte (Frankfurt am Main: Johann Gottfried Zubrodt's heirs, 1691);

Der Teutschen Sprache Stammbaum und Fortwachs, oder Teutscher Sprachschatz, worinnen alle und iede teutsche Wurzeln oder Stammwörter, so viel deren annoch bekant und ietzo im Gebrauch seyn, nebst ihrer Ankunft, abgeleiteten, duppelungen, und vornemsten Redarten mit guter lateinischen Tolmetschung und kunstgegründeten Anmerkungen befindlich. Samt einer Hochteutschen Letterkunst, Nachschuß und *teutschem Register. So Lehrenden als Lernenden zu beider Sprachen Kundigkeit, nötig und nützlich, durch unermüdeten Fleiß in vielen Jahren gesamlet,* as der Spate (Nuremberg: Published by Johann Hofmann, printed in Altdorf by Heinrich Meyer, 1691);

Zeitungs-Lust und Nutz: Oder derer so genanten Novellen oder Zeitungen, wirkende Ergetzlichkeit, Anmut, Notwendigkeit und Frommen, auch was bey deren Lesung zu lernen, zu beobachten und zu bedenken sey? Samt einem Anhang, bestehend: Jn Erklärung derer in den Zeitungen vorkommenden fremden Wörter, as der Spate (Hamburg: Benjamin Schiller, 1695);

Des Spaten Politischer Briefverfasser (Hamburg: Benjamin Schiller, 1695);

Der Allerneust-ankommende Secretarius, mit sich bringend einen grossen Vorrath derer durch das gantze menschlichen Leben vorkomenden Briefe, als nehmlich: Fürstliche- Ambts- Krieges- Rechts- Hauß- Lehr- Kauffmanns- Reichs- Höfliche- Verliebte- Traurige- Boßirliche und Lustige Brieffe, as der Spate (Hamburg: Gottfried Liebernickel, 1699);

Die Dichtkunst des Spaten 1685, edited by Herbert Zeman, Wiener Neudrucke, 5 (Vienna: Österreichische Bundesverlag, 1975).

Editions: *Geharnschte Venus 1660* [erroneously attributed to Jakob Schwieger], edited by Theobald Raehse, Neudrucke deutscher Litteraturwerke des 16. und 17. Jahrhunderts, no. 74/75 (Halle: Niemeyer, 1888);

Die Geharnschte Venus, edited by Conrad Höfer, Jahresgabe der Gesellschaft der Münchner Bücherfreunde für ihre 75 Mitglieder (Munich: Wolf, 1925);

"Die Wittekinden. Singe- und Freuden-Spiel," in *Oratorium: Festspiel,* edited by Willi Flemming, Deutsche Literatur in Entwicklungsreihen, Reihe Barock, Barockdrama, 6 (Leipzig: Reclam, 1933);

Die Geharnschte Venus oder Liebes-Lieder im Kriege gedichtet, edited by Herbert Zeman (Munich: Kösel, 1968);

Der Teutschen Sprache Stammbaum und Fortwachs oder Teutscher Sprachschatz, 3 volumes, edited by Stefan Sonderegger (Munich: Kösel, 1968);

Der Teutschen Sprache Stammbaum und Fortwachs, 3 volumes, edited by Gerhard Ising, Documenta Linguistica, Reihe II (Hildesheim: Olms, 1968–1969);

Zeitungs Lust und Nutz, edited by Gert Hagelweide (Bremen: Schünemann, 1969);

Die Geharnschte Venus, edited by Ferdinand van Ingen (Stuttgart: Reclam, 1970).

OTHER: Basilius Förtsch, *Neu-entsprungene Wasser-Quelle, vor Gottes ergebene, und Geistlich-dürstige Seelen, worinnen, Vorbereit- Zeit- Arbeit- Leid- Freud- Streit- und Ewigkeit-Gebete zu befinden, aufgeraumet von dem Spahten. Nebst einem vollständigen Evangelischen Gesangbuch,* edited by Stieler (Weimar: Joachim Heinrich Schmidt, 1670);

Trifolium Sacrum: Sive Exercitium Pietatis quadripartitum. S. Scripturae dictis Precationibus, Psalmis & Hymnis constans. Pro Pueris. Collectore Serotino, edited by Stieler (Nuremberg: Johann Hofmann, 1676);

Der bußfertige Sünder oder Geistliches Handbüchlein, vor, in, und nach der Beicht und dem heiligen Abendmahl . . . zugebrauchen. Nebst darzu gehörigen Psalmen und Christlichen Liedern. Neu eingerichtet, edited by Stieler (Nuremberg: Published by Johann Hofmann, printed in Jena by Johann Nisius, 1679);

Balthasar Kindermann, *Herrn Baltasar Kindermanns Teutscher Wolredener auf allerhand Begebenheiten im Stats- und Hauswesen gerichtet, als das sind: Hochzeit- Kindtauf- Begräbniß- Empfah- Huldigungs- Glückwunsch- und viel andere wichtige Sachen, Anbring- Handel- und Beantwortungen, bey Abschickungen, Gesantschaften, Befehligen, auch in eigenen, offen- und sonderbaren Amts- und Bürgerlichen Geschäfften nachrichtlich zugeberauchen. Nach heutiger Politischen Redart gebessert und mit vielen Komplimenten, Vorträgen, Beantwortungen, wie nicht weniger mit unterschiedlichen nohtwendigen und nützlichen Anmerkungen und Haupt-Erinnerungen gemehret von dem Spaten,* edited by Stieler (Wittenberg: Published by Hiob Wilhelm Fincelius, printed in Jena by Samuel Krebs's heirs, 1680);

Bernhard Schotanus, *Vade-mecum juridicum sive Compendium scientiae juris privati. praeeunte D. Bernhardo Schotano . . . Adjecta sunt . . . opuscula ex ore Dn. Serotini, des Spaten,* edited by Stieler (Nuremberg: Published by Johann Hofmann, printed in Jena by Johann Nisius, 1683);

Les plus belles Lettres des meilleurs Auteurs François de ce tems Receuillies et traduites en Allemand par le Tard. Die feineste Schreiben der besten Frantzösischen Brief-Verfasser dieser Zeit . . . zusammengetragen samt der Teutschen Ubersetzung, außgefertiget von dem Spaten, translated and edited by Stieler (Hamburg: Benjamin Schiller, 1696).

Caspar Stieler was an important seventeenth-century lyric poet, a pathbreaker in the development of German-language verse forms suitable for musical settings (both song and musical drama), the creator of an early German dictionary, and the author of many books on letter writing and other skills expected of a courtly bureaucrat. Himself a *Kammersekretarius* (court secretary) at various Middle and North German courts between 1662 and 1690, he was a standard setter for the profession, and several of his handbooks were reprinted until well into the eighteenth century. He may have contributed more substantively and in more diverse ways to the development of German prose and verse style than any other single member of the Fruchtbringende Gesellschaft (Fruit-bringing Society), the society created for the purpose of fostering the German language in all of its various contexts. He was a master of style and language, whether poetic or pragmatic.

Stieler was born in Erfurt in 1632, the son of the pharmacist Ernst Stieler and Regina Stieler, née Quernt. As his grandfather had also been a pharmacist, and as his stepfather, Johann Martini, whom his mother married after the death of Ernst Stieler when Caspar was four years old, was likewise of this profession, one might expect that Stieler would have followed this family tradition. Instead, after graduating from the Ratsgymnasium in his hometown in 1648 he studied medicine at the Universities of Leipzig, Erfurt, Marburg, and Gießen. But he never completed his medical studies; in 1650 he was expelled from the University of Gießen for dueling, resisting arrest, and escaping from custody.

Perhaps in search of a distant site in which to reestablish himself, he first attempted to earn a living as a tutor in the East Prussian university city of Königsberg (today Kaliningrad, Russia). He matriculated at the university after a few years and continued his studies, adding theology, rhetoric, and law to medicine. The rhetoric professor Valentin Thilo, a colleague and friend of the professor of poetics and lyric poet Simon Dach, seems to have introduced Stieler to the circle of poets around Dach, the *Kurbishütte* (Pumpkin-Hut) group that included the important lied composer Heinrich Albert. From them Stieler absorbed the notions that lyric poetry was synonymous with song and that the forms of poetic language had a musical basis that required collaboration with a composer for completion. The events of the Königsberg years — lectures, musical and theatrical performances, close friendships, dalliance and perhaps at least one more serious love affair, a military campaign in which Stieler served as

an *Auditeur* (military court official) from 1655 to 1657, and a life-threatening illness — all find depiction in anecdotes in his works, beginning with his chief contribution to the continuo Lied tradition, *Die Geharnschte Venus* (Armored Venus).

Die Geharnschte Venus, complete by 1657, when he wrote the preface, although not published until 1660, is a structured collection or cycle comprising seven groups of ten lyric poems, each with an isostrophic musical setting for solo voice and basso continuo accompaniment. The title sets the theme: love poems written in wartime. These worldly — often bawdy — songs come with a sly disclaimer warning readers whose prudery would lead them to disapprove: "Wer Ernst und Eyffer liebt und nie bey Lust gewesen, / hat meine Venus noch zu singen, noch zu lesen" (He who loves earnestness and zeal and never indulges in pleasure / should neither sing nor read my Venus).

The musical settings were provided by several composers, among them prominent representatives of the North German school based in Hamburg, where the collection was published. Some — which Stieler modestly termed *übelkingend* (bad-sounding) — were by the poet himself, who was apparently an amateur musician of respectable talent. As was generally the case in the seventeenth century, these secular songs were published under a pseudonym, Filidor der Dorfferer (Filidor the Villager), a name with connotations of the pastoral tradition that also cloaks the author's identity in spite of what sounds like autobiographical accounts. Stieler never claimed this song cycle, and the identity of the poet — if it was ever known to the many enthusiastic readers (and, presumably, singers or hearers) of the seventeenth century — was lost by the time Johannes Moller listed it under another's name in 1744. It took the clever detective work of Albert Köster in his *Der Dichter der Geharnschten Venus* (The Poet of the Armored Venus, 1897), based on deciphered anagrams, dialect studies, and circumstantial evidence, to discover that Stieler was the author.

After handing over the song cycle to the publisher in Hamburg, Stieler embarked on a poor man's grand tour of Europe, with significant stops in France and Italy. His relatives being either unable or unwilling to finance his travels — he had still not completed any useful university education, an accomplishment that might have elicited family support for such a journey — Stieler signed on with a series of noblemen as companion or translator. As such positions normally went to experienced travelers, the poet must have been an individual of com-

*Frontispiece for the collection of songs that Stieler published
under a pseudonym in 1660. His authorship was not
established until the 1890s.*

pelling charm and supreme self-confidence. In any case, his travels enabled him to become fluent in French and Italian, to experience theatrical performances at some of the great theaters of Europe, and to acquire the polished manners (and mannerisms) that would make him a welcome courtier at any court in Europe. Though a Protestant, he gained an audience with the Pope during his stay in Rome and carried on a short conversation with him. Anecdotes such as this episode would pepper his handbooks and contribute to their popularity.

On his return to Erfurt in 1661 he fell in love with a patrician woman, Regina Sophie Breitenbach, and set about making himself worthy of her hand in marriage. He resumed his studies at

Jena, concentrating on the remunerative profession of law, and even before completing these studies landed a respectable post in 1662 as *Sekretär* to the young, newly installed count of the small principality of Schwarzburg-Rudolstadt, Albert Anton. This position made Stieler's proposal acceptable to Regina Breitenbach's family, and the marriage took place in 1663.

The Rudolstadt post included an enormous variety of activities and responsibilities. In addition to handling correspondence for the count, Stieler tutored pages and noble children in style and foreign languages, read news reports aloud at the count's table, organized and produced musical entertainments, wrote occasional poems, and wrote and produced six musical dramas for dynastic celebrations between 1665 and 1667. His relationship with the count and his family was one of mutual respect. Two children were born to Regina during the Rudolstadt years, Caspar Ernst in 1664 and Caspar Friedrich in 1665.

The most significant works from Stieler's pen during the Rudolstadt period were the so-called *Rudolstädter Festspiele,* six musical dramas for performance at occasions of dynastic importance. Unlike many occasional plays of the period, which were mythological masques, Stieler's were full-length comedies and tragicomedies based on Romance-language models. The two produced for the celebration of Count Albert Anton's wedding in 1665, *Der Vermeinte Printz* (The Assumed Prince) and *Ernelinde,* a translation of an Italian tragicomedy, are romantic comedies culminating in happy endings complete with royal marriages. Nor does the parallelism to the dynastic occasion stop there: each plot alludes to a parallel situation in the personal or political events surrounding the count's marriage. Yet neither play is limited to the context of the occasion for which it was designed, which may account for the wide success of the edition prepared for sale. In addition to a rather risqué plot, each play has a subplot with comic characters whose cheerfully frank sexuality reminds one of the lusty songs of *Die geharnschte Venus.* Each play consists of prose acts with *Singende Zwischenspiele* (musical intermezzi); in *Der Vermeinte Printz* these intermezzi are miniature operatic scenes on a mythological plane.

One of the plays for 1666, *Die Wittekinden* (The Wittekinds), a romantic comedy based on the lives of some of the count's ancestors, is actually an opera, with a recitative text designed to be sung in its entirety. One of the plays for 1667, *Der betrogene Betrug* (Deceived Deception), has sung intermezzi that form an independent miniature opera with a plot based on Greco-Roman mythology. But all these theatrical performances rely heavily on the contributions of music, as might be expected from a lyric poet whose notion of poetry is synonymous with song and who dabbled in composition himself. The six plays were apparently marketed quite widely, for two or more of them can be found in dozens of libraries of what was then the German-speaking area of Europe.

The last two Rudolstadt plays apparently postdate Stieler's presence there, for he accepted a new and better-paying post in late 1666 in Eisenach as secretary to the ducal brothers of Saxe-Weimar. His family was growing – another son, Carl Christian Heinrich, was born in 1667 – and his need for money was becoming acute; in addition to accepting the higher-paying position, Stieler began at this time to publish works designed to provide income. A first important step was entrance into the Fruchtbringende Gesellschaft; with the sponsorship of his Weimar colleague and friend Georg Neumark, former secretary of the society, he was successful in his request for membership and joined the society in late 1668 as Der Spate (The Late One), a name he used as his pseudonym in most subsequent publishing ventures (it is sometimes spelled *Der Spahte*). In 1669 he translated at the behest of his employer the best-known Italian-language opera of the period, Francesco Sbarra's *Il Pomo d'oro* (The Golden Apple), as *Der göldene Apfel;* the original had been created for the imperial wedding in Vienna in 1668 with a musical score by Marc'antonio Cesti. Stieler's charming German text, which attests to the his skill as a German poet and librettist as well as to his abilities in Italian, was not published but survives in its manuscript presentation copy in Weimar. Other important freelance writing ventures during Stieler's Eisenach period include two edited collections of spiritual songs, *Neuentsprungene Wasser-Quelle* (Newly Flowing Fountain, 1670) and *Trifolium Sacrum* (1676), and his best-selling handbook on the art of being a secretary, *Teutsche Sekretariat-Kunst* (German Art of the Secretary, 1673), which was to be reprinted and revised well into the eighteenth century.

Four more children were born in the Eisenach years: Maria Regina, Georg Christoph, Heinrich Gottfried, and, in 1676, Melusina Benigna; but Regina died from complications of giving birth to the last child. Stieler's contribution to the memorial pamphlet for his wife is a compelling expression of his grief:

Mein Kind, du weichst von mir
    und lässet mich alleine,
    und meine sieben kleine,
die minder nicht sind deine?
Wir arme; Weh! recht Arme; bleiben hier.
Ach! nimm mich mit, mein Herz!
Wart! Ich bin fertig dir zu folgen.
Umsonst; sie hört nicht mehr. Nu! Schmerz!
Tritt her an ihre Statt! die Freud' ist todt.
Laß mich mit meinen kleinen,
bis wir uns einst (ach! wenn wirds seyn?) vereinen,
uns satt zerweinen.

(My child, you fade away from me
    and leave me all alone
    with my seven little ones
who are no less your own?
We miserable ones – woe, right miserable – remain
    here.

Oh! take me along, my heart!
Wait! I'm ready to follow you.
In vain; she hears no more. Now! Pain!
Come take her place! My joy is dead.
Let me, together with my little ones,
until we someday (oh! when might that be?) meet
    again,
cry ourselves out until we can no more.)

The irregular form of the Italian madrigal tradition, which he had explored in a selection of short epigrammatic pieces at the end of *Die Geharnschte Venus,* here approaches the more realistic emotionality of operatic arioso.

The depth of his grief and his inability to cope with life in Regina's absence are reflected in his rushed marriage in May 1677 to Christine Margaretha Cotta to provide a stepmother for his children, unfulfilled publishing contracts and angry letters from his publishers, and apparently unfulfilled duties in his secretarial position, which he had to give up in 1677. The loss of his position compelled him to finish several freelance projects. The legal handbook *Der teutsche Advocat* (The German Lawyer) appeared in 1678 and *Der allzeitfertige Secretarius* (The Ever-Ready Secretary), another handbook on the secretarial profession, in 1679. One freelance project, the edited song collection *Der bußfertige Sünder* (The Penitent Sinner, 1679), however, may have been more than an effort designed for financial gain. In the dedicatory epistle addressed to Ahasverus Fritsch, spiritual adviser to the countesses of Schwarzburg-Rudolstadt, Stieler records what may be the resolution of the spiritual crisis brought about by the death of his wife. His gratitude to his *Gevatter und Patron* (mentor and patron) seems to indicate that the proto-Pietist Fritsch had helped him find the courage to face up to his youthful worldliness, much like the bußfertiger Sünder of the title. In any case, the lighthearted, sensual, and humorous poet of *Die geharnschte Venus* and the Rudolstadt plays disappears forever, to be replaced by a serious, dignified, even moralistic author with a Pietistic streak.

Stieler found a position in 1678 as secretary of the University of Jena, where he also privately taught German style. By 1680, perhaps partly because of two dramatic texts he wrote to attract a patron, his search for a new position at a central German court was successful, and he obtained the coveted post as secretary in Weimar, replacing his friend Neumark. After Duke Johann Ernst II of Saxe-Weimar died in 1683, Stieler continued to serve under his sons, the coregents Duke Wilhelm Ernst and Duke Johann Ernst III. The Weimar

plays, *Bellemperie* (1680) and *Willmut* (1680), although similar to his earlier works in form, are striking expressions of his new serious persona. *Bellemperie,* based on Thomas Kyd's *The Spanish Tragedie* (1592), is a highly moralistic tragedy of retribution; even Stieler's usual comic figure, Scaramutza, has acquired a tendency to heavy-handed satire and black humor that provides a tone different from that found in the Rudolstadt plays. *Willmut,* an allegory of sin and salvation in pastoral guise, is also heavily moralistic. Yet both retain the effective theatricality of Stieler's earlier works and must have endeared him to his new patron, who soon put him to work on two new operas of 1684 that are apparently adaptations of libretti by others – he changed titles and character names and added comic scenes with Scaramutza in versions that have not survived. One of these operas, *Krieg und Sieg der Keuschheit* (Chastity's War and Victory), may well have derived from Stieler's pen in its earlier manifestation as *Floretto* in Hamburg the year before. The libretto for this opera is an adaptation of Christian Weise's prose play *Die triumphierende Keuschheit* (Chastity Triumphant, 1668).

The Weimar years also saw new freelance efforts: *Der Auditeur* (The Military Hearing Officer, 1683); another edited song collection, *J. N. J. Jesus-Schall und Wiederhall* (Sound and Reverberation in the Name of Jesus, 1684), with proto-Pietistic elements that show continuing influence from Fritsch; and a geography handbook, *A. Z. Schattenriß der Welt* (Outline of World Geography, 1684), which provoked an exchange of criticism and response that lasted for several years. In 1685 he completed a poetical treatise in alexandrine verse, *Die Dichtkunst des Spahten* (Poetical Treatise of the Late One), which was not published until 1975; it survives in a presentation manuscript copy in Copenhagen.

In 1685 Stieler was appointed *Hofrat* (adviser) to Duke Philip Ludwig of Holstein-Wiesenburg. After the death of the duke in 1689 Stieler retired to his hometown, Erfurt, where he continued his freelance writing activities. At his request, in 1705 his family's patent of nobility was renewed, enabling him to call himself Caspar von Stieler. Most significant of the publications of this final period of productivity is his great dictionary, *Der Teutschen Sprache Stammbaum und Fortwachs* (The German Language's Family Tree and Its Growth, 1691), a work he must have been preparing for decades. The dictionary arranges German vocabulary by stem or root, rather than in alphabetical order, and provides Latin definitions for thousands of words and phrases, many of them highly colloquial. It was the basis for all later German dictionaries. Many of the colorful colloquialisms defined in Jacob Grimm's *Deutsches Wörterbuch* (German Dictionary, 1852–1960) come from Stieler's collection. Other late handbooks include *Relationes Curiosae* (Curious Relations, 1691), *Zeitungs-Lust und Nutz* (Pleasure and Uses to Be Derived from Newspapers, 1695), *Politischer Briefverfasser* (Political Letter-Writer, 1695), and *Der Allerneust-ankommende Secretarius* (The Very Newest Secretary, 1699). Rreprints and revised editions of his earlier handbooks also continued to emerge during Stieler's final two decades of life. He died on 24 June 1707.

Stieler's early works – those whose author termed himself Filidor or Filidor der Dorfferer – have only been attributed to him since the late nineteenth century. These works were never acknowledged by the poet; it is assumed that his disparagement of his early works in the *Sekretariat-Kunst* edition of 1705 refers to these products of his youth: "So muß ich bekennen, daß so oft ich meine vorige Schreiberey lese, darob einen Ekel empfinde und mich meiner misbrauchten Übereiling schäme" (This I must confess that as often as I read my earlier writings I feel revulsion and shame for my hasty misspent efforts). Nearly all works by Stieler after 1668 are signed with his official pen name in the Fruchtbringende Gesellschaft, Der Spate or Der Spahte. The motto that accompanies this name in the membership records explains it as signifying "Übertrifft den Frühzeitigen" (Overcomes the Earlier One) – perhaps a criticism of his earlier efforts. In 1744 Johannes Moller attributed *Die Geharnschte Venus* to Jacob Schwieger; the ignorance of Stieler's authorship continued through 1888, when Theobald Raehse published *Die Geharnschte Venus* as a product of that minor North German poet. As late as 1933 Willi Fleming proposed that Stieler's replacement in Rudolstat, Georg Bleyer, had written Filidor's works. But the correctness of the thorough analyses of Köster and of his student Conrad Höfer, whose *Die Rudolstädter Festspiele aus den Jahren 1665–67 und ihr Dichter* (The Rudolstadt Festival Plays of the Years 1665–67 and Their Author) appeared in 1904, should not be doubted. These significant poems and plays by "Filidor" are, indeed, by the youthful Caspar Stieler.

As a versifier who understood the demands of musical settings more fully than perhaps any other poet of the century, Stieler contributed in substantive ways to the development of poetic forms for continuo Lied and for opera – especially recitative. As a master of prose style – whether in prose plays,

official letters, journalistic accounts, or highly personable and colorful expository prose in his handbooks – Stieler contributed also to the development of a lucid and precise modern German style, a style that could still be appreciated during the Age of the Enlightenment. And as an amateur linguist and a connoisseur of the building blocks of language and style – words and phrases – he enriched the appreciation of the German language, including its most colloquial forms, as an effective conveyer of meaning. But above all, in his poetic works – particularly those youthful products he signed "Filidor" – he recorded himself indelibly as a personality of enormous charm and as a sensitive human being whose self-expression was less obscured by traditional rhetorical stances than was common during the seventeenth century in Germany.

Bibliography:

Gerhard Dünnhaupt, *Personalbibliographie zu den Drucken des Barock,* volume 9, part 6 (Stuttgart: Hiersemann, 1993), pp. 3951–3972.

Biographies:

Johann Heinrich von Falckenstein, "Caspars von Stieler, ehemahligen Herzog-Holstein-Wiesenburgischen Hof-Raths, insgemein Serotinus, oder der Spate genannt, Lebens-Beschreibung," in his *Analecta Nordgaviensia* (Schwabach, 1738), pp. 253–280;

Ferdinand van Ingen, "Kaspar Stieler," in his *Deutsche Dichter: Leben und Werk deutschsprachiger Autoren,* volume 2: *Reformation, Renaissance und Barock* (Stuttgart: Reclam, 1988), pp. 313–320.

References:

Judith P. Aikin, "The Audience within the Play: Clues to Intended Audience Reaction in German Baroque Tragedies and Comedies," *Daphnis: Zeitschrift für Mittlere Deutsche Literatur,* 13, no. 1–2 (1984): 187–201;

Aikin, "Authorial Self-Consciousness in the Theater of Caspar Stieler," in *Literary Culture in the Holy Roman Empire,* edited by James A. Parente Jr. and others (Chapel Hill: University of North Carolina Press, 1990), pp. 247–258;

Aikin, "Creating a Language for German Opera: The Struggle to Adapt Madrigal Versification in Seventeenth-Century Germany," *Deutsche Vierteljahrsschrift für Literaturwissenschaft und Geistesgeschichte,* 62 (June 1988): 266–289;

Aikin, "'Fertigkeit' – A Millennialist Conceit in a Dedicatory Epistle by Caspar Stieler," in *Opitz und seine Welt: Festschrift für George Schulz-Behrend zum 12. Februar 1988,* edited by Barbara Becker-Cantarino and Jörg-Ulrich Fechner (Amsterdam: Rodopi, 1989), pp. 5–20;

Aikin, "Libretti without Scores: Problems in the Study of Early German Opera," in *Music and German Literature,* edited by James M. McGlathery (Columbia, S.C.: Camden House, 1992), pp. 51–64;

Aikin, "Practical Uses of Comedy at a Seventeenth-Century Court: The Political Polemic in Caspar Stieler's *Der Vermeinte Printz," Theatre Journal,* 35 (December 1983): 519–532;

Aikin, "Romantic Comedy as Religious Allegory: The Millennial Kingdom in Caspar Stieler's *Die erfreuete Unschuld," German Quarterly,* 57 (Winter 1984): 59–74;

Aikin, "Satire, Satyr Plays, and German Baroque Comedy," *Daphnis: Zeitschrift für Mittlere Deutsche Literatur,* 14 (1985): 759–778;

Aikin, *Scaramutza in Germany: The Dramatic Works of Caspar Stieler* (University Park: Pennsylvania State University Press, 1980);

Johannes Bolte, "Eine ungedruckte Poetik Kaspar Stielers," *Sitzungsberichte der preußischen Akademie der Wissenschaften, phil.-hist. Classe,* 15 (1926): 97–122;

Conrad Höfer, *Die Rudolstädter Festspiele aus den Jahren 1665–67 und ihr Dichter: Eine literar-historische Studie* (Leipzig: Voigtländer, 1904);

Gerhard Ising, *Die Erfassung der deutschen Sprache des ausgehenden 17. Jahrhunderts in den Wörterbüchern Matthias Kramers und Kaspar Stielers* (Berlin: Akademie-Verlag, 1956);

Harold Jantz, "Helicon's Harmonious Springs – Kaspar Stieler and Poetic Form," in *Deutsche Barocklyrik: Gedichtinterpretationen von Spee bis Haller,* edited by Martin Bircher and A. Haas (Bern, 1973), pp. 135–152;

Albert Köster, *Der Dichter der Geharnschten Venus* (Marburg: Elwert, 1897);

Johannes Moller, *Cimbria Literata,* volume 2 (Copenhagen: G. F. Kisel, 1744), pp. 870–871;

Rudolf Schoenwerth, *Die niederländischen und deutschen Bearbeitungen von Thomas Kyds "Spanish Tragedy"* (Leipzig: Voigtländer, 1903);

Herbert Zeman, "Kaspar Stieler," in *Deutsche Dichter des 17. Jahrhunderts: Ihr Leben und Werk,* edited by Harald Steinhagen and Benno von Wiese (Berlin: Schmidt, 1984), p. 576;

Zeman, "Kaspar Stielers 'Die Geharnschte Venus': Aspekte literaturwissenschaftlicher Deutung," *Deutsche Vierteljahrsschrift für Literaturwissenschaft und Geistesgeschichte,* 48 (September 1974): 478–527;

Zeman, *Kaspar Stieler – Versuch einer Monographie,* dissertation, University of Vienna, 1965;

Zeman, "Philipp von Zesens literarische Wirkungen auf Kaspar Stielers 'Geharnschte Venus' (1660)," in *Philipp von Zesen 1619–1969: Beiträge zu seinem Leben und Werk,* edited by Ferdinand van Ingen (Wiesbaden: Steiner, 1972), pp. 231–245.

Johann Wilhelm von Stubenberg

(22 April 1619 – 15 March 1663)

Albrecht Classen
University of Arizona

BOOKS: *Deutsches Hochzeitsgedicht zur Vermählung Georg Neumarks mit Anna Margaretha geb. Werner* (Jena: Georg Sengenwald, 1655);

Norma seu Regula Armentorum Equinorum (Vienna: Printed by Susanna Rickes, published by Johann Georg Hertz, 1662).

TRANSLATIONS: Giovanni Francesco Biondi, *Eromena: Das ist, Liebes- und Heldengedicht, jn welchem, nechst seltenen Begebenheiten viel kluge Gedancken, merckwürdige Lehren, verständige Gespräche und verborgene Geschichte zu beobachten* (Nuremberg: Printed by Michael Endter, 1650); modern edition, edited by Martin Bircher (Bern, Frankfurt am Main, New York & Paris: Peter Lang, 1989);

Biondi, *Das vertriebene Fräulein, oder der Eromena zweiter Theil* (Nuremberg: Printed by Michael Endter, 1651);

Biondi, *Koralbo: oder der Eromena dritter Theil* (Nuremberg: Michael Endter, 1651);

Giovanni Ambrogio Marini, *Wettstreit der Verzweifelten: Ein sehr anmuhtiges und künstliches Liebs-Geschicht* (Frankfurt am Main: Johann Hüttner, 1651);

Biondi, *Der Eromena vierdter und letzter Theil* (Nuremberg: Michael Endter, 1652);

Giovanni Francesco Loredano, *Geschicht-reden: Das ist, Freywillige Gemüths-Schertze* (Nuremberg: Michael Endter, 1652);

Luca Assarino, *König Demetrius. Eine warhaffte, aber mit vielen Sinnreichen, zur Wolredenheit, Lesens-anmutigheit, auch nutzlicher Sittenlehre, dienlichen Beygedichten vermehrte und geschmükkte Geschicht* (Nuremberg: Michael Endter, 1653);

François de Grenaille, *Frauenzimmer Belustigung. Ein so wol zu Geistlicher Sittenlehre als zierlicher Wolredenheit nutz- und ergötzliches Wercklein* (Nuremberg: Michael Endter, 1653);

Francis Bacon, *Getreue Reden: die Sitten- Regiments- und Haußlehre betreffend, aus dem Lateinischen gedolmetscht* (Nuremberg: Michael Endter, 1654);

Bacon, *Fürtrefflicher Staats- Vernunfft- und Sitten-Lehr-Schrifften* (Nuremberg: Michael Endter, 1654);

Loredano, *Andachten über die Sieben Busz-Psalm deß Königlichen Propheten Davids. Zu Gottes Ehre aus dem Jtaliänischen gedolmetscht* (Ulm: Georg Wildeisen, 1654);

Marini, *Printz Kaloandro. Zu mehrer Ausübung und Ausschmückung unserer hochdeutschen Sprache, in selbiger aus dem Jtaliänischen übersetzt* (Nuremberg: Michael Endter, 1656);

Marini, *Endjmjro, oder des Kalloandro Zweyter Theil* (Nuremberg: Michael Endter, 1656);

Ferrante Pallavicino, *Geteutschter Samson* (Nuremberg: Michael Endter, 1657);

Charles Sorel, Sieur de Souvigny, *Von menschlicher Vollkommenheit, worbey die waaren Güter betrachtet werden, insonderheit der Seelen ihre; Samt den Lehr-Arten der Wissenschaften* (Nuremberg: Michael Endter, 1660);

George de Scudéry (actually, Madeleine de Scudéry), *Clelja: Eine Römische Geschichte,* 5 volumes (Nuremberg: Michael & Johann Friedrich Endter, 1664);

Loredano, *Andachten, vber die 15. Staffel-Psalmen deß Königlichen Propheten Davids. Zu Gottes Ehre auß dem Jtaliänischen gedolmetscht* (Frankfurt am Main: Johann Conrad Emmerich, 1669);

Giovanni Battista Manzini, *Dem Weisen ist verboten zu dienen, ein sehr zierlich und wolgesetztes Wercklein* (Frankfurt am Main & Regensburg: Published by Johann Conrad Emmerich, 1671).

Johann Wilhelm von Stubenberg's contribution to German baroque literature consists not in creative work but in his translations of major literary, moralistic, and practical treatises from French, Italian, and English into German. He was honored for these achievements by being invited to become a member of the Fruchtbringende Gesellschaft (Fruitbringing Society) in Nuremberg. He had close con-

Johann Wilhelm von Stubenberg; engraving by
Georg Christoph Eimmart

tacts with writers such as Catharina Regina von Greiffenberg and Johann Beer and influenced their work through his translations. Stubenberg was one of the first to recognize Greiffenberg's poetic talent, and he recommended her to the well-known Nuremberg poet Sigmund von Birken.

Stubenberg was born on 22 April 1619 in Neustadt in Bohemia to Rudolf von Stubenberg and his third wife, Justina, née von Zelking, both of whom came from old Austrian aristocratic families. The Thirty Years' War deeply affected the Stubenbergs. Rudolf was killed in an explosion on 1 February 1620; at about the same time the so-called Winter King, Friedrich von der Pfalz (of the Palatinate), who ruled in Bohemia, was defeated, leaving the Protestant aristocracy in Austria unprotected from persecution by the Hapsburg monarchy in Vienna. Stubenberg's father was posthumously accused of having participated in a conspiracy, and his properties were confiscated. The widow and her one-year-old son found refuge with her husband's brother, Georg von Stubenberg the Elder, at his estate,

Schallaburg on the Danube, near Melk in Lower Austria. Johann Wilhelm attended the country school in Loosdorf. But pressure from the Catholic Hapsburgs on the Protestant landed gentry increased, and in 1629 Georg was forced to leave his home and move to Regensburg, where he died in 1630. Justina and her son went to Pirna in Saxony, near the border with Bohemia. She died in 1632, leaving her son in the care of a man named Georg Krschinetzky in Dresden.

Stubenberg embarked on his educational tour of Europe in 1636, acquiring an excellent knowledge of foreign languages, sciences, and courtly manners. When he spent some time with Count Anton Günther in Oldenburg, a strong interest in horses was awakened in him that later translated into his Latin treatise *Norma seu Regula Armentorum Equinorum* (Norms or Rules for the Keeping of Horses, 1662).

After Stubenberg returned to Dresden in 1639, his relatives succeeded in giving him access to his inheritance from his uncle Georg; his father's property seems to have been lost entirely. In 1641 the estates of Schallaburg and Sichtenberg were transferred to Stubenberg. He continued to travel extensively and met his future wife, Felicitas Dorothea von Eibiswald, a descendant of an old Styrian family, at the court of Brunswick. They married in 1642 and settled in Protestant Preßburg (Hungary) for religious reasons. The first of their two children, a son, was born on 2 January 1643.

After reading a book by Karl Gustav von Hille about the Fruchtbringende Gesellschaft in 1647, Stubenberg tried to make contact with members of the first and most important language society in Germany, which had been founded by Duke Ludwig of Anhalt-Köthen in 1617. Stubenberg became a member in 1648 with the sobriquet Der Unglückliche "in zarter Jugend" (The Unfortunate One "in Fragile Youth") and established close friendships with the important poets Birken and Georg Philipp Harsdörffer. The latter would become the major source of inspiration for the translations that would establish Stubenberg's fame. Apart from some short poems in anthologies, he wrote no original works in German.

One of the major motivations for translating important treatises into German was to demonstrate the intellectual sophistication of the language. In this practice Stubenberg followed some of the greatest baroque writers, such as Harsdörffer, Birken, Martin Opitz, Johann Rist, and Justus Georg Schottelius. He seems, however, to have gone overboard in the effort, which was quite typical of members of the *Sprachgesellschaften* (language associations), to find German words for all foreign expressions. This is not to diminish his idealism, which he expresses vigoriously in the prologue to his translation *König Demetrius* (King Demetrius, 1653), from Luca Assarino's *Il Demetrio* (1643): "Derohalben, so du, Deutsch-liebender Leser . . . aus meinen Dolmetschungen, hier oder da, nach Art der nutzbaren Bienen, irgend ein schön-fügliches Wort, dich dessen in nutzbaren Sachen zubedienen, einsammlen wirst, so wirst du mir meine wolgemeinte Lust-mühe in etwas bezahlen, und benutzen helffen" (If you, German-loving reader . . . will collect, here and there in the manner of useful bees, any beautiful and fitting word out of my translations, then you will reward me and help me use my well-intended loving efforts).

The interest in the "cleaning up" of the German language went along with strong concern for the improvement of readers' morals, as can be seen by the explicit references to virtue and honor in the subtitles of Stubenberg's translations. Frus-

trated by the condition of his society, he perceived his role as that of teacher and moralist, following the model of other members of the Fruchtbringende Gesellschaft such as Harsdörffer. Since he belonged to the Protestant nobility in Austria, however, he seems to have felt a particular affiliation with a literary society there, the Isternymphen (Ister Nymphs), of which Greiffenberg was a member. Stubenberg often dedicated his translations to women, considering himself a sort of minnesinger in the service of ladies, admiring their beauty and writing on behalf of their honor. He aimed for the education of noblewomen at large, as he stresses in the foreword to *Frauenzimmer Belustigung* (Entertainment for Women, 1653), his translation of François de Grenaille's *Les plaisirs des Dames* (1641). And in the prologue to *Geschicht-reden* (Discussions on History, 1652), his translation of Giovanni Francesco Loredano's *Scherzi geniali* (1632), he emphasizes women's need to find help from men to maintain "die von uns von diesem zarten Geschlechte, so streng-erfordert- und hoch-verlangte schwere Tugenden, der Keuschheit, Beständigkeit, Sittsamkeit, Mäßigkeit, und d.g." (the highly desired, difficult virtues of chastity, constancy, proper behavior, modesty, and so on that are so strictly demanded by us [men]). Particularly here, in his dedication to Margareta Maria von Buwinghausen und Wallmerode, Stubenberg advocates women's right to education. Margareta is said to have been an excellent poet and translator, but none of her texts or letters to Stubenberg appear to have survived.

Between 1650 and 1652 Stubenberg produced, apart from some dedicatory poems in books by others, what is probably his most important work: the translation in four parts of Giovanni Francesco Biondi's *La Eromena* (1624), one of the first novels in the new courtly style describing the adventures of a knight errant. The translation was published in Nuremberg by Michael Endter, who took great pains to embellish the volumes with illustrations and with beautiful copperplates for the title pages; Harsdörffer supplied a foreword. The translation was reprinted several times, appearing as late as 1667. Although Stubenberg did not gain any financial benefit from this or any other of his publications, it brought him into close contact with Birken, who was to become his main source of inspiration and help in his later life. Stubenberg, who did not see himself as a poet, admired this literary skill in Birken and asked him to contribute a dedicatory poem to *Printz Kaloandro* (1656), Stubenberg's translation of *Il Calloandro* (1640), by Giovanni Ambrogio Marini. *Printz Kaloandro,* like *Eromena,* was a massive work; the former comprised almost thirteen hundred printed pages, the latter about two thousand. Stubenberg was a highly energetic and industrious writer, but the publication of his translations was frequently delayed because the publishers could not keep up with him and sometimes were not inclined to accept his manuscripts.

On 4 January 1652 Emperor Friedrich III issued a law that called for all Protestants to be exiled from Austria. Stubenberg hoped to buy an estate in the area of Weimar and to convince the new head of the Fruchtbringende Gesellschaft, Duke Wilhelm IV of Saxe-Weimar (Duke Ludwig of Anhalt-Köthen had died in 1650), to intervene on behalf of the Austrian aristocrats who belonged to the Lutheran Church. He traveled to Weimar at the end of the year but returned to Schallaburg, where he would stay until 1657.

Stubenberg dedicated *Getreue Reden: die Sitten-Regiments- und Haußlehre betreffend* (Honorable Speeches Concerning the Teachings on Morality, Government, and Domestic Issues, 1654), a translation of Francis Bacon's *Essayes* (1591–1625), to the new emperor Ferdinand IV, hoping that the work might influence the young man. But Ferdinand died in 1654, and Stubenberg's situation worsened. The sale of his castle did not proceed because of administrative objections; differences between him and the buyer, the abbot of the Melk monastery; and political conflicts. He continued his translation projects: between 1653 and 1654 he translated a Latin treatise by the eminent North German historian Hermann Conring and two treatises by Bacon, and in 1658 Hugo Grotius's magnum opus *De veritate religionis Christianae* (On the Truth of the Christian Religion, 1627). None of those translations was ever published, and the manuscripts have apparently been lost. Religious texts such as *Andachten über die Sieben Busz-Psalm deß Königlichen Propheten Davids* (Meditations on the Seven Penitence Psalms by the Kingly Prophet David, 1654), translated from Loredano's *Senei di devotione i sette salmi* (1642), and *Geteutschter Samson* (Samson Translated into German, 1657), his translation of Ferrante Pallavicino's *Il Sansone* (1638), were more appropriate to his skills.

After Leopold I was crowned emperor in 1658 Stubenberg attempted to improve his relationship with the court in Vienna and spent considerable time there. He even applied for a position as a court councillor but was turned down because of his Protestantism. The sale of his castle was finally completed on 11 December 1662, when Reichardt Augustin Klezle of Altenach bought the estate. Since

Stubenberg was not allowed to transfer his money to Germany, he could not move into a Protestant area, and he settled in Vienna. He kept up an intensive correspondence with his many friends, particularly Greiffenberg and Wolfgang Helmhard of Hohberg, both of whom he helped in their early literary enterprises; he recommended the former to his friend Birken and supported the latter in his attempts to publish his massive epic in alexandrine verse, *Der Habspurgische Ottobert* (1663, 1664). His treatise on raising horses, *Norma seu Regula Armentorum Equinorum,* was written in Latin because the Hungarian nobility mostly spoke that language; the work reflects Stubenberg's unrelenting attempts to move to Hungary, where he could be among his friends.

Stubenberg's last major translation project was the French novel *Clelia: Eine Römische Geschichte* (Clelia: A Roman Story, 1664), written by Madeleine de Scudéry but originally published in 1654 under her brother's name. Although the voluminous work was not much to his liking, he completed it to please the aristocratic women readers of Vienna; the members of the Isternymphen had urged him to carry out this task. *Clelia* consisted of five volumes, each of around one thousand pages. Stubenberg dedicated it to Empress Eleonore, Emperor Ferdinand III's widow, and included some poems by Greiffenberg and others who praised the quality of the work.

Since 1653 Stubenberg had developed a special concern with literary and philosophical works that included a broad spectrum of information about historical or scientific fields. *Clelia* fulfilled this interest as well, because it enabled the reader to educate himself or herself about Roman history without collecting the knowledge "aus ganz grossen Büchereyen erst mit unsäglicher Mühe-Schweiß" (out of very large libraries with indescribably painful efforts). On the other hand, Stubenberg refused to accept the task of translating Tacitus's *Germania,* despite the urgings of the Counts Montecuccoli and Strozzi. This incident shows that he still had some important contacts with the court and yet had strength enough to refrain from becoming a servant of the court.

Stubenberg made many attempts to help younger poets be accepted as members of the Fruchtbringende Gesellschaft, but he could not prevent the society's steady decline and ultimate downfall. He died on 15 March 1663 and was buried in Kittsee. A few years later his remains were transferred to a grave in Regensburg next to his wife, son, and daughter-in-law.

Bibliography:

Gerhard Dünnhaupt, *Personalbibliographien zu den Drucken des Barock,* volume 9, part 6 (Stuttgart: Hiersemann, 1993), pp. 3989–4003.

Biography:

Johann Loserth, "Der Unglückselige: Ein Mitglied der Fruchtbringenden Gesellschaft aus dem Hause Stubenberg," *Mitteilungen des Vereins für die Geschichte der Deutschen in Böhmen,* 48 (1910): 247–291.

References:

F. W. Barthold, *Geschichte der Fruchtbringenden Gesellschaft: Sitten, Geschmacksbildung und schöne Redekünste deutscher Vornehmen vom Ende des XVI. bis über die Mitte des XVII. Jahrhunderts* (Berlin: Duncker, 1848; reprinted, Hildesheim: Olms, 1969);

Martin Bircher, *Johann Wilhelm von Stubenberg (1619–1663) und sein Freundeskreis: Studien zur österreichischen Barockliteratur protestantischer Edelleute,* Quellen und Forschungen zur Sprach- und Kulturgeschichte der gemanischen Völker, new series 25 (Berlin: De Gruyter, 1968);

Bircher and Peter M. Daly, "Catharina Regina von Greiffenberg und Johann Wilhelm von Stubenberg: Zur Frage der Autorschaft zweier anonymer Widmungsreden," *Literaturwissenschaftliches Jahrbuch,* 7 (1966): 17–35;

Otto Brunner, *Adeliges Landleben und europäischer Geist: Leben und Werk Wolf Helmhards von Hohberg 1612–1688* (Salzburg: Müller, 1949);

Georg Loesche, "Die böhmischen Exulanten in Sachsen," *Jahrbuch der Gesellschaft für die Geschichte des Protestantismus in Österreich,* 42–44 (1923).

Papers:

Johann Wilhelm von Stubenberg's letters and other manuscripts can be found in the Archiv des Pegnesischen Blumenordens in the Germanisches National-Museum, Nuremberg; in the Akten der Fruchtbringenden Gesellschaft in the Staatsarchiv in Weimar; in the Akten der Fruchtbringenden Gesellschaft in the Heimat-Museum der Stadt Köthen; in the Stubenberg-Archiv in Graz; in the Niederösterreichisches Landesarchiv and the Finanz- und Hofkammerarchiv in Vienna; and in the Stiftsarchiv in Melk.

Andreas Tscherning

(18 November 1611 – 27 September 1659)

David Halsted

University of Cincinnati

SELECTED BOOKS: *LobGesang vber den frewdenreichen GeburtsTag vnsers Herrn vnd Heylands Jesu Chrjstj* (Rostock: Johann Richel's heirs, 1635);

Lob des Weingottes (Rostock: Printed by Joachim Fuess's widow, 1636);

Lob der Buchdruckerey (Breslau: Printed by Georg Baumann, 1640);

Andreas Tschernings Deutscher Getichte Früling (Breslau: Published by Georg Baumann, 1642; enlarged edition, Rostock: Printed by Johann Richel, published by Joachim Wild, 1646);

Semicenturia Schediasmatum Andreae Tscherningii Siles (Rostock: Printed by Johann Richel, 1643); enlarged as *Schediasmatum Liber Unus* (Rostock: Johann Richel, 1644);

Schediasmatum pars altera (Rostock: Printed by Johann Richel, 1650);

Vortrab des Sommers Deutscher Getichte (Rostock: Printed by Nicolaus Keil, published by Joachim Wild, 1655);

Anacreon Latinus Universae Studiosorum Coronae In Almae ad Varnum Sacer. Auctore Andrea Tscherningio, Prof. Poet. (Rostock: Nicolaus Keil's heirs, 1656);

Democritus (Rostock: Nicolaus Keil's heirs, 1656);

Andreas Tschernings unvorgreiffliches Bedencken über etliche mißbräuche in der deutschen Schreib- und Sprach-Kunst, insonderheit der edlen Poeterey (Lübeck: Published by Michael Volck, printed by Valentin Schmalhertz's heirs, 1658); republished as *Unvorgreiffliches Bedencken über etliche mißbräuche in der deutschen Schreib- und Sprach-Kunst, insonderheit der edlen Poeterey. Wie auch Kurtzer Entwurff oder Abrieß einer deutschen Schatzkammer, von schönen und zierlichen Poëtischen redens-arten, umbschreibungen, und denen dingen, so einem getichte sonderbaren glantz und anmuht geben können* (Lübeck: Published by Michael Volck, printed by Valentin Schmalhertz's heirs, 1659).

OTHER: Daniel Heinsius and Caspar Barlaeus, *Rachel Deplorans Infanticidium Herodis,* translated and adapted by Tscherning (Breslau, 1635);

Centuria Proverbiorum Alis Imperatorum Muslimici distichis Latino-Germanicis expressa, ab Andrea Tscherningio, Cum Notis brevioribus, translated by Tscherning (Breslau: Georg Baumann, 1641);

Martin Opitz, *Judith, auffs neu aussgefertiget; worzu das vördere theil der Historie sampt den Melodeyen auf iedwedes Chor beygefüget,* edited by Tscherning (Rostock: Johann Richel, 1646);

Proverbia Arabica Germanicé expressa, translated by Tscherning (Rostock: Johann Richel, 1654).

Andreas Tscherning was one of the leading members of the school of poets who sought to follow the path laid out by Martin Opitz. Tscherning was well regarded in the seventeenth and eighteenth centuries. Augustus Buchner, professor of poetics and rhetoric at the University of Wittenberg and teacher of an extraordinary number of the seventeenth century's finest poets, admired him; Matthäus Apelles von Löwenstern supported him financially and joined him in writing and dramatic projects; the teacher and poet Christophorus Colerus in Breslau (now Wrocław) helped launch his career; he followed Nathan Chrytäus and the Laurembergs in the chair for poetics at Rostock University and taught his eventual successor, Daniel Georg Morhof; he was admired by Colerus's student Johann Peter Titz, professor of poetry and rhetoric at the gymnasium in Danzig (today Gdansk, Poland). In his *Versuch einer Critischen Dichtkunst* (Essay on a Critical Poetics, 1730) Johann Christoph Gottsched named Tscherning, along with Opitz, Simon Dach, Andreas Gryphius, and Paul Fleming, as one of the exemplary poets young people should be encouraged to imitate, and Gotthold Ephraim Lessing also thought highly of his work. Yet the sole book-length study of this poet, rhetorician, poetic theorist, and early translator of Arabic literature dates from

1912; essays on Tscherning, too, have been in short supply.

Andreas Tscherning was born in 1611 in Bunzlau (now Boleslawiec) in Silesia. Tscherning began his education in Bunzlau but was not able to finish school there; by 1629 the city had been subjected to the rigors of Hapsburg Counter-Reformation policy. After a brief stay in Görlitz, Tscherning arrived at the celebrated Elisabethgymnasium in Breslau in 1630 or 1631. His first published poems date from 1631. Like so much of the poetry of the day, they were written in Latin for particular occasions – births, deaths, weddings, promotions to new offices, and name days. School instruction included practice in composing Latin poems for these purposes. Tscherning's first preserved German poem dates from 1632.

In Breslau, Tscherning became friendly with Opitz and Colerus, both of whom were also from Bunzlau. In 1635 Tscherning enrolled at the university at Rostock, where, among his other pursuits, he studied oriental languages. This interest led to the publication of *Centuria Proverbiorum Alis Imperatorium Muslimici distichis Latino-Germanicis expressa . . . Cum Notis brevioribus* (One Hundred Proverbs of Ali, Ruler of the Muslims, Put into Latin and German Distichs . . . with Brief Notes, 1641) and *Proverbia Arabica Germanicé expressa* (Arabic Proverbs Translated into German, 1654). In 1636 he returned to Breslau, where he remained until 1642, when he set off again for Rostock.

During the 1630s Tscherning became an active poet in both Latin and German. In 1635 and 1636 three important poems were published: *Rachel Deplorans Infanticidum Herodis* (Rachel Lamenting the Infanticide of Herod, 1635), a translation and adaptation of poems by Daniel Heinsius and Caspar Barlaeus; *LobGesang über den frewdenreichen Geburts-Tag unsers Herrn und Heylands Jesu Christi* (Song of Praise on the Joyful Birth of Our Lord and Savior Jesus Christ, 1635); and *Lob des Weingottes* (Praise of the God of Wine, 1636). The last two are written in imitation of Opitz's translations from Heinsius. During this period Tscherning began his friendship with Buchner, since 1616 professor of poetry and since 1632 professor of rhetoric at Wittenberg University. In 1640 Tscherning dedicated a long poem to Buchner, *Lob der Buchdruckerey* (In Praise of the Art of Printing). The friendship reflected and helped foster Buchner's and Tscherning's shared views about the nature, purposes, and ideals of German poetry.

The year 1642 was a watershed in Tscherning's life, for in this year he both resumed his ori-

ental studies at the University of Rostock and published a large collection of his German poetry, the *Deutscher Getichte Früling* (The Springtime of German Verse). A second edition, including the proverbs of Ali, was published in 1646. This book established Tscherning's reputation as a poet, while his studies prepared him to accept the post of professor of poetry at Rostock. To qualify for the chair, Tscherning had to get a master's degree, prove that he was not a Calvinist, and establish his abilities in Latin poetry and poetics. He finished his degree in 1644 and was appointed to the chair, though his salary would not begin for another three years. One year later, though, he married Katerina Marsilius, a lawyer's widow, and with this step his finances were put on solid footing. The couple had a son, Andreas, on 25 December 1645, and a daughter, Anna Catherina, on 2 June 1647. As a professor, Tscherning lectured on such authors as Juvenal, Virgil, and Horace. In this period university education was centered on Latin poetry and literature; Tscherning, however, also taught German poetry.

Tscherning's literary activities continued alongside his teaching duties. In 1644 the first of two volumes of his Latin occasional poetry, *Schediasmatum Liber Unus* (A Book of Extemporaneous Verse) appeared. In 1646 Tscherning published an expanded version of Opitz's opera *Judith* (1635) with music by Tscherning's patron, Apelles von Löwenstern; the opera had been performed in Thorn (today Torun) in 1642. By extending Opitz's libretto from three acts to five, Tscherning recast the piece in the form of a classical tragedy. The extra material he added had its source in a Latin school play by Sixt Birk of Strasbourg (1539). In 1650 the second volume of *Schediasmatum* appeared. The year 1655 saw the publication of Tscherning's second large collection of German verse, the *Vortrab des Sommers Deutscher Getichte* (The Vanguard of the Summer of German Verse). This work was not as successful as *Deutscher Getichte Früling*. In 1658, only a year before Tscherning's death, he published a theoretical treatise on the art of writing German poetry, *Andreas Tschernings unvorgreiffliches Bedencken über etliche mißbräuche in der deutschen Schreib- und Sprach-Kunst, insonderheit der edlen Poeterey* (Andreas Tscherning's Essay of Misgivings about Several Abuses in German Orthography and Speaking, Especially in the Noble Art of Poetry). This work presents a systematic treatment of German orthographic and poetic practice in the spirit of Opitz and includes a poetic thesaurus. Tscherning died on 27 September 1659.

Frontispiece for the collection that established Andreas Tscherning's reputation as a poet

Tscherning learned to write Latin and German poetry in an age that was marked by artistic convention. It was the custom to write poetry in exchange for payment, and much of Tscherning's output took the form of occasional verse. He complained in the foreword to *Deutscher Getichte Früling* and in the opening poem of *Schediasmatum Liber Unus* of the necessity of writing poetry at the behest of another rather than as an act of free inspiration. Also in Tscherning's day the humanist tradition of literary imitation was still a vital force. *Schatzkammern* (thesauri), such as the one published by Tscherning, were lists of formulaic treatments of images or themes, such as "the still port" to mean "death" or "the heavenly lamp" for "sun," and the repetition of such phrases makes much seventeenth-century poetry look clichéd to a twentieth-century eye. Tscherning's reputation among his contemporaries and among scholars of the baroque rests primarily

on his formal skill. For all these virtues, however, Tscherning's poetry does not appeal immediately to the modern ear as do Philipp von Zesen's or Georg Philipp Harsdörffer's experiments in meter and sound, Christian Hoffmann von Hoffmannswaldau's psychological and erotic meditations, Daniel Casper von Lohenstein's political pathos, or Andreas Gryphius's existential anxiety. Paradoxically, it is just those areas in which Tscherning's skill and significance are revealed most clearly that are least accessible to a taste shaped by modernity.

These formal virtues are what help define Tscherning's place in the history of German verse. Several scholars, among them Hans Heinrich Borcherdt and Willi Flemming, have described Tscherning's poetry as part of an Opitzian "middle way." This line of poetic influence connects Opitz to his admirer Buchner and his poetic imitators Tscherning and Titz, continuing through Tscherning's student and successor Morhof. Running between the stylistic excesses of Zesen and the antiquarian interests of the Fruchtbringende Gesellschaft (Fruit-bringing Society), this line connects the Renaissance to the early eighteenth century, as Gottsched's praise indicates. The classical restraint and measured quality of Tscherning's verse corresponds, as Manfred Windfuhr points out, to Tscherning's praise of reason in his *Lob der Buchdruckerey*. The poetry and the theoretical treatises of the *Opitzianer* condemn rhetorically swollen metaphors and metrical experiments, emphasizing purity in language and regularity of form. In Buchner and Tscherning this emphasis on purity takes the form of a conscious avoidance of or embarrassment over the erotic.

That Tscherning's reputation as a close follower of Opitz was justified can readily be seen in his verse. The poetic forms and meters Tscherning uses in his two major collections had been popularized in German by Opitz; like Opitz, Tscherning shows a preference for the long alexandrine line and for iambic and trochaic lines of three or four feet, with occasional use of *vers communs*. Experiments with other meters, such as the dactyl and anapest, or with such set forms as sonnets and the rondeau occur, though exceptionally, in Tscherning's poetry. In Latin, Tscherning uses meters and forms common to Latin occasional verse of the day, especially the elegiac couplet – a hexameter line followed by a pentameter. Tscherning examined many of the poems of particular formal interest years in his poetics, showing his awareness of and interest in the possibilities for formal innovation that even the relatively restrictive rules of Opitzian poetics offered.

The thematic range of Tscherning's poetry is, to the modern eye, somewhat limited. Occasional poems form the bulk of his collections in both German and Latin. These poems had often been printed before, either as individual titles or in collections of poems by groups of authors on a specific event. His nonoccasional verse includes allegorical representations, fables, religious and moral meditations, and several examples of poetry inclining to social or political satire. The few poems on love objects are clumsy. Of special interest to the student of literary history are the poems decrying bad poets and a poem on the persecution of rhetoric called "The Tongue Speaks." *Deutscher Getichte Früling* includes several translations into German from contemporary poets working in Latin: Heinsius, Barlaeus, Jan Gruter, and members of Silesia's learned elite, such as Opitz, Bernhard Nüssler, Caspar Kirchner, and Andreas Senftleben. There is also a translation from Dutch poems by Heinsius and, as Ulrich Bornemann has shown, by Dirk Volkerstzoon Coornhert. These translations are to be thought of as a kind of imitation, a way for the poet to learn how to re-create in German what had been accomplished in more established poetic traditions. There are also several poems that follow models in German by Opitz.

Tscherning's poems cover a variety of tones and colors. His capacity for humor appears in "Dactylische Ode. Auff einen Aussbund eines Lustigen und Possirlichen Hündleins" (A Dactylic Ode on the Example of a Merry and Comical Pup), which opposes, in a lively meter indicating the vivacity of its subject, the animal's infectious gaiety to the earnestness of the literature it was Tscherning's profession to study, and in "Lagopus wil ein Edelman sein" (Lagopus Wants to Be a Nobleman), a short satire on a commoner who tries to give out that he is an aristocrat but is caught. "Auff Hn. Johann Heermanns P.L.C. Pfarrers zu Köben Deutsche Epigrammata" (On the Publication of the German Epigrams of Herr Johann Heerman, Imperial Poet Laureate and Minister at Köben) and a particularly engaging poem, "Auff die Music," (On Music), are constructed of lines combining a dactyl and a trochee.

Tscherning's understanding of his relationship to the world of learning in his day appears in several poems. *Lob der Buchdruckerey* begins by drawing a connection between reason and the rise of new sciences and technologies:

Wer spricht dass fort vnd für die Welt nur ärger werde?
Er sieht gewiss nicht an den Himmel noch die Erde
Mit Augen der Vernunfft.

(Who says the world grows only worse and worse?
He certainly does not see heaven or earth
With eyes made clear by reason.)

The poem goes on to argue that the German invention of book publishing ranks with the great cultural achievements of the ancients and the moderns, including Galileo's invention of the telescope and the discovery of the New World. The negotiation between the ancients and modernity was a popular and important theme in seventeenth-century thought, resting as it did on the tense relation between scientific and technical progress, in which a sense of superiority to the Greco-Roman world was clearly felt, on the one hand, and the world of literary culture, in which the means of measuring "progress" were less clear, on the other.

The presence of neo-Stoic elements in his work also marks Tscherning as typical of his time. Neo-Stoicism, a late humanist application of ancient moral and political precepts to the modern world and an amalgamation of Stoic with Christian teachings, developed in the Netherlands in the late sixteenth century, became popular across Europe, and remained an important cultural force until the end of the seventeenth century. Tscherning's friend and teacher Colerus had been trained at Strasbourg by Matthias Bernegger, an important representative of neo-Stoic political thought; Colerus himself had taught neo-Stoicism in Breslau, and Tscherning surely absorbed some of his enthusiasm. In poems such as "Gedult ist allen Menschen nötig" (Patience Is Necessary for All), "Güter des Gemütes" (Wealth of the Spirit), and "Uberwinde dich selbst" (Overcome Thyself) Tscherning explores explicitly neo-Stoic themes. "Gedult ist allen Menschen nötig" ties Stoic suffering to Christian virtue, a theme perhaps most famously treated in Gryphius's martyr plays and one that both the founder of neo-Stoicism, Justus Lipsius, and Heinsius had considered in their prose works. "Güter des Gemütes" tells the story of a wise man who, having lost his goods in a shipwreck, declares that in losing mere material possessions he has lost nothing truly his own, a theme that echoes the Roman philosopher Seneca's stories of Stilbo, a philosopher whose goods and family were destroyed in war – parallels to the story of Job lay, naturally, close at hand. "Uberwinde dich selbst" explores the image of the soul as a site of contest to describe the process of moral self-discipline. The

Title page for Tscherning's treatise on poetic theory

poem echoes Lipsius's dialogue *De constantia* (On Constancy, 1584).

Tscherning's poetic theory, *Unvorgreiffliches Bedencken,* follows and expands on points covered in the poetics of Opitz and Buchner. Tscherning's poetics, a compendium of his views gathered over years of writing poetry and teaching the writing of poetry, represent one of the more important statements in Opitzian poetic theory and taste and may be compared in this regard to Titz's poetics of 1642, *Zwey Bücher von der Kunst Hochdeutsche Verse und Lieder zu machen* (Two Books on the Art of Making High German Verses and Songs). Tscherning's poetic examples come mostly from Opitz, from Fleming, and from his own work; in matters of theory he refers again and again to Opitz and to Buchner, quoting letters from the Wittenberg professor and referring

to Buchner's influential lectures on poetics. Other contemporary German scholars and poets to whom Tscherning refers or whom he cites, not always approvingly, include Harsdörffer, Zesen, Heermann, Justus Georg Schottelius, Johann Rist, Johannes Plavius, Johannes Freinsheim, and Zacharias Lund. Figures from earlier generations, such as Melchior Goldast, Martin Luther, Ambrosius Lobwasser, and Buchner's predecessor Friedrich Taubmann, join past and present luminaries of the international literary and academic community: Lipsius; Hugo Grotius; Guillaume de Salluste, Seigneur du Bartas; Julius Caesar Scaliger; Balthasar Venator; Gerardus Johannes Vossius; and Marc-Antoine Muretus.

As an Opitzian, Tscherning was concerned both with preserving the "purity" of the German language and with not allowing its literature to slip below a level at which it could compete with classical literature. The relationship to the classics is significant in light of the move away from classical models that was already taking place in Germany in the 1640s. Even as Colerus, Buchner, Titz, and Tscherning were seeking to preserve Opitz's achievements after his death, writers such as Harsdörffer were calling for an aesthetics of German poetry separate from poetic theory based on Roman and modern Latin verse, while new currents from abroad, such as Marinism, had begun to make their presence felt. The classical rhetorical and poetic tradition, with which Tscherning's work stands in an often quite close dialogue, has been broken to such an extent that his poems (and those of many of his contemporaries) may seem to be scholastic exercises today, and the conventionality of his verse may make it seem stilted or unoriginal. Much of his verse was written on demand, often under time pressure. Since occasional verse is now out of fashion, it is hard for the modern reader to overcome the feeling that the bulk of Tscherning's output, because it was written in praise of specific individuals and often in exchange for payment, is not "artistic." In this sense Tscherning himself analyzed one of the fundamental reasons for the waning of interest in his verse.

Letters:

Epistulae Celebrium Eruditissimorumque virorum varii argumenti, praesertim C. Coleri, H. Grotii, J. B. Venatoris, Jani Gruteri, N. Rittershusii, C. Barthii, Joh. H. Boecleri, J. Mochingeri, et aliorum ex Museo A. I askii, edited by Andreas Jaski (Amsterdam: Jansson-Waesberg, 1705);

August Buchner, *Augusti Buchneri Epistolarum Partes Tres . . . Opera M. Joh. Jacobi Stübelii . . .* (Frankfurt am Main & Leipzig: Gottfried Lesch, 1720);

Alexander Reifferscheid, *Briefe G. M. Lingelsheims, M. Berneggers und ihrer Freunde; Quellen zur Geschichte des geistigen Lebens in Deutschland während des 17. Jahrhunderts,* volume 1 (Heilbronn: Henninger, 1889).

Bibliographies:

Karl Goedeke, *Grundriss zur Geschichte der deutschen Dichtung,* volume 3 (Dresden: Ehlermann, 1887), p. 51;

Franz Heiduk, *Die Dichter der galanten Lyrik* (Bern: Francke, 1971), p. 126;

Sergio Lupi, ed., *Dizionario critico della letteratura tedesca,* volume 2 (Turin: Unione tipgrafico-editrice torinese, 1976), p. 1184;

Erdmann Neumeister, *De Poetis Germanicis Hujus seculi praecipuis Dissertatio compendiaria,* translated by G. Merwald (Bern: Francke, 1978), p. 483;

Gerhard Dünnhaupt, *Personalbibliographien zu den Drucken des Barock,* volume 9, part 6 (Stuttgart: Hiersemann, 1993).

Biography:

Hans Heinrich Borcherdt, *Andreas Tscherning: Ein Beitrag zur Literatur- und Kultur-Geschichte des 17, Jahrhunderts* (Munich & Leipzig: Hans-Sachs Verlag Gotthilf Haist, 1912).

References:

Wilfried Barner, *Barockrhetorik: Untersuchungen zu ihren geschichtlichen Grundlagen* (Tübingen: Niemeyer, 1970);

Adalheid Beckmann, *Motive und Formen der deutschen Lyrik des 17. Jahrhunderts und ihre Entsprechungen in der französischen Lyrik seit Ronsard: Ein Beitrag zur vergleichenden Literaturgeschichte* (Tübingen: Niemeyer, 1960);

Hans Heinrich Borcherdt, *Augustus Buchner und seine Bedeutung für die deutsche Literatur des 17. Jahrhunderts* (Munich: Beck, 1919);

Ulrich Bornemann, *Ablehnung und Abgrenzung: Untersuchungen zur Rezeption der niederländischen Literatur in der deutschen Dichtungsreform des siebzehnten Jahrhunderts* (Assen & Amsterdam: Van Gorcum, 1976);

Bornemann, "Dirck Volckertszoon Coornhert und Andreas Tscherning über Reichtum, Armut, Almosen und Bettler: Zu den niederländisch-deutschen Literaturbeziehungen," *Daphnis: Zeitschrift für Mittlere Deutsche Literatur,* 19, no. 3 (1990): 493–509;

Gerhard Dünnhaupt, "Der barocke Eisberg: Überlegungen zur Erfassung des Schrifttums des 17. Jahrhunderts," *Aus dem Antiquariat,* 10 (1980): 441–446;

David Halsted, "Koexistenz, Kontinuität, Transformation: Die lateinische und deutsche pindarishe Ode (1616–1642)," *Daphnis: Zeitschrift für Mittlere Deutsche Literatur* (forthcoming);

Halsted, "*Poetry and Politics in the Silesian Baroque: Neo-Stoicism in the Work of Christophorus Colerus and His Circle,*" dissertation, University of Michigan, 1992;

Helmut Henne, *Hochsprache und Mundart im schlesischen Barock: Studien zum literarischen Wortschatz in der ersten Hälfte des 17. Jahrhunderts,* Mitteldeutsche Forschungen, no. 44 (Cologne & Graz: Böhlau, 1966);

Renate Hildebrandt-Günther, *Antike Rhetorik und deutsche literarische Theorie im 17. Jahrhundert,* Marburger Beiträge zur Germanistik, no. 13 (Marburg: Elwert, 1966);

Max Hippe, *Christoph Köler, ein schlesischer Dichter des siebzehnten Jahrhunderts: Sein Leben und eine Auswahl seiner deutschen Gedichte,* Mittheilungen aus dem Stadtarchiv und der Stadtbibliothek zu Breslau, no. 5 (Breslau: Morgenstern, 1902);

Arno Lubos, *Geschichte der Literatur Schlesiens,* volume 1 (Munich: Korn, 1960);

Günther Müller, *Geschichte des deutschen Liedes vom Zeitalter des Barock bis zur Gegenwart* (Darmstadt: Wissenschaftliche Buchgesellschaft, 1959);

Marian Szyrocki, *Die deutsche Literatur des Barock: Eine Einführung* (Stuttgart: Reclam, 1979);

Karl Viëtor, *Geschichte der deutschen Ode,* Geschichte der deutschen Literatur nach Gattungen, no. 1 (Munich: Drei Masken, 1923);

Manfred Windfuhr, *Die barocke Bildlichkeit und ihre Kritiker: Stilhaltungen in der deutschen Literatur des 17. und 18. Jahrhunderts,* Germanistische Abhandlungen, no. 15 (Stuttgart: Metzler, 1966).

Niclas Ulenhart

(*flourished circa 1600*)

Gerhart Hoffmeister
University of California, Santa Barbara

BOOK: *Zwo kurtzweilige, lustige, und lächerliche Historien, Die Erste, von Lazarillo de Tormes, einem Spanier, was für Herkommens er gewesen, wo, und was für abenthewerliche Possen, er in seinen Herrendiensten getriben, wie es jme auch darben, biß er gehenrat, ergangen, vnnd wie er letstlich zu erlichen Teutschen in Kundschaft gerathen. Auß Spanischer Sprach ins Teutsche ganz trewlich transferirt. Die ander, von Isaac Winckelfelder, vnd Jobst von der Schneid, Wie es disen beyden Gesellen in der weitberühmten Statt Prag ergangen, was sie daselbst für ein wunderseltzame Bruderschafft angetroffen, vnd sich in dieselbe verleiben lassen* (Augsburg: Printed by Andreas Aperger, published in Munich by Nicolaus Heinrich, 1617).

Editions: *Sonderlich-Curieuse Historia von Jsaac Winckelfelder und Jobst von der Schneidt,* edited by August Sauer (Prague: Gesellschaft deutscher Bücherfreunde in Böhmen, 1923);

Sonderbare Geschichte von Isaac Winckelfelder und Jobst von der Schneid, edited by Gutta Veidl (Munich: Langen-Müller, 1941);

Historia von Isaac Winckeldelder und Jobst von der Schneid 1617, edited by Gerhart Hoffmeister, Literatur-Kabinett, no. 1 (Munich: Fink, 1983).

Although nothing at all is known about Niclas Ulenhart himself, his *Historia von Isaac Winckelfelder und Jobst von der Schneid* (History of Isaac Winckelfelder und Jobst von der Schneid, 1617), published half a dozen times during the seventeenth century, has an important place in the reception of Miguel de Cervantes in Germany and the inauguration of a native *Schelmenroman* (picaresque novel). Not only was Ulenhart the first German author to adapt a Cervantes work into a language other than Spanish, but he adapted it so successfully to a German environment that it took until 1868 to discover Ulenhart's model.

Several generations of scholars have speculated about Ulenhart's life, but no information has come to light apart from the internal evidence the text of his novel provides. Early in the twentieth century Ulenhart was thought to be the grandson of the Augsburg Reformation printer Philipp Ulhart, but no record of an Ulenhart family has been found in Augsburg archives. Nicolaus Heinrich, the publisher of the novel, was located in Munich; *Historia von Isaac Winckelfelder und Jobst von der Schneid* was, however, printed in Augsburg. Since Munich was the only significant publishing center in the southeastern region of the empire, it does not necessarily follow that Ulenhart must have been a citizen of either of the two towns. Much more likely is the hypothesis of Ulenhart's origin in Prague, the setting of his work. The name Niclas Ulenhart may even be a pseudonym.

It took until 1648 for the first incomplete translation of *Don Quixote,* Cervantes's masterpiece of 1605 and 1615, to appear in German translation. Since 1613 Don Quixote had, however, gained wide acclaim as a legendary figure through Dutch and French intermediaries. Even more popular in the first half of the seventeenth century were the twelve tales in Cervantes's *Novelas ejemplares* (Exemplary Stories, 1613), among them *Rinconete y Cortadillo,* the story of two youths who strike up a friendship in a country inn and decide to become vagabonds and travel to Seville. On the road they rob some travelers; but when they steal purses from people in town, they learn that they must be licensed by Monipodio, the underworld boss of Seville. After an initiation the two thieves are admitted to the beggars' fraternity, which observes strict principles of religious behavior and thus serves as an ironic mirror of the legitimate Christian society. *Rinconete y Cortadillo* is considered the earliest Cervantes *novela,* conceived most likely during the poet's stay in Seville in 1602–1603, as well as the most accomplished one: it is full of life, memorable scenes, and ambiguities, bordering on an objective portrayal of manners and customs.

Ulenhart does not mention Cervantes, although he concedes that his version may have an equivalent "in forma authentica" (in authentic form). He did not translate the original but made an ingenious adaptation of it to German requirements. He followed the outlines of the plot of *Rinconete y Cortadillo* but changed the setting, the characters of the leading figures, and the style to such a degree that he ended up using twice as many pages as Cervantes.

Ulenhart's novel is set not in staunchly Catholic Seville but in Prague's Old Town, which teems with Jews, Catholics, Hussites, and Protestants. The plot unfolds in a district bounded by the Jewish quarter, the Hradschin Palace, the cathedral, and the marketplace. The fourteen- and fifteen-year-old picaros of Cervantes's story turn into twenty-one- or twenty-two-year-old vagrants. Ulenhart also changes his protagonists' backgrounds: Rinconete's father, a seller of indulgences in the struggle against the Moors, has been turned into a Calvinist vicar, whose strictness becomes unbearable to his son Isaac and pushes him onto the road of absolute freedom. Cortadillo's father is a deceitful tailor who taught his son the art of picking pockets, whereas Jobst can no longer stand to live in a Moravian Anabaptist community. Like their Spanish models, the youngsters meet on the road, living from hand to mouth but surviving on different foods: Cervantes's wine from the Guadacanal region, citrus fruit, white bread with cheese, olives, and crabs are replaced by Rhine or Franconian wine, bratwurst, bratfisch, roast pig, loin of veal, and goose. The underworld boss Monipodio and his female counterpart Señora Pipota also undergo considerable changes. Monipodio reemerges as Zuckerbastel (sugar daddy), somewhat more congenial and also more demonic than his model, a mix of incongruous features as his leather pants and slippers clash with his black face. The best example of Ulenhart's successful transposition is his renaming of Pipota: she becomes Maruschka, an endearing pet name for this thieving old woman with a big heart and a strong sense of piety who before and after successful thefts prays fervently to her saints.

Title page for the first edition of Niclas Ulenhart's translation and adaptation of Miguel de Cervantes's Rinconete y Cortadillo. *The translation of* Lazarillo de Tormes *in the same volume is not thought to be by Ulenhart.*

Cervantes's diction is elegant and precise; no word is superfluous. Prominent among his stylistic features is his elliptic speech, modeled after the terseness of classical Roman authors. Transferring the Sevillian story to a German-speaking Bohemian environment, Ulenhart lost this Spanish brevity; his readers needed explanations, interpretations, and arguments. The result is a vibrant, popular, yet poetic style, which in its diversity and amplitude perfectly mirrors the Bohemian milieu and in its own way matches Cervantes. Ulenhart is a master of the German language; he even adapts the jargon of the Spanish picaros to the corresponding terms of German *Rotwelsch* (thieves' cant). On account of his involved periods, his diction has been compared to a *poetischer Kanzleistil* (poeticized chancery style) typical of the early baroque period around 1600. But whereas Aegidius Albertinus translated from Spanish in the service of the Counter-Reformation, and Hans Ludwig Kuffstein did so for the sake of improved courtly manners, Ulenhart's novel has no extraliterary purpose. He wrote not for courtly society but for anyone who would enjoy a tale about genuinely German rogues.

With its many editions, *Historia von Isaac Winckelfelder und Jobst von der Schneid* was so successful that Johann Jakob Christoffel von Grimmelshausen could open his novel *Der abenteuerliche Simplicissimus Teutsch* (The Adventurous Simplicissimus German, 1669) with a reference to the "Zuckerbastels Zunfft zu Prag" (Zuckerbastel's guild in Prague), as if his readers would know about it fifty years after the first edition of Ulenhart's work. The popularity of *Historia von Isaac Winckelfelder und Jobst von der Schneid* prompted another author, La Zelande, to transfer the same plot from Prague to Lisbon in *Der Alten und Newen Spitzbuben . . . Practiquen* (The Tricks . . . of Old and New Rogues, 1682). Willibald Alexis (pseudonym of Georg Wilhelm Häring) probably went back to Cervantes's original or a close translation of it when he composed his youthful short story "Die ehrlichen Leute" (Honest People, 1825), recasting the plot in the Berlin underworld.

References:

Richard Alewyn, "Die ersten deutschen Übersetzer des 'Don Quijote' und des 'Lazarillo de Tormes,' " *Zeitschrift für deutsche Philologie,* 54 (1929): 203–216;

Lienhard Bergel, "Cervantes in Germany," in his *Cervantes across the Centuries* (New York: Dryden, 1947), pp. 305–342;

Gerhart Hoffmeister, "Grimmelshausens *Simplicissimus* und der spanisch-deutsche Schelmenroman," *Daphnis,* 5 (1976): 275–294;

Hoffmeister, *Spanien und Deutschland: Geschichte und Dokumentation der literarischen Beziehungen,* Grundlagen der Romanistik, no. 9 (Berlin: Schmidt, 1976);

Hubert Rausse, "Die ersten deutschen Übertragungen von Cervantes' *Novelas ejemplares,*" *Studien für vergleichende Literaturgeschichte,* 9 (1909): 385–405;

Paul Richter, "Cervantes und Alexis: Untersuchungen zum Fortleben der Cervantesschen Gaunernovelle *Rinconete y Cortadillo* in der deutschen Literatur," *Jahrbuch der Alexis-Fontane-Gesellschaft* (1937): 22–29;

Reiner Schulze-van Loon, "Niclas Ulenharts 'Historia': Beiträge zur deutschen Rezeption der 'Novela picaresca' und zur Frühgeschichte der barocken Prosa," dissertation, University of Hamburg, 1955.

Georg Rodolf Weckherlin

(14 September 1584 – 13 February 1653)

Richard E. Schade
University of Cincinnati

BOOKS: *Triumf newlich bey der F. Kindtauf zu Stuttgart gehalten* (Stuttgart: Printed by Johann Weyrich Rösslin, 1616); English version published as *Trivmphall Shews set forth lately at Stutgart. Written first in German, and now in English* (Stuttgart: Printed by Johann Weyrich Rösslin, 1616);

Kurtze Beschreibung, deß zu Stutgarten, bey den Fürstlichen Kindtauf vnd Hochzeit, Jüngst-gehaltenen Frewden-Festes (Tübingen: Dietrich Werlin, 1618);

Oden vnd Gesänge (Stuttgart: Printed by Johann Weyrich Rösslin the Elder, 1618);

Das ander Buch Oden vnd Gesäng (Stuttgart: Printed by Johann Weyrich Rösslin the Elder, 1619);

A Panegyricke to the most honourable and renowned Lord, the Lord Hays Vicount of Doncaster His Majesties of Great-Brittaine Ambassadour in Germanie sung by the Rhine (Stuttgart: Printed by Johann Weyrich Rösslin the Elder, 1619);

Gaistliche und Weltliche Gedichte (Amsterdam: Johannes Jansson, 1641; enlarged, 1648).

Editions and Collections: *Gedichte von Georg Rodolf Weckherlin,* edited by Karl Goedeke (Leipzig: Brockhaus, 1873);

Georg Rudolf Weckherlins Gedichte, 3 volumes, edited by Hermann Fischer (Tübingen: Litterarischer Verein, 1894–1907; reprinted, Darmstadt: Wissenschaftliche Buchgesellschaft, 1968);

Gedichte, edited by Christian Wagenknecht (Stuttgart: Reclam, 1972);

Stuttgarter Hoffeste, edited by L. Krapf and C. Wagenknecht (Tübingen: Niemeyer, 1979), pp. 1–296.

Edition in English: *The German Lyric of the Baroque in English Translation,* translated by George C. Schoolfield (New York: AMS Press, 1966), pp. 300–307.

"GEntle reader, Behold here a small booke written in English by a German, and printed in Germanie. Therefore if thou art too daintie a reader, I doe intreat thee, to seeke somewhere els fit

Georg Rodolf Weckherlin; engraving by William Faithorne after an oil painting, now lost, by Daniel Mytens

food, to bee pleased withall, as I know, there is greater store of in England, then in any other countrie." Even today the introductory words of *Triumphall Shews set forth lately at Stutgart. Written first in German, and now in English* (1616) by Georg Rodolf Weckherlin fascinate. At a time when the Elizabethan Age had receded and the Stuart monarchy was consolidating absolutist control over England, a poet from the southwest German duchy of Württemberg was dedicating a court festival book

Frontispiece for the first edition of Weckherlin's "spiritual and worldly poems." An enlarged edition appeared seven years later.

Weckherlin matriculated in the faculty of law at the University of Tübingen in 1599. The young man was being groomed for political service, and to this end his father admonished him to seek only the company of the God-fearing and to exercise propriety at every turn. Weckherlin sought the favor of young noblemen enrolled in Tübingen's Collegium illustre, a newly created ducal academy that attracted the best sons of the Holy Roman Empire. It was there that he met his later benefactor, Johann Friedrich, the princely heir to the Duchy of Württemberg. Even as a student he was establishing a network among the influential, connections that soon paid off: from 1604 until 1615 he accompanied various nobles on missions through Germany, into France, and to England. In France he mastered the language and became familiar with French literary culture; in England he became engaged to Elizabeth Raworth. On his return to Stuttgart in May 1615 the thirty-year-old Weckherlin had experienced much and had developed linguistic skills unusual for a German writer of the day, all of which he dedicated to the service of Duke Johann Friedrich. He and Raworth were married in 1616.

Weckherlin's first major literary project was a description of the festivities attendant to the baptism of the duke's son, events he was also involved in organizing. *Triumf Newlich bey der F. Kindtauf zu Stuttgart gehalten* (Triumph Recently Held in Stuttgart for the Princely Baptism, 1616) and its English version, *Triumphall Shews,* were astounding in the sumptuous complexity of allegorical conception designed to "dazzle the eyes of the beholders." Weckherlin's 125-page prose festival book was interlaced with celebratory verse:

> FAire Princess, glory of this season,
> The truth of your praise (vertues price)
> Doth so farre passe all humane reason,
> That he, whose hand would enterprise
> T'augment your fame by his deserving quill,
> Must either have much rashnesse or much skill.

Such literary creativity in the praise of princes assured the poet a job as often as it was required; *Kurtze Beschreibung, deß zu Stutgarten, bey den Fürstlichen Kindtauf und Hochzeit, Jüngst-gehaltenen Frewden-Festes* (Brief Description of the Joyous Festival in Stuttgart for the Princely Baptism and Wedding, 1618) is another example. Whether in German, French, Italian, English, Latin, or the local Swabian dialect, Weckherlin proved himself an adept master of verse forms fit for princes.

to "Elisabeth, onely davghter to his most excellent Majestie of Great-Britaine [James I]." In word and deed it was a signal event for the young Weckherlin, one defining the character of a literary career largely determined by equal loyalties to two realms but by a single sociocultural context – the absolutist court.

Weckherlin was born into a family of some importance in Stuttgart, the capital of the Duchy of Württemberg. His father, Johannes, was an aristocratic official of the duchy. From 1593 to 1599 Weckherlin attended the Padagogium, the elementary school that was the training ground for the sons of the best families. Latin, religion, and sacred music were the boy's daily fare, and the recitations, playacting, and songs would leave an indelible mark on his imagination.

Further proof of his ability came in the two books of *Oden und Gesänge* (Odes and Songs, 1618, 1619), collections filled with panegyrics of the highest style and with Petrarchan amatory verse, impressive odes, and ribald drinking songs. Weckherlin thereby documented the adaptability of the German language to all verse forms, from whatever national tradition. Shortly before his younger contemporary Martin Opitz would promulgate new rules for German poetry, Weckherlin was practicing what was to be preached; Opitz would include eight of Weckherlin's exemplary texts in his important *Teutsche Pöemata und Aristarchus* (German Poetry and Aristarchus, 1624). The Stuttgart poet had crossed the threshold to literary fame, only to leave Germany forever in 1619.

Mr. Wakerley, or Weckerling, as he was variously called in England, crossed the English Channel in the diplomatic service of Württemberg, subsequently switching his allegiance to the court of the exiled elector palatine, Friedrich V. In 1626 he was appointed secretary in the service of the Stuart monarchy, responsible for court correspondence and, as a "licenser," for reviewing current periodicals and recent publications on history. He became a British subject in 1630. At fifty he sat for a portrait in which he appeared every inch a servant to King Charles I, from the style of his beard to his fashionable dress.

Weckherlin continued to write German poetry, publishing a collection, *Gaistliche und Weltliche Gedichte* (Spiritual and Worldly Poems), in 1641; an enlarged edition appeared in 1648. Though far from the ravages of the Thirty Years' War of 1618 to 1648, the poet suffered along with his homeland:

> Zerbrich das schwere Joch, darunder du
>   gebunden,
> O Teutschland, wach doch auff, fass wider einen
>   muht,
> Gebrauch dein altes hertz, und widersteh der wuht,
> Die dich, und die freyheit durch dich sebs
>   uberwunden!
>
> (Destroy the heavy yoke beneath which you are
>   bound!
> Oh Germany, awake! Again your courage claim!
> Employ your time-tried heart and seek the rage to tame
> Which by your aid yourself and freedom would con-
>   found!)

In this sonnet, "An das Teutschland" (To Germany), he implored the country to ally itself with the Protestant princes and to resist the entreaties of the imperial side. In other poems he praised the hope of the Protestant cause, the Swedish king Gustav Adolf:

> O König, dessen Haupt den Weltkreis zu regieren
> Und dessen Faust die Welt zur siegen allein gut,
> O Herrscher, dessen Herz, Herr, dessen grossen Mut
> Gottsforscht, Gerechtigkeit, Stärk, mass und Weisheit
>   zieren!
>
> (Oh king, whose head alone can rule Earth's company,
> Whose hand alone the world in victory can embrace,
> Oh chief, whose heart, oh lord, whose courage knows
>   the grace
> Of fear of God, restraint, strength, wisdom, equity!)

The death of the king in 1632 elicited a 606-line poetic lamentation, "Der Groß Gustav ist tod! Tod ist Gustav der Groß!" (Great Gustav is dead! Dead is Gustav the Great!), a work of grand scope that is moving in its intensity. Ever an ardent monarchist, ever a Protestant patriot, ever a politically astute poet, Weckherlin hoped for the triumph of divine right and armed might in his tortured homeland.

The spiritual poems of the two collections were conceived as self-consolation in troubled times. Weckherlin's rendering of the Psalms into German was part of a tradition started by Martin Luther's translations and taken up by many other poets. Born a Lutheran, familiar with Catholicism and Calvinism, and embroiled in the complexities of the Anglican-Puritan conflict in England, Weckherlin expressed in his Psalms a view of God as an absolutist seventeenth-century prince and of himself as the Lord's court poet.

Gaistliche und Weltliche Gedichte had little impact in his homeland. The texts lacked the elegant refinements of verse schooled on Opitz's dicta, and the poet was geographically isolated. Even though he had corresponded with Opitz in 1637, the times had passed Weckherlin by. After Charles I fled Oliver Cromwell's forces in 1642, the old man served the Puritan government as secretary for foreign affairs, relinquishing the post shortly after the execution of Charles I in 1649. He briefly served as an assistant to his successor in office, the blind poet John Milton. His wife had died in 1645; his daughter followed in 1652. Weckherlin himself died on 13 February 1653; he was survived by a son, Rudolph.

Letters:

Leonard W. Forster, *Sources for G. R. Weckherlin's Life in England: The Correspondence* (London: Cambridge University Press, 1946);

Forster, "Dichterbriefe aus dem Barock," *Euphorion*, 47 (1953): 405–411.

Biographies:

Carl Philipp Conz, *Nachrichten von dem Leben und den Schriften Rudolph Weckherlins* (Ludwigsburg, 1803);

Leonard W. Forster, *Georg Rudolf Weckherlin: Zur Kenntnis seines Lebens in England* (Basel: Schwabe, 1944);

Ernst Ribbat, "Georg Rodolf Weckherlin," in *Deutsche Dichter des 17. Jahrhunderts: Ihr Leben und Werk,* edited by Harald Steinhagen and Benno von Wiese (Berlin: Schmidt, 1984), pp. 74–89;

Dieter Breuer, "Georg Rodolf Weckherlin," in *Deutsche Dichter: Leben und Werk deutschsprachiger Autoren,* volume 2, edited by Gunter E. Grimm and Frank R. Max (Stuttgart: Reclam, 1988), pp. 119–127.

References:

Adolf Beck, "Über ein Gedicht von Georg Rudolf Weckherlin," *Jahrbuch der deutschen Schiller-Gesellschaft,* 6 (1962): 14–20;

Leonard Forster, "Kleine Schriften zur deutschen Literatur im 17. Jahrhundert: III. Zu Georg Rudolf Weckherlin," *Daphnis: Zeitschrift für Mittlere Deutsche Literatur,* 6 (1977): 163–234;

Flora Kimmich, "Weckherlin, Petrarchism and the Renewal of Vernacular Poetry," *Daphnis: Zeitschrift für Mittlere Deutsche Literatur,* 7 (1978): 181–197;

Ingrid Laurien, *"Höfische" und "bürgerliche" Elemente in den Gaistlichen und Weltlichen Gedichten Georg Rodolf Weckherlins (1648)* (Stuttgart: Heinz, 1981);

Hans Lentz, *Zum Verhältnis von Versiktus und Wortakzent im Versbau G. R. Weckherlins* (Munich: Fink, 1966);

Volker Meid, "Ein politischer Deutscher: Zu Weckherlins Sonett *An das Teutschland,*" in *Gedichte und Interpretationen,* volume 1, edited by Meid (Stuttgart: Reclam, 1982), pp. 148–158;

Ernst Ribbat, "'Tastend nach Autonomie': Zu Weckherlins *Geistlichen und Weltlichen Gedichten,*" in *Rezeption und Produktion zwischen 1570 und 1730,* edited by Wolfdietrich Rasch and others (Bern: Francke, 1972), pp. 73–92;

Aaron Schaffer, *Georg Rudolf Weckherlin: The Embodiment of a Transitional Stage in German Metrics* (Baltimore: Johns Hopkins University Press, 1918);

Christian Wagenknecht, *Weckherlin und Opitz: Zur Metrik der deutschen Renaissancepoesie* (Munich: Beck, 1971);

Sylvia Weimar-Kluser, *Die höfische Dichtung G. R. Weckherlins* (Bern: Lang, 1971).

Papers:

Georg Rodolf Weckherlin's papers, including letters and his diary, are in the archives of Weckherlin's descendant, the lord of Downshire, Easthampstead Park, near London. Documents on Weckherlin's diplomatic and court activities are in the Hauptstaatsarchiv Stuttgart and in the Public Record Office, London.

Diederich von dem Werder

(17 January 1584 – 18 December 1657)

Dieter Merzbacher
Herzog August Bibliothek

Translated by Nicola McGregor

BOOKS: *Selbst eigene Gottselige Tränen Dieterichs von dem Werder die Er der weiland WholEdlen [sic] Vielehr vnd Tugentreichen Frawen Dorotheen Catharinen, gebornen von Waldaw auß dem Hause Schanowitz, seinem hertzvielgeliebten Ehegemahl, als dieselbe in seinem abwesen den 12. Februarii Selig von dieser Welt abgeschieden, vnd er ihren Cörper folgendes tages zu seiner anheimkunfft verblichen gefunden, zu Jhrem Lob von Hertzen nachgesandt hat. Geschehen im Jahr vnsers Erlösers M. DC. XXV* (Zerbst: Printed by Zacharias Dörffer, 1625); revised as *Selbst eigene Gottselige Thränen. Einer Vornehmen Hoch-Adelichen Ritter-Stands-Person: Jhrer vielgeliebten Hertzens-Freundin, als dieselbe in Jhres Ehewirts Abwesen von dieser Welt abgeschieden, vnd Er folgenden Tags jhren Cörper zu seiner Ankunfft Todtsverblichen gefunden; Seine Eheliche Liebe männiglich zubezeugen auff jmmerwendes Gedechtnüß nachgesandt,* anonymous (N.p., 1636);

Krieg vnd Sieg Christi gesungen jn 100. Sonetten da in jedem vnd jeglichem Verse die beyden wörter Krjeg vnd Sjeg auffs wenigste einmahl, befindlich seyn, anonymous (Wittenberg: Printed by Johann Röhner, 1631);

Die BuszPsalmen, in Poesie gesetzt. Sampt angehengtem TrawerLied vber die klägliche Zerstörung der Löblichen vnd Vhralten Stadt Magdeburg, anonymous (Leipzig: Published by Elias Rehefeld, printed by Abraham Lamberg's heirs, 1632);

Friedens-Eede [i.e., *-Rede*], *jn Gegenwart vieler Fürsten, Fürstinnen vnd Fräwlein, auch grosser Anzahl Hochadelicher gelehrter vnd anderer vornehmen Manns- Frawen- vnd Jungfräwlichen Personen: Mit recht abgewechselter Stimme vnd Außrede, wie auch tappffern schön bequembten Bewegungen vnd zierlichsten Gebärden aller Leibsgliedmassen* (Hamburg: Tobias Gundermann, 1639);

Kurtzer Bericht von der Fruchtbringenden Geselschaft Vorhaben, auch dero Namen, Gemählde und Wörter jn achtzeilige Reimgesetze verfasset, by Werder and *Duke Ludwig of Anhalt-Köthen* (Köthen, 1641; enlarged edition, Frankfurt am Main, 1646);

Lob und Ehren-Gedächtnüß der Weiland Durchleuchtigen Hochgebornen Fürstin und Frauen, Frauen, Johannetten-Elisabeth: Fürstin zu Anhald (Zerbst: Printed by Andreas Betzel, 1647);

Vier und zwantzig Freuden-reiche Trost-Lieder, oder Trostreiche Freuden-Gesänge, auff die Stunde des Todes, oder tödtlicher Schmertzen, vermittelst gewisser Sprüche Göttlicher Schrifft, nach schönen und sehr beweglichen Melodeyen bequemet und eingerichtet (Leipzig: Published by Tobias Riese, printed by Timotheus Ritzsch, 1653);

Erster Theil, Seufftzender Andachten, auff die Stunde des Todes, oder tödlicher Schmertzen, eingerichtet nach dem Fürbilde der Gesunden Wortte (Frankfurt an der Oder: Printed by Andreas Beckmann, 1667).

OTHER: Torquato Tasso, *Gottfried von Bulljon, oder Das Erlösete Jerusalem,* translated by Werder (Frankfurt am Main: Published by Daniel & David Aubrj & Clemens Schleich, 1626; revised edition, Frankfurt am Main: Printed by Caspar Rötel, published by Johann Pressen, 1651); edited by Gerhard Dünnhaupt, Deutsche Neudrucke, Reihe Barock 24 (Tübingen, 1974);

Lodovico Ariosto, *Drey Gesänge vom Rasenden Rolandt, aus dem Jtalianischen Poëten Ariosto zur Prob vnd Anfang vbergesetzt,* translated by Werder (Leipzig: Published by Elias Rehefeld, printed by Abraham Lamberg's heirs, 1632); republished as *Die Historia vom Rasenden Roland* (Leipzig: Published by Elias Rehefeld, Printed by Henning Köler, 1636);

Ariosto, *Fernerer Verlauff der History vom Rasenden Roland,* translated by Werder (Leipzig: Published by Elias Rehefeld, printed by Gregor Ritzsch, 1634);

Ariosto, *Noch weiterer Verlauff der History vom Rasenden Roland,* translated by Werder (Leipzig: Elias Rehefeld, 1634);

Ariosto, *Folge der History vom Rasenden Roland,* translated by Werder (Leipzig: Elias Rehefeld, 1636);

Guillaume de Salluste, seigneur du Bartas, *Die Erste und Andere Woche Wilhelms von Saluste Herren zu Bartas,* translated by Tobias Hübner, edited by Werder (Köthen, 1640);

Wilhelm von Kalckheim, *Der verfolgete David . . . Aufs neüe übersehen und verbessert,* edited by Werder and Duke Ludwig of Anhalt-Köthen (Köthen, 1643);

Giovanni Francesco Loredano, *Djanea oder Rähtselgedicht, in welchem, vnter vielen anmuhtigen Fügnussen, hochwichtige Staatsachen, denklöbliche Geschichte, und klugsinnige Rahtschläge, vermittelst der Majestätischen Deutschen Sprache, kunstzierlich verborgen,* translated by Werder (Nuremberg: Published by Wolfgang Endter, 1644); edited by Dünnhaupt, Nachdrucke deutsche Literatur des 17. Jahrhunderts, no. 22 (Bern, 1984).

Diederich von dem Werder typifies the courtly culture of the first half of the century of German baroque, which was characterized by an interest in literature and by the chivalrous value system of the nobility. In the service of the houses of Hessen, Anhalt, Sweden, and finally Brandenburg, Werder came into contact with many renowned statesmen. Brought up at the court of the landgrave of Hessen-Kassel, Moritz der Gelehrte (the Learned), he knew Romance languages and their literatures and, under the cognomen Der Vielgekörnte (The Many-Seeded One), took a prominent place in the Fruchtbringende Gesellschaft (Fruit-bringing Society), which sought to defend virtue and nurture the German mother tongue. He is important as the first to translate Lodovico Ariosto's *L'Orlando furioso* (1516) and Torquato Tasso's *Il Goffredo, overo Gerusalemme liberata* (Godfrey; or, The Liberation of Jerusalem, 1575) into German.

Werder belonged to an Anhalt family of ancient nobility: he was born on 17 January 1584 at the estate Werdershausen near Grobzig, the fourth and youngest son of Gebhard von dem Werder and Katharina von dem Werder, née von Hahn. His education began in the house of his relative Hans von Bodenhausen, tutor to the prince's sons and director of the prince's court school in Kassel. By 1597 Werder was attending the school for pages, which was reorganized by Moritz der Gelehrte into the grammar-school-style Collegium Mauritianum. The

Reformed Humanistic learning that he encountered there laid the foundations of Werder's unshakable Reformed faith. He studied at the University of Leipzig in the summer semester of 1596, at the University of Jena in 1598, and at the University of Marburg, where he received his degree in theology and law in 1605.

After the customary educational tour of France and Italy, Werder was appointed equerry and footman by Landgrave Moritz. In 1610 he participated in the siege of Jülich as a cavalry captain under the command of Prince Christian I of Anhalt-Bernburg; fighting alongside him was the Anhalt councillor Tobias Hübner, with whom Werder would later work on literary projects. In 1612 Werder attended Emperor Matthias's coronation in Frankfurt am Main, as well as the marriage of Markgrave Joachim Ernst of Brandenburg to Countess Sophie zu Solms in Ansbach; also in 1612 he inherited the estates of Reinsdorf, Görzig, Gerlebogk, Werdershausen, and Ziebig. A year later he was present at the wedding of Electoral Prince Friedrich V to the English princess Elizabeth in Heidelberg, an alliance for which the Reformed nobility had high hopes. In the entertainment for the occasion, for which Hübner contributed poetical texts, Werder assumed the role of King Midas. He married Dorothea Katharina von Waldau on 21 June 1618. Werder was admitted into the Fruchtbringende Gesellschaft as its thirty-first member in 1620.

In Kassel, Werder's career enjoyed a rapid rise. As privy councillor and head majordomo he was responsible for the education of the princes in a time of profound political and cultural reforms, in which the Reformed faith was implemented and the educational system was reorganized. The court became open to European culture: English actors made appearances in Kassel, teachers of modern languages were appointed, and literary genres and material of predominantly Italian provenance were taken up, including the works of Tasso and Ariosto. But the exceptional learning of the landgrave stood in great contrast to his political misfortunes. When the estates forced him into negotiations with the Austrian general Johann Tserklaes, Graf von Tilly, he passed the governorship to his son Wilhelm V. It was in these circumstances that Werder resigned from his offices on 21 June 1622 and withdrew to his Reinsdorf estate, not far from Köthen in the principality of Anhalt.

The urgent encouragement of the members of the Fruchtbringende Gesellschaft and Hübner's translation of Guillaume de Sallusts, seigneur du

Bartas's creation epic *Les Sepmaines* (The Weeks, 1619), the first publication of the society, prompted Werder to translate Tasso's epic into German. Christian II of Anhalt-Bernburg, the nephew of Prince Ludwig of Anhalt-Köthen, the founder of the Fruchtbringende Gesellschaft, sent an edition of *Goffredo, overe Gerusalemme liberata* from Italy for Werder in 1623. The manuscript for *Gottfried von Bulljon, oder Das Erlösete Jerusalem,* (Godfrey of Bullion; or, Freed Jerusalem) was completed in 1624, but the making of the copperplate engravings by Matthaus Merian the elder delayed its publication until 1626.

Tasso's *Gerusalemme liberata* was ubiquitous at this time. In 1624, for example, Claudio Monteverdi composed the opera *Combattimento di Tancredi e Clorinda,* based on the twelfth canto of the epic. The work marked the high point of Italian chivalric epic, and Werder's translation became the exemplary model of national literature in the German language. While he changed Tasso's hendecasyllabic line into an alexandrine with the obligatory caesura, he left the rhyme scheme, *abababcc,* intact. In addition, he showed his modernity in having the accent of the meter accord with natural German word accent; the manuscript for *Gottfried* was already complete when this crucial rule of German prosody was promulgated by Martin Opitz in his *Buch der Deutschen Poeterey* (Book of German Poetry, 1624). But it is above all in the poem "Herrligkeit Christi" (The Glory of Christ), which he inserted into the preface, that Werder shows his knowledge of verse reform. Augustus Buchner, the Wittenberg University professor of rhetoric and poetics, praised this short religious verse epic to Opitz in 1626; in the body of *Gottfried,* on the other hand, he saw grammatical faults and dated vocabulary. Opitz himself placed less emphasis on Werder's poetic achievement than on the noble ethos of the translation. Two years later Opitz praised Werder in the dedication of his sermon *Über das leyden unseres Heylands* (On the Suffering of Our Savior, 1628) as "O Werder, werther Held, / Der Ritter Blum und Zier" (O Werder, worthy hero, / Flower and ornament of knights). Epic power, wordplay, chiasmus, sustained anaphora, onomatopoeic effects, and cumulations of asyndetic clauses distinguish Werder's translation. It has, however, been superseded by the 1802 translation by Johann Diederich Gries, which also preserved the octave verse form, and the 1978 translation by Emil Staiger and is now only of historical value.

When Hübner, writing to Buchner, emphasized that the new way of writing poetry was not to

Title page for Diederich von dem Werder's translation of Giovanni Francesco Loredano's La Dianea. The work was misattributed to Georg Philipp Harsdörffer until 1973.

be credited exclusively to Opitz, he enclosed Werder's *Selbst eigene Gottselige Tränen* (Even My Own Blessed Tears, 1625) as evidence. This poem of 214 lines of alexandrine verse had been composed by Werder after his wife died in childbirth, together with a baby daughter, on 12 February 1625, while Werder was away. His description of the final farewell makes a strong impression, although he says himself that he lacks the ability to communicate the pain adequately. The poem proclaims not a secularized idea of *vanitas* or stoic fatalism but a certainty of faith that informs his everyday life. The same stylistic devices are used to rhetorical effect as in *Gottfried:* wordplay in the form of *ars combinatoria,* listing, *amplificatio,* emphatic repetition, and *parallelismus membrorum,* all borne on an epic alexandrine verse form. A 1636 revision frees this poem of lament from its biographical base. *Selbst eigene Gottselige Thränen. Einer Vornehmen Hoch-*

Adelichen Ritter-Stands-Person (My Own Blessed Tears. A Refined Person of High Noble Knightly Rank) is a poem of praise for love within marriage. The slightly coarse concluding remark seems out of character with the rest of the text when it warns "Weibsvolck nicht für Fuß-Schemel zu halten" (not to regard womenfolk as footstools). After Dorothea's death, Werder married Juliane Ursula von Peblis, a widow.

In 1626 Werder represented Anhalt interests before the electoral prince in Dresden and in 1627 before Emperor Ferdinand II in Vienna, to whom he presented a copy of his Tasso translation. The Anhalt principality was particularly hard hit by the warring parties in the so-called Danish/Lower Saxony phase of the Thirty Years' War, in particular by the demands for contributions from the imperial troops stationed at the Elbe crossing near Dessau.

Werden wrote the cycle *Krieg und Sieg Christi gesungen in 100. Sonetten* (The War and Victory of Christ Sung in 100 Sonnets, 1631), he says in the preface, "Diweil aus gerechtem Gerichte Gottes fast alle Chur-Fürstenthümer, Herrschaften und Provintzen unsers armen Vaterlandes durch den leidigen Krieg nunmehr in grund verheeret, verderbet, ausgeplündert, versengt, verbrennet, und wüste gemacht; der leute viel ermordet, geschändet, verarmet, und ins euserste elend gesetzet sein" (Because by the just judgment of God nearly all the electoral princes' lands, the dominions and the provinces of our poor fatherland have, through the burdensome war, now been utterly devastated, ruined, plundered, scorched, burned, and laid waste; many of the people murdered, violated, impoverished, and placed in the most extreme misery), and "auch bey uns Teutschen jetzo nichts anders als seufftzen, trawren, heulen, weinen, schreyen, sich ängsten, klage und beklagen" (now also among us Germans there was met with nothing but sighing, grieving, wailing, weeping, moaning, fearing, lamenting, and mourning). It was, he says, the last words of a dying relative, "Victoria, Victoria" (Victory, Victory), that prompted him to write his first sonnet, although he had "nie besondere beliebung zu den Sonetten getragen" (never borne a particular liking toward sonnets); with variations on the word *victoria,* the sonnet appears in the preface. The cycle begins with the fall of the angels and ends with the events of the Passion; its stylistic features include *ars combinatoria,* emphatic repetition, *inventio,* and *amplificatio,* all supported by the strict form of the alexandrine verse. A variation of the sestina in the concluding sonnet personalizes the cycle:

Verleih' O aller Krieg- und Siegesreichster Gott,
Weil du mich jeztund auch zu deinen Kriegen vnd
    Siegen
So starck beruffen lest, das Sieghafft ich in Kriegen,
Als dein Kriegs-Siegesman, nicht schewe not vnd todt.
Auff daß ich auch mit helff im Kriege Sieg erringen,
Vnd vnser Land vom Krieg' in Sieg vnd Friede bringen.

(Grant, oh God most warlike and victorious,
Since you have now to your war and victories,
Summoned me so clearly, that, victorious in wars,
I might not as your victorious warrior fear tribulation
    and death.
So that I may also help win victory in war
And bring our land from war into victory and peace.)

On 3 January 1632 Werder entered the army of Gen. Johan Banér and took command of a regiment whose upkeep Anhalt had to finance. Truly a product of the time is his *Die Busz Psalmen, in Poesie gesetzt* (The Psalms of Penance, Versified, 1632), to which is added a "TrawerLied" (song of mourning) about the destruction of Magdeburg by Tilly on 20 May 1631. Werder's reworkings of the Psalms, with their direct and personal touch, are an attempt to strengthen the anti-Hapsburg front. In the song of repentance Werder mounts a strong attack against Tilly, the "gottlosen Bulenknecht" (godless lecher) and "alten Kahlkopf" (old bald-head) who raped the maiden (Magdeburg) and for that deed deserves "daß das Schiff Charonis mit [ihm] stracks in seinen Abgrundt lieff" (that Charon's ship take [him] straight into the abyss).

Werder's translation of Ariosto's *L'Orlando furioso* appeared in installments; the first volume was titled *Drey Gesänge vom Rasenden Rolandt, aus dem Italianischen Poëten Ariosto zur Prob und Anfang ubergesetzt* (Three Cantos of the Frenzy of Roland, Translated from the Italian Poet Ariosto as a Sample and Beginning, 1632). The Italian epic did not appeal just to the educated courtly audience addressed in the opening lines: "VOn Frawen, Rittern, Lieb', vnd Waffen wil ich singen, / Wie auch von Höffligkeit vnd vielen tapffern Dingen" (Of ladies, knights, love and weapons will I sing, / And of courtliness and many bold things). Seventeen further cantos appeared in 1634, and cantos 21 to 30 followed in 1636. There is no evidence that a manuscript for the remainder ever existed; thus, those parts of the work are missing that tell of Roland's recovering his senses and that also contain, along with the poet's self-reflection in the last canto, the genealogical-etiological passages addressed to the court of Ferrara. But it is only these last cantos that give the romance, overburdened with changes in time, place, and characters, its narrative and functional coherence. In addition to being incomplete, the German work constantly diverges from the original. Werder extends the twenty-third canto by 640 lines taken from Matteo Maria Boiardo's *Orlando innamorato,* skips passages, omits catalogues of names, summarizes, and does away with the mythological apparatus and, with it, its unnecessary scholarly ballast. Nothing is allowed to interrupt the reader's hunt for new adventures. The Old French *Chanson de Roland* (Song of Roland) provides Ariosto's poem with its framework of the fantastic, fairy-tale world of knights and their adventures in love and war; Werder, with his Reformed faith, must have struggled to do justice to a work of such libertine tendencies and erotic permissiveness.

The political situation undoubtedly interfered with Werder's work on *Rasenden Roland,* for he was intensively involved in the events of the war. After the Swedes' unsuccessful storming of the Alte Veste (Old Fortress) near Nuremberg, in which Albrecht Eusebius Wenzel von Wallenstein's troops were barricaded, in August 1632, Werder set off to join Gustav Adolph, who was killed at Lützen on 16 November 1632. In February 1634 he arrived in Dresden in the service of Axel Oxenstierna, seeking to dispose the electoral prince favorably toward the Swedes; it was there that he informed Oxenstierna of Wallenstein's assassination on 26 February.

The atrocities of the war and the threatening collapse of the territorial structure of society could no longer be dealt with through reflective wordplay and meditative, puzzling verse alone. To the pointlessness of war Werder opposed his pacifistic "Teilimitatio" (part imitation) of the *Querela Pacis* of Desiderius Erasmus of Rotterdam, titled *Friedens-Rede* (Words of Peace, 1639). His fifteen-year-old son Paris, whose nickname in the Fruchtbringende Gesellschaft was Der Friedfertige (The Peacemaker), declaimed the work before an audience of high-ranking persons. Werder does not imitate the learned discourse of Erasmus but uses emotive rhetorical devices to articulate the yearning for peace. The figure of Peace makes an urgent appeal to the controlling powers of society to be mindful once more of Christian values:

Ich bitte euch jhr Christliche Fürsten, wann jhr anderst in Warheit Christliche Fürsten seydt, beschawet vnd betrachtet das Bildnuß ewers Fürsten, Schawet wie Er sein Reich angefangen, wie Er darinnen fortgefahren, vnd wie Er von hinnen geschieden, so werdet jhr bald verstehen, wie Er von euch haben will, daß Fried und Einigkeit ewer höchste Sorge seyn solte.

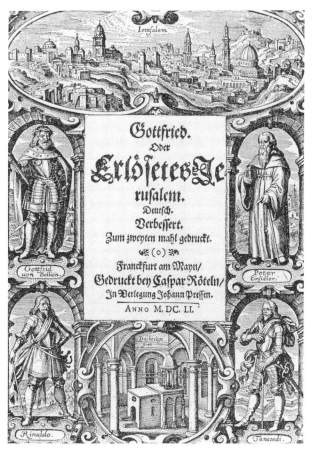

Title page for the revised edition of Werder's translation of Torquato Tasso's Il Goffredo, overo Gerusalemme liberata

(I ask you, you Christian princes, if you are in truth Christian princes, look upon and consider the portrait of your Prince. Look how He began His realm, how He continued in it, and how He departed from here. Then you will soon understand how He seeks of you that peace and unity should be your first care.)

With the end of the Swedish-Anhalt alliance Werder's primary concern, as subdirector of the principality of Anhalt, was to stave off the heavy financial costs of the war, and he entered into negotiations with leading military figures on both the Swedish and imperial sides. Frequently those involved were also members of the Fruchtbringende Gesellschaft: Octavio Piccolomini d'Aragona, Der Zwingende (The Forceful One); Oxenstierna, Der Gewünschte (The Desired One); Alexandre Erskein, Der Fürsichtige (The Provident One); and Banér, Der Haltende (The Constant One). He also corresponded with Karl Gustav Wrangel, Der Obsiegende (The Victorious One). Werder's final position was as privy councillor and colonel in the service of Brandenburg.

Werder returned to Italian literature in 1644 with his translation of Giovanni Francesco Loredano's *La Dianea* (1635). Following John Barclay's *Argenis* (1621) and indebted to the late Hellenistic narrative structure, the work was called by Werder a *Rähtselgedicht* (riddle poem). Against the background of old chivalric motifs it works in contemporary events, people, and places. Thus, for example, the second book deals with the assassination of Wallenstein. The main plot concerns the separation and reunion of lovers. An appendix lists neologisms, some of which are still in use today: *Gunstzeichen* (token of favor), *Vermummen* (muffle up; disguise; mask), *Umfang* (extent, scope), *Vorwurf* (reproach), *Wechselreden* (dialogue), and *Wink* (nod, sign). The misattribution of the work, which was published anonymously, to Georg Philipp Harsdörffer goes back to Johann Herdeger, the chronicler of the Nuremberg language society Löblicher Hirten- und Blumenorden an der Pegnitz (Eminent Order of Shepherds and Flowers of the Pegnitz River); Gerhard Dünnhaupt showed in 1973 that Werder was the author.

The end of his military obligations allowed Werder to become heavily involved in the Fruchtbringende Gesellschaft at a time when Prince Ludwig, freed from his duties as Swedish governor, was also able to devote more time to literary interests. Werder acted as Ludwig's adviser: he saw to mottoes, produced drafts of coats of arms, and fostered *conversatio* in *Gesellschaftsbrieflein* (society letters), in which, alongside humorous poems, there was no lack of irony and mild sarcasm. He appraised the works of fellow society members, including Buchner's *Weg-Weiser zur Deutschen Tichtkunst* (Guide to the Art of German Poetry, 1663); the *Deutscher Sprachlehre Entwurf* (Outline of German Grammar, 1641) of Christian Gueintz, the tutor of Werder's son Paris; and Philipp von Zesen's work on poetics, *Deutscher Helikon* (German Helicon, 1641). He corrected Prince Ludwig's biblical poems and composed poems of dedication for the prince's *Denckwürdige Geschichte des grossen Tamerlanis* (The Memorable Story of Tamerlane the Great, 1639), for Prince Christian II of Anhalt-Bernburg's *Unterweisung eines christlichen Fürsten* (Instruction for a Christian Prince, 1639), and for Harsdörffer's *Frauenzimmer Gesprechspiele* (Playful Colloquies for the Ladies, 1641–1657). The most important of his epicedia (mourning poems) is the funeral ode for Prince Ludwig, who died on 7 January 1650. Printed in the eulogy, it was also engraved on the prince's sarcophagus.

When, as in the case of Harsdörffer or Justus Georg Schottelius, Werder felt that he had to curb the capriciousness of would-be innovators in orthography, word formation, or metrics and prosody, he admonished them "sich in Schrancken zuhalten, und nicht so nach ihrem blossen wahn ... regeln vnd neue arten, ohne erheblich ursachen, zusezten vnd zufüren" (to stay within limits, and not to introduce and practice ... rules and new methods merely according to their whims, without good reason). Nonetheless, Harsdörffer, citing Opitz, accorded Werder first place in his otherwise alphabetical *Specimen Philologiae Germaniae* (1646). Still, the relationship between the two authors – the one a courtly noble, the other a patrician town bourgeois – was at times a prickly one. When Harsdörffer recruited far too many new members for the society – including Johann Michael Moscherosch, "wan gleich Herr Moscherosch sonst nichts würdiges bey der deutschen Sprache bisher gethan" (even if Herr Moscherosch has not thus far done anything else worthy for the German language), as Werder smugly noted – Werder did not conceal from the Nuremberger his aristocratic elitism and sarcastic indignation. One conflict between the two was settled in the *Wechselschreiben* (Written Exchanges) of the Fruchtbringende Gesellschaft through the mediation of Der Unveränderliche (The Unchanging One), Prince Christian II of Anhalt-Bernburg: Werder had seen in the simile of Holy Communion with which Harsdörffer introduced his anthology of didactic poems, *Nathan und Jotham* (1659), a debasing of the Reformed faith.

In May 1651 Werder was one of the twenty-four members who elected Duke Wilhelm IV of Saxe-Weimar, Der Schmackhafte (The Tasteful One), as the new head of the society, after the position had been vacant for a year. Thereafter, with the exception of the revision of *Gottfried* (1651), he devoted himself to the idea of the Christian *ars moriendi* (art of dying). He composed three thousand *Todesandachten* (Meditations on Death), the first thousand of which appeared posthumously in 1667; the second part is lost, while the last thousand are preserved in a manuscript. Published in his lifetime was *Vier und zwantzig Freuden-reiche Trost-Lieder, oder Trostreiche Freuden-Gesänge, auff die Stunde des Todes, oder tödtlicher Schmertzen* (Twenty-four Joyful Songs of Consolation or Consoling Hymns of Joy upon the Hour of Death or of Mortal Pain, 1653). The texts, which Werder says, "eine innerliche Freudigkeit zum Sterben ... erregen können" (can ... arouse an inner joyfulness about dying), fell victim to the censorship of the senior court chaplain of Saxony, Johannes Hülsemann, who replaced three stanzas. Once again the interpretation of Holy Communion caused disagreement: Werder had referred to it as a purely symbolic event. The last known poem by Werder appears in *Panegyricus funebris,* written to commemorate the death of Duke Friedrich the Elder of Saxe-Weimar (Der Friedenreiche [The Peaceable One] in the Fruchtbringende Gesellschaft), who died on 19 August 1656.

Werder died on 18 December 1657 at his Reinsdorf estate. He was buried at the local church on 13 May of the following year. Duke Wilhelm IV of Saxe-Weimar composed an elegy for Der Vielgekörnte: "Jhr habet Ehr und Ruhm, so wohl im Buch als Schwert gesucht" (You sought honor and renown in book as well as sword). The duke also praised Werder's piety. *Arma et littera* but also *pietas* were the three components of the life of Diederich von dem Werder, the "Zier der Zeit" (ornament of the age), as Opitz called him in the dedication to his *Übersetzung ethlicher Psalmen* (Translation of Several Psalms, 1634).

Letters:

Der Fruchtbringenden Gesellschaft ältester Ertzschrein, edited by Gottlieb Krause (Leipzig: Dyk, 1855; reprinted, Hildesheim & New York: Olms, 1973), pp. 141–190;

Martin Bircher, "Autographen barocker Autoren," *Chloe: Beihefte zum Daphnis,* volume 6 (Amsterdam: Rodopi, 1987): 291–356;

Briefe der Fruchtbringenden Gesellschaft und Beilagen: Die Zeit Fürst Ludwigs von Anhalt-Köthen, edited by Klaus Conermann and Dieter Merzbacher (Tübingen: Niemeyer, 1992).

Bibliographies:

Karl Goedeke, *Grundriß zur Geschichte der deutschen Dichtung: Aus den Quellen,* volume 3 (Dresden: Ehlermann, 1887);

Gerhard Dünnhaupt, *Personalbibliographien zu den Drucken des Barock,* volume 9, part 6 (Stuttgart: Hiersemann, 1993), pp. 4251–4267.

Biography:

Georg Witkowski, *Diederich von dem Werder* (Leipzig: Veit, 1887).

References:

Achim Aurnhammer, "Diederich von dem Werder," in *Literatur-Lexikon: Autoren und Werke deutscher Sprache,* edited by Walther Killy, volume 12 (Munich: Bertelsmann, 1992), pp. 252–253;

Johann Christoff Beckmann, *Historie des Fürstenthums Anhalt* (Zerbst: Zimmermann, 1710);

Klaus Conermann, *Fruchtbringende Gesellschaft: Der Fruchtbringenden Gesellschaft geöffneter Erzschrein. Das Köthener Gesellschaftsbuch Fürst Ludwigs I. von Anhalt-Köthen 1617–1650,* 3 volumes (Leipzig & Weinheim: Edition Leipzig, 1985), III: 34–36;

Gerhard Dünnhaupt, *Diederich von dem Werder: Versuch einer Neuwertung seiner Hauptwerke* (Bern: Peter Lang, 1973);

Gottlieb Krause, "Diederich von dem Werder," *Mitteilungen des Vereins für anhaltische Geschichte und Altertumskunde,* 4 (1884): 30–54;

Krause, *Ludwig, Fürst zu Anhalt-Köthen und sein Land vor und während des Dreißigjährigen Krieges* (Neusalz, 1877–1879);

Krause, ed., *Urkunden, Aktenstücke und Briefe zur Geschichte der Anhaltischen Lande und ihrer Fürsten unter dem Drucke des dreißigjährigen Krieges,* 5 volumes (Leipzig: Dyk, 1861–1866);

Friedrich Wilhelm Strieder, "Dieterich von dem Werder," in *Grundlage zu einer Hessischen Gelehrten- und Schriftsteller-Geschichte seit der Reformation bis auf gegenwärtige Zeiten,* volume 16, edited by L. Wachler (Marburg, 1812), pp. 534–539.

Papers:

Letters and other autographs of Diederich von dem Werder are in the Landeshauptarchiv Sachsen-Anhalt/Oranienbaum und Heimatmuseum, Köthen; the Murhardsche Bibliothek, Kassel; the Koninklijke Bibliotheek, The Hague; Sammlung Martin Bircher, Germanisches Nationalmuseum, Nuremberg; the Staatsarchiv, Hamburg; the Staatsarchiv, Merseburg; the Hessisches Staatsarchiv; the Thüringisches Hauptstaatsarchiv, Weimar; the Herzog August Bibliothek Wolfenbüttel; the Riksarkivet, Stockholm; the Niedersachsische Landesbibliothek, Hannover; and the Bibliotecka Jagiellónska, Kraków.

Paul Winckler

(13 November 1630 – 1 March 1686)

Lynne Tatlock
Washington University

BOOKS: *Ehren-Gedächtnis des weyland Hoch- und Wolgebohrenen Herrn Herrn Hansens von Schönaich Freyherrens zu Beuten Carolath Ambtitz Mellendorf Schlaupitz und Tarnau etc. Lobwürdigsten Andenckens* (N.p., 1676);

Statua Triumphatrici Fortissimorum Viennen (Liegnitz: Christoph Wätzoldt, 1683);

Fama Lotharingica, sive Serenissimi Principis et Domini, Domini Caroli V. Lotharingiae Ducis, Burriae Domini. Trophoea. Aeternitati. Suspensa (Liegnitz: Christoph Wätzoldt, 1683);

Zwey Tausend gutte Gedancken zusammen gebracht von Dem Geübten (Görlitz: Christoph Zipper, 1685);

Guter Gedancken Drey Tausend zusammen gebracht von Dem Geübten (Görlitz: Christoph Zipper, 1685);

Der Edelmann (Lüneburg: Johann Georg Lipper, 1696; republished, Nuremberg: Published by Christoph Riegel, 1697).

Edition: *Der Edelmann,* edited by Lynne Tatlock, Nachdrucke deutscher Literatur des 17. Jahrhunderts, no. 64 (Bern: Peter Lang, 1988).

OTHER: "Sonneto," in *Geteutschter Samson des Fürtrefflichsten Italiänischen Schreiber-Liechtes unserer Zeiten Herrn Ferrante Pallavicini. Durch Ein Mitglied der Hochlöblichen Fruchtbringenden Gesellschaft Den Unglückseligen,* by Johann Wilhelm von Stubenberg (Nuremberg: Michael Endter, 1657), pp. 12^a–12^b;

"Gryphius ut cecidit, Cytharam projecit Apollo," in *Last- und Ehren- auch Daher immerbleibende Danck- und Denck-Seule Bey vollbrachter Leich-Bestattung Des Weiland Wol-Edlen Groß-Achtbarn und Hochgelehrten Herrn Andreae Gryphii, Des Fürstenthums Glogau treugewesenen von vielen Jahren Syndici, In einer Abdanckungs-Sermon,* edited by Baltzer Siegmund von Stosch (N.p., 1664), pp. 81–82;

"Aus dem Leben des niedern Adels," in *Aus dem Jahrhundert des großen Krieges,* volume 3 of *Bilder aus der deutschen Vergangenheit,* edited by Gustav Freytag (Leipzig: Hirzel, 1896–1898), pp. 320–336.

SELECTED PERIODICAL PUBLICATIONS – UNCOLLECTED: "Bilder aus der deutschen Vergangenheit: Fortüne eines Bürgerlichen nach dem dreißigjährigen Kriege," edited by Gustav Freytag, *Die Grenzboten: Zeitschrift für Politik, Literatur und Kunst,* 2, no. 19 (1860): 329–348;

"Bilder aus der deutschen Vergangenheit: Pfeffersäcke und Krippenreiter um 1660," edited by Freytag, *Die Grenzboten: Zeitschrift für Politik, Literatur und Kunst,* 3, no. 19 (1860): 1–26;

"Paul Winckler's Selbstbiographie," edited by August Kahlert, *Zeitschrift des Vereins für Geschichte und Altertum Schlesiens,* 3 (1860): 82–146.

Paul Winckler left three remarkable pieces of writing to posterity: his autobiography (1860); two collections of aphorisms (1685); and a lengthy novel, *Der Edelmann* (The Nobleman, 1696). Only the aphorisms and a few short occasional pieces were published during his lifetime. Like many professional bourgeois men of the late seventeenth century, the ambitious Silesian Winckler was a self-made man who rose from a lowly station as the abused ward of his sister's father-in-law to a prominent position as a successful lawyer and *Kurfürstliche Rat* (electoral councillor) of Brandenburg. All of Winckler's works reflect his involvement in public affairs; they are firmly rooted in the here and now of seventeenth-century Silesia. Winckler's lively, eclectic writing reveals common sense; psychological acumen; encyclopedic erudition; close attention to the workings of social, economic, and legal systems; historical curiosity; and a sense of wonder about the natural world. While the vicissitudes of Winckler's life are perhaps not atypical of the times, his novel and autobiography constitute a rarity: fiction and nonfiction by the same author that to some extent overlap in content but differ in form. These works provide unique insight into the workings of a seventeenth-century bourgeois mind as it seeks to reconstruct the contemporary world with prose.

Winckler was born on 13 November 1630 in Groß-Glogau in Silesia (now in Poland). His father, Paul Winckler, was a merchant, and his mother, Anna Winckler, was the sister of the most famous German poet of the age, Andreas Gryphius. Although Winckler's parents were Protestants, Hapsburg law required that the child be baptized Catholic. When Winckler was about four, his father died. As there were no available Protestant schools, Winckler received instruction at home. His mother died in 1641; her second husband quickly remarried, and Winckler became the ward of the maltster Mathias Nitsche, his sister's father-in-law. Nitsche neglected Winckler and was on the verge of putting the boy into service with a Polish officer when the principal of the Fraustadt school took an interest in him. Thus, in the spring of 1645 Winckler went to school for the first time. A year and a half later he was promoted to the senior class, and in April 1649 he enrolled in the university in Frankfurt an der Oder. After additional short sojourns at the Universities of Leipzig and Wittenberg, his means gave out, and he returned to Glogau in the fall of 1650 and acquired a position as a tutor for a noble family.

Three years later he left this reasonably secure post, against the advice of his uncle Gryphius. He had pressing reasons: for three years he had participated in his patron's constant carousing, and he feared that such activities would eventually be his undoing – his posthumous novel would include satiric vignettes of riotous nobility whose drinking bouts end in brawls. After resigning his position he set off on a journey down the Oder River, along the Baltic coast, and up the Elbe River, which took him through Frankfurt an der Oder, Küstrin, Stettin, Greifswald, Rostock, Stralsund, Wismar, Lübeck, Hamburg, Magdeburg, and Leipzig to the imperial city of Regensburg, where, in 1653, he witnessed the coronation of the Hapsburg Ferdinand IV as German king. Shortly after the coronation, acute hunger forced him to sell his best clothes to an actor.

His attempts to find a position as a secretary in Regensburg failed, and he traveled on to Ingolstadt, Augsburg, Ulm, Tübingen, and Strasbourg, where, penniless and without connections, he became ill. With the aid of his Strasbourg landlord he was able to return to Stuttgart, where he became acquainted with a fellow Silesian, Johann

Heinrich Calisius, who recommended him to the Nuremberg intellectual Sigmund von Birken as a pious, quiet, and learned man, sorely in need of financial support; Calisius also pointed out to Birken that Winckler was a close relative of Gryphius. Birken had been asked by the Austrian nobleman Johann Wilhelm von Stubenberg to find a tutor for Stubenberg's eleven-year-old son, Rudolf Wilhelm. Winckler reported to Birken in Nuremberg, as he himself later expressed it, the picture of death. Birken reluctantly sent him on to Schallaburg, Stubenberg's estate in Lower Austria.

In March 1654 Winckler, still ailing – he was, among other complaints, infected with scabies – set out on foot from Nuremberg, caught a ship in Regensburg, and arrived in Schallaburg seriously ill and exhausted. Although Winckler's appearance must have been shocking, the Stubenbergs welcomed him, and Frau von Stubenberg nursed him back to health. Soon, however, further difficulties beset Winckler, this time in the form of imperial politics. In the sixteenth century the nobility of Lower and Upper Austria had proved particularly receptive to the Reformation and had resisted the Counter Reformation. Throughout the seventeenth century the Hapsburgs had attempted to reestablish Catholicism and, simultaneously, their hegemony over the estates in their hereditary lands – roughly, modern Austria and parts of northern Italy. At the time of Winckler's arrival in Lower Austria the Protestant nobility was all but extinguished in Upper Austria; Stubenberg and his circle represented a last cultural flowering of the Protestant nobility in Lower Austria. In keeping with Hapsburg policy, a Catholic commission ordered the exile of all non-Catholic employees of the Lower Austrian Protestant nobility. Thus, the newly recovered Winckler was ordered to report to the monastery of Melk to be instructed in the Catholic faith, after which he was sent to a priest in the nearby village of Loosdorf for further instruction. As Winckler reports in his autobiography, he and the priest got on well and amused themselves with eating and drinking. Winckler eventually received a certification of religious instruction, but, as the document stated, he had refused to convert. Stubenberg, therefore, had no choice but to send the young tutor out of Austria.

In the company of his pupil, Rudolf Wilhelm, and Frau von Stubenberg, Winckler traveled up the Danube River to Pressburg (then the capital of Hungary; today Bratislava, Slovakia), where, in July 1655, he witnessed the coronation of the new Hapsburg ruler, Leopold I, as king of Hungary. Fol-

Fold-out frontispiece and title page for the second edition of Paul Winckler's posthumously published novel

lowing an outbreak of the plague in Pressburg, Winckler and Rudolf Wilhelm retreated to a village on Schütt, an island in the Danube. The enterprising Winckler soon organized a society of shepherds to entertain the noble company gathered there. As a result of this activity Stubenberg nominated Winckler in 1661 for membership in the most distinguished German-language society of the century, the Fruchtbringende Gesellschaft (Fruit-bringing Society). Winckler received the name Der Geübte (The Practiced One), the motto "In der Haushaltung" (In the Household), and the plant insignia flax.

In the fall of 1655 Winckler and Rudolf Wilhelm returned secretly to Schallaburg, where Winckler spent the winter. The following spring he resigned his post. In June 1656 Stubenberg wrote to Birken, "Paul Winkler [*sic*] ist gewisslich ein gelehrter Kerl, aber die Jugendbelehrung seinem Weltsinne zu ver-driesslich" (Paul Winckler is certainly a learned fellow, but the instruction of youth is too tiresome for his worldly inclinations). On Schütt, Winckler had fallen in love with a young noblewoman, whom he identifies in his autobiography only as his shepherdess Dorinda – twenty-four years later he notes that the poems he had written for her are still among his papers. Winckler returned to Pressburg, where he lingered until Dorinda was finally forced to marry a Viennese merchant. He traveled to Vienna and then – via

Prague (where he witnessed the coronation of Leopold I as king of Bohemia in 1656), Dresden, and Wittenberg – to the northern German city of Kiel, where he acquired a post as secretary to a Danish officer.

In 1658 he resigned his position and returned to his homeland, but he was so repulsed by his first glimpse of Glogau that he decided to go to Vienna. Instead, he wound up in the vicinity of Breslau (today Wroclaw, Poland), where he became legal adviser to a nobleman, Hans von Schönaich. Shortly after accepting the position he was sent to the imperial court in Vienna, where he successfully defended Schönaich's interests. After six years with Schönaich, Winckler again quit and moved into the city of Breslau, where he began in earnest to build a legal practice.

After the mayor of Breslau – Winckler's uncle Gryphius – died in 1664, the imperial authorities in Vienna insisted that his successor, Wolff Alexander von Stosch, resign and that a Catholic, Erasmus Krug from Vienna, replace him. Winckler returned to Vienna, where he was able to ensure that the Protestant Stosch remained in office. In 1664 Winckler became engaged to Christina Bergmann, a wealthy widow from Fraustadt, but he dissolved the engagement in 1667. Winckler later noted that he was particularly glad to be free of Bergmann, as her father had nearly been brought to trial for witchcraft; indeed, Winckler himself could tell of two strange occurrences that he attributed to Bergmann's father's black magic. Winckler's practice was flourishing, yet in 1668 he gave it up for a position with a nobleman in Groß Peterwitz, five miles from Breslau. He soon regretted his decision and returned to Breslau, where he again prospered. In 1671 the elector of neighboring Brandenburg, Friedrich Wilhelm, made Winckler his agent in Breslau. In 1668 Winckler married Christina von Logau, a distant relative of the Silesian poet and epigrammatist Friedrich von Logau; they had three children – Anna Christina, Christian Wilhelm, and Ferdinand – before Christina died in 1678. On 23 December 1678 Friedrich Wilhelm granted Winckler the title of Kurfürstliche Rat.

During the 1670s Winckler began suffering ever-more-frequent attacks of gout. Around 1678 they became so severe that he feared that he would die. This presentiment of death prompted him to write his autobiography for his children. The autobiography would remain in manuscript form until 1860, when a Silesian professor, August Kahlert, edited it for publication in a local scholarly journal. Winckler's narration of his life story links the story of the self-made man to contemporary world events. While Winckler perfunctorily professes humility before God's mysterious ways, he expresses considerable pride in his success – indeed, he dramatizes low points in his life so as to make the high points all the more remarkable. The autobiography is largely written in prose but is punctuated by four poems; the opening poem is dated 25 April 1678, and the final page of the manuscript bears the date 1 June 1679. Winckler frequently interrupts the narrative to reproduce in full documents important to his life story: for example, the certificate of instruction from the priest in Loosdorf, the paper dissolving his engagement to Bergmann, and his commission from the elector of Brandenburg. In footnotes he tells amusing and sensational anecdotes, and in the main text he flavors his account of the milestones in his public life with ghost stories, recollections of dreams, an account of his fortunate meeting with a long-lost uncle, tales of persons who changed their sex, and relations of catastrophes and adventures; he frequently exhorts his readers to wonder at and ponder the strangeness of these events. Scholars, noting the liveliness of Winckler's narrative, have compared it to a novel. Indeed, Winckler himself reworked portions of it in his own novel, and the anonymous author (thought to be Christian Stieff) of *Schlesischer Robinson oder Frantz Anton Wentzels v. C** eines Schlesischen Edelmanns*

Denkwürdiges Leben (Silesian Robinson; or, The Notable Life of Frantz Anton Wentzel von C**, a Silesian Nobleman, 1723, 1724), who must have had access to a manuscript copy of the autobiography, included two lengthy and only slightly altered passages, as well as other information gleaned from the autobiography. Winckler appears under his own name and plays a large role in the education of the protagonist.

The autobiography concludes in 1679, and almost nothing is known about Winckler's last seven years other than that, two years after his first wife's death, he married Maria Aßmann, with whom he had a daughter who died in infancy. Winckler's acute suffering from gout provided not only the impetus for his autobiography but apparently also the leisure to write his novel and his aphorisms, as well as his two Latin occasional pieces celebrating the defeat of the Turks by the imperial army in 1683. Winckler's collections of aphorisms appeared in 1685, shortly before his death, and his novel was published posthumously. Internal evidence from the novel suggests that it was completed sometime after 1682. The introduction to *Der Edelmann* reports that the author wrote the novel for his own entertainment, to ease the pain of his gout, and to put these "Hencker-mässige Stunden" (torturous hours) to good use. Whether the introduction was actually written by Winckler or by an anonymous editor remains unknown.

Winckler's collections of aphorisms, *Zwey Tausend gutte Gedancken* (Two Thousand Good Thoughts, 1865) and *Guter Gedancken Drey Tausend* (Three Thousand Good Thoughts, 1865) have received little scholarly attention, but those who have examined them have termed them elegant, clever, and pithy. Winckler's undertaking echoes similar projects from the early modern period, notably Desiderius Erasmus's *Adagiorum Chiliades* (1508). The collection is eclectic, including sayings on a wide variety of topics. Some of them may be original with Winckler; at least, he is credited as the first written source for them. Others were gleaned from existing collections. Many of the aphorisms comment sharply on contemporary social and political matters, and they range from the crude to the poetic. In the final analysis, Winckler's aphorisms emphasize experience, realism, and common sense.

Winckler died in Breslau on 1 March 1686. When his 810-page novel, which is set in and around a thinly disguised Breslau, appeared ten years later, it was not published in that city; the sharply satiric portraits of the nouveaux riches and the impoverished landed gentry were undoubtedly still all too readily identifiable. Winckler's name does not appear on the title page, and for many years the identity of the author remained unknown. The editor of the manuscript, as well as the extent to which it may have been altered, are unknown to this day.

Although the title of the novel as well as the colloquium of its middle section vaguely recall Baldassare Castiglione's influential *Il Cortegiano* (The Courtesan, 1528), the court plays no role here; it is replaced by the seventeenth-century provincial town and its inhabitants and the neighboring landed gentry. Moreover, noblemen usually serve as negative examples, and the author makes no concerted attempt to describe the perfect nobleman. The novel consists of a satiric frame, focusing on the town of Belissa (Breslau) and its environs, and a voluminous middle section. This middle section takes place on a neighboring country estate, Ritterfeld, where a learned company, including a doctor, a lieutenant colonel, a lawyer, a pastor, and the aristocratic hosts, the Kronbergs, spends several days discussing all manner of things, from human reproduction to contemporary politics. Winckler maintains the thin fiction of the conversation throughout this middle section, punctuating the talk sporadically with the interlocutors' meals, naps, and walks. Besides the actual conversation, Winckler inserts written texts – a Latin lampoon, the catalogue of the imperial treasury in Vienna, long passages from the German translation (1680) by Christian Knorr von Rosenroth of Thomas Browne's *Pseudodoxia Epidemica* (1646), and reports that are allegedly taken from newspapers – that the participants read aloud to one another.

The publisher went to the considerable expense of supplying the book with an index of topics discussed, an elaborate frontispiece, and seventeen original copper engravings; presumably the book was expected to sell well, and the appearance of a second edition a year later indicates that such expectations were met. While the novel was all but forgotten by the second half of the following century, the nationalism and resultant new interest in local history of the nineteenth century brought Winckler's work once again before the reading public. The Silesian journalist, novelist, and popular historian Gustav Freytag included excerpts from it in his five-part history, *Bilder aus der deutschen Vergangenheit* (Pictures from the German Past, 1859–1866). He praised the realism of Winckler's writing, maintaining that the work offers a true picture of the past. While, in contrast to Freytag, twentieth-century scholars note the satiric, and hence exaggerated, side of Winckler's novel, the book remains an important cultural document as well as a fascinating example of the German novel in the late seventeenth century.

References:

Friedrich Andreae, "Aus der guten alten Zeit: 2. Urteile des Reichsfreiherrn Johann Michael v. Loen," *Schlesische Geschichtsblätter* (1916): 64–71;

Martin Bircher, *Johann Wilhelm von Stubenberg (1619–1663) und sein Freundeskreis,* Quellen und Forschungen zur Sprach- und Kulturgeschichte der germanischen Völker, new series 25 (Berlin: De Gruyter, 1968), pp. 118–126;

Bircher, "Paul Winckler (1630–1686)," in *Dizionario critico della letteratura tedesca,* volume 2 (Turin: Unione tipografico-editrice torinese, 1976), pp. 1298–1299;

Wolfgang van der Briele, *Paul Winckler, ein Beitrag zur Literaturgeschichte des 17. Jahrhunderts* (Rostock: Hinstorff, 1918);

Gustav Freytag, "Aus dem Leben des niedern Adels," in his *Aus dem Jahrhundert des großen Krieges,* volume 3 of *Bilder aus der deutschen Vergangenheit* (Leipzig: Hirzel, 1898), pp. 294–347;

Karl Goedeke, *Grundriß zur Geschichte der deutschen Dichtung,* second edition, 15 volumes (Dresden: Ehlermann, 1886), II: 17; III: 10, 260;

Terry Rey Griffin, "Paul Winckler's 'Der Edelmann': A Study in a 17th Century German Novel," dissertation, University of Tennessee, 1976;

August Kahlert, "Paul Winckler: Ein Lebensbild aus dem 17. Jahrhundert," *Deutsches Museum: Zeitschrift für Literatur, Kunst und öffentliches Leben,* 9 (1859): 641–653;

Karl Konrad, "Paul Winckler: Zum 250. Todestag eines Schlesiers 1686–1. März–1936," *Schlesische Monatshefte,* 13 (1936): 103–109;

Konrad, "Der 'schlesische Robinson' und sein Verfasser," *Mitteilungen der schlesischen Gesellschaft für Volkskunde,* 37 (1938): 203–214;

[Christian Stieff?], *Schlesischer Robinson oder Frantz Anton Wentzels v. C** eines Schlesischen Edelmanns Denkwürdiges Leben, seltsame Unglücks-Fälle und ausgestandene Abentheuer, aus übersendeten glaubwürdigen Nachrichten, so wol zur Belustigung des Lesers, als Unterricht adelicher Jugend in Druck gegeben,* 2 volumes (Breslau & Leipzig: Ernst Christian Brachvogel, 1723, 1724);

Wilhelm Wattenbach, "Miscellen: Noch etwas über Paul Winckler," *Zeitschrift des Vereins für Geschichte und Altertum Schlesiens,* 3 (1860–1861): 221–222.

Papers:
Six letters from Paul Winckler to Sigmund von Birken are in the archives of the Pegnitz Gesellschaft in Nuremberg.

Philipp von Zesen

(8 October 1619 – 13 November 1689)

Karl F. Otto Jr.
University of Pennsylvania

BOOKS: *Melpomene oder Trauer- und Klaggedichte, vber das vnschuldigste vnd bitterste Leiden vnd Sterben Jesu Chrjstj* (Halle: Printed by Peter Schmidt, 1638);

Charitinnen oder Danck-Lob vnd Abschieds-Gedichte vom Nutz und Werth des Saltzes welches im Hällischen Parnaß öffentlich gehalten (Halle, 1639);

Deütscher Helikon, oder Kurtze verfassung aller Arten der Deütschen jetzt üblichen Verse, wie dieselben ohne Fehler recht zierlich zu schreiben, bey welchem zu besserm fortgang vnserer Poesie Ein Richtiger Anzeiger der Deütschen gleichlautenden vnd einstimmigen, so wohl Männlichen, als Weiblichen Wörter (nach dem abc. Reimweise gesetzt,) zu finden (Wittenberg: Printed by Johann Röhner, 1640); enlarged as *Deutsches Helikons Erster und Ander Teil, oder Unterricht, wie ein Deutscher Vers und Getichte auf mancherley Art ohne fehler recht zierlich zu schreiben* (Wittenberg: Printed by Johann Röhner, 1641); enlarged as *Durch-aus vermehrter und zum dritt- und letzten mal in dreien teilen aus gefärtigter Hochdeutscher Helikon, oder Grundrichtige anleitung zur hochdeutschen Dicht- und Reimkunst* (Wittenberg: Published by Johann Seelfisch, 1649); enlarged as *Durch-aus vermehrter und zum viert- und letzten mahl in vier teilen ausgefärtigter Hoch-Deutscher Helikon, oder Grundrichtige Anleitung zur Hochdeutschen Dicht- und Reimkunst* (Berlin: Published by Daniel Reichel, printed in Jena by Georg Sengenwald, 1656);

Himlische Kleio oder Freuden-Gedichte auff die hocherfreuliche und verwunderliche Geburths-Nacht unsers neugebohrnen Jesuleins (Hamburg: Printed by Heinrich Werner, 1641);

FrühlingsLust oder Lob- und Liebes-Lieder (Hamburg, 1642);

Poetischer Rosen-Wälder Vorschmack oder Götter- und Nymfen-Lust, wie sie unlängst in dem Heliconischen Gefilde vollbracht auff Lieb- und Lobseeliges Ansuchen einer dabey gewesenen Nymfen kürtzlich entworffen (Hamburg: Tobias Gundermann, printed by Heinrich Werner, 1642);

Philipp von Zesen; engraving by Christian von Hagen

Hooch-Deutsche Spraach-Übung oder unvorgreiffliches Bedenken über die Hooch-deutsche Haupt-Spraache und derselben Schreibrichtigkeit (Hamburg: Heinrich Werner, 1643);

Scala Heliconis Tevtonici: seu Compendiosa omnium Carminum Germanicorum simplicium, tum hactenus usitatorum, tum recens ad Graecorum & Latinorum formas effictorum, delineatio (Amsterdam: Johannes Jansson, 1643);

Adriatische Rosemund. Last hägt Lust, as Ritterhold von
  Blauen (Amsterdam: Ludwig Elzevier, 1645);
*Dichterische Jugend-Flammen, in etlichen Lob- Lust- und
  Liebes-Liedern zu lichte gebracht* (Hamburg: Johann Naumann, 1651);
*Rosen-mând: das ist in ein und dreissig gesprächen eröfnete
  Wunderschacht zum unerschätzlichen Steine der
  Weisen* (Hamburg: Georg Pape, 1651);
*Gekreutziger Liebsflammen. oder Geistlicher Gedichte
  Vorschmak* (Hamburg: Georg Pape, 1653);
*Güldener Regen, über die Deutsche durch den göttlichen
  Ferdjnanden, den alzeit friedfärtigen Vater des
  Vaterlandes, itzund in Regensburg berufene Danae
  von oben herab ausgegossen* (Regensburg: Printed
  by Christoph Fischer, 1653);
*Moralia Horatiana: Das ist Die Horatzische Sitten-Lehre,
  aus der Ernst-sittigen Geselschaft der alten Weise-
  meister gezogen* (Amsterdam: Printed by
  Cornelis de Bruyn, published by Cornelis
  Danckerts, 1656);
*Frauenzimmers Buß- Beicht- und Beht-Büchlein vor, in,
  und nach genießung, des heiligen Nachtmahls* (Amsterdam: Printed by Christoph Conrad, sold
  in Hamburg by Zacharias Dose, 1657);
Frauenzimmers Gebeht-Buch (Amsterdam: Printed by
  Christoph Conrad, sold in Hamburg by
  Zacharias Dose, 1657);
Neues Buß- und Gebätt-buch (Schaffhausen: Johann
  Caspar Suter, 1660);
*Leo Belgicus, Hoc est, Succincta, ac dilucida Narratio Ex-
  ordii, progressus, ac denique ad summam perfectionem
  redacti stabiliminis, & interioris formae, ac status,
  Reipublicae foederatarum Belgii Regionum: Cui
  accesserunt & Additamenta* (Amsterdam: Ludwig
  & Daniel Elzevier, 1660); revised and pub-
  lished in German as *Niederländischer Leue das ist,
  kurtzer, doch grundrichtiger Entwurf der innerlichen
  Gestalt und Beschaffenheit des Staht-wesens der
  sieben Vereinigten Niederländer* (Nuremberg: Johann Hoffmann, 1677);
*Die verschmähete, doch wieder erhöhete Majestäht; das ist,
  Kurtzer Entwurf der Begäbnüsse Karls des Zweiten,
  Königs von Engelland, Frankreich, Schotland und
  Jrland* (Amsterdam: Joachim Nosche, 1661);
*Coelvm Astronomico-Poeticvm sive Mythologicvm Stellarvm
  fixarvm. hoc est, Signorum coelestium, sive Con-
  stellationum omnium ad certas imagines redactarum,
  inque Coelo fictitio sive Organo Globi Astronomici
  continui, mythologico nomine & picturâ, ab Antiquis
  repraesetarum svccincta descriptio* (Amsterdam: Johannes Blaeu, 1662);
Beschreibung der Stadt Amsterdam (Amsterdam:
  Joachim Nosch, 1664; Amsterdam: Marcus
  Wilhelmsen Doornick, 1664);

*Des Geistlichen Standes Vrteile wider den Gewissenszwang
  in Glaubenssachen, aus den alten der fürnehmsten
  Kirchenlehrer, und neuen nachmahliger selbst heutiges
  tages Gottsgelehrter Geistlichen Schriften zusammen
  gesamlet* (Amsterdam: Printed by Christoph
  Conrad, 1665);
*Des Weltlichen Standes Handlungen, und Vrteile wider den
  Gewissenszwang in Glaubenssachen, aus den Ge-
  schichten der Keiser, Könige, Fürsten und anderer
  Weltlichen Obrigkeiten* (Amsterdam: Printed by
  Christoph Conrad, 1665);
*Hochdeutsche Helikonische Hechel, oder des Rosenmohndes
  zweite Woche* (Hamburg: Christian Guth,
  1668);
Die Reinweisse Hertzogin, auf Gnädigsten befehl besungen
  (Hamburg: Georg Rebenlein, 1668);
Schöne Hamburgerin (N.p., 1668);
*Das Hochdeutsche Helikonische Rosentahl, das ist, Der
  höchstpreiswürdigen Deutschgesinneten Genossen-
  schaft Erster oder Neunstämmiger Rosen-Zunft
  Ertzschrein* (Amsterdam: Printed by Christoph
  Conrad, 1669);
*Assenat; das ist derselben, und des Josefs heilige Stahts-
  Lieb- und Lebens-geschicht* (Amsterdam: Christian van Hagen, 1670);
*Dichterisches Rosen- und Liljen-tahl, mit mancherlei Lob-
  lust- schertz- schmertz- leid- und freuden-liedern
  gezieret* (Hamburg: Georg Rebenlein, 1670);
*Kriegs-Lieder, bei Betrachtung der Himlischen Kriegs-
  helden, am heiligen Engelsfeste, verfasset, und den
  Jrdischen Kriegsleuten zur übung der Gottsäligkeit,
  vorgesungen* (Hamburg: Arnold Lichtenstein,
  1676);
*Der Hoch-preis-würdigen Deutschgesinneten Genossenschaft
  Erster zwo Zünfte, nähmlich der Rosen- und Liljen-
  Zunft sämtlicher Zunftgenossen Zunft- Tauf- und
  Geschlächts-Nahmen, samt ihren Zunftzeichen, und
  Zunftsprüchen* (Hamburg: Printed by Arnold
  Lichtenstein, 1676);
*Reise-Lieder zu Wasser und Lande, für Schif- Fuhr- und
  Handels-Leute, wie auch andere über Land und
  Wasser Reisende* (Hamburg: Arnold Lichtenstein, 1677);
Simson, eine Helden- und Liebes-Geschicht (Nuremberg:
  Published by Johann Hofmann, printed by
  Andreas Knorz, 1679);
*Des Hochdeutschen Helikonischen Liljentahles, das ist der
  Hochpreiswürdigen Deutschgesinneten Genossenschaft
  Zweiter oder Siebenfacher Liljen-Zunft Vorbericht,
  ausgefärtigt durch den Färtigen* (Amsterdam: Pub-
  lished by the Genossenschaft, printed by
  Christoph Conrad, 1679);

Prirau, oder Lob des Vaterlandes (Amsterdam: Published by the Genossenschaft, printed by Christoph Conrad, 1680);

Die frühleuchtende Dichterkunst des sonderlich wohlgeahrteten und mit dem Lichte des Verstandes herlich ausgeschmükten Jünglings, Esdras Markus Lichtensteines, der die Gottesgelehrtheit, samt der Ebräischen Ertz- und anderen Haupt-Sprachen, zum Grundziele seiner Geflissenheit erkohren, kröhnete und belehnete, kraft verliehener Röm. Keiserl. Volmacht, am hochheiligen Jesus Tage des 1684sten Heiljahrs, mit dem immergrühnenden Lorbeerkrantze und herrlichleuchtendem Dichterglantze Der Färtig-Wohlsetzende (Hamburg: Printed by Arnold Lichtenstein, 1684);

Des Hochdeutschen Helikonischen Nägleintahles, das ist der Hochpreiswürdigen Deutschgesinten Genossenschaft Dritter oder Fünffacher Näglichen-Zunft Vorbericht, as Der Färtige (Hamburg: Printed by Arnold Lichtenstein, 1687);

Der erdichteten heidnischen Gottheiten, wie auch Als- und Halb-Gottheiten Herkunft und Begäbnisse, den Liebhabern nicht allein der Dicht- Bild- und Mahler-Kunst, sondern auch der gantzen Welt- und Gottes-gelehrtheit zu erleuterung ihres verstandes zu wissen nöthig, kurtzbündig beschrieben (Nuremberg: Johann Hoffmann, 1688).

Editions and Collections: *Moralia Horatiana,* 2 volumes, edited by W. Brauer (Wiesbaden: Pressler, 1963);

Zugelassenes Liebes-Übung, edited by Klaus Kaczerowsky (Berlin: Hessling, 1966);

Assenat, edited by Volker Meid (Tübingen: Niemeyer, 1967);

Moralia Horatiana, edited by Kaczerowsky (Bremen: Dieterich, 1970);

Sämtliche Werke, 15 volumes published, edited by Ferdinand van Ingen (Berlin: De Gruyter, 1970–   );

Europas erster Baedeker: Filip von Zesens Amsterdam 1664, edited by Christian Gellinek, Culture of European Cities, no. 2 (Frankfurt am Main: Peter Lang, 1988).

TRANSLATIONS: Vital d'Audiguier, *Liebes-beschreibung Lysanders und Kalisten* (Amsterdam: Ludwig Elzevier, 1644);

Madeleine de Scudéry, *Ibrahims oder des Durchleuchtigen Bassa und der beständigen Jsabellen Wunder-Geschichte* (Amsterdam: Ludwig Elzevier, 1645);

Torquato Tasso, *Der herzlich-verliebte schmerzlich-betrübte beständige Roselieb: oder Waldspiel* (Hamburg: Heinrich Werner, 1646);

François de Soucy, Sieur de Gerzan, *Die afrikanische Sofonisbe* (Amsterdam: Ludwig Elzevier, 1647);

Matthias Dögen, *Heutiges tages Übliche Kriges-Bau-kunst mit vilen außerläsenen so wol alten als neuen geschichten bewährt: und mit den vornämsten Fästungen der Christenheit lehr-bilds-weise ausgezieret,* translated by Zesen and Gottfried Hegenitz (Amsterdam: Ludwig Elzevier, 1648);

Augustus Buchner, *Was Karl der erste, König in Engelland, bei dem über Jhn gefälltem todesuhrteil hette fürbringen können. Zwei-fache Rede* (Wittenberg, 1649);

Salomons, des Ebreischen Königes, Geistliche Wohl-lust, oder Hohes Lied; jn Palmen- oder dattel-Reimen, mit bei-gefügten neun, vom fürtreflichen J. Schopen gesetzten sang-weisen, auch kurtzen erklährungen des geistlichen verstandes: beides nach art der gespräch-spiele auff öffentlicher schau-burg fürgestellet (Amsterdam: Christoph Conrad, 1657);

Johann Arndt, *Paradys-Hofken vol Christlijke Deugden* (Amsterdam: Jan van Ravestein, 1658);

Georges Fournier, S.J., *Handbuch der itzt üblichen Kriegs-baukunst, aus den gestalten der besten und itziger Zeit berühmtesten Festungen gezogen* (Amsterdam: Johannes Jansson & Eliseus Weyerstraten's widow, 1667);

Willem Goeree, *Anweisung zur algemeinen Reis- und Zeichenkunst* (Hamburg: Johann Naumann & Georg Wolff, 1669);

Arnold Montanus, *Denkwürdige Gesandtschafften der Ost-Jndischen Geselschaft in den Vereinigten Niederländern, an unterschiedliche Keyser von Japan* (Amsterdam: Jacob van Meurs, 1669);

Jan van Beverwijck, *Schatz der Gesundheit, das ist, Kurtzer Begrif der algemeinen Bewahrkunst* (Amsterdam: Johannes Blaeu, 1671);

van Beverwijck, *Schatz der Ungesundheit, das ist, Kurtzer Begrif der algemeinen Artzneikunst* (Amsterdam: Johannes Blaeu, 1671);

Alain Manesson Mallet, *Kriegsarbeit oder Neuer Festungsbau, so wol der Lehrsatzmäßige, als Unlehrsatzmäßige, in drei Teilen abgehandelt,* 3 volumes (Amsterdam: Jacob von Meurs, 1672);

Jan A. Komensky (Johann Amos Comenius), *Eerste Deel Prima Pars Erster Teil Der School-Geleertheyd, scholasticae Eruditionis, der Schvhl-Gelehrthejt, genoemt dicta genennet Het Portael: Vestibulum: Dje Vortvhre* (Amsterdam: Printed by Jan van Ravenstein, 1673);

Thomas à Kempis, *Andächtiger Lehr-Gesänge von Kristus Nachfolgung und Verachtung aller eitelkeiten der Welt, erstes Mandel* (Nuremberg: Published by Johann Hoffmann, printed in Magdeburg, 1675).

Only since the 1960s has an overall positive picture emerged regarding Philipp von Zesen's contributions to German language and literature. For hundreds of years, beginning during his own lifetime, Zesen was scorned and mocked; he seemed destined forever to be an outsider. Recent studies of his contributions in several fields, however, including poetry, poetics, novels, history, devotional literature, and coinage of new words, as well as his participation in language and literature societies, show him in a new light; he deserves still further study so that his rightful place in literary history will be secure.

Zesen was born on 8 October 1619 in the village of Priorau, approximately equidistant from Dessau and Bitterfeld, to Philipp and Dorothea Zesen. He is one of the early representatives of the many German authors whose fathers were Lutheran pastors: his father served as pastor in Priorau from 1616 to 1668. Zesen received his earliest education at home, then, beginning in 1637, he attended the gymnasium in Halle directed by Christian Gueintz. Zesen later claimed that he completed a rhyme lexicon by the time he was twelve years old; as a young scholar scarcely twenty years old he published that lexicon in his poetic handbook, *Deütscher Helikon* (German Helicon, 1640). This was not his first publication, however; his first work in print was *Melpomene* (1638), a brief selection of religious poems dealing with the Passion and death of Christ. In the next year he wrote a lengthier work dealing with salt, long an important part of the economy in Halle, and this work appeared in (differing) Latin and German versions, the former containing a few remarks on poetics that were later incorporated into his *Deütscher Helikon*.

Zesen's *Deütscher Helikon* was the first German-language poetic handbook since Martin Opitz's *Buch von der deutschen Poeterey* (Book of German Poetry, 1624). After Opitz's, it was also the most successful (there were four editions, as well as excerpts published by others) and probably the most innovative, because it was only after Zesen strongly supported the use of dactyls in German that they became an integral part of regularly used metric forms. Opitz had recommended against them; August Buchner had sanctioned them in his lectures at the University of Wittenberg in the 1630s; Zesen seems to have been the first to put into print the suggestion that they be used, although recent scholarship suggests a closer look at Martin Rinckart's contribution to this discussion. Zesen had attended the University of Wittenberg – he was awarded an M.A. de-

Illustration for Zesen's translation of François de Soucy, Sieur de Gerzan's Die afrikanische Sofonisbe: *Masinissa orders the execution of Kleomedes; Sofonisbe has fainted*

gree there in April 1641 – and had heard Buchner lecture; other students had also heard Buchner, of course, and his lectures on poetics were well known.

The impact of the "new" verse forms can scarcely be overestimated: Zesen showed that such forms were useful and appropriate not only in secular but also in religious poetry, perhaps most poignantly in his translation and reworking of the Song of Songs. In the second edition of his *Helikon* (1641) Zesen suggested that one could mix various meters, such as the iambic, trochaic, and dactylic. The musicality of German verse began to blossom as ever more poets used these forms, and scholars have pointed out their relationship to the joyful meter of dance. Zesen's poetic handbook differs from that of Opitz in many other ways, of which perhaps the extensive selection of "sample" poems showing various meters and rhyme schemes is the most obvious.

Almost immediately after receiving his degree Zesen headed for Hamburg. Occasional poems honoring births, deaths, birthdays, or name days indicate that Zesen had arrived in Hamburg at the latest in September 1641. In the next year he published his first pastoral work, *Poetischer Rosen-Wälder Vorschmack* (Foretaste of Poetic Rose-Forests), and the first collection of his poems, *FrühlingsLust* (Spring Joy).

In the fall of 1642 Zesen was in Amsterdam, where he remained until 1648. Amsterdam was a gathering place for many foreigners in the seventeenth century, among them students and those fleeing religious persecution; by 1648 the population had risen to approximately 150,000. There was a considerable publishing trade in Amsterdam, and hundreds of books in German were published there. Zesen quickly made contact with publishers of such books and probably worked as a proofreader in one or more of their houses.

The origins of Zesen's language and literature society, the Deutschgesinnete Genossenschaft (German-Minded Society), are rather unclear; Zesen himself presents contradictory evidence in his works. The idea for the society was probably conceived in 1642 – Zesen claims that he and two companions founded the society in that year – but first carried out in 1643, after Zesen had moved to Amsterdam; the fourth member, and thus the first member other than the founders, was not admitted until 1644. Many of the earliest members were Germans who were attending universities in Holland, such as those in Utrecht and Amsterdam. The society flourished until after Zesen's death. Like other similar societies, it had as its goals both the preservation of the traditional German virtues and the transformation of German into a respectable literary language. The members were frequently engaged in the translation of books from various languages into German. Zesen headed the society until his death in 1689.

Zesen himself quickly became involved in translating various works into German. One of the early translations in which he participated was that of Matthias Dögen's work on fortifications, *Architectura militaris moderna* (1647), which he produced, together with another member of the society, Gottfried Hegenitz, as *Heutiges tages Übliche Kriges-Bau-kunst* (Modern Common Military Architecture, 1648). Zesen's interest in translating such works

on the art of war continued throughout his life; he later translated lengthy works on fortifications by Georges Fournier (1667) and Alain Manesson Mallet (1672).

During Zesen's first stay in Amsterdam he was also busy translating novels from the French: Vital d'Audiguier's *Liebes-beschreibung Lysanders und Kalisten* (Portrayal of the Love of Lysander and Caliste, 1644), Madeleine de Scudéry's *Ibrahims oder des Durchleuchtigen Bassa und der beständigen Isabellen Wunder-Geschichte* (The Marvelous Story of Abraham; or, Of the Illustrious Bassa and the Faithful Isabel, 1645), and François de Soucy, Sieur de Gerzan's *Die afrikanische Sofonisbe* (The African Sophonisbe, 1647) appeared in quick succession. The influence these literary translations had on Zesen's work and on that of his contemporaries has never been thoroughly investigated, although it is clear that some elements, such as having a third party relate events that occurred prior to the action of a novel, found their way into Zesen's later works. And conversely, many innovations characteristic of Zesen's original works, particularly in terms of vocabulary, orthography, and style, appear in these three translations.

Zesen's first original novel, *Adriatische Rosemund* (The Adriatic Rosemund), appeared in 1645. Of his three novels, *Adriatische Rosemund* has kept scholars busiest as they try to determine whether it is a pastoral work, a courtly-historical piece, an autobiographical novel, or simply a symbolic representation of his language and literature society. One of the first nonpicaresque novels in German not to be based on an earlier source, *Adriatische Rosemund* does not fit neatly into any of the types of novel prevalent in the seventeenth century. Even the orthography, which is perhaps the clearest example of Zesen's preoccupation with extensive and full-fledged orthographic reforms (the only possible exception is his *Hooch-Deutsche Spraach-Übung* [High German Orthography, 1643]), sets it apart from all other novels of the era, including those by Zesen himself. The work appeared under a pseudonym, Ritterhold von Blauen, which his contemporaries soon penetrated: *Ritterhold* and the name of the novel's hero, *Markhold,* are both linguistically or etymologically related to *Philipp,* and *Blauen* is related to *Caesius,* the Latinized form of *Zesen.*

In 1648 Zesen returned to Germany, where he visited Prince Ludwig of Anhalt-Cöthen in Dessau in an attempt to secure acceptance into the most prestigious of the seventeenth-century language and literature societies, the Fruchtbringende Gesellschaft (Fruit-bringing Society), of which Ludwig was the founder and head. Zesen did become a member that same year, with the society name Der Wohlsetzende (The Well-Bred One), even though some of the other members opposed Zesen and his orthographic reforms in letters to Ludwig. In the spring of 1649 Zesen was back in Holland. He remained there until 1653, when he went to the court in Dessau; the purpose of this trip has never been determined. From Dessau he traveled to Regensburg, where he was raised into the nobility by Emperor Ferdinand III. His panegyrical poem *Güldener Regen* (Golden Rain, 1653) was written as a thank-you to the emperor.

In the 1650s Zesen seems to have had a feud with Johann Rist, the Lutheran pastor in Wedel. The details are sketchy, but it has been claimed that Rist founded his Elbschwanenorden (Order of Swans on the Elbe) as a rival to Zesen's Deutschgesinnte Genossenschaft.

In 1655 Zesen traveled to see Heinrich, Count of Thurn, who had become governor of what is today Estonia and was a member of Zesen's language and literature society. Zesen then traveled back to Holland, arriving early in 1656; he remained until 1667. The fourth, and last, edition of his *Helikon* had appeared in 1656, probably just before his return to the Netherlands. His *Moralia Horatiana,* poems based on ethical statements in various works of Horace, also appeared in 1656; it is the only emblem book Zesen ever published. In the same year he completed a lengthy historical work in Latin about Holland, *Leo Belgicus* (The Netherlandic Lion), which was not published until 1660. Zesen published a somewhat modified German version of this history many years later as *Niederländischer Leue* (The Netherlandic Lion, 1676).

It was during this lengthy sojourn in the Netherlands that Zesen began writing devotional literature. His *Frauenzimmers Buß- Beicht- und Beht-Büchlein vor, in, und nach genießung, des heiligen Nachtmahls* (Women's Prayer-Book, for Use before, during, and after the Reception of Holy Communion) and *Frauenzimmers Gebeht-Buch* (Women's Prayer-Book) both appeared in 1657. That same year he published a separate translation of the Song of Songs, which had been included in his poetic handbook; the next year the first edition of his Dutch translation of Johann Arndt's *Paradiesgärtlein* (The Little Garden of Paradise) appeared. Editions and reprintings of this little prayer book continued to appear well into the next century.

In 1664, to express his gratitude to Amsterdam for making him an honorary citizen, Zesen produced his profusely illustrated *Beschreibung der*

Illustration for Zesen's novel Assenat: *the betrothal of Assenat and Joseph*

Stadt Amsterdam (Description of the City of Amsterdam). The book was brought out in a large quarto and in a duodecimo edition by prominent Amsterdam publishing houses. It is still consulted because of its accuracy. Recent scholarship has suggested that *Beschreibung der Stadt Amsterdam* was not written by Zesen but by others, whose work he edited; there is no convincing proof for this theory, and Zesen identifies himself on the title page as the author.

By December 1667 Zesen had returned to Hamburg, where the twenty-fifth anniversary celebration for the Deutschgesinnete Genossenschaft was held in 1668 (lending credence to the sugges-

Illustration for Zesen's novel Simson: *Delila ties up the sleeping Simson*

tion that the society was founded in 1643, rather than in 1642). By 1669 he was back in Amsterdam, where his first programmatic work on his language and literature society, *Das Hochdeutsche Helikonische Rosentahl* (The German Rose Valley on the Helicon), appeared that year. The work explains some of the symbolism connected with the society; discusses the first subgroup within the society, the Rosenzunft (Brethren of the Rose); and lists all the members, together with their society sobriquets. It also includes several poems by Zesen and by Friedrich Scherertz, a member of the society from Lüneburg who was in Amsterdam at the time.

Zesen's second novel and first biblical novel, *Assenat,* appeared the next year. In terms of editions and translations, it was by far Zesen's most successful novel: there were two more editions in German, in 1672 and 1679, and six editions of a Danish

translation from 1711 to 1776, as well as another manuscript translation into Danish. There has always been discussion of the relationship between this novel and a similar novel by Hans Jakob Christoffel von Grimmelshausen, *Exempel der unveränderlichen Vorsehung Gottes. Unter einer anmutigen und ausführlichen Histori vom Keuschen Joseph in Egypten* (Example of the Unchanging Providence of God: In a Charming and Detailed History of the Chaste Joseph in Egypt, 1666). Zesen's work, however, clearly belongs in the category of the novels of state that were so often written in the seventeenth century; it has been referred to as the "literary realization of contemporary absolutistic thought."

Zesen's most comprehensive collection of lyric poetry also appeared in 1670. *Dichterisches Rosen- und Lilien-tahl* (Poetic Valley of Roses and Lilies) includes many examples of Zesen's occasional poetry and covers many years of his writing; it also includes the best examples of poetry in Dutch by Zesen.

Zesen married Maria Beckers, from Stade in Germany, in Amsterdam on 13 May 1672; the marriage was childless. They soon traveled to Germany, but in the spring of 1674 Zesen returned to Holland, this time for only a short stay. Except for a few short trips within Germany, Zesen remained in Hamburg until the summer of 1679, when he and his wife returned to the Netherlands so that she could start a business. The venture seems to have been unsuccessful; around this time Zesen began to complain in letters to David Hanisius, a member of the Deutschgesinnete Genossenschaft (and the first commoner to become librarian at the ducal library in Wolfenbüttel), about financial worries and his lack of a position at court.

Zesen's second biblical novel, *Simson* (Samson, 1679), is inferior to his other attempt in that genre; stylistically it is characterized by constant repetition and rephrasing. In this work, as in his previous biblical novel, the prefiguration of Jesus Christ in the main male figure is clear. This idea is not original with Zesen but can be found in much of the devotional literature of the time. Zesen's complaints about the state of his health were becoming more frequent (there is one, for example, in the preface to *Simson*), and it is perhaps for that reason that he began to think more and more about the town in which he was born. The next year he wrote a lengthy poem about his native town, *Prirau [sic], oder Lob des Vaterlandes* (Priorau; or, Praise of the Fatherland), stressing that no matter where he was in reality, he was always in his hometown in spirit.

The exact date of Zesen's return to Hamburg is not clear, but after 1684 his name again appears on occasional poetry for various residents of the city, although not as frequently as when he first arrived in 1640. His last work, *Der erdichteten heidnischen Gottheiten* (The Fabricated Heathen Gods, 1688), harks back to one of his earliest works: a short treatise within his poetic handbook dealing with the question of whether one should invent German names for the gods and goddesses or whether one ought instead to use the original "foreign" names.

Zesen died on 13 November 1689 in Hamburg. His literary remains have never been found; whatever library he might have owned seems to have been auctioned off shortly after his death.

Letters:
Etlicher der hoch-löblichen Deutsch-gesinneten Genossenschaft Mitglieder, wie auch anderer hoch-gelehrten Männer Sende-schreiben Erster Teil, edited by Johann Bellin (Hamburg: Heinrich Werner, 1647);
Wohlgegründete Bedenkschrift über die Zesische sonderbahre Ahrt Hochdeutsch zu Schreiben und zu Reden, edited by Andreas Daniel Habichhorst (Hamburg: Arnold Lichtenstein, 1678);
Augusta Steinberg, "Ein Brief Philipp Zesens," *Neue Zürcher Zeitung und schweizerisches Handelsblatt,* 130 (11 March 1909): 1;
Ferdinand Josef Schneider, "Ein Brief Philipp von Zesens," *Zeitschrift für deutsche Philologie,* 53 (1928): 153–155;
Leonard Forster, "Dichterbriefe aus dem Barock," *Euphorion,* 47 (1953): 390–411.

Bibliographies:
Karl F. Otto Jr., *Philipp von Zesen: A Bibliographical Catalogue,* Bibliographien zur deutschen Barockliteratur, no. 1 (Bern & Munich: Francke, 1972);
Joseph Leighton, "Zu drei wiederaufgefundenen Gedichten von Philipp von Zesen," *Daphnis: Zeitschrift für Mittlere Deutsche Literatur,* 6 (1977): 367–373;
Otto, "Wiederaufgefundene Zeseniana I," *Wissenschaftliche Zeitschrift der Martin Luther Universität Halle-Wittenberg: Gesellschaft- und Sprachwissenschaftliche Reihe,* 30, no. 4 (1981): 113–127;
Anthony J. Harper, "Drei neuaufgefundene frühe Gelegenheitsgedichte Philipp von Zesens," *Wolfenbütteler Barock-Nachrichten,* 10 (December 1983): 543–547;

Otto, "Wiederaufgefundene Zeseniana II," *Wissenschaftliche Zeitschrift der Martin Luther Universität Halle-Wittenberg: Gesellschaft- und Sprachwissenschaftliche Reihe,* 33, no. 5 (1984): 79–90;
Leonard Forster, "Zeseniana in der Domkapitelbibliothek zu Durham," in *Festschrift zum 60. Geburtstag von Hans-Gert Roloff,* edited by James Hardin and Jorg Jungmayr (Bern: Peter Lang, 1992), pp. 893–903;
Gerhard Dünnhaupt, *Personalbibliographien zu den Drucken des Barok,* volume 9, part 6 (Stuttgart: Hiersemann, 1993), pp. 4272–4331.

Biographies:
Max Gebhardt, *Untersuchungen zur Biographie Philipp Zesens* (Berlin: Rehm, 1888);
E. W. Moes, "Philipp von Zesen," *Jaarboek der Vereeniging Amstelodamum,* 5 (1907): 113–127;
Cornelia Bouman, *Philipp von Zesens Beziehungen zu Holland* (Bonn: Ludwig, 1916);
Jan Hendrik Scholte, "Philipp von Zesen," *Jaarboek van het Genootschap Amstelodamum,* 14 (1916): 37–143;
Herbert Blume, "Beiträge zur Biographie Zesens," *Daphnis: Zeitschrift für Mittlere Deutsche Literatur,* 3 (1974): 196–202.

References:
Paul Baumgartner, *Die Gestaltung des Seelischen in Zesens Romanen* (Frauenfeld & Leipzig: Huber, 1942);
Willi Beyersdorff, *Studien zu Philipp von Zesens biblischen Romanen Assenat und Simson* (Leipzig: Eichblatt, 1928);
Martin Bircher, "Zesen und Zürich," in *From Wolfram and Petrarch to Goethe and Grass: Studies in Literature in Honor of Leonard Forster,* edited by D. H. Green, L. P. Johnson, and Dieter Wuttke (Baden-Baden: Koerner, 1982), pp. 501–509;
Herbert Blume, "Die dänischen Übersetzungen von Zesens Roman *Assenat,*" *Nerthus,* 2 (1969): 79–93;
Blume, *Die Morphologie von Zesens Wortneubildungen* (Clausthal & Zellerfeld: Bönnecke, 1967);
Karl Dissel, *Philipp von Zesen und die Deutschgesinnte Genossenschaft,* Wissenschaftliche Beilage zum Osterprogramm des Wilhelm-Gymnasiums in Hamburg 1890, no. 715 (Hamburg: Lütcke & Wulff, 1890);
Willem Graadt van Roggen, *Een Stichtsche Sleutelroman uit de zeventiende eeuw* (Utrecht: Bruna, 1943);
Alfred Gramsch, *Zesens Lyrik* (Kassel: Edda, 1922);

Margarete Gutzeit, *Darstellung und Auffassung der Frau in den Romanen Philipps von Zesen* (Anklam: Poettcke, 1917);

Hugo Harbrecht, *Philipp von Zesen als Sprachreiniger* (Karlsruhe: Gillardon, 1912);

Harbrecht, "Verzeichnis der von Zesen verdeutschten Lehn- oder Fremdwörter," *Zeitschrift für deutsche Wortforschung,* 14 (1912): 71–81;

Hendrika Hasper, "Das Gründungsjahr der Deutschgesinnten Genossenschaft," *Neophilologus,* 10 (1925): 249–260;

Ferdinand van Ingen, "Frauentugend and Tugendexempel: Zum Frauenzimmer-Spiegel des Hieronymus Ortelius and Philipp von Zesens biblischen Frauenporträts," in *Barocker Lust-Spiegel: Studien zur Literatur des Barock. Festschrift für Blake Lee Spahr,* edited by Martin Bircher, Jorg-Ulrich Fechner, and Gerd Hillen (Amsterdam: Rodopi, 1984), pp. 345–383;

Ingen, *Philipp von Zesen* (Stuttgart: Metzler, 1970);

Ingen, "Philipp von Zesen," in *Deutsche Dichter des 17. Jahrhunderts: Ihr Leben und Werk,* edited by Harald Steinhagen and Benno von Wiese (Berlin: Schmidt, 1984), pp. 497–516;

Ingen, "Philipp von Zesens zehte Muse: Dorothea Eleonora von Rosenthal (Poetische Gedancken und Poetischer Rosen-Wälder Vorschmack)," in *Grenz-Gänge: Literatur und Kultur im Kontext,* edited by Guillaume van Gemert and Hans Ester (Amsterdam: Rodopi, 1990), pp. 85–110;

Ingen, ed., *Philipp von Zesen 1619–1969: Beiträge zu seinem Leben und Werk* (Wiesbaden: Steiner, 1972);

Klaus Kaczerowsky, *Bürgerliche Romankunst im Zeitalter des Barock: Philipp von Zesens* Adriatische Rosemund (Munich: Fink, 1969);

Hans Körnchen, *Zesens Romane: Ein Beitrag zur Geschichte des Romans im 17. Jahrhundert,* Palaestra, no. 115 (Berlin: Mayer & Müller, 1912);

Leo Lensing, "A Philosophical Riddle: Philipp von Zesen und Alchemy," *Daphnis: Zeitschrift für Mittlere Deutsche Literatur,* 6, no. 1–2 (1977): 123–146;

Ulrich Maché, "Zesen als Poetiker," *Deutsche Vierteljahrsschrift für Literaturwissenschaft und Geistesgeschichte,* 41 (August 1967): 391–423;

Werner Volker Meid, *Zesens Romankunst* (Darmstadt: Studentenwerk, 1966);

Thomas John Minnes, "Zesens Rosen-Mând und kleinere poetologische Schriften: Ein Kommentar," dissertation, State University of New York at Stony Brook, 1981;

Karl F. Otto Jr., "Bemerkungen zu Zesens Frühlingslust," *Daphnis: Zeitschrift für Mittlere Deutsche Literatur,* 1, no. 1 (1972): 777–787;

Otto, "Philipp von Zesen: Magister?," *Wolfenbütteler Barock-Nachrichten,* 17 (June 1990): 13–15;

Otto, "Sub-Groups of the Deutschgesinnte Genossenschaft," *Daphnis: Zeitschrift für Mittlere Deutsche Literatur,* 17, no. 3 (1988): 627–632;

John Roger Paas, "Philipp von Zesen's Work with Amsterdam Publishers of Engravings 1650–1670," *Daphnis: Zeitschrift für Mittlere Deutsche Literatur,* 13, no. 1–2 (1984): 319–341;

Ursula Rausch, "Philipp von Zesens *Adriatische Rosemünd* und C. F. Gellerts *Leben der schwedischen Gräfin von G.*: Eine Untersuchung zur Individualitätsentwicklung im deutschen Roman," dissertation, University of Freiburg, 1961;

Birger Säterstrand, *Die Sprache Zesens in der* Adriatische Rosemund (Greifswald: Adler, 1923);

Jan Hendrik Scholte, "Datierungsprobleme in der Zesenforschung," *Neophilologus,* 10 (1925): 260–265;

Scholte, "Dertig jaar Zesen-Onderzoek in Nederland," *Jaarboek van het Genootschap Amstelodamum,* 41 (1947): 67–109;

Scholte, "Utrecht in het oeuvre van Philipp von Zesen," *Jaarboekje van "Oud-Utrecht"* (1945): 126–149;

Scholte, "Zesens 'Adriatische Rosemund,'" *Deutsche Vierteljahrsschrift für Literaturwissenschaft und Geistesgeschichte,* 23, no. 2–3 (1949): 288–305;

Scholte, "Zesen's *Adriatische Rosemund* als symbolische Roman," *Neophilologus,* 30 (1945): 20–30;

Franz G. Sieveke, "Philipp von Zesens *Assenat:* Doctrina und Eruditio im Dienst des Exemplificare," *Jahrbuch der Deutschen Schiller-Gesellschaft,* 13 (1969): 115–136;

Ingeborg Spriewald, "Die Anwaltschaft für den Menschen im Roman bei Zesen und Grimmelshausen," in *Studien zur deutschen Literatur im 17. Jahrhundert,* edited by Werner Link (Berlin: Aufbau, 1984), pp. 352–438;

Clara Stucki, *Grimmelshausens und Zesens Josephromane: Ein Vergleich zweier Barockdichter* (Horgen-Zurich & Leipzig: Münster-Presse, 1933);

Gary Craig Thomas, "Dance Music and the Origins of the Dactylic Meter," *Daphnis: Zeitschrift für Mittlere Deutsche Literatur,* 16, no. 1–2 (1987): 107–146;

Thomas, "Philipp von Zesen and Music," dissertation, Harvard University, 1973;

Renate Weber, "Die Lieder Philipp von Zesens," dissertation, University of Hamburg, 1962.

Julius Wilhelm Zincgref

(3 June 1591 – 12 November 1635)

Jonathan P. Clark
Concordia College

BOOKS: *Facetiæ Pennalivm, Das ist, Allerley lustige Schulbossen, auß Hieroclis facetiis Philosophorum zum theil verdeutschet, vnd zum theil auß dem täglichen Prothocollo der heutigen Pennal zusammen getragen. Mit sampt etlichen angehengten vnterschiedlichen Charakterismis oder Beschreibungen des Pennalismi, Pedantismi, vnd Stupiditatis oder der Stockheiligkeit,* anonymous (N.p., 1618); enlarged as *Vermehrete Schuelbossen* (N.p., 1624, enlarged, 1627); enlarged as *Newlich vermehrte Pennal- vnd Schul-Possen* (N.p., 1636);

Triga amico-poetica siue Iulii Gvlielmi Zincgrefi Heidelbergensis Iuuenilia Poetica: Friderici Lingelshemii Heidelbergensis p. m. Reliquiae Poeticae. Ioannis Leonhardi Weidneri Palatini Conatuum Poeticorum Prodomus, by Zincgref, Friedrich Lingelsheim, and Johann Leonhard Weidner, edited by Weidner (N.p., 1619);

Emblematvm Ethico-Politicorvm Centuria (Frankfurt am Main: Johann Theodor de Bry, 1619); republished as *Sapientia picta. Das ist, Künstliche Sinnreiche Bildnussen vnd Figuren, darinnen denkwürdige Sprüch vnd nützliche Lehren im Politischen vnd gemeinen Wesen durch hundert schöne newe Kupferstück vorgebildet, entworffen, vnd durch deutsche Reymen erkläret werden. So auch zu einem Stamm oder Wappen Büchlein füglich zugebrauchen* (Frankfurt am Main: Peter Marschall, 1624); republished as *Fahnenbilder, das ist, Sinnreiche Figuren vnd Sprüch, von Tugenden vnd Tapfferkeit Heroischer Persohnen, in Fahnen, Cornetten, Libereyen, Trompeten, vnd dergleichen zu gebrauchen* (Frankfurt am Main: Johann Ammon, 1633);

Newe Zeitungen von vnterschiedlichen Orten: Das ist, Die alte Warheit mit eim newen Titul, anonymous (N.p., 1619); enlarged as *Warhaffte Newe Zeitungen, von vnterschiedlichen Orten vnd Landen. Das ist: Die alte Warheit mit eim newen Titul. Vermehrt vnd auch verbessert* (N.p., 1620);

Quotlibetisches Weltkefig. Darinn gleichsam, alß in einem Spiegel, daß gegenwärtige Weltgetümmel, gehümmel vnd getrümmel, wüten vnd toben, liegen triegen vnd kriegen, jrren wirren vnd sinceriren, Schwarm vnd Alarm, zusehen, anonymous (N.p., 1623, enlarged, 1623); enlarged as *Quotlibetisches Welt und Hummel Kefig* (N.p., 1632);

Eine Vermahnung zur Dapfferkeit, nach form, vnd art der Elegien des Griechischen Poeten Tyrtaei, welche der Lacedaemonier Feldst Obersten jhren Bürgern vnd Soldaten, ehe sie ins Treffen giengen, vorzulesen pflegten (N.p., 1625); republished as *Soldaten Lob, oder Vnvberwindlicher Soldaten Trutz, Von Eigenschafften, vnd vortrefflichen, vnvberwindlichen Dapfferkeit der Edlen Soldaten* (Frankfurt am Main: Published by Johann Friedrich Weiss, 1632);

Der Teutschen Scharpfsinnige kluge Sprüch (Strasbourg: Josiah Rihel's heirs, 1626); enlarged as *Der Teutschen Scharpfsinnige kluge Sprüch, Apophthegmata genant,* 2 volumes (Strasbourg: Josias Rihel, 1628, 1631); enlarged as *Teutscher Nation Klug-außgesprochene Weißheit,* 3 volumes (Leiden: Frans Heger, 1644–1645; enlarged edition, 5 volumes, Amsterdam: Ludwig Elzevier, 1653–1655).

Editions and Collections: *Scharfsinnige Sprüche der Teutschen, Apophthegmata genannt,* edited by B. F. Guttenstern (Mannheim: Hoff, 1835);

Gesammelte Schriften, edited by Dieter Mertens and Theodor Verweyen, 3 volumes (Tübingen: Niemeyer, 1978–1993).

OTHER: Martin Opitz, *Martini Opicii Teutsche Poëmata vnd Arjstarchvs wieder die verachtung Teutscher Sprach, Item Verteutschung Danielis Heinsij Lobgesangs Iesu Christi, vnd Hymni in Bachem sampt einem anhang mehr außerlesener geticht anderer Teutscher Pöeten. Der gleichen in dieser Sprach hiebeuor nicht auß kommen,* edited by Zincgref (Strasbourg: Published by Eberhard Zetzner, 1624).

Auserlesene Gedichte Deutscher Poeten gesammelt von Julius Wilhelm Zinkgref. 1624, edited by W. Braune, Neudrucke deutscher Litteraturwerke

Frontispiece for the 1653–1655 edition of Julius Wilhelm Zincgref's collection of apothegms. The title as given here differs somewhat from that on the title page.

des XVI. und XVII. Jahrhunderts, no. 15 (Halle: Niemeyer, 1879).

Julius Wilhelm Zincgref was a patriot as well as a reformer. He believed that national identity finds its source and sustenance in a common language and in educational and linguistic reforms that guarantee national and religious freedoms.

Zincgref was born on 3 June 1591 in Heidelberg to Laurentius Zincgref, legal counselor to the elector palatine, and Margaretha Zincgref, née Dresch; by the time of his mother's death in 1620 he would be the only one of their six children — three daughters and three sons — still alive. At sixteen he enrolled at the University of Heidelberg to continue in his father's footsteps by earning a law degree. After completing the humanistic part of his studies in 1612 he undertook a five-year course of travel to study in Basel, Orléans, Marseilles, England, the Netherlands, and Italy. During his travels he became acquainted with many jurists and professors of law, and he also may have met the writer Georg Rodolf Weckherlin. On his return to Heidelberg in 1617, Zincgref was awarded a doctorate of law.

For part of his journey through Europe, Zincgref was accompanied by his friend Friedrich Lingelsheim. Though Lingelsheim died shortly before Zincgref's return to Heidelberg, the importance of this relationship can not be underestimated. Lingelsheim's house served as a gathering place for the most influential poets of the early seventeenth century and, as such, became a starting point for Zincgref's own poetic development and a lightning rod for what would be seen as the beginnings of German poetic reform. Lingelsheim's father, Georg Michael, had brought together around 1600 a group of poets influenced by German Renaissance humanism. They included Paul Melissus Schede, poet laureate at the ducal court and director of the court library, and Peter Denaisius, who lived at Laurentius Zincgref's house from 1584 to 1590. A second group of poets formed around Martin Opitz, who spent a year as a tutor at Lingelsheim's house in 1619–1620. This circle of poets included Janus Gebhardt, Balthasar Venator, Jacob Creutz, and Heinrich Albert Hamilton, as well as Zincgref.

Before his return to Heidelberg, Zincgref's poetic endeavors were directed at his friends Lingelsheim and Johann Leonhard Weidner. Weidner, a teacher in Neuhausen, published a collection of Zincgref's, Lingelsheim's, and his own early poetry as *Triga amico-poetica* (Poetry by Three Friends) in 1619. The poems in the volume had been written for a small circle of friends. The works written after Zincgref's return from his travels reflect a newfound political engagement and are meant for a larger audience. Arising at a time of war in the Palatinate, Zincgref's early works — *Facetiae Pennalium* (Facetiousness of Feathery Things, 1618), *Emblematum Ethico-Politicorum Centuria* (One Hundred Ethical-Political Emblemata, 1619), and the flyer *Newe*

Zeitungen (New Reports, 1619) – address two intertwined issues: the freedom of the Palatinate from foreign domination and the purity of the German language. *Facetiae Pennalium* is a collection of anecdotes and moral sentences critical of contemporary pedagogy and of scholarship that is erudite but impractical. At issue in this work is a stagnant educational system that does not allow for constructive criticism or change. Many educators – though not all, as Zincgref would point out in an apology in the second edition of the work (1627) – have attained their degrees in an ossified educational system and have brought the inefficiencies of that system into government offices, where scholarly disputes and continual finger-pointing render government ineffectual. More effort has been spent, according to Zincgref, on saving face than in helping "Land und Leuth" (country and people). As an example of how governmental paralysis is a result of an educational system that produces cowards, corrupt and bankrupt students, and scribes, Zincgref points to an inefficient armament policy that contributed to the inadequate defenses of the Palatinate. Zincgref calls for a moral renewal in government through the reform of an educational system mired in Scholastic traditions.

Fleeing Heilbronn, where he was stationed as general auditor of the Heidelberg garrison, in 1622, Zincgref went to Strasbourg via Frankfurt am Main. He became an interpreter for Wilhelm Marescot, the French envoy to the German elector princes. Zincgref's service ended not long afterward in Stuttgart, when he fell ill and was forced to return to Strasbourg.

Zincgref continued his criticism of the injustices of the war in *Quotlibetisches Weltkefig* (World Cage, Any Way You Will, 1623). A moral satire in the tradition of the works of Johann Fischart, *Quotlibetisches Weltkefig* demonstrates that the goals of the war are the extermination of the Calvinists and the unrestrained expansion of Spanish, Austrian, and Bavarian power. Zincgref makes explicit reference of the events of 1622, accusing imperial troops led by Johann Tserklaes, Graf von Tilly, of murdering pregnant women, children, and old people.

When Opitz fled Heidelberg in 1620 because of Tilly's advance on the city, he left Zincgref a collection of his poetry in manuscript form. Zincgref had these works published in 1624 as *Teutsche Poëmata und Aristarchus* (German Poems and "Aristarchus"), but he reordered the poems and made other editorial changes in them. Though Zincgref incurred Opitz's wrath for making these changes, he received praise from his contemporaries for making

public a uniquely German poetry. Zincgref says in the dedication that he had three reasons for publishing the volume: to illustrate that the claims by other nations to poetic superiority were unfounded; to impress upon his countrymen that German should be valued as a poetic language; and to demonstrate that language and national character are inextricably linked. To belittle one's mother tongue, according to Zincgref, is tantamount to denigrating one's own identity.

Zincgref's edition pays tribute to Opitz as a leader in German poetic reform; it also recognizes other contributions to a German poetic voice by appending to Opitz's work poems by other poets: Schede, Denaissus, Weckherlin, Creutz, Gebhardt, Hamilton, Venator, Isaac Habrecht, Caspar Kirchner, Balthasar Wesselius, and Christoph von Schallenberg. Zincgref also includes twenty-two of his own poems. Zincgref not only introduced the poetry of Opitz and the others to a wider audience but also placed these works in the context of a national identity. He says in the introduction that German will only take the place of Latin when German poetry becomes a recognized artistic exercise, and poets writing in German turn from being simple rhyme makers to become true poets. In arguing for a new poetic ethos Zincgref implicitly criticizes the state of education in Germany and the place of Latin within that system. The new Latin poetry of the day was produced largely by teachers and preachers and was inextricably linked to the objects of their professional attention and calling, demanding an elevated poetic style that tended toward pedantry. Zincgref argues that the poetry of the new class of poets, who prefer the vernacular, is not tied to a particular profession; thus, poetic form and motifs can break from tradition.

The first three poems in the appendix address the difficulties in achieving this task. Habrecht questions whether Greece and Rome will continue to garner poetic fame and admonishes the German muse to step forward to claim her share of the glory. Zincgref responds to the question by pointing out that while the way to the laurels may be long and fraught with difficulties, the reward will make it worthwhile. Finally, Schede places the blame for an undeveloped German poetry on German self-deprecation and foreign influences. More than a comment on the present state of German poetic production, Zincgref's collection is an attempt to lead the way in the development of a uniquely German poetry. *Teutsche Poëmata und Aristarchus,* with its appendix, traces a German poetic revival that found its beginning with the humanist poets, carried over to a new generation of poets represented by Zincgref and his friends, and culminated in Opitz. Zincgref's patriotism is especially evident in his promotion of a uniquely German poetic tradition.

One of Zincgref's poems in the appendix to *Teutsche Poëmata und Aristarchus* describes the consequences of a government bureaucracy that works counter to the good of the people, and it speaks to the depth of Zincgref's patriotic fervor as it extends beyond language to the practical realities of armed defense. "Vermanung zur Dapfferkeit" (Call to Courage) was written both as a call to arms and as a defense of the soldiers of the Heidelberg garrison, who were called cowards by the citizens during Tilly's siege. Zincgref's poem begins with a tribute to the fatherland:

> KEin Tod ist löblicher, kein Tod wird mehr geehret,
> > Als der, durch den das Heil deß Vatterlandts sich
> > > nehret,
> > Den einer willkom heist, dem er entgegen lacht,
> Ihn inn die Arme nimpt, und doch zugleich veracht.
> . . . .
> Ein solcher Mann der ist der Statt gemeines gut,
> Der Wiedersacher grauß deß Landts wehrhaffte Hut. . . .
>
> (No death is more praiseworthy, no deed more honorable
> > Than the one by which the fatherland is nourished,
> > A death one welcomes, one laughs in the face of,
> Holds by the arm and yet despises.
> . . . .
> Such a man is the common good of the city,
> The bane of the oppressor, the true defender of the country.)

Zincgref goes on to argue that a people that does not value its soldiers has no hope for survival; indeed, it has already died. The soldier, in return for unqualified support, must fight for the common good without thought of death. The only crime is in not trying. The poem establishes Zincgref as a patriot whose poetry assumes a social function in its condemnation of the foreign invasion of Germany and in its praise of the country.

In Strasbourg, Zincgref met Agnete Nordeck Patrick, a widow. They were married in Worms in 1626. Before leaving Strasbourg in 1627, Zincgref published what would become his most popular work, *Der Teutschen Scharpfsinnige kluge Sprüch* (Witty, Clever Aphorisms of the Germans, 1626), generally known as *Apophthegmata,* a collection of witty pieces, aphorisms, dialogues, anecdotes, and wordplays. His *Emblematum Ethico-Politicorum Centuria* can be seen as the predecessor to the *Apophthegmata*

(1628, 1631): illustrated by the Swiss publisher and engraver Matthäus Merian, who worked with his father in Heidelberg in 1620, the *Emblematum* is a collection of moral sentences primarily drawn from classical sources. *Apophthegmata,* however, draws strictly from German sources. Many of the passages come from Zincgref's friends and acquaintances, such as the Lingelsheims or Weidner, but they also come from better-known personalities such as Fischart, Desiderius Erasmus, Martin Luther, and Sebastian Franck. Zincgref tries in this collection, first, to illustrate that wisdom is as abundant in German writings as in those of any other language and, second, to maintain the honor and respectability of German by avoiding the obscene quotations found in collections from the sixteenth century. Most important, however, Zincgref hopes to show that the Germans are not barbarians and that they are not mute. In case all freedoms are extinguished as a result of the war, Zincgref wants to preserve reasoned words and thoughtful speeches of German origin.

Both the praise heaped upon Zincgref in the dedicatory poems by such writers as Venator, Creutz, and Johann Michael Moscherosch and the many editions attest to the popularity of the work and the chord it struck at a time when Germany was beset by foreign invasion. Before the end of the war the work went through seven editions; it also proved to be popular after the war, with four further editions between 1649 and 1693. Thus, it contributed to the construction of a national identity in the wake of the devastation of the war. Moreover, it influenced new generations of German writers, including Hans Jakob Christoffel von Grimmelshausen, Georg Philipp Harsdörffer, and Quirinus Kuhlmann.

Zincgref lived in Saint Goar until he was called to Kreuznach as a magistrate's clerk by the Palatine duke Philipp Ludwig. After the Swedish king Gustav Adolph and his troops moved on to Creutzlingen, Zingref's job was expanded under the electoral prince, Karl. After the defeat of the Protestant forces in the Battle of Nördlingen on 6 September 1634, Zincgref tried to return to Saint Goar; on the way he was wounded and robbed by soldiers from Weimar. Though he did eventually make it home, he never fully recovered from his wounds, and he died of the plague on 12 November 1635 at the age of forty-four. He was survived by Agnete and two sons; a third son had died shortly before Zincgref.

Zincgref's works provide a transition between the humanist traditions of the late sixteenth century and the beginning of a German national literature that continued to develop throughout the seventeenth century. Rather than deny the past he builds on its foundation, bringing two generations together in his collections of sayings and poetry. As he writes in the preface to his *Apophthegmata:*

Ich hab das mein gethan, so vil mir Gott beschert:
Ein ander thue das sein, so wirdt die Kunst gemehrt.

(I have done what I could, as much as God bestowed upon me,
Let others do their part and art will flourish.)

The continual popularity of his works throughout the seventeenth century attests to the degree to which he was successful.

Bibliography:

Gerhard Dünnhaupt, *Personalbibliographien zu den Drucken des Barock,* volume 9, part 6 (Stuttgart: Hiersemann, 1993), pp. 4356–4372.

Biography:

Franz Schnorr von Carolsfeld, "Julius Wilhelm Zincgrefs Leben und Schriften," *Archiv für Literaturgeschichte,* 8 (1879): 1–58, 446–490.

References:

Curt von Faber du Faur, "The Author of *Sapientia Picta," Yale University Library Gazette,* 28 (April 1954): 156–160;

Oskar Fischl, "Quelle und Nachwirkung von Julius Wilhelm Zincgrefs 'Vermanung zur Dapfferkeit,' " *Euphorion,* 18 (1911): 27–41;

Werner Paul Friederich, "Julius Wilhelm Zinkgref and His Fellow-Poets," *Germanic Review,* 9 (October 1934): 219–238;

Dieter Mertens, "Zu Heidelberger Dichtern von Schede bis Zincgref," *Zeitschrift für deutsches Altertum und deutsche Literatur,* 103, no. 3 (1974): 200–241;

Theodor Verweyen, *Apophthegmata und Scherzrede: Die Geschichte einer einfachen Gattungsform und ihrer Entfaltung im 17. Jahrhundert,* Linguistica et Litteraria, no. 5 (Bad Homburg: Gehlen, 1970);

Emil Weller, "Der Dichter Zincgref als Verfasser des Welt- und HummelKäfigs," *Anzeiger für Kunde der deutschen Vorzeit,* 4 (1856): 297–300;

Günter Weydt, "Apophthegmata Teutsch," in *Festschrift für Jost Trier zum 70. Geburtstag,* edited by William Foerste and Karl Heinz Borck (Cologne: Böhlau, 1964), pp. 364–385.

Books for Further Reading

Aikin, Judith P. *German Baroque Drama.* Boston: Twayne, 1982.

Alewyn, Richard, ed. *Deutsche Barockforschung. Dokumentation einer Epoche,* second edition. Cologne: Kiepenheuer & Witsch, 1965.

Bahner, Werner, ed. *Renaissance, Barock, Aufklärung: Epochen- und Periodisierungsfragen.* Berlin: Akademie Verlag, 1976.

Bahr, Erhard, ed. *Geschichte der deutschen Literatur: Kontinuität und Veränderung. Vom Mittelalter bis zur Gegenwart,* volume 1: *Vom Mittelalter bis zum Barock.* Tübingen: Francke, 1987.

Barner, Wilfried. *Barockrhetorik: Untersuchungen zu ihren geschichtlichen Grundlagen.* Tübingen: Niemeyer, 1970.

Barner, ed. *Der Literarische Barockbegriff.* Darmstadt: Wissenschaftliche Buchgesellschaft, 1975.

Bircher, Jörg-Ulrich Fechner, and Gerd Hillen, eds. *Barocker Lust-Spiegel: Studien zur Literatur des Barock; Festschrift für Blake Lee Spahr.* Amsterdam: Rodopi, 1984.

Bircher, Martin, and Ferdinand van Ingen, eds. *Sprachgesellschaften – Sozietäten – Dichtergruppen. Arbeitsgespräch in der Herzog August Bibliothek Wolfenbüttel 28. bis 30. Juni, 1977.* Hamburg: Hauswedell, 1978.

Brinker-Gabler, Gisela, ed. *Deutsche Literatur von Frauen,* volume 1: *Vom Mittelalter bis zum Ende des 18. Jahrhunderts.* Munich: Beck, 1988.

Browning, Robert M. *German Baroque Poetry. 1618–1723.* University Park: Pennsylvania State University Press, 1971.

Buck, August. *Renaissance und Barock: Die Emblematik. Zwei Essays.* Frankfurt am Main: Athenaion, 1971.

Buck, ed. *Neues Handbuch der Literaturwissenschaft: Renaissance und Barock,* volumes 9 and 10. Frankfurt am Main: Athenaion, 1972.

Buck, Georg Kauffmann, Blake Lee Spahr, and C. Wiedemann, eds. *Europäische Hofkultur im 16. und 17. Jahrhundert: Vorträge und Referate gehalten anläßlich des Kongresses des Wolfenbütteler Arbeitskreises für Renaissanceforschung und des internationalen Arbeitskreises für Barockliteratur in der Herzog August Bibliothek Wolfenbüttel vom 4. bis 8. September, 1979.* Hamburg: Hauswedell, 1981.

Bukofzer, Manfred F. *Music in the Baroque Era: From Monteverdi to Bach.* New York: Norton, 1947.

Campe, Rüdiger. *Affekt und Ausdruck: Zur Umwandlung der literarischen Rede im 17. und 18. Jahrhundert.* Tübingen: Niemeyer, 1990.

Capua, A. G. de. *German Baroque Poetry: Interpretive Readings.* Albany: State University of New York Press, 1973.

Curtius, Ernst Robert. *European Literature and the Latin Middle Ages.* New York: Pantheon, 1953.

Cysarz, Herbert. *Deutsche Barockdichtung: Renaissance, Barock, Rokoko.* Leipzig: Haessel, 1924.

Cysarz. *Deutsche Barocklyrik,* second enlarged edition. Stuttgart: Reclam, 1970.

De Boor, Helmut. *Die deusche Literatur vom Späthumanismus zur Empfindsamkrit, 1570–1750,* volume 5 of *Geschichte der deutschen Literatur,* fourth edition, edited by de Boor and Richard Newald. Munich: Beck, 1951.

Emrich, Wilhelm. *Deutsche Literatur der Barockzeit, 1600–1700.* Königstein im Taunus: Athenäum, 1981.

Engels, Heinz. *Die Sprachgesellschaften des 17. Jahrhunderts.* Giessen: Schmitz, 1983.

Faber du Faur, Curt von. *German Baroque Literature: A Catalogue of the Collection in The Yale University Library,* 2 volumes. New Haven: Yale University Press, 1958, 1969.

Foerster, Rolf Helmut. *Die Welt des Barock.* Munich: Desch, 1970.

Forster, Leonard. *Studien zur europäischen Rezeption deutscher Barockliteratur.* Wiesbaden: Harrassowitz, 1983.

Friedrich, Carl Joachim. *The Age of the Baroque, 1610–1660.* New York: Harper & Row, 1952.

Gaede, Friedrich W. *Humanismus, Barock, Aufklärung: Geschichte der deutschen Literatur vom. 16. bis zum 18. Jahrhundert.* Bern: Francke, 1971.

Garber, Klaus, ed. *Europäische Barock-Rezeption: Voträge und Referate gehalten anläßlich des 6. Jahrestreffens des Internationalen Arbeitskreises für Barockliteratur in der Herzog August Binbliothek Wolfenbüttel vom 22. bis 25. August 1988.* Wiesbaden: Harrassowitz, 1991.

Gillespie, Gerald. *Garden and Labyrinth of Time: Studies in Renaissance and Baroque Literature.* New York: Lang, 1988.

Grimm, Günter, and Frank Rainer Max, eds. *Deutsche Dichter: Leben und Werk deutschsprachiger Autoren,* volume 2: *Reformation, Renaissance und Barock.* Stuttgart: Reclam, 1989.

Grimminger, Rolf, ed. *Hansers Sozialgeschichte der deutschen Literatur vom 16. Jahrhundert bis zur Gegenwart,* volume 3. Munich: Hanser, 1980.

Gumbrecht, Hans Ulrich, and Ursula Link-Heer, eds. *Epochenschwellen und Epochenstrukturen im Diskurs der Literatur- und Sprachhistorie.* Frankfurt am Main: Suhrkamp, 1985.

Hankamer, Paul. *Deutsche Gegenreformation und deutsches Barock; die deutsche Literatur im Zeitraum des 17. Jahrhunderts.* Stuttgart: Metzler, 1935.

Hankamer. *Die Sprache, ihr Begriff und ihre Deutung im 16. und 17. Jahrhundert.* Bonn: Cohen, 1927.

Hederer, Edgar. *Deutsche Dichtung des Barock,* fourth edition. Munich: Hanser, 1965.

Hofmeister, Gerhart, ed. *German Baroque Literature: The European Perspective.* New York: Ungar, 1983.

Kaczerowsky, Klaus, ed. *Schäferromane des Barock,* Rowohlts Klassiker, volume 530/531. Reinbek bei Hamburg: Rowohlt, 1970.

Kemper, Hans Georg. *Deutsche Lyrik der frühen Neuzeit,* volume 3: *Barock-Mystik.* Tübingen: Niemeyer, 1988.

Könneker, Barbara, and Conrad Wiedemann. *Deutsche Literatur in Humanismus und Barock*. Frankfurt am Main: Athenaion, 1973.

Kühlmann, Wilhelm. *Gelehrtenrepublik und Fürstenstaat: Entwicklung und Kritik des deutschen Späthumanismus in der Literatur des Barockzeitalters*. Tübingen: Niemeyer, 1982.

Meid, Volker. *Barocklyrik*. Stuttgart: Metzler, 1986.

Merkel, Ingrid. *Barock*. Bern: Francke, 1971.

Müller, Richard. *Dichtung und Bildende Kunst im Zeitalter des deutschen Barock*. Leipzig: Huber, 1937.

Nelson, Lowry. *Baroque Lyric Poetry*. New Haven: Yale University Press, 1961.

Neumeister, Sebastian, and Conrad Widemann, eds. *Res publica litteraria: Die Institutionen der Gelehrsamkeit in der frühen Neuzeit*. Wiesbaden: Harrossowitz, 1987.

Pascal, Roy. *German Literature in the Sixteenth and Seventeenth Centuries: Renaissance – Reformation – Baroque*. New York: Barnes & Noble, 1968.

Powell, Hugh. *Trammels of Tradition. Aspects of German Life and Culture in the 17th Century and their Impact on the Contemporary Literature*. Tübingen: Niemeyer, 1988.

Pyritz, Hans, and Ilse Pyritz. *Bibliographie zur deutschen Literaturgeschichte des Barockzeitalters,* 2 volumes. Bern: Francke, 1985.

Schone, Albrecht. *Emblematik und Drama im Zeitalter des barock,* revised edition. Munich: Beck, 1964.

Schulz-Behrend, George. *The German Baroque: Literature, Music, Art*. Austin: University of Texas Press, 1972.

Skrine, Peter. *The Baroque: Literature und Culture in Seventeenth-Century Europe*. London: Methuen / New York: Holmes & Meier, 1978.

Spahr, Blake Lee, ed. *Problems and Perspectives: A Collective of Essays on German Baroque Literature*. Frankfurt am Main: Lang, 1981.

Stamm, Rudolf, ed. *Die Kunstformen des Barockzeitalters*. Bern & Munich: Francke, 1956.

Stammler, Wolfgang. *Von der Mystik zum Barock, 1400–1600,* revised and enlarged edition. Stuttgart: Metzler, 1950.

Steffen, Hans, ed. *Formkräfte der deutschen Dichtung vom Barock bis zur Gegenwart,* second edition. Göttingen: Vadenhoeck & Ruprecht, 1967.

Steinhagen, Harald, and Benno von Wiese. *Deutsche Dichter des 17. Jahrhunderts: Ihr Leben und Werk*. Berlin: Schmidt, 1984.

Szyrocki, Marian. *Die Deutsche Literatur des Barock. Eine Einführung,* second edition. Reinbek bei Hamburg: Rowohlt, 1970.

Szyrocki. *Lyrik des Barock*. Reinbek bei Hamburg: Rowohlt, 1971.

Vivian, Kim, ed. *A Concise History of German Literature to 1900*. Columbia, S.C.: Camden House, 1992.

Von Wiese, Benno. *Das deutsche Drama vom Barock bis zur Gegenwart.* Düsseldorf: Bagel, 1975.

Wagener, Hans. *The German Baroque Novel.* Boston: Twayne, 1973.

Warnke, Frank. *Versions of Baroque: European Literature in the Seventeenth Century.* New Haven: Yale University Press, 1972.

Wolf, A. *A History of Science, Technology, and Philosophy in the 16th and 17th Centuries.* London: Allen & Unwin, 1935.

Wollflin, Heinrich. *Renaissance und Barock.* Ithaca, N.Y.: Cornell University Press, 1967.

Contributors

Judith P. Aikin ....*University of Iowa*
Sigmund J. Barber ....*Grinnell College*
Barbara Becker-Cantarino ....*Ohio State University*
Stanley W. Beeler ....*University of Calgary*
Jill Bepler..*Herzog August Bibliothek*
Günter Berghaus..*University of Bristol*
Thomas W. Best..*University of Virginia*
Barton W. Browning ....*Pennsylvania State University*
Jonathan P. Clark..*Concordia College*
Albrecht Classen...*University of Arizona*
G. Richard Dimler ....*Fordham University*
Joscelyn Godwin..*Colgate University*
David Halsted ....*University of Cincinnati*
Anthony J. Harper ....*University of Strathclyde*
Andreas Herz ....*Herzog August Bibliothek*
Peter Hess ....*University of Texas at Austin*
Gerhart Hoffmeister..*University of California, Santa Barbara*
Lawrence S. Larsen...*University of Oklahoma*
Dieter Merzbacher..*Herzog August Bibliothek*
Erika A. Metzger ....*State University of New York at Buffalo*
Karl F. Otto Jr...*University of Pennsylvania*
John Roger Paas ....*Carleton College*
John Pustejovsky ....*Marquette University*
Max Reinhart ....*University of Georgia*
Hans-Gert Roloff ....*Freie Universität Berlin*
Jeffrey L. Sammons...*Yale University*
Richard E. Schade ....*University of Cincinnati*
George C. Schoolfield..*Yale University*
Sara Smart..*Exeter University*
Blake Lee Spahr ....*University of California at Berkeley*
Lynne Tatlock...*Washington University*
Mara R. Wade ....*University of Illinois at Urbana-Champaign*
Renate Wilson..*University of South Carolina*

Cumulative Index

Dictionary of Literary Biography, Volumes 1-164
Dictionary of Literary Biography Yearbook, 1980-1995
Dictionary of Literary Biography Documentary Series, Volumes 1-13

Cumulative Index

DLB before number: *Dictionary of Literary Biography,* Volumes 1-164
Y before number: *Dictionary of Literary Biography Yearbook,* 1980-1995
DS before number: *Dictionary of Literary Biography Documentary Series,* Volumes 1-13

D

F

413

I

K

M

Maass, Joachim 1901-1972 . . . . DLB-69

Mabie, Hamilton Wright
1845-1916 . . . . DLB-71

Mac A'Ghobhainn, Iain (see Smith, Iain Crichton)

MacArthur, Charles
1895-1956 . . . . DLB-7, 25, 44

Macaulay, Catherine 1731-1791 . . . . DLB-104

Macaulay, David 1945- DLB-61

Macaulay, Rose 1881-1958 . . . . DLB-36

Macaulay, Thomas Babington
1800-1859 . . . . DLB-32, 55

Macaulay Company DLB-46

MacBeth, George 1932- DLB-40

Macbeth, Madge 1880-1965 . . . . DLB-92

MacCaig, Norman 1910- DLB-27

MacDiarmid, Hugh 1892-1978 . . . . . . DLB-20

MacDonald, Cynthia 1928- DLB-105

MacDonald, George
1824-1905 . . . . DLB-18, 163

MacDonald, John D.
1916-1986 . . . . DLB-8; Y-86

MacDonald, Philip 1899?-1980 . . . . . DLB-77

Macdonald, Ross (see Millar, Kenneth)

MacDonald, Wilson 1880-1967 . . . . . DLB-92

Macdonald and Company
(Publishers) DLB-112

MacEwen, Gwendolyn 1941- DLB-53

Macfadden, Bernarr
1868-1955 . . . . DLB-25, 91

MacGregor, Mary Esther (see Keith, Marian)

Machado, Antonio 1875-1939 . . . . . DLB-108

Machado, Manuel 1874-1947 . . . . . . DLB-108

Machar, Agnes Maule 1837-1927 . . . . DLB-92

Machen, Arthur Llewelyn Jones
1863-1947 . . . . DLB-36, 156

MacInnes, Colin 1914-1976 . . . . DLB-14

MacInnes, Helen 1907-1985 . . . . DLB-87

Mack, Maynard 1909- DLB-111

Mackall, Leonard L. 1879-1937 . . . . DLB-140

MacKaye, Percy 1875-1956 . . . . DLB-54

Macken, Walter 1915-1967 . . . . DLB-13

Mackenzie, Alexander 1763-1820 . . . DLB-99

Mackenzie, Compton
1883-1972 . . . . DLB-34, 100

Mackenzie, Henry 1745-1831 . . . . . . DLB-39

Mackey, William Wellington
1937- DLB-38

Mackintosh, Elizabeth (see Tey, Josephine)

Mackintosh, Sir James
1765-1832 . . . . DLB-158

Maclaren, Ian (see Watson, John)

Macklin, Charles 1699-1797 . . . . DLB-89

MacLean, Katherine Anne 1925- DLB-8

MacLeish, Archibald
1892-1982 . . . . DLB-4, 7, 45; Y-82

MacLennan, Hugh 1907-1990 . . . . . . DLB-68

Macleod, Fiona (see Sharp, William)

MacLeod, Alistair 1936- DLB-60

Macleod, Norman 1906-1985 . . . . DLB-4

Macmillan and Company DLB-106

The Macmillan Company DLB-49

Macmillan's English Men of Letters,
First Series (1878-1892) DLB-144

MacNamara, Brinsley 1890-1963 . . . . DLB-10

MacNeice, Louis 1907-1963 . . . . . . DLB-10, 20

MacPhail, Andrew 1864-1938 . . . . . . DLB-92

Macpherson, James 1736-1796 . . . . . DLB-109

Macpherson, Jay 1931- DLB-53

Macpherson, Jeanie 1884-1946 . . . . . DLB-44

Macrae Smith Company DLB-46

Macrone, John
[publishing house] DLB-106

MacShane, Frank 1927- DLB-111

Macy-Masius DLB-46

Madden, David 1933- DLB-6

Maddow, Ben 1909-1992 . . . . DLB-44

Maddux, Rachel 1912-1983 . . . . Y-93

Madgett, Naomi Long 1923- DLB-76

Madhubuti, Haki R.
1942- DLB-5, 41; DS-8

Madison, James 1751-1836 . . . . DLB-37

Maginn, William 1794-1842 . . . DLB-110, 159

Mahan, Alfred Thayer 1840-1914 . . . DLB-47

Maheux-Forcier, Louise 1929- DLB-60

Mahin, John Lee 1902-1984 . . . . DLB-44

Mahon, Derek 1941- DLB-40

Maikov, Vasilii Ivanovich
1728-1778 . . . . DLB-150

Mailer, Norman
1923- DLB-2, 16, 28; Y-80, 83; DS-3

Maillet, Adrienne 1885-1963 . . . . . . DLB-68

Maimonides, Moses 1138-1204 . . . . . DLB-115

Maillet, Antonine 1929- DLB-60

Maillu, David G. 1939- DLB-157

Main Selections of the Book-of-the-Month
Club, 1926-1945 . . . . DLB-9

Main Trends in Twentieth-Century Book
Clubs DLB-46

Mainwaring, Daniel 1902-1977 . . . . . DLB-44

Mair, Charles 1838-1927 . . . . DLB-99

Mais, Roger 1905-1955 . . . . DLB-125

Major, Andre 1942- DLB-60

Major, Clarence 1936- DLB-33

Major, Kevin 1949- DLB-60

Major Books DLB-46

Makemie, Francis circa 1658-1708 . . . DLB-24

The Making of a People, by
J. M. Ritchie DLB-66

Maksimović, Desanka 1898-1993 . . . . DLB-147

Malamud, Bernard
1914-1986 . . . . . . DLB-2, 28, 152; Y-80, 86

Malet, Lucas 1852-1931 . . . . DLB-153

Malleson, Lucy Beatrice (see Gilbert, Anthony)

Mallet-Joris, Françoise 1930- DLB-83

Mallock, W. H. 1849-1923 . . . . . . DLB-18, 57

Malone, Dumas 1892-1986 . . . . DLB-17

Malone, Edmond 1741-1812 . . . . DLB-142

Malory, Sir Thomas
circa 1400-1410 - 1471 . . . . DLB-146

Malraux, André 1901-1976 . . . . DLB-72

Malthus, Thomas Robert
1766-1834 . . . . DLB-107, 158

Maltz, Albert 1908-1985 . . . . DLB-102

Malzberg, Barry N. 1939- DLB-8

Mamet, David 1947- DLB-7

Manaka, Matsemela 1956- DLB-157

Manchester University Press DLB-112

Mandel, Eli 1922- DLB-53

Mandeville, Bernard 1670-1733 . . . . DLB-101

Mandeville, Sir John
mid fourteenth century DLB-146

Mandiargues, André Pieyre de
1909- DLB-83

Manfred, Frederick 1912-1994 . . . . . . DLB-6

Mangan, Sherry 1904-1961 . . . . DLB-4

Mankiewicz, Herman 1897-1953 . . . . DLB-26

Mankiewicz, Joseph L. 1909-1993 . . . DLB-44

Mankowitz, Wolf 1924- DLB-15

P

Q

R

S

445

ISBN 0-8103-9359-X